Economics and Liability for Environmental Problems

T0304182

International Library of Environmental Economics and Policy

General Editors: Tom Tietenberg and Wendy Morrison

Titles in the Series

Fisheries Economics, Volumes I and II
Lee G. Anderson

Green Accounting
Peter Bartelmus and Eberhard K. Seifert

**The Economics of International
Environmental Agreements**
Amitrajeet A. Batabyal

Agro-Environmental Policy
Sandra S. Batie and Rick Horan

**Direct Environmental Valuation Methods,
Volumes I and II**
Richard T. Carson

**International Trade and the
Environment**
Judith M. Dean

**Economic Costs and Consequences of
Environmental Regulation**
Wayne B. Gray

**The Theory and Practice of Command
and Control Regulation**
Gloria E. Helfand and Peter Berck

**The Economics of Residential Solid Waste
Management**
Thomas C. Kinnaman

**Property Rights and Environmental
Problems, Volume I and II**
Bruce Larson

Indirect Valuation Methods
Robert Mendelsohn

The Economics of Land Use
Peter J. Parks and Ian W. Hardie

The Economics of Sustainability
John C.V. Pezzey and Michael A. Toman

**The Economics of Biodiversity
Conservation**
Stephen Polasky

**The Economics of Environmental
Monitoring and Enforcement**
Clifford S. Russell

Discounting and Environmental Policy
Joel D. Scheraga

Economics of Forestry
Roger A. Sedjo

**Economics and Liability for Environmental
Problems**
Kathleen Segerson

**Experiments in Environmental Economics,
Volumes I and II**
Jason F. Shogren

**Emissions Trading Programs,
Volumes I and II**
Tom Tietenberg

Economics and Liability for Environmental Problems

Edited by

Kathleen Segerson

University of Connecticut, USA

Routledge
Taylor & Francis Group

LONDON AND NEW YORK

First published 2002 by Dartmouth Publishing Company and Ashgate Publishing

Reissued 2018 by Routledge
2 Park Square, Milton Park, Abingdon, Oxon OX14 4RN
711 Third Avenue, New York, NY 10017, USA

Routledge is an imprint of the Taylor & Francis Group, an informa business

Publisher's Note
The publisher has gone to great lengths to ensure the quality of this reprint but points out that some imperfections in the original copies may be apparent.

Disclaimer
The publisher has made every effort to trace copyright holders and welcomes correspondence from those they have been unable to contact.

A Library of Congress record exists under LC control number: 2001022938

ISBN 13: 978-1-138-73063-2 (hbk)
ISBN 13: 978-1-138-73060-1 (pbk)
ISBN 13: 978-1-315-18813-3 (ebk)

Contents

PART II   APPLICATIONS

Acknowledgements

The editor and publishers wish to thank the following for permission to use copyright material.

Academic Press for the essays: Kathleen Segerson (1990), 'Liability for Groundwater Contamination from Pesticides', *Journal of Environmental Economics and Management*, **19**, pp. 227–43. Copyright © 1990, Elsevier Science (USA), reprinted by permission of the publisher; Kathleen Segerson and Tom Tietenberg (1992), 'The Structure of Penalties in Environmental Enforcement: An Economic Analysis', *Journal of Environmental Economics and Management*, **23**, pp. 179–200. Copyright © 1992, Elsevier Science (USA), reprinted by permission of the publisher; Steven Garber and James K. Hammitt (1998), 'Risk Premiums for Environmental Liability: Does Superfund Increase the Cost of Capital?', *Journal of Environmental Economics and Management*, **36**, pp. 267–95. Copyright © 1998, Elsevier Science (USA), reprinted by permission of the publisher; Anna Alberini and David H. Austin (1999), 'Strict Liability as a Deterrent in Toxic Waste Management: Empirical Evidence from Accident and Spill Data', *Journal of Environmental Economics and Management*, **38**, pp. 20–48. Copyright © 1999, Elsevier Science (USA), reprinted by permission of the publisher.

American Economic Association for the essay: A. Mitchell Polinsky (1980), 'Strict Liability vs. Negligence in a Market Setting', *American Economic Review*, **70**, pp. 363–67. Copyright © 1980 American Economic Association.

Blackwell Publishers Ltd for the essay: Anthony G. Heyes (1996), 'Lender Penalty for Environmental Damage and the Equilibrium Cost of Capital', *Economica*, **63**, pp. 311–23. Copyright © 1996 The London School of Economics and Political Science.

Elsevier Science for the essays: Keith N. Hylton (1990), 'The Influence of Litigation Costs on Deterrence under Strict Liability and under Negligence', *International Review of Law and Economics*, **10**, pp. 161–71. Copyright © 1990 Butterworth-Heineman; Harry A. Newman and David W. Wright (1990), 'Strict Liability in a Principal-Agent Model', *International Review of Law and Economics*, **10**, pp. 219–31. Copyright © 1990 Butterworth-Heineman.

Harvard Law Review Association for the essay: Guido Calabresi and A. Douglas Melamed (1972), 'Property Rules, Liability Rules, and Inalienability: One View of the Cathedral', *Harvard Law Review*, **85**, pp. 1089–128. Copyright © 1972 Harvard Law Review Association.

Journal of Legal Studies for the essays: Steven Shavell (1984), 'Liability for Harm versus Regulation of Safety', *Journal of Legal Studies*, **13**, pp. 357–74. Copyright © 1984 University of Chicago; Michele J. White and Donald Wittman (1983), 'A Comparison of Taxes, Regulation, and Liability Rules under Imperfect Information', *Journal of Legal Studies*, **12**, pp. 413–25. Copyright © 1983 University of Chicago; Steven Shavell (1980), 'Strict Liability versus Negligence', *Journal of Legal Studies*, **9**, pp. 1–25. Copyright © 1980 University of Chicago;

Series Preface

The *International Library of Environmental Economics and Policy* explores the influence of economics on the development of environmental and natural resource policy. In a series of twenty five volumes, the most significant journal essays in key areas of contemporary environmental and resource policy are collected. Scholars who are recognized for their expertise and contribution to the literature in the various research areas serve as volume editors and write an introductory essay that provides the context for the collection.

Volumes in the series reflect the broad strands of economic research including 1) Natural and Environmental Resources, 2) Policy Instruments and Institutions and 3) Methodology. The editors, in their introduction to each volume, provide a state-of-the-art overview of the topic and explain the influence and relevance of the collected papers on the development of policy. This reference series provides access to the economic literature that has made an enduring contribution to contemporary and natural resource policy.

TOM TIETENBERG
WENDY MORRISON
General Editors

Introduction

What is Environmental Liability?

Many of the most pressing environmental concerns today relate to contamination resulting from the disposal or release of toxic or hazardous substances. Examples include oil spills, accidental releases of hazardous chemicals, leaching of contaminants into groundwater, nuclear accidents and nuclear waste disposal. Unlike traditional pollutants that are released regularly into the air or water (such as sulphur dioxide or NO_x), these contamination problems stem from 'events' or 'environmental accidents' that occur unexpectedly. Because these events are unpredictable, they pose a particular challenge for the design of environmental policy.

With event-based pollution problems, environmental policy instruments can take one of two possible forms. The first form are *ex ante* policy instruments, such as regulation or taxation of activities that could lead to environmental contamination. These instruments are applied to the potentially hazardous activity at the time it is undertaken, and are imposed regardless of whether a contamination event eventually occurs. Under the second form, *ex post* policy instruments, imposition of the instrument is triggered by the contamination event itself. Environmental liability is an example of an *ex post* policy instrument, under which a party (or parties) responsible for the contamination event becomes liable for the damages that result from that event. Typically, liability takes the form of payment of compensation to the victim(s) who suffered the resulting damages or, if this is not practical, then to a fund with a designated use. Responsible parties ('injurers') can also be held liable for the cost of cleaning up the contamination or restoring certain environmental services.

Liability for environmental damages can be imposed either statutorily or under common law. For example, in the United States, the Comprehensive Environmental Response, Compensation and Liability Act of 1980 (CERCLA or the 'Superfund' Act) statutorily holds responsible parties liable for the costs of cleaning up hazardous waste sites. However, third-party victims who suffer damages as a result of the contamination must seek compensation under common law. Other examples of statutory environmental liability include the US Oil Pollution Act of 1990 and the 1991 German Environmental Liability Act.

The two main types of liability for damages are strict liability and negligence. Under strict liability, an injurer is held liable for damages regardless of the conduct that led to the event. In particular, he is held liable regardless of the amount of care exercised in conducting the activities that ultimately caused the damages. In contrast, under a negligence rule of liability, an injurer is held liable for damages resulting from his activities only if, in conducting those activities, he did not exercise sufficient care – that is, he was deemed to have conducted the activities in a negligent way. Because, under strict liability, injurers must pay whenever damages occur, strict liability is comparable to a 'price instrument' or Pigouvian tax (Cooter, 1984; Segerson, 2000). In contrast, because a negligence rule sets a standard for sufficient or 'due' care, and liability is imposed only if that standard is not met, negligence-based liability is comparable to a 'quantity instrument'. It acts like a regulation; failure to comply with a regulation can trigger the imposition of fines and penalties, and failure to comply with the due standard of care triggers liability for damages.

Although strict liability and negligence are the two main types of liability, other related rules exist as well. For example, under a rule of contributory negligence, an injurer would not be held liable for damages if it were found that the victim also acted negligently and the victim's negligence contributed to the accident. Under contributory negligence, the injurer would be relieved of liability entirely regardless of the extent of the victim's negligence. In contrast, under a rule of comparative negligence, the victim's negligence would reduce but not eliminate the injurer's liability. The extent of the injurer's liability would depend on the relative contributions of the injurer's and the victim's negligence.

Because environmental liability relates to the occurrence of environmental accidents, the economic models of environmental liability draw heavily from the general literature on the economics of accident law (see, for example, Shavell, 1987). For this reason, the first part of this volume (Part I) is devoted to this more general literature, with a focus on essays that have particular relevance for the study of environmental accidents and environmental liability. The essays in Part I are divided into two groups. The first group examines the appropriate role for liability as a policy instrument *vis-à-vis* other instruments. The second group examines in detail the incentive effects created by the imposition of liability, with particular emphasis on the incentive issues that are likely to arise in the context of environmental accidents (for example, bankruptcy, litigation costs, delegation of responsibility and insurance). The essays in Part II then use this general theory to study specific environmental issues, such as hazardous waste disposal and oil spills, industrial accidents and spills, contamination from agricultural pesticides and nuclear accidents. These applications include theoretical or conceptual models of alternative liability rules, empirical studies of the impact of liability and studies of environmental liability reform.

Theory

The Role of Liability

In general, liability can serve three main goals: compensation, corrective justice and deterrence (Dewees *et al.*, 1996). The compensation goal holds that liability should be designed so as to spread the risks associated with risky activities and ensure that victims who suffer damages as a result of those activities receive compensation for their losses. This goal tends to favour strict liability over negligence, since strict liability generally provides for greater victim compensation. In contrast, those who believe that the main goal of liability is corrective justice tend to favour negligence rules since they are more closely linked to punishment for socially unacceptable actions. The deterrence goal is concerned not with correcting past wrongs or ensuring compensation for victims, but rather with deterring future behaviour that leads to unacceptable risks. As discussed below, whether this 'risk reduction' goal is better served by strict liability or a negligence rule depends on the nature of the risk.

Most of the economic analysis of liability focuses on the deterrence goal, or, equivalently, on creating incentives for risk reduction (see, for example, Shavell, 1987). These incentives can relate to any of the factors that can ultimately affect damages, including:

- injurer care levels
- injurer activity levels
- injurer response or clean-up
- victim care levels
- victim activity levels.

For example, the risks associated with groundwater contamination from agricultural pesticides can depend on:

- the amount of care exercised by the farmer in applying the pesticide (injurer care)
- the amount of the pesticide applied (injurer activity level)
- the removal of the plume if contamination occurs (injurer response)
- the victim's use of a water filter to filter out contaminants (victim care)
- the victim's amount of water consumption (victim activity level).

Likewise, the risks associated with oil spills depend not only on the care taken in transporting the oil (for example, tanker construction and navigation safety) but also on the amount of oil transported (the activity level). Policies designed to reduce these risks can create incentives that affect any one or more of these risk-related factors.

Regardless of the factor, the benchmark used in economic analyses of the incentive effects of liability is *economic efficiency*. Incentives are economically efficient if injurers and/or victims are induced to choose the amount of care, activity or response that maximizes the expected net social benefit from a given activity, where the net social benefit incorporates not only the gains from conducting the activity but also the associated costs, including the damages that can result from that activity. When one or more parties are risk-averse, the definition of costs must also include the costs associated with bearing risks. For a given level of risk, efficient risk-sharing requires that costs be allocated so as to minimize the total costs associated with bearing risks. Note that, in some cases, it may not be possible to achieve both efficient risk reduction incentives and efficient risk sharing simultaneously. In such cases, there is a trade-off between the two efficiency goals (Shavell, 1979; Segerson, 1987).

If the goal is efficient deterrence, then an evaluation of liability requires a comparison of how effective liability rules are in achieving efficient deterrence relative to other policy instruments. Many scholarly papers have been devoted to a comparison of alternative policy instruments. Some of these look more generally at controlling externalities, sometimes with particular emphasis on environmental externalities (for example, Bohm and Russell, 1985). Others focus specifically on the relative advantages and disadvantages of legal liability.

In a seminal essay on the use of liability, Calabresi and Melamed (Chapter 1) present a model of how liability rules and property rules constitute different means of protecting entitlements or rights. Under a general liability rule, whether based on strict liability or negligence, the injurer has the right to engage in an activity that might cause damage to another (that is, a victim) without the victim's consent, but the injurer must pay compensation to the victim for damages that he causes (negligently, if the appropriate rule is negligence). Thus, the victim does not have the right to be free from damages, but he has the right to compensation for those damages. In contrast, when rights are protected by a property rule (for example, an injunction under nuisance law), a potential victim has the right to prohibit an injurer from engaging in that activity. The injurer would have to seek the consent of (and presumably bribe) the victim to allow the activity to take place. The basic question that Calabresi and Melamed ask is: when should entitlements be protected by a liability rule rather than a property rule? In their answer, they emphasize the role of avoidance (that is, deterrence) costs, as well as transactions costs.

The choice between liability rules and property rules is a key issue when disputes are between a relatively small set of easily identifiable injurers and victims so that bargaining between the parties is possible. In these contexts, the alternative to liability is another common law remedy. In other contexts, the alternative to liability may be some form of government regulation, under which the government effectively acts on behalf of victims to limit or prohibit activities that could lead to third-party damages. Shavell (Chapter 2) identifies four factors that determine the relative desirability of liability vs. regulation. They are:

1. the difference in knowledge about risky activities
2. the likelihood that injurers will have the assets to pay for harms caused
3. the likelihood that injurers will face the threat of a suit for harm done
4. the relative magnitudes of the administrative costs associated with using the two systems.

Liability is more desirable the greater is the private knowledge about risky activities relative to the knowledge of regulators; the greater are private assets that could be used to pay for damages, the greater is the likelihood that harmed parties would sue for damages, and the smaller are the administrative costs of using the liability system.

As noted by Shavell in Chapter 4, one of the issues that determines the desirability of controlling externalities through liability rather than government regulation is information asymmetries – that is, the fact that private parties may have better information than regulators about risky activities. The effect of information asymmetries or imperfect information on the relative merits of alternative policy instruments has been widely recognized in the literature on instrument choice. In a seminal essay on the choice between price-based instruments (that is, taxes) and quantity-based instruments (that is, regulations or permits), Weitzman (1974) showed that, although the two instruments have identical welfare properties when the marginal costs and marginal benefits of pollution abatement are known with certainty, their welfare effects differ when the regulator does not know the marginal costs of abatement. In Chapter 3 White and Wittman extend the Weitzman analysis to include liability as a possible alternative instrument. Even though under conditions of certainty strict liability is very similar to a Pigouvian tax and a negligence rule resembles a regulation (Cooter, 1984; Segerson, 2000), White and Wittman show that, under uncertainty about the costs and benefits of pollution control, the liability rules dominate taxes and regulations. For example, strict liability for 'reasonable' damages – that is, damages to the average victim – is preferred to either taxation or regulation because, under strict liability, the firm's marginal cost for polluting is the same as society's marginal cost, rather than being horizontal (as under a tax) or vertical (as under a regulatory standard). This same feature of strict liability makes it more efficient than a Pigouvian tax in the long run, since injurers are forced to pay the social costs of their activities not only at the margin but in total as well (Segerson, 2000).

The above comparisons of liability with alternative policy instruments presume that liability would be a substitute for another instrument (for example, taxes or regulation). However, in many cases, liability is coupled with other traditional policy instruments. For example, in the US hazardous waste sites are governed both by liability for clean-up imposed under CERCLA and the regulations imposed under the Resource Conservation and Recovery Act (RCRA). In this case, the role of liability is to complement other policy instruments rather than substitute for them. This can be particularly effective when each instrument can compensate for the limitations of the other instrument. For example, liability can compensate for the fact that not all actions that contribute to potential damages are easily monitored and hence regulated, while regulation can compensate for the limitations in the effectiveness of liability caused by limited assets or limited incentives to sue. Shavell (Chapter 4) shows that, because of the limitations of both systems, the joint use of liability and regulation is generally more efficient than the use of either system alone.

The Incentive Effects of Liability

To achieve its deterrence goal, liability must provide an incentive for injurers or victims to take steps to reduce either the probability of an accident or the damages that would result. The economic literature on liability has identified a number of factors that determine the effectiveness of the risk-reduction incentives created by alternative liability rules (for example, Segerson, 1995). One important factor is *whether the magnitude of the risk created by a given activity is influenced primarily by the actions of the injurer (the case of 'unilateral care') or instead it is also significantly affected by the actions of the victim (the case of 'bilateral care').* In cases of bilateral care, the liability rule must create proper risk-reduction incentives not only for the injurer but also for the victim. Some rules are effective in creating incentives for one party but not the other. For example, strict liability creates risk-reduction incentives for the injurer but not for the victim.

A second important factor is *whether the risk is influenced primarily by decisions regarding care (by the injurer or the victim) or instead the parties' activity (or output) levels are significant determinants of risk as well.* Examples where activity or output levels are important include waste disposal risks, which depend not only on the care taken in disposal but also on the amount of waste disposed, and oil spill risks, which depend on both the care taken in transport and the amount of oil transported. In such cases, the liability rule must create proper incentives not only for care but also for reductions in activity levels or output. Again, some rules provide effective incentives for one type of risk reduction but not the other. For example, a negligence rule creates proper incentives for injurers to meet the due standard of care (if it is set at the efficient level), but it does not create an incentive for reductions in risk-generating activities.

While many accidents involve a single injurer, in some cases the actions of multiple parties combine to create risks in a non-separable way – that is, in such a way that the risk attributable to any individual injurer cannot be easily identified. For example, when many firms dispose of their waste in a single waste disposal facility, the risk of contamination from that facility is a function of the combined contributions of all of the firms. When multiple injurers exist, the liability rule must create incentives for efficient risk reduction by each injurer. A simple apportionment rule (for example, each injurer pays 1/nth of the damages if there are n firms) will not create efficient incentives since each injurer will bear 100 per cent of the cost of his own risk reduction but receive only 1/nth of the benefit (in the form of reduced liability). Thus, the third factor influencing the incentive effects of alternative liability rules is *whether there are multiple injurers.*

Fourth, the incentive effects of alternative liability rules depend on *whether the parties involved in the liability action are linked through some form of market or other contractual relationship.* For example, when an employee of a firm suffers from exposure to an environmental contaminant in the workplace, the injurer (employer) is the purchaser of services from the victim (employee). Similarly, when risks arise from consumption of a product (such as pesticide residues on food), the injurer (producer) sells the product to the victim (consumer). In cases involving multiple injurers, two or more of those injurers might have a contractual relationship, as, for example, when contamination at a waste disposal site is affected by the actions of both the waste generator and the owner of the waste disposal facility. In this case, one injurer (the owner of the facility) sells waste disposal services to the other injurer (the waste generator). When the injurer and victim or multiple injurers are linked through a market relationship, the incentive effects of alternative liability rules will be affected by the extent to which one party can shift costs on to the other party through changes in the market or contract price.

The incentive effects of liability are created by the requirement that liable parties pay for the damages for which they are responsible. In some cases, responsible parties do not actually pay for damages. This can occur either because victims do not bring suit against the injurer or because the injurer does not have the assets to pay the damage award. Because litigation is costly, under a system where victims must pay their own litigation costs, they will not find it economically beneficial to bring a suit if the associated litigation costs exceed the damage award they can expect to receive. Similarly, in cases where the damage award exceeds the injurer's assets or the injurer is otherwise judgment-proof (for example, the firm whose activity created the contamination problem no longer exists), or when the victim cannot prove that the injurer was responsible for the damages (for example, when a given cancer case may or may not have been caused by previous exposure to a hazardous substance), the injurer cannot be forced to pay the full damage award. Thus, a fifth factor determining the incentive effect of liability is *whether the injurer is likely to be forced to pay the full damages, should his activities result in an accident.*

The economic literature on liability rules has examined the incentive effects of alternative liability rules under different scenarios defined by the above five factors. Some basic principles have emerged from the literature, which have implications for the incentive effects of those rules. These include the following:

- *Principle 1: Parties who bear damages have an incentive to reduce those damages.*
  This basic principle drives many of the results regarding both injurer and victim incentives. For example, it implies that a strict liability rule, under which injurers bear the full amount of damages and victims do not bear any damages, creates incentives for injurer care but not for victim care. Thus, a strict liability rule is efficient in the context of unilateral accidents, but not in the context of bilateral accidents where victim care is an important determinant of risk. However, a negligence rule will create efficient incentives for victim care because, provided the injurer is non-negligent, victims will bear their own losses.
- *Principle 2: Incentives for care can be created by imposing sufficiently large penalties for failure to take care.*
  This principle underlies many of the results related to negligence-based rules, under which there is effectively a penalty for insufficient care. In the context of unilateral

accidents, it implies that a standard negligence rule with the due standard of care set at the efficient level will induce the injurer to undertake that level of care. Similarly, in a bilateral care context, strict liability with a defence of contributory negligence (under which the injurer is relieved of liability if the victim was negligent as well) will provide efficient incentives for victim care since, if victims are negligent, they will pay a penalty by having to bear their own losses. Thus, a defence of contributory negligence can eliminate the inefficient victim care incentives that exist when strict liability is applied to bilateral care accidents.

- *Principle 3: If a party does not pay the full social cost of engaging in an activity, they tend to 'overengage' in the activity (for example, produce too much since prices are too low).* This principle drives many of the results regarding incentives to reduce risks through reductions in activity levels or output. For example, since under a strict liability rule injurers bear the full damages and victims do not, a strict liability rule creates efficient incentives for reductions in injurer activity levels but not for reductions in victim activity levels. However, because injurers do not bear the full damages under a negligence rule, they tend to overengage in the risk-generating activity (for example, overproduce) when liability is governed by a negligence rule.

- *Principle 4: Market or contractual relationships provide opportunities for shifting costs (including liability) from one party to another.* When shifting is possible, the party who is legally liable for damages can pass some or all of those costs on to the other party through adjustments in the contract price. For example, a seller of a product can pass some or all of the costs of liability for damages caused by that product on to consumers of the product through an increase in the product price. Similarly, an employer can pass some of his liability on to workers whose actions result in damages through reductions in wages if wages can be linked to whether an accident has occurred. When shifting is perfect, the assignment of liability between the two parties to the relationship is 'irrelevant' in the sense that changes in the assignment of liability will not change the allocation of resources (for example, decisions about care or activity levels).

- *Principle 5: For efficient risk-sharing, risks should be placed on the parties that are best able to bear them (because of risk preference or risk-spreading opportunities), or shared until the marginal cost of additional risk is equal for all parties.* Because under strict liability the risks associated with the uncertainty of damages are borne by injurers, this principle implies that the allocation of risk under strict liability is efficient if injurers are better able to bear risks than victims (due, for example, to the existence of first-party insurance). Alternatively, a negligence rule leads to an efficient allocation of risk if victims are better able to bear risk than injurers. However, overall efficiency requires consideration of both risk-sharing and risk-reduction incentives. Depending on the risk preferences of the parties involved, there is a potential trade-off between efficient risk-sharing and providing efficient incentives for risk reduction.

- *Principle 6: Factors that reduce the amount of liability an injurer would face (and hence the marginal benefit of care) without also reducing the marginal cost of care will reduce the incentive for injurers to take care.* Factors that tend to reduce the amount of liability an injurer faces include the presence of victim litigation costs, limited injurer assets or, equivalently, the probability that the injurer will be insolvent (that is, bankrupt) or otherwise judgment-proof at the time of trial, and uncertainty over whether the injurer was, in fact, responsible for the damages suffered by the victim. Similar effects result from apportionment rules, under which injurers bear only a fraction of damages. Since these factors decrease liability and hence the marginal benefit of care, they generally lead to underdeterrence unless the marginal cost of care is simultaneously reduced (as is possible with asset limits).

The above summary gives an introduction to some of the results that have emerged from the economic literature on the incentive effects of alternative liability rules and the basic principles that drive those results. Many of those results were originally presented or developed in the collection of essays included in this volume. For example, Shavell (Chapter 5) presents economic models of accidents in a number of contexts, including both unilateral and bilateral care models, models where both care and activity levels affect risks, and models in which the injurer and victim have a contractual or market relationship. He establishes the basic results discussed above (Principles 1, 2 and 3) regarding the incentive effects of strict liability and negligence rules in these contexts, including the efficient injurer care incentives created by both strict liability and negligence, the inefficient victim care incentives under strict liability, the impact of both strict liability and negligence on incentives for reductions in both injurer and victim activity levels, and the irrelevance of the assignment of liability in the context of market relationships where shifting is perfect (for example, because risks are perfectly perceived).

In his analysis of the effect of liability on activity levels, Shavell assumes that there is a fixed number of potential injurers. In this sense, his analysis of market behaviour is a short-run analysis. However, Polinsky (Chapter 6) extends Shavell's analysis to consider the long-run effects of liability, where in the long run firms can enter or exit an industry in response to changes in profitability. Differences in profitability under alternative rules create different entry/ exit incentives and hence industries of different sizes. He shows that the industry is efficient under strict liability but inefficiently large under a negligence rule (Principle 3).

In Polinsky's model there is no market relationship between injurers and victims since the victims are not the purchasers of the firms' products. Thus, there is no possibility that parties could bargain around the assignment of liability, as assumed in Coase (1967) and Calabresi and Melamed (Chapter 1). Elaborating on the Coase theorem, Demsetz (Chapter 7) compares the long-run impacts of alternative liability rules (strict liability versus no liability) when parties can bargain. The ability to bargain effectively creates a market-like relationship between the two parties, whereby the assignment of liability affects the returns of both parties. Thus, as Demsetz's essay concludes, the basic 'irrelevance' results from models where the parties have a market relationship also hold in the context where parties can bargain (Principle 4).

In some cases, the market relationship is not between the injurer and the victim, but rather between two parties related to the cause of the damages. As noted above, an important class of such problems are those where a firm hires an employee, and the employee, acting as an 'agent' of the firm, undertakes activities that could cause harm to a third party. In this context, liability could be imposed on either the firm itself (possibly including the officers of the firm) or on the employee. The firm and the employee have a market relationship through the employment contract. Using a principal-agent model of the firm, Newman and Wright (Chapter 8) show that, as long as the employee's wage can be contingent on the occurrence of an accident, a mechanism for shifting costs exists. Hence, even though the care decision is made by the employee, imposing strict liability on the firm will still result in an optimal level of care because the liability costs imposed on the firm are shifted to the employee through the wage contract. Thus, given perfect shifting, Newman and Wright show that the basic irrelevance result from the models that include market relationships holds in this context as well (Principle 4).

In the model of Newman and Wright, the firm is assumed to be risk-neutral, while the employee is assumed to be risk-averse. Given this, imposing strict liability on the firm leads both to an optimal level of care and to efficient risk-sharing, since risks are borne by the risk-neutral party (the firm) when the employee is induced to choose the optimal level of care. Shavell (Chapter 9) considers a scenario in which there are no market relationships among the parties but both the injurer and the victim are risk-averse. He shows that, in the absence of insurance, there is a trade-off between risk-sharing and incentives when both parties are risk-averse, and a first-best outcome cannot be achieved under either strict liability or a negligence rule (Principle 5). This trade-off can be eliminated by insurance, provided that the insurer can observe the injurer's care level and make the insurance contract contingent on the injurer's care. The existence of such an insurance contract effectively creates a market relationship between the insurer and the injurer that provides a mechanism for shifting the expected liability costs that the insurer would pay back on to the injurer through changes in the insurance premium. Again, this is analogous to the results in the accident models with market relationships between injurers and victims (Principle 4). However, when perfect shifting cannot occur – that is, when the insurer cannot base the insurance premium on the injurer's care (for example, when care is not observable) – then the presence of insurance reduces the injurer's incentive to take care.

The reduction in injurer care incentives that can result from the existence of insurance occurs because, with insurance, the injurer does not ultimately bear the full damages resulting from his activities. As noted above, similar reductions in care incentives can result from other factors that reduce the injurer's cost below total damages, including insufficient incentives for victims to sue for damages, insufficient injurer assets and difficulty in proving causation of damages (Principle 6). Shavell (Chapter 4) presents a simple model in which firms have limited assets and the probability of a suit could be less than one. As expected, the result is that, under strict liability, the injurer's care incentives are diluted and hence underdeterrence occurs.

In Shavell's model, the probability of a suit is exogeneous. Hylton (Chapter 10) explicitly models the victim's decision to bring suit, given the expected damage award and the costs of litigation. He shows that the underdeterrence under strict liability stems from two sources: first, the fact that injurers do not bear the losses of victims who choose not to sue because their litigation costs exceed their losses and, second, the fact that, in making their care decisions, injurers do not consider the litigation costs of victims who choose to sue when those costs must be borne by the plaintiff rather than by the defendant.

A similar underdeterrence result can occur when injurers have limited assets (see Shavell, Chapter 4). If the damage award they could face exceeds their assets, injurers will be held liable only up to the extent of their assets and hence will not face the full cost of damages. However, this underdeterrence result assumes that the probability that an injurer would be unable to pay the full amount of damages is exogenous. In Chapter 11 Beard develops a model in which the probability of bankruptcy is endogenous; increased expenditures on care reduce the injurer's assets and hence increase the likelihood that the remaining assets will be insufficient to cover any damage award that might have to be paid. This, in turn, creates a subsidy to spending since it reduces the marginal cost of spending, which tends to increase expenditures on care relative to the optimal level, *ceteris paribus*. This reduction in marginal cost combines with the usual reduction in marginal benefit (in the form of reduced liability payment) to determine the overall impact of potential bankruptcy on injurer care. The net result is that, with an endogenous level of assets, the possibility of bankruptcy can lead to either over- or underdeterrence.

The potential for underdeterrence due to limited assets or the difficulty of proving that an injurer's actions are responsible for a loss ultimately suffered by a victim (for example, cancer) seems particularly problematic in the context of catastrophic personal injuries, where a large number of victims are killed or seriously injured. Landes and Posner (Chapter 12) extend the standard accident model to the case of catastrophic accidents in which there are a large number of potential victims. They argue that, in such cases, the effect of bankruptcy on the marginal benefit of care is likely to be greater than the effect on the marginal cost of care (since the probability of an accident is small), and hence that the combined effect is still one of underdeterrence under strict liability. They argue, however, not only that the underdeterrence effect can be reduced by using a negligence rule, but also that the underdeterrence that can stem from the difficulty of proving causation can be reduced by allowing all exposed individuals to sue for expected damages at the time of exposure – in other words, sue for the increased risk of future illness.

Applications

The above results were derived in the context of general models of accidents. However, interest in the use of liability specifically in the context of environmental accidents developed in the 1980s and still continues. In the United States, much of this interest stemmed from the passage of CERCLA in 1980, which imposed liability for the clean-up of hazardous waste sites on the responsible parties. This volume contains a number of applications of these general principles to environmental accidents. These applications include conceptual models of environmental liability, empirical studies of the effect of liability on environmental risks, and studies of environmental liability reform.

Conceptual Models

Because much of the interest in environmental liability stems from the liability provisions in CERCLA, which have been mimicked by many individual states and other countries, much of the literature on environmental liability focuses on the specific liability provisions of this act. One controversial feature of liability under CERCLA is the broad definition of the responsible parties. For example, if a piece of contaminated property is sold, the new owner can be considered a responsible party and hence inherit liability for clean-up. Many have argued that the transfer of liability to the new owner discourages land sales. There is particular concern that it will discourage the redevelopment of old industrial sites or 'brownfields' and instead encourage developers to build on pristine sites ('greenfields'). In Chapter 13 Boyd *et al.* examine the effect of liability transfers on the real estate market. They show that, in the presence of perfect information, the expected liability costs will be capitalized into land prices, and hence the transfer of liability will not distort the incentives to buy and sell property (an application of

Principle 4). However, when sellers have better information about the extent of contamination than buyers or detection is otherwise imperfect, then perfect shifting will not occur and real estate markets will be distorted. In particular, they show that, in this context, liability shifting can create an adverse selection problem that leads to too little redevelopment of industrial sites.

Under the original provisions of CERCLA, if a site owner were insolvent, liability could also be shifted to banks and other institutions that were financially tied to a contaminated site. This potential for 'lender liability' prompted significant concerns, particularly since banks were often viewed as 'deep pockets' that did not suffer from asset limitations. As expected, if the site owner's care decisions are made prior to the bank's involvement – for example, prior to receiving a loan – and there is perfect information about the extent of contamination (and hence liability), then the potential transfer of liability to lending institutions will not affect the availability of capital (an application of Principle 4) since the interest rate will simply adjust to reflect the lender's expected liability (Segerson, 1993). In particular, an increase in the extent of the lender's liability will increase the equilibrium interest rate for loans. However, perfect shifting cannot occur if there is asymmetric information between the firm and the lender about the likely returns from investment projects (causing an adverse selection problem of the type discussed by Boyd *et al.* in Chapter 13) or if the firm's abatement decisions are made after the loan is received (thereby causing a moral hazard problem similar to the one described in Principle 6). Heyes (Chapter 14) shows that, in the presence of both adverse selection and moral hazard, a shift in liability to the lender has an ambiguous effect on the equilibrium rate of return on capital. Because of adverse selection, the lender wants to increase the interest rate to 'weed out' riskier projects. However, to reduce the moral hazard problem, it will want to decrease the interest rate to decrease the firm's costs and thereby decrease incentives for cost-cutting through reductions in care. Regardless of which of these effects dominates, though, the net effect is a greater proportion of potential borrowers are excluded from the capital market. Thus, a shift of liability to the lender unambiguously reduces the amount of credit available in the market.

In addition to the concerns about the extension of liability to new site owners and lenders, concerns have also been expressed about the use of joint and several liability for environmental contamination. Under joint and several liability, if multiple polluters contributed to a contamination problem, any one of them can be held liable for the full amount of damages. This rule has been heavily criticized for being unfair, since a single party can be held liable for the entire damage even if his contribution to that damage was relatively small. Kornhauser and Revesz (Chapter 15) present a detailed analysis of the efficiency of joint and several liability under both negligence and strict liability. They show that joint and several liability can lead to efficient care under a negligence rule if the due standard of care is set optimally, but that this rule is not efficient under strict liability when the apportionment rules usually applied are used. The explanation is simply that, even under joint and several liability, the negligence rule can impose a sufficiently high penalty on polluters to induce efficient care (Principle 2), while under strict liability the apportionment rules imply that polluters bear only a fraction of the damages caused by their actions and hence face inefficient incentives for care (Principle 6). Tietenberg (Chapter 16) draws similar conclusions based on a model that considers explicitly the role of the government's litigation strategy – that is, the fact that, in order to maximize the amount of revenue available for clean-up, the government has an incentive to target certain responsible parties (for example, firms with more cash reserves) for liability.

The analysis of CERCLA liability implies that the effect of alternative liability rules depends on those parties that are, or expect to be, targeted for liability. The importance of how broadly the liability net is cast is also apparent in the analysis of the effect of liability for damages that result from the use of hazardous products. In Chapter 17 Segerson examines liability for groundwater contamination resulting from the use of agricultural pesticides. She shows that, when the only potentially liable party is the farmer, then exempting farmers from liability leads to underdeterrence since farmers would not face the full amount of damages resulting from their pesticide use (Principle 6). However, if the producers of the pesticide are also potentially liable, then a farmer exemption can still lead to efficient farmer incentives. If liability is instead imposed on pesticide producers, they can shift some of the cost of liability on to farmers through increases in pesticide prices. The ability to shift costs through the price of pesticides provides a mechanism for inducing farmers to reduce contamination risks through reduced use of pesticides (Principle 4). Thus, if the exemption is limited to farmers who are non-negligent in their use of pesticides and liability is then shifted to the pesticide producers, the exemption will still lead to efficient farmer behaviour.

The appropriate scope of liability is also an issue in environmental accidents that result from corporate activity, where the actions of both managers and employees combine to determine potential damages. In a general accident context, Newman and Wright (Chapter 8) examine the special case where only employee actions affect damages. Segerson and Tietenberg (Chapter 18) present a similar model where damages are affected by both the firm's production level and the care undertaken by employees. They show that, if actions are fully observable and wages can be adjusted to reflect the firm's environmental performance, then the combination of forward and backward shifting ensures that corporate and individual (that is, employee) liability are perfect substitutes (Principle 4). However, many environmental contamination events involve long lag times that make perfect shifting impossible. In such cases, the standard irrelevance result does not hold, and the imposition of liability on both parties may be necessary to induce efficient incentives.

Empirical Models

The theoretical literature on liability suggests that, in the presence of market relationships, liability costs can be shifted from one party to another through adjustments in prices (Principle 4). The available empirical evidence provides some support for this hypothesis. For example, Opaluch and Grigalunas (Chapter 19) found evidence that liability for the environmental risks associated with oil exploration was capitalized into bids for Outer Continental Shelf leases. They estimated that the perceived liability stemming from environmental risks reduced total high bids by 20 per cent. Similarly, Garber and Hammitt (Chapter 20) found evidence that potential Superfund liability increased the cost of capital for large firms, although they could not detect a similar effect for small firms.

While these findings suggest that potential liability is being capitalized into prices (at least in some cases), they do not provide direct evidence of a behavioural response to the imposition of liability. There are very few empirical studies of the impact of liability on polluter behaviour, since data suitable for testing behavioural hypotheses regarding the impact of liability are often not available (see Segerson, 2000). In a recent study, Alberini and Austin (Chapter 21) were able to examine the deterrence effect of liability by studying the accident and spill rates of states that have adopted a strict liability rule (rather than a negligence rule or regulation alone) for the clean-up of hazardous releases or sites not covered by the federal Superfund. They are not able to find any evidence that strict liability leads to greater deterrence and hence fewer spills and accidents than a negligence-based rule. In fact, for some chemicals they find that strict liability states tend to have higher spill rates.

One explanation for this finding is that strict liability creates a greater incentive than negligence for risky activities to be concentrated in small firms that can avoid liability through bankruptcy. In Chapter 22 Ringleb and Wiggins provide evidence suggesting that firms may respond to the imposition of liability by shielding their assets through divestiture. Using data on small-firm entry into the US economy, they show that entry rates were significantly higher, *ceteris paribus*, in industries that were likely to face greater environmental liability for workplace-related exposures. This suggests that the imposition of increased liability could actually lead to greater environmental risk if it induces firms to reduce their liability not through increased care but rather through corporate restructuring.

Liability Reform

Concerns about the effectiveness of current liability laws have led to calls for reforms aimed at increasing the deterrence, compensation and/or fairness of the liability system. The insights from the theoretical and empirical literature on the incentive effects of liability have been used to guide recommendations for liability reform. For example, drawing on the results from the theoretical literature on liability transfers and on the relative merits of strict liability versus negligence, Boyd (Chapter 23) discusses the appropriate design of liability for environmental contamination in Central and Eastern Europe. He argues that liability for existing contamination should not be transferred to new property owners, because of the uncertainties and information asymmetries regarding the extent of contamination. In addition, because of the limited assets of many firms and the overburdened judicial system in these countries, he advocates the use of a negligence rule rather than strict liability for prospective contamination.

Similarly, in the final chapter of this volume Faure draws on the economic principles of accident law to analyse the shortcomings of international conventions regarding compensation for nuclear accidents and to recommend policy reforms. He argues that caps on the amount of compensation under these conventions can lead to underdeterrence in the same way that limited assets do and he proposes, as an alternative, the use of an industry-wide risk-sharing pool, which would allow individual plant owners to diversify risk while at the same time creating a collective industry interest in reducing risks and hence monitoring individual members of the pool.

Conclusion

The essays contained in this volume, and the literature on liability more generally, suggest that, with regard to the role of liability as a means of reducing environmental risks, in principle liability has the potential to create strong incentives to reduce environmental risks through increased precaution and reductions in risky activities. However, this potential will be realized only when the likelihood that a responsible party will actually pay for the damages that result from his (negligent) behaviour is sufficiently high. The incentive effects of liability are often reduced as a result of the nature of the risk (for example, the difficulty of proving causation), the nature of the polluter (for example, the existence of insufficient assets), the constraints on the use of the legal system (for example, the high cost of litigation), or the design of the liability policy (for example, the imposition of liability caps). While liability rules can be designed to reduce these disincentive effects, it is likely that the joint use of liability and safety regulation will lead to more effective reduction of environmental risks than the use of liability alone.

References

Bohm, Peter and Russell, Clifford (1985), 'Comparative Analysis of Alternative Policy Instruments', in Allen V. Kneese and James L. Sweeney (eds), *Handbook of Natural Resource and Energy Economics*, Amsterdam: North-Holland.

Coase, Ronald (1960), 'The Problem of Social Cost', *Journal of Law and Economics*, **3**, pp. 1–44.

Cooter, Robert (1984), 'Prices vs. Sanctions', *Columbia Law Review*, **84**, pp. 1523–60.

Dewees, Don, Duff, David and Trebilcock, Michael (1996), *Exploring the Domain of Accident Law: Taking the Facts Seriously*, New York and Oxford: Oxford University Press.

Segerson, Kathleen (1987), 'Risk-sharing and Liability in the Control of Stochastic Externalities', *Marine Resource Economics*, **4**, pp. 175–92.

Segerson, Kathleen (1993), 'Liability Transfers: An Economic Assessment of Buyer and Lender Liability', *Journal of Environmental Economics and Management*, **25**, pp. S46–S63.

Segerson, Kathleen (1995), 'Liability and Penalty Structures in Policy Design', in Daniel W. Bromley (ed.), *Handbook of Environmental Economics*, Oxford and Cambridge, MA: Blackwell Publishers.

Segerson, Kathleen (2000), 'Liability for Environmental Damages', in Henk Folmer and H. Landis Gabel (eds), *Principles of Environmental and Resource Economics: A Guide for Students and Decision Makers*, Aldershot: Edward Elgar Publishers.

Shavell, Steven (1979), 'Risk-sharing and Incentives in the Principal and Agent Relationship', *Bell Journal of Economics*, **10** (1), pp. 55–73.

Shavell, Steven (1987), *Economic Analysis of Accident Law*, Cambridge, MA: Harvard University Press.

Weitzman, Martin (1974), 'Prices vs. Quantities', *Review of Economic Studies*, **41**, pp. 477–91.

Part I
Theory

The Role of Liability

[1]

PROPERTY RULES, LIABILITY RULES, AND INALIENABILITY: ONE VIEW OF THE CATHEDRAL

Guido Calabresi * and A. Douglas Melamed **

Professor Calabresi and Mr. Melamed develop a framework for legal analysis which they believe serves to integrate various legal relationships which are traditionally analyzed in separate subject areas such as Property and Torts. By using their model to suggest solutions to the pollution problem that have been overlooked by writers in the field, and by applying the model to the question of criminal sanctions, they demonstrate the utility of such an integrated approach.

I. INTRODUCTION

ONLY rarely are Property and Torts approached from a unified perspective. Recent writings by lawyers concerned with economics and by economists concerned with law suggest, however, that an attempt at integrating the various legal relationships treated by these subjects would be useful both for the beginning student and the sophisticated scholar.[1] By articulating a concept of "entitlements" which are protected by property, liability, or inalienability rules, we present one framework for such an approach.[2] We then analyze aspects of the pollution problem and of

---

* John Thomas Smith Professor of Law, Yale University. B.S. Yale, 1953; B.A. Oxford, 1955; LL.B. Yale, 1958; M.A. Oxford, 1959.

** Member of the District of Columbia Bar. B.A. Yale University, 1967; J.D. Harvard University, 1970.

[1] *See, e.g.,* Michelman, *Pollution as a Tort: A Non-Accidental Perspective on Calabresi's* COSTS, 80 YALE L.J. 647 (1971) (analysis of three alternative rules in pollution problems); Demsetz, *Toward a Theory of Property Rights,* 57 AM. ECON. REV. 347 (1967) (Vol. 2 — Papers and Proceedings) (analysis of property as a means of cost internalization which ignores liability rule alternatives).

[2] Since a fully integrated approach is probably impossible, it should be emphasized that this article concerns only one possible way of looking at and analyzing legal problems. Thus we shall not address ourselves to those fundamental legal questions which center on what institutions and what procedures are most suitable for making what decisions, except insofar as these relate directly to the problems of selecting the initial entitlements and the modes of protecting these entitlements. While we do not underrate the importance, indeed perhaps the primacy, of legal process considerations, *see* pp. 1116–17 *infra*, we are merely interested in the light

1090   *HARVARD LAW REVIEW*   [Vol. 85:1089

criminal sanctions in order to demonstrate how the model enables us to perceive relationships which have been ignored by writers in those fields.

The first issue which must be faced by any legal system is one we call the problem of "entitlement." Whenever a state is presented with the conflicting interests of two or more people, or two or more groups of people, it must decide which side to favor. Absent such a decision, access to goods, services, and life itself will be decided on the basis of "might makes right" — whoever is stronger or shrewder will win.[3] Hence the fundamental thing that law does is to decide which of the conflicting parties will be entitled to prevail. The entitlement to make noise versus the entitlement to have silence, the entitlement to pollute versus the entitlement to breathe clean air, the entitlement to have children versus the entitlement to forbid them — these are the first order of legal decisions.

Having made its initial choice, society must enforce that choice. Simply setting the entitlement does not avoid the problem of "might makes right"; a minimum of state intervention is always necessary.[4] Our conventional notions make this easy to compre-

---

that a rather different approach may shed on problems frequently looked at primarily from a legal process point of view.

As Professor Harry Wellington is fond of saying about many discussions of law, this article is meant to be only *one* of Monet's paintings of the Cathedral at Rouen. To understand the Cathedral one must see all of them. *See* G. HAMILTON, CLAUDE MONET'S PAINTINGS OF ROUEN CATHEDRAL 4–5, 19–20, 27 (1960).

[3] One could of course look at the state as simply a larger coalition of friends designed to enforce rules which merely accomplish the dominant coalition's desires. Rules of law would then be no more than "might makes right" writ large. Such a view does not strike us as plausible if for no other reason than that the state decides too many issues in response to too many different coalitions. This fact, by itself, would require a different form of analysis from that which would suffice to explain entitlements resulting from more direct and decentralized uses of "might makes right."

[4] For an excellent presentation of this general point by an economist, see Samuels, *Interrelations Between Legal and Economic Processes*, 14 J. LAW & ECON. 435 (1971).

We do not intend to imply that the state relies on force to enforce all or most entitlements. Nor do we imply that absent state intervention only force would win. The use by the state of feelings of obligation and rules of morality as means of enforcing most entitlements is not only crucial but terribly efficient. Conversely, absent the state, individuals would probably agree on rules of behavior which would govern entitlements in whole series of situations on the basis of criteria other than "might makes right." That these rules might themselves reflect the same types of considerations we will analyze as bases for legal entitlements is, of course, neither here nor there. What is important is that these "social compacts" would, no less than legal entitlements, give rise to what may be called obligations. These obligations in turn would cause people to behave in accordance with the compact in particular cases regardless of the existence of a predominant force. In this article

hend with respect to private property. If Taney owns a cabbage patch and Marshall, who is bigger, wants a cabbage, he will get it unless the state intervenes.[5] But it is not so obvious that the state must also intervene if it chooses the opposite entitlement, communal property. If large Marshall has grown some communal cabbages and chooses to deny them to small Taney, it will take state action to enforce Taney's entitlement to the communal cabbages. The same symmetry applies with respect to bodily integrity. Consider the plight of the unwilling ninety-eight-pound weakling in a state which nominally entitles him to bodily integrity but will not intervene to enforce the entitlement against a lustful Juno. Consider then the plight — absent state intervention — of the ninety-eight-pounder who desires an unwilling Juno in a state which nominally entitles everyone to use everyone else's body. The need for intervention applies in a slightly more complicated way to injuries. When a loss is left where it falls in an auto accident, it is not because God so ordained it. Rather it is because the state has granted the injurer an entitlement to be free of liability and will intervene to prevent the victim's friends, if they are stronger, from taking compensation from the injurer.[6] The loss is shifted in other cases because the state has granted an entitlement to compensation and will intervene to prevent the stronger injurer from rebuffing the victim's requests for compensation.

---

we are not concerned as much with the workings of such obligations as with the reasons which may explain the rules which themselves give rise to the obligations.

[5] "Bigger" obviously does not refer simply to size, but to the sum of an individual's resources. If Marshall's gang possesses superior brain and brawn to that of Taney, Marshall's gang will get the cabbages.

[6] Different cultures deal with the problem in different ways. Witness the following account:

"Life Insurance" Fee is 4 Bulls and $1200. Port Moresby, New Guinea. Peter Howard proved that he values his life more than four bulls and $1200. But he wants $24 and one pig in change.

Mr. Howard gave the money and livestock to members of the Jiga tribe, which had threatened to kill him because he killed a tribe member in an auto accident last October 29.

The police approved the extortion agreement after telling the 38 year old Mr. Howard they could not protect him from the sworn vengeance of the tribe, which lives at Mt. Hagen, about 350 miles Northeast of Port Moresby.

Mr. Howard, of Cambridge, England, was attacked and badly beaten by the tribesmen after the accident.

They said he would be killed unless the payment of money and bulls was made according to the tribal traditions. It was the first time a white man in New Guinea had been forced to bow to tribal laws.

After making the payment, Mr. Howard demanded to be compensated for the assault on him by the tribesmen. He said he wanted $24 and one pig. A Jiga spokesman told him the tribe would "think about it." New York Times, Feb. 16, 1972, at 17, col. 6.

The state not only has to decide whom to entitle, but it must also simultaneously make a series of equally difficult second order decisions. These decisions go to the manner in which entitlements are protected and to whether an individual is allowed to sell or trade the entitlement. In any given dispute, for example, the state must decide not only which side wins but also the kind of protection to grant. It is with the latter decisions, decisions which shape the subsequent relationship between the winner and the loser, that this article is primarily concerned. We shall consider three types of entitlements — entitlements protected by property rules, entitlements protected by liability rules, and inalienable entitlements. The categories are not, of course, absolutely distinct; but the categorization is useful since it reveals some of the reasons which lead us to protect certain entitlements in certain ways.

An entitlement is protected by a property rule to the extent that someone who wishes to remove the entitlement from its holder must buy it from him in a voluntary transaction in which the value of the entitlement is agreed upon by the seller. It is the form of entitlement which gives rise to the least amount of state intervention: once the original entitlement is decided upon, the state does not try to decide its value.[7] It lets each of the parties say how much the entitlement is worth to him, and gives the seller a veto if the buyer does not offer enough. Property rules involve a collective decision as to who is to be given an initial entitlement but not as to the value of the entitlement.

Whenever someone may destroy the initial entitlement if he is willing to pay an objectively determined value for it, an entitlement is protected by a liability rule. This value may be what it is thought the original holder of the entitlement would have sold it for. But the holder's complaint that he would have demanded more will not avail him once the objectively determined value is set. Obviously, liability rules involve an additional stage of state intervention: not only are entitlements protected, but their transfer or destruction is allowed on the basis of a value determined by some organ of the state rather than by the parties themselves.

An entitlement is inalienable to the extent that its transfer is not permitted between a willing buyer and a willing seller. The state intervenes not only to determine who is initially entitled and to determine the compensation that must be paid if the en-

---

[7] A property rule requires less state intervention only in the sense that intervention is needed to decide upon and enforce the initial entitlement but not for the separate problem of determining the value of the entitlement. Thus, if a particular property entitlement is especially difficult to enforce — for example, the right to personal security in urban areas — the actual amount of state intervention can be very high and could, perhaps, exceed that needed for some entitlements protected by easily administered liability rules.

titlement is taken or destroyed, but also to forbid its sale under some or all circumstances. Inalienability rules are thus quite different from property and liability rules. Unlike those rules, rules of inalienability not only "protect" the entitlement; they may also be viewed as limiting or regulating the grant of the entitlement itself.

It should be clear that most entitlements to most goods are mixed. Taney's house may be protected by a property rule in situations where Marshall wishes to purchase it, by a liability rule where the government decides to take it by eminent domain, and by a rule of inalienability in situations where Taney is drunk or incompetent. This article will explore two primary questions: (1) In what circumstances should we grant a particular entitlement? and (2) In what circumstances should we decide to protect that entitlement by using a property, liability, or inalienability rule?

II. The Setting of Entitlements

What are the reasons for deciding to entitle people to pollute or to entitle people to forbid pollution, to have children freely or to limit procreation, to own property or to share property? They can be grouped under three headings: economic efficiency, distributional preferences, and other justice considerations.[8]

A. Economic Efficiency

Perhaps the simplest reason for a particular entitlement is to minimize the administrative costs of enforcement. This was the reason Holmes gave for letting the costs lie where they fall in accidents unless some clear societal benefit is achieved by shifting them.[9] By itself this reason will never justify any result except that of letting the stronger win, for obviously that result minimizes enforcement costs. Nevertheless, administrative efficiency may be relevant to choosing entitlements when other reasons are taken into account. This may occur when the reasons accepted are indifferent between conflicting entitlements and one entitlement is cheaper to enforce than the others. It may also occur when the reasons are not indifferent but lead us only slightly to prefer one over another and the first is considerably more expensive to enforce than the second.

But administrative efficiency is just one aspect of the broader concept of economic efficiency. Economic efficiency asks that we

---

[8] *See generally* G. Calabresi, The Costs of Accidents 24–33 (1970) [hereinafter cited as Costs].

[9] *See* O.W. Holmes, Jr., The Common Law 76–77 (Howe ed. 1963). For a criticism of the justification as applied to accidents today, see Costs 261–63. *But cf.* Posner, *A Theory of Negligence*, 1 J. Legal Stud. 29 (1972).

choose the set of entitlements which would lead to that allocation
of resources which could not be improved in the sense that a
further change would not so improve the condition of those who
gained by it that they could compensate those who lost from it and
still be better off than before. This is often called Pareto optimality.[10] To give two examples, economic efficiency asks for that
combination of entitlements to engage in risky activities and to be
free from harm from risky activities which will most likely lead
to the lowest sum of accident costs and of costs of avoiding
accidents.[11] It asks for that form of property, private or communal, which leads to the highest product for the effort of producing.

Recently it has been argued that on certain assumptions,
usually termed the absence of transaction costs, Pareto optimality
or economic efficiency will occur regardless of the initial entitlement.[12] For this to hold, "no transaction costs" must be under-

[10] We are not here concerned with the many definitional variations which en-
circle the concept of Pareto optimality. Many of these variations stem from the
fact that unless compensation actually occurs after a change (and this itself assumes
a preexisting set of entitlements from which one makes a change to a Pareto optimal arrangement), the redistribution of wealth implicit in the change may well
make a return to the prior position also seem Pareto optimal. There are any number of variations on this theme which economists have studied at length. Since in
the world in which lawyers must live, anything close to Pareto efficiency, even if
desirable, is not attainable, these refinements need not detain us even though they
are crucial to a full understanding of the concept.

Most versions of Pareto optimality are based on the premise that individuals
know best what is best for them. Hence they assume that to determine whether
those who gain from a change could compensate those who lose, one must look
to the values the individuals themselves give to the gains and losses. Economic
efficiency may, however, present a broader notion which does not depend upon
this individualistic premise. It may be that the state, for paternalistic reasons, *see*
pp. 1113-14 *infra*, is better able to determine whether the total gain of the winners
is greater than the total loss of the losers.

[11] The word "costs" is here used in a broad way to include all the disutilities
resulting from an accident and its avoidance. As such it is not limited to monetary costs, or even to those which could in some sense be "monetizable," but rather
includes disutilities or "costs" — for instance, the loss to an individual of his leg
— the very expression of which in monetary terms would seem callous. One of the
consequences of not being able to put monetary values on some disutilities or
"costs" is that the market is of little use in gauging their worth, and this in turn
gives rise to one of the reasons why liability, or inalienability rules, rather than
property rules may be used.

[12] This proposition was first established in Coase's classic article, *The Problem
of Social Cost*, 3 J. LAW & ECON. 1 (1960), and has been refined in subsequent
literature. *See, e.g.,* Calabresi, *Transaction Costs, Resource Allocation and Liability Rules — A Comment*, 11 J. LAW & ECON. 67 (1968); Nutter, *The Coase
Theorem on Social Cost: A Footnote*, 11 J. LAW & ECON. 503 (1968). *See also*
G. STIGLER, THE THEORY OF PRICE 113 (3d ed. 1966); Mishan, *Pareto Optimality
and the Law*, 19 OXFORD ECON. PAPERS 255 (1967).

stood extremely broadly as involving both perfect knowledge and
the absence of any impediments or costs of negotiating. Negotiation costs include, for example, the cost of excluding would-be
freeloaders from the fruits of market bargains.[13] In such a fric-
tionless society, transactions would occur until no one could be
made better off as a result of further transactions without making
someone else worse off. This, we would suggest, is a necessary,
indeed a tautological, result of the definitions of Pareto optimality
and of transaction costs which we have given.

Such a result would not mean, however, that the *same* allocation of resources would exist regardless of the initial set of entitlements. Taney's willingness to pay for the right to make noise
may depend on how rich he is; Marshall's willingness to pay for
silence may depend on his wealth. In a society which entitles
Taney to make noise and which forces Marshall to buy silence
from Taney, Taney is wealthier and Marshall poorer than each
would be in a society which had the converse set of entitlements.
Depending on how Marshall's desire for silence and Taney's for
noise vary with their wealth, an entitlement to noise will result in
negotiations which will lead to a different quantum of noise than
would an entitlement to silence.[14] This variation in the quantity

---

[13] The freeloader is the person who refuses to be inoculated against smallpox
because, given the fact that almost everyone else is inoculated, the risk of smallpox
to him is less than the risk of harm from the inoculation. He is the person who
refuses to pay for a common park, though he wants it, because he believes that
others will put in enough money to make the park available to him. *See* Costs
137 n.4. The costs of excluding the freeloader from the benefits for which he re-
fused to pay may well be considerable as the two above examples should suggest.
This is especially so since these costs may include the inefficiency of pricing a good,
like the park once it exists, above its marginal cost in order to force the freeloader
to disclose his true desire to use it — thus enabling us to charge him part of the
cost of establishing it initially.

It is the capacity of the market to induce disclosure of individual preferences
which makes it theoretically possible for the market to bring about exchanges leading to Pareto optimality. But the freeloader situation is just one of many where
no such disclosure is achieved by the market. If we assume perfect knowledge,
defined more broadly than is normally done to include knowledge of individual
preferences, then such situations pose no problem. This definition of perfect knowledge, though perhaps implicit in the concept of no transaction costs, would not
only make reaching Pareto optimality easy through the market, it would make it
equally easy to establish a similar result by collective fiat.

For a further discussion of what is implied by a broad definition of no transaction costs, see note 59 *infra*. For a discussion of other devices which may induce
individuals to disclose their preferences, see note 38 *infra*.

[14] *See* Mishan, *Pareto Optimality and the Law*, 19 Oxford Econ. Papers 255
(1967). Unless Taney's and Marshall's desires for noise and silence are totally
unaffected by their wealth, that is, their desires are totally income inelastic, a
change in their wealth will alter the value each places on noise and silence and
hence will alter the outcome of their negotiations.

of noise and silence can be viewed as no more than an instance of the well accepted proposition that what is a Pareto optimal, or economically efficient, solution varies with the starting distribution of wealth. Pareto optimality is optimal *given* a distribution of wealth, but different distributions of wealth imply their own Pareto optimal allocation of resources.[15]

All this suggests why distributions of wealth may affect a society's choice of entitlements. It does not suggest why *economic efficiency* should affect the choice, if we assume an absence of any transaction costs. But no one makes an assumption of no transaction costs in practice. Like the physicist's assumption of no friction or Say's law in macro-economics, the assumption of no transaction costs may be a useful starting point, a device which helps us see how, as different elements which may be termed transaction costs become important, the goal of economic efficiency starts to prefer one allocation of entitlements over another.[16]

Since one of us has written at length on how in the presence of various types of transaction costs a society would go about deciding on a set of entitlements in the field of accident law,[17] it is enough to say here: (1) that economic efficiency standing alone would dictate that set of entitlements which favors knowledgeable choices between social benefits and the social costs of obtaining them, and between social costs and the social costs of avoiding them; (2) that this implies, in the absence of certainty as to whether a benefit is worth its costs to society, that the cost should be put on the party or activity best located to make such a cost-benefit analysis; (3) that in particular contexts like accidents or pollution this suggests putting costs on the party or activity which

---

[15] There should be no implication that a Pareto optimal solution is in some sense better than a non-Pareto optimal solution which results in a different wealth distribution. The implication is only that given the *same* wealth distribution Pareto optimal is in some meaningful sense preferable to non-Pareto optimal.

[16] *See* Demsetz, *When Does the Rule of Liability Matter?*, 1 J. LEGAL STUD. 13, 25-28 (1972); Stigler, *The Law and Economics of Public Policy: A Plea to the Scholars*, 1 J. LEGAL STUD. 1, 11-12 (1972).

The trouble with a term like "no transaction costs" is that it covers a multitude of market failures. The appropriate collective response, if the aim is to approach Pareto optimality, will vary depending on what the actual impediments to full bargaining are in any given cases. Occasionally the appropriate response may be to ignore the impediments. If the impediments are merely the administrative costs of establishing a market, it may be that doing nothing is preferable to attempting to correct for these costs because the administrative costs of collective action may be even greater. Similarly, if the impediments are due to a failure of the market to cause an accurate disclosure of freeloaders' preferences it may be that the collective can do no better.

[17] *See* COSTS 135-97.

can most cheaply avoid them; (4) that in the absence of certainty as to who that party or activity is, the costs should be put on the party or activity which can with the lowest transaction costs act in the market to correct an error in entitlements by inducing the party who can avoid social costs most cheaply to do so; [18] and (5) that since we are in an area where by hypothesis markets do not work perfectly — there are transaction costs — a decision will often have to be made on whether market transactions or collective fiat is most likely to bring us closer to the Pareto optimal result the "perfect" market would reach.[19]

Complex though this summary may suggest the entitlement choice to be, in practice the criteria it represents will frequently indicate which allocations of entitlements are most likely to lead to optimal market judgments between having an extra car or taking a train, getting an extra cabbage and spending less time working in the hot sun, and having more widgets and breathing the pollution that widget production implies. Economic efficiency is not, however, the sole reason which induces a society to select a

---

[18] In *The Costs of Accidents*, the criteria here summarized are discussed at length and broken down into subcriteria which deal with the avoidance of different types of externalization and with the finding of the "best briber." Such detailed analysis is necessary to the application of the criteria to any specific area of law. At the level of generality of this article it did not seem to us necessary.

[19] In accident law this election takes the form of a choice between general or market deterrence and specific deterrence, in which the permitted level and manner of accident causing activities is determined collectively. For example, society may decide to grant an entitlement to drive and an entitlement to be compensated for accidents resulting from driving, and allow decisions by individual parties to determine the level and manner of driving. But a greater degree of specific deterrence could be achieved by selecting a different set of initial entitlements in order to accord with a collective cost-benefit analysis — by, for example, prohibiting cars of more than a certain horsepower.

The primary disadvantage of specific deterrence, as compared with general deterrence, is that it requires the central decisionmaker not only to determine the costs of any given activity, but also to measure its benefits, in order to determine the optimum level of activity. It is exceedingly difficult and exceedingly costly for any centralized decisionmaker to be fully informed of the costs and benefits of a wide range of activities. The irony is that collective fiat functions best in a world of costless perfect information; yet in a world of costless transactions, including costless information, the optimum allocation would be reached by market transactions, and the need to consider the alternative of collective fiat would not arise. One could, however, view the irony conversely, and say that the market works best under assumptions of perfect knowledge where collective fiat would work perfectly, rendering the market unnecessary. The fact that both market and collective determinations face difficulties in achieving the Pareto optimal result which perfect knowledge and no transaction costs would permit does not mean that the same difficulties are always as great for the two approaches. Thus, there are many situations in which we can assume fairly confidently that the market will do better than a collective decider, and there are situations where we can assume the opposite to be true. *See* COSTS 103–13.

set of entitlements. Wealth distribution preferences are another, and thus it is to distributional grounds for different entitlements to which we must now turn.

B. *Distributional Goals*

There are, we would suggest, at least two types of distributional concerns which may affect the choice of entitlements. These involve distribution of wealth itself and distribution of certain specific goods, which have sometimes been called merit goods.

All societies have wealth distribution preferences. They are, nonetheless, harder to talk about than are efficiency goals. For efficiency goals can be discussed in terms of a general concept like Pareto optimality to which exceptions — like paternalism — can be noted.[20] Distributional preferences, on the other hand, cannot usefully be discussed in a single conceptual framework. There are some fairly broadly accepted preferences — caste preferences in one society, more rather than less equality in another society. There are also preferences which are linked to dynamic efficiency concepts — producers ought to be rewarded since they will cause everyone to be better off in the end. Finally, there are a myriad of highly individualized preferences as to who should be richer and who poorer which need not have anything to do with either equality or efficiency — silence lovers should be richer than noise lovers because they are worthier.[21]

Difficult as wealth distribution preferences are to analyze, it should be obvious that they play a crucial role in the setting of entitlements. For the placement of entitlements has a fundamental effect on a society's distribution of wealth. It is not enough, if a society wishes absolute equality, to start everyone off with the same amount of money. A financially egalitarian society which gives individuals the right to make noise immediately makes the would-be noisemaker richer than the silence

---

[20] For a discussion of paternalism, see pp. 1113–14 *infra.*

[21] The first group of preferences roughly coincides with those notions which writers like Fletcher, following Aristotle, term distributive justice. The second and third groups, instead, presumably deal with Fletcher's "corrective" justice — rewards based on what people do rather than what they are. *See* Fletcher, *Fairness and Utility in Tort Theory*, 85 HARV. L. REV. 537, 547 n.40 (1972).

Within the "corrective" justice category our second and third groupings distinguish those preferences which are transparently linked to efficiency notions from those whose roots are less obvious. If there were a generally accepted theory of desserts, one could speak in general terms about the role the third group plays just as one tends to speak about the role of either the first or second group. We do not believe that an adequate theory of desserts — even if possible — is currently available. *See also* pp. 1102–05 *infra.*

loving hermit.[22] Similarly, a society which entitles the person with brains to keep what his shrewdness gains him implies a different distribution of wealth from a society which demands from each according to his relative ability but gives to each according to his relative desire. One can go further and consider that a beautiful woman or handsome man is better off in a society which entitles individuals to bodily integrity than in one which gives everybody use of all the beauty available.

The consequence of this is that it is very difficult to imagine a society in which there is complete equality of wealth. Such a society either would have to consist of people who were all precisely the same, or it would have to compensate for differences in wealth caused by a given set of entitlements. The former is, of course, ridiculous, even granting cloning. And the latter would be very difficult; it would involve knowing what everyone's tastes were and taxing every holder of an entitlement at a rate sufficient to make up for the benefits the entitlement gave him. For example, it would involve taxing everyone with an entitlement to private use of his beauty or brains sufficiently to compensate those less favorably endowed but who nonetheless desired what beauty or brains could get.

If perfect equality is impossible, a society must choose what entitlements it wishes to have on the basis of criteria other than perfect equality. In doing this, a society often has a choice of methods, and the method chosen will have important distributional implications. Society can, for instance, give an entitlement away free and then, by paying the holders of the entitlement to limit their use of it, protect those who are injured by the free entitlement. Conversely, it can allow people to do a given thing only if they buy the right from the government. Thus a society can decide whether to entitle people to have children and then induce them to exercise control in procreating, or to require people to buy the right to have children in the first place. A society can also decide whether to entitle people to be free of military service and then induce them to join up, or to require all to serve but enable each to buy his way out. Which entitlement a society decides to sell, and which it decides to give away, will likely depend in part on which determination promotes the wealth distribution that society favors.[23]

---

[22] This assumes that there is not enough space for the noisemaker and the silence lover to coexist without intruding upon one another. In other words, this assumes that we are dealing with a problem of allocation of scarce resources; if we were not, there would be no need to set the initial entitlement. *See generally* Mishan, *supra* note 12.

[23] Any entitlement given away free implies a converse which must be paid for. For all those who like children, there are those who are disturbed by children;

If the choice of entitlements affects wealth distribution generally, it also affects the chances that people will obtain what have sometimes been called merit goods.[24] Whenever a society wishes to maximize the chances that individuals will have at least a minimum endowment of certain particular goods — education, clothes, bodily integrity — the society is likely to begin by giving the individuals an entitlement to them. If the society deems such an endowment to be essential regardless of individual desires, it will, of course, make the entitlement inalienable.[25] Why, however, would a society entitle individuals to specific goods rather than to money with which they càn buy what they wish, unless it deems that it can decide better than the individuals what benefits them and society; unless, in other words, it wishes to make the entitlement inalienable?

We have seen that an entitlement to a good or to its converse is essentially inevitable.[26] We either are entitled to have silence or entitled to make noise in a given set of circumstances. We either have the right to our own property or body or the right to share others' property or bodies. We may buy or sell our-

---

for all those who detest armies, there are those who want what armies accomplish. Otherwise, we would have no scarce resource problem and hence no entitlement problem. Therefore, one cannot simply say that giving away an entitlement free is progressive while selling it is regressive. It is true that the more "free" goods there are the less inequality of wealth there is, if everything else has stayed the same. But if a free entitlement implies a costly converse, entitlements are *not* in this sense free goods. And the issue of their progressivity and regressivity must depend on the relative desire for the entitlement as against its converse on the part of the rich and the poor.

Strictly speaking, even this is true only if the money needed to finance the alternative plans, or made available to the government as a result of the plans, is raised and spent in a way that is precisely neutral with respect to wealth distribution. The point is simply this: even a highly regressive tax will aid wealth equality if the money it raises is all spent to benefit the poorest citizens. And even a system of outdoor relief for the idle rich aids wealth equality if the funds it requires are raised by taxing only the wealthiest of the wealthy. Thus whenever one speaks of a taxing program, spending program, or a system of entitlements as progressive or regressive, one must be assuming that the way the money is spent (if it is a tax) or the way it is raised (if it is a spending program) does not counter the distributive effect of the program itself.

[24] *Cf.* R. Musgrave, The Theory of Public Finance 13–14 (1959).

[25] The commonly given reasons why a society may choose to do this are discussed *infra* at pp. 1111–15. All of them are, of course, reasons which explain why such goods are often categorized as merit goods. When a society subsidizes a good it makes a similar decision based on similar grounds. Presumably, however, in such cases the grounds only justify making possession of the good less costly than would be the case without government intervention, rather than making possession of the good inevitable.

[26] This is true unless we are prepared to let the parties settle the matter on the basis of might makes right, which itself may also be viewed as a form of entitlement.

selves into the opposite position, but we must start somewhere. Under these circumstances, a society which prefers people to have silence, or own property, or have bodily integrity, but which does not hold the grounds for its preference to be sufficiently strong to justify overriding contrary preferences by individuals, will give such entitlements according to the collective preference, even though it will allow them to be sold thereafter.

Whenever transactions to sell or buy entitlements are very expensive, such an initial entitlement decision will be nearly as effective in assuring that individuals will have the merit good as would be making the entitlement inalienable. Since coercion is inherent because of the fact that a good cannot practically be bought or sold, a society can choose only whether to make an individual have the good, by giving it to him, or to prevent him from getting it by giving him money instead.[27] In such circumstances society will pick the entitlement it deems favorable to the general welfare and not worry about coercion or alienability; it has increased the chances that individuals will have a particular good without increasing the degree of coercion imposed on individuals.[28] A common example of this may occur where the good involved is the present certainty of being able to buy a future benefit and where a futures market in that good is too expensive to be feasible.[29]

---

[27] For a discussion of this inevitable, and therefore irrelevant degree of coercion in the accident context, see COSTS 50–55, 161–73.

[28] The situation is analogous to that which involves choosing between systems of allocation of accident costs which minimize rapid changes in wealth, through spreading, and those that do not. Indeed, if the avoidance of rapid changes in wealth is, itself, viewed as a merit good, the analogy is complete. In the accident field a great deal of attention has been devoted to the problem of rapid changes in wealth. *See, e.g.,* Morris & Paul, *The Financial Impact of Automobile Accidents,* 110 U. PA. L. REV. 913, 924 (1962). *But see* W. BLUM & H. KALVEN, PUBLIC LAW PERSPECTIVES ON A PRIVATE LAW PROBLEM — AUTO COMPENSATION PLANS (1965).

[29] A full discussion of this justification for the giving of goods in "kind" is well beyond the scope of this article. An indication of what is involved may be in order, however. One of the many reasons why the right to vote is given in kind instead of giving individuals that amount of money which would assure them, in a voteless society, of all the benefits which having the vote gives them, is that at any given time the price of those benefits in the future is totally uncertain and, therefore, virtually no amount of money would assure individuals of having those future benefits. This would not be the case if an entrepreneur could be counted on to guarantee those future benefits in exchange for a present money payment. That is what happens in a futures market for, say, sow's bellies. The degree of uncertainty in the cost of the future benefits of the vote is such, however, that a futures market is either not feasible, or, what is the same thing, much too costly to be worthwhile. In such circumstances the nonmarket alternative of giving of the good in kind seems more efficient. Many of the merit goods which are, in fact, given in kind in our society — for example, education — share this character-

1102   *HARVARD LAW REVIEW*   [Vol. 85:1089]

C. *Other Justice Reasons*

The final reasons for a society's choice of initial entitlements we termed other justice reasons, and we may as well admit that it is hard to know what content can be poured into that term, at least given the very broad definitions of economic efficiency and distributional goals that we have used. Is there, in other words, a reason which would influence a society's choice of initial entitlements that cannot be comprehended in terms of efficiency and distribution? A couple of examples will indicate the problem.

Taney likes noise; Marshall likes silence. They are, let us assume, inevitably neighbors. Let us also assume there are no transaction costs which may impede negotiations between them. Let us assume finally that we do not know Taney's and Marshall's wealth or, indeed, anything else about them. Under these circumstances we know that Pareto optimality — economic efficiency — will be reached whether we choose an entitlement to make noise or to have silence. We also are indifferent, from a general wealth distribution point of view, as to what the initial entitlement is because we do not know whether it will lead to greater equality or inequality. This leaves us with only two reasons on which to base our choice of entitlement. The first is the relative worthiness of silence lovers and noise lovers. The second is the consistency of the choice, or its apparent consistency, with other entitlements in the society.

The first sounds appealing, and it sounds like justice. But it is hard to deal with. Why, unless our choice affects other people, should we prefer one to another?[30] To say that we wish, for

---

istic of involving present rights to future benefits in circumstances where a futures market does not exist and at first glance seems very difficult to organize cheaply. We do not suggest that this is the sole explanation for the way voting is handled in our society. For instance, it does not explain why the vote cannot be sold. (An explanation for that may be found in the fact that Taney's benefit from the vote may depend on Marshall's not having more of it than he.) It does, however, add another, not frequently given, explanation for the occasional allocation of goods rather than money to individuals.

[30] The usual answer is religious or transcendental reasons. But this answer presents problems. If it means that Chase, a third party, suffers if the noise-maker is preferred, because Chase's faith deems silence worthier than noise, then third parties *are* affected by the choice. Chase suffers; there is an external effect. But that possibility was excluded in our hypothetical. In practice such external effects, often called moralisms, are extremely common and greatly complicate the reaching of Pareto optimality. *See* pp. 1112–13 *infra*.

Religious or transcendental reasons may, however, be of another kind. Chase may prefer silence not because he himself cares, not because he suffers if noise-makers get the best of it when his faith deems silence lovers to be worthier, but because he believes God suffers if such a choice is made. No amount of compensation will help Chase in this situation since he suffers nothing which can be

instance, to make the silence lover relatively wealthier because we prefer silence is no answer, for that is simply a restatement of the question. Of course, if the choice does affect people other than Marshall and Taney, then we have a valid basis for decision. But the fact that such external effects are extremely common and greatly influence our choices does not help us much. It does suggest that the reaching of Pareto optimality is, in practice, a very complex matter precisely because of the existence of many external effects which markets find hard to deal with. And it also suggests that there often are general distributional considerations between Taney-Marshall and the rest of the world which affect the choice of entitlement. It in no way suggests, however, that there is more to the choice between Taney-Marshall than Pareto optimality and distributional concerns. In other words, if the assumptions of no transaction costs and indifference as to distributional considerations, made as between Taney and Marshall (where they are unlikely), could be made as to the world as a whole (where they are impossible), the fact that the choice between Taney's noise or Marshall's silence might affect other people would give us no guidance. Thus what sounds like a justice standard is simply a handy way of importing efficiency and distributional notions too diverse and general in their effect to be analyzed fully in the decision of a specific case.

The second sounds appealing in a different way since it sounds like "treating like cases alike." If the entitlement to make noise in other people's ears for one's pleasure is viewed by society as closely akin to the entitlement to beat up people for one's pleasure, and if good efficiency and distributional reasons exist for not allowing people to beat up others for sheer pleasure, then there may be a good reason for preferring an entitlement to silence rather than noise in the Taney-Marshall case. Because the two entitlements are apparently consistent, the entitlement to silence strengthens the entitlement to be free from gratuitous beatings which we assumed was based on good efficiency and distributional reasons.[31] It does so by lowering the enforcement costs of the entitlement to be free from gratuitous beatings; the entitlement to silence reiterates and reinforces the values protected by the entitlement to be free from gratuitous beatings and reduces the number of discriminations people must make between one activity and another, thus simplifying the task of obedience.

compensated, and compensating God for the wrong choice is not feasible. Such a reason for a choice is, we would suggest, a true nonefficiency, nondistribution reason. Whether it actually ever plays a role may well be another matter.

[31] The opposite would be true if noisemaking were thought to be akin to industry, and drive and silence to lethargy and laziness, and we had good efficiency or distributional reasons for preferring industry to lethargy.

The problem with this rationale for the choice is that it too comes down to efficiency and distributional reasons. We prefer the silence maker because *that* entitlement, even though it does not of itself affect the desired wealth distribution or lead us away from efficiency in the Taney-Marshall case, helps us to reach those goals in other situations where there are transaction costs or where we do have distributional preferences. It does this because people do not realize that the consistency is only apparent. If we could explain to them, both rationally and emotionally, the efficiency and distributional reasons why gratuitous beating up of people was inefficient or led to undesirable wealth distribution, and if we could also explain to them why an entitlement to noise rather than silence in the Taney-Marshall case would not lead to either inefficiency or maldistribution, then the secondary undermining of the entitlement to bodily integrity would not occur. It is only because it is expensive, even if feasible, to point out the difference between the two situations that the apparent similarity between them remains. And avoiding this kind of needless expense, while a very good reason for making choices, is clearly no more than a part of the economic efficiency goal.[32]

Still we should admit that explaining entitlements solely in terms of efficiency and distribution, in even their broadest terms, does not seem wholly satisfactory. The reasons for this are worth at least passing mention. The reason that we have so far explained entitlements simply in terms of efficiency and distribution is ultimately tautological. We defined distribution as covering *all* the reasons, other than efficiency, on the basis of which we might prefer to make Taney *wealthier* than Marshall. So defined, there obviously was no room for any other reasons. Distributional grounds covered broadly accepted ideas like "equality" or, in some societies, "caste preference," and highly specific ones like "favoring the silence lover." We used this definition because there is a utility in lumping together all those reasons for preferring Taney to Marshall which cannot be explained in terms of a desire to make everyone better off, and in contrasting them with efficiency reasons, whether Paretian or not, which can be so explained.

Lumping them together, however, has some analytical dis-

---

[32] We do not mean to underestimate the importance of apparent consistency as a ground for entitlements. Far from it, it is likely that a society often prefers an entitlement which even leads to mild inefficiencies or maldistribution of wealth between, say, Taney and Marshall, because that entitlement tends to support other entitlements which are crucial in terms of efficiency or wealth distribution in the society at large and because the cost of convincing people that the situations are, in fact, different is not worth the gain which would be obtained in the Taney-Marshall case.

advantages. It seems to assume that we cannot say any more about the reasons for some distributional preferences than about others. For instance, it seems to assume a similar universality of support for recognizing silence lovers as relatively worthier as there is for recognizing the relative desirability of equality. And that, surely, is a dangerous assumption. To avoid this danger the term "distribution" is often limited to relatively few broad reasons, like equality. And those preferences which cannot be easily explained in terms of these relatively few broadly accepted distributional preferences, or in terms of efficiency, are termed justice reasons. The difficulty with this locution is that it sometimes is taken to imply that the moral gloss of justice is reserved for these residual preferences and does not apply to the broader distributional preferences or to efficiency based preferences. And surely this is wrong, for many entitlements that properly are described as based on justice in our society can easily be explained in terms either of broad distributional preferences like equality or of efficiency or of both.

By using the term *"other* justice reasons" we hope to avoid this difficulty and emphasize that justice notions adhere to efficiency and broad distributional preferences as well as to other more idiosyncratic ones. To the extent that one is concerned with contrasting the difference between efficiency and other reasons for certain entitlements, the bipolar efficiency-distribution locution is all that is needed. To the extent that one wishes to delve either into reasons which, though possibly originally linked to efficiency, have now a life of their own, or into reasons which, though distributional, cannot be described in terms of broad principles like equality, then a locution which allows for "other justice reasons" seems more useful.[33]

III. Rules For Protecting and Regulating Entitlements

Whenever society chooses an initial entitlement it must also determine whether to protect the entitlement by property rules, by liability rules, or by rules of inalienability. In our framework, much of what is generally called private property can be viewed as an entitlement which is protected by a property rule. No one can take the entitlement to private property from the holder unless the holder sells it willingly and at the price at which he subjectively values the property. Yet a nuisance with sufficient public utility to avoid injunction has, in effect, the right to take property with compensation. In such a circumstance the entitlement to the property is protected only by what we call a liability rule:

---

[33] *But see* Fletcher, *supra* note 21, at 547 n.40.

an external, objective standard of value is used to facilitate the transfer of the entitlement from the holder to the nuisance.[34] Finally, in some instances we will not allow the sale of the property at all, that is, we will occasionally make the entitlement inalienable.

This section will consider the circumstances in which society will employ these three rules to solve situations of conflict. Because the property rule and the liability rule are closely related and depend for their application on the shortcomings of each other, we treat them together. We discuss inalienability separately.

A. Property and Liability Rules

Why cannot a society simply decide on the basis of the already mentioned criteria who should receive any given entitlement, and then let its transfer occur only through a voluntary negotiation? Why, in other words, cannot society limit itself to the property rule? To do this it would need only to protect and enforce the initial entitlements from all attacks, perhaps through criminal sanctions,[35] and to enforce voluntary contracts for their transfer. Why do we need liability rules at all?

In terms of economic efficiency the reason is easy enough to see. Often the cost of establishing the value of an initial entitlement by negotiation is so great that even though a transfer of the entitlement would benefit all concerned, such a transfer will not occur. If a collective determination of the value were available instead, the beneficial transfer would quickly come about.

Eminent domain is a good example. A park where Guidacres, a tract of land owned by 1,000 owners in 1,000 parcels, now sits would, let us assume, benefit a neighboring town enough so that the 100,000 citizens of the town would each be willing to pay an average of $100 to have it. The park is Pareto desirable if the owners of the tracts of land in Guidacres actually value their entitlements at less than $10,000,000 or an average of $10,000 a tract. Let us assume that in fact the parcels are all the same and all the owners value them at $8,000. On this assumption, the park is, in economic efficiency terms, desirable — in values foregone it costs $8,000,000 and is worth $10,000,000 to the buyers. And yet it may well not be established. If enough of the owners hold-out for more than $10,000 in order to get a share of the $2,000,000 that they guess the buyers are willing to pay over the

---

[34] *See, e.g.,* Boomer v. Atlantic Cement Co., 26 N.Y.2d 219, 309 N.Y.S.2d 312, 257 N.E.2d 870 (1970) (avoidance of injunction conditioned on payment of permanent damages to plaintiffs).

[35] The relationship between criminal sanctions and property entitlements will be examined *infra* pp. 1124–27.

value which the sellers in actuality attach, the price demanded will be more than $10,000,000 and no park will result. The sellers have an incentive to hide their true valuation and the market will not succeed in establishing it.

An equally valid example could be made on the buying side. Suppose the sellers of Guidacres have agreed to a sales price of $8,000,000 (they are all relatives and at a family banquet decided that trying to hold-out would leave them all losers). It does not follow that the buyers can raise that much even though each of 100,000 citizens *in fact* values the park at $100. Some citizens may try to free-load and say the park is only worth $50 or even nothing to them, hoping that enough others will admit to a higher desire and make up the $8,000,000 price. Again there is no reason to believe that a market, a decentralized system of valuing, will cause people to express their true valuations and hence yield results which all would *in fact* agree are desirable.

Whenever this is the case an argument can readily be made for moving from a property rule to a liability rule. If society can remove from the market the valuation of each tract of land, decide the value collectively, and impose it, then the holdout problem is gone. Similarly, if society can value collectively each individual citizen's desire to have a park and charge him a "benefits" tax based upon it, the freeloader problem is gone. If the sum of the taxes is greater than the sum of the compensation awards, the park will result.

Of course, one can conceive of situations where it might be cheap to exclude all the freeloaders from the park, or to ration the park's use in accordance with original willingness to pay. In such cases the incentive to free-load might be eliminated. But such exclusions, even if possible, are usually not cheap. And the same may be the case for market methods which might avoid the holdout problem on the seller side.

Moreover, even if holdout and freeloader problems can be met feasibly by the market, an argument may remain for employing a liability rule. Assume that in our hypothetical, freeloaders can be excluded at the cost of $1,000,000 and that all owners of tracts in Guidacres can be convinced, by the use of $500,000 worth of advertising and cocktail parties, that a sale will only occur if they reveal their true land valuations. Since $8,000,000 plus $1,500,000 is less than $10,000,000, the park will be established. But if collective valuation of the tracts and of the benefits of the prospective park would have cost less than $1,500,000, it would have been inefficient to establish the park through the market — a market which was not worth having would have been paid for.[36]

---

[36] It may be argued that, given imperfect knowledge, the market is preferable because it places a limit — the cost of establishing a market — on the size of the

1108   *HARVARD LAW REVIEW*   [Vol. 85:1089

Of course, the problems with liability rules are equally real. We cannot be at all sure that landowner Taney is lying or holding out when he says his land is worth $12,000 to him. The fact that several neighbors sold identical tracts for $10,000 does not help us very much; Taney may be sentimentally attached to his land. As a result, eminent domain may grossly undervalue what Taney would actually sell for, even if it sought to give him his true valuation of his tract. In practice, it is so hard to determine Taney's true valuation that eminent domain simply gives him what the land is worth "objectively," in the full knowledge that this may result in over or under compensation. The same is true on the buyer side. "Benefits" taxes rarely attempt, let alone succeed, in gauging the individual citizen's relative desire for the alleged benefit. They are justified because, even if they do not accurately measure each individual's desire for the benefit, the market alternative seems worse. For example, fifty different households may place different values on a new sidewalk that is to abut all the properties. Nevertheless, because it is too difficult, even if possible, to gauge each household's valuation, we usually tax each household an equal amount.

The example of eminent domain is simply one of numerous instances in which society uses liability rules. Accidents is another. If we were to give victims a property entitlement not to be accidentally injured we would have to require all who engage in activities that may injure individuals to negotiate with them before an accident, and to buy the right to knock off an arm or a leg.[37] Such pre-accident negotiations would be extremely ex-

---

possible loss, while the costs of coercion cannot be defined and may be infinite. This may be true in some situations but need not always be the case. If, for example, we know that the holdouts would sell for $500,000 more than is offered, because they recently offered the land at that higher price, coercing them to sell at an objectively determined price between the seller's offer and the purchaser's offer cannot result in more than $500,000 in harm. Thus, the costs of coercion would also not be infinite. Nor is it an answer to say that the man who would sell for a higher price but is coerced for a lower one suffers an indefinite nonmonetary cost in addition to the price differential simply because he is coerced and resents it. For while this may well be true, the same nonmonetary resentment may also exist in those who desire the park and do not get it because the market is unable to pay off those who are holding out for a greater than actual value. In other words, unascertainable resentment costs may exist as a result of either coercion or market failure.

[37] Even if it were possible, it should be clear that the good which would be sold would not be the same as the good actually taken. If Taney waives for $1,000 the right to recover for the loss of a leg, should he ever lose it, he is negotiating for a joint product which can be described as his "desire or aversion to gamble" and "his desire to have a leg." The product actually taken, however, is the leg. That the two goods are different can be seen from the fact that a man who demands $1,000 for a 1 in a 1,000 chance of losing a leg may well demand more

pensive, often prohibitively so.[38] To require them would thus preclude many activities that might, in fact, be worth having. And, after an accident, the loser of the arm or leg can always very plausibly deny that he would have sold it at the price the buyer would have offered. Indeed, where negotiations after an accident do occur — for instance pretrial settlements — it is largely because the alternative is the collective valuation of the damages.

It is not our object here to outline all the theoretical, let alone the practical, situations where markets may be too expensive or fail and where collective valuations seem more desirable. Economic literature has many times surrounded the issue if it has not

than $100,000 for a 1 in 10 chance of losing it, and more than $1,000,000 for the sale of his leg to someone who needs it for a transplant. *See generally* Costs 88–94. This does not mean that the result of such transactions, if feasible, would *necessarily* be worse than the result of collective valuations. It simply means that the situation, even if feasible, is different from the one in which Taney sells his house for a given price.

[38] Such preaccident negotiations between potential injurers and victims are at times not too costly. Thus in a typical products liability situation the cost of negotiation over a potential injury need not be prohibitive. The seller of a rotary lawn mower may offer to sell at a reduced price if the buyer agrees not to sue should he be injured. Nevertheless, society often forbids such negotiations because it deems them undesirable. This may occur because of the reasons suggested in note 37 *supra*, or for any of the other reasons which cause us to make some entitlements wholly or partly inalienable, *see infra* pp. 1111–15.

Attempts have been made to deal with situations where ex ante negotiations are not feasible by fiscal devices designed to cause people to reveal their preferences. One of these contemplates requiring individuals to declare a value on their properties, or even limbs, and paying a tax on the self assessed value. That value would be the value of the good if it were taken in an accident or by eminent domain. *See generally* N. Tideman, Three Approaches to Improving Urban Land Use, ch. III (1969) (unpublished Ph.D. dissertation submitted to U. of Chicago Economics Department, on file in Yale Law Library). Of course, if the good is only taken as a result of an accident or eminent domain, the problem of gambling described in note 37 *supra* would remain. If, instead, the property or limb could be taken at will at the self assessed value, serious problems would arise from the fact that there are enormous nonmonetizable, as well as monetizable, costs involved in making people put money values on all their belongings and limbs.

An additional, though perhaps solvable, problem with self assessed taxes is the fact that the taking price would exclude any consumer surplus. This may have no significance in terms of economic efficiency, but if the existence of consumer surplus in many market transactions is thought to have, on the whole, a favorable wealth distribution effect, it might well be a reason why self assessed taxes are viewed with skepticism. *Cf.* Little, Self-Assessed Valuations: A Critique (1972) (unpublished paper, on file in Harvard Law School Library). The reader might reasonably wonder why many individuals who view self assessed taxes with skepticism show no similar concerns for what may be a very similar device, optional first party insurance covering pain and suffering damages in automobile injuries. *See, e.g.,* Calabresi, *The New York Plan: A Free Choice Modification,* 71 Colum. L. Rev. 267, 268 n.6 (1971).

always zeroed in on it in ways intelligible to lawyers.[39] It is enough for our purposes to note that a very common reason, perhaps the most common one, for employing a liability rule rather than a property rule to protect an entitlement is that market valuation of the entitlement is deemed inefficient, that is, it is either unavailable or too expensive compared to a collective valuation.

We should also recognize that efficiency is not the sole ground for employing liability rules rather than property rules. Just as the initial entitlement is often decided upon for distributional reasons, so too the choice of a liability rule is often made because it facilitates a combination of efficiency and distributive results which would be difficult to achieve under a property rule. As we shall see in the pollution context, use of a liability rule may allow us to accomplish a measure of redistribution that could only be attained at a prohibitive sacrifice of efficiency if we employed a corresponding property rule.

More often, once a liability rule is decided upon, perhaps for efficiency reasons, it is then employed to favor distributive goals as well. Again accidents and eminent domain are good examples. In both of these areas the compensation given has clearly varied with society's distributive goals, and cannot be readily explained in terms of giving the victim, as nearly as possible, an objectively determined equivalent of the price at which he would have sold what was taken from him.

It should not be surprising that this is often so, even if the original reason for a liability rule is an efficiency one. For distributional goals are expensive and difficult to achieve, and the collective valuation involved in liability rules readily lends itself to promoting distributional goals.[40] This does not mean that distributional goals are always well served in this way. Ad hoc decision-making is always troublesome, and the difficulties are especially acute when the settlement of conflicts between parties is used as a vehicle for the solution of more widespread distributional problems. Nevertheless, distributional objectives may be better attained in this way than otherwise.[41]

---

[39] For a good discussion of market failure which is intelligible to lawyers, see Bator, *The Anatomy of Market Failure*, 72 Q. J. ECON. 351 (1958).

[40] Collective valuation of costs also makes it easier to value the costs at what the society thinks they should be valued by the victim instead of at what the victim would value them in a free market if such a market were feasible. The former kind of valuation is, of course, paternalism. This does not mean it is undesirable; the danger is that paternalism which is not desirable will enter mindlessly into the cost valuation because the valuation is necessarily done collectively. See pp. 1113–14 *infra*.

[41] For suggestions that at times systematic distributional programs may cause

B. *Inalienable Entitlements*

Thus far we have focused on the questions of when society should protect an entitlement by property or liability rules. However, there remain many entitlements which involve a still greater degree of societal intervention: the law not only decides who is to own something and what price is to be paid for it if it is taken or destroyed, but also regulates its sale — by, for example, prescribing preconditions for a valid sale or forbidding a sale altogether. Although these rules of inalienability are substantially different from the property and liability rules, their use can be analyzed in terms of the same efficiency and distributional goals that underlie the use of the other two rules.

While at first glance efficiency objectives may seem undermined by limitations on the ability to engage in transactions, closer analysis suggests that there are instances, perhaps many, in which economic efficiency is more closely approximated by such limitations. This might occur when a transaction would create significant externalities — costs to third parties.

For instance, if Taney were allowed to sell his land to Chase, a polluter, he would injure his neighbor Marshall by lowering the value of Marshall's land. Conceivably, Marshall could pay Taney not to sell his land; but, because there are many injured Marshalls, freeloader and information costs make such transactions practically impossible. The state could protect the Marshalls and yet facilitate the sale of the land by giving the Marshalls an entitlement to prevent Taney's sale to Chase but only protecting the entitlement by a liability rule. It might, for instance, charge an excise tax on all sales of land to polluters equal to its estimate of the external cost to the Marshalls of the sale. But where there are so many injured Marshalls that the price required under the liability rule is likely to be high enough so that no one would be willing to pay it, then setting up the machinery for collective valuation will be wasteful. Barring the sale to polluters will be the most efficient result because it is clear that avoiding pollution is cheaper than paying its costs — including its costs to the Marshalls.

Another instance in which external costs may justify inalienability occurs when external costs do not lend themselves to collective measurement which is acceptably objective and nonarbitrary. This nonmonetizability is characteristic of one category of external costs which, as a practical matter, seems frequently to

greater misallocation of resources than ad hoc decisions, see Ackerman, *Regulating Slum Housing Markets on Behalf of the Poor: Of Housing Codes, Housing Subsidies and Income Redistribution Policy*, 80 YALE L.J. 1093, 1157–97 (1971); Calabresi, *supra* note 12.

1112   *HARVARD LAW REVIEW*   [Vol. 85:1089

lead us to rules of inalienability. Such external costs are often called moralisms.

If Taney is allowed to sell himself into slavery, or to take undue risks of becoming penniless, or to sell a kidney, Marshall may be harmed, simply because Marshall is a sensitive man who is made unhappy by seeing slaves, paupers, or persons who die because they have sold a kidney. Again Marshall could pay Taney not to sell his freedom to Chase the slaveowner; but again, because Marshall is not one but many individuals, freeloader and information costs make such transactions practically impossible. Again, it might seem that the state could intervene by objectively valuing the external cost to Marshall and requiring Chase to pay that cost. But since the external cost to Marshall does not lend itself to an acceptable objective measurement, such liability rules are not appropriate.

In the case of Taney selling land to Chase, the polluter, they were inappropriate because we *knew* that the costs to Taney and the Marshalls exceeded the benefits to Chase. Here, though we are not certain of how a cost-benefit analysis would come out, liability rules are inappropriate because any monetization is, by hypothesis, out of the question. The state must, therefore, either ignore the external costs to Marshall, or if it judges them great enough, forbid the transaction that gave rise to them by making Taney's freedom inalienable.[42]

Obviously we will not always value the external harm of a moralism enough to prohibit the sale.[43] And obviously also, external costs other than moralisms may be sufficiently hard to value to make rules of inalienability appropriate in certain circumstances; this reason for rules of inalienability, however, does seem most often germane in situations where moralisms are involved.[44]

---

[42] Granting Taney an inalienable right to be free is in many respects the same as granting most of the people a property entitlement to keep Taney free. The people may bargain and decide to surrender their entitlement, *i.e.*, to change the law, but there are limits on the feasibility of transactions of this sort which make the public's entitlements virtually inalienable.

[43] For example, I am allowed to buy and read whatever books I like, or to sell my house to whomever I choose, regardless of whether my doing so makes my neighbors unhappy. These entitlements could be a form of self paternalism on the part of the neighbors who fear a different rule would harm them more in the long run, or they could be selected because they strengthen seemingly similar entitlements. *See* pp. 1103–04 *supra*. But they may also reflect a judgment that the injury suffered by my neighbors results from a moralism shared by them but not so widespread as to make more efficient their being given an entitlement to prevent my transaction. In other words, people who are hurt by my transaction are the cheapest cost avoiders, *i.e.*, the cost to them of my being allowed to transact freely is less than the cost to me and others similarly situated of a converse entitlement.

[44] The fact that society may make an entitlement inalienable does not, of

There are two other efficiency reasons for forbidding the sale of entitlements under certain circumstances: self paternalism and true paternalism. Examples of the first are Ulysses tying himself to the mast or individuals passing a bill of rights so that they will be prevented from yielding to momentary temptations which they deem harmful to themselves. This type of limitation is not in any real sense paternalism. It is fully consistent with Pareto efficiency criteria, based on the notion that over the mass of cases no one knows better than the individual what is best for him or her. It merely allows the individual to choose what is best in the long run rather than in the short run, even though that choice entails giving up some short run freedom of choice. Self paternalism may cause us to require certain conditions to exist before we allow a sale of an entitlement; and it may help explain many situations of inalienability, like the invalidity of contracts entered into when drunk, or under undue influence or coercion. But it probably does not fully explain even these.[45]

True paternalism brings us a step further toward explaining such prohibitions and those of broader kinds — for example the prohibitions on a whole range of activities by minors. Paternalism is based on the notion that at least in some situations the Marshalls know better than Taney what will make Taney better off.[46] Here we are not talking about the offense to Marshall from Taney's choosing to read pornography, or selling himself into slavery, but rather the judgment that Taney was not in the position to choose best for himself when he made the choice for erotica or servitude.[47]

---

course, mean that there will be no compensation to the holder of the entitlement if it is taken from him. Thus even if a society forbids the sale of one's kidneys it will still probably compensate the person whose kidney is destroyed in an auto accident. The situations are distinct and the kidney is protected by different rules according to which situation we are speaking of.

[45] As a practical matter, since it is frequently impossible to limit the effect of an inalienable rule to those who desire it for self paternalistic reasons, self paternalism would lead to some restraints on those who would desire to sell their entitlements. This does not make self paternalism any less consistent with the premises of Pareto optimality; it is only another recognition that in an imperfect world, Pareto optimality can be approached more closely by systems which involve some coercion than by a system of totally free bargains.

[46] This locution leaves open the question whether Taney's future well-being will ultimately be decided by Taney himself or the many Marshalls. The latter implies a further departure from Paretian premises. The former, which may be typical of paternalism towards minors, implies simply that the minors do not know enough to exercise self paternalism.

[47] Sometimes the term paternalism is used to explain use of a rule of inalienability in situations where inalienability will not make the many Marshalls or the coerced Taney any better off. Inalienability is said to be imposed because the many Marshalls believe that making the entitlement inalienable is doing God's

The first concept we called a moralism and is a frequent and important ground for inalienability. But it is consistent with the premises of Pareto optimality. The second, paternalism, is also an important economic efficiency reason for inalienability, but it is not consistent with the premises of Pareto optimality: the most efficient pie is no longer that which costless bargains would achieve, because a person may be better off if he is prohibited from bargaining.

Finally, just as efficiency goals sometimes dictate the use of rules of inalienability, so, of course, do distributional goals. Whether an entitlement may be sold or not often affects directly who is richer and who is poorer. Prohibiting the sale of babies makes poorer those who can cheaply produce babies and richer those who through some nonmarket device get free an "unwanted" baby.[48] Prohibiting exculpatory clauses in product sales makes richer those who were injured by a product defect and poorer those who were not injured and who paid more for the product because the exulpatory clause was forbidden.[49] Favoring the specific group that has benefited may or may not have been the reason for the prohibition on bargaining. What is important is that, regardless of the reason for barring a contract, a group did gain from the prohibition.

This should suffice to put us on guard, for it suggests that direct distributional motives may lie behind asserted nondistributional grounds for inalienability, whether they be paternalism, self paternalism, or externalities.[50] This does not mean that giving

---

will, that is, that a sale or transfer of the entitlement would injure God. Assuming this situation exists in practice, we would not term it paternalism, because that word implies looking after the interests of the coerced party. *See* note 30 *supra*.

[48] This assumes that a prohibition on the sale of unwanted babies can be effectively enforced. If it can, then those unwanted babies which are produced are of no financial benefit to their natural parents and bring an increase in well-being to those who are allowed to adopt them free and as a result of a nonmarket allocation. Should the prohibition on sales of babies be only partially enforceable, the distributional result would be more complex. It would be unchanged for those who could obtain babies for adoption legally, *i.e.*, for those who received them without paying bribes, as it would for the natural parents who obeyed the law, since they would still receive no compensation. On the other hand, the illegal purchaser would probably pay, and the illegal seller receive, a higher price than if the sale of babies were legal. This would cause a greater distributive effect within the group of illegal sellers and buyers than would exist if such sales were permitted.

[49] *See* note 37 *supra*.

[50] As a practical matter, it is often impossible to tell whether an entitlement has been made partially inalienable for any of the several efficiency grounds mentioned or for distributional grounds. Do we bar people from selling their bodies for paternalistic, self paternalistic, or moralistic cost reasons? On what basis do we prohibit an individual from taking, for a high price, one chance in three of having

weight to distributional goals is undesirable. It clearly is desirable where on efficiency grounds society is indifferent between an alienable and an inalienable entitlement and distributional goals favor one approach or the other. It may well be desirable even when distributional goals are achieved at some efficiency costs. The danger may be, however, that what is justified on, for example, paternalism grounds is really a hidden way of accruing distributional benefits for a group whom we would not otherwise wish to benefit. For example, we may use certain types of zoning to preserve open spaces on the grounds that the poor will be happier, though they do not know it now. And open spaces may indeed make the poor happier in the long run. But the zoning that preserves open space also makes housing in the suburbs more expensive and it may be that the whole plan is aimed at securing distributional benefits to the suburban dweller regardless of the poor's happiness.[51]

IV. THE FRAMEWORK AND POLLUTION CONTROL RULES

Nuisance or pollution is one of the most interesting areas where the question of who will be given an entitlement, and how it will be protected, is in frequent issue.[52] Traditionally, and very ably in the recent article by Professor Michelman, the nuisance-pollution problem is viewed in terms of three rules.[53] First, Taney

---

to give his heart to a wealthy man who needs a transplant? Do we try to avoid a market in scarce medical resources for distributional or for some or all of the efficiency reasons discussed?

[51] There is another set of reasons which causes us to prohibit sales of some entitlements and which is sometimes termed distributional; this set of reasons causes us to prohibit sales of some entitlements because the underlying distribution of wealth seems to us undesirable. These reasons, we would suggest, are not true distributional grounds. They are, rather, efficiency grounds which become valid because of the original maldistribution. As such they can once again be categorized as due to externalities, self paternalism, and pure paternalism: (1) Marshall is offended because Taney, due to poverty, sells a kidney, and therefore Marshall votes to bar such sales (a moralism); (2) Taney, seeking to avoid temporary temptation due to his poverty, votes to bar such sale (self paternalism); and (3) the law prohibits Taney from the same sale because, regardless of what Taney believes, a majority thinks Taney will be better off later if he is barred from selling than if he is free to do so while influenced by his own poverty (pure paternalism). We do not mean to minimize these reasons by noting that they are not strictly distributional. We call them nondistributional simply to distinguish them from the more direct way in which distributional considerations affect the alienability of entitlements.

[52] It should be clear that the pollution problem we discuss here is really only a part of a broader problem, that of land use planning in general. Much of this analysis may therefore be relevant to other land use issues, for example exclusionary zoning, restrictive covenants, and ecological easements. *See* note 58 *infra.*

[53] Michelman, *supra* note 1, at 670. *See also* RESTATEMENT (SECOND) OF TORTS

may not pollute unless his neighbor (his only neighbor let us assume), Marshall, allows it (Marshall may enjoin Taney's nuisance).[54] Second, Taney may pollute but must compensate Marshall for damages caused (nuisance is found but the remedy is limited to damages).[55] Third, Taney may pollute at will and can only be stopped by Marshall if Marshall pays him off (Taney's pollution is not held to be a nuisance to Marshall).[56] In our terminology rules one and two (nuisance with injunction, and with damages only) are entitlements to Marshall. The first is an entitlement to be free from pollution and is protected by a property rule; the second is also an entitlement to be free from pollution but is protected only by a liability rule. Rule three (no nuisance) is instead an entitlement to Taney protected by a property rule, for only by buying Taney out at Taney's price can Marshall end the pollution.

The very statement of these rules in the context of our framework suggests that something is missing. Missing is a fourth rule representing an entitlement in Taney to pollute, but an entitlement which is protected only by a liability rule. The fourth rule, really a kind of partial eminent domain coupled with a benefits tax, can be stated as follows: Marshall may stop Taney from polluting, but if he does he must compensate Taney.

As a practical matter it will be easy to see why even legal writers as astute as Professor Michelman have ignored this rule. Unlike the first three it does not often lend itself to judicial imposition for a number of good legal process reasons. For example, even if Taney's injuries could practicably be measured, apportionment of the duty of compensation among many Marshalls would present problems for which courts are not well suited. If only those Marshalls who voluntarily asserted the right to enjoin Taney's pollution were required to pay the compensation, there would be insuperable freeloader problems. If, on the other

---

§§ 157–215 (1965). Michelman also discusses the possibility of inalienability. Michelman, *supra*, at 684. For a discussion of the use of rules of inalienability in the pollution context, see pp. 1123–24 *infra*.

[54] *See, e.g.*, Department of Health & Mental Hygiene v. Galaxy Chem. Co., 1 ENVIR. REP. 1660 (Md. Cir. Ct. 1970) (chemical smells enjoined); Ensign v. Walls, 323 Mich. 49, 34 N.W. 2d 549 (1948) (dog raising in residential neighborhood enjoined).

[55] *See, e.g.*, Boomer v. Atlantic Cement Co., 26 N.Y. 2d 219, 309 N.Y.S. 2d 312, 257 N.E.2d 870 (1970) (avoidance of injunction conditioned on payment of permanent damages to plaintiffs).

[56] *See, e.g.*, Francisco v. Department of Institutions & Agencies, 13 N.J. Misc. 663, 180 A. 843 (Ct. Ch. 1935) (plaintiffs not entitled to enjoin noise and odors of adjacent sanitarium); Rose v. Socony-Vacuum Corp., 54 R.I. 411, 173 A. 627 (1934) (pollution of percolating waters not enjoinable in absence of negligence).

hand, the liability rule entitled one of the Marshalls alone to enjoin the pollution and required all the benefited Marshalls to pay
their share of the compensation, the courts would be faced with
the immensely difficult task of determining who was benefited how
much and imposing a benefits tax accordingly, all the while observing procedural limits within which courts are expected to function.[57]

The fourth rule is thus not part of the cases legal scholars
read when they study nuisance law, and is therefore easily ignored
by them. But it is available, and may sometimes make more sense
than any of the three competing approaches. Indeed, in one
form or another, it may well be the most frequent device employed.[58] To appreciate the utility of the fourth rule and to com-

---

[57] This task is much more difficult than that which arises under rule two, in
which the many Marshalls would be compensated for their pollution injuries.
Under rule two, each victim may act as an individual, either in seeking compensation in the first instance or in electing whether to be a part of a class seeking compensation. If he wishes to and is able to convince the court (by some
accepted objective standard) that he has been injured, he may be compensated.
Such individual action is expensive, and thus may be wasteful, but it presents no
special problems in terms of the traditional workings of the courts. But where the
class in question consists, not of those with a right to enjoin, but of those who
must pay to enjoin, freeloader problems require the court to determine that an unwilling Marshall has been benefited and should be required to pay. The basic
difficulty is that if we begin with the premise which usually underlies our notion
of efficiency — namely, that individuals know what is best for them — we are
faced with the anomaly of compelling compensation from one who denies he has
incurred a benefit but whom we require to pay because *the court* thinks he has
been benefited.

This problem is analogous to the difficulties presented by quasi-contracts. In
terms of the theory of our economic efficiency goal, the case for requiring compensation for unbargained for (often accidental) benefits is similar to the argument for compensating tort victims. Yet courts as a general rule require compensation in quasi-contract only where there is both an indisputable benefit (usually of a pecuniary or economic nature) and some affirmative acknowledgment
of subjective benefit (usually a subsequent promise to pay). *See* A. CORBIN, CON-
TRACTS §§ 231–34 (1963). This hesitancy suggests that courts lack confidence in
their ability to distinguish real benefits from illusions. Perhaps even more importantly, it suggests that the courts recognize that what may clearly be an objective "benefit" may, to the putative beneficiary, not be a subjective benefit —
if for no other reason than that unintended changes from the status quo often
exact psychological costs. If that is the case, there has been no benefit at all in
terms of our efficiency criterion.

[58] *See* A. KNEESE & B. BOWER, MANAGING WATER QUALITY: ECONOMICS, TECH-
NOLOGY, INSTITUTIONS 98–109 (1968); Krier, *The Pollution Problem and Legal
Institutions: A Conceptual Overview*, 18 U.C.L.A.L. REV. 429, 467–75 (1971).

Virtually all eminent domain takings of a nonconforming use seem to be examples of this approach. Ecological easements may be another prime example. A
local zoning ordinance may require a developer to contribute a portion of his
land for purposes of parkland or school construction. In compensation for taking

pare it with the other three rules, we will examine why we might choose any of the given rules.

We would employ rule one (entitlement to be free from pollution protected by a property rule) from an economic efficiency point of view if we believed that the polluter, Taney, could avoid or reduce the costs of pollution more cheaply than the pollutee, Marshall. Or to put it another way, Taney would be enjoinable if he were in a better position to balance the costs of polluting against the costs of not polluting. We would employ rule three (entitlement to pollute protected by a property rule) again solely from an economic efficiency standpoint, if we made the converse judgment on who could best balance the harm of pollution against its avoidance costs. If we were wrong in our judgments and if transactions between Marshall and Taney were costless or even very cheap, the entitlement under rules one or three would be traded and an economically efficient result would occur in either case.[59] If we entitled Taney to pollute and Marshall valued clean air more than Taney valued the pollution, Marshall would pay Taney to stop polluting even though no nuisance was found. If we entitled Marshall to enjoin the pollution and the right to pollute was worth more to Taney than freedom from pollution was to Marshall, Taney would pay Marshall not to seek an injunction or would buy Marshall's land and sell it to someone who would agree not to seek an injunction. As we have assumed no one else was hurt by the pollution, Taney could now pollute even though the initial entitlement, based on a wrong guess of who was the cheapest avoider of the costs involved, allowed the pollution to be enjoined. Wherever transactions between Taney and Marshall are easy, and wherever economic efficiency is our goal, we could employ entitlements protected by property rules even though we would not be sure that the entitlement chosen was the right one. Transactions as described above would cure the error. While the entitlement might have important distributional effects, it would not substantially undercut economic efficiency.

---

the developer's entitlement, the locality will pay the developer "damages": it will allow him to increase the normal rate of density in his remaining property. The question of damage assessment involved in ecological easements raises similar problems to those raised in the benefit assessment involved in the question of quasi-contract. *See* note 57 *supra*.

[59] For a discussion of whether efficiency would be achieved in the long, as well as the short, run, see Coase, *supra* note 12; Calabresi, *supra* note 12 (pointing out that if "no transaction costs" means no impediments to bargaining in the short or long run, and if Pareto optimality means an allocation of resources which cannot be improved by bargains, assumptions of no transaction costs and rationality necessarily imply Pareto optimality); Nutter, *supra* note 12 (a technical demonstration of the applicability of the Coase theorem to long run problems). *See also* Demsetz, *supra* note 16, at 19–22.

The moment we assume, however, that transactions are not cheap, the situation changes dramatically. Assume we enjoin Taney and there are 10,000 injured Marshalls. Now *even if* the right to pollute is worth more to Taney than the right to be free from pollution is to the sum of the Marshalls, the injunction will probably stand. The cost of buying out all the Marshalls, given holdout problems, is likely to be too great, and an equivalent of eminent domain in Taney would be needed to alter the initial injunction. Conversely, if we denied a nuisance remedy, the 10,000 Marshalls could only with enormous difficulty, given free-loader problems, get together to buy out even one Taney and prevent the pollution. This would be so even if the pollution harm was greater than the value to Taney of the right to pollute.

If, however, transaction costs are not symmetrical, we may still be able to use the property rule. Assume that Taney can buy the Marshalls' entitlements easily because holdouts are for some reason absent, but that the Marshalls have great freeloader problems in buying out Taney. In this situation the entitlement should be granted to the Marshalls unless we are sure the Marshalls are the cheapest avoiders of pollution costs. Where we do not know the identity of the cheapest cost avoider it is better to entitle the Marshalls to be free of pollution because, even if we are wrong in our initial placement of the entitlement, that is, even if the Marshalls are the cheapest cost avoiders, Taney will buy out the Marshalls and economic efficiency will be achieved. Had we chosen the converse entitlement and been wrong, the Marshalls could not have bought out Taney. Unfortunately, transaction costs are often high on both sides and an initial entitlement, though incorrect in terms of economic efficiency, will not be altered in the market place.

Under these circumstances — and they are normal ones in the pollution area — we are likely to turn to liability rules whenever we are uncertain whether the polluter or the pollutees can most cheaply avoid the cost of pollution. We are only likely to use liability rules where we are uncertain because, if we are certain, the costs of liability rules — essentially the costs of collectively valuing the damages to all concerned plus the cost in coercion to those who would not sell at the collectively determined figure — are unnecessary. They are unnecessary because transaction costs and bargaining barriers become irrelevant when we are certain who is the cheapest cost avoider; economic efficiency will be attained without transactions by making the correct initial entitlement.

As a practical matter we often are uncertain who the cheapest cost avoider is. In such cases, traditional legal doctrine tends to find a nuisance but imposes only damages on Taney payable to the Marshalls.[60] This way, if the amount of damages Taney is made to pay is close to the injury caused, economic efficiency will have had its due; if he cannot make a go of it, the nuisance was not worth its costs. The entitlement to the Marshalls to be free from pollution unless compensated, however, will have been given *not* because it was thought that polluting was probably worth less to Taney than freedom from pollution was worth to the Marshalls, nor even because on some distributional basis we preferred to charge the cost to Taney rather than to the Marshalls. It was so placed *simply because we did not know* whether Taney desired to pollute more than the Marshalls desired to be free from pollution, and the only way we thought we could test out the value of the pollution was by the only liability rule we thought we had. This was rule two, the imposition of nuisance damages on Taney. At least this would be the position of a court concerned with economic efficiency which believed itself limited to rules one, two, and three.

Rule four gives at least the possibility that the opposite entitlement may also lead to economic efficiency in a situation of uncertainty. Suppose for the moment that a mechanism exists for collectively assessing the damage resulting to Taney from being stopped from polluting by the Marshalls, and a mechanism also exists for collectively assessing the benefit to each of the Marshalls from such cessation. Then — assuming the same degree of accuracy in collective valuation as exists in rule two (the nuisance damage rule) — the Marshalls would stop the pollution if it harmed them more than it benefited Taney. If this is possible, then even if we thought it necessary to use a liability rule, we would still be free to give the entitlement to Taney or Marshall for whatever reasons, efficiency or distributional, we desired.

Actually, the issue is still somewhat more complicated. For just as transaction costs are not necessarily symmetrical under the two converse property rule entitlements, so also the liability rule equivalents of transaction costs — the cost of valuing collectively and of coercing compliance with that valuation — may not be symmetrical under the two converse liability rules. Nuisance damages may be very hard to value, and the costs of informing all the injured of their rights and getting them into court may be prohibitive. Instead, the assessment of the objective damage to Taney from foregoing his pollution may be cheap and so might the as-

---

[60] *See, e.g.*, City of Harrisonville v. W.S. Dickey Clay Mfg. Co., 289 U.S. 334 (1933) (damages appropriate remedy where injunction would prejudice important public interest); Madison v. Ducktown Sulphur, Copper & Iron Co., 113 Tenn. 331, 83 S.W. 658 (1904) (damages appropriate because of plaintiff's ten year delay in seeking to enjoin fumes).

sessment of the relative benefits to all Marshalls of such freedom from pollution. But the opposite may also be the case. As a result, just as the choice of which property entitlement may be based on the asymmetry of transaction costs and hence on the greater amenability of one property entitlement to market corrections, so might the choice between liability entitlements be based on the asymmetry of the costs of collective determination.

The introduction of distributional considerations makes the existence of the fourth possibility even more significant. One does not need to go into all the permutations of the possible tradeoffs between efficiency and distributional goals under the four rules to show this. A simple example should suffice. Assume a factory which, by using cheap coal, pollutes a very wealthy section of town and employs many low income workers to produce a product purchased primarily by the poor; assume also a distributional goal that favors equality of wealth. Rule one — enjoin the nuisance — would possibly have desirable economic efficiency results (if the pollution hurt the homeowners more than it saved the factory in coal costs), but it would have disastrous distribution effects. It would also have undesirable efficiency effects if the initial judgment on costs of avoidance had been wrong and transaction costs were high. Rule two — nuisance damages — would allow a testing of the economic efficiency of eliminating the pollution, even in the presence of high transaction costs, but would quite possibly put the factory out of business or diminish output and thus have the same income distribution effects as rule one. Rule three — no nuisance — would have favorable distributional effects since it might protect the income of the workers. But if the pollution harm was greater to the homeowners than the cost of avoiding it by using a better coal, and if transaction costs — holdout problems — were such that homeowners could not unite to pay the factory to use better coal, rule three would have unsatisfactory efficiency effects. Rule four — payment of damages to the factory after allowing the homeowners to compel it to use better coal, and assessment of the cost of these damages to the homeowners — would be the only one which would accomplish both the distributional and efficiency goals.[61]

An equally good hypothetical for any of the rules can be constructed. Moreover, the problems of coercion may as a

---

[61] Either of the liability rules may also be used in another manner to achieve distributional goals. For example, if victims of pollution were poor, and if society desired a more equal distribution of wealth, it might intentionally increase "objective" damage awards if rule two were used; conversely, it might decrease the compensation to the factory owners, without any regard for economic efficiency if rule four were chosen. There are obvious disadvantages to this ad hoc method of achieving distributional goals. *See* p. 1110 *supra*.

practical matter be extremely severe under rule four. How do the homeowners decide to stop the factory's use of low grade coal? How do we assess the damages and their proportional allocation in terms of benefits to the homeowners? But equivalent problems may often be as great for rule two. How do we value the damages to each of the many homeowners? How do we inform the homeowners of their rights to damages? How do we evaluate and limit the administrative expenses of the court actions this solution implies?

The seriousness of the problem depends under each of the liability rules on the number of people whose "benefits" or "damages" one is assessing and the expense and likelihood of error in such assessment. A judgment on these questions is necessary to an evaluation of the possible economic efficiency benefits of employing one rule rather than another. The relative ease of making such assessments through different institutions may explain why we often employ the courts for rule two and get to rule four — when we do get there — only through political bodies which may, for example, prohibit pollution, or "take" the entitlement to build a supersonic plane by a kind of eminent domain, paying compensation to those injured by these decisions.[62] But

---

[62] Of course, variants of the other rules may be administered through political institutions as well. Rule three, granting a property entitlement to a polluter, may be effectuated by tax credits or other incentives such as subsidization of nonpolluting fuels offered for voluntary pollution abatement. In such schemes, as with rule four, political institutions are used to effect comprehensive benefit assessment and overcome freeloader problems which would be encountered in a more decentralized market solution. However, this centralization — to the extent that it replaces voluntary payments by individual pollution victims with collective payments not unanimously agreed upon — is a hybrid solution. The polluter must assent to the sale of his entitlement, but the amount of pollution abatement sought and the price paid by each pollution victim is not subjectively determined and voluntarily assented to by each.

The relationship of hybrids like the above to the four basic rules can be stated more generally. The buyer of an entitlement, whether the entitlement is protected by property or liability rules, may be viewed as owning what is in effect a property right not to buy the entitlement. But when freeloader problems abound, that property right may instead be given to a class of potential buyers. This "class" may be a municipality, a sewer authority, or any other body which can decide to buy an entitlement and compel those benefited to pay an objective price. When this is done, the individuals within the class have themselves only an entitlement not to purchase the seller's entitlement protected by a liability rule.

As we have already seen, the holder of an entitlement may be permitted to sell it at his own price or be compelled to sell it at an objective price: he may have an entitlement protected by a property or liability rule. Since, therefore, in any transaction the buyer may have a property or liability entitlement not to buy and the seller may have a property or a liability entitlement not to sell, there are, in effect, four combinations of rules for each possible original location of the en-all this does not, in any sense, diminish the importance of the fact that an awareness of the possibility of an entitlement to pollute, but one protected only by a liability rule, may in some instances allow us best to combine our distributional and efficiency goals.

We have said that we would say little about justice, and so we shall. But it should be clear that if rule four might enable us best to combine efficiency goals with distributional goals, it might also enable us best to combine those same efficiency goals with other goals that are often described in justice language. For example, assume that the factory in our hypothetical was using cheap coal *before* any of the wealthy houses were built. In these circumstances, rule four will not only achieve the desirable efficiency and distributional results mentioned above, but it will also accord with any "justice" significance which is attached to being there first. And this is so whether we view this justice significance as part of a distributional goal, as part of a long run efficiency goal based on protecting expectancies, or as part of an independent concept of justice.

Thus far in this section we have ignored the possibility of employing rules of inalienability to solve pollution problems. A general policy of barring pollution does seem unrealistic.[63] But rules of inalienability can appropriately be used to limit the levels of pollution and to control the levels of activities which cause pollution.[64]

One argument for inalienability may be the widespread exist-

---

titlement: voluntary seller and voluntary buyer; voluntary seller and compelled buyer; compelled seller and voluntary buyer; compelled seller and compelled buyer. Moreover, since the entitlement to that which is being bought or sold could have been originally given to the opposite party, there are, in effect, eight possible rules rather than four.

We do not mean by the above to suggest that political institutions are used only to allocate collectively held property rights. Quite the contrary, rule two, for instance, gives pollution victims an entitlement protected by a liability rule to be free from pollution. This rule could be administered by decentralized damage assessment as in litigation, or it could be effected by techniques like effluent fees charged to polluters. The latter type of collective intervention may be preferred where large numbers are involved and the costs of decentralized injury valuation are high. Still, under either system the "sale price" is collectively determined. so the basic character of the victims' entitlement is not changed.

[63] *See* Michelman, *supra* note 1, at 667.

[64] This is the exact analogue of specific deterrence of accident causing activities. *See* Costs at 95–129.

Although it may seem fanciful to us, there is of course the possibility that a state might wish to grant a converse entitlement — an inalienable entitlement to pollute in some instances. This might happen where the state believed that in the long run everyone would be better off by allowing the polluting producers to make their products, regardless of whether the polluter thought it advantageous to accept compensation for stopping his pollution.

ence of moralisms against pollution. Thus it may hurt the Marshalls — gentleman farmers — to see Taney, a smoke-choked city dweller, sell his entitlement to be free of pollution. A different kind of externality or moralism may be even more important. The Marshalls may be hurt by the expectation that, while the present generation might withstand present pollution levels with no serious health dangers, future generations may well face a despoiled, hazardous environmental condition which they are powerless to reverse.[65] And this ground for inalienability might be strengthened if a similar conclusion were reached on grounds of self paternalism. Finally, society might restrict alienability on paternalistic grounds. The Marshalls might feel that although Taney himself does not know it, Taney will be better off if he really can see the stars at night, or if he can breathe smogless air.

Whatever the grounds for inalienability, we should reemphasize that distributional effects should be carefully evaluated in making the choice for or against inalienability. Thus the citizens of a town may be granted an entitlement to be free of water pollution caused by the waste discharges of a chemical factory; and the entitlement might be made inalienable on the grounds that the town's citizens really would be better off in the long run to have access to clean beaches. But the entitlement might also be made inalienable to assure the maintenance of a beautiful resort area for the very wealthy, at the same time putting the town's citizens out of work.[66]

V. THE FRAMEWORK AND CRIMINAL SANCTIONS

Obviously we cannot canvass the relevance of our approach through many areas of the law. But we do think it beneficial to examine one further area, that of crimes against property and bodily integrity. The application of the framework to the use of criminal sanctions in cases of theft or violations of bodily integrity is useful in that it may aid in understanding the previous material, especially as it helps us to distinguish different kinds of legal problems and to identify the different modes of resolving those problems.

Beginning students, when first acquainted with economic efficiency notions, sometimes ask why ought not a robber be simply charged with the value of the thing robbed. And the same question

---

[65] *See* Michelman, *supra* note 1, at 684.

[66] *Cf.* Frady, *The View from Hilton Head*, HARPER's, May, 1970, at 103–112 (conflict over proposed establishment of chemical factory that would pollute the area's beaches in economically depressed South Carolina community; environmental groups that opposed factory backed by developers of wealthy resorts in the area, proponents of factory supported by representatives of unemployed town citizens).

is sometimes posed by legal philosophers.[67] If it is worth more to the robber than to the owner, is not economic efficiency served by such a penalty? Our answers to such a question tend to move quickly into very high sounding and undoubtedly relevant moral considerations. But these considerations are often not very helpful to the questioner because they depend on the existence of obligations on individuals not to rob for a fixed price and the original question was why we should impose such obligations at all.

One simple answer to the question would be that thieves do not get caught every time they rob and therefore the costs to the thief must at least take the unlikelihood of capture into account.[68] But that would not fully answer the problem, for even if thieves were caught every time, the penalty we would wish to impose would be greater than the objective damages to the person robbed.

A possible broader explanation lies in a consideration of the difference between property entitlements and liability entitlements. For us to charge the thief with a penalty equal to an objectively determined value of the property stolen would be to convert all property rule entitlements into liability rule entitlements.

The question remains, however, why *not* convert all property rules into liability rules? The answer is, of course, obvious. Liability rules represent only an approximation of the value of the object to its original owner and willingness to pay such an approximate value is no indication that it is worth more to the thief than to the owner. In other words, quite apart from the expense of arriving collectively at such an objective valuation, it is no guarantee of the economic efficiency of the transfer.[69] If this is so with property, it is all the more so with bodily integrity, and we would not presume collectively and objectively to value the cost of a rape to the victim against the benefit to the rapist even if economic efficiency is our sole motive. Indeed when we approach bodily integrity we are getting close to areas where we do not let the entitlement be sold at all and where economic efficiency enters

---

[67] One of the last articles by Professor Giorgio Del Vecchio came close to asking this question. *See* Del Vecchio, *Equality and Inequality in Relation to Justice*, 11 NAT. LAW FORUM 36, 43–45 (1966).

[68] *See, e.g.*, Becker, *Crime and Punishment: An Economic Approach*, 76 J. POL. ECON. 169 (1968).

[69] One might also point out that very often a thief will not have the money to meet the objectively determined price of the stolen object; indeed, his lack of resources is probably his main motivation for the theft. In such cases society, if it insists on a liability rule, will have to compensate the initial entitlement holder from the general societal coffers. When this happens the thief will not feel the impact of the liability rule and hence will not be sufficiently deterred from engaging in similar activity in the future. *Cf.* COSTS at 147–48.

in, if at all, in a more complex way. But even where the items taken or destroyed are things we do allow to be sold, we will not without special reasons impose an objective selling price on the vendor.

Once we reach the conclusion that we will not simply have liability rules, but that often, even just on economic efficiency grounds, property rules are desirable, an answer to the beginning student's question becomes clear. The thief not only harms the victim, he undermines rules and distinctions of significance beyond the specific case. Thus even if in a given case we can be sure that the value of the item stolen was no more than X dollars, and even if the thief has been caught and is prepared to compensate, we would not be content simply to charge the thief X dollars. Since in the majority of cases we cannot be sure of the economic efficiency of the transfer by theft, we must add to each case an undefinable kicker which represents society's need to keep all property rules from being changed at will into liability rules.[70] In other words, we impose criminal sanctions as a means of deterring future attempts to convert property rules into liability rules.[71]

The first year student might push on, however, and ask why we treat the thief or the rapist differently from the injurer in an auto

---

[70] If we were not interested in the integrity of property rules and hence we were not using an indefinable kicker, we would still presumably try to adjust the amount of damages charged to the thief in order to reflect the fact that only a percentage of thieves are caught; that is, we would fix a price-penalty which reflected the value of the good and the risk of capture.

[71] A problem related to criminal sanctions is that of punitive damages in intentional torts. If Taney sets a spring gun with the purpose of killing or maiming anyone who trespasses on his property, Taney has knowledge of what he is doing and of the risks involved which is more akin to the criminal than the negligent driver. But because Taney does not know precisely which one of many Marshalls will be the victim of his actions, ex ante negotiations seem difficult. How then do we justify the use of criminal sanctions and of more than compensatory damages? Probably the answer lies in the fact that we assume that the benefits of Taney's act are not worth the harm they entail if that harm were fully valued. Believing that this fact, in contrast with what is involved in a simple negligence case, should be, and in a sense can be, made known to the actor at the time he acts, we pile on extra damages. Our judgment is that most would act differently if a true cost-benefit burden could be placed. Given that judgment and given the impossibility of imposing a true cost-benefit burden by collective valuations — because of inadequate knowledge — we make sure that if we err we will err on the side of overestimating the cost.

There may be an additional dimension. Unlike fines or other criminal sanctions, punitive damages provide an extra compensation for the victim. This may not be pure windfall. Once the judgment is made that injuries classified as intentional torts are less desirable than nonintentional harms — either because they are expected to be less efficient or because there is less justification for the tortfeasor's not having purchased the entitlement in an ex ante bargain — then it may be that the actual, subjective injury to the victim from the tort is enhanced. One

accident or the polluter in a nuisance case. Why do we allow
liability rules there? In a sense, we have already answered the
question. The only level at which, before the accident, the driver
can negotiate for the value of what he might take from his
potential victim is one at which transactions are too costly. The
thief or rapist, on the other hand, could have negotiated without
undue expense (at least if the good was one which we allowed to be
sold at all) because we assume he knew what he was going to do
and to whom he would do it. The case of the accident is different
because knowledge exists only at the level of deciding to drive
or perhaps to drive fast, and at that level negotiations with potential victims are usually not feasible.

The case of nuisance seems different, however. There the
polluter knows what he will do and, often, whom it will hurt. But
as we have already pointed out, freeloader or holdout problems
may often preclude any successful negotiations between the
polluter and the victims of pollution; additionally, we are often
uncertain who is the cheapest avoider of pollution costs. In
these circumstances a liability rule, which at least allowed the
economic efficiency of a proposed transfer of entitlements to be
tested, seemed appropriate, even though it permitted the non-
accidental and unconsented taking of an entitlement. It should
be emphasized, however, that where transaction costs do not bar
negotiations between polluter and victim, or where we are sufficiently certain who the cheapest cost avoider is, there are no efficiency reasons for allowing intentional takings, and property rules,
supported by injunctions or criminal sanctions, are appropriate.[72]

VI. CONCLUSION

This article has attempted to demonstrate how a wide variety
of legal problems can usefully be approached in terms of a specific
framework. Framework or model building has two shortcomings.

whose automobile is destroyed accidentally suffers from the loss of his car; one
whose automobile is destroyed intentionally suffers from the loss of the car, and
his injury is made greater by the knowledge that the loss was intentional, wilful,
or otherwise avoidable.

[72] *Cf.* pp 1111–13.

We have not discussed distributional goals as they relate to criminal sanctions. In part this is because we have assumed the location of the initial entitlement — we have assumed the victim of a crime was entitled to the good stolen or
to his bodily integrity. There is, however, another aspect of distributional goals
which relates to the particular rule we choose to protect the initial entitlement.
For example, one might raise the question of linking the severity of criminal sanctions to the wealth of the criminal or the victim. While this aspect of distributional goals would certainly be a fruitful area of discussion, it is beyond the scope
of the present article.

The first is that models can be mistaken for the total view of phenomena, like legal relationships, which are too complex to be painted in any one picture. The second is that models generate boxes into which one then feels compelled to force situations which do not truly fit. There are, however, compensating advantages. Legal scholars, precisely because they have tended to eschew model building, have often proceeded in an ad hoc way, looking at cases and seeing what categories emerged. But this approach also affords only one view of the Cathedral. It may neglect some relationships among the problems involved in the cases which model building can perceive, precisely because it does generate boxes, or categories. The framework we have employed may be applied in many different areas of the law. We think its application facilitated perceiving and defining an additional resolution of the problem of pollution. As such we believe the painting to be well worth the oils.

[2]

LIABILITY FOR HARM VERSUS REGULATION OF SAFETY

STEVEN SHAVELL*

I. INTRODUCTION

LIABILITY in tort and the regulation of safety represent two very different approaches for controlling activities that create risks of harm to others. Tort liability is private in nature and works not by social command but rather indirectly, through the deterrent effect of damage actions that may be brought once harm occurs. Standards, prohibitions, and other forms of safety regulation, in contrast, are public in character and modify behavior in an immediate way through requirements that are imposed before, or at least independently of, the actual occurrence of harm.

As a matter of simple description, it is apparent that liability and safety regulation are employed with an emphasis that varies considerably with the nature of the activity that is governed. Whether I run to catch a bus and thereby collide with another pedestrian will be influenced more by the possibility of my tort liability than by any prior regulation of my behavior (informal social sanctions and risk to self aside). Similarly, whether I cut down a tree that might fall on my neighbor's roof will be affected more by the prospect of a tort suit than by direct regulation. But other decisions—whether I drive my truck through a tunnel when it is loaded with explosives or mark the fire exits in my store, or whether an electric utility incorporates certain safety features in its nuclear power plant—are apt to be determined substantially, although not entirely, by safety regulation. There are also intermediate cases, of course; consider, for instance, the

* Professor of Law and Economics, Harvard Law School. I wish to thank Bruce Ackerman, Susan Rose Ackerman, Lucian Bebchuk, Paul Burrows, Louis Kaplow, Mark Kelman, and Richard Stewart for comments and the National Science Foundation (grant no. SES-8014208) for financial support. A formal version of the main argument of this article is made in my Harm as a Prerequisite for Liability (1979) (unpublished manuscript, Harvard Univ. Dep't of Econ.); and in A Model of the Optimal Use of Liability and Safety Regulation (forthcoming, Rand J. Econ.). The present article will provide the basis for a chapter in the part on torts of *A Theoretical Analysis of Law*, a book on which I am at work.

behavior of ordinary drivers on the road and the effects of tort sanctions and regulation of automobile use.

What has led society to adopt this varying pattern of liability and safety regulation? What is the socially desirable way to employ the two means of alleviating risks? These are the questions to be addressed here, and in answering them I use an instrumentalist, economic method of analysis, whereby the effects of liability rules and direct regulation are compared and then evaluated on a utilitarian basis, given the assumption that individual actors can normally be expected to act in their own interest.[1] In making this evaluation, I have not counted compensation of injured parties as an independent factor on the grounds that first-party insurance (augmented if necessary by a public insurance program) can discharge the compensatory function no matter what the mix of liability and regulation. Likewise, for simplicity I ignore the complications that would be introduced by considering interest group theories of regulation.[2] Also, I do not make an explicit attempt to determine the extent to which the conclusions reached may be separately attributable to either of the two dimensions in which liability and safety regulation differ: employed only after harm is done versus beforehand; employed only at the initiative of private parties versus a public authority.[3]

Subject to these caveats and assumptions, this article first discusses four general determinants of the relative desirability of liability and regulation. It then argues in light of the determinants that the actual, observed use of the two methods of reducing risks may be viewed as socially desirable, or roughly so. The article concludes with several qualifying remarks and with comments on how the analysis could be extended to incorporate additional means of social control including the fine and the injunction.

II.   THEORETICAL DETERMINANTS OF THE RELATIVE DESIRABILITY OF LIABILITY AND SAFETY REGULATION

To identify and assess the factors determining the social desirability of liability and regulation, it is necessary to set out a measure of social welfare; and here that measure is assumed to equal the benefits parties

---

[1] This is the general approach adopted by two influential legal scholars in their analyses of tort law; see Guido Calabresi, The Costs of Accidents, 1970; and Richard Posner, Economic Analysis of Law (2d ed. 1977), ch. 6.

[2] See, for example, George Stigler, The Theory of Economic Regulation, 2 Bell J. Econ. 3 (1971); and Sam Peltzman, Toward a More General Theory of Regulation, 19 J. Law & Econ. 211 (1976).

[3] But the concluding discussion may help the reader to make a judgment about this issue.

derive from engaging in their activities, less the sum of the costs of precautions, the harms done, and the administrative expenses associated with the means of social control. The formal problem is to employ the means of control to maximize the measure of welfare.

We can now examine four determinants that influence the solution to this problem. The first determinant is the possibility of a *difference in knowledge about risky activities* as between private parties and a regulatory authority. This difference could relate to the benefits of activities, the costs of reducing risks, or the probability or severity of the risks.

Where private parties have superior knowledge of these elements, it would be better for them to decide about the control of risks, indicating an advantage of liability rules, other things being equal. Consider, for instance, the situation where private parties possess perfect information about risky activities of which a regulator has poor knowledge. Then to vest in the regulator the power of control would create a great chance of error. If the regulator overestimates the potential for harm, its standard will be too stringent, and the same will be the case if it underestimates the value of the activity or the cost of reducing risk. If the regulator makes the reverse mistakes, moreover, it will announce standards that are lax.

Under liability, however, the outcome would likely be better. This is clear enough under a system of strict liability—whereby parties have to pay damages regardless of their negligence—for then they are motivated to balance the true costs of reducing risks against the expected savings in losses caused. Now assume that the form of liability is the negligence rule—according to which parties are held responsible for harm done only if their care falls short of a prescribed level of "due" care—and suppose further that once harm occurs, the courts could acquire enough information about the underlying event to formulate the appropriate level of due care. Then parties, anticipating this, would be led in principle to exercise due care.[4] The situation is altered for the worse if the courts are unable to acquire sufficient information to determine the best level of due care; but the outcome would still be superior to that achievable under regulation if the information obtained ex post at trial would be better than that which a regulator could acquire and act upon ex ante.

These conclusions are reversed, of course, if the information possessed by a regulator is superior to private parties' and the courts'; converse reasoning then shows that the use of direct regulation would be more attractive than liability.

[4] See John Prather Brown, Toward an Economic Theory of Liability, 2 J. Legal Stud. 323 (1973).

The question that remains, therefore, is when we can expect significant differences in information between private parties and regulators to exist. And the answer is that private parties should generally enjoy an inherent advantage in knowledge. They, after all, are the ones who are engaging in and deriving benefits from their activities; in consequence, they are in a naturally superior position to estimate these benefits and normally are in at least as good a position to estimate the nature of the risks created and the costs of their reduction. For a regulator to obtain comparable information would often require virtually continuous observation of parties' behavior, and thus would be a practical impossibility. Similarly, the courts—when called upon under a negligence system—should have an advantage, though a less decisive one, over a regulator. One would indeed expect courts to adjust the due care level to take into account the facts presented by litigating parties more easily than a regulator could individualize its prior standards or modify them to reflect changed conditions.

Yet this is not to say that private parties or the courts will necessarily possess information superior to that held by a regulatory authority. In certain contexts information about risk will not be an obvious by-product of engaging in risky activities but rather will require effort to develop or special expertise to evaluate. In these contexts a regulator might obtain information by committing social resources to the task, while private parties would have an insufficient incentive to do this for familiar reasons: A party who generates information will be unable to capture its full value if others can learn of the information without paying for it. For parties to undertake individually to acquire information might result in wasteful, duplicative expenditures, and a cooperative venture by parties might be stymied by the usual problems of inducing all to lend their support.[5] Continuing, once a regulator obtains information, it may find the information difficult to communicate to private parties because of its technical nature or because the parties are hard to identify or are too numerous. Thus we can point to contexts where regulators might possess better information than private parties to whom it cannot easily be transmitted, even if the usual expectation would be for these parties to possess the superior information.

The second of the determinants of the relative desirability of liability and regulation is that *private parties might be incapable of paying for the full magnitude of harm done*. Where this is the case, liability would not furnish adequate incentives to control risk, because private parties would treat losses caused that exceed their assets as imposing liabilities only

---

[5] See generally Kenneth J. Arrow, Essays in the Theory of Risk Bearing (1971), ch. 6.

equal to their assets.[6] But under regulation inability to pay for harm done would be irrelevant, assuming that parties would be made to take steps to reduce risk as a precondition for engaging in their activities.[7]

In assessing the importance of this argument favoring regulation over liability, one factor that obviously needs to be taken into account is the size of parties' assets in relation to the probability distribution of the magnitude of harm; the greater the likelihood of harm much larger than assets, the greater the appeal of regulation.

Another factor of relevance concerns liability insurance. Here the first point to make is that a party's motive to purchase liability insurance against damage judgments exceeding his assets will be a diminished one, as the protection will in part be for losses that the party would not otherwise have to bear.[8] A party with assets of $20,000 might not be eager to purchase coverage against a potential liability of $100,000, as four-fifths of the premium would be in payment for the $80,000 amount that he would not bear if he did not buy coverage. Hence, it might be rational for the party not to insure against the $100,000 risk. If this is the case, then the assertion that liability does not create an adequate motive to reduce risk is clearly unrebutted.

Suppose, however, that the party does choose to purchase liability insurance covering losses substantially exceeding his assets or is required by statute to do so. What then is his incentive to take care? The answer depends on whether insurers can easily determine risk-reducing behavior—so that they can link the premium charged or the other terms or conditions of coverage to the party's precautions. Where this linkage can be established, the party's incentive to take care should be tolerably good. But if insurers find it too costly to verify insureds' efforts at risk reduction, then their incentives to take care may be insufficient; plausibly, they could be lower than if no insurance coverage had been obtained. Consider a requirement that the party facing a $100,000 risk purchase full coverage against it and assume that the insurer cannot observe anything about the party's exercise of care. Then as the party would not have to pay a higher premium or be otherwise penalized for failure to take

[6] See more generally Steven Shavell, The Judgment Proof Problem (1984) (unpublished manuscript, Harvard Law School).

[7] The parties could be made to do this through the exercise of the state's police powers; force could be used to prevent a business from operating that disobeyed safety regulations. Where, however, monetary penalties are relied upon to induce parties to satisfy regulations, the fact that their assets are limited might lead to problems.

[8] See William Keeton & Evan Kwerel, Externalities in Automobile Insurance and the Underinsured Driver Problem, 27 J. Law & Econ. 149 (1984); and Shavell, *supra* note 6.

proper care, he would have no reason to do this. Yet if he had not owned the liability coverage, at least his $20,000 assets would have been at risk, supplying him with some motive to take care. Thus, it appears that the problem of inadequacy of incentives to take care which arises when parties' assets are less than potential harms can either be mitigated or exacerbated by the (mandatory or voluntary) purchase of liability insurance, depending on insurers' ability to monitor insureds.

An additional factor of relevance in considering the effects of inability to pay for harm done concerns firms and their employee decisionmakers. What is of special interest in this regard is that the activities of firms are prone to result in liabilities much larger than the assets of their employees—quite apart from whether firms themselves have assets sufficient to cover their liabilities.[9] This means that employees' personal liability or ex post sanctions imposed on them of a firm's devise may not result in proper incentives to reduce risks; an employee with assets of $50,000 might not take suitable precautions to reduce the risk of a $1 million corporate liability if only his assets or his job is at stake.[10] Hence, some sort of regulation of employees may be necessary to reduce risks appropriately.

But as firms themselves would wish to avoid large liabilities, they would have good reason to establish, ex ante, internal controls over the behavior of their employees. Thus we cannot conclude that there ought to be social regulation without supplying an argument for why it would be superior to a firm's own form of regulation. Now such an argument can be given in respect to the highest level of management—those individuals whose activities are overseen only by the board of directors and the shareholders—assuming that the board and the shareholders lack the time and the necessary expertise to control management's behavior as effectively as a regulator. This argument cannot be made, however, in respect to members of lower-level management, for they have superiors within the firm who presumably have better knowledge than a regulator and are thus able to set up a better scheme of ex ante controls. On the other hand, the desire of these superiors to regulate lower-level management might be inadequate precisely because the assets of the superiors could be less than the firm's potential liability. Thus, the situation is complex, but especially

[9] For a general discussion of closely related issues, see Christopher D. Stone, The Place of Enterprise Liability in the Control of Corporate Conduct, 90 Yale L. J. 1 (1980); and see also Lewis A. Kornhauser, An Economic Analysis of the Choice between Enterprise and Personal Liability for Accidents, 70 Calif. L. Rev. 1345 (1982).

[10] Risk aversion is a qualifying factor here. If the individual is sufficiently risk averse (and does not own liability coverage), he might still take adequate care; but beyond some magnitude of corporate liability—perhaps $2 million if not $1 million—the appropriate level of care would exceed that which the individual would be led to take.

in relation to the decisions of higher-level management we can see that there exist arguments in favor of social regulation independently of whether firms' assets are large enough to cover their liabilities.

Let us turn next to the third of the four general determinants, the chance that *parties would not face the threat of suit for harm done*. Like incapacity to pay for harm, such a possibility results in a dilution of the incentives to reduce risk created by liability, but it is of no import under regulation.

The weight to be attached to this factor depends in part upon the reasons why suit might not be brought. One reason that a defendant can escape tort liability is that the harms he generates are widely dispersed, making it unattractive for any victim individually to initiate legal action. This danger can be offset to a degree if victims are allowed to maintain class actions, whose application has problematic features, however. A second cause of failure to sue is the passage of a long period of time before harm manifests itself. This raises the possibility that by the time suit is contemplated, the evidence necessary for a successful action will be stale or the responsible parties out of business. A third reason for failure to sue is difficulty in attributing harm to the parties who are in fact responsible for producing it. This problem could arise from simple ignorance that a given harm or disease was caused by a human agency (as opposed to being "natural" in origin) or from inability to identify which one or several out of many parties was the cause of harm.[11]

The problems here are aggravated when the potential liability rests on large firms, where complications analogous to those mentioned before exist. Namely, even if the harms can be attributed to an individual firm, the prospect of a successful suit may exert only slight influence on the behavior of corporate decisionmakers. With the passage of time, for example, there might be no clear way of determining which were the responsible employees, or those who were responsible may no longer be with the firm. The actual decisionmakers therefore may be beyond both the threat of suit and the prospect of sanctions internal to the firm.

The last of the determinants is the magnitude of the *administrative costs incurred by private parties and by the public* in using the tort system or direct regulation. Of course, the costs of the tort system must be

[11] Discussion of modifications of the tort system that would alleviate this problem of attribution—notably, imposing liability in proportion to the probability of causation—is beyond the scope of the present article. On this matter, see Comment, DES and a Proposed Theory of Enterprise Liability, 46 Fordham L. Rev. 963 (1978); David Rosenberg, The Causal Connection in Mass Exposure Cases: "Public Law" Vision of the Tort System, 97 Harv. L. Rev. 851 (1984); Steven Shavell, Uncertainty over Causation and the Determination of Civil Liability (1983) (unpublished manuscript, Harvard Law School).

broadly defined to include the time, effort, and legal expenses borne by private parties in the course of litigation or in coming to settlements, as well as the public expenses of conducting trials, employing judges, empaneling juries, and the like. Similarly, the administrative costs of regulation include the public expense of maintaining the regulatory establishment and the private costs of compliance.

With respect to these costs, there seems to be an underlying advantage in favor of liability, for most of its administrative costs are incurred only if harm occurs. As this will usually be infrequent, administrative costs will be low. Indeed, in the extreme case where the prospect of liability induces parties to take proper care and this happens to remove all possibility of harm, there would be no suits whatever and thus no administrative costs (other than certain fixed costs). Moreover, there are two reasons to believe that even when harm occurs administrative costs should not always be large. First, under a well-functioning negligence rule, defendants should in principle generally have been induced to take due care; injured parties should generally recognize this and thus should not bring suit. Second, suits should usually be capable of being settled cheaply by comparison to the cost of a trial. A final cost advantage of the liability system is that under it resources are naturally focused on controlling the behavior of the subgroup of parties most likely to cause harm; for because they are most likely to cause harm (and presumably most likely to be negligent), they are most likely to be sued.

Under regulation, unlike under liability, administrative costs are incurred whether or not harm occurs; even if the risk of a harm is eliminated by regulation, administrative costs will have been borne in the process. Also, in the absence of special knowledge about parties' categories of risk, there is no tendency for administrative costs to be focused on those most likely to cause harm, again because these costs are incurred before harm occurs. On the other hand, a savings in administrative costs can typically be achieved through the use of probabilistic means of enforcement.[12] But there is a limit to these savings because there is some minimum frequency of verification necessary to insure adherence to regulatory requirements.[13]

[12] See Donald Wittman, Prior Regulation versus Post Liability: The Choice between Input and Output Monitoring, 6 J. Legal Stud. 193 (1977), for a discussion of probabilistic enforcement in a setting similar to that of this article.

[13] This minimum frequency of verification is determined by the maximum fine—the size of parties' assets—that can be paid for noncompliance. To induce a party with assets of $10,000 to make a precautionary expenditure of $500, for example, his compliance must be verified with a probability of at least 5 percent; for otherwise, even were the fine to equal his entire assets, the probability-discounted fine would be less than $500. But if the likelihood of harm were negligible or lower than 5 percent, then under liability administrative costs could easily be smaller than under regulation, despite its probabilistic enforcement.

Joint Use of Liability and Regulation

Examination of the four determinants has thus shown that two generally favor liability—administrative costs and differential knowledge—and the other two favor regulation—incapacity to pay for harm done and escaping suit. This suggests not only that neither tort liability nor regulation could uniformly dominate the other as a solution to the problem of controlling risks, but also that they should not be viewed as mutually exclusive solutions to it. A complete solution to the problem of the control of risk evidently should involve the joint use of liability and regulation, with the balance between them reflecting the importance of the determinants.

If, then, some combination of liability and regulation is likely to be advantageous, two questions immediately arise: Should a party's adherence to regulation relieve him of liability in the event that harm comes to pass? On the other hand, should a party's failure to satisfy regulatory requirements result necessarily in his liability? Our theory suggests a negative answer to both questions.

As to the first, if compliance with regulation were to protect parties from liability, then none would do more than to meet the regulatory requirements. Yet since these requirements will be based on less than perfect knowledge of parties' situations, there will clearly be some parties who ought to do more than meet the requirements—because they present an above-average risk of doing harm, can take extra precautions more easily than most, or can take precautions not covered by regulation. As liability will induce many of these parties to take beneficial precautions beyond the required ones, its use as a supplement to regulation will be advantageous.[14] At the same time, just because this is true, regulatory requirements need not be as rigorous as if regulation were the sole means of controlling risks.

A similar analysis is appropriate for the second question. If failure to satisfy regulatory requirements necessarily resulted in a finding of negligence, then some parties would be undesirably led to comply with them when they would not otherwise have done so. In particular, there will be some parties (*a*) who ought not to meet regulatory requirements because they face higher than usual costs of care or because they pose lower risks

---

[14] To illustrate, suppose that a $500 expenditure is desirable for typical firms to make to prevent $1,000 in losses, but for atypical firms, an additional $500 expenditure will prevent another $1,000 in losses. If the regulator is unable to tell the atypical firms apart and tailor regulations to them, then only through the deterrent of liability will these firms be led to make the extra $500 expenditure. Note, however, that use of liability alone would not be desirable, as then firms with low assets or ones likely to escape suit might not make even the first $500 expenditure.

than normal and (*b*) who will not have been forced to satisfy regulatory requirements due to flaws in or probabilistic methods of enforcement. By allowing these parties to escape liability in view of their circumstances, the possibility that they would still be led to take the wasteful precautions can be avoided.[15]

III.   ACTIVITIES CONTROLLED MAINLY BY LIABILITY: THE TYPICAL TORT

In this section and the next I will attempt to show that the theoretically desirable uses of tort liability and regulation correlate roughly with their uses in fact. In speaking first about activities controlled primarily by liability rules, I will for concreteness make reference to two activities mentioned earlier—to my chopping down a tree that might fall on my neighbor's home and to my running to catch a bus and possibly colliding with another person. A consideration of the relevance of the four determinants to activities such as these will suggest strong advantages of the liability system and acute drawbacks of regulation.

As regards the first determinant, there is ample reason to believe that private parties would possess much better information about risks and whether and how to reduce them than would a regulator. Because I would know the precise position of my tree and of my neighbor's home, I would likely have superior insight into the chance of an accident and the opportunity to lower it by use of guy wires, or by cutting down the tree in stages. Likewise, I would presumably be better able to determine whether I should do the work myself or hire an independent contractor to do it. Similarly, my knowledge of the probability of knocking someone down when running for a bus at that particular corner under these particular conditions of visibility and weather would be better than a regulator's, and I would surely know more about the importance of catching the bus.

In these situations private parties possess the better information because they apparently do obtain it as an ordinary by-product of their

---

[15] Suppose that, unlike in note 14 *supra,* the atypical parties ought not to make the first $500 expenditure because for them it would not reduce losses at all. Then, assuming that the regulator is unable to identify atypical parties, a single regulatory standard must be used, and suppose that it corresponds to the $500 expenditure (as the typical parties for whom this is appropriate are so numerous). Now consider the question whether an atypical party who for some reason was not made to satisfy the standard should be found negligent for that, if he happens to cause an accident. Clearly, if such an atypical party were not found negligent, then he would not make the $500 expenditure, the desirable result; but if he were found negligent, he might be led to make the expenditure. Hence it is best for atypical parties to escape liability for negligence if they did not adhere to the regulatory standard. (And note again that the use of liability alone would not be desirable, for without regulation typical parties with low assets or who would escape suit would fail to make the $500 expenditure.)

activities and can take into account the changes in circumstance that influence the risks and the value of their activities. Consequently, parties should make reasonably satisfactory decisions under liability, while costly mistakes would be unavoidable under regulation. Were the regulatory authority to set forth rules on the felling of trees or the pursuit of buses, it is a certainty that the rules would sometimes be too restrictive, imposing needless precautions that would not be taken due to a concern only over liability; conversely, the rules would fail to identify desirable precautions that parties would obviously be motivated to take to avoid liability.

Turning next to the ability to pay for harm done, there is admittedly a potential problem, but sometimes not one of great magnitude. The damage to my neighbor's roof, for example, will probably be limited in scope, and I am likely to have assets plus liability insurance sufficient to cover it whether I own or rent my house. While inability to pay for harm counts as a weakness of liability in respect to the typical tort, it does not stand out as a problem of unusual dimension, at least by comparison to many of the situations to be discussed in the next part of the article.

The likelihood that suit would be brought against a liable defendant, moreover, appears to be relatively high for the typical tort, as none of the reasons for failure to bring suit seems to apply. Harms generally will not be dispersed among victims; my tree will fall on one, not many, roofs; I will collide with one or at most several pedestrians. Harms will not take a long period of time to manifest themselves; rather, any injury that I cause to a pedestrian or any damage to my neighbor's roof will be an immediate and direct consequence of my behavior. Further, harms will normally be readily attributed to responsible parties; there will be no mystery over whose tree damaged my neighbor's roof or over how the damage came about. There is thus no argument favoring regulation for fear that proper defendants would systematically escape suit.

Finally, liability should enjoy a significant administrative cost advantage over regulation in controlling the risks of typical torts. One does have the impression that it should be much less costly for society to incur administrative costs only when falling trees happen to descend on neighbors' homes and only when individuals chasing buses happen to collide with pedestrians, fairly unlikely events, than for society to formulate and enforce regulations on when and how trees may be cut down and on when individuals may be allowed to hurry after a bus.[16] Indeed, virtually all our

---

[16] Suppose, for instance, that the likelihood of my tree's striking my neighbor's roof is 0.1 percent; that should this happen, the chance there would be a dispute over my negligence is 50 percent; that given this, the probability of a settlement before trial would be 75 percent;

routine activities—walking, mowing a lawn, playing catch—are perfectly innocuous in the overwhelming majority of instances, so that the savings achieved by limiting the bearing of administrative costs to those few occasions when harm occurs must be great.

The notion of effective regulation of the activities of everyday life even seems fanciful to contemplate, particularly because it would necessitate the use of extremely frequent and intrusive verification procedures. This is because what would usually need to be determined by a regulatory authority are aspects of modifiable behavior rather than "fixed" physical objects. While it may be enough to inspect elevator cables annually, because their condition will change little over that period, effective regulation of ordinary behavior such as whether I chase after buses clearly requires much more frequent monitoring.

Also of importance is the tendency for administrative costs to be incurred primarily in controlling the parties most likely to cause harm. Because those who fail to prevent their trees from falling on their neighbors' roofs must be a disproportionately awkward group, it is a good thing that the liability system's costs be concerned only with them; it would be a waste for society to incur costs to monitor the majority of careful individuals whose trees fall safely to the ground; yet that is just what the regulatory approach requires.

Let us now summarize our discussion. Of the four determinants, differential knowledge and the size of administrative costs pointed strongly in favor of use of liability to reduce the risk of the typical tort, while inability to pay for harm done worked with only moderate force against it, and the possibility of escaping suit did not constitute an argument against it. Thus, the use in practice of liability to control the familiar category of risks known as torts seems to be the theoretically preferred solution to the problem.

IV.   ACTIVITIES SUBJECT TO SIGNIFICANT REGULATION

This section will argue that it is desirable that society resort to safety regulation where it generally does—in controlling the risks of fire, the production and sale of many foods and drugs, the generation of pollu-

---

that the administrative costs of a settlement would be $100 and those of a trial $1,000. Then the likelihood of a dispute ending in settlement would be 0.0375 percent, of one ending in litigation 0.0125 percent, so that the expected administrative costs associated with my chopping down my tree would be .000375 × $100 + .000125 × $1,000, or about 16 cents. It is hard to think of any regulatory scheme that could, ex ante, verify satisfaction of safety requirements at comparable cost.

tants, and the transport and use of explosives and other dangerous materials. A consideration of the four determinants in these areas will lead to the conclusion that substantial regulation is not a coincidence but rather is needed, both because liability alone would not adequately reduce risks and because the usual disadvantages of regulation are not as serious as in the tort context.

First, what typifies much of regulation in the areas of concern is that its requirements can be justified by common knowledge or something close to it. Presumably most of us would agree that it is well worthwhile for explosives to be transported over designated routes that avoid the drastic risks of explosions in tunnels or in densely populated locations; that expenditures on very strong elevator cables are warranted by the resulting reduction in the probability of fatal accidents; that milk should be pasteurized to decrease the chances of bacterial contamination. In these and similar cases, the regulatory authority can be reasonably confident that its requirements are justified in the great majority of situations. To be sure, they will not always be justified; there will be some occasions when milk will be consumed soon enough that failure to pasteurize it would lead to no significant risk. But these occasions will be few in number, and the error due to inappropriate regulation will be small.

Furthermore, even where the proper design of regulation must be based on much more than common knowledge, the regulatory authority may not suffer an informational disadvantage, but instead may enjoy a positive advantage relative to private parties. Notably, in dealing with many health-related and environmental risks, a regulatory agency may have better access to, or a superior ability to evaluate, relevant medical, epidemiological, and ecological knowledge. A small fumigating company, for example, might know little about, and have limited ability to understand, the nature of the risks that the chemicals it uses create. The same might be true of a large producer of pesticides; it may be uneconomical for the producer to develop and maintain expert knowledge about the dangerous properties of pesticides, especially where there are economies of scale in acquiring this knowledge and where it would benefit others.

Consideration of the determinant concerning inability to pay for harm done also suggests why we regulate the activities that we do. A fire at a nightclub or hotel could harm a large number of individuals and create losses greater than the worth of the owner. The harm caused by mass consumption of spoiled food or by inoculation with vaccines with adverse side effects could easily exhaust the holdings of even a large corporation, and so too with the losses resulting from explosions, oil spills, or the release of toxic agents or radioactive substances. Clearly, in many areas of regulation, potential liability could exceed the assets of the firms involved (certainly of their employees), and the deterrent effect of tort law is therefore diluted.

Deterrence is similarly diluted by the likelihood that responsible parties would not be sued for a wide class of environmental and health-related harms. Many of these harms are sufficiently dispersed that individual victims do not find it worth their while to bring suit. In addition, these harms often become apparent only after the passage of years, either because ecological damage or the disease process itself is slow (as with asbestosis) or because the substance generating the risk retains its potency for a long period (as with anthrax bacillus or radioactive wastes). In consequence, it may be difficult for victims to assemble the evidence necessary to succeed in a suit, the responsible individuals may have retired or died, or the firms themselves may have gone out of business. Last, it is frequently hard to trace environmental and health-related harms to particular causes and then to particular firms. Many different substances may combine to produce a given type of harm, and the mechanism that links cause to effect may be complex and incompletely understood. There are, then, a variety of reasons to believe that parties responsible for environmental and health-related harms would not be sued, and hence to find the use of regulation attractive.

Finally, regarding administrative costs, several factors may offset the underlying advantage of liability in the major regulated areas. First, what regulation often requires is the presence of particular safety devices—fire extinguishers, guard rails, lifeboats—making enforcement less costly than if regulation demanded particular modes of behavior. And where regulation does demand a type of behavior, there may be features of the situation making lack of compliance hard to conceal. How easy would it be for a dairy to keep secret its failure to pasteurize milk when samples can be tested at low cost and when numbers of employees would be aware of the violation? Second, probabilistic methods of enforcement of regulation are often employed; firms are subject to spot visits by regulatory authorities; products and services are randomly selected and examined. Thus, the administrative costs of verifying adherence to regulatory requirements appear sometimes to be low per party, while other times some savings are realized by verifying compliance on a probabilistic basis.

We conclude that the importance of the four determinants is different for the major regulated areas from what it is for the typical tort. In the regulated areas, there is a larger likelihood that responsible parties will be unable to pay for or will escape detection and suit for harms that they bring about; and the disadvantages of regulation involving administrative costs and differential knowledge are less troublesome. Of course, the relative weights of these determinants will change from one case to the next—the possibility of escaping suit, for example, is of significant concern for harms due to pesticides although of little concern for damage caused by fire. But the overall balance of the determinants in the various cases should indicate the desirability of substantial regulation.

This general claim of theoretical consistency is further supported by considering the "second-order" choices society has made over which *aspects* of an activity to regulate given the initial choice that the activity is one that should be subject to important controls. While fire regulations will often contain requirements concerning the installation of smoke alarms and sprinkler systems, they inevitably will not cover many routine practices, such as whether to store flammable furniture polish in a closet through which a heating pipe passes. Regulating these practices would usually be very expensive (closets would have to be checked frequently) or require a highly contextual sort of knowledge (type of polish and of heating pipe). It therefore appears that the two disadvantages of regulation—the magnitude of administrative costs and the regulator's inferior information about risk—help explain what aspects of a regulated activity are left unregulated.

The claim of theoretical consistency is also confirmed by the observed interrelationship between regulation and imposition of liability, especially in the basic rule that compliance with regulation does not necessarily relieve a party of liability.[17] Moreover, the cases often say that it is "unusual circumstances" or "increased danger" that makes additional precautions desirable, which is exactly what our theory suggested ought to give rise to liability despite satisfaction of regulation.[18] Similarly, the failure to conform to regulation does not in fact automatically result in liability.[19] And the explanation that is furnished here—that a party's "violation of the [statutory] law" does not imply his negligence if the special circumstances justify the apparent disobedience—again comports with the theory.[20]

---

[17] See William L. Prosser, Handbook of the Law of Torts (4th ed. 1971), at 203.

[18] See *id.* at 204. Also, at 203, Prosser writes, "The statutory standard is no more than a minimum, and it does not necessarily preclude a finding that the actor was negligent in failing to take additional precautions. Thus the requirement of a hand signal on a left turn does not mean that . . . a driver . . . is absolved from all obligation to slow down, keep a proper lookout, and proceed with reasonable care." This statement is in perfect agreement with our explanation from Section II, *supra,* where we said that the statutory standard ought to be regarded as a minimum since there would be parties who ought to take greater care and would not do so were they to escape liability on account of simply complying with the statutory standard.

[19] *Id.* at 197.

[20] *Id.* at 198. At 198 and 199, Prosser writes that "it has been held not to be negligence to violate . . . a statute because of physical circumstances beyond the driver's control, as

V. CONCLUDING COMMENTS

a) The basic purpose of the last two sections of this article has been to demonstrate how the observed use of liability and regulation can be explained by looking to the four determinants discussed at the outset. As would be true of any simple theory, however, the fit between the theory presented here and reality is only approximate.

Indeed, we often encounter the view that major mistakes have been made in the use of liability and regulation. On the one hand, it may be asserted that regulation has proved inadequate, as for instance in controlling the disposal of toxic wastes. This particular claim may well have merit, for until recently toxic wastes were little regulated, while the threat of tort liability probably provided an insufficient deterrent against improper disposal—due to manifold problems faced by victims in establishing causation and to the possibility that responsible parties would be unable to pay for harm done.[21] Conversely, there are frequent charges that certain regulations are too restrictive, as in complaints that various OSHA requirements and antipollution standards are unduly constraining or impose excessive costs on industry.[22]

That there are such examples of apparent social irrationality is to be expected, for the choices actually made about regulation and liability are obviously influenced by factors lying outside the framework of this analysis, and in any event often will not reflect a conscious, careful use of a cost-benefit calculus. Moreover, the complexity of the relationship between liability and regulation and the many unanswered empirical questions also afford ready explanations for differences between observed and ideal results.

b) The theoretical determinants examined here would be of relevance to

---

where his lights suddenly go out on the highway at night . . . . Another valid excuse is that of emergency, as where one drives on the left because the right is blocked, or a child dashes to the street . . ." Such results obviously agree with what we said in Section II. That is, we do not want the driver to stay on the right-hand side of the road when the child dashes out; holding him liable for being on the left would give him a socially undesirable incentive to drive on the right.

[21] See, for example, Note, Allocating the Costs of Hazardous Waste Disposal, 94 Harv. L. Rev. 584 (1981) and references cited therein; Richard A. Epstein, The Principles of Environmental Protection: The Case of Superfund, 2 Cato J. 9 (1982); and "Public Threat Feared in Loopholes in Laws on Toxic Waste Dumping," New York Times, June 6, 1983, at 1.

[22] See, for example, Stephen Breyer, Regulation and Its Reform (1982), ch. 14; Albert L. Nichols & Richard Zeckhauser, Government Comes to the Workplace: An Assessment of OSHA, 49 Public Interest 39 (1977); and, for a general introduction to the issues, ch. 5 of Environmental Law and Policy (Richard B. Stewart & James E. Krier eds. 2d ed. 1978).

a more comprehensive analysis of the social control of risk, and specifically to one allowing for the use of public fines measured by harm done,[23] and of the private right to enjoin others from engaging in harmful activities. The general conclusions that would emerge from such an analysis seem clear.

First, the fine is identical to liability in that it creates incentives to reduce risk by making parties pay for the harm they cause. Thus the fine enjoys essentially the same advantages as liability rules—the private parties balance the costs of reducing risks against the benefits, while society bears administrative costs only when harm occurs. Also, the fine suffers from similar disadvantages—inability to pay for harm done dilutes its effectiveness, as does the possibility that violators would escape detection.

But the fine differs from liability in its public nature; private parties do not institute suits to collect fines nor benefit financially when they are paid. The principal implication of this difference is that the likelihood of imposition of a fine may be less than the likelihood of a private suit. Private parties should ordinarily be more likely to know when harm occurs than a public agency and, as just observed, will not profit from reporting harm but may from bringing suit. Nevertheless, in some circumstances the advantage may lie with the fine. A fine could be imposed where suits would not be brought due to difficulty in establishing causation or where harms are widely dispersed, as in many environmental and health cases.

The injunction, unlike the fine, resembles safety regulation, for it works in a direct way to control risk; the injunction prevents harm simply by proscribing certain behavior. Hence the injunction shares the main advantages of safety regulation. Its use is in no way impeded by the possibility that a party would not be able to pay for the harm he does,[24] or by the chance that the harm would be highly dispersed or hard to attribute to him under tort principles. Just as, for instance, the regulation of nuclear power plants might be justified by both these factors, so too might enjoining their operations in certain circumstances.

The injunction, however, differs from safety regulation in that it is brought at the behest of private parties. The injunction accordingly has an advantage where private parties would have superior information about

---

[23] Thus, from the point of view of parties who pay fines, it is as if they were strictly liable for harm done.

[24] This point is made in Robert C. Ellickson, Alternatives to Zoning: Covenants, Nuisance Rules, and Fines on Land Use Controls, 40 U. Chi. L. Rev. 681 (1973).

the harm they might suffer, as is perhaps true of ordinary nuisances. But safety regulation would be more attractive where parties are not easily able to assess dangers or where many parties are involved and "free rider" and associated problems make it difficult to coordinate a collective action.

As this discussion indicates, the injunction and safety regulation may be viewed as substitutes, but not perfect ones, and similarly with the fine and liability. Thus, although an analysis of all four methods of controlling risk would be complicated, the conclusions would parallel our own. Where the theoretical determinants had indicated a relative advantage of regulation over liability, they would now indicate an advantage of regulation or the injunction over liability or the fine.

[3]

A COMPARISON OF TAXES, REGULATION, AND LIABILITY RULES UNDER IMPERFECT INFORMATION

MICHELLE J. WHITE and DONALD WITTMAN*

I. Introduction

Economists have devoted a great deal of ink and effort over the past several years to analyzing the effects of existing and alternate government regulatory programs in the pollution area and asking what type of program can best achieve the government's regulatory goals. Much of the debate has focused on comparing the effects of price incentive approaches (effluent taxes or subsidies), quantity controls or liability rules as alternate regulatory instruments for achieving the same goals.[1] Much of the literature makes the assumption of perfect information. However the choice among regulatory instruments depends in practice not only on their theoretical qualities, but also on the costs of translating theory into practice. Different programs may be more or less costly to administer because information requirements differ, because uncertainty affects them in different ways, or because more or less difficult administrative decisions need to be made more or less frequently.

In this paper we present a simple general framework for analyzing the costs of operating different types of pollution control programs under the assumption of imperfect information. Within this framework we analyze

* New York University and University of California, Santa Cruz. This research was supported by the NSF Law and Social Sciences Program under grants 79-28428 and 78-25721 and by a grant from the Sloan Foundation to New York University.

[1] See, for example, John Prather Brown, Toward an Economic Theory of Liability, 2 J. Legal Stud. 323 (1973); A. Mitchell Polinsky, Controlling Externalities and Protecting Entitlements: Property Right, Liability Rule and Tax-Subsidy Approaches, 8 J. Legal Stud. 1 (1979); Susan Rose-Ackerman, Effluent Changes: A Critique, 6 Canad. J. Econ. 512 (1973); James M. Buchanan & Gordon Tullock, Polluters' Profits and Political Response: Direct Controls versus Taxes, 65 Am. Econ. Rev. 139 (1975); John Prather Brown & William L. Holahan, Taxes and Legal Rules for the Control of Externalities When There Are Strategic Responses, 9 J. Legal Stud. 165 (1980).

four different programs: a fixed price incentive for pollution abatement (or effluent tax), a system of quantity controls, and two types of liability rules. Our model is similar to that proposed by Weitzman and extended by Yohe to analyze the desirability of quantity versus price controls in a centralized economy under uncertainty.[2] Our results are striking in comparison to theirs, however. Both our model and that of Yohe show that the choice between simple price versus quantity controls depends on the relative slopes of the marginal benefit versus cost curves, leaving little a priori ground for preferring one method over the other. However, the strict liability rule which we consider is shown to be preferable to both quantity and price controls.[3]

II. Administrative Costs

In this section we present our basic model of welfare costs. Suppose a polluter—a factory—produces smoke, s, which damages a victim—an orchard—nearby. We assume that the cost of smoke to the victim consists of either reduced revenues from lower output quality (smoke-damaged apples sell for less) or increased costs due to the need to take smoke abatement measures (spraying the apples to make them smoke resistant or planting a variety of apple not susceptible to smoke damage), or both. The smoke damage function is defined to include the cost of smoke abatement measures by the victim if they are economically efficient.

The marginal cost of smoke damage to the victim, $C(s)$, is assumed to be linear, or

$$C(s) = C_0 + C_1 s + u, \tag{1}$$

where $C_1 > 0$ and $|u| < C_0$. Here u is a random variable with an expected value of zero and a symmetric distribution.[4] Equation (1) implies that the total cost of pollution to the victim increases at an increasing rate.

---

[2] See Martin L. Weitzman, Prices vs. Quantities, 41 Rev. Econ. Stud. 50 (1974); Gary W. Yohe, Towards a General Comparison of Price Controls and Quantity Controls under Uncertainty, 45 Rev. Econ. Stud. 229 (1978); Zvi Adar and James M. Griffin, Uncertainty and the Choice of Pollution Control Instruments, 3 J. Environmental Econ. & Management 178 (1976).

[3] We assume high transaction costs; however, on those occasions when transaction costs are low, liability (or a property right system) is strictly superior to the other alternatives. Regulation does not allow transactions between the polluter and pollutee to correct for incorrect standards. Under effluent taxes (which are not returned to the victims), if transaction costs are low the pollutee and polluter will decide on less than the optimal amount of smoke because at the optimal amount the tax plus marginal cost is greater than the marginal benefit (equal to marginal cost).

[4] We use the word victim, but $C_0 + C_1 s + u$ could also stand for the marginal damage to *all* the pollutees. A linear curve is a first-order approximation to a nonlinear curve. Our

Turning to the polluter, we assume that it is costly for it to abate smoke or, equivalently, that it derives benefit from producing (or not abating) smoke. The marginal benefit of smoke to the polluter is assumed to be linear, or

$$B(s) = B_0 + B_1 s + v, \tag{2}$$

where $B_1 < 0$ and $|v| < B_0$. Here v is also a random variable with an expected value of zero and a symmetric distribution.[5]

Thus we assume that both the marginal cost to the victim of smoke damage and the marginal benefit to the polluter of smoke production are linear functions with stochastic terms. The uncertainty problem is structured as follows. The pollution control agency is assumed to know the cost and benefit parameters C_0, C_1, B_0, and B_1. These nonstochastic parameters might be obtained by surveying a sample of firms or by determining the costs of particular pollution abatement technologies from engineering specifications. The information might be obtained on a more disaggregated level. For example, nonstochastic parameters may be separately determined for firms in different industries or in different regions, since firms in different industries use different pollution abatement methods and since different control technologies may be more or less effective depending on local climatic or congestion conditions. On a still more refined level the agency might attempt to learn information concerning the particular polluter or victim but still not know the cost curves with certainty; that is, it does not know u or v. This is both because the cost of obtaining 100 percent accurate information would be prohibitive and also because firms have incentives to give inaccurate information. Polluters would exaggerate the benefits from smoke production and victims the

---

assumptions concerning $C(s)$ are virtually the same as those made by Weitzman (*supra* note 2) and Yohe (*supra* note 2), who use a third-order Taylor expansion of the total cost function. (Thus only the slope and intercept of the marginal cost curve are known.) For infinitesimal changes the approximation error is negligible and therefore can be ignored entirely. For larger changes, the maximum degree of error can be calculated. Our assumptions concerning the stochastic term differ from Yohe's. We make the typical econometric assumption of heteroscedasticity in the error term.

[5] Note that long-run and short-run costs and benefits may differ if polluters' and pollutees' locations are fixed in the short run but not in the long run. In the long run, for example, the benefits of pollution abatement may be defined for the best user of the site rather than the current user of the site. See Michelle J. White & Donald Wittman, Long-Run versus Short-Run Remedies for Spatial Externalities: Liability Rules, Pollution Taxes, and Zoning, in Essays on the Law and Economics of Local Governments (Daniel L. Rubinfeld ed. 1979) No. 3, COUPE Papers on Pub. Econ.; Michelle J. White & Donald Wittman, Optimal Spatial Location under Pollution: Liability Rules and Zoning, 10 J. Legal Stud. 249 (1981); Donald Wittman, Pigovian Taxes, Liability Rules and Regulation of the Inputs (Working paper, Univ. California, Santa Cruz 1981); and Michelle J. White & Donald Wittman, Pollution Taxes and Optimal Spatial Location, 49 Economica 297 (1982), for different analyses and solutions to the long-run entry problems.

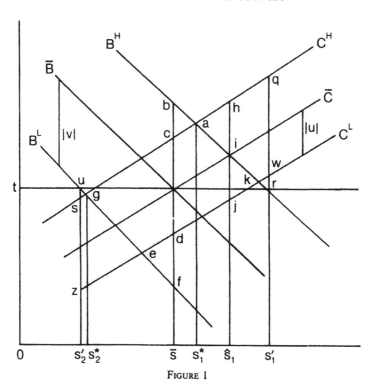

FIGURE 1

costs, each to induce the agency to set a control program that shifts more of the burden onto the other party.[6] Because there is little reason to believe that the stochastic term of the particular polluter is related to the stochastic term of a particular pollutee, we assume that u and v are distributed independently.

Figure 1 shows the expected cost and benefit curves for the expected polluter and victim, $\bar{B}$ and $\bar{C}$, and for polluters and victims with high and low marginal cost and benefit curves, denoted with superscripts H and L. Because u and v are symmetric distributions, only two values of each need to be considered: $u = \pm|u|$ and $v = \pm|v|$. As shown in the diagram,

---

[6] Thus the government may over- or underestimate the total cost or benefits of pollution summed over everyone in society. Evan Kwerel, To Tell the Truth: Imperfect Information and Optimal Pollution Control, 44 Rev. Econ. Stud. 595 (1977); Marc J. Roberts & Michael Spence, Effluent Charges and Licenses under Uncertainty, 5 J. Pub. Econ. 193 (1976), discuss a mixed effluent tax and licensing pollution and control program. These surmount the information problem by giving firms incentives to reveal truthful information concerning their abatement costs. However, their models only deal with polluters' incentives, not the victims'.

$|u| < |v|$, but the opposite could also hold. In the subsections below we analyze separately the effects of the different regulatory regimes: quantity regulation, an effluent tax, and liability rules.

Quantity Regulation

Under quantity regulation, the authority is assumed to determine the level of smoke production for which expected marginal benefit from smoke abatement equals expected marginal cost. This level is denoted by $\bar{s}$. Thus $C_0 + C_1\bar{s} = B_0 + B_1\bar{s}$, or

$$\bar{s} = \frac{B_0 - C_0}{C_1 - B_1}. \tag{3}$$

The authority then requires that polluters abate smoke to $\bar{s}$. However, the optimal smoke level is where actual marginal cost equals actual marginal benefit. This level is denoted s^*. Thus $C_0 + C_1 s^* + u = B_0 + B_1 s^* + v$ or

$$s^* = \frac{B_0 - C_0 + v - u}{C_1 - B_1}. \tag{4}$$

Quantity regulation thus causes deadweight losses to be incurred whenever $\bar{s} \neq s^*$ or when $u \neq v$. Examining Figure 1, four cases can be distinguished, corresponding to the possibilities $B^H - C^H$, $B^H - C^L$, $B^L - C^H$, and $B^L - C^L$. For $B^H - C^H$, the efficient level of smoke production is s_1^*, and the use of quantity regulation leads to a deadweight cost corresponding to triangle *abc*. Similarly, for $B^L - C^L$, the deadweight cost is triangle *def*, which is equal to *abc*. For $B^L - C^H$, the efficient smoke level is s_2^* and the deadweight cost is triangle *gcf*, while for $B^H - C^L$ the deadweight cost is the same.

We can characterize the deadweight cost more generally for any of the triangles as

$$\tfrac{1}{2}|s^* - \bar{s}| \cdot |B(\bar{s}) - C(\bar{s})|. \tag{5}$$

Substituting from (1)–(4) into (5), we have

$$\tfrac{1}{2}(v - u)^2 / (C_1 - B_1). \tag{6}$$

The expected deadweight cost is therefore

$$\tfrac{1}{2} \cdot \frac{1}{C_1 - B_1} [\sigma_v^2 + \sigma_u^2 - 2\,\text{cov}(v,u)]. \tag{7}$$

Because by assumption u and v are distributed independently, cov (v,u) = 0. Note that the denominator of (7) is positive because $C_1 \geq 0$ and $B_1 \leq 0$. The expected deadweight cost from quantity regulation therefore increases as either the marginal benefit or marginal cost curves become more steeply sloped. It also increases with the variance of the stochastic terms u and v. The level of marginal benefit and cost, B_0 and C_0, does not enter into the deadweight cost determination.[7]

Effluent Tax

Under an effluent tax, the authority levies a tax on the polluter equal to t dollars per unit of smoke output. The price is determined in our model as the level needed to induce efficient smoke production for the polluter and victim having expected levels of marginal benefit and cost, or $u = v = 0$. Because $\bar{s}$ is the efficient smoke output in this case, the tax $t = B_0 + B_1\bar{s} = C_0 + C_1\bar{s}$ becomes

$$t = B_0 + \frac{B_1 (B_0 - C_0)}{C_1 - B_1}. \tag{8}$$

Thus the per unit tax equals the expected marginal benefit and cost at $\bar{s}$. The tax is shown as a horizontal line in Figure 1.

From Figure 1, the level of smoke output chosen by a polluter with marginal benefit B^H facing tax t is s_1'. If the victim has marginal cost C^H, then the efficient level of smoke output is s_1^*. This implies a deadweight cost triangle aqr. Similarly, the level of smoke output chosen by a polluter with marginal benefit B^L is s_2', while if the victim has marginal cost C^H, then the efficient smoke level is s_2^*. The resulting deadweight cost is triangle gus. For $B^H - C^L$ the cost is also $wkr = gus$, while for $B^L - C^L$ it is $zue = aqr$.

The deadweight cost triangles can be characterized generally as

$$\tfrac{1}{2}|s^* - s'| \cdot |B(s') - C(s')|, \tag{9}$$

where the asterisk indicates the efficient level of smoke output for the polluter and victim and the prime sign indicates the level chosen under the effluent tax. To solve for s', we find the level of smoke output for which the polluter's actual marginal benefit equals the tax, or

$$B(s') = t = B_0 + B_1 \frac{(B_0 - C_0)}{C_1 - B_1}. \tag{10}$$

---

[7] We derived (7) assuming implicitly that the four triangles in Figure 1 occur with equal probability. This follows from our assumption that the distributions of u and v are symmetric and independent. The measure of deadweight cost remains the same, however, if the distribution of u and/or v is generalized: for example, there might be two values of u, $|u_1|$ and $|u_2|$, occurring with probability λ and $(1 - \lambda)$, respectively. Then $\pm u_1$ would each occur with $\lambda/2$ probability and $\pm u_2$ would each occur with $(1 - \lambda)/2$ probability. The expected welfare loss from quantity regulation would still be (7). Further generalizations of this type also leave (7) unaffected.

A COMPARISON OF TAXES 419

Thus $s' = [(B_0 - C_0)/(C_1 - B_1)] - v/B_1$. Substituting (4) and (10) into (9), we get the expected deadweight cost of an effluent tax:

$$\frac{1}{2}\left| \frac{B_1u - C_1v}{B_1(C_1 - B_1)} \right| \cdot \left| \frac{-B_1u - C_1v}{B_1} \right| = \\ \frac{1}{2}\frac{[B_1^2\sigma_u^2 + C_1^2\sigma_v^2 - 2B_1C_1\text{cov}(u,v)]}{B_1^2(C_1 - B_1)}. \tag{11}$$

If u and v are independent, this becomes

$$\frac{1}{2}\frac{(B_1^2\sigma_u^2 + C_1^2\sigma_v^2)}{B_1^2(C_1 - B_1)}. \tag{12}$$

The expected deadweight cost of an effluent tax again rises with u and v, but now the slope terms B_1 and C_1 have contrary effects.

From (7) and (12) we can determine the expected deadweight cost of quantity controls relative to an effluent tax (price regulation). The cost ratio is

$$\frac{\sigma_u^2 + \left(\frac{C_1^2}{B_1^2}\right)\sigma_v^2}{\sigma_u^2 + \sigma_v^2}. \tag{13}$$

The effluent tax is the more efficient control method if (13) exceeds unity, while quantity control is more efficient in the opposite case. Which is the more desirable pollution control method thus depends only on the relative slopes of the marginal benefit and cost functions: if $|C_1| > |B_1|$, then quantity controls are preferred, while if $|C_1| < |B_1|$, then the effluent tax is preferred.[8]

This is illustrated in Figure 2, which shows an example in which the slope of the marginal cost curve is very steep, while the slope of the marginal benefit curve is relatively flat. Quantity regulation produces deadweight loss triangles in the $B^H - C^H$ and $B^H - C^L$ cases of *amc* and *cbd*, respectively. The effluent tax produces the much larger deadweight loss triangles of *afg* and *bhf* in the same two cases. Intuitively, the tax works badly here because the marginal cost to the firm (effluent tax) is horizontal while the marginal cost to society is nearly vertical. Under regulation, the smoke constraint can be viewed as a vertical marginal cost curve to the firm which more closely approximates the nearly vertical

---

[8] See Ronald Grieson & Donald Wittman, Regulation May Be No Worse Than the Alternatives, in Housing and Externalities (Ronald Grieson ed. 1982), for a comparison of regulation to taxes and liability rules regarding incentives for the relevant authorities to act efficiently, information requirements, and long-run effects.

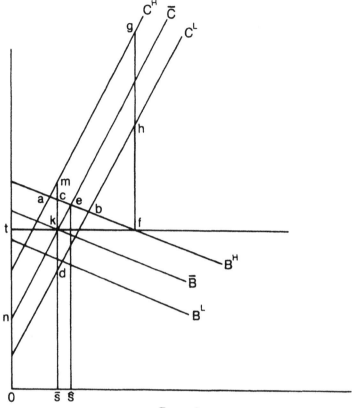

FIGURE 2

social marginal cost. We could similarly illustrate the opposite case in which the effluent tax is preferred.[9]

Liability Rules

An alternative approach to pollution control is via a liability system rather than by quantity or price regulation. Under a liability rule, the

[9] These results generalize much of the literature on price versus quantity regulation. Because some of this work was not directly concerned with externalities, we reinterpret the results in the context of pollution control. Weitzman (*supra* note 2); Adar & Griffin (*supra* note 2); Gideon Fishelson, Emission Control Policies under Uncertainty, 3 J. Environmental Econ. & Mgmt. 189 (1976); and Yohe (*supra* note 2) derive the cost of a quantity standard by assuming either that the marginal cost of smoke to the polluter is fixed or that the marginal benefit of smoke to the victim is fixed; thus their results are special cases of our more general formulation. Yohe (*supra* note 2) considers uncertainty in both curves.

polluter is obligated to pay the victim compensation for damages suffered. The obligation to pay may depend on the polluter's behavior: under a negligence liability standard, the polluter only pays if it fails to take reasonable measures to abate its smoke, while under a strict liability standard, the polluter pays regardless. Strict liability is the traditional legal doctrine applied in nuisance (externality) cases, while negligence applies generally in tort (injury) cases. Strict liability is generally less efficient than regulation or effluent taxes in cases where there are large numbers of victims, each having a small claim. Unless class action suits are allowed, the transactions costs of litigating many small claims are usually prohibitive. There are also important administrative differences between liability rules and quantity regulation or effluent taxes. The latter two systems are administered ex ante by an administrative agency and polluters' payments go to the government. In contrast, liability rules are administered ex post by the Courts and polluters' payments go to the victim.[10] We discuss both strict liability and negligence liability rule systems separately below.

Strict Liability. Under a conventional strict liability system, the polluter is liable for a "reasonable" level of damages.[11] In our context, this is assumed to be the relevant area under the victim's expected marginal damage curve, $C_0 + C_1 \hat{s}$, where $\hat{s}$ is the smoke level chosen by the polluter under the liability rule.[12] Thus the marginal liability per unit of smoke produced paid by the polluter is

$$L = C_0 + C_1 \hat{s}. \tag{14}$$

The liability rule forces the polluter to internalize the value of pollution damage for the average victim. The polluter minimizes his total private

[10] For a discussion of the relative merits of input versus output monitoring, see Donald Wittman, Prior Regulation versus Post Liability: The Choice between Input and Output Monitoring, 6 J. Legal Stud. 193 (1977).

[11] The determination of effluent taxes and standards also relies on "reasonable" costs to the victim. Under strict liability for reasonable costs, the polluter is liable for costs encountered by the pollutee under the assumption that the pollutee responds optimally to the *given* amount of smoke produced by the polluter. The polluter is liable for this amount independent of what the pollutee actually does. Thus in nuisance law, when sulfur fumes make his land useless for growing crops, the farmer can collect for lost profits due to not growing a crop. (See United Verde Extension Mining Co. v. Ralston, 296 P. 262 (1931).) He collects the same amount whether he plants a hopeless crop or not. This is known as the doctrine of avoidable consequences. As Donald Wittman, in Optimal Pricing of Sequential Inputs: Last Clear Chance, Mitigation of Damages, and Related Doctrines in the Law, 10 J. Legal Stud. 65 (1981), has shown, this liability rule (unlike other formulations of strict liability) results in optimal behavior by both the polluter and pollutee when there is perfect information. Here we consider its properties under imperfect information.

Under strict liability for optimal costs, the polluter is liable for the expected marginal cost curve. The polluter maximizes profits by setting his actual marginal benefit curve to the expected marginal cost curve, which under strict liability is his actual marginal cost curve.

[12] These could be increased or decreased by a constant term without affecting the results.

costs at the point where his marginal liability equals marginal benefit, or where (14) equals (2).

Turning again to Figure 1, the level of smoke output chosen by a polluter with marginal benefit B^H facing liability rule L (14) is $\hat{s}_1$, where actual marginal benefit equals average marginal cost. This gives rise to deadweight costs of *ahi* in the $B^H - C^H$ case and *ijk* in the $B^H - C^L$ case. The other two possibilities are similar.

More generally, deadweight costs in the strict liability case are

$$\tfrac{1}{2}|\hat{s} - s^*| \cdot |B(\hat{s}) - C(\hat{s})| = \tfrac{1}{2}|\hat{s} - s^*| \cdot |u|. \tag{15}$$

The polluter determines the amount of smoke s by equating the marginal benefit from smoke to the liability per unit of smoke, or

$$L = C_0 + C_1\hat{s} = B_0 + B_1\hat{s} + v. \tag{16}$$

Thus

$$\hat{s} = \frac{B_0 - C_0 + v}{C_1 - B_1}. \tag{17}$$

Substituting (17) and (4) into (15) we get the expected loss from strict liability:

$$\tfrac{1}{2}\,\frac{\sigma_u^2}{(C_1 - B_1)}. \tag{18}$$

Under strict liability we find that expected deadweight costs increase with u, are independent of v, and are negatively related to the slopes of both the marginal cost and benefit curves.

Comparing expected deadweight cost levels for strict liability to the effluent tax and to quantity controls, (18), (12), and (7), we find that strict liability appropriately defined has unambiguously lower costs than either quantity regulation or the effluent tax in all cases. Intuitively, the liability rule is preferred because the marginal cost (liability payment) curve to the firm has the same slope as the marginal cost curve to society. In contrast, the marginal cost curve to the firm under an effluent tax is horizontal, while under a regulation it is implicitly vertical. Thus we have the surprising result that while economists have belabored the choice between quantity regulation and fixed-per-unit price regulation (the effluent tax), they have neglected a very simple third alternative, strict liability, which dominates both.

Further, the liability rule alternative has lower information costs than either of the two other methods. The liability rule requires that the authority inform the polluter of two parameters, C_0 and C_1, whereas quantity regulation and the effluent tax each require only one parameter, s or t, respectively. Nonetheless, less information is needed to determine both

C_0 and C_1 than is needed to determine either s or t. Determining C_0 and C_1 requires surveying only a group of victims of pollution, while determining either s or t requires surveying groups of both victims and polluters. Under a liability rule the victim sues the polluter in court and the court, ex post, determines and assesses a reasonable level of damages $C_0 + C_1\hat{s}$. Polluters thus anticipate in advance that they will be held liable for damages equal to the level suffered by the average victim and they internalize the amount $C_0 + C_1\hat{s}$ as part of their costs in determining a level of smoke output. This liability rule is actually used by the courts, suggesting that such an approach is administratively feasible.

Negligence Liability.   Negligence as a liability system has a potential advantage over strict liability in that fewer cases are brought and litigated because victims cannot collect from injurers who take reasonable measures to reduce damage (although the social cost of each court case may be higher because information is required to determine the appropriate standard of care). Thus court costs are likely to be lower in total. However, negligence rules have higher expected deadweight costs than strict liability rules.

Suppose the polluter is made liable for damage only if he fails to take reasonable abatement measures, defined as producing no more smoke than would be efficient for the average polluter in the presence of the average victim. Such a "reasonableness" standard would mean that the courts, like the authority, would only have to determine marginal cost and benefit levels for the expected polluter and victim, not for the particular polluter and victim in question. Such a standard, however, would typically give the polluter an incentive to produce no more (and no less) smoke than $\bar{s}$. It therefore would typically have the same expected deadweight cost results as quantity regulation (and sometimes lower deadweight costs than under quantity regulation when the polluter chooses to be negligent).[13]

---

[13] If the polluter chooses more smoke than $\bar{s}$, he is liable for damages. As before, he will choose the smoke level where actual marginal benefit equals expected marginal cost ($\hat{s}$ in Figure 2). $\hat{s} > \bar{s}$ only if $v > 0$ (that is, the B^H curve holds). If the polluter is strictly liable, he must pay the pollutee an amount equal to the area under the marginal cost curve between 0 and $\hat{s}$ (trapezoid $0ne\hat{s}$). If the polluter chooses $\bar{s}$, he is no longer liable. By choosing $\bar{s}$, his benefits of smoke are reduced (that is, his abatement costs are increased) by the trapezoid $c\bar{s}\hat{s}e$, but at the same time his liability is decreased from $0ne\hat{s}$ to zero. Thus for the polluter to choose $\bar{s}$, triangle cek must be bigger than trapezoid $0nk\bar{s}$. This could conceivably occur if the marginal benefit of more smoke was falling rapidly (that is, additional smoke prevention was very costly) and the standard, $\bar{s}$, was much closer to zero smoke than to $\hat{s}$ (that is, there were very high standards of smoke abatement). Even under these circumstances such an occurrence would only happen half the time, because the error term must be positive in order for $\hat{s} > \bar{s}$. When $\hat{s}$ is less than $\bar{s}$, the polluter will choose $\bar{s}$ under a negligence system,

An alternative negligence rule would make the polluter liable for the average victim's damage if it produced more smoke than is efficient given the average victim's marginal costs and its own marginal benefit, or s. Such a system would have the same expected deadweight cost as strict liability but would not require that every case be litigated. However, it would be difficult to administer because determination of whether or not the polluter is negligent would require information concerning the particular polluter's own (rather than the expected) marginal benefit level; but this is exactly the kind of information error we are discussing.

Thus, while a negligence rule based on $\bar{s}$ has lower administrative costs than a strict liability rule because fewer cases are litigated, it has higher expected deadweight costs. The same negligence rule has an advantage over quantity regulation in that under negligence not all instances of pollution damage are litigated, while under quantity regulation the authority must set quantity controls for each instance of pollution. When the polluter adheres to the negligence rule expected deadweight costs are the same for both systems. On the rarer occasions when the polluter chooses to be negligent, expected deadweight cost is less than that for quantity regulation.

III. Conclusion

We have presented a simple general framework for analyzing the deadweight costs of various types of pollution regulation, including quantity regulation, an effluent tax, and liability rules. Our major results are the following:

1. The expected deadweight cost of administering quantity regulation relative to price regulation (where price regulation is in the form of a fixed per unit effluent tax) depends only on the relative slopes of the marginal benefit and cost curves for pollution abatement. Quantity regulation is preferred if the slope of the marginal benefit curve from pollution abatement is steeper and price regulation if the slope of the marginal cost curve is steeper.

2. An appropriately defined strict liability approach to pollution control has lower expected deadweight costs than either quantity regulation or the effluent tax. This type of liability rule is actually used by the courts, thus demonstrating its feasibility.

---

because he is not liable if he chooses $\bar{s}$ and all that a reduction to $\bar{s}$ does is to increase the polluter's abatement costs.

Thus a negligence rule will have the same characteristics as a quantity regulation at least 50 percent of the time under any circumstances and will have the same welfare loss under typical circumstances.

A COMPARISON OF TAXES 425

3. A negligence liability approach has expected deadweight cost less than or equal to the expected deadweight costs obtained under quantity controls. The former also has an advantage in that fewer instances of pollution are litigated in court under negligence than must be regulated by the pollution authority under quantity controls.

In conclusion, while economists have devoted considerable effort to debating the relative merits of quantity versus price controls in nonmarket allocation contexts, our analysis suggests that existing liability rules dominate both of these.

[4]

A model of the optimal use of liability and safety regulation

Steven Shavell*

A model of the occurrence of accidents is used to examine liability and safety regulation as means of controlling risks. According to the model, regulation does not result in the appropriate reduction of risk—because the regulator lacks perfect information—nor does liability result in that outcome—because the incentives it creates are diluted by the chance that parties would not be sued for harm done or would not be able to pay fully for it. Thus, neither liability nor regulation is necessarily better than the other, and as is stressed, their joint use is generally socially advantageous.

1. Introduction

■ This article considers the use of liability and safety regulation as means of controlling accident risks.[1] In the model that is studied, parties may reduce these risks by taking care; and because the risks vary among parties, the socially desirable levels of care that they should exercise vary as well.

Neither regulation nor liability, however, leads all parties to exercise the socially desirable levels of care. Regulation does not result in this outcome because the regulatory authority's information about risk is imperfect, while liability does not create sufficient incentives to take appropriate care because of the possibility that parties would not be able to pay fully for harm done or would not be sued for it.[2] Depending on the importance of these factors, either regulation or liability could turn out to be preferred when considered as an alternative to the other.

But as is stressed, it is often socially advantageous for the two means of controlling risk to be jointly employed—for parties to be required to satisfy a regulatory standard and also to face possible liability.[3] Moreover, in this case, parties causing other than relatively

---

* Harvard Law School.

I wish to thank L. Bebchuk and A.M. Polinsky for comments and the National Science Foundation (grant no. SES-8014208) for financial support.

[1] A more general but informal discussion of liability and regulation is presented in Shavell (1984); two other articles of relevance (see footnote 4) are Wittman (1977) and Weitzman (1974). See also Calabresi (1970) for an early discussion of closely connected issues.

[2] These two causes of dilution of incentives under liability are not unimportant. It is frequently the case that a party's potential for doing harm is great in relation to its assets, even if the party is a large firm (consider the risk of fires and explosions and environmental and health-related risks such as oil spills, accidents at nuclear power plants, and mass exposure to carcinogens). It is also often true that a party would not be sued, for the harm might be difficult to trace to its source or it might be highly dispersed (consider again many environmental and health-related risks).

[3] This is the situation in fact: satisfaction of regulatory requirements usually does not insulate parties from liability; see Prosser (1971, pp. 203–204).

Economics and Liability for Environmental Problems

low risks are led to do more than to satisfy the regulatory standard, for their potential liability makes that worth their while. At the same time, just because these parties take more care than is required, it is socially desirable for the regulatory standard to be lower than if regulation were used alone. In effect, a reduction of the regulatory standard can be afforded because liability is present to take up some of the "slack" associated with the lower standard.[4]

2. The model

■ Risk-neutral parties may reduce the probability of causing an accident by making expenditures on care. Define

x = level of care; $x \geq 0$;
$p(x)$ = probability of causing an accident; $0 < p(x) < 1$; $p'(x) < 0$; $p''(x) > 0$; and
h = magnitude of harm if an accident occurs,

where h differs among parties, each of whom knows his own h. The regulator is aware only of the distribution of h.[5] Let

$f(h)$ = probability density of h; $f(h) > 0$ on and only on $[a, b]$, $0 < a < b$.

Assume that the social welfare criterion is the minimization of the expected sum of the costs of care and of harm done. Thus, the welfare-maximizing or first-best level of care as a function of a party's h is determined by minimizing over x

$$x + p(x)h. \tag{1}$$

The first-order condition is therefore[6]

$$1 = -p'(x)h, \tag{2}$$

which, of course, means that the marginal cost of care, 1, equals the expected marginal benefits, $-p'(x)h$. Denote by $x^*(h)$ the first-best level of care and observe that it is increasing in h.[7]

---

[4] Wittman (1977), the only previous article of which I am aware on the subject of liability and safety regulation, analyzes the probabilistic use of fines to enforce regulation and liability law. Thus what is of concern is quite different from the issues of interest here.

In Weitzman (1974), regulation is compared to use of a price or tax. Thus, for instance, in the context of pollution, regulation of the quantity of an effluent is compared to use of a tax per unit of the effluent; and what is stressed is the possibility that the social authority might err not only in regulating the quantity of the effluent—owing to lack of information about the costs and benefits of preventing pollution—but also in setting a pollution tax—for the authority would not be expected to know ahead of time the amount of damage that would be done by the effluent.

In this article, on the other hand, it is not use of a pollution tax that is compared to regulation; it is liability for harm done. The significance of this difference is that whereas the pollution tax is imposed *before* harm occurs and therefore naturally involves uncertainty as to its amount, liability is imposed by its nature only *after* harm has occurred, and therefore presumably involves little (and in the model, no) uncertainty over its amount. In other words, the problem here with liability does not involve lack of information on the part of the social authority; instead, as explained, it has to do with dilution of incentives.

[5] Shavell (1983) also considers the assumption that h is the sum of a random component h_1 known only by parties and of another component h_2 known only by the regulator. Thus, it was possible to study the use of regulation to correct for a systematically low level of care that would otherwise result if parties underestimated the component h_2 of risk.

[6] We assume that the condition (2) holds for the first-best x for all h in $[a, b]$, that is, that $1 < -p'(0)a$.

[7] Differentiate (2) with respect to h to get $0 = -p''(x)x'(h)h - p'(x)$, so that $x'(h) = -p'(x)/(p''(x)h) > 0$ (since $p'(x) < 0$ and $p''(x) > 0$).

☐ **Liability as the sole means of controlling risk.** Assume that the harm some parties might do exceeds their assets; and assume also that parties might escape suit. Thus, define

y = level of assets; $0 \leq y < b$; and
q = probability of suit, given that harm has been done; $0 \leq q < 1$,

where y and q are the same for each party. Now if a party causes harm h and is sued, he will be liable for h,[8] but will pay that amount only if $h \leq y$. Hence, his problem is to choose his level of care x to minimize

$$x + p(x)q\min\{h, y\},\tag{3}$$

and let the solution to this be denoted

$$x_l(h) = \text{care selected by a party, given } h.$$

Then we have

Proposition 1. Under liability, the care taken by parties as a function of the harm they might do is

$$x_l(h) = x^*(q\min\{h, y\}) < x^*(h).\tag{4}$$

Hence, as shown in Figure 1, the level of care is less than first-best, but it increases with the magnitude of the potential harm so long as this is less than the level of assets.[9]

Proof. The equality in (4) is obvious, since (3) is of the form of (1). The inequality and shape of the graph of x_l follow, since (as was observed) x^* is increasing in its argument, while $q\min\{h, y\} < h$ and is increasing for $h < y$ and then constant for $h \geq y$.

☐ **Regulation as the sole means of controlling risk.** Because the regulator cannot observe h, the standard it sets—which each party satisfies to engage in his activity—must be the same for all parties. Hence, if

$$s = \text{regulatory standard},$$

the regulator's problem is to minimize over s

$$s + p(s) \int_a^b hf(h)dh = s + p(s)E(h),\tag{5}$$

where E is the expectation operator. Let

$$s^* = \text{optimal regulatory standard},$$

the solution to (5). Hence, we have the following proposition.

Proposition 2. The optimal regulatory standard equals the level of care that would be first-best for a party posing the average risk of harm,

$$s^* = x^*(E(h)).\tag{6}$$

---

[8] In saying here that a party is liable for harm done, we are implicitly assuming that the form of liability is strict. Were we to consider instead the negligence rule—under which a party would be liable only if his level of care was inadequate, that is, less than $x^*(h)$—the qualitative character of the results to be obtained would be essentially unaltered. For instance, referring to the next proposition, the incentive to take care would still generally be diluted. The only difference is that $x_l(h)$ would be determined by a slightly different equation. (Actually, $x_l(h)$ would equal $x^*(q\min\{h, y\})$ unless q and y were sufficiently high, in which case it would equal $x^*(h)$.)

[9] We ignore the possibility of increasing liability from the harm h to h/q. Were this done, expected liability would be h despite the fact that $q < 1$. Thus, care would be optimal where $h/q \leq y$, but it would still be suboptimal where $h/q > y$, so that the essential nature of our results would be the same.

274   /   THE RAND JOURNAL OF ECONOMICS

FIGURE 1

FIRST–BEST LEVEL OF CARE VS. CARE TAKEN UNDER LIABILITY

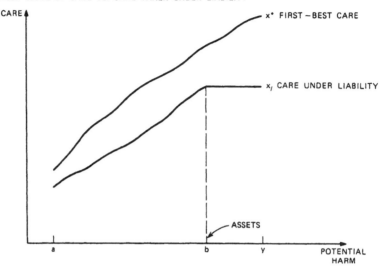

In particular, parties presenting a risk of harm less than $E(h)$ take more care than is first-best, and those presenting a risk higher than $E(h)$ take less care than is first-best.

Proof. Since the right-hand side of (5) is of the form of (1), (6) is correct.

☐ **Regulation vs. liability.** The difference in expected social costs between the situation where liability alone is employed and that where only the optimal regulatory standard is used is

$$\int_a^b \{[x_l(h) + p(x_l(h))h] - [s^* + p(s^*)h]\} f(h)dh. \qquad (7)$$

From this, we obtain the following proposition.

Proposition 3. Use of regulation is superior to use of liability if the factors that dilute the incentive to take care under liability are sufficiently important (q or y sufficiently low) or if the variability among parties is sufficiently small (h sufficiently concentrated about $E(h)$); otherwise liability is superior to regulation.

Note. The statement about the desirability of regulation and the dilution of incentives is obviously true. The other statement is also clearly valid: Figure 2 shows that regulation is superior to liability in a region R about $E(h)$; and hence regulation is superior if h is sufficiently likely to be close to $E(h)$.

Proof. We first want to show that, given y, there is a $q(y)$ where $0 < q(y) \leq 1$ such that regulation is superior to liability for $q \leq q(y)$, but not otherwise. Now if q or y equals 0, then (4) implies that $x_l(h)$ is identically equal to 0, and thus the situation is as if $s = 0$. But since s^* is the (unique) optimal s and is positive, social costs must be lower under regulation than when q or y equals 0. This fact and the continuity of social costs in q imply that for any y, regulation is superior to liability for all q sufficiently small. Moreover, if liability is superior to regulation for some q_1, then the same must be true for any $q_2 > q_1$, for social costs are easily shown to be decreasing in q under liability, but are unaffected by q under regulation.

FIGURE 2

COMPARISON OF REGULATION AND LIABILITY

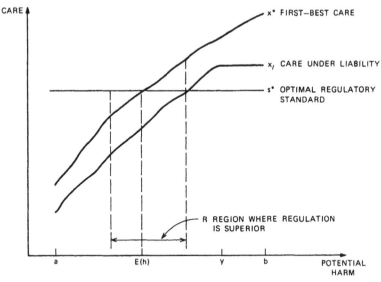

We similarly establish the analogous claim that, given q, there is a $y(q)$, where $0 < y(q) \leqq b$, with regulation being superior when $y \leqq y(q)$.

To prove the claim about variability in h, note from (4) that

$$x_l(E(h)) < x^*(E(h)) = s^*.$$

Hence, by continuity, there must exist a nondegenerate interval including $E(h)$ in which $s^* + p(s^*)h < x_l(h) + p(x_l(h))h$. Thus, if enough probability mass is within this interval, (7) will be positive, and regulation will be superior to liability.

□ **Joint use of regulation and liability.** Assume now that parties must satisfy a regulatory standard and are also subject to liability. Then their levels of care will be given by $\max\{s, x_l(h)\}$, and the situation will be as shown in Figure 3. For an s such as s_1, all parties with $h \leqq h(s_1)$ will take care of s_1, and others will take care of $x_l(h)$.[10] On the other hand, for an s such as s_2 that exceeds $x_l(b)$, all parties will take care of s_2. With this in mind, it is evident that the problem of the regulatory authority is to minimize over s

$$\int_b^a [\max\{s, x_l(h)\} + p(\max\{s, x_l(h)\})h] f(h)dh, \tag{8}$$

or, equivalently,

$$\min\left\{ \min_{0 \leqq s < x_l(b)} \int_a^{h(s)} [s + p(s)h] f(h)dh + \int_{h(s)}^b [x_l(h) + p(x_l(h))h] f(h)dh, \right.$$

$$\left. \min_{s \geqq x_l(b)} s + p(s) \int_a^b hf(h)dh \right\}. \tag{8a}$$

---

[10] Here $h(\ )$ denotes the inverse of $x_l(\ )$, where the latter is rising.

FIGURE 3

JOINT USE OF REGULATION AND LIABILITY

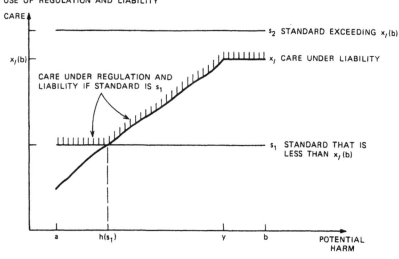

Let s^{**} denote the solution to this.[11] Then we have the following proposition.

Proposition 4. Under optimal joint use of regulation and liability, there are two possible types of outcome:

(a) The optimal regulatory standard is less than the optimal standard were regulation used alone, but it exceeds the first-best level of care for those parties posing the least risk of harm; that is,

$$x^*(a) < s^{**} < s^*. \tag{9}$$

Furthermore, in this case some parties are induced by liability to take more care than the required standard s^{**}. A sufficient condition for (9) to hold is

$$x_l(b) > s^*, \tag{10}$$

or, equivalently, that the incentive to take care is not excessively diluted (q sufficiently close to 1, y sufficiently close to b).

(b) The optimal regulatory standard equals the optimal standard where regulation alone was employed; that is,

$$s^{**} = s^*. \tag{11}$$

In this case no party is induced by liability to take more care than s^{**}. This will obtain if $x_l(b)$ is sufficiently low, or, equivalently, if the incentive to take care is sufficiently diluted (q or y sufficiently low).

Note. (a) To explain this result and the reason that s^{**} may be less than s^* (perhaps the typical case), consider Figure 4 and condition (10), which means that some parties are induced by liability to take more care than s^*. The reason that this condition implies $s^{**} < s^*$ is essentially that when regulation alone was used, reducing the standard below

---

[11] A solution exists since (8) is continuous in s and it is clear (and will be shown in step (i) of the proof) that s may be taken to lie in a closed and bounded interval.

FIGURE 4

OPTIMAL JOINT USE OF REGULATION AND LIABILITY: CASE WHERE SOME PARTIES TAKE MORE
CARE THAN IS REQUIRED BY REGULATION

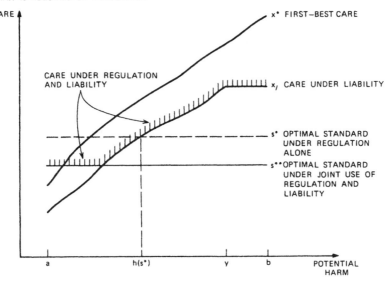

s^* was not worthwhile because it resulted in *all* parties' taking less care than s^*; but here it results *only* in those parties' with $h < h(s^*)$ taking less care: parties with higher h are induced by liability to take more care than s^*. Thus, we said in the Introduction that liability could take up some of the slack resulting from lowering the regulatory standard below s^*.

On the other hand, to understand why $s^{**} > x^*(a)$, observe that raising the standard from the level $x^*(a)$ does not lead to any first-order change in expected social costs with respect to parties with $h = a$; but it does result in a first-order reduction in expected social costs with respect to all other parties with higher h who would not have been induced by liability to take so much care as $x^*(a)$.

In addition, we shall show in the proof that s^{**} is determined by the condition

$$1 = -p'(s)\left[\int_a^{h(s)} hf(h)dh \Big/ \int_a^{h(s)} f(h)dh\right],$$ (12)

the interpretation of which is that the marginal cost of care equals the expected reduction in harm, where the expectation is over only those parties who are not affected by liability and thus are affected by the regulatory standard.[12]

(b) It is evident from Figure 5 why this case arises when $x_l(b)$ is sufficiently low: then the incentive to take care created by liability is too weak to take up any of the slack due to lowering the standard below s^*. It is therefore best to leave the standard at s^*. Also, it should be noted that in this case, the use of liability is superfluous, since the outcome is the same as if regulation alone is employed.

Proof. See the Appendix.

---

[12] Condition (12) is the analogue of (6), as is apparent when the latter is rewritten as $1 = -p'(s)E(h)$.

FIGURE 5

OPTIMAL JOINT USE OF REGULATION AND LIABILITY: CASE WHERE ALL PARTIES TAKE ONLY THE REQUIRED LEVEL OF CARE

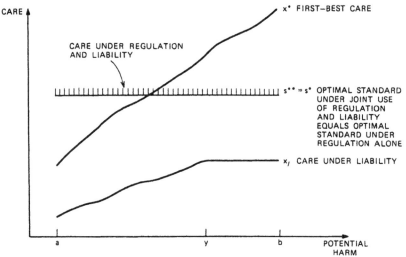

Appendix

■ **Proof of Proposition 4.** The argument consists of a series of steps, the first four of which establish (a) and the last two of which show (b).

(i) s^{**} must lie in $[x^*(a), s^*]$: It is easy to verify that for every h, expected social costs are lower at $s = x^*(a)$ than at smaller s, so that $s^{**} \geq x^*(a)$.

To show that $s^{**} \leq s^*$, let $C(s; r)$ be expected social costs, given s, when regulation alone is employed, and let $C(s; rl)$ be expected social costs when regulation and liability are jointly employed. Then for any $s_1 < s_2$, we claim that

$$C(s_1; r) - C(s_2; r) \geq C(s_1; rl) - C(s_2; rl). \qquad (A1)$$

This will follow from demonstrating the corresponding weak inequality for each h:

$$[s_1 + p(s_1)h] - [s_2 + p(s_2)h]$$
$$\geq [\max\{s_1, x_i(h)\} + p(\max\{s_1, x_i(h)\})h] - [\max\{s_2, x_i(h)\} + p(\max\{s_2, x_i(h)\})h]. \qquad (A2)$$

To verify (A2), consider Figure A1, which shows in the regions A, B, and C the different relations that may hold among s_1, s_2, and $x_i(h)$. It is easy to check that for h in A, equality obtains in (A2), and that for h in B or in C, (A2) holds strictly.

As s^{**} minimizes $C(s; rl)$ over s, $C(s^*; rl) - C(s^{**}; rl) \geq 0$. But then if $s^{**} > s^*$, (A1) would imply $C(s^*; r) - C(s^{**}; r) \geq 0$, which would contradict the fact that s^* is the unique optimum under regulation alone. Hence $s^{**} \leq s^*$.

(ii) $s^{**} < s^*$ implies that some parties choose care exceeding s^{**}, that is, $x_i(b) > s^{**}$: If $x_i(b) \leq s^{**}$, then for $s \geq s^{**}$, the second term in braces in (8a) is relevant. Since this term has a unique minimum over *all* s at s^*, and $s^* > s^{**}$, the term must have a unique minimum over $s \geq s^{**}$ at s^*. But this means that the term cannot have had a minimum at s^{**}, which is a contradiction.

(iii) $s^{**} < s^*$ implies that s^{**} is determined by the first-order condition (12) and that $s^{**} > x^*(a)$: From (ii) we know that if $s^{**} < s^*$, then the first term in braces in (8a) is relevant for all s in an interval properly including $x^*(a)$ and s^{**}. In particular, then, at s^{**} the derivative of the term with respect to s must be zero. But the derivative is

$$\int_a^{h(s)} f(h)dh + p'(s) \int_a^{h(s)} hf(h)dh. \qquad (A3)$$

FIGURE A1

CARE TAKEN UNDER LIABILITY AND UNDER TWO DIFFERENT STANDARDS

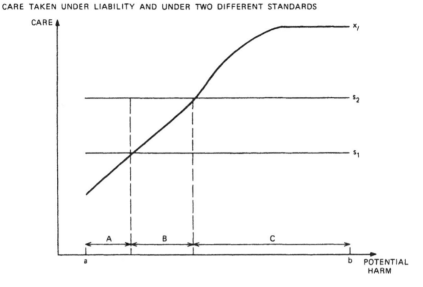

The first term of (A3) is positive since, from (i), $s^{**} \geq x^*(a)$, since $h(x^*(a)) > a$,[13] and since $h(\ )$ is increasing in its argument. Hence (A3) is equivalent to

$$\left\{ \int_a^{h(s)} f(h)dh \right\} \left\{ 1 + p'(s) \left[\int_a^{h(s)} hf(h)dh \Big/ \int_a^{h(s)} f(h)dh \right] \right\}. \tag{A3a}$$

Since (A3a) equals zero at s^{**}, (12) follows.

To prove that $s^{**} > x^*(a)$, we need only show that $s^{**} \neq x^*(a)$ (for by (i), $s^{**} \geq x^*(a)$) which in turn will follow if we show that (A3a) is unequal to zero when evaluated at $s = x^*(a)$. To do this, note that since $h(x^*(a)) > a$, the first term in (A3a) is positive; and observe that

$$\int_a^{h(s)} hf(h)dh \Big/ \int_a^{h(s)} f(h)dh \tag{A4}$$

is the mean of h conditional on its being in the interval $[a, h(s)]$. This tends to a as $h(s)$ tends to a and is strictly increasing in $h(s)$. Thus, since $h(x^*(a)) > a$, (A4) must exceed a at $s = x^*(a)$. From this and the fact that $1 + p'(x^*(a))a = 0$ it follows that the second term in braces in (A3a) is negative when evaluated at $x^*(a)$.

(iv) If (10) holds, then $s^{**} < s^*$: Suppose otherwise. Then, by (i), $s^{**} = s^*$. But suppose (10) implies that the first expression in braces in (8a) is relevant at s^*; we need only show that (A3a) is positive at s^* to contradict the presumed optimality of $s^{**} = s^*$. To do this, note from (6) and (2) that $1 + p'(s^*) \int_a^b hf(h)dh = 0$. Since (A4) is strictly less than $\int_a^b hf(h)dh$ when evaluated at s^*, however, it follows that the second term in braces in (A3a) is positive at s^*. Since the first term in (A3a) is clearly positive at s^*, (A3a) must be positive.

We remark also that it is obvious that (10) will hold if q and y are sufficiently high, for as q approaches 1 and y approaches b, $x_l(b)$ approaches $x^*(b) > s^*$.

(v) If $s^{**} = s^*$: then no party chooses care exceeding s^*: Otherwise, $x_l(b) > s^*$, which by (iv) implies $s^{**} < s^*$, a contradiction.

(vi) If $x_l(b)$ is sufficiently low, then $s^{**} = s^*$: Assume the contrary. Then in particular it must be possible that $s^{**} < s^*$ for an $x_l(b) \leq x^*(a)$. But by (ii) we know that if $s^{**} < s^*$, then $x_l(b) > s^{**}$. Hence, $x^*(a) > s^{**}$. This, however, contradicts (i), so that certainly for all $x_l(b)$ as low as $x^*(a)$, $s^{**} = s^*$.

---

[13] For any h such that $x^*(h)$ lies in the domain of the function $h(\ )$, we have $h(x^*(h)) > h$; this is obvious from Figure 1.

We remark also that it is clear that as q decreases, so does $x_i(b)$, and it approaches 0 as q approaches 0; and similarly, as y decreases and approaches a. Hence, if q or y is sufficiently small, $s^{**} = s^*$.

References

CALABRESI, G. *The Costs of Accidents.* New Haven: Yale University Press, 1970.

PROSSER, W. *Handbook of the Law of Torts,* 4th ed. St. Paul: West Publishing Co., 1971.

SHAVELL, S. "A Model of the Socially Optimal Use of Liability and Regulation." Working Paper No. 1220, National Bureau of Economic Research, 1983.

———. "Liability for Harm versus Regulation of Safety." *Journal of Legal Studies,* Vol. 13 (1984), pp. 357–374.

WEITZMAN, M. "Prices vs. Quantities." *Review of Economic Studies,* Vol. 41 (1974), pp. 447–491.

WITTMAN, D. "Prior Regulation versus Post Liability: The Choice between Input and Output Monitoring." *Journal of Legal Studies,* Vol. 6 (1977), pp. 193–212.

The Incentive Effects of Liability

[5]

STRICT LIABILITY VERSUS NEGLIGENCE

*STEVEN SHAVELL**

I. INTRODUCTION AND DISCUSSION

T HE aim of this article is to compare strict liability and negligence rules on the basis of the incentives they provide to "appropriately" reduce accident losses. It will therefore be both convenient and clarifying to abstract from other issues in respect to which the rules could be evaluated. In particular, there will be no concern with the bearing of risk—for parties will be presumed risk neutral—nor with the size of "administrative costs"—for the legal system will be assumed to operate free of such costs—nor with distributional equity—for the welfare criterion will be taken to be the following aggregate: the benefits derived by parties from engaging in activities less total accident losses less total accident prevention costs.

Because the analysis of the rules will employ a mathematical model, it seems desirable to consider first in an informal way the points to be made and the logic behind them. Since this discussion will not serve as a complete summary, readers will probably also want to at least look at the statements of the propositions in the later parts of the paper and will almost certainly wish to read the concluding comments (which are not focused on the details of the model).

Accidents will be conceived of as involving two types of parties, "injurers" and "victims," only the latter of which are assumed to suffer direct losses. The category of accidents that will be examined initially are *unilateral* in nature, by which is meant that the actions of injurers but not of victims are assumed to affect the probability or severity of losses. The unilateral case is studied for two reasons. First, it is descriptive of situations in which whatever changes in the behavior of victims that could reasonably be expected to result from changes in liability rules would have only a small influence on accident losses.[1] The second reason is pedagogical; it is easier to understand the general *bilateral* case after having studied the unilateral case.

* Associate Professor of Economics, Harvard University, and Visiting Professor, Harvard Law School. I wish to thank the National Science Foundation (NSF grant SOC-76-20862) for financial support and Peter Diamond, Douglas Ginsburg, Henry Hansmann, Duncan Kennedy, and, especially, A. Mitchell Polinsky and Richard Posner for comments.

[1] Examples of accidents occurring in such situations and which therefore might be considered

Unilateral Case

This case (as well as the bilateral case) will be considered in each of several situations distinguished by the nature of the relationship between injurers and victims.

Accidents between strangers (see Proposition 1): In this subcase it is supposed that injurers and victims are strangers, that neither are sellers of a product, and that injurers may choose to engage in an activity which puts victims at risk.

By definition, under the negligence rule all that an injurer needs to do to avoid the possibility of liability is to make sure to exercise due care if he engages in his activity.[2] Consequently *he will not be motivated to consider the effect on accident losses of his choice of whether to engage in his activity or, more generally, of the level at which to engage in his activity;* he will choose his level of activity in accordance only with the personal benefits so derived. But surely any increase in his level of activity will typically raise expected accident losses (holding constant the level of care). Thus he will be led to choose too high a level of activity;[3] the negligence rule is not "efficient."

Consider by way of illustration the problem of pedestrian-automobile accidents (and, as we are now discussing the unilateral case, let us imagine the behavior of pedestrians to be fixed). Suppose that drivers of automobiles find it in their interest to adhere to the standard of due care but that the possibility of accidents is not thereby eliminated. Then, in deciding how much to drive, they will contemplate only the enjoyment they get from doing so. Because (as they exercise due care) they will not be liable for harm suffered by pedestrians, drivers will not take into account that going more miles will mean a higher expected number of accidents. Hence, there will be too much driving; an individual will, for example, decide to go for a drive on a mere whim despite the imposition of a positive expected cost to pedestrians.

However, under a rule of strict liability, the situation is different. Because

---

unilateral are not hard to imagine: a water main breaks and floods the basement of a home; a plane crashes into a house; a surgeon performs the wrong procedure on an anaesthetized patient. Concededly, even in these examples the victim could have taken *some* protective action (the surgeon's patient could have hired another surgeon to watch over the operation), but, we may plausibly assume, not at a cost nearly low enough to make it worthwhile.

[2] It is assumed for ease of exposition that courts have no difficulty in determining if a party did in fact exercise due care; the reader will have no trouble in appropriately modifying the arguments to be made so as to take into account relaxation of such simplifications as this.

[3] Specifically, while he will choose to engage in the activity just up to the level at which the personal benefit from a marginal increase would equal zero, it would be best from society's viewpoint for him to engage in the activity only up to the level at which his benefit from a marginal increase would equal the (positive) social marginal cost in terms of accident losses.

an injurer must pay for losses whenever he is involved in an accident,[4] he will be induced to consider the effect on accident losses of both his level of care *and* his level of activity. His decisions will therefore be efficient. Because drivers will be liable for losses sustained by pedestrians, they will decide not only to exercise due care in driving but also to drive only when the utility gained from it outweighs expected liability payments to pedestrians.

Accidents between sellers and strangers (see Proposition 2): In this subcase it is assumed that injurers are sellers of a product or service and that they conduct their business in a competitive market. (The assumption of competition allows us to ignore monopoly power, which is for the purposes of this article a logically tangential issue.) Moreover, it is assumed that victims are strangers; they have no market relationship with sellers either as their customers or as their employees.

Under the negligence rule the outcome is inefficient, but the reasoning is slightly different from that of the last subcase. While it is still true that all a seller must do to avoid liability is to take due care, why this results in too high a level of activity has to do with market forces. Because the seller will choose to avoid liability, the price of his product will not reflect the accident losses associated with production. This means that buyers of the product will face too low a price and will purchase too much, which is to say that the seller's level of activity will be too high. Imagine that the drivers are engaged in some business activity—let us say that they are taxi drivers. Then, given that they take due care, the taxi drivers will not have liability expenses, will set rates equal to "production" cost (competition among taxi drivers is assumed), will experience a greater demand than if rates were appropriately higher, and will therefore carry too many fares and cause too many accidents.

Under strict liability, the outcome is efficient, and again the reasoning is a little different from that in the last subcase. Since sellers have to pay for accident losses, they will be led to take the right level of care. And since the product price will reflect accident losses, customers will face the "socially correct" price for the product; purchases will therefore be appropriately lower than what they would be if the product price did not reflect accident losses. Taxi drivers will now increase rates by an amount equal to expected accident losses suffered by pedestrians, and the demand for rides in taxis will fall.

Accidents between sellers and customers—or employees (see Proposition 3 and Part III. B (iii)): It is presumed here that victims have a market relationship with sellers as either their customers or their employees; and since both situations are essentially the same, it will suffice to discuss only that when victims are customers. In order to understand the role (which is important)

---

[4] Causal or other reasons for limiting the scope of liability are ignored.

of customers' knowledge of risk, three alternative assumptions will be considered: customers know the risk presented by each seller; they do not know the risk presented by each seller but they do know the average seller's risk;[5] they misperceive even this average risk.

Under the negligence rule, the outcome is efficient only if customers correctly perceive risks. As before, when the victims were strangers, sellers will take due care in order to avoid liability, so that the product price will not reflect accident losses. However, now the accident losses are borne by the customers. Thus, the "full" price in the eyes of customers is the market price plus imputed perceived accident losses. Therefore, if risks are correctly perceived, the full price equals the socially correct price, and the quantity purchased will be appropriate. But if risks are not correctly perceived, the quantity purchased will be inappropriate; if customers underestimate risks, what they regard as the full price is less than the true full price and they will buy too much of the product, and conversely if they overestimate risks.[6]

Think, for example, of the risk of food poisoning from eating at restaurants. Under the negligence rule, restaurants will decide to avoid liability by taking appropriate precautions to prepare meals under sanitary conditions. Therefore, the price of meals will not reflect the expected losses due to the (remaining) risk of food poisoning. If customers know this risk, they will correctly consider it in their decisions over the purchase of meals. But if they underestimate the risk, they will purchase too many meals; and if they overestimate it, too few.

Under strict liability, the outcome is efficient regardless of whether customers misperceive risks. As in the last subcase, because sellers have to pay for accident losses, they will decide to take appropriate care and will sell the product at a price reflecting accident losses. Thus customers will face the socially correct price and will purchase the correct amount. Their perception of the risk is irrelevant since it will not influence their purchases; as they will be compensated under strict liability for any losses, the likelihood of losses will not matter to them. Restaurant-goers will face a price that reflects expected losses due to food poisoning when meals are prepared under sanitary conditions; they will buy the same—and appropriate—number of meals whether they think the probability of food poisoning is low or high, for they will be compensated for any losses suffered.[7]

---

[5] If sellers are assumed to be identical (as they are in the formal model) and therefore to act identically, the average risk will in fact be the risk presented by each seller. But it will be seen from the discussion of the situation when sellers are not liable that the first and second assumptions are nevertheless different.

[6] It may be instructive to mention the parallel situation in regard to employee victims. If employees correctly perceive risks at the workplace, then they will (appropriately) choose to work for a firm only if the "net" wage—the market wage less the expected accident losses they bear—is at least equal to their opportunity elsewhere. But if, say, they underestimate risks, they might choose to work for a firm when the net wage is in fact below their opportunity elsewhere.

[7] However, it is worthwhile noticing that if they could not possibly be compensated for a kind

STRICT LIABILITY VERSUS NEGLIGENCE 5

When sellers are simply not liable for accident losses, then the outcome is efficient only if customers know the risk presented by each seller. For, given this assumption, because customers will seek to buy products with the lowest full price (market price plus expected accident losses), sellers will be induced to take appropriate care (since this will lower the accident-loss component of the full price). While it is true that if a restaurant took inadequate precautions to prevent food poisoning, it could offer lower-priced meals, it is also true that customers would respond not just to the market price of meals but also to the likelihood of food poisoning—which they are presumed to know. Therefore customers would decide against giving the restaurant their business. Consequently, restaurants will be led to take adequate precautions and to charge accordingly. Moreover, because customers will base purchases on the correctly perceived full price, they will buy the correct amount.

If, however, customers do not know the risk presented by individual sellers, there are two sources of inefficiency when sellers are not liable. The first is that, given the risk of loss, the quantity purchased by customers may not be correct; of course, this will be true if customers misperceive the risk. The second source of inefficiency is that sellers will not be motivated by market forces to appropriately reduce risks. To understand why, consider the situation when customers do correctly perceive the average risk (when they do not correctly perceive this risk, an explanation similar to the one given here could be supplied). That is, assume that customers know the risk presented by sellers as a group but do not have the ability to "observe" the risk presented by sellers on an individual basis. Then sellers would have no inducement to exercise adequate care. Suppose that restaurant-goers know the risk of food poisoning at restaurants in general and it is, say, inappropriately high. Then if a *particular* restaurant were to take sufficient precautions to lower the risk, customers would not recognize this (except insofar as it eventually affected the average risk—but under the assumption that there are many competing restaurants, this effect would be negligible). Thus the restaurant could not charge a higher price for its meals—customers would have no reason not to go to the cheaper restaurants. In consequence, a situation in which sellers take inadequate care to reduce risks would persist; and similar reasoning shows that a situation in which they take adequate care would not persist. (Notice, however, that since customers are assumed to correctly perceive the average risk, at least they will purchase the correct number of meals—correct, given the high risk.)

---

of loss from food poisoning, then misperception of risk certainly would matter. For instance, if there were a risk of death from food poisoning and if restaurant-goers underestimated it, then they would expose themselves to a higher risk of death by eating restaurant meals than they would truly want to bear. Thus, the conclusion of this paragraph that misperception of risk does not matter under strict liability holds only in respect to risks compensable by payment of money damages.

Finally, it should be observed that the discussion of liability in the present subcase bears on the role of tort law in a contractual setting. When customers make purchases, they are willingly entering into a kind of contract—in which they agree to a price and pay it, receive goods, and expose themselves to a risk (in the absence of liability).[8] Therefore, our conclusions may be generally expressed by the statement that, when customers' knowledge of risks is perfect, the rule of liability does not matter; the "contractual" arrangement arrived at in the market is appropriate. But when the knowledge is not perfect, there is generally scope for the use of liability, and the relative performance of liability rules depends on the precise nature of the imperfection in knowledge. The force of this point, and the fact that it is not always an obvious one, is perhaps well illustrated by the situation described in the previous paragraph. In that situation, customers did correctly perceive average risk, so that there was "assumption of risk," but this did not lead to a desirable result. The situation was one therefore in which, under our assumptions, courts ought not to allow the defense of assumption of risk to be successfully asserted.

Bilateral Case

In this case, account is taken of the possibility that potential victims as well as injurers may influence the probability or magnitude of accident losses by their choices of both level of care and of level of activity.

Accidents between strangers (see Propositions 4 and 5):[9] Under the negligence rule,[10] the outcome is not efficient. As was true in the unilateral case, since all that an injurer needs to do to avoid liability is to exercise due care,

---

[8] It should be remarked that the possibility of contractual arrangements that go beyond mere agreement on price is not considered here; for example, the possibility that sellers might give customers some form of guarantee is not allowed for in the discussion or in the analysis. However, our conclusions do have some relevance to what contractual arrangements might be made. This is because what is "efficient" is, by definition, what maximizes benefits minus costs, which is in turn what is in the mutual interest of the sellers and customers to do. (To illustrate, if customers *realize* that they do not know the risk of loss, then they might wish for, and insist on, a blanket guarantee, in effect making the seller strictly liable, and thereby giving him an incentive to reduce the risk of loss.) Of course, the reason this is not considered here is that a satisfactory treatment would require us to study at the least the value of explicit arrangements over the arrangements that inhere in the applicable tort and contract law, the costs of making explicit arrangements as opposed to the expected costs of reliance on the applicable law, and the willingness of courts to enforce what is at variance with the applicable law.

[9] The explanation given in this and in the next subcase for why neither strict liability with a defense of contributory negligence nor the negligence rule results in an efficient outcome is in its essence that given by Richard Posner, Economic Analysis of Law 139-40 (2d ed. 1977). See also Duncan Kennedy, A History of Law and Economics or the Fetishism of Commodities (1979) (unpublished mimeographed paper at Harvard University) which makes related points at 54-63.

[10] In the present discussion, it will make no difference whether or not the reader thinks of this rule as incorporating the defense of contributory negligence.

he will choose too high a level of activity. In regard to victims, however, the situation is different. Since a victim bears his accident losses, he will choose an appropriate level of care *and* an appropriate level of his activity, given the (inefficient) behavior of injurers. The drivers will exercise due care but will go too many miles. And the pedestrians, knowing that they must bear accident losses, will exercise due care (in crossing streets and so forth) and they will also reduce the number of miles they walk in accordance with expected accident losses per mile.

Under strict liability with a defense of contributory negligence, the outcome is symmetrical to the last—and again inefficient.[11] Because all that a victim needs to do to avoid bearing accident losses is to take due care, he will have no motive to appropriately reduce *his* level of activity; this is the inefficiency. However, because injurers now bear accident losses, they will take the appropriate amount of care and choose the right level of activity, given the inefficient behavior of victims. Drivers will exercise due care and go the correct number of miles. Pedestrians will also exercise due care but will walk too many miles.

From this discussion it is apparent that the choice between strict liability with a defense of contributory negligence and the negligence rule is a choice between the lesser of two evils. Strict liability with the defense will be superior to the negligence rule when it is more important that injurers be given an incentive through a liability rule to reduce their activity level than that victims be given a similar incentive; that is to say, when it is more important that drivers go fewer miles than that pedestrians walk fewer miles.

Because neither of the familiar liability rules induces efficient behavior, the question arises, *"Is there any conceivable liability rule depending on parties' levels of care and harm done that induces efficient behavior?"* It is proved below (Proposition 5) that the answer is *"No."* The problem in essence is that for injurers to be induced to choose the correct level of activity, they must bear all accident losses; and for victims to choose the correct level of their activity, they also must bear all accident losses. Yet it is in the nature of a liability rule that both conditions cannot hold simultaneously; clearly, injurers and victims cannot each bear all accident losses.[12]

Accidents between sellers and strangers (see Proposition 6): Because the reader will be able to appeal to arguments analogous to those already made and in order to avoid tedious repetition, explanation of the results stated in this and the next subcase will be abbreviated or will be omitted.

[11] It is of course clear that under strict liability without the defense the outcome is inefficient, for victims would have no motive to take care.

[12] However, when other means of social control are also employed, it is possible to achieve an efficient outcome. For example, if use of the negligence rule were supplemented by imposition of a tax on the level of injurer activity, an efficient outcome could be achieved.

Under both the negligence rule and strict liability with a defense of contributory negligence, the outcome is inefficient, as was true in the last subcase. Under the negligence rule, sellers will take appropriate care, but since the product price will not reflect accident losses, too much will be purchased by customers. Also, since victims bear accident losses, they will take appropriate care and choose the right level of activity. Under strict liability with the defense, sellers will take appropriate care and the product price will reflect accident losses, so the right amount will be purchased. Victims will exercise due care but will choose too high a level of activity. In addition, as in the last subcase, there does not exist any liability rule that induces efficient behavior.

Accidents between sellers and customers—or employees (see Propositions 7a and 7b and Part IV.B (iii)): As before it will be enough to discuss here only the situation when victims are customers. If customers have perfect knowledge of the risk presented by each seller, then the outcome is efficient under strict liability with a defense of contributory negligence or the negligence rule or if sellers are not subject to liability at all. For instance, in the latter situation, since customers wish to buy at the lowest full price, sellers will be led to take appropriate care; and since customers will make their purchases with the full price in mind, the quantity they buy will be correct; and since they bear their losses, they will take appropriate care.

There is, however, a qualification that needs to be made concerning the way in which it is imagined that customers influence accident losses. If one assumes that customers influence losses only by their choice of level of care and of the amount purchased, then what was stated in the previous paragraph is correct; and in regard to services and nondurables (such as meals at restaurants) this assumption seems entirely natural. But in regard to durable goods, it might well be thought that customers influence accident losses not only by their choice of level of care and of purchases, but also by their decision as to frequency of use per unit purchased. The expected number of accidents that a man will have when using a power lawn mower would seem to be influenced not only by whether he in fact purchases one (rather than, say, a hand mower) and by how carefully he mows his lawn with it, but also by how frequently he chooses to mow his lawn. In order for customers to be led to efficiently decide the frequency of use, they must bear their own accident losses. Thus, in regard to durables, the outcome is efficient under the negligence rule or if sellers are not liable, but the outcome is inefficient under strict liability with a defense of contributory negligence; for then if the man buys a power lawn mower, he will have no motive to appropriately reduce the number of times he mows his lawn.

Now suppose that customers correctly perceive only average risks. Then, subject again to a qualification concerning durables, the results are as follows. The outcome is efficient under strict liability with a defense of contributory negligence or under the negligence rule, but the outcome is not efficient if sellers are not liable, for then they will not take sufficient care. The qualification is that if the sellers produce durables, strict liability with the defense is inefficient, leaving the negligence rule as the only efficient rule.

Last, suppose that customers misperceive risks. Then the outcome is efficient only under strict liability with a defense of contributory negligence; and the qualification to this is that, if sellers produce durables, even strict liability with the defense is inefficient, so that there does not exist a liability rule which is efficient.

II. The Model

The assumptions here are much as described in the introduction. There is a single physical good, called "income." The utility (or disutility) of any action which a party takes is assumed to have a well-defined equivalent in terms of income; and, henceforth, when reference is made to income, what will be meant is the amount of literal income plus income equivalents. The (von Neumann-Morgenstern) utility of income is assumed to be equal to income. Thus, parties are risk-neutral; expected utility is expected income. Since the social-welfare function is taken to be the sum of expected utilities, social welfare is the sum of expected incomes.

Accidents are assumed to involve two types of parties, injurers and victims. The number of injurers is assumed equal to the number of victims (and equal to the number of customers in the market case described below); this assumption is inessential and could obviously be modified. In the absence of liability rules, all accident losses fall on victims. The class of injurers and the class of victims are themselves each comprised of identical parties.

Injurers either engage in a nonmarket activity—the "nonmarket" case—or are sellers of a product or service—the "market" case. In the market case, sellers are expected to be profit-maximizing price takers and to face constant production costs per unit. Thus, they earn zero profits in competitive equilibrium. Victims are either strangers, customers, or employees. If victims are customers or employees, three alternative assumptions (which were discussed in the introduction) are made about their knowledge of accident risks.

Parties take liability rules as given; they do not circumvent the rules by contractual arrangement.[13] They also take the behavior of others as given.

---

[13] The justification is the familiar one, that some "transaction cost" stands in the way. In the nonmarket case and the market case involving strangers, it is that it would be very difficult for each potential injurer to get together with and make a contractual arrangement with each of his potential victims. In the market case, the assumption is that the costs of

10   THE JOURNAL OF LEGAL STUDIES

Under these assumptions, the (Nash) equilibrium associated with the use of a liability rule can be determined.

An analysis of equilibrium outcomes under liability rules for the nonmarket and market cases is made both in the part of the paper concerned with unilateral accidents and in the one dealing with bilateral accidents. In the nonmarket case, victims are assumed to engage in their activity at a fixed level and to exercise a fixed level of care. Their only role in the market case is, if they are customers, to decide how much to buy or, if they are employees, to decide where to work. The liability rules examined are no liability, strict liability, and the negligence rule. In the bilateral case, two additional liability rules are considered, strict liability with a defense of contributory negligence and the negligence rule with that defense.

If a liability rule results in the outcome that maximizes social welfare, it will be called efficient. The efficient values of variables will be denoted with an "*".

Because the notation used changes somewhat in the different cases analyzed, it will be easiest to present it and to modify it as needed.

III.   Unilateral Accidents

Define the following variables,

$$x \geqq 0 \quad \text{care level of an injurer.}$$
$$y \geqq 0 \quad \text{activity level of an injurer,}$$
$$l(x) \quad \text{expected accident losses per}$$
$$\text{unit of injurer activity level.}^{[14]}$$

Expected accident losses are assumed to fall with care, so $l' < 0$, but at a decreasing rate, so $l'' > 0$. Notice that the model allows for the possibility that injurers may choose not to engage in their activity at all; this corresponds to $y = 0$.

Under strict liability, an injurer is assumed to pay for all accident losses suffered by victims of accidents in which he is involved. Under the negligence rule an injurer has to pay for accident losses only if his care level is less than a due care level. Define

$$\bar{x} = \text{injurer's due care level.}$$

---

bargaining and perhaps of recording an agreement make it easier for the involved parties to rely on a liability rule.

[14] We are implicitly assuming that increasing the activity level corresponds to a physical repetition of an activity and causes a proportional rise in expected accident losses. For example, doubling the activity level would double expected accident losses (the level of care held constant). This assumption often seems to be the natural one to make, but it will be clear that the qualitative nature of our results would not be altered if expected accident losses were a more general function of x and y.

STRICT LIABILITY VERSUS NEGLIGENCE   11

Thus, as emphasized in the introduction, y does not enter into a determination about negligence.

A. The Nonmarket Case: Accidents between Strangers

Recall that in this case, injurers are not sellers of a product or service but they may decide to engage in an activity which puts victims at risk. Define

$$a(x,y) = \text{income equivalent of the utility to}$$
$$\text{an injurer of engaging in his activity at}$$
$$\text{level } y \text{ and exercising care } x.\text{[15]}$$

Assume that taking more care reduces this, so $a_x < 0$.[16] Assume also that, given the care level, increases in the activity level up to some point result in increases in utility; beyond that point, however, utility falls with increases in the activity level. Specifically, for any x, $a_y(x,y) > 0$ for $y < y(x)$ and $a_y(x,y) < 0$ for $y > y(x)$. Here $y(x)$ is (uniquely) defined by either $a_y(x,y) = 0$ or, if this never holds, by $y(x) = 0$.

Social welfare W is given by[17]

$$W(x,y) = a(x,y) - yl(x). \tag{1}$$

Note that what enters into W is not only expected accident losses (through yl) and prevention costs (through a_x), but also the benefits of participating in the activity (through a_y). The efficient values x^* and y^* maximize W.

Since under strict liability an injurer must pay for accident losses to possible victims, an injurer's position is

$$a(x,y) - yl(x). \tag{2}$$

The injurer's problem, maximizing (2) over x and y, is the social problem. Strict liability is therefore efficient.

Under the negligence rule, assume that the due care level $\bar{x}$ is sufficiently low so that injurers decide to act in a nonnegligent way, that is, to choose $x = \bar{x}$.[18] Thus, the injurer's problem becomes one of choosing y to maximize

---

[15] The reader might find it convenient to think about the case $a(x,y) = z(y) - v(x)y$, where $z(y)$ is the benefit of engaging in the activity at level y and $v(x)$ is the cost of taking care x per unit of activity.

[16] Subscripts denote partial derivatives. The arguments of derivatives will frequently be suppressed in the notation.

[17] We need only consider social welfare for a "representative" injurer and victim pair—recall that we have assumed for simplicity that their numbers are equal. An injurer's expected income is $a(x,y)$ − expected liability payments, and a victim's expected liability payments − $yl(x)$. Adding these gives W.

[18] If $\bar{x}$ were so high that injurers decided to be negligent, they would be, in effect, strictly liable. It does not seem natural to analyze this possibility as one having to do with the negligence rule.

$$a(\bar{x}, y). \tag{3}$$

The injurer therefore increases y to the point at which it yields no marginal benefit; in other words, he selects $y(\bar{x})$. Let $y^*(\bar{x})$ be the efficient y given $\bar{x}$ (that is, $y^*(\bar{x})$ maximizes W over y given $\bar{x}$). Then the injurer's activity level is excessive in the sense that $y(\bar{x}) > y^*(\bar{x})$, and for this reason one can immediately conclude that the negligence rule is not efficient.[19] The socially optimal due care level, say $\bar{x}^*$, is determined by maximizing

$$W(\bar{x}, y(\bar{x})) = a(\bar{x}, y(\bar{x})) - y(\bar{x})l(\bar{x}) \tag{4}$$

over $\bar{x}$ (where $\bar{x}$ must be in the range low enough so that injurers decide to set $x = \bar{x}$). Under fairly weak assumptions, it is true that $\bar{x}^* > x^*$.[20] The optimal due care standard exceeds the efficient care level because it is socially desirable to compensate for inability to control the activity level by forcing injurers to exercise special care (and because this in itself reduces the value of the activity, inducing injurers to lower the activity level).

If there is no liability, the outcome is generally worse than that under the negligence rule (with $\bar{x}^*$ as the due care standard), since injurers exercise no care. That is, $x = 0$ and $y = y(0)$ is the outcome.[21]

The conclusions about the welfare comparison of liability rules may be summarized as follows.

PROPOSITION 1. *Suppose that injurers and victims are strangers. Then strict liability is efficient and is superior to the negligence rule, which is superior to not having liability at all.*

B. *The Market Case: Accidents between Sellers and Victims*

Injurers are now assumed to be sellers of a product or service. The precise interpretation of care x will be explained in the various subcases, which are distinguished by whether the victims are strangers, customers, or employees. The activity level y will be interpreted as the seller's output.

---

[19] Assume that W is concave in y, that $\bar{x} > 0$, and that $y(\bar{x}) > 0$. Then $y(\bar{x})$ is identified by the first-order condition $a_y = 0$. But $y^*(\bar{x})$ is determined by $a_y = l$. Since $l > 0$ and W is concave, $y^*(\bar{x}) < y(\bar{x})$. Note, however, that the concavity assumption is not needed to show that the negligence rule is not efficient; without it we can still conclude that $y^*(\bar{x}) \neq \bar{y}(\bar{x})$.

[20] Let $[0, \hat{x}]$ be the range of $\bar{x}$ such that injurers would choose $x = \bar{x}$. It is easy to show that $\hat{x} > x^*$. Thus, assuming concavity of (4) in $\bar{x}$, we need only argue that $dW/d\bar{x} > 0$ when evaluated at x^*. But $dW/D\bar{x} = W_x - y'l$ and it is plausible that both terms should be positive at x^*. Assuming that W is concave in x and that the optimal x given $\bar{y}(x^*)$ exceeds x^*, we have $W_x > 0$. Also, assuming that $y' < 0$, $-y'l > 0$.

[21] To show that the negligence rule would be better, we need only demonstrate that $\bar{x}^* > 0$ (for $\bar{x} = 0$ corresponds to no liability). This is plausible for the reasons given in the previous footnote: A sufficient condition for $dW/d\bar{x} > 0$ at $\bar{x} = 0$ is that $W_x(0, y(0)) > 0$ and $y'(0) < 0$.

STRICT LIABILITY VERSUS NEGLIGENCE   13

Before considering the subcases, additional notation is needed, as is a description of competitive market equilibrium. Define

$$c(x) = \text{production cost per unit given } x,$$
$$p = \text{product price,}$$

and assume that $c' > 0$ and $c'' > 0$. The seller's full cost per unit produced and sold is

$$c(x) + \text{expected liability payments per unit.} \tag{5}$$

Since sellers maximize expected profits and are price takers,

$$x \text{ is chosen by sellers to minimize } c(x) + \text{expected}$$
$$\text{liability payments per unit.} \tag{6}$$

Also, in equilibrium, price must equal full cost,

$$p = c(x) + \text{expected liability payments per unit.} \tag{7}$$

(However, (6) and (7) will be slightly modified when the victims are customers and can observe x.) Now define

$$b(y) = \text{income equivalent of gross benefits enjoyed by}$$
$$\text{a customer who purchases } y.$$

These benefits are gross of any expected accident losses he has to bear. We assume $b' > 0$ and $b'' < 0$. The customer's position u is

$$u(y) = b(y) - py - \text{any expected accident losses he}$$
$$\text{has to bear.} \tag{8}$$

The customer's demand is therefore determined by

$$u(y) \text{ is maximized over } y. \tag{9}$$

Equilibrium p, x, and y are determined by (6), (7), and (9).
  Social welfare W is given by

$$W = b(y) - yc(x) - yl(x), \tag{10}$$

the gross value of output to customers minus production costs—note that the increase in c with x corresponds to prevention costs—minus expected accident losses. As in the nonmarket case, maximizing W requires taking into account the benefits of y as well as accident costs and prevention costs. From (10), it is clear that the efficient value x^* is determined by

$$\text{minimize } c(x) + l(x) \text{ over } x \tag{11}$$

and that y^* is then determined by

$$\text{maximize } b(y) - y(c(x^*) + l(x^*)) \text{ over } y. \tag{12}$$

(i) *Victims are strangers*. Here x is interpreted as the care the seller exercises in the conduct of his operations.

Under strict liability sellers are induced to choose the care level that minimizes production costs plus accident losses. Moreover because customers pay a price that reflects production costs plus accident losses, they are induced to purchase the socially correct output. To prove this, note that full cost per unit is $c(x) + l(x)$, which (see (6)) sellers minimize. Hence (see (11)), x^* is the care level. Therefore (see (7)), price p equals $c(x^*) + l(x^*)$. Hence (see (8) and (9)), consumers maximize $b(y) - py = b(y) - (c(x^*) + l(x^*))y$. This implies (see (12)) that y^* is chosen. Consequently, strict liability is efficient.

Under the negligence rule, an efficient outcome is not achieved. This is because sellers escape liability by acting nonnegligently. Hence the price charged customers reflects production costs but not accident losses. Since customers face too low a price, output is too high. To demonstrate this, assume (for the reason given in the nonmarket case) that $\bar{x}$ is low enough so that sellers decide to be nonnegligent. Then production cost and price must be $c(\bar{x})$. Consequently, customers choose y to maximize $b(y) - py = b(y) - c(\bar{x})y$. Let $y(\bar{x})$ be the customers' choice and $y^*(\bar{x})$ the efficient y given $\bar{x}$. Then $y(\bar{x}) > y^*(\bar{x})$, output is excessive, which also implies that the negligence rule cannot be efficient. The optimal due care level $\bar{x}^*$ is determined by maximizing

$$W(\bar{x}, y(\bar{x})) = b(y(\bar{x})) - c(\bar{x}) - y(\bar{x})l(\bar{x}) \tag{13}$$

over $\bar{x}$ (in the range such that sellers choose to be nonnegligent). As in the nonmarket case, it can be shown that $\bar{x}^* > x^*$, and for analogous reasons.[22]

If there is no liability, sellers have no motive to prevent accidents nor do customers have a motive to buy a socially appropriate quantity, since price does not reflect accident losses. Therefore, the outcome is worse than under the negligence rule. Specifically, production cost and price are $c(0)$ and customers choose $y(0)$.[23]

In summary, the conclusions are just as in the nonmarket case.

PROPOSITION 2. *Suppose that injurers are sellers and that victims are strangers. Then strict liability is efficient and is superior to the negligence rule, which is superior to not having liability at all.*

(ii) *Victims are customers*. In this subcase x might still be interpreted as the care the seller exercises in the conduct of his operations. This would be

---

[22] This and other claims made in this paragraph can be proved using arguments analogous to those in notes 19 & 20 *supra*.

[23] That no liability is inferior to the negligence rule can be shown by establishing, as in note 21 *supra*, that $\bar{x}^* > 0$.

appropriate if one is thinking about accidents which occur at the time and place of sale of a product or service. On the other hand, if one is considering accidents which occur after the time of purchase and involve a product that the customer takes away with him (a car, a piece of industrial machinery), then x should be interpreted as an index of the safety and reliability of the product.

Under strict liability, an argument virtually identical to that given in (i) shows that the efficient outcome results. Sellers again choose x in accord with (11). Thus price is $c(x^*) + l(x^*)$, and as customers do not bear accident losses, they select y in accord with (12). Note that this argument in no way depends on customers' knowledge of the risk of accident losses.

However, under the negligence rule, the analysis changes. Assume first that customers know what expected accident losses are either for particular sellers or only on average. Then the efficient outcome results if the due care level $\bar{x}$ is set equal to the efficient level x^*. To prove this, suppose that sellers choose x^*. Then, as they are nonnegligent, price equals $c(x^*)$. Since customers bear losses $l(x^*)$ per unit and know their magnitude, they maximize over y their utility position, $b(y) - py - l(x^*)y = b(y) - (c(x^*) + l(x^*))y$. Thus, they choose y^*. Therefore, to complete the proof, we need only show that sellers would choose x^* or, more precisely, that no seller would have a motive to choose an x other than x^* if there were an equilibrium in which x^* was the commonly chosen care level. To show this, suppose, on the contrary, that some seller chooses $x > x^*$. If customers can't observe *his x*, then he gets no benefit in the price from raising x but does incur greater production costs. On the other hand, if customers can observe his x, it is easy to show they wouldn't purchase from him if he charged his cost of production. If he did that, a customer's utility position would be the maximum over y of $b(y) - (c(x) + l(x))y$ which (since $x \neq x^*$) must be less than $b(y^*) - (c(x^*) + l(x^*))y^*$, the utility position of the customer if he buys from a seller who chooses x^*. Now assume that some seller chooses $x < x^*$. Then, as he will be liable for accident losses, his problem is to minimize full unit costs, namely $c(x) + l(x)$. But this implies that he chooses x^*, a contradiction.

Consider now the outcome under the negligence rule given the assumption that customers misperceive risks. Specifically, suppose that if expected accident losses are really $l(x)$, customers think they are $(1 + \lambda)l(x)$. Thus $\lambda > 0$ means that customers overestimate risk and $\lambda < 0$ that they underestimate risk. Assume that $\bar{x}$ is such that sellers choose $x = \bar{x}$. The price is therefore $c(\bar{x})$ and customer purchases are determined by maximizing over y the perceived utility position $b(y) - py - (1 + \lambda)l(\bar{x}) = b(y) - (c(\bar{x}) + (1 + \lambda)l(\bar{x}))y$. Therefore customers buy too little (less than $y^*(\bar{x})$) if they overestimate risk and too much if they underestimate risk. In particular, an efficient outcome cannot result.

Finally, consider the situation if there is no liability. Assume initially that customers can identify expected accident losses for particular sellers. Then competitive forces would induce sellers to choose an efficient care level and customers' purchases would be efficient. To show this we demonstrate that a situation in which sellers choose x^* is an equilibrium which results in an efficient outcome. Assuming that x^* is chosen by sellers, price must equal $c(x^*)$. Thus, customers (recognizing that they bear $l(x^*)$) choose y to maximize $b(y) - py - l(x^*)y = b(y) - (c(x^*) + l(x^*))y$. Consequently, they choose y^*. If a seller chose $x \neq x^*$, no customer would choose to buy from him. For if the customer were charged the production cost, his utility would be the maximum over y of $b(y) - (c(x) + l(x))y$. Since $x \neq x^*$, this must be less than $b(y^*) - (c(x^*) + l(x^*))y^*$, which is the customer's alternative.

If there is no liability and customers know expected accident losses only on average, then an efficient outcome would not result, for sellers would have no motive to take care. That is, $x = 0$ would hold. Also price would equal $c(0)$. Since they would realize that they bear $l(0)$, customer purchases would be determined by maximizing $b(y) - py - l(0)y = b(y) - (c(0) + l(0))y$. Thus, at least purchases would be efficient given the inefficiently low care level.

When there is no liability and customers misperceive average risks, then, as in the last paragraph, sellers choose $x = 0$, but in this instance customers purchase the wrong amount given that $x = 0$. Thus the outcome is worse than in the previous paragraph.

These results are summarized below.

PROPOSITION 3. *Suppose that injurers are sellers and that victims are customers. Then the relative performance of liability rules depends on the knowledge customers have about risk.* (See Table 1.)

As for the ranking of the inefficient outcomes in Table 1, it was shown that (a) is superior to (c) and it can also be shown that (b) is superior to (c) (using the argument of note 21 *supra*); however there is no necessary relationship between (a) and (b).

(iii) *Victims are employees.* In this subcase the results and their proofs are exactly parallel to those in the last subcase (in Proposition 3 merely substitute the word "employee" for "customer"). Therefore, it will not be necessary to verify all the results. However, it will be described how the model changes and, to provide a pattern for the reader, a proof that strict liability is efficient will be given.

The variable x is interpreted as the care the seller exercises in his production process.

It is assumed that an employee's wage minus the expected accident losses that he has to bear must equal his "opportunity wage," which is set by economy-wide forces of supply and demand and is therefore taken as exogenous. Define

TABLE 1

Knowledge of risk of accident loss	Form of Liability		
	Strict Liability	Negligence	No Liability
Accurate knowledge about each seller's risk	efficient	efficient	efficient
Accurate knowledge only of the average risk	efficient	efficient	inefficient (a)
Misperception of average risk	efficient	inefficient (b)	inefficient (c)

w = wage paid to employee,

$\bar{w}$ = opportunity wage,

so that[24]

$\bar{w}$ = w − expected accident losses borne.   (14)

The seller's unit cost of production is

$$c(x) = w + k(x),$$ (15)

where $k(x)$ are nonlabor production costs given x.

Under strict liability the efficient outcome results because, on the one hand, firms are induced to choose a care level that minimizes nonlabor production costs plus expected accident losses and, on the other, because customers face a price that reflects total production costs plus expected accident losses. To see this, note that since employees do not bear accident losses, $\bar{w} = w$. Hence, firms minimize $c(x) + l(x) = \bar{w} + k(x) + l(x)$, which means that they choose x^*. Price therefore equals $c(x^*) + l(x^*)$ and customers choose y to maximize (12).

IV. BILATERAL ACCIDENTS

Define the following additional notation,

$s \geqq 0$ care level of a victim,

$t \geqq 0$ activity level of a victim.

Expected accident losses are assumed to fall with victims' care and to rise with victims' activity levels. Also, if victims do not engage in their activity (t

---

[24] The wage is normalized so that it is the amount paid per unit of labor time necessary to produce one unit of output.

Economics and Liability for Environmental Problems

$= 0$), then losses are zero. More will be said later about how expected accident losses are related to s and t.

As previously noted, along with the liability rules examined in the last section, both strict liability and the negligence rule will be considered when there is a defense of contributory negligence. Therefore, define

$$\bar{s} = \text{due care level for victims.}$$

However, there will never be need to distinguish between the negligence rule with and without the defense. This is because in this model the two negligence rules are equivalent (as is true in most models which assume that injurers are identical).[25]

The results and proofs of this section closely parallel those of the last. Therefore, although formal statements of the results will be given, proofs will usually either be omitted or only sketched.

A. *The Nonmarket Case: Accidents between Strangers*

Define

$$h(s,t) = \text{income equivalent of the utility to a}$$
$$\text{victim of engaging in his activity at}$$
$$\text{level } t \text{ and exercising care } s$$

and assume that h has properties analogous to those of the function $a(x,y)$ (namely, assume that $h_s < 0$, $h_t(s,t) > 0$ for $t < t(s)$, etc.). Also define

$$l(x,s) = \text{expected accident losses per victim per}$$
$$\text{unit of injurer activity and of victim ac-}$$
$$\text{tivity,}$$

where $l_x < 0$ and $l_s < 0$. Thus, expected accident losses as a function of x, y, s, and t are $ytl(x,s)$.[26]

Social welfare is

$$W(x,y,s,t) = a(x,y) + h(s,t) - ytl(x,s), \tag{16}$$

the sum of the benefits of engaging in their activities for victim and injurer less the expected cost of accidents.

[25] While it is true that if an injurer is negligent, whether there is a defense of contributory negligence matters, it turns out that, in the situations which we consider, all injurers decide to act in a nonnegligent way. Therefore, whether there is a defense of contributory negligence is irrelevant.

[26] Expected accident losses have this form if we make the same assumption about the victim's activity level as we have made about the injurer's: an increase in the activity level is a physical repetition of an activity which causes a proportional rise in expected accident costs. This makes analysis easier (principally, the proof to Proposition 5), and it will be clear that the qualitative nature of the results would not change were expected accident costs to depend in a more general way on x,y,s, and t.

Under strict liability with a defense of contributory negligence, an efficient outcome cannot be achieved, for assume otherwise. Then, in particular, it must be that $s = \bar{s} = s^*$. This means victims will never have to bear losses. Consequently they will have no motive to reduce accident losses by lowering their activity level, and t will exceed t^*.

An argument similar to this one (and to the basic argument made in the last part) shows that an efficient outcome cannot be achieved under the negligence rule. Under the negligence rule injurers are not given an incentive to reduce accident losses by lowering their activity level.

Thus, as stated before, the choice between strict liability with a defense of contributory negligence and the negligence rule is a choice in favor of the lesser of two evils.

However, a rule of strict liability without a defense of contributory negligence would never be desirable, as it would always be dominated by strict liability with the defense. (The argument showing this is essentially that of note 21 *supra*). Similarly, it would never be desirable not to have liability, for this would result in an outcome inferior to that under the negligence rule. No welfare comparison can be made between strict liability and not having liability without knowing whether it is more important to control victim or injurer behavior.

In summary,

PROPOSITION 4. *Suppose that injurers and victims are strangers. Then none of the usual liability rules is efficient. Strict liability with a defense of contributory negligence is superior to the negligence rule if it is sufficiently important to lower injurer activity levels. Strict liability without the defense and no liability are each inferior to whichever rule is better: either strict liability with the defense or the negligence rule.*

The next result states that there is no conceivable liability rule that induces parties to act efficiently.

PROPOSITION 5. *Suppose that injurers and victims are strangers and consider any liability rule which may depend on any or all of the following variables: the victim's losses, the care he exercises, the care the injurer exercises. Then the liability rule is not efficient.*

To prove this, note that under a liability rule of the type under consideration, expected payments by the injurer must be of the form $ytq(x,s)$. Now suppose that the rule is efficient. If the injurer is to select the efficient activity level, then y^* must be the solution to

$$\text{maximize } a(x^*,y) - yt^*q(x^*,s^*). \tag{17}$$
$$y$$

On the other hand, since y^* maximizes $W(x^*,y,s^*,t^*)$, y^* must be the solution to

$$\text{maximize } a(x^*,y) - yt^*l(x^*,s^*). \tag{18}$$
$$y$$

Consequently, it must be that $q(x^*,s^*) = l(x^*,s^*)$. Similarly, if the victim is to choose his efficient activity level, then t^* must solve

$$\text{maximize } h(s^*,t) + y^*t(q(x^*,s^*) - l(x^*,s^*)). \tag{19}$$
$$t$$

But since t^* must also solve

$$\text{maximize } h(s^*,t) - y^*tl(x^*,s^*), \tag{20}$$
$$t$$

it must be that $q(x^*,s^*) = 0$, which is a contradiction.

B.   *The Market Case: Accidents between Sellers and Victims*

The same assumptions are made about the market as in Part III.B. However, victims now play a role in accidents.

(i)   *Victims are strangers.* In this subcase, the results are just like those described in the nonmarket case, and for reasons which combine the arguments given there and in Part III.B(i). (See also the discussion in the introduction.)

PROPOSITION 6. *Suppose that injurers are sellers and that victims are strangers. Then the results are as given in Propositions 4 and 5.*

(ii)   *Victims are customers.* In this subcase, the customer care level will have the usual interpretation. However, the customer activity level could be interpreted in several ways. First, think of it as the quantity of the good the customer purchases. This is the interpretation that will be made in regard to purchases of services or of products which are not durables. In this situation, then, the victim's activity level and the injurer's activity level are one and the same, namely, the level of output (so $t = y$); expected accident losses are given by $yl(x,s)$; and the following result holds.

PROPOSITION 7a. *Suppose that injurers are sellers of a nondurable good or service and that victims are customers. Then the relative performance of liability rules depends on the knowledge customers have about risks.* (See Table 2.)

Now consider the situation when customers buy durable goods—say lawn mowers or, if the customer is a firm, industrial machinery. In this situation,

STRICT LIABILITY VERSUS NEGLIGENCE

TABLE 2

Knowledge of risk of accident loss	Form of Liability			
	Strict Liability with Defense of Contributory Negligence	Negligence	Strict Liability	No Liability
Accurate knowledge about each seller's risk	efficient	efficient	inefficient	efficient
Accurate knowledge only of the average risk	efficient	efficient	inefficient	inefficient
Misperception of average risk	efficient	inefficient	inefficient	inefficient

it is assumed that the customer contributes to expected accident losses not only through the choice of care level and quantity purchased but also by the rate of use, denoted by r, of each unit purchased (number of times a mower is used per week, the frequency of operation of a machine). Therefore, the income equivalent of the utility of use to the customer will be written $h(s,t,r)$ (with $h_r > 0$) and the expected accident losses, $yrl(x,s)$. The results must now be modified as follows.

PROPOSITION 7b. *Suppose that injurers are sellers of a durable good and that victims are customers. Then the relative performance of liability rules depends on the knowledge customers have about risks.* (See Table 3.)

The point to be noticed here is (as explained before) that strict liability with a defense of contributory negligence never leads to an efficient outcome. It is true that in order to avoid being contributorily negligent, customers exercise due care and, because price reflects accident losses, they purchase the socially correct amount. However, they have no motive to lower expected accident losses by reducing their frequency of use of the product they buy. In contrast, under the negligence rule, provided that customers have knowledge of accident risks, an efficient outcome is achieved. Sellers exercise due care to avoid being found negligent. Customers choose the socially desirable care level, quantity to purchase, *and* rate of use since they bear accident losses.

(iii) *Victims are employees.* In this subcase, there is some difficulty in interpreting what the activity level would mean. In many situations, there is no obvious aspect of the discretionary behavior of the employee that would not come under the rubric of care. If so, the results turn out to be identical to

TABLE 3

| | Form of Liability | | | |
Knowledge of risk of accident loss	Strict Liability with Defense of Contributory Negligence	Negligence	Strict Liability	No Liability
Accurate knowledge about each seller's risk	inefficient	efficient	inefficient	efficient
Accurate knowledge only of the average risk	inefficient	efficient	inefficient	inefficient
Misperception of average risk	inefficient	inefficient	inefficient	inefficient

those reported in Proposition 7a. However, in situations where there is a type of employee decision that fits the description of activity level given here, then the results are those of Proposition 7b.

V.   Concluding Comments

1. A question which is in a sense logically prior to the analysis of this article must be mentioned, namely, *"Why isn't the level of activity usually considered in the formulation of a due care standard?"* After all, the inefficiencies discussed here were viewed in the main as deriving from the fact that in order to avoid being found negligent (or contributorily negligent), parties are not motivated to alter their level of activity.[27] The answer to the question appears to be that the courts would run into difficulty in trying to employ a standard of due care expanded in scope to include the level of activity. In formulating such a broadened due care standard, courts would, by definition, have to decide on the appropriate level of activity, and their competence to do this is problematic. How would courts decide the number of

[27] Were the level of activity included in the "due care" standard, a party would, by definition of due care, have to choose both the level of activity and the level of care appropriately in order to avoid liability; thus the inefficiencies analyzed in this article would be eliminated. However, A. Mitchell Polinsky, Strict Liability versus Negligence in a Market Setting (1979) (unpublished mimeographed paper, Stanford University) makes a point of qualification to this. He observes that in the market case it is not enough for the level of activity to be incorporated in the due care standard for each firm within the industry, for then too many firms would enter it; rather, the level of activity would somehow have to be made part of the due care standard for the industry as a whole. He also notes a similar point in respect to the nonmarket case.

miles an individual ought to drive or how far or how often a pedestrian ought to walk?[28] How would courts decide the level of output an industry—much less a firm within an industry—ought to produce? To decide such matters, courts would likely have to know much more than would normally have to be known to decide whether care, conventionally interpreted, was adequate.[29]

2. From the logic of the arguments presented here, it can be seen that what is important about the variable "level of activity" is only that it is not included in the due care standard. Any other variable omitted from the standard would also be inappropriately chosen in many of the circumstances in which we said the same of the level of activity. For example, in regard to accidents involving firms and strangers it has been noted that, if the scale of a firm's research in safety technology is not comprehended by the standard of due care, then under the negligence rule the firm would not be expected to invest sufficiently in such research.[30]

3. Commentators on tort law have in recent years frequently pointed to the reciprocal nature of harm, especially in the sense that the victim must be present in order to suffer harm. This has unfortunately engendered a misleading piece of folklore: that the very concept of harm is rendered ambiguous. While it is undeniable that for harm to occur there must be a victim, I can see no sense in which this truism leads to conceptual problems in instrumentalist analysis. Here, under the heading of bilateral accidents, the situation when victims as well as injurers could vary their level of activity (and of care) was studied; and one such possibility for victims was a level of activity of zero, which is to say, the "victims" are not around to be harmed. Thus, for example, the result (Proposition 4) concerning strict liability (with the defense of contributory negligence) versus negligence in regard to accidents between strangers might be expressed by saying that strict liability is preferable if it is more desirable to control whether injurers are present than it is to control whether victims are present; and the next result (Proposition 5) might be expressed by saying that there is no liability rule which generally induces both victims and injurers to make the efficient decision as to whether they should be present.[31]

    [28] There might also be evidentiary problems. The courts might find it difficult to learn how many miles an individual drives or a pedestrian walks.

    [29] On this argument, we would expect that when courts could easily discern what the level of activity ought to be, then it would be incorporated into the standard of due care. One legal doctrine which appears to confirm this is that of "coming to the nuisance," for the doctrine is applied in precisely those situations when the *activity* of coming to the nuisance—which is quite distinct from the level of *care* exercised once one is near the nuisance—may be seen as clearly socially undesirable.

    [30] See Posner, *supra* note 9, at 139 & 140.

    [31] It should be noted that Proposition 5 holds if one thinks of the level of activity as a binary variable (and/or if there is no variable "care"), for the proof does not depend on the level of activity being a continuous variable (nor on the existence of the variable care).

4. The analysis presented here does appear to help to explain certain features of tort law. A notable example is provided by the so-called pockets of strict liability: for ultrahazardous activities, ownership of wild animals, and so forth. These areas of strict liability seem to have two characteristics. First, they are such that injurer activity has a distinctive aspect (which makes the activity easy for the law to single out) and imposes nonnegligible risks on victims (which makes the activity worthwhile controlling). And, second, they are such that victim activity is usually not at all special—on the contrary, it is typically entirely routine in nature, part of what it is to carry on a normal life—and is therefore activity that cannot and ought not be controlled. Consequently, it is appealing to explain the pockets of strict liability by the idea (expressed in Propositions 4 and 6) that strict liability is preferable if it is more desirable to control injurers' activity than victims'.[32]

However, there are many features of tort law which the analysis by itself does not seem to satisfactorily explain. And this is not unexpected, for it is in the nature of the formal approach to isolate selected factors of interest by ignoring others; the formal approach aims for a particular kind of insight, not for true balance or comprehensiveness.[33] Two examples will illustrate various limitations in our ability to employ in a direct way the results of this article. The first concerns the trend in decisions in product-liability cases toward expansion of manufacturer's liability. If this trend can be likened to one toward holding manufacturers strictly liable, we may be tempted to explain it as broadly rational given some of our results (Propositions 2, 3, 6,

[32] Posner, *supra* note 9, at 140-41, makes essentially this point. Also George P. Fletcher, Fairness and Utility in Tort Theory, 85 Harv. L. Rev. 537 (1972), explains the pockets of strict liability (at 547-49) by appeal to the notion that strict liability is imposed when parties create "nonreciprocal" risks. Our discussion might be viewed as helping to explain why it is that when parties create nonreciprocal risks, they should be strictly liable (but Fletcher would probably not welcome this interpretation).

[33] Of course, the informal instrumentalist approach is more flexible, aims for, and achieves greater balance and generality. But, whether formal or informal, the instrumentalist approach has been subject to the limitation that it does not refer to "moralist" argument or explanation— that which sounds in terms of what is "right" or "fair" or "just" to do in the particular situation at hand. (Fletcher, *supra* note 32, is a recent and valuable discussion of the contrast between the instrumentalist and moralist approaches. See also Richard Epstein, A Theory of Strict Liability, 2 J. Legal Stud. 151 (1973).) Perhaps a few tentative remarks about this will not be out of order. Given that (i) we believe that to an important extent legal institutions are/should be shaped by moralist notions and that legal decisions are/should be made in consideration of them; and that (ii) the instrumentalist approach has some merit (I am not saying how much) in descriptive and normative analysis of law, it seems plausible (by implicit reasoning) that (iii) moralist notions must encapsulate instrumentalist goals (and, of course, there are explicit arguments for this, such as those of the utilitarian ethical theorists). Yet it also seems that (iv) to an important extent the moralist notions (or many of them) must be viewed as having a life of their own—cannot be fruitfully, or at least naturally, viewed as embodying what would normally be conceived of as instrumentalist goals. One would hope that discussion of such issues in the future might help to clarify the extent to which the division between instrumentalists and moralists merely reflects use of a different mode of discourse, and is therefore not "real," and the extent to which the division is in fact substantive.

7a). However, realism requires us to look at other, complementary explanations of the trend, such as that strict liability may provide a better means of risk sharing than the negligence rule, or that strict liability may be easier to apply than the negligence rule. Moreover, realism requires us to ask whether there even is an explanation of the trend based on its social rationality—whether in fact the trend might be socially undesirable, say on the ground that the expansion in the scope of liability has led to an excessively costly volume of disputes. Similar questions may be asked in respect to the second example, which concerns the fact that the negligence rule is the dominant form of tort liability in Anglo-American and in Western European legal systems today. Our analysis certainly does not suggest why this should be so, since, at least as often as otherwise, strict liability (with a defense of contributory negligence) is superior to the negligence rule. We are therefore led to ask again about such matters as risk sharing, administrative simplicity, and (especially) the social costs of expansion of the scope of liability.

5. Many of the points made in this article have been discussed before, and doubtless numerous times.[34] For example, the literature on enterprise liability virtually always considers the effect of such liability on product price, and the influence of this on purchases. The contribution made here would therefore seem to lie principally in the attention given to context—to the specifics of the relationship obtaining between injurers and victims—and in the unified way in which the variety of problems is viewed.

[34] But it is hard to find the points stated in explicit and general form. However, the reader should certainly refer to "Strict Liability vs. Negligence" in Posner *supra* note 9, at 137-42, which is the clearest discussion of our subject of which I am aware, and on which this article may properly be regarded as building. The reader should also refer to Guido Calabresi, Optimal Deterrence and Accidents, 84 Yale L. J. 656 (1975). And the reader might also want to look at the following papers by economists: John Prather Brown, Toward an Economic Theory of Liability, 2 J. Legal Stud. 323 (1973); Peter A. Diamond, Single Activity Accidents, 3 J. Legal Stud. 107 (1974); Jerry Green, On the Optimal Structure of Liability Laws, 7 Bell J. Econ. 553 (1976); and Steven Shavell, Accidents, Liability, and Insurance (forthcoming in Am. Econ. Rev.). In these papers liability rules are studied when parties can affect accident losses only by altering their levels of care; levels of activity are implicitly regarded as fixed (but see Section 11 of Diamond's paper). The reader may also find relevant Michael Spence, Consumer Misperceptions, Product Failure, and Producer Liability, 44 Rev. Econ. Stud. 561 (1977). He studies the use of strict liability and fines in the case of unilateral accidents; and he allows for sellers to offer guarantees and for consumers to be risk averse and to misperceive risks.

[6]

Strict Liability vs. Negligence in a Market Setting

By A. Mitchell Polinsky*

There are two competing rules of liability for controlling activities like speeding or polluting which cause harm to others. The rule of strict liability shifts the victim's harm to the injurer regardless of the injurer's behavior, while the rule of negligence shifts the burden to the injurer only if the injurer does not take some specified amount of care.

Most formal analyses of strict liability and negligence have been in a nonmarket context like automobile accidents.[1] These studies conclude (or imply) that both rules are efficient when the administering authority has sufficient information to set the negligence standard properly (in each case a defense of contributory negligence may be required). According to these analyses, strict liability is efficient because it fully internalizes the harm, and negligence is efficient because the injurer can be induced to take exactly the specified amount of care and this amount can be set efficiently. For reasons which will become apparent, it is important to note that these models have assumed a fixed number of injurers—for example, a predetermined number of drivers.

Interestingly, most informal discussions of strict liability and negligence have suggested that in a market setting negligence may be inefficient even when the administering authority has perfect information. The argument is stated clearly in a discussion of environmental control by Richard Stewart and James Krier:

> If strict liability is not imposed for the residual damages caused by partially controlled polluting activity, these damages will not be reflected in the price of commodities produced by such activity. As a result, commodities with whose production pollution is associated will be underpriced relative to commodities whose production causes no pollution, resulting in resource misallocation. [p. 227][2]

This paper formally analyzes strict liability and negligence in a market setting. The discussion emphasizes the impact of the rules on the market price and on the number of firms in the industry. For simplicity, the damage caused by each firm is assumed to be determined only by that firm's "care" (and not also by the firm's output or the victim's behavior).[3]

The argument that both strict liability and negligence are efficient is correct in the short run when the number of firms causing harm is fixed. The market price in the short run is the same under strict liability and negligence despite the fact that under the rule of negligence firms do not bear the cost of their harmful activity. The argument that only strict liability is efficient is correct in the long run when the number of firms is variable. When the negligence standard corresponds to the efficient level of care, the market price in the long run under negligence is too low and too many firms enter the industry. However, when the standard is

*Law School and economics department, Stanford University; and National Bureau of Economic Research. Work on this paper was supported by the National Science Foundation through a grant (SOC 78-20159) to the law and economics program of the National Bureau of Economic Research. Any opinions expressed are my own and not those of the NBER. Helpful comments were received from participants in a number of seminars.

[1] See, for example, the paper by John Brown. The only exceptions are discussed in fn. 4 below. There are also a number of formal studies of products liability in a market context which do not compare strict liability to negligence.

[2] See also the discussions by Guido Calabresi (pp. 500–17), Duncan Kennedy (pp. 54–61), and Richard Posner (pp. 137–42). Michael Spence and Martin Weitzman (pp. 216–17) make a similar point in the context of comparing taxes to standards.

[3] See comments (e) and (f) in Section IV below for a discussion of how the results are affected if harm also depends on output or the victim's behavior.

chosen optimally, taking into account the inefficiency of the negligence rule, the standard exceeds the efficient level of care, the price rises, and the number of firms falls. The optimal second best standard may actually result in the same price and number of firms under negligence as under strict liability.[4]

I. The Model

The analysis of strict liability and negligence is undertaken in a very simple partial-equilibrium model of a competitive industry composed of n identical firms. Each firm's cost of producing q units of output is $C(q)$. The average cost function is assumed to be U-shaped. Each firm's cost of taking z units of care is z (care is defined so that one unit costs one dollar). Associated with each firm's level of care is an external damage $D(z)$. Damages decrease with care. Let $P(s)$ be the industry's inverse demand function, where $s = nq$ is aggregate output. Social welfare W equals the benefits to consumers of output nq (assumed to be approximated by the area under the industry's inverse demand curve), less the cost of producing nq, the external damages, and the cost of taking care:

$$(1) \quad W = \int_0^{nq} P(s)\,ds - nC(q) - nD(z) - nz$$

In the short run, the number of firms is fixed.[5] The social optimum is defined by the q and z which maximize social welfare. From (1) the first-order condition (all solutions are assumed to be unique interior local optima) with respect to q may be written as

$$(2) \quad P(nq) = C'(q)$$

[4]A recent paper by Čento Veljanovski (pp. 17–22) uses a diagrammatic model to show that negligence is inefficient in the long run, but he does not consider the second best problem. The paper by Steven Shavell develops some closely related issues (see comment (e) in Section IV below). Barry Weingast, Mark McBride, and John Conant compare strict liability and negligence when, in effect, only the consumer of a product affects the harm.

[5]If the number of firms is effectively variable in the short run due to exit, the results may be different (see comment (d) in Section IV below).

This has the usual interpretation that price equals marginal cost. The first-order condition with respect to z is

$$(3) \quad -D'(z) = 1$$

This states that the marginal benefits from an increase in care—reduced damages—equals the marginal cost of greater care.

In the long run, the number of firms is variable. The social optimum is now defined by the q, z, and n which maximize social welfare. From (1) the first-order condition with respect to n can be written as

$$(4) \quad P(nq) = [C(q) + D(z) + z]/q$$

This has the usual interpretation that price equals average cost.

The social welfare-maximizing values of the variables will be indicated by an asterisk.

II. Short-Run Analysis

Under strict liability, each firm's problem is to maximize revenues less production costs, external damages, and the cost of taking care:

$$(5) \quad \underset{q,z}{\text{Max}}\; Pq - C(q) - D(z) - z$$

The first-order conditions with respect to q and z are, respectively,

$$(6) \quad P = C'(q)$$

$$(7) \quad -D'(z) = 1$$

which coincide with the social optimum. This is not surprising since strict liability fully internalizes the externality.

Under negligence, let $\bar{z}$ be the standard of care. Each firm's problem is

$$(8) \quad \underset{q,z}{\text{Max}}\; Pq - C(q) - \bar{D}(z) - z$$

where
$$\bar{D}(z) = \begin{cases} 0 & \text{if} \quad z \geqslant \bar{z}, \\ D(z) & \text{if} \quad z < \bar{z} \end{cases}$$

The first-order condition with respect to q is the same as (6). It is easily shown that when

$\bar{z} = z^*$, the level of care chosen by each firm is $\bar{z}$ (see fn. 8 below). Thus, the social optimum can be reached under negligence if the standard is chosen properly, equal to the efficient level of care.

III. Long-Run Analysis

Under strict liability, each firm chooses output and care to maximize profits as indicated by (5), so that (6) and (7) are satisfied (implying at least that $z = z^*$). In addition, equilibrium is characterized by zero profits:

$$(9) \quad P(nq)q - C(q) - D(z^*) - z^* = 0$$

This is equivalent to the condition for the social optimum that price equals average cost. Thus, strict liability is efficient in the long run.

Under negligence, assume initially that the standard is set at the efficient level of care. Firms maximize profits by choosing output and care according to (8), so that (6) is satisfied and $z = z^*$. The zero profit condition under negligence is, therefore,

$$(10) \quad P(nq)q - C(q) - z^* = 0$$

This condition, along with (6), implies that the output of each firm under negligence is too low, that the market price is too low, and that too many firms enter the industry.[6]

Since the negligence outcome is not efficient when the standard equals the efficient level of care, the optimal second best standard is of some interest. It can be demonstrated that, optimally chosen, $\bar{z} > z^*$.[7] The reason for this is not hard to understand. Consider a slight increase in the standard starting at $\bar{z} = z^*$. Since firms will continue to meet the standard (they will

over some range), their costs will rise and, as a consequence, so will the market price. This has the beneficial effect of raising the output of each firm (which was too low when $\bar{z} = z^*$) and of reducing the number of firms. The inefficiency created by inducing firms to take care just above the efficient level is negligible since the effect on social welfare of a marginal change in firms' care is zero at the optimal level of care. Thus, it is desirable to increase the standard to some extent.

There is a limit to how high the standard can be set and still induce firms to meet the standard. It is easy to show that the highest feasible standard leads to the same price under negligence as under strict liability; given this standard and the resulting price, the output of each firm and the number of firms is efficient under negligence.[8] By reasoning similar to that used in the previous paragraph, it might seem, therefore, that the optimal second best standard should not be this high: the effect on social welfare from lowering the level of care slightly (by lowering the standard) would be beneficial, while the effect on social welfare due to the resulting marginal changes in firm output and the number of firms would seem to be negligible. Perhaps surprisingly, this argument is not correct. It can be demonstrated that the optimal second best standard under negligence might in fact lead to the same price, firm output, and number of firms as under strict liability.[9]

---

[6]Let q^0 and n^0 be the equilibrium values of q and n under negligence. Substituting $P(nq) = C'(q)$ into (9) and (10) gives expressions of the form $C'(q)q - C(q) - K = 0$, where K is some constant. It follows from $C'' > 0$ (rising marginal costs are assumed) that $dq/dK > 0$. Thus, $q^0 < q^*$. Since $P(nq) = C'(q)$ and $C'' > 0$, $P(n^0 q^0) < P(n^* q^*)$. Thus, $n^0 q^0 > n^* q^*$ and $n^0 > n^*$.

[7]Firms will just meet the standard if and only if $\bar{z}$ is between zero and some $\hat{z} > z^*$ (see fn. 8 below). Given $\bar{z}$ in this range, it follows from substituting (6) into (10) (with $\bar{z}$ replacing z^*) that the equilibrium q minimizes $(C(q) + \bar{z})/q$. Let $q(\bar{z})$ be the solution to this problem. Given $q(\bar{z})$, the price is $(C(q(\bar{z})) + \bar{z})/q(\bar{z})$. Thus, $nq(\bar{z}) = P^{-1}[(C(q(\bar{z})) + \bar{z})/q(\bar{z})]$. Let $n(\bar{z})$ be the solution of

this expression for n. Substituting $q(\bar{z})$ and $n(\bar{z})$ into (1) gives social welfare solely as a function of the standard, $W(\bar{q})$. After some manipulation, it can be seen that $\text{sgn}\{W'\} = \text{sgn}\{-n'D - n(D'+1)\}$. Since $n' < 0$ it follows from assuming that $D(z) + z$ is U-shaped that $W'(\bar{z}) > 0$ for $\bar{z} < z^*$.

[8]If $\bar{z} < \hat{z}$, where $\hat{z} = D(z^*) + z^*$, firms will choose $\bar{z}$ because $\bar{z} < z + D(z)$ for all $z < \bar{z}$. If $\bar{z} = \hat{z}$, firms are indifferent between $\bar{z}$ and z^*. If $\bar{z} > \hat{z}$, firms will choose z^*. Thus, the highest feasible standard is $\hat{z}$ (or arbitrarily close to it). Given $\bar{z} = \hat{z}$, it follows from the discussion in fn. 7 above that $q(\hat{z}) = q^*$ and that the price is $(C(q^*) + D(z^*) + z^*)/q^*$; since q and $P(nq)$ are the same as under strict liability, n must also be the same.

[9]It is sufficient to show that it is possible that $W'(\bar{z}) > 0$ for all $\bar{z} < \hat{z}$. Recall from fn. 7 above that $\text{sgn}\{W'\} = \text{sgn}\{-n'D - n(D'+1)\}$. Since $D'(z)$, $n(z)$, and $n'(z)$ are continuous functions on $0 < z < \hat{z}$, they are bounded. Thus, if $D(\hat{z})$ is sufficiently large, the result follows.

The basis for this conclusion can be explained as follows. It is true that lowering the standard slightly from its highest feasible level improves social welfare through its effect on the level of care and leaves social welfare unchanged by its effect on firm output. It is not true, however, that lowering the standard leaves social welfare unchanged through its effect on the number of firms even though the number of firms was previously efficient. This is because the optimal number of firms *given* an inefficiently high level of care is less than the efficient number of firms. Since lowering the standard reduces firms' costs and consequently increases the number of firms, this effect on social welfare is undesirable. Therefore, whether the standard should be lowered depends on the strength of this effect relative to the beneficial effect on care.

IV. Discussion

(a) The model used here can be interpreted in two ways. The most natural interpretation is that the damage from each firm's output harms individuals who are not consumers of that output (for example, a chemical industry pollutes a lake used for recreation). The other interpretation is that the damage falls on the consumers of the firm's output but they underestimate it (for example, food producers sell products with misperceived carcinogenic effects). Under the second interpretation the model applies as it stands if the consumers are totally ignorant of the harm. However, it is easy to modify it to allow the demand curve for the output to shift, depending on who bears the damage. As long as consumers underestimate the damages, the basic results will apply.

(b) In a sense, the problem discussed here with the negligence rule in a market setting is that it is not possible to apply the rule to the industry as a whole. Courts are allowed to determine only whether any particular firm is negligent with respect to the activities over which it has control. This is not sufficient to correctly regulate the number of firms in the long run since all firms are acting the same way. No firm can be held responsible for the number of firms in the industry.

(c) The same type of observation would apply in a nonmarket setting in which there is free entry into the injuring activity. For example, consider individuals who must decide whether to drive to a nearby city—and thereby risk hitting innocent pedestrians —or to not make the trip at all. Under a negligence rule, too many individuals will make the trip even if all who do so take the proper amount of care in driving. The earlier formal analyses of strict liability and negligence in a nonmarket context which concluded that both rules were efficient assumed a fixed number of injurers.

(d) A version of the entry problem with the negligence rule also can arise in a market setting in the short run. For example, suppose there are a certain number of firms operating in the short run in the absence of any regulation and that these firms have different costs of production (but, for simplicity, the same damage functions and cost of taking care). The rule of strict liability—which would still be efficient with this generalization—may drive some of the costlier firms out of business. The rule of negligence, however, may induce some firms which would have gone out of business under strict liability to stay in business. As in the long run, this will result in too low a price and too many firms.[10]

(e) The main point of this paper would not be affected if each firm's total damage depends both on that firm's level of care and its output. If the negligence standard is then appropriately defined both with respect to the firm's care level and its output, the present analysis would apply essentially unchanged. If, however, the negligence standard is still defined just in terms of care (as is usual in practice), there would be an additional problem with the negligence rule besides the entry problem: it would distort the firm's choice between care and output.[11]

---

[10]This point is illustrated diagrammatically in the context of comparing taxes to subsidies in my 1979 paper.

[11]See Steven Shavell's paper. Since he treats the industry as composed of one competitively behaving

(f) Some of the conclusions of this paper may be affected if the total damage depends both on the firm's actions and the victim's behavior (for example, the care exercised in using a lawn mower). If the number of potential victims is fixed—so there is no "entry issue" on the victim's side—then the present results would be essentially unchanged (putting aside the separate issue discussed in the previous comment). An appropriate defense of contributory negligence—in which the firm would be free of liability if the victim did not take his efficient amount of care—should in principle be added to both the strict liability and negligence rules. In equilibrium the victim would take the correct amount of care, so the strict liability and negligence rules would operate as described in this paper. If, however, the number of victims is variable, then in general neither liability rule (with a defense of contributory negligence) would be expected to be efficient. Negligence would lead to excessive entry on the injurer side, while strict liability would encourage too much entry on the victim side.[12]

---

firm whose harm depends on care and output, he does not raise the problem of controlling the number of firms.

[12]An analogous result is shown by Shavell when the damage depends on the levels of care and activity of one injurer and one victim. The same point should apply when damages depend on care and the number of injurers and victims.

REFERENCES

J. P. Brown, "Toward an Economic Theory of Liability," *J. Legal Stud.*, June 1973, *2*, 323–49.

G. Calabresi, "Some Thoughts on Risk Distribution and the Law of Torts," *Yale Law J.*, Mar. 1961, *70*, 499–553.

D. Kennedy, "A History of Law and Economics, or the Fetishism of Commodities," unpublished paper, Harvard Univ., Sept. 1978.

A. M. Polinsky, "Notes on the Symmetry of Taxes and Subsidies in Pollution Control," *Can. J. Econ.*, Feb. 1979, *12*, 75–83.

Richard A. Posner, *Economic Analysis of Law*, 2d ed., Boston 1977.

S. Shavell, "Strict Liability versus Negligence," *J. Legal Stud.*, Jan. 1980, *9*, 1–25.

A. M. Spence and M. L. Weitzman, "Regulatory Strategies for Pollution Control," in Ann F. Friedlaender, ed., *Approaches to Controlling Air Pollution*, Cambridge 1978.

Richard B. Stewart and James E. Krier, *Environmental Law and Policy: Readings, Materials and Notes*, 2d ed., Indianapolis 1978.

Č. G. Veljanovski, "'Economic' Myths about Common Law Realities—Economic Efficiency and the Law of Torts," work. paper no. 5, Centre Socio-Legal Stud., Oxford Univ., Mar. 1979.

B. R. Weingast, M. E. McBride, and J. L. Conant, "Product Safety and Consumer Information: The Impact of Liability Assignment and Standards Regulation," work. paper no. 45, Center Stud. Amer. Bus., Washington Univ. (St. Louis), June 1979.

[7]

WHEN DOES THE RULE OF LIABILITY MATTER?

*HAROLD DEMSETZ**

THE active interface between law and economics has been limited largely to antitrust and regulation, but recent work, primarily in economics, has revealed a much wider area of common interest. The new development, which deals with the definition and structure of property rights, has implications for central areas of the law, such as real property, torts, and contracts, although it originated in an economic analysis of the divergence between private and social cost. While still in its embryonic stage, the analysis has proceeded far enough for it to be called to the attention of a wider audience.

The questions with which we shall be concerned are whether and under what conditions a legal decision about liability affects the uses to which resources will be put and the distribution of wealth between owners of resources. If ranchers are held liable for the damage done by their cattle to corn fields, how will the outputs of meat and corn be affected? If drivers or pedestrians, alternatively, are held liable for automobile-pedestrian accidents, how will the accident rate be affected? What implications for extortion (an extreme form of wealth redistribution) are found in the decision about who is liable for damages?

I.

Recent developments in this area began with an article by Professor R. H. Coase.[1] Coase's work presented a penetrating criticism of the conventional treatment by economists of divergences between private and social cost. The social cost of furthering an economic activity is the resulting reduction in the value of production that is obtainable from other activities. Such reductions occur because the resources required to further an activity are scarce and must be diverted from other possible uses. According to the view that Coase challenged, social cost, being the sum total of the costs incurred to carry on any activity, might very well differ from private cost. For example, the so-

*Professor of Business Economics, Law School and Graduate School of Business, University of Chicago. The author wishes to thank the Charles R. Walgreen Foundation for financial aid through its grant to the University of Chicago, and, also, the Lilly Endowment through its grant to the University of California.

[1] R. H. Coase, The Problem of Social Cost, 3 J. Law & Econ. 1 (1960).

cial cost of running steam locomotives properly includes the fire damage done to surrounding farm crops by sparks from the locomotive. If the railroad is not required to pay for these damages, perhaps through a tax per train, then, according to the conventional analysis, the railroad would not take account of crop damage costs in deciding how many trains to run. In the absence of a specific public policy to intervene, the rate at which an activity is carried forth, which is determined solely by private cost, would diverge from the optimum rate, which is determined by social cost. In the present example, the private cost of running additional trains, being less than the social cost because crop damage is not taken into account, would encourage the railroad to run too many trains per day. The conventional economic analysis called for the levy of a tax per train, equivalent to the damages, in order to bring social cost and private cost into equality.

Coase demonstrated that the imposition of such a tax could, in some circumstances, aggravate the difficulty, but two other aspects of his work are of more concern to us. Coase (1) showed that powerful market forces exist that tend to bring private and social cost into equality without the use of a tax, and (2) discussed the conditions under which the legal position toward liability for damages would and would not alter the allocation of resources. Coase discusses an interaction between two productive activities, ranching and farming, in the context of a competitive regime in which the cost of transacting (or negotiating) is assumed to be zero.[2] His analysis concludes that social cost and private cost will be brought into equality through market negotiations—and this regardless of which party is assigned the responsibility for bearing the cost that results from the proximity of ranching and farming.

The law, reasoning that crops *stand in the way* of a neighbor's cattle, can leave the farmer to bear the cost of crop damage; alternatively, reasoning that cattle *stray errantly* across farm fields, the law can assign liability for crop damages to ranchers. Coase's work demonstrates that either legal position will result in the same resource allocation—*i.e.*, in the same quantities of corn and meat—and, also, that negotiations between the parties to the damage will, with either legal position, eliminate any divergence between private and social cost. If the law favors ranchers by leaving farmers to bear the cost of crop damage, then there exist incentives for farmers to pay ranchers to reduce the sizes of the herds, or to take other measures that will reduce the amount of damage. A summary arithmetic example reveals how such market transactions lead to Coase's results.

Suppose that the net return to an owner of ranchland would be increased by $50 if herd size were increased by one head of cattle but that the additional

---

[2] *Id.* at 2–8.

head of cattle would impose corn damage on the owner of neighboring farm-land that reduced his net return by $60. If the law did *not* require the rancher to compensate the farmer, the farmer would offer to pay the rancher a sum up to $60, the damage he would suffer if the rancher increased his herd by one head. The rancher would accept the offer since any amount above $50 would be more than ample compensation for the reduction in net returns associated with the smaller herd size.

Negotiations would continue until the net return to the rancher of a head of cattle exceeded the reduction in net return to the farmer associated with the damage done by that head of cattle. Such negotiations would bring the total value of corn and beef produced to a maximum since herd size would be reduced only when the consequent increase in the net value of corn output ($60 in the above example) exceeded the decrease in the net value of beef output ($50 in the example) required to reduce crop damage.

If the rule of liability were the reverse, requiring the owner of ranchland to compensate the farmer for the crop damage, the same equilibrium would be reached. Since the rancher earns a net return of only $50 and must pay damages of $60 if he raises an additional head of cattle, he would find it in his interest not to increase the size of his herd. Moreover, he would reduce the size of his herd as long as the net return forgone was smaller than the result-ing increase in the net return to farming since this would be the liability to him if he did not reduce herd size by another unit. He would be led to settle upon the same herd size, with the same consequence for crop size, as he would have chosen in the absence of liability. The mix of output is not changed[3] because negotiations between the parties eliminate all divergence between private and social cost.

The resulting equality between social and private cost is important enough to warrant a few more words. The conventional analysis of the farmer-rancher interaction would have concluded that in the absence of liability for damage (or of an appropriate tax per head of cattle) the social cost of increasing herd size would have exceeded the rancher's private cost by the $60 damage done to the neighboring farmer's crops. The rancher, if he were neither held liable nor taxed, would have no reason to take account of this damage and would

[3] I ignore other possibilities such as building a fence. These are discussed by Coase (*id.* at 3). Consideration of them changes the exposition but not the results.

One further assumption is required for the mix of output to remain unchanged. Any re-distribution of wealth resulting from a change in the rule of liability is assumed to have no consequences for the demands for the products produced. Owners of farmland and ranchland should be vegetarians in equal proportions, for otherwise a redistribution of wealth between these two groups would alter the market demands for corn and beef and thereby indirectly alter the mix of output produced. The wealth redistribution problem will be discussed later when we turn to the subject of extortion.

therefore be led to raise too many cattle and impose too much damage on farm crops. It is the supposed existence of this gap between private and social cost that seems to call for a tax per head of cattle or for an assignment of liability to the rancher. Coase's reasoning shows this logic to be in error. Even in the absence of a tax or liability for damage, the harmful effects of his activities on surrounding crops would be brought to bear on the private calculations of the owner of ranchland, for he must reckon as a true (but implicit) cost of increasing herd size the payment from the farmer that he must forgo if he refuses to agree to the farmer's request for a reduction in herd size. Market negotiations bring the full cost of his decision to bear on him through the offers made by the farmer and thereby eliminate any difference between private and social cost. This, as Coase recognized, would not be true if the cost of negotiating could not be assumed to be negligible. We shall return to this problem later.

It is not generally appreciated that Coase's reasoning has legal applications that extend beyond problems of the divergence between social and private cost as these typically are conceived. What is at issue in the farmer-rancher case is which party has a particular property right. In the one case the farmer has the right to allow or prohibit cattle grazing on certain specified lands, while in the other case it is the rancher who has the right. Private property takes the form of a bundle of rights, of which different components may be held by different persons. In the absence of significant negotiating cost, the use to which these property rights is put is independent of the identities of the owners since each owner will be given market incentives to use his property right in the most valuable way. Just what is the most valuable way depends on market conditions and not owner identities.

The analysis can be extended to many types of property right problems. One that is of current interest to lawyers is the continuing litigation about the legal status of the reserve clause in organized baseball. An important defense of the reserve clause has been the assertion that it prevents wealthy baseball clubs from acquiring too large a share of the good players. By applying the above analysis to this problem it is possible to refute the assertion, especially since the cost of negotiations would seem to be negligible in this case. For what is at issue is whether the identity of the owner of a player's baseball services will alter the location of his playing activities. An application of Coase's analysis to this problem suggests that the reserve clause should have no effect on the identity of the team for which a player plays.

When signing initially with a major league organization, a player owns his baseball talent in the sense that he has the right to offer his services for sale to any ball club. But once he signs with a major league club, he can no longer negotiate with other clubs for the sale of his services, although he retains the right to refuse to play. The reserve clause, which is written into every major league contract, requires major league clubs who wish to acquire the services of a player who is already under contract to purchase his contract from the club currently owning it. Thus, once a player signs with a major league organization, part of the bundle of property rights to his services are transferred from the player to the club with which he signs. The right to play on various teams passes via the reserve clause from the player to the club owning his contract, and this club can reserve the player for its own use even though other teams might be willing to pay the player more than he is receiving.

The question considered here is *not* whether there exists a correlation between the wealth of a club and the quality of its players. The relevant question is whether the distribution of players among teams would change were the reserve clause to be declared illegal. Would wealthier clubs acquire more good players if the right to negotiate with other teams always resided with the player?[4]

In the absence of the reserve clause, a player would change clubs only if he found it in his interest to do so. With the reserve clause, a player will change clubs only if the club that owns his contract finds it in its interest. It appears that a different pattern of player migration between clubs might exist with the reserve clause than without it. But the appearance is deceptive. No matter who owns the right to sell the contract for the services of a baseball player, the distribution of players among teams will remain the same.

To see why this is so, assume that a player *not* subject to the reserve clause receives a $15,000 per annum wage from club A for which he currently plays. Club B offers him $16,000 to play for them. If this amount exceeds the value of the player to club A, the club will not find it in its interest to make a counteroffer large enough to retain the player's services and he will join club B. However, if his services are worth more than $16,000 to club A, the club will find it in its interest to make a counteroffer large enough to retain his services. With no reserve clause the player plays for the club that most highly values[5] his services.

Let us now suppose that the reserve clause is effective and, as before, that

---

[4] The reserve clause and other aspects of organized baseball are discussed in Simon Rottenberg, The Baseball Players' Labor Market, 64 J. Pol. Econ. 242 (1956). The reasoning employed by Rottenberg is similar but not identical to the above argument. Rottenberg's argument is based partly on the premise, not used here, that it takes two fairly well matched teams to produce a good game.

[5] Nonpecuniary aspects of his employment are discussed later, but it should be noted that the argument for retention of the reserve clause is not based on nonpecuniary job amenities.

the player is currently paid $15,000 by club A. Club B now offers club A $1,000 per annum (or its present value equivalent) for the player's contract, so that if the negotiations succeed club B will pay $16,000 for the player's services of which $15,000 is paid to the player under the terms of the purchased contract and $1,000 is paid to club A. If $1,000 per annum exceeds the player's net value to club A after it pays his $15,000 annual salary, then it will be in club A's interest to sell his contract to club B, but if the player is worth more to club A than $16,000 (equal to the $1,000 offer from club B plus the player's $15,000 salary), it will refuse to sell his contract.

The condition under which the player is transferred to club B when he is subject to the reserve clause is precisely the condition under which he will elect to transfer to club B when he is not subject to the reserve clause. He transfers to club B if club B finds his services more valuable than does club A whether or not the reserve clause is in effect. The reserve clause, therefore, cannot be expected to result in a different distribution of players among teams than would prevail in its absence.

The reader may object, suggesting that nonpecuniary considerations might make the distribution of players different depending on the legal status of the reserve clause. But this objection also would be in error. Suppose that the player, presently owned by a California club, has developed a preference for working in California. If there were no reserve clause, his preference would lead him to ask at least $1,000 more to play ball with a Chicago club than he earns playing for a California club; and, in the absence of a reserve clause, a Chicago club would need to bid $1,000 more than a California club to obtain his services. But this is also true with the reserve clause. Under reserve clause arrangements, suppose that the Chicago club offers the California club only $500 more than the player's net value to the California club. The California club, indeed, will be tempted to sell the player's contract to Chicago. It appears that the $500 increment, which would be too small to move the player were there no reserve clause, is large enough to move him if there is a reserve clause. This is incorrect because the player, when working under the reserve clause arrangement, would be willing to offer a sum of up to $1,000 (the value of the nonpecuniary amenities to him of California) to the California club to induce it to refuse to sell his contract to Chicago. Any amount above $500 would be sufficient to make the California club reject Chicago's offer since Chicago is offering only $500 more than the player is worth to the California club. (The player can "offer" such an amount by accepting a pay reduction.) With or without the reserve clause, then, the player will locate where the value he places on amenities plus the value of his baseball talent is greatest.

II

The significance of Coase's work quickly led to critical responses by Wellisz,[6] Calabresi,[7] and others, although Calabresi withdrew his criticism in a later paper.[8] The criticism centered around two allegations—that the Coase theorem neglects long-run considerations that negate it and that the spirit of the work endorses the use of resources for the undesirable purpose of "extortion." The long-run issue is discussed here and the "extortion" problem in Part III. In Part IV, I discuss the problems introduced when the assumption of negligible transaction cost is dropped.

The question of long-run considerations has been raised because it would seem that different liability rules would alter the profitability of remaining inside or outside each industry. It is alleged that if farmers are left to bear the cost that arises from proximity to cattle, the rate of return to farming will fall and resources will therefore leave the farming industry. Alternatively, if ranchers are left to bear the cost, the resulting reduction in rate of return to ranching will lead to the exit of resources from that industry. Hence, even if transaction cost is zero, the market will allocate resources differently in the long run depending upon which rule of liability is chosen.

But short-run versus long-run considerations should have no bearing on the Coase theorem, which is based on the proposition that an implicit cost (the forgone payment from the farmer) is just as much a cost as is an explicit cost (the liability damage), and this proposition surely must hold in the long run as well as in the short run. One way of demonstrating this is by allowing the two activities to be merged under a common owner. A detailed example of this is given by G. Warren Nutter.[9] If there is no special cost to operating a multiproduct firm, the costly interaction between farming and ranching will be fully brought to the owner's attention in his operation of a farming-ranching enterprise. The mix of output that he produces will be that which maximizes his earnings. The rule of liability that is chosen can have no effect on his decisions because the owner of such a firm must bear the interaction cost whichever legal rule is adopted. The cost interdependence is a technical-economic interdependence, not a legal one. Since such merged operations are possible, the rule of liability is rendered irrelevant to the

[6] Stanislaw Wellisz, On External Diseconomies and the Government Assisted Invisible Hand, 31 Economica (N.S.) 345 (1964).

[7] Guido Calabresi, The Decision for Accidents: An Approach to Nonfault Allocation of Costs, 78 Harv. L. Rev. 713 (1965).

[8] Guido Calabresi, Transaction Costs, Resource Allocation and Liability Rules—A Comment, 11 J. Law & Econ. 67 (1968).

[9] G. Warren Nutter, The Coase Theorem on Social Cost: A Footnote, 11 J. Law & Econ. 503 (1968).

choice of output mix. But a refutation of the criticism that is based on the use of the joint product enterprise gives rise to the (incorrect) suspicion that the basic problem has been begged, since the rule of liability that is chosen cannot in this case alter the wealth of the owner of a farming-ranching enterprise. The spirit of the argument can be preserved, while the suspicion is allayed, by assuming that the advantages offered by specialization of ownership are so great that it is uneconomic to merge the two activities into a single ranching-farming firm.

If owners of farmland bear the cost of crop damage, what must be the cost conditions that are associated with an equilibrium allocation of land to farming, ranching, and other uses? For such damage to arise there must be a sufficient scarcity of land to force farms and ranches into proximity. Marginal farm acreage (acreage that just "breaks even") must earn revenue sufficient to cover all cost, including the cost of crop damage done by straying cattle. Suppose the proximity of ranching and farming reduces the net return to the owner of farmland by $100 as compared with what could be earned were there no neighboring ranch. If ranching continues on the neighboring acres, it must be true that the net return to the owner of the ranchland exceeds $100, for otherwise the farmer would have been able to purchase the removal of cattle from neighboring land by offering $100 to the neighboring ranchers. The reduction in net return to farming brought about because of crop damage is thus implicitly taken into account by the owner of the ranchland when he refuses the offer of the owner of the neighboring farmland. The money offered by the farmer is refused by the rancher precisely because the continued use of the land for grazing brings in additional net revenue in excess of $100.

Land that is submarginal as farm or ranchland (land that cannot be profitably farmed or ranched) is unable to earn revenue sufficient to cover the explicit $100 damage cost if it is put to the plough or the $100 implicit cost if it is employed in ranching. Were this land to be employed in farming, its owner would suffer losses attributable in part to the damage done to his crops by straying cattle, whereas if it were employed in ranching its owner would suffer the implicit loss of forgoing a $100 payment from the neighboring farmer (the owners of farmland bearing the cost of crop damage). Submarginal land by definition can be neither farmed nor ranched profitably.

Now let the rule of liability be changed so that ranchers become liable for crop damage. If there is to be a long-run effect, it must be true that the cost interrelationships change in a manner that causes either the conversion of ranchland to farmland or submarginal land to farmland. But neither conversion can be made profitable by the change in liability.

Acreage that was marginally profitable in ranching must remain ranch-land because it had been earning net revenues in excess of the $100 damages done by cattle to surrounding farmland. If a producing ranch were to be switched from ranching to farming to avoid the new liability its owner would forgo revenues (in excess of $100) that exceeded the resulting reduction in liability ($100). The owner of what was marginal ranchland, therefore, will continue to employ his land in ranching under the new liability rule.

The land that previously was submarginal must remain submarginal. The changed liability rule will not attract this land into farming. Submarginal lands under the original rule of liability earned insufficient revenues in farm-ing to cover the $100 cost of crop damage. Under the new rule of liability, neighboring ranchers will succeed in negotiating with the owners of this land to keep it out of farming. Operating ranches, under the old rule of liability, had been yielding net revenues in excess of $100; therefore it will be possible and profitable for ranchers, in order to avoid the $100 crop damage that otherwise would result, to offer an amount to the owners of submarginal land that is sufficient to keep the land out of farming.

There is a temptation at this point in the argument to believe that an error has been made. Suppose that the farmer suffers damages equal to $100 and the rancher enjoys a net return equal to $110. If the rancher is not liable he will choose to continue ranching and to refuse a payment from a neighboring farmer of $100 to stop ranching. But if the rule of liability is reversed, he will continue ranching only if his $110 net return is sufficient to cover the cost imposed on the farmer ($100) *plus* the payment required to keep sub-marginal land (which can be assumed to border on another boundary of the ranch) out of farming. There has been no error in the argument, but there is an error in introducing the second neighbor halfway through the analysis. With the rancher not liable, he would have elected to remain in ranching only if the net return to ranching exceeded the payments to leave ranching offered to him by *both* his neighbors. If the rancher finds it remunerative to remain in ranching in the face of both these offers he must earn a sufficient net return from ranching, after the rule of liability is changed and he is held liable, to be able to pay damages to his neighboring farmer *and* to pay the owner of neighboring submarginal land to keep that land out of production.

The change in the rule of liability does not lead to a conversion of ranch-land or submarginal land to farming. The use of land that maximized re-turns before the change in liability rule continues to maximize returns after the new rule is adopted, and the mix of output is unaffected by the choice of liability rule even when long-run considerations are analyzed. To understand the effect of altering the rule of liability it is important to recognize that the owner of a resource who finds it in his interest to employ that resource in a particular way when he bears the cost of an interaction will be paid to employ that resource *in the same way* when the rule of liability is reversed. What can happen, and in this case does happen, when the rule of liability is changed is that present owners of land having a comparative advantage in ranching suffer a *windfall* loss in the value of their land while owners of farmland enjoy a *windfall* gain. But this redistribution of wealth cannot alter the uses of these lands.

III

The problem of "extortion" is part of the larger problem of wealth redistribution that may accompany a change in the rule of liability. Our concern here is with situations in which such a redistribution takes place. However, it should be noted that, when there is no restriction on contracting, a change in the rule of liability need not be accompanied by wealth redistribution. If owners of firms are made liable for industrial accidents, for example, then the equilibrium wage will move downward to reflect the shifting of this explicit cost from workers to employers. Employers no longer will need to cover the cost of industrial accidents in the wages they pay since this cost will be paid by them in the form of industrial accident insurance or self-insurance required by the new rule of liability. The general effect of shifting accident liability directly to firms will be merely to change the classification, not the amount, of remuneration. What under no employer liability were simply wages become under employer liability wages plus accident benefits. No redistribution of wealth accompanies the change in liability. Workers who, when they had to bear the cost of accidents directly, received $X in wages will, under the new rule of liability, receive part of the $X in the form of accident compensation and the remainder in wages, but there will be no change in their total income after taking account of expected accident costs under the two systems.

This holds strictly only if workers and employers are allowed to enter into voluntary contractual arrangements for reshifting the explicit cost back to workers, a matter that need not be discussed in detail here. If such agreements are disallowed by the law—*i.e.*, if the costs of making such agreements is prohibitively high because of their illegality—then some wealth may be redistributed from those workers who would have found it advantageous to self-insure to workers who find it advantageous to buy insurance; such a law would force workers, in the wage reductions they must accept, to purchase insurance for industrial accidents from their employers.

The problem of "extortion" arises when a change in liability gives rise to a redistribution in wealth. In the farmer-rancher case, the relative values of nearby farm and ranchlands will be changed when the rule of liability is altered. Under one rule of liability, with farmers required to bear the cost of crop damage, farmers will need to pay ranchers to reduce herd size; under the other rule ranchers will have to pay farmers for damages or for any alteration in the quantity of corn grown nearby. The change in the direction of payments must affect the rents that can be collected by owners of these lands and thus the market values of these lands.

In these cases the owner of the specialized resource, ranchland or farmland, that is not required to bear the cost of the interaction may threaten to increase the intensity of the interaction in an attempt to get his neighbor to pay him a larger sum than would ordinarily be required to obtain his cooperation in adjusting the intensity of the interaction downward. The owner of ranchland, if he is not liable for crop damage done by straying cattle, might, in the absence of a neighboring farmer, raise only 1,000 head of cattle. With proximity between farming and ranching, a neighboring owner of farmland might be willing to pay the rancher the sum required to finance a 200-head reduction in herd size. However, if the owner of ranchland *threatens* to raise 1,500 head, he may be able to secure more than this sum from the farmer because of the additional crop damage that would be caused by the larger herd size. With or without this "extortion" threat, the size of the herd will be reduced to 800 because that is the size, by assumption, that maximizes the total value of both activities. Given the interrelationship between the two activities, that is the herd size that will maximize the return to the farmer and, indirectly, the sum available for possible transfer to the rancher. What is at issue is the sharing of this maximum return.

To the extent that there exist alternative farm sites, the ability of the owner of ranchland to make such a threat credible is compromised. Competition among such owners will reduce the payment that farmers make to ranchers to that sum which is just sufficient to offset the revenue forgone by ranchers when herd size is reduced. No rancher could succeed in a threat to increase herd size above normal numbers because other ranchers would be willing to compete to zero the price that farmers are asked to pay to avoid abnormally large herd sizes. Abnormally large herd size, in itself, will generate losses to owners of ranchland and, for this reason, competition among such owners will reduce the price that owners of farmland must pay to avoid such excessive herd sizes to zero.

But if a ranchland owner has a locational monopoly, in the sense that there are no alternative sites available to farmers, then the rancher may succeed in acquiring a larger sum from his neighboring farmer in order to avoid abnormally large herd sizes. The acquisition of a larger sum by the owner of ranchland generally will require him to incur some cost to make his threat credible, perhaps by actually beginning to increase herd size beyond normal levels. If the cost of making this threat credible is low relative to the sum available for transfer from the owner of farmland, the rancher will be in a good position to accomplish the transfer. The sum available for transfer will be the amount by which the value of the neighboring land when used as farmland exceeds its value in the next best use. If the rancher were to demand a larger payment from his neighbor, the neighboring land would be switched to some other use.

The temptation to label such threats extortion or blackmail must be resisted by economists for these are legal and not economic distinctions. The rancher merely attempts to maximize profits. If his agreements with neighboring farmers are marketed in competition with other ranchers, profit maximization constrained by competition implies that an agreement to reduce herd size can be purchased for a smaller payment than if effective competition in such agreements is absent. The appropriate economic label for this problem is nothing more nor less than monopoly. It takes on the cast of such legal classifications as extortion only because the context seems to be one where the monopoly return is received by threatening to produce something that is not wanted—excessively large herds. The conventional monopoly problem involves a reduction or a threat to reduce the output of a desired good. In the unconventional monopoly problem presented here, there is a threat to increase herd size beyond desirable levels. But this difference is superficial. The conventional monopoly problem can be viewed as one in which the monopolist produces more scarcity than is desired, and the unconventional monopoly problem discussed here can be considered one in which the monopolist threatens to produce too small a reduction in crop damage. Any additional sum that the rancher succeeds in transferring to himself from the farmer is correctly identified as a monopoly return.

The temptation to resolve this monopoly problem merely by reversing the rule of liability must be resisted. Should the liability rule be reversed and the owner of ranchland now be held liable for damage done by his cattle to surrounding crops, the specific monopoly problem that we have been discussing would be resolved. But if the farmer enjoys a locational monopoly such that the rancher has nowhere else to locate, the shoe will now be on the other foot. The farmer can threaten to increase the number of bushels of corn planted, and hence the damage for which the rancher will be liable, unless the rancher pays the farmer a sum greater than would be required under competitive conditions. The potential for monopoly and the wealth redistribution implied by monopoly is present in principle whether or not the owner of ranchland is held liable for damages. Both the symmetry of the problem and its disappearance under competitive conditions refute the allegation that Coase's analysis implicitly endorses the use of resources in undesirable activities.

Should the law treat such classes of monopoly problem as "extortion" or "blackmail"? It may not be useful for the law to take this step because the threat is made credible by increasing the output of an economic good—cattle if the rancher is not liable, corn if he is. Because it is difficult to sort desirable from undesirable increases in herd or crop size, there is a real danger of penalizing desirable increases in herd or crop size by mistake if such wealth transfers are treated as extortion. Activities to which anti-extortion laws normally apply typically involve the use of violence or the threat to take some action that falls within a general class of actions considered socially undesirable. The application of anti-extortion legal measures in such cases is less likely to penalize socially desirable actions by mistake. In other cases, it may be possible for the courts to limit the amount of payments to levels that are reasonable compensations for costs incurred (or profits forgone), although it is not clear how easily such determinations can be made by courts. Alternatively, it is possible to attempt to eliminate the source of the problem—monopoly—but the wisdom of relying on antitrust in this context is a matter on which the author is unprepared to speak.

IV

The costly interaction between farming and ranching is not properly attributed to the actions of either party individually, being "caused," instead, by resource scarcity, the scarcity of land and fencing materials. If transaction cost is negligible, it would seem that the choice of liability rule cannot depend on who "causes" the damage since both jointly do, or on how resource allocation will be altered, since no such alteration will take place, but largely on judicial or legislative preferences with regard to wealth distribution.

Once significant transacting or negotiating cost is admitted into the analysis, the choice of liability rule will have effects on resource allocation, and it no longer follows that wealth distribution is the main or even an important consideration in choosing the liability rule. The assumption of negligible transacting cost can be only a beginning to understanding the economic consequences of the legal arrangements that underlie the operations of the economy, but little more can be done here than to illustrate the nature of the considerations.[10]

The most obvious effect of introducing significant transacting cost is that

[10] Other considerations that arise when the cost of transacting is positive are discussed in Harold Demsetz, Some Aspects of Property Rights, 9 J. Law & Econ. 61 (1966).

negotiations will not be consummated in those situations where the expected benefits from exchange are less than the expected cost of exchanging. Exchange opportunities will be exploited only up to the point where the marginal gain from trade equals the marginal cost of trade. Of course, there is nothing necessarily inefficient in halting exchange at this point. If this were all that could be said on the subject, there would be little more to do than call the reader's attention to the similar analytical roles of transport cost in international trade and transacting cost in exchange generally. But there is more to say.

Significant transacting cost implies that the rule of liability generally will have allocative effects (as Coase recognizes). Consider the problem of liability for automobile-pedestrian accidents. To the extent that "accident" has any economic meaning it must mean that circumstances are such that voluntary negotiations between the driver and the pedestrian are prohibitively costly in many driving situations. The parties to an accident, either because of the speed with which the accident occurs or because of a failure to notice the presence of a competing claimant for the right-of-way, cannot conclude an agreement over the use of the right-of-way at costs that are low enough, *ex ante*, to make the effort worthwhile.

Partly as a consequence of the costliness of such negotiations, rules of the road are developed. Speed limits, traffic signals, and legal constraints on passing are substituted for the development of saleable private rights. In a specific case it may be possible to assign private rights to use the road in a way that makes the exchange of these rights feasible, but, in general, if these rules make economic sense it is precisely because the cost of transacting is expected to be too high in most cases to warrant the development of saleable private rights to the use of roads.

The practicality of such rules is not an argument for or against government action, but a rationale for the substitution of rules for negotiation. The use of rules to eliminate costly negotiations can be found in the management of privately owned parking lots and toll roads as well as in those that are publicly owned.

Such rules notwithstanding, accidents do take place. Assuming that the cost of transacting is too high to make negotiated agreements practical in such cases, we can compare the effect on resource allocation of the rule of liability that is chosen. If drivers are held liable in automobile-pedestrian accidents, the incentives for pedestrians to be careful about how and where they cross streets will be reduced. The incentives for drivers to be careful will be increased. Indeed, if each pedestrian could be guaranteed *full* compensation for all financial, physical, and psychological costs suffered in an accident, then pedestrians would become indifferent between being struck by an auto and not being struck. Drivers, however, would actively seek to avoid accidents since they would always be liable, whereas if it were possible to have a system of complete and full pedestrian liability it would be the drivers who became indifferent between accidents and no accidents and it would be the pedestrians who actively sought to avoid accidents.

In a regime in which transacting cost was zero, either system of liability would generate the same accident-avoiding behavior, as the Coase analysis suggests. With driver liability, drivers would themselves avoid accidents or, if such avoidance could be purchased at lower cost from pedestrians, drivers would pay pedestrians to avoid accidents. Under a scheme of pedestrian liability it would be the pedestrians who took direct action to avoid accidents or indirect action by paying drivers to avoid accidents. Under either rule of liability those accidents are avoided for which the accident cost exceeds the least cost method of avoiding accidents, where the least cost is the lesser of either the driver or pedestrian cost of avoiding accidents. Both rules of liability, assuming zero transacting cost, yield the same accident rate and the same accident-avoiding behavior. The effect of switching from one rule of liability to another is limited to wealth redistribution.

In a situation in which transacting cost is prohibitively high, driver liability leads to the avoidance only of those accidents for which the cost of avoidance to the *driver* is less than the expected accident cost, and pedestrian liability leads to the avoidance of only those accidents for which the cost of avoidance to the *pedestrian* is less than the expected accident cost. In general, the accident rate that results will differ under these two systems since the cost of avoiding accidents will not be the same for drivers and pedestrians. Both systems will lead to higher accident rates than would be true if transacting costs were zero. The effect of positive transacting cost is to raise the cost of avoiding accidents through the foreclosure of the use of possibly cheaper cost-avoidance techniques when these can be employed only by the other party to the accident. A similar conclusion can be reached for all liability problems when transacting cost is prohibitive and when the law cannot particularize the rule of liability to take account of who is the least-cost damage avoider in every instance.

One liability rule may be superior to another if transacting costs are more than negligible precisely because the difficulty of avoiding costly interactions is not generally the same for the interacting parties. It may be less costly for pedestrians to avoid accidents or for farmers to relocate their crops than it is for drivers to avoid accidents or ranchers to reduce the number of cattle they raise. If information about this were known, it would be possible for the legal system to improve the allocation of resources by placing liability on that party who in the usual situation could be expected to avoid the costly interaction most cheaply.

The use of words such as "blame," "responsible," and "fault" must be treated with care by the economist because they have no useful meanings in an economic analysis of these problems other than as synonyms for the party who could have most easily avoided the costly interaction. Whether the interaction problem involves crop damage, accidents, soot, or water pollution, the qualitative relationship between the interacting parties is symmetrical. It is the *joint* use of a resource, be it geographic location, air, or water that leads to these interactions. It is the demand for scarce resources that leads to conflicting interests.

The legal system does produce rules for determining *prima facie* "fault," but in this context "fault" means only according to some acceptable and applicable legal precedent. In an accident involving a rear-end collision, the court generally will place the burden for proving the absence of negligence on the party driving the following car. If a car strikes a person running across a fenced expressway at night the burden of proving the absence of negligence is likely to be placed on the pedestrian. In treating such cases differently, the law bases its decisions on acceptable and appropriate precedents, but the acceptability of these precedents should not be confused with the morality of the interacting parties. A deeper analysis of these precedents may reveal that they generally make sense from the economic viewpoint of placing the liability on that party who can, at least cost, reduce the probability of a costly interaction happening. Less care need be taken by the driver of the following car in a rear-end collision than would need to be taken by the lead driver to avoid the accident, and less care is needed by a pedestrian to refrain from running across an expressway than is needed by a driver to avoid striking the pedestrian. Nor need the acceptability of such precedents be based on restitution since, as these precedents become known, their long-run effect is to deter accidents at least cost. If courts are to ignore wealth, religion, or family in deciding such conflicts, if persons before the courts are to be treated with regard only to the cause of action and available proof, then, as a normative proposition, it is difficult to suggest any criterion for deciding liability other than placing it on the party able to avoid the costly interaction most easily.

[8]

International Review of Law and Economics (1990), *10*(219–231)

STRICT LIABILITY IN A PRINCIPAL-AGENT MODEL

HARRY A. NEWMAN

Assistant Professor, University of Illinois at Chicago, College of Business Administration, Chicago, IL 60680

AND

DAVID W. WRIGHT

Assistant Professor, The University of Michigan, School of Business Administration, Ann Arbor, MI 48109

1. INTRODUCTION

Previous analytical work examining strict liability has generally ignored the existence of moral hazard problems within the firm. In this work, the firm has been implicitly modeled as a single individual (for example, Shavell [1980, 1982], Landes and Posner [1981], Polinsky [1980], Polinsky and Rogerson [1983], and Mantell [1984]).[1] However, it is often the case that an owner of a firm (principal) hires an employee (agent) to perform activities which could result in the harm of a third party. For example, in the recent industrial accident case of the 1984 Bhopal, India gas leak, Union Carbide Corporation had established the subsidiary Union Carbide India Ltd., which in turn hired Indian employees to operate a chemical plant. In general, if the preferences of the agent differ from those of the owner and if the agent's effort is unobservable, then a moral hazard problem may exist within the firm. This study examines the socially optimal level of care and the care taken under strict liability in the presence of moral hazard through the application of principal-agent economic models.[2]

Since this paper examines environments in which a principal hires an agent to engage in a productive activity, the influence that strict liability has on firm behavior can be analyzed in settings where firm ownership is separated from management (for example, as in the Union Carbide Bhopal, India accident). While previous research has considered the direct influence of liability rules on the care taken by an owner-manager, this paper examines the influence that strict liability

We are grateful for the insightful comments of Greg Niehaus, Jim Noel, Ted Snyder, and Robert Thomas.

[1] In the prior literature, the firm could be viewed as a collection of individuals whose preferences are identical. Analytically, there is no substantive difference between a firm comprised of a single individual and a firm consisting of a collection of individuals with identical preferences. The economics literature has long recognized that preferences may, in fact, differ across individuals. This paper demonstrates that moral hazard arising from a difference in preferences and effort unobservability can affect the level of care taken by the firm.

[2] Essentially, under a strict liability rule, a party which causes a loss for a victim must pay damages whether or not the party was negligent.

has on the choice of employment contracts offered by the owner to the agent, which in turn, influences the agent's choice of care.[3]

This paper finds that strict liability induces the owner to offer employment contracts that motivate the agent to take a socially optimal level of care. It is also found that the care exerted by the agent when moral hazard is present can be less than or greater than the care taken when moral hazard is absent.

The remainder of this paper is organized as follows. Section 2 presents the fundamental principal-agent model employed in the paper. Section 3 considers the social welfare maximization problem. Section 4 uses the model developed in section 2 to compare the level of care taken by the agent under strict liability with the social welfare maximizing level of care. Section 5 compares the effort exerted when moral hazard is absent with the effort exerted when moral hazard is present under strict liability. The section also examines how the presence of moral hazard affects the socially optimal level of care. Conclusions and implications are given in section 6.

2. THE PRINCIPAL-AGENT MODEL OF A FIRM ENGAGED IN HAZARDOUS ACTIVITIES

Suppose a risk neutral principal hires a risk averse agent for his productive effort. Both the principal and agent act to maximize their respective individual expected utilities. The agent manages a potentially hazardous endeavor (for example, blasting activities or the operation of a chemical plant) where there is a probability that such activities can result in off-site property damage.[4] The level of effort chosen by the agent affects the likelihood of an accident. Thus, effort can be interpreted as care. It is also assumed that it is too costly for a potential victim to unilaterally avoid damages caused by an accident. Thus, the socially optimal solution will involve the exercise of care by the firm in the prevention of an accident. The following notation is used in the paper.

a = the level of care taken by the agent in managing the hazardous activity.

$p(a)$ = the probability of an accident given the agent's level of care.

$W(I)$ = the agent's compensation as a function of I, where I is some mutually observable variable upon which an enforceable contract can be based.

$H(W(I), a)$ = the agent's utility function as a function of compensation and effort.

u = the agent's reservation level of utility, where $u > 0$.

R = the firm's (principal's) net profits prior to compensation payments to the agent and any legal damages that might be payable to the victim if an accident occurs.[5]

[3] Principal-agent models have been used to examine the economic effects of the imposition of a vicarious liability rule on firm behavior (Sykes 1981, 1984; Kornhauser, 1982). Throughout this paper a vicarious liability rule is employed since it is the extant rule of law. Thus, principals are assumed to be held liable for the torts of their agents.

[4] Damages for personal harm can also be incorporated into the model if there is a monetary equivalent for personal harm incurred as a result of an accident.

[5] The results of the paper would not change if R is made dependent on whether an accident occurs (i.e., the firm might incur costs resulting from an accident due to the loss of assets and impairment of operations).

$G(\cdot)$ = the potential victim's utility function where the argument is the level of total wealth.

y = the potential victim's initial wealth endowment (that is, wealth prior to any accident).

L = the monetary loss sustained by a victim if an accident occurs.

The following assumptions will be employed in the paper.

(A1) *The agent's feasible action set:* The agent chooses an action from a set of actions represented by a closed real interval, $[\underline{a}, \bar{a}]$.

(A2) *The accident prevention technology:* Regardless of the level of care taken by the agent, an accident is never certain nor impossible. Furthermore, the probability of an accident is strictly decreasing in care, but at a decreasing rate. Thus, $0 < p(a) < 1$, $p'(a) < 0$, and $p''(a) > 0$ for all $a \in [\underline{a}, \bar{a}]$ where $p'(a)$ and $p''(a)$ are the first and second derivatives of $p(a)$, respectively. This assumption is consistent with the prior literature (for example, Shavell [1980, 1982, 1984]).

(A3) *The agent's utility:* The agent is risk and effort averse and has a utility function which is separable in wealth and effort. Thus, $H(W(I), a) = U(W(I)) - a$, with $U'(\cdot) > 0$ and $U''(\cdot) < 0$ where $U'(\cdot)$ and $U''(\cdot)$ are the first and second derivatives of $U(\cdot)$, respectively.[6] Let U^{-1} represent the inverse of $U(\cdot)$ with $U^{-1'}(\cdot)$ and $U^{-1''}(\cdot)$ denoting the first and second derivatives of $U^{-1}(\cdot)$, respectively.[7]

(A4) *The principal's utility:* The principal is risk neutral.

(A5) *The victim's utility:* The victim is risk averse so that $G'(\cdot) > 0$ and $G''(\cdot) < 0$ where $G'(\cdot)$ and $G''(\cdot)$ are the first and second derivatives of $G(\cdot)$, respectively.

(A6) *Moral hazard:* The agent's efforts cannot be observed.

(A6') *No Moral hazard:* The agent's efforts are observable.

In order to introduce moral hazard into the principal-agent model, it will generally be assumed that the agent's efforts cannot be observed (A6). Thus, the employment contract offered to the agent must be based on some other variable which is observable. Since an accident is observable and its likelihood is influenced by the agent's effort, the occurrence of an accident itself can serve as a variable upon which an enforceable and motivational contract can be based. Thus, let $I = 1$ if an accident occurs and $I = 0$ otherwise.

The analysis of section 5 will at times utilize assumption (A6') in order to examine the impact moral hazard has on optimal employment contracts and levels of care compared to what occurs when moral hazard is absent.

The principal's task is to offer an incentive compatible contract to the agent which maximizes the principal's expected utility given the firm operates under a strict liability system. Solutions to the problem are considered in section 4.

3. THE SOCIAL WELFARE MAXIMIZATION PROBLEM

The social welfare maximization problem is provided so that the social welfare maximizing level of care can be compared with the care taken under strict liability. A social planner would maximize a weighted average of the victim's and the

---

[6]The assumption that the agent's utility is linear in effort is made without loss of generality since units of effort can always be chosen so that this is true.

[7]Since $U' > 0$ and $U'' < 0$, U^{-1} exists and is strictly increasing and convex.

principal's utility functions.[8] This is equivalent to maximizing one party's expected utility subject to the other earning his reservation level of utility as in Shavell [1982]. If the agent's level of care is unobservable, the tools available to the social planner for this task consist of the choice of social welfare maximizing employment contracts and the direct transfer of wealth between the principal and victim, contingent upon the occurrence of an accident. Let $t_1(t_2)$ represent the wealth transfer between the principal and potential victim if an accident occurs (does not occur). Let c and $1 - c$ be the weights applied to the principal's utility function and the agent's utility function, respectively, where $0 < c < 1$.

The socially optimal level of care is found by solving the following maximization problem:

$$\max_{W(I).a.t_1.t_2} \quad c[R - E(W(I)) - p(a)t_1 - (1 - p(a))t_2]$$

$$+ (1 - c)[p(a)G(y + t_1 - L) + (1 - p(a))G(y + t_2)] \quad (1)$$

Subject to

$$E[U(W(I))] - a \geq u$$

$$a \in argmax \ E[U(W(I))] - á$$

$$á \in [\underline{a}, \bar{a}]$$

where E is the expectation operator.

It is useful to note several points about this social welfare problem and its solution. First, the objective function is linearly decreasing in the expected compensation of the agent, $E(W(I))$. Second, the first order conditions, with respect to t_1 and t_2, imply $t_2 = t_1 - L$. Consequently, the potential victim's wealth will be $y + t_2 = y + t_1 - L$ whether an accident occurs or not, a well-known result of optimal risk sharing imposing no risk on the risk averse potential victim. Therefore, the objective function can be rewritten as

$$c[R - E(W(I)) - p(a)L - t_2] + (1 - c)G(y + t_2).$$

Third, t_2 solves the expression $G'(y + t_2) = c/(1 - c)$ and hence does not depend on the contract, $W(I)$, or the agent's level of care, a. If the social planner does not desire to transfer wealth in the absence of an accident, c can be chosen so that the optimal value for t_2 is 0. Finally, the assumptions that (1) the probability of an accident decreases as more care is taken ($p' < 0$), (2) the marginal benefits from additional care are decreasing ($p'' > 0$), and (3) the agent is risk averse (also employed by Shavell [1980, 1982, 1984]) meet the sufficient conditions given in Rogerson [1985] to guarantee that the agent's effort choice is unique (that is, given an employment contract, the set of actions maximizing the agent's expected utility consists of a single element).

Intuitively, the optimal employment contract equates society's expected marginal benefits from additional care with society's expected marginal costs. The expected marginal benefits consist of the change in the probability of an accident multiplied by L. The expected marginal costs consist of the additional expected

---

[8]In fact, the social welfare between the principal, agent and potential victim is being managed. The welfare of the agent is governed by u and can be interpreted as a variable under the control of the social planner.

compensation necessary to induce the agent to exert greater effort in the prevention of an accident.

4. STRICT LIABILITY UNDER MORAL HAZARD

This section compares the effort exerted under strict liability with the socially optimal level of care. Under strict liability the principal must pay damages, L, in the event of an accident regardless of the level of care taken by the agent. Thus, the principal's maximization problem can be stated as:

$$\max_{W(I),a} R - E(W(I)) - p(a)L \tag{2}$$

Subject to

$$E[U(W(I))] - a \geq u$$

$$a \in argmax\, E[U(W(I))] - á$$

$$á \in [\underline{a}, \bar{a}]$$

Proposition 1 compares the effort exerted by the agent under strict liability with the socially optimal level of care.

Proposition 1 *Given (A1)–(A5) and the existence of moral hazard (A6), a strict liability rule induces the principal to offer an employment contract which motivates the agent to provide a socially optimal level of care.*

Proof: The constraints in the social welfare optimization problem (1) and in the principal's maximization problem under strict liability (2) are identical. Thus, solutions to one problem are feasible in the other. As noted earlier since $y + t_2 = y + t_1 - L$, the social welfare objective function reduces to:

$$\max_{a,W(I),t_2} \{c[R - E(W(I)) - p(a)L]\} + \{(1 - c)G(y + t_2) - ct_2\}.$$

Since t_2 was shown not to depend on a or $W(I)$, the objective function is separable into two independent terms:

$$\max_{a,W(I)} c[R - E(W(I)) - p(a)L]$$

$$\max_{t_2} (1 - c)G(y + t_2) - ct_2$$

The first of these two expressions is the principal's objective function multiplied by the weighting factor, c. Thus, optimizing contracts in the principal's problem (2) also serve to maximize the social welfare function in (1).

The following lemma characterizes the optimal employment contract under strict liability and will be useful in section 5 when examining the effects of moral hazard on strict liability models. Let an employment contract in the presence of moral hazard be of the form $W(I) = \{W(0), W(1)\}$ where $W(0)$ is the compensation paid to the agent if no accident occurs and $W(1)$ is the compensation in the event of an accident.

Lemma 1 *Given (A1)–(A4) and the existence of moral hazard (A6),*

(1)   The employment contract, $W_á(I)$, inducing the level of care, á, that minimizes expected labor costs, $EC(á) = [p(á)w(1) + (1 - p(á))w(0)]$ is:

$$W_á(I) = w(0) = w(1) = U^{-1}(u + \underline{a}) \qquad \text{for } á = \underline{a}$$

$$W_á(I) = \begin{cases} w(0) = U^{-1}\left(u + á - \dfrac{p(á)}{p'(á)}\right) \\[2mm] w(1) = U^{-1}\left(u + á + \dfrac{1 - p(á)}{p'(á)}\right) \end{cases} \qquad \text{for } á \neq \underline{a}$$

(2) $EC(á)$ is strictly increasing in the induced level of care, á.

Proof: See Appendix 1.

5. THE EFFECTS OF MORAL HAZARD ON STRICT LIABILITY MODELS

The previous section examined the influence of strict liability on firm behavior in the presence of moral hazard. This section examines how the results in the presence of moral hazard compare with those when moral hazard is absent.

The first step is to derive principal-agent models of the accident problem where moral hazard is absent. This is accomplished by relaxing assumption A6 and assuming the agent's effort is observable (A6'). It is then seen how the presence of moral hazard affects the socially optimal level of care and the care taken under strict liability.

An enforceable employment contract can be based on effort when it is observable. Denote a contract in which the agent's compensation is a function of (possibly) both the agent's action and the occurrence of an accident by $S(a, I)$.

The socially optimal level of care, when the agent's effort is observable, is found by solving the following maximization problem:

$$\max_{S(a,\, I), a, t_1, t_2} c[R - E(S(a, I)) - p(a)t_1 - (1 - p(a))t_2]$$

$$+ (1 - c)[p(a)G(y + t_1 - L) + (1 - p(a))G(y + t_2)] \quad (3)$$

Subject to

$$E[U(S(a, I))] - a \geq u$$

$$a \in argmax\, E[U(S(á, I))] - á$$

$$á \in [\underline{a}, \bar{a}]$$

The principal's maximization problem under strict liability is given by:

$$\max_{S(a,\, I), a} R - E[S(a, I)] - p(a)L \quad (4)$$

Subject to

$$E[U(S(a, I))] - a \geq u$$

$$a \in argmax \; E[U(S(á, I))] - á$$

$$á \in [\underline{a}, \bar{a}]$$

The following lemma regarding the optimal employment contract between the principal and the agent is used in proving the main results of this section.

Lemma 2 *Given (A1)–(A4) and the absence of moral hazard (A6'):*

(1) *The employment contract, $S_á(a, I)$, inducing a given level of care, á, that minimizes expected labor costs is the forcing contract:*

$$S_á(a, I) = \begin{cases} s(a, I) = U^{-1}(u + á) & \text{if } a = á \\ 0 & \text{otherwise} \end{cases}$$

(2) *$s(á, I) = U^{-1}(u + á)$ is strictly increasing and convex in á.*

Proof: See Appendix 1.

The following proposition is a restatement of Proposition 1 from section 4 but for firm environments in which moral hazard is absent. It is provided for completeness and for use in proving the main results of this section.

Proposition 2 *Given (A1)–(A5) and the absence of moral hazard (A6'), a strict liability rule induces the principal to offer an employment contract which motivates the agent to provide a socially optimal level of care.*

The proof for Proposition 2 is identical to the proof for Proposition 1, except for notation. It is omitted for purposes of brevity.

Proposition 3 states the main result of this section. Proposition 3 compares the socially optimal level of care in the presence of moral hazard with the socially optimal level of care in the absence of moral hazard. The proposition also compares the level of care induced by the principal under strict liability when moral hazard is present and absent. The proof of Proposition 3 assumes that the induced action under strict liability is interior to the feasible action set, so that the first derivatives of the objective functions equal zero. Let a_u^* denote the level of care induced by the optimal employment contract in the solution to the principal's strict liability problem (2) when effort is unobservable. Let a_o^* denote the level of care induced by the optimal employment contract in the solution to the principal's strict liability problem (4) when effort is observable.

Proposition 3 *Given (A1)–(A5),*

(1) *Under strict liability, the care induced by the optimal employment contract offered in the presence of moral hazard, a_u^*, can be either greater than, equal to, or less than the care induced by the optimal employment contract in the absence of moral hazard, a_o^*.*

    (i) *If $\dfrac{d}{da} EC(a_u^*) > U^{-1\prime}(u + a_u^*)$, then the induced level of care will be*

smaller in the presence of moral hazard.

(ii) *If* $\dfrac{d}{da} EC(a_u^*) = U^{-1\prime}(u + a_u^*)$, *then the induced level of care will be the same in the presence and absence of moral hazard.*

(iii) *If* $\dfrac{d}{da} EC(a_u^*) < U^{-1\prime}(u + a_u^*)$, *then the induced level of care will be greater in the presence of moral hazard.*

(2) *The socially optimal level of care in the presence of moral hazard can be either greater than, equal to, or less than the socially optimal level of care in the absence of moral hazard.*

(i) *If* $\dfrac{d}{da} EC(a_u^*) > U^{-1\prime}(u + a_u^*)$, *then the socially optimal level of care will be smaller in the presence of moral hazard.*

(ii) *If* $\dfrac{d}{da} EC(a_u^*) = U^{-1\prime}(u + a_u^*)$, *then the socially optimal level of care will be the same in the presence and absence of moral hazard.*

(iii) *If* $\dfrac{d}{da} EC(a_u^*) < U^{-1\prime}(u + a_u^*)$, *then the socially optimal level of care will be greater in the presence of moral hazard.*

Proof:

(1) (i) Since a_u^* and a_o^* maximize the principal's expected utility for the two strict liability problems, they satisfy the first order conditions from the two maximization problems:

$$-p'(a_u^*)L - \frac{d}{da} EC(a_u^*) = 0$$

$$-p'(a_o^*)L - U^{-1\prime}(u + a_o^*) = 0$$

However, if

$$\frac{d}{da} EC(a_u^*) > U^{-1\prime}(u + a_u^*)$$

then

$$-p'(a_u^*)L - U^{-1\prime}(u + a_u^*) > 0.$$

This implies $a_o^* > a_u^*$ since the principal's expected utility in the absence of moral hazard is concave in a.

The proofs for parts (1) (ii) and (1) (iii) of the proposition follow in similar fashion and are omitted for the sake of brevity.

(2)   The proof is immediate from Propositions 1, 2, and 3(1).

It is, of course, true that for any given level of care, $á$, the expected compensation costs in the presence of moral hazard, $EC(á)$, exceed the compensation costs in the absence of moral hazard, $U^{-1}(u + á)$. In fact, the excess of $EC(á)$ over $U^{-1}(u + á)$ can be regarded as the costs of moral hazard. However, the fact that moral hazard is "costly" at any induced effort level does not imply that the equilibrium solution to the agency problem produces a lower level of care in the presence of moral hazard than when moral hazard is absent. Proposition 3 demonstrates that the level of effort exerted under strict liability in the presence of moral hazard can be either greater than, equal to, or less than the effort exerted in the absence of moral hazard.

The intuition behind this result is as follows. The equilibrium solutions to the two principal-agent problems equate the marginal benefits from effort with their marginal costs. The marginal benefit of a unit of additional effort on the part of the agent is represented by the reduced expected loss from an accident, $p'(\acute{a})L$. For any given level of effort, $\acute{a}$, these marginal benefits are the same in the presence or absence of moral hazard. However, the marginal costs of inducing additional effort differ, depending upon the presence or absence of moral hazard. If at a_u^* the marginal costs of effort in the presence of moral hazard are increasing at a faster rate than in the absence of moral hazard $\left(\dfrac{d}{da} EC(a_u^*) > U^{-1}{}'(u + a_u^*) \right)$,

then the costs of moral hazard are increasing in effort. In other words, the marginal costs of inducing an additional unit of effort would be less in the absence of moral hazard than in the presence of moral hazard. This implies that the induced effort in the presence of moral hazard is less than the induced effort in the absence of moral hazard, since the marginal benefits of additional effort are the same in both circumstances. Of course, when the marginal costs of moral hazard at a_u^* are decreasing $\left(\dfrac{d}{da} EC(a_u^*) < U^{-1}{}'(u + a_u^*) \right)$, then the reverse is true. This implies

$a_o^* < a_u^*$, since the loss in benefits by inducing lower effort is less than the savings in compensation. Further, since Propositions 1 and 2 demonstrate that the socially optimal level of care and the induced level of care under strict liability are the same (either in the presence or absence of moral hazard) it follows immediately that the socially optimal level of care can either increase or decrease with the introduction of moral hazard in the firm. Finally, since the case involving higher induced effort in the presence of moral hazard ($a_o^* < a_u^*$) may be counterintuitive, an example is provided in Appendix 2.

6. SUMMARY AND CONCLUSIONS

This paper uses a principal-agent economic model of the firm to analytically examine issues surrounding the use of strict liability for the accident problem. This includes examining the consequences of the presence of moral hazard within the firm on the level of care induced by the principal under strict liability and on the socially optimal level of care.

The results show that strict liability motivates the principal to offer a contract which induces a socially optimal level of care. This is true either in the presence or absence of moral hazard within the firm. The analysis demonstrates that the care exerted under strict liability when moral hazard is present is generally different from the care taken when moral hazard is absent. The induced level of care can be either greater or lower in the presence of moral hazard than in its absence— depending on the marginal costs of moral hazard with respect to increases in effort. Similarly, the socially optimal level of care can be either higher or lower in the presence of moral hazard than when moral hazard is absent.

APPENDIX 1

This appendix provides proofs to Lemmas 1 and 2.

Proof of Lemma 1:

The principal's employment contract inducing the level of care, $\acute{a}$, that minimizes expected labor costs is derived by solving the following minimization problem:

$$\min_{w(0),w(1)} \quad p(\acute{a})w(1) + (1 - p(\acute{a}))w(0)$$

Subject to

$$p(\acute{a})U(w(1)) + (1 - p(\acute{a}))U(w(0)) - \acute{a} \geq u \qquad (c1)$$

$$p(\acute{a})U(w(1)) + (1 - p(\acute{a}))U(w(0)) - \acute{a}$$
$$\geq p(a)U(w(1)) + (1 - p(a))U(w(0)) - a \text{ for all } a \in [\underline{a}, \bar{a}] \quad (c2)$$

(1)   (i)   Consider $\acute{a} = a$. Since $p' < 0$ and $p'' > 0$, a necessary and sufficient condition for satisfying the second constraint (c2) is

$$p'(\underline{a})[U(w(1)) - U(w(0))] - 1 \leq 0. \qquad (c3)$$

Thus, (c3) can replace (c2) to produce an equivalent minimization problem. Now, at $w(0) = w(1) = U^{-1}(u + \underline{a})$ constraint (c1) is binding while (c3) is not. Therefore, the Kuhn-Tucker sufficient condition for minimization is that there exists an $s \geq 0$ such that:

$$p(\underline{a}) - sp(\underline{a})U'(w(1)) = 0$$

$$1 - p(\underline{a}) - s(1 - p(\underline{a}))U'(w(0)) = 0$$

which is satisfied by $s = 1/U'(w(1)) = 1/U'(w(0))$.

(ii)   Consider $\acute{a} \in (a, \bar{a})$. Since $p' < 0$ and $p'' > 0$, a necessary and sufficient condition for satisfying the second constraint (c2) is

$$p'(\acute{a})[U(w(1)) - U(w(0))] - 1 = 0. \qquad (c4)$$

Thus, (c4) can replace (c2) to produce an equivalent minimization problem. Now, at

$$w(0) = U^{-1}\left(u + \acute{a} - \frac{p(\acute{a})}{p'(\acute{a})}\right)$$

$$w(1) = U^{-1}\left(u + \acute{a} + \frac{1 - p(\acute{a})}{p'(\acute{a})}\right)$$

constraint (c4) is satisfied and (c1) is binding. Therefore, the Kuhn-Tucker sufficient conditions for minimization are that there exist an $s \geq 0$ and a t such that:

$$p(\acute{a}) - sp(\acute{a})U'(w(1)) - tp'(\acute{a})U'(w(1)) = 0$$

$$1 - p(\acute{a}) - s(1 - p(\acute{a}))U'(w(0)) + tp'(\acute{a})U'(w(0)) = 0$$

which are satisfied by:

$$s = \frac{(1 - p(\acute{a}))U'(w(1)) + p(\acute{a})U'(w(0))}{U'(w(0))U'(w(1))}$$

$$t = -\frac{p(\acute{a})(1 - p(\acute{a}))[U'(w(1)) - U'(w(0))]}{p'(\acute{a})U'(w(0))U'(w(1))}$$

(iii) Consider $\acute{a} = \bar{a}$. Since $p' < 0$ and $p'' > 0$, a necessary and sufficient condition for satisfying the second constraint (c2) is

$$p'(\bar{a})[U(w(1)) - U(w(0))] - 1 \geq 0. \tag{c5}$$

Thus, (c5) can replace (c2) to produce an equivalent minimization problem. Now, at

$$w(0) = U^{-1}\left(u + \bar{a} - \frac{p(\bar{a})}{p'(\bar{a})}\right)$$

$$w(1) = U^{-1}\left(u + \bar{a} + \frac{1 - p(\bar{a})}{p'(\bar{a})}\right)$$

both constraints (c1) and (c5) are binding. Therefore, the Kuhn-Tucker sufficient conditions for minimization are that there exist $s, t \geq 0$ such that:

$$p(\bar{a}) - sp(\bar{a})U'(w(1)) - tp'(\bar{a})U'(w(1)) = 0$$

$$1 - p(\bar{a}) - s(1 - p(\bar{a}))U'(w(0)) + tp'(\bar{a})U'(w(0)) = 0$$

which are satisfied by:

$$s = \frac{(1 - p(\bar{a}))U'(w(1)) + p(\bar{a})U'(w(0))}{U'(w(0))U'(w(1))}$$

$$t = -\frac{p(\bar{a})(1 - p(\bar{a}))[U'(w(1)) - U'(w(0))]}{p'(\bar{a})U'(w(0))U'(w(1))}$$

(2) The first derivative of expected labor costs with respect to $\acute{a}$ is:

$$\frac{d}{d\acute{a}}\left\{p(\acute{a})U^{-1}\left(u + \acute{a} + \frac{1 - p(\acute{a})}{p'(\acute{a})}\right) + (1 - p(\acute{a}))U^{-1}\left(u + \acute{a} - \frac{p(\acute{a})}{p'(\acute{a})}\right)\right\}$$

$$= p'(\acute{a})\left[U^{-1}\left(u + \acute{a} + \frac{1 - p(\acute{a})}{p'(\acute{a})}\right) - U^{-1}\left(u + \acute{a} - \frac{p(\acute{a})}{p'(\acute{a})}\right)\right]$$

$$+ \frac{p(\acute{a})p''(\acute{a})(p(\acute{a}) - 1)}{(p'(\acute{a}))^2}\left[U^{-1\prime}\left(u + \acute{a} + \frac{1 - p(\acute{a})}{p'(\acute{a})}\right)\right.$$

$$\left. - U^{-1\prime}\left(u + \acute{a} - \frac{p(\acute{a})}{p'(\acute{a})}\right)\right]$$

which is strictly greater than zero by $0 < p(\acute{a}) < 1$, $p' < 0$, $p'' > 0$ and U^{-1}

230   *Strict liability in a principal-agent model*

·strictly increasing and convex in $\acute{a}$.

Proof of Lemma 2:

(1) The employment contract, $S_{\acute{a}}(a, I)$, inducing the level of care, $\acute{a}$, that minimizes expected labor costs is derived by solving the following minimization problem:

$$\min_{s(\acute{a},0),s(\acute{a},1)} \quad p(\acute{a})s(\acute{a}, 1) + (1 - p(\acute{a}))s(\acute{a}, 0)$$

Subject to

$$p(\acute{a})U(s(\acute{a}, 1)) + (1 - p(\acute{a}))U(s(\acute{a}, 0)) - \acute{a} \geq u$$

$$p(\acute{a})U(s(\acute{a}, 1)) + (1 - p(\acute{a}))U(s(\acute{a}, 0)) - \acute{a}$$
$$\geq p(a)U(s(a, 1)) + (1 - p(a))U(s(a, 0)) - a \text{ for all } a \in [\underline{a}, \bar{a}]$$

From Harris and Raviv [1979], any contract based on a and I is equivalent to a forcing contract of the form:

$$S_{\acute{a}}(a, I) = \begin{cases} s(a, I) = t(I) & \text{if } a = \acute{a} \\ 0 & \text{otherwise} \end{cases}$$

which induces the agent to take action $\acute{a}$ such that

$$p(\acute{a})U(t(1)) + (1 - p(\acute{a}))U(t(0)) - \acute{a} \geq u.$$

Therefore, the contract minimizing expected labor costs is $t(1) = t(0) = U^{-1}(u + \acute{a})$ since $U(\cdot)$ is concave. Hence, the agent's actual and expected compensation will be $U^{-1}(u + \acute{a})$.

(2) Since U is strictly increasing, U^{-1} is as well. Therefore, the first derivative of $s(\acute{a}, I) = U^{-1}(u + \acute{a})$ with respect to $\acute{a}$ is positive.

APPENDIX 2

The purpose of this appendix is to provide an example that demonstrates that the level of care induced under strict liability can be larger when moral hazard is present than when moral hazard is absent.

Let $p(a) = (1 - a)^{1.05}$ where $a \in [.01, .99]$, $U(Z) = (1/10,000)Z^{.8}$ where Z is the agent's wealth, $u = .2$, $R = \$5,000,000$, $L = \$120,020$.

In this example, the optimal employment contract in the presence of moral hazard is $W(I) = \{\$124,974, \$7,555\}$ which induces the agent to exert effort $a_u^* = .9$. When moral hazard is absent, the optimal contract pays the agent \$80,537 if effort level $a = .641$ is chosen and \$0 otherwise. The agent will then choose $a_o^* = .641$, of course. Therefore, in this example the effort induced in the presence of moral hazard is greater than in the absence of moral hazard.

REFERENCES

Brown, J. P., "Toward an Economic Theory of Liability," *The Journal of Legal Studies*, Vol. 2 (1973), pp. 323–49.

Harris, M. and A. Raviv, "Optimal Incentive Contracts with Imperfect Information,"

Journal of Economic Theory, Vol. 20 (1979), pp. 231–59.

Kornhauser, L. A., "An Economic Analysis of the Choice Between Enterprise and Personal Liability for Accidents," *California Law Review*, Vol. 70 (1982), pp. 1345–92.

Landes, W. M. and R. A. Posner, "The Positive Economic Theory of Tort Law," *Georgia Law Review*, Vol. 15 (1981), pp. 851–924.

Mantell, E. H., "Allocative and Distributive Efficiency of Products Liability Law in a Monopolistic Market," *Journal of Products Liability*, Vol. 7 (1984), pp. 143–52.

Polinsky, A. M., "Strict Liability vs. Negligence in a Market Setting," *The American Economic Review*, Vol. 70 (1980), pp. 363–67.

Polinsky, A. M. and W. P. Rogerson, "Products Liability, Consumer Misperceptions, and Market Power," *The Bell Journal of Economics*, Vol. 14 (1983), pp. 581–89.

Rogerson, W. P., "The First-Order Approach to Principal-Agent Problems," *Econometrica*, Vol. 53 (1985), pp. 1357–67.

Shavell, S., "Risk Sharing and Incentives in the Principal and Agent Relationship," *The Bell Journal of Economics*, Vol. 10 (1979), pp. 55–73.

———, "Strict Liability Versus Negligence," *Journal of Legal Studies*, Vol. 9 (1980), pp. 1–25.

———, "On Liability and Insurance," *The Bell Journal of Economics*, Vol. 13 (1982), pp. 120–32.

———, "A Model of the Optimal Use of Liability and Safety Regulation," *Rand Journal of Economics*, Vol. 15 (1984), pp. 271–80.

Sykes, A. O., "An Efficiency Analysis of Vicarious Liability Under the Law of Agency," *The Yale Law Journal*, Vol. 91 (1981), pp. 169–206.

———, "The Economics of Vicarious Liability," *The Yale Law Journal*, Vol. 93 (1984), pp. 1231–80.

[9]

On liability and insurance

Steven Shavell*

The question considered in this article is how liability rules and insurance affect incentives to reduce accident risks and the allocation of such risks. This question is examined when liability is strict or based on the negligence rule; and, if first-party and liability insurance are available, when insurers have information about insured parties' behavior and when they do not have such information. The conclusions are in essence that although both of the forms of liability create incentives to take care, they differ in respect to the allocation of risk; that, of course, the presence of insurance markets mitigates this difference and alters incentives to take care; and that despite the latter effect, the sale of insurance is socially desirable.

1. Introduction

■ This article is concerned with identifying how liability rules and insurance affect incentives to reduce accident risks and the allocation of such risks.[1] Two principal forms of liability will be examined: *strict liability*, under which a party who has caused a loss must pay damages whether or not he was negligent; and the *negligence rule*, under which a party who has caused a loss is required to pay damages only if he was negligent. The two major types of insurance coverage will also be considered: *first-party insurance*, that is, coverage against direct loss; and *liability. insurance*, coverage against having to pay damages.

It is clear that liability rules influence accident avoidance as well as the allocation of accident risks. It is evident too that insurance has both effects, for by its nature insurance spreads losses; and it also alters incentives—in a way that depends on the extent of coverage and on the connection, if any, between the terms of a policy and actions taken by an insured party to reduce risk.

Moreover, the effects of liability rules and of insurance are mutually dependent. The allocation of risk associated with the use of a liability rule depends on insurance coverage, and the latter depends on the liability rule since the rule determines in part the risks parties face. Likewise, the incentives to avoid accidents created by liability rules influence and are influenced by insurance coverage; and this raises a question of interest, namely, could liability insurance be socially disadvantageous on account of its dulling the incentive to reduce accident risks?[2]

---

* Harvard Law School.
    I wish to thank G. Calabresi, P. A. Diamond, A. Klevorick, A. M. Polinsky, and R. Posner for comments and the National Science Foundation (Grant nos. SOC-76-20862 and SES-80-14208) for financial support.
[1] The term "accident" is to be given the broadest interpretation. It will refer to instances of loss arising in most any type of situation in which the actions of a party (an individual or a firm) affect the probability distribution of loss suffered by others.

[2] This question was seriously discussed when liability insurance was first offered for sale in England and in the United States. As one commentator writes, "For a time . . . there was considerable uncertainty as to whether any contract by which an insured was to be protected against the consequences of his own negligence . . . was not void as contrary to public policy. . . . [But] when it became apparent that no dire consequences

In view of these remarks about the relationship between liability rules and insurance, the main features of the model and the analysis to be presented may be briefly indicated before proceeding.[3] In the model, accidents are assumed to involve two types of parties, "injurers" and "victims," only the former of which are assumed to be able to affect the likelihood of accidents, and only the latter of which are assumed to suffer direct losses in the event of accidents. Given this model, the following conclusions are reached.

(i) Strict liability and negligence both create incentives to reduce accident risk, but they differ with respect to the allocation of risk.[4] Under strict liability injurers bear risk and victims are protected against risk, whereas under the negligence rule injurers do not bear risk—if they are not negligent, they will not have to pay damages when involved in accidents—and victims do bear risk. In consequence, if insurance is unavailable, then strict liability will be attractive when injurers are risk neutral (or, more generally, are better able to bear risk than victims), and the negligence rule will be appealing in the reverse situation.[5]

(ii) The availability of insurance alters this conclusion and suggests that with respect to the bearing of risk, strict liability and negligence should be equally attractive; for victims can avoid the risk that they would bear under the negligence rule by purchasing first-party insurance, and injurers can shift the risk that they would bear under strict liability by purchasing liability insurance. However, matters are complicated if liability insurers cannot monitor injurer behavior, since problems of "moral hazard" would then result in injurers' purchasing only partial coverage.

(iii) The availability of liability insurance does not have an undesirable effect on the working of liability rules. Although the purchase of liability insurance changes the incentives created by liability rules, the terms of the insurance policies sold in a competitive setting would be such as to provide an appropriate substitute (but not necessarily

---

in fact resulted, these objections passed out of the picture . . ." (Prosser, 1971, p. 543). However, it is worth noting that liability insurance is not sold in the Soviet Union, where the view is held that the insurance would interfere unduly with the role of liability as a deterrent (Tunc, 1973).

[3] The analysis builds in two important respects on Brown (1973), Diamond (1974), Green (1976), and Shavell (1980), which study accidents and liability when parties are risk neutral and thus when there are no insurance markets. The first respect in which the model of this article differs from those in the articles cited is in its portrayal of the functioning of liability rules. In the cited articles, a liable party pays any judgment rendered against him out of his own pocket, whereas in the model studied here—and as is usually the case in fact—a liable party pays little or none of a judgment against him; instead his liability insurer pays. This means that the way in which liability rules are envisioned here to create incentives to reduce accident risks is to a considerable degree indirect, being associated with the terms of liability insurance policies.

The second respect in which the present model differs from the others is simply that because account is taken of attitudes toward risk, the normative comparison of liability rules involves considerations of the allocation of risk as well as of reduction of accident losses. Indeed, this means that liability rules are sometimes not equivalent here when they would have been had parties been assumed risk neutral. Similarly, because this article considers the possibility of risk aversion and, therefore, the presence of insurance markets, the social desirability of liability insurance can be examined.

In addition to the articles cited above, the reader may wish to refer to Spence (1977) and to Epple and Raviv (1978), which study strict product liability but not the negligence rule and which, in any event, focus on different issues (Spence on warranties; Epple and Raviv on market structure). Finally, the reader should refer to Calabresi (1970) and to Posner (1977), which contain interesting and suggestive, informal analysis of accidents and liability.

[4] The model abstracts from considerations other than those of incentives and the allocation of risk. In particular, there is no account taken of administrative costs (but see the concluding comments).

[5] Moreover, it will be shown that were strict liability the form of liability in this situation, it would be best for the level of liability to be less than losses caused, as if to insure partially the risk averse injurers. In other words, when the generator of an externality is risk averse, "fully internalizing" the externality is not desirable.

equivalent) set of incentives to reduce accident risks. In other words, it is not socially beneficial for the government to intervene in the operation of competitive liability insurance markets (thus answering the question posed above).[6]

2. The model

■ It is assumed in the model that injurers are identical and act so as to maximize the expected utility of wealth, and the same is presumed about victims. Under one interpretation to be made, injurers are taken to be sellers of a product for which each victim has an inelastic demand for a single unit;[7] under the other interpretation, injurers are assumed to be engaged in a private, nonmarket activity.[8] Now define the following notation:

U = utility function of injurers—who are risk neutral or risk averse;

u = initial wealth of injurers; $0 < u$;

V = utility function of victims—who are risk neutral or risk averse;

v = initial wealth of victims; $0 < v$;

x = level of injurers' expenditures on accident prevention activity;

$p(x)$ = probability of an accident, given x; $0 < p < 1$ and p is decreasing and strictly convex in x;

l = loss[9] sustained by a victim if there is an accident; $0 < l < u$[10];

r = under the first interpretation of the model, the price paid by victims for the product sold by injurers; under the other interpretation, a "lump sum" amount paid (before an accident might occur) by victims and received, as a lump sum, by injurers.

The problem to be solved using this model and notation is to choose "policy variables" in a Pareto efficient way, that is, in a way such that no alternative choice would raise the expected utility of both injurers and victims.[11] It is assumed that given the choice of policy variables, injurers select a level of prevention activity and a liability insurance policy (if available) to maximize their expected utility EU, while taking as fixed the behavior of victims and the value of r;[12] and victims select a first-party insurance policy (if available) to maximize their expected utility EV, while taking as fixed injurers' behavior and the value of r. Formally, then, the problem is:

to choose policy variables to maximize EV subject to the constraints: (1)

victims maximize EV (taking injurers' behavior and r as given);   (2)

---

[6] It will be seen that this fact cannot be interpreted as an application of the theorem of welfare economics stating that a competitive equilibrium with complete markets is Pareto efficient.

[7] Under this interpretation, victims may either be imagined to suffer a loss due to a production-related accident (oil spill ruins beach front property), or else to suffer a loss due to failure of the product purchased (explosion of purchased boiler causes damage to plant).

[8] We do not ask whether (or to what extent) the injurer would engage in his activity. That question is among those considered in Shavell (1980).

[9] The possibility of nonmonetary losses is not considered.

[10] In other words, it is assumed that injurers are able to pay for the losses they might cause.

[11] In the various versions of the problem that will be considered, the relevant policy variables will be obvious from context. They may include parameters of a liability rule, a choice among alternative liability rules, or, possibly, a decision about intervention in insurance markets.

[12] For the assumption that injurers take r as fixed to make sense under the interpretation that r is the price of the product they sell and that loss is caused by product failure, it must be assumed that victim/consumers of the product cannot determine the accident probabilities of sellers on an individual basis. (Otherwise, the level of prevention activity would affect the price r through its influence on the accident probability.)

injurers maximize EU (taking victims' behavior and r as given);   (3)

$$r \text{ satisfies } EU = \bar{U};$$ (4)

and, sometimes, subject also to the constraint that

competitive first party and liability insurance markets operate.   (5)

Under the interpretation whereby injurers are sellers of a product, the price r may be viewed as market determined: Suppose that there is free entry into the product market and that $\bar{U}$ is the injurers' "opportunity level" of utility (injurers may engage in an alternative activity that yields $\bar{U}$). Then, in equilibrium, r must be such that their expected utility is $\bar{U}$. Under the other interpretation, when injurers are not sellers of a product, the reference level of expected utility $\bar{U}$, and thus the amount r, may be regarded as reflecting a social decision about their welfare.

3. The first-best solution to the accident problem

■ Before considering liability rules and insurance, it will be of interest to know what an omniscient and benevolent dictator would do to solve the accident problem. The dictator would choose in a Pareto efficient way the level of injurers' prevention activity and the levels of wealth for both injurers and victims, contingent on accident involvement and subject to a resource constraint. More precisely, denoting by v_n the wealth of a victim if he is not involved in an accident, v_a his wealth if he is, and similarly for u_n and u_a, the dictator would

$$\underset{x, v_n, v_a, u_n, u_a}{\text{maximize}} \; EV = (1 - p(x))V(v_n) + p(x)V(v_a) \tag{6}$$

subject to:

$$EU = (1 - p(x))U(u_n) + p(x)U(u_a) = \bar{U}; \tag{7}$$

$$[(1 - p(x))v_n + p(x)v_a] + [(1 - p(x))u_n + p(x)u_a] + [p(x)l + x] = u + v. \tag{8}$$

Note that equation (8) states that expected resource use equals the available resources.[13] We then have

Proposition 1. A first-best solution to the accident problem is achieved if and only if (a) the level of prevention activity minimizes expected accident losses plus the costs of prevention activity (i.e., $p(x)l + x$); and (b) risk averse parties (injurers or victims) are left with the same level of wealth regardless of whether an accident actually occurs.

Note: The explanation for this is, of course, that the dictator can fully insure risk averse parties and, thus, it becomes desirable to maximize total expected resources, which means minimizing expected accident losses plus prevention costs.

Proof: Note first that given any x, a necessary and sufficient condition for optimality of $v_n, v_a, u_n,$ and u_a is that they satisfy (7) and (8), that $v_n = v_a$ if the victim is risk averse, and that $u_n = u_a$ if the injurer is risk averse.[14]

     Consequently, we may set $\gamma = v_n = v_a$ and $\mu = u_n = u_a$. (If the victim is risk neutral, we may always take $v_n = v_a$; and similarly if the injurer is risk neutral, we may always take $u_n = u_a$.) Thus the problem (6)–(8) is equivalent to

$$\underset{\gamma, \mu, x}{\text{maximize}} \; V(\gamma) \tag{9}$$

---

[13] The justification for writing the resource constraint in terms of expected values is the conventional one, that accident risks are small and independent. Note that the constraint makes sense only if the number of injurers equals the number of victims, an assumption which would be easy to modify.

[14] This is a standard result in the theory of Pareto-efficient sharing of risk (see for example Borch (1962)) and can easily be verified from the Kuhn-Tucker conditions for the problem (6)–(8).

subject to:

$$U(\mu) = \bar{U}, \tag{10}$$

$$\gamma + \mu + p(x)l + x = u + v. \tag{11}$$

But (10) determines a value, say $\bar{\mu}$, of μ, so that the two constraints reduce to

$$\gamma = (u + v - \bar{\mu}) - (p(x)l + x). \tag{12}$$

Hence, the problem is simply to maximize over x the quantity $V(u + v - \bar{\mu} - (p(x)l + x))$, which is equivalent to minimizing $p(x)l + x$. *Q.E.D.*

Note that the first-best level of prevention activity, to be denoted x^*, must be unique (by strict convexity of $p(x)$). Since the situation of interest is where $x^* > 0$, this will be assumed to be true below.

4. The achievable solution to the accident problem

■ To determine the solution to the accident problem when liability rules are used— that is, to determine Pareto efficient solutions to the problem (1)–(5)—the rules must first be formally defined. Under strict liability, whenever an injurer is involved in an accident, he must pay the victim an amount in damages. Denote damages by d, and observe that in principle damages need not equal the victim's loss. Under the negligence rule, an injurer must pay damages to the victim only if the court determines that the injurer's prevention activity fell short of a *standard of due care*. Denote the standard of due care by $\bar{x}$. It will be assumed that the courts' information about the injurer's behavior is accurate, so that an injurer will be found negligent if and only if he was in fact negligent.[15]

The operation of liability rules will now be studied both when insurance is assumed to be available and when it is not. The latter case is of interest both because it will allow us to see more easily the difference that insurance makes and also because in reality insurance might be unavailable.

□ **Functioning of liability rules when insurance is not available.** Let us first show

Proposition 2. Under strict liability, suppose that injurers are risk neutral. Then, according to a Pareto efficient solution, (a) damages paid by an injurer equal a victim's losses (i.e., $d = l$) and (b) a first-best outcome is achieved. On the other hand, if injurers are risk averse, then under an efficient solution (c) damages paid are less than a victim's losses (i.e., $d < l$) and (d) a first-best outcome is not achieved.

Note: Parts (a) and (b) are true for familiar reasons: When $d = l$, the "externality" of accident losses is "fully internalized," so that the injurers choose an appropriate level of prevention activity. Also, since injurers are risk neutral, it does not matter that they bear risk. Finally, victims, who might be risk averse, bear no risk since they are compensated for accident losses.

With regard to (c), it is not surprising that when injurers are risk averse, the externality they generate should not be fully internalized. (Under the first interpretation of the model, this means that buyers of a risky product are better off if risk averse sellers are subject to less than full liability for harm done.) Were d set equal to l, injurers would be exposed to "excessive" risk, with the consequence that they would have to be compensated excessively for bearing the risk or for engaging in excessive accident prevention activity. (The actual magnitude of the efficient d would depend on the victims' attitude toward risk as well; presumably, the more risk averse the victims, the higher would be

---

[15] The importance of this assumption is noted in the concluding comments.

this d.) Part (d) is true because if the efficient d is positive (as one would expect), then injurers bear risk; and if the efficient d is 0,[16] then injurers will choose x equal to 0, which is not first-best (as $x^* > 0$).

Proof: Assume first that injurers are risk neutral. Then if a first-best outcome is achieved when $d = l$, certainly $d = l$ must be a Pareto efficient solution to the problem of concern. We shall therefore assume that $d = l$ and shall show that a first-best outcome would result. If $d = l$, injurers will select x to maximize[17]

$$EU = (1 - p(x))(u + r - x) + p(x)(u + r - x - l) = u + r - (x + p(x)l). \quad (13)$$

Therefore, they will select x to minimize $x + p(x)l$. Moreover, since victims (who might be risk averse) will receive l whenever there is an accident, their income will be constant. Thus, if r is such that $EU = \bar{U}$, the "if" part of Proposition 1 implies that the first-best solution (corresponding to $\bar{U}$) is achieved. This proves parts (a) and (b).

Assume now that injurers are risk averse, so that

$$EU = (1 - p(x))U(u + r - x) + p(x)U(u + r - x - d). \quad (14)$$

Victims' expected utility is then

$$EV = (1 - p(x))V(v - r) + p(x)V(v - r - l + d), \quad (15)$$

and the problem (1)-(5) reduces to

$$\text{maximize } EV \quad (16)$$
$$\scriptsize d,r,x$$

subject to:[18]

$$EU_x = 0 \quad (17)$$

$$EU = \bar{U}. \quad (18)$$

Since the constraints (17) and (18) determine (and, let us assume, uniquely) r and x as functions of d, the problem may be written as

$$\text{maximize } EV(d) = (1 - p(x(d)))V(v - r(d)) + p(x(d))V(v - r(d) - l + d). \quad (19)$$

Now observe that[19]

$$EV'(d) = -p'x'[V(v - r) - V(v - r - l + d)]$$
$$\qquad\qquad - r'(1 - p)V'(v - r) + p(1 - r')V'(v - r - l + d). \quad (20)$$

To show that $d < l$, we shall verify that $EV'(l) < 0$. (A similar series of steps will verify that $EV'(d) < 0$ for $d > l$.) From (20), we have that $EV'(l) = (p - r')V'(v - r)$, so that we need to verify that $r' > p$. To do this, differentiate (18) to get

$$EU_x x'(d) + EU_r r'(d) + EU_d = 0, \quad (21)$$

and using (17), solve for r',

$$r'(d) = \frac{-EU_d}{EU_r} = \frac{p(x)U'(u + r - x - d)}{(1 - p(x))U'(u + r - x) + p(x)U'(u + r - x - d)} \quad (22)$$

$$= p(x)/[(1 - p(x))\frac{U'(u + r - x)}{U'(u + r - x - d)} + p(x)].$$

---

[16] Examples can be constructed in which the efficient d is 0.

[17] Since the injurer is risk neutral, we may assume that the utility function is just $U(w) = w$ for any wealth w.

[18] It will be assumed that the first-order condition (17) determines the injurer's choice of x for the values of r and d to be considered.

[19] In the next expression and several later ones, certain functions will for convenience be written without their arguments (e.g., p' rather than $p'(x(d))$).

It is clear from (22) that $r' > p$ for any $d > 0$ (and thus for $d = 1$). This establishes part (c), and part (d) is clear from the Note. *Q.E.D.*

The next result is

Proposition 3. Under the negligence rule, suppose that victims are risk neutral. Then, according to a Pareto efficient solution, (a) the standard of due care equals the first-best level (i.e., $\bar{x} = x^*$), and (b) a first-best outcome is achieved. However, if victims are risk averse, then under a Pareto efficient solution (c) the standard of due care is generally different from the first-best level, and (d) a first-best outcome is not achieved.

Note: Parts (a) and (b) are true because if $\bar{x} = x^*$, injurers will find it in their interest to choose $x = \bar{x}$, that is, to act in a nonnegligent way. Thus, the injurers, who might be risk averse, bear no risk. As victims are risk neutral, the fact that they bear risk does not matter. But, of course, when victims are risk averse, that they bear risk does matter, so that, as stated in (d), a first-best outcome would not be achieved. Moreover, in this case it will be seen that it would often be desirable that $\bar{x} > x^*$, so as to further reduce the likelihood of accidents.

Proof: To establish (a) and (b), let us show that when victims are risk neutral, a first-best outcome will result if $\bar{x} = x^*$ and $d = 1$. To see this, consider first the possibility that injurers choose an $x \geq x^*$. Then, clearly, it must be that they choose $x = x^*$. On the other hand, if the injurers choose an $x < x^*$, then, since they would be found negligent if involved in accidents,

$$EU = (1 - p(x))U(u + r - x) + p(x)U(u + r - x - l)$$

$$\leq U(u + r - x - p(x)l) < U(u + r - x^* - p(x^*)l) < U(u + r - x^*). \quad (23)$$

(Use was made here of the fact that x^* minimizes $x + p(x)l$.) Thus injurers would choose x^*, would not be found negligent if involved in accidents, and would bear no risk. As victims are risk neutral, Proposition 1 then implies that a first-best outcome would be achieved.

Now assume that victims are risk averse and consider only $\bar{x}$ such that injurers would choose $x = \bar{x}$.[20] (Even if we restrict attention to the case when $d = 1$, the set of such $\bar{x}$ properly includes $[0, x^*]$ since (23) is a strict inequality.) For such $\bar{x}$, $EV = (1 - p(\bar{x}))V(v - r) + p(\bar{x})V(v - r - l)$ and $EU = U(u + r - \bar{x})$. The problem of concern is therefore to maximize EV over r and $\bar{x}$ subject to $EU = \bar{U}$. But from the latter constraint, it follows that r and $\bar{x}$ are determined by $r = \bar{x} + k$, where k is an appropriate constant, so that the problem reduces to

$$\underset{\bar{x}}{\text{maximize}} \; (1 - p(\bar{x}))V(v - k - \bar{x}) + p(\bar{x})V(v - k - \bar{x} - l). \quad (24)$$

If V were linear, the solution to (24) would be $\bar{x} = x^*$, but since V is concave we would, as remarked, expect the solution to exceed x^*. It is possible, however, that the solution to (24) would be less than x^*.[21] In any event, since victims are risk averse and bear risk, Proposition 1 implies that a first-best outcome is not achieved. *Q.E.D.*

□ **Functioning of liability rules when insurance is available.** It will be assumed here that parties can purchase insurance at actuarially fair rates from a competitive insurance industry. Thus, if victims are risk averse, they will choose to buy full coverage against any risk they bear.

---

[20] Otherwise, the liability rule reduces to strict liability.

[21] The intuition is that even though a risk averse injurer has a greater motive to reduce the probability of a loss than does a risk neutral injurer, spending to reduce the probability exposes him to a larger risk (for if he loses l, his final income will be lower by l *plus* his expenditure).

In contrast, whether risk averse injurers will purchase full coverage depends on whether liability insurers can "observe" the levels of prevention activity of individual injurers. If liability insurers cannot do this, then, clearly, they cannot link the premium or terms of the policy to the level of prevention activity. Consequently, were injurers to purchase complete coverage, there would be a problem of moral hazard: Injurers would have no reason to avoid accidents, would therefore be involved in accidents with high probability, and would find themselves paying a high premium per dollar of coverage. But if injurers purchased policies with incomplete coverage, they would be exposed to some risk, would thus have some inducement to avoid accidents, would be involved in accidents with a lower probability than before, and would therefore pay a lower premium per dollar of coverage (though still an actuarially fair premium—given their altered behavior). Hence, it should seem plausible and can be shown under quite general assumptions that injurers would in fact purchase policies with incomplete coverage.[22]

On the other hand, if liability insurers can observe prevention activity, then they can make the premium or other policy terms depend on such activity, thereby giving injurers an incentive to avoid accidents even if they purchase full coverage. Hence, it should seem plausible in this case that risk averse injurers would purchase complete coverage and would be motivated to act so as to minimize expected damages plus prevention costs (i.e., $p(x)d + x$).[23]

The next result can now be stated and proved.

Proposition 4. Under strict liability, according to a Pareto efficient solution, (a) damages paid by an injurer equal a victim's losses (i.e., $d = l$), (b) government intervention in the liability insurance market is not desirable, and (c) a first-best outcome is achieved unless injurers are risk averse and liability insurers cannot observe their level of prevention activity.

Note: In the case when injurers are risk neutral and liability insurers cannot observe prevention activity, injurers would decide against purchase of liability insurance. The reason is that because of moral hazard, the cost of insurance coverage would exceed an injurer's expected cost were he not to purchase coverage; and since protection against risk is of no consequence to him, he would not buy coverage. Hence, the situation will be essentially that in the first part of Proposition 2, and a first-best outcome will be achieved. Note also that the issue of intervention in insurance markets is moot since no one buys insurance.

If injurers are risk neutral and liability insurers can observe prevention activity, then injurers will be indifferent as to whether and in what amount to purchase liability coverage and will, if $d = l$, be induced to choose x^* by their exposure to liability or by the terms of their insurance policy, should they have one. Also, since victims will bear no risk (although they could always purchase insurance if they needed it), Proposition 1 implies that a first-best outcome will be achieved and, thus, that government intervention in insurance markets could not be desirable.

---

[22] The formal problem that yields this result is

$$\max_{x,q} EU = (1 - p(x))U(u + r - \pi - x) + p(x)U(u + r - \pi - x + q - d)$$

subject to (i) EU is maximized over x and (ii) $\pi = p(x)q$, where π is the insurance premium and q is the level of coverage. Constraint (i) says that the insured chooses x in a personally optimal way, given his insurance policy, and constraint (ii) is the condition of actuarial fairness. Shavell (1979b) discusses conditions under which the solution has $q < d$, which we shall assume to be true; Arrow (1971) and Pauly (1974) also analyze the general problem of moral hazard.

[23] The formal problem that yields this result is $\max_{q,x} EU = (1 - p(x))U(u + r - p(x)q - x) + p(x)U(u + r - p(x)q - x + q - d)$. Note that in this problem the individual takes into account that his choice of x affects the premium he pays, whereas in the problem described in note 22 that was not true. It is well known and easy to verify that the solution to this problem is $q = d$ and the x that minimizes $p(x)d + x$.

If injurers are risk averse and liability insurers can observe prevention activity, injurers will purchase full coverage against damages, will therefore not bear risk and, if $d = l$, will be induced by the terms of their policy to choose x^*. Thus, Proposition 1 again implies our result.

In the last case (which is complex), when liability insurers cannot observe the prevention activity of risk averse injurers, the injurers will purchase incomplete coverage against damages (as explained in the paragraph preceding the Proposition). If we let q denote their level of coverage, this means that the injurers will bear a positive residual risk of $d - q$, so that a first-best outcome will not be achieved. Moreover, it becomes obvious that the argument that liability insurance eliminates the incentive to avoid accidents is mistaken. Because injurers will still bear a risk after purchase of liability coverage, they will make some effort to avoid accidents. But, of course, what is asserted in the Proposition is a stronger claim than that liability insurance does not eliminate incentives. What is asserted is that if $d = l$ and injurers purchase liability coverage, there are no measures the government can take to improve welfare. Why this should be so may be put informally as follows. One supposes that there would be scope for beneficial government intervention in the liability insurance market only if the sale of liability coverage were to worsen the welfare of victims. But if $d = l$, the welfare of victims is unaffected by the occurrence of accidents because the victims are fully compensated for losses. Thus there is no apparent opportunity for beneficial intervention in the insurance market.[24]

At the same time, it is important to point out (and will be shown at the end of the proof) that in this last case under discussion an efficient solution could also be achieved by the government's banning liability insurance and reducing liability from l to $l - q$, leaving risk averse victims to purchase first-party coverage of q.[25] (Note that this does not contradict the Proposition, for the banning of liability insurance and reduction of liability do not raise welfare; they leave it unchanged.)

Proof: If injurers are risk neutral and liability insurers cannot observe x, suppose that injurers were to purchase coverage $q > 0$. Then they would select x to maximize $u + r - \pi - x - p(x)(d - q)$, where π is the actuarially fair premium. If we denote the solution to this problem by x_1, then π must equal $p(x_1)q$, so that the expected wealth of injurers would be

$$u + r - p(x_1)q - x_1 - p(x_1)(d - q) = u + r - x_1 - p(x_1)d. \qquad (25)$$

On the other hand, if injurers do not purchase any coverage, they will select x to maximize $u + r - x - p(x)d$, so that denoting the solution to this by x_2, their expected wealth would be

$$u + r - x_2 - p(x_2)d. \qquad (26)$$

Since, as is easily verified, $x_1 < x_2$, and since x_2 maximizes $u + r - x - p(x)d$ and is unique (for $p(x)$ is strictly convex), the expression in (26) is larger than that in (25). Hence, the injurers will not purchase liability insurance coverage, and we may appeal to the argument proving Proposition 2 (a) and (b) to establish Proposition 4 in the present case.

If injurers are risk neutral, $d = l$, and liability insurers can observe x, then whatever level of coverage injurers select (they are in fact indifferent among all levels of coverage,

---

[24] But if there were a nonmonetary component to the loss suffered by victims for which compensation could not possibly be made (perhaps blindness or paralysis), then the victims' welfare would be affected by the occurrence of accidents. Thus, limiting the purchase of liability insurance might in principle be desirable.

[25] This describes a solution which resembles the situation in the Soviet Union. As mentioned in note 2, liability insurance is not available there.

including none), they will be induced to choose x^*. This follows because their premium for coverage $q \geq 0$ will depend on x and equal $p(x)q$, so that they will choose x to maximize

$$u + r - p(x)q - x - p(x)(l - q) = u + r - x - p(x)l. \tag{27}$$

Since if $d = l$, x^* will be chosen, and since victims will bear no risk, Proposition 1 implies our result.

If injurers are risk averse and liability insurers can observe x, the remark in the Note following the proposition supplies the argument for the result.

We shall use a two-part argument to establish (a) and (b) for the case in which injurers are risk averse and liability insurers cannot observe x. First, we shall consider what would be done by a benevolent dictator whose powers are limited only by inability to observe x and, therefore, by inability to set x directly. Then we shall show in a series of steps that under strict liability, with $d = l$, the operation of the liability insurance market leads to the same result that the dictator would have chosen. This will complete the argument establishing (a) and (b).

The problem of the benevolent dictator who cannot observe x is

$$\underset{v_n, v_a, u_n, u_a}{\text{maximize } EV} = (1 - p(x))V(v_n) + p(x)V(v_a) \tag{28}$$

subject to

$$EU = (1 - p(x))U(u_n - x) + p(x)U(u_a - x) = \bar{U} \tag{29}$$

$$EU \text{ is maximized over } x \tag{30}$$

$$[(1 - p(x))v_n + p(x)v_a] + [(1 - p(x))u_n + p(x)u_a] + p(x)l = u + v. \tag{31}$$

Here the variables are defined as in Section 3, except that now u_n and u_a are gross of the costs of prevention activity. Constraint (30) is introduced because injurers are free to select x. As in the proof of Proposition 1, it is easy to show that we may take $v_n = v_a$. Thus, setting $\gamma = v_n = v_a$, the dictator's problem becomes

$$\underset{\gamma, u_n, u_a}{\text{maximize } EV} = V(\gamma) \tag{32}$$

subject to (29), (30), and to

$$\gamma + (1 - p(x))u_n + p(x)u_a + p(x)l = u + v. \tag{33}$$

Now let us show that the above problem is equivalent to the following one: liability is strict, with $d = l$; liability insurance is sold at an actuarially fair price; but the government, rather than the competitive insurance market, determines the extent of coverage q. This latter problem is (where π, recall, is the premium for insurance)

$$\underset{q, \pi, r}{\text{maximize } V(v - r)} \tag{34}$$

subject to

$$EU = (1 - p(x))U(u + r - \pi - x) + p(x)U(u + r - \pi - x + q - l) = \bar{U} \tag{35}$$

$$EU \text{ is maximized over } x, \tag{36}$$

$$\pi = p(x)q. \tag{37}$$

Under the change of variables $\gamma = v - r$, $u_n = u + r - \pi$, $u_a = u + r - \pi + q - l$, direct substitution shows that the problem (34)–(37) is, as claimed, the same as the problem (32), (29), (30), (33).

Now write (34)–(37) in the equivalent form

$$\underset{q, \pi, r}{\text{maximize } EU} = (1 - p(x))U(u + r - \pi - x) + p(x)U(u + r - \pi - x + q - l) \tag{38}$$

subject to

$$EU \text{ is maximized over } x, \tag{39}$$

$$\pi = p(x)q, \tag{40}$$

$$EV = V(v - r) = \bar{V}, \tag{41}$$

where $\bar{V}$ is the optimal value of V in (34)–(37). Observe that (41) alone determines r. Thus, (38)–(41) reduce to

$$\underset{q,\pi}{\text{maximize }} EU \tag{42}$$

subject to (39) and (40). But (see note 22) this is exactly the problem that is solved by the liability insurance market. Hence, we have completed our proof of (a) and (b) for the case in which injurers are risk averse and liability insurers cannot observe x. Part (c) also follows since liability coverage will be partial.

With regard to the claim made in the Note about the banning of liability insurance, suppose that such insurance cannot be purchased and let $\hat{d} = l - q$, and $\hat{r} = r - \pi$, where r, q, and π are the values from the efficient solution when liability insurance can be purchased. The reader may easily verify that the injurer would then select the same level of prevention activity and enjoy the same expected utility as in the efficient solution with the purchase of liability insurance allowed; the same is true of the victim, who, if risk averse, buys first party insurance, paying π for coverage of q. *Q.E.D.*

The last result is

Proposition 5. Under the negligence rule, a Pareto-efficient solution is such that: (a) the standard of due care equals the first-best level (i.e., $\bar{x} = x^*$); (b) a first-best outcome is achieved; and (c) government intervention in the liability insurance market is not desirable.

Note: As in Proposition 3, if $\bar{x} = x^*$, injurers will decide to be nonnegligent and will choose $x = x^*$, but now this is true despite their opportunity to act negligently and to protect themselves by purchase of liability insurance. And although this also means that victims will bear risk, they can purchase full coverage from first-party insurers. Thus a first-best solution will be achieved and, therefore, government intervention in insurance markets could not be desirable.

Proof: It will suffice to show that liability insurance would not be purchased, for then an argument virtually identical to that of parts (a) and (b) of Proposition 3 may be employed to show (a) and (b) here; and (c) follows from (b). Let us therefore assume that when $\bar{x} = x^*$, injurers purchase coverage, and show that this leads to a contradiction. If they purchase coverage, it must be that $x < x^*$ (for otherwise injurers would never be found negligent if involved in accidents and would have no reason to insure). Thus, the injurers' premium must be $p(x)q$, so that

$$EU = (1 - p(x))U(u + r - p(x)q - x) + p(x)U(u + r - p(x)q - x + q - l))$$

$$\leq U((1 - p(x))(u + r - p(x)q - x) + p(x)(u + r - p(x)q - x + q - l))$$

$$= U(u + r - x - p(x)l) < U(u + r - x^* - p(x^*)l)$$

$$< U(u + r - x^*). \tag{43}$$

But this is a contradiction, since it means that injurers would prefer to choose x^* and to be nonnegligent. *Q.E.D.*

5. Concluding comments

■ Because the object here was to isolate the roles of liability rules and of insurance in providing incentives and in allocating risk, it was of course necessary to exclude much from the analysis. Hence, we shall close with brief comments on several of the more important omissions, pointing out how, if at all, they affect our results.

Perhaps the most noticeable simplification of the model was the assumption that victims could not alter accident risks. Were that assumption relaxed, however, appropriate analogues to our results would remain true.[26] Consider, for instance, the situation under strict liability with a defense of contributory negligence (allowing the injurer to escape liability if the victim was shown to have acted negligently), when insurers can observe the level of prevention activity of risk averse insureds, be they injurers or victims. In this situation it can be demonstrated that a first-best outcome can be achieved (in Nash equilibrium). Victims are induced to act in a nonnegligent way despite their opportunity to purchase first-party insurance, and injurers, realizing that victims will not be found contributorily negligent, are induced under the terms of their liability policies to choose the socially optimal level of prevention activity. The arguments applied with respect to victims to show these and other results in the more general case are essentially those we presented with respect to injurers, for not only may victims alter accident risks, but also first-party coverage (like liability coverage) involves potential elements of moral hazard.

Another simplifying assumption of the model was that there were no "administrative" costs connected with the supply of insurance or with the operation of the legal system. Consideration of administrative costs would have made a difference to our study, especially with regard to the closely related issues of the type of insurance coverage offered by the market and the comparison of liability rules. Suppose, for example, that it would be very expensive to determine injurers' prevention activity. Then liability insurers would not do so, and therefore, as explained, the policies they sell would involve incomplete coverage. Consequently, as stated in Proposition 4, under strict liability risk averse injurers would be left bearing a risk, which is socially undesirable. On the other hand, according to Proposition 5, under the negligence rule the socially undesirable bearing of risk would be avoided, for the injurers would act in a nonnegligent way. Yet it should not be concluded from this that the negligence rule would be superior to strict liability, for the application of the negligence rule requires the courts to ascertain injurers' prevention activity—an undertaking that was assumed in the first place to have been sufficiently costly to make it less than worthwhile for liability insurers. This should illustrate both the complexities that would be involved in an analysis of our subject incorporating administrative costs and the need for caution in interpretation of results.

A third simplifying assumption of the model was that there were no errors or uncertainty as to legal outcomes. Thus, under strict liability, an injurer who caused a loss was always found liable, and under the negligence rule, an injurer's fault or lack of fault was always correctly determined. Were these assumptions altered, certain unnatural features of equilibrium in our model would disappear: under strict liability, victims would no longer be completely protected against risk, and, if risk averse, they would purchase first-party coverage; and under the negligence rule, nonnegligent injurers would no longer be sure that they would be found free of fault, and, if risk averse, they would purchase liability coverage. These new elements of uncertainty under the liability rules would generally mean that our results would hold only in an approximate sense.

References

ARROW, K. "Insurance. Risk, and Resource Allocation" in *Essays in the Theory of Risk-Bearing*, Chicago: Markham, 1971, pp. 134–143.

BORCH, K. "Equilibrium in a Reinsurance Market." *Econometrica*, Vol. 30 (1962), pp. 424–444.

BROWN, J. "Toward an Economic Theory of Liability." *Journal of Legal Studies*, Vol. 2 (1973), pp. 323–350.

---

[26] In Shavell (1979a), an earlier version of this article, the possibility that victims can alter accident risks is taken into account.

132 / THE BELL JOURNAL OF ECONOMICS

CALABRESI, G. *The Costs of Accidents.* New Haven: Yale University Press, 1970.

DIAMOND, P. "Single Activity Accidents." *Journal of Legal Studies,* Vol. 3 (1974), pp. 107–164.

EPPLE, D. AND RAVIV, A. "Product Safety: Liability Rules, Market Structure, and Imperfect Information." *American Economic Review,* Vol. 68 (1978), pp. 80–95.

GREEN, J. "On the Optimal Structure of Liability Laws." *Bell Journal of Economics,* Vol. 7 (1976), pp. 553–574.

PAULY, M. "Overinsurance and Public Provision of Insurance." *Quarterly Journal of Economics,* Vol. 87 (1974), pp. 44–62.

POSNER, R. *Economic Analysis of Law,* 2nd ed. Boston: Little, Brown & Co., 1977.

PROSSER, W. *Law of Torts.* St. Paul: West Publishing Co., 1971.

SHAVELL, S. "Accidents, Liability, and Insurance." Mimeographed, Harvard Institute of Economic Research, Discussion Paper No. 685, 1979a.

———. "On Moral Hazard and Insurance." *Quarterly Journal of Economics,* Vol. 93 (1979b), pp. 541–562.

———. "Strict Liability vs. Negligence." *Journal of Legal Studies,* Vol. 9 (1980), pp. 1–25.

SPENCE, A.M. "Consumer Misperceptions, Product Failure, and Product Liability." *Review of Economic Studies.* Vol. 64 (1977), pp. 561–572.

TUNC, A. *Torts,* Introduction to Volume XI, *International Encyclopedia of Comparative Law.* The Hague: Mouton, 1973.

[10]

THE INFLUENCE OF LITIGATION COSTS ON DETERRENCE UNDER STRICT LIABILITY AND UNDER NEGLIGENCE

KEITH N. HYLTON

Assistant Professor, Northwestern University School of Law, and Research Fellow, American Bar Foundation, USA

1. INTRODUCTION

This paper examines the influence of litigation costs on deterrence under strict liability and under negligence. By deterrence, I refer to the effect of the threat of liability on the care exercised by potential injurers.[1] More precisely, this paper takes litigation costs as given and examines the social desirability of the levels of care exercised under negligence and under strict liability.[2]

The relationship of this paper to the existing literature examining the influence of litigation costs on incentives under a liability system can best be described by comparing its focus to two fairly recent papers.[3] Shavell (1982) examines whether plaintiffs bring suit when bringing suit is socially desirable in a regime in which litigation is costly. Polinsky and Rubinfeld (1988) examine whether the level of liability is socially optimal in a regime in which litigation is costly. This paper examines whether the level of care is socially optimal in a regime in which litigation is costly.

The major result presented in this paper is that strict liability leads to underdeterrence when litigation costs are taken into account. The intuition behind this conclusion is straightforward. Optimal deterrence requires that all external costs resulting from the injurer's failure to take care be "internalized" to the injurer. But if litigation is costly, two types of external cost will not be internalized under strict liability: the litigation cost "imposed" on victims who choose to sue; and the losses suffered by victims who choose not to sue because the cost of litigating exceeds the anticipated damage award.

The negligence rule also leads to underdeterrence when litigation costs are taken into account. Specifically, if agents have rational expectations and the jury is perfectly informed, then in equilibrium a negligence regime must underdeter. The

I thank Steven Shavell for many valuable discussions. I also thank Ian Ayres, Richard Craswell, John Donohue, Daniel Rubinfeld, Peter Siegelman, and an anonymous referee for helpful comments on this paper. I have benefited from the support of the Program in Law and Economics at Harvard Law School, which is itself supported by a grant from the John M. Olin Foundation.

[1] This paper does not discuss the level of care exercised by potential victims, nor does it address the activity levels of injurers or victims.

[2] The socially optimal level of care is the level that minimizes the sum of expected accident losses, the cost of accident avoidance, and litigation costs. "Optimal deterrence" results when actors take care when and only when it is socially desirable.

[3] On the influence of litigation costs on incentives see, e.g., Ordover (1978), Ordover (1981), Shavell (1982), Menell (1983), Kaplow (1986), Rose-Ackerman and Geistfeld (1987), Polinsky and Rubinfeld (1988).

reason for this was, for the most part, provided in Ordover (1978): if under negligence all injurers obey the due care standard, no one will have an incentive to sue because the expected award will be zero; and if no one will sue, no one has an incentive to take care. Thus, an equilibrium under negligence requires the presence of a subset of potential injurers who do not obey the due care standard. It is shown in this paper that this subset is made up of potential injurers for whom taking care is socially desirable; thus, negligence underdeters.

Part A of section 2 of this paper presents the model. Part B of the same section presents the basic deterrence proposition under strict liability and discusses implications of the model for the literature on the social versus private incentives to bring suit.[4] Part C discusses deterrence under negligence.

2. THE MODEL

A. Basic structure and assumptions

All actors are assumed to be risk neutral. It is also assumed that victims (plaintiffs) are the only parties who suffer loss from an accident, that the risk of loss to victims can be reduced by the exercise of caution by potential injurers (potential defendants), and that it is costly for injurers to take care.

Let p = the probability of loss if potential injurers do not take care, $p > 0$; and q = the probability of loss if injurers do take care, $p > q > 0$. Let v = the (dollar) loss suffered by an accident victim, $v > 0$. The variable v is assumed to be random, with distribution function $H(v)$. Specifically, it is assumed that the potential injurer randomly experiences accidents with victims, each of whom is capable of realizing a specific dollar loss, and these losses are distributed over the population in accordance with the distribution function H.[5] Thus, if the potential injurer takes care, the expected loss suffered by victims is $qE(v)$; and if the injurer does not take care the expected loss is $pE(v)$, where

$$E(v) = \int_0^\infty v dH(v). \tag{1}$$

Let x = the cost to a potential injurer of taking care, where $x > 0$. The variable x is assumed to be random, with distribution function $G(x)$. The value of x is unobservable to potential victims; however, it is observed by the injurer and is known to him before he commits an offense. Further, in a negligence regime in which jurors have perfect information, the value of x is, in effect, observed by the jury. The typical injurer will choose not to take care if the expected cost of taking care exceeds the expected cost of not doing so. Thus unless the injurer is required to pay damages for either committing an offense or failing to take care, precaution will not be exercised.

I assume that victims can sue for no more than the value of their loss, v.[6] Let c_v = the litigation cost borne by a victim, $c_v > 0$; and c_o = the litigation cost borne by an injurer in defending himself against a claim, $c_o > 0$.

---

[4]See Shavell (1982), Menell (1983), Kaplow (1986), Rose-Ackerman and Geistfeld (1987).

[5]An alternative explanation is that the accident loss imposed on every victim is itself a random variable governed by $H(v)$.

[6]The assumption that victims generally can sue for no more than the loss from injury has a great deal of support. See McCormick (1935), p. 85. There are, of course, cases in which victims are awarded more than their losses (e.g., punitive damages, treble damages in antitrust). Conversely, there are examples in which suits are brought by the government but where victims are awarded damages (e.g., enforcement of the National Labor Relations Act).

B. Strict liability

1. Basic Propositions

In this section I consider the influence of litigation costs on deterrence under strict liability.

Two basic assumptions determine the effect of litigation costs on deterrence. The first is that suit is brought when it is privately profitable, that is, when $v > c_v$. Thus, once an accident has occurred, the probability that the victim will bring suit is $1 - H(c_v)$. The second assumption is that a potential injurer will take care if, after observing x, the expected cost of doing so is less than the expected cost of not doing so. Under these assumptions, the injurer will take care, under strict liability, when

$$x + q[1 - H(c_v)][c_o + E(v|v > c_v)] < p[1 - H(c_v)][c_o + E(v|v > c_v)], \quad (2)$$

where

$$E(v|v > c_v) = \int_{c_v}^{\infty} v dH(v)/[1 - H(c_v)]. \quad (3)$$

Note that $E(v|v > c_v)$ is the expectation of v given that $v > c_v$. Thus, $c_o + E(v|v > c_v)$ is the injurer's expected liability given that the victim brings suit. Equivalently, (2) can be written

$$x < (p - q)[1 - H(c_v)][E(v|v > c_v) + c_o]. \quad (4)$$

Taking care is socially desirable if, after the realization of x,

$$pE(v) + p[1 - H(c_v)](c_o + c_v) > x + qE(v) + q[1 - H(c_v)](c_o + c_v). \quad (5)$$

Note that (5) can be rewritten

$$x < (p - q)E(v) + (p - q)[1 - H(c_v)](c_o + c_v). \quad (6)$$

If private enforcement (that is, the bringing of suits by plaintiffs) causes some actors for whom (5) is not satisfied to take care, then such enforcement "overdeters." Similarly, if there are actors, for whom (5) is satisfied, who do not take care, then there is an "underdeterrence" problem. Finally, "optimal deterrence" occurs when enforcement causes actors to take care if and only if (5) is satisfied. With this in mind, we can state the following:

Proposition 1: Strict liability underdeters.

The proof relies on (4) and (6). Using (4) and (6), strict liability underdeters if and only if

$$(p - q)E(v) + (p - q)[1 - H(c_v)](c_o + c_v)$$
$$> (p - q)[1 - H(c_v)][E(v|v > c_v) + c_o],$$

or equivalently

$$E(v) + [1 - H(c_v)]c_v > \int_{c_v}^{\infty} v dH.$$

However, from the definition of $E(v)$

$$E(v) = \int_0^{c_v} v dH + \int_{c_v}^{\infty} v dH,$$

and the proposition follows.

Thus, if the socially optimal level of care is the level that minimizes the sum of expected accident losses, accident avoidance costs, and litigation costs, a strict liability regime will always result in potential injurers, as a group, taking too little care relative to the social optimum. More precisely, there will be potential injurers for whom taking care is socially desirable who will not take care. The intuition behind this result is straightforward. In a regime in which litigation is costly, the social cost generated by the injurer's failure to take care is the sum of the expected loss imposed on a victim and the litigation costs imposed on society. Only part of this social cost is internalized under strict liability: the expected loss imposed on a victim who will bring suit plus the litigation cost borne by the injurer. As a result, strict liability must underdeter.

The intuition behind proposition 1 suggests a policy for achieving the socially optimal level of care under a strict liability regime. Optimal deterrence can be achieved by making the injurer pay, in the form of a tax added to the injurer's litigation cost, the expected loss imposed on a non-suing victim, plus the victim's litigation cost.[7] This argument is stated in a more rigorous fashion in the following proposition.

Proposition 2: Under strict liability, the socially optimal level of care is achieved by adding to the injurer's expected litigation cost the victim's expected litigation cost plus the expected loss suffered by non-suing victims.

To prove proposition 2, let t be a tax that is added to the injurer's cost of litigating. Given this, $(p - q)[1 - H(c_v)]t$ is the marginal tax incurred by the potential injurer in failing to take care. Using (4) and (6), deterrence is optimal if and only if

$(p - q)v + (p - q)[1 - H(c_v)](c_o + c_v)$

$$= (p - q)[1 - H(c_v)][E(v|v > c_v) + c_o + t].$$

The solution requires that t satisfy

$$\int_0^{c_v} v dH + [1 - H(c_v)]c_v = [1 - H(c_v)]t, \qquad (7)$$

where the term on the right-hand side of (7) is the expected tax, given that an

K. N. HYLTON   165

accident has occurred. The terms on the left-hand side of (7) are, respectively, the expected loss imposed of non-suing victims and the expected cost to the victim of litigating, given that an accident has occurred.

An alternative way of stating proposition 2 is suggested by rewriting (7) as follows:

$$\int_0^{c_v} v dH/[1 - H(c_v)] + c_v = t. \tag{8}$$

Thus, optimal deterrence is achieved by making the injurer pay a tax, in addition to the cost of the injurer of litigating, that is equal to the sum of two terms: the expected loss of non-suing victims, divided by the probability that suit will be brought, and the victim's litigation cost.

This unambiguously upward adjustment in the injurer's liability should be compared with Polinsky and Rubinfeld (1988), which suggests that the optimal adjustment to compensatory damages might be positive or negative. The conclusion differs here largely because this paper examines a different question. The Polinsky and Rubinfeld paper determines the level of damages, to be paid to the victim, that minimizes the sum of expected accident losses, avoidance costs, and expected litigation costs. This paper, in proposition 2, determines the level of liability that causes the injurer to exercise the socially optimal level of care. The key difference between the approaches is that the adjustment to damages is a tax that is not transferred to the victim in this model, while the adjustment becomes part of the victim's award in the Polinsky and Rubinfeld paper. In addition, in the Polinsky and Rubinfeld paper, the injurer is able to preclude suit by exercising a level of care that makes it unprofitable for the victim to bring suit. The injurer cannot do this in this model because the decision to sue itself depends on a random event: whether the victim's loss exceeds the cost of litigating.[8]

2. Implications of the Model for the Literature on the Social Desirability of Suit

The treatment of the typical victim's loss as random, which this paper adds to the basic model developed in Shavell (1982), has interesting implications for the literature on the social desirability of suit.[9] Nothing in the model disturbs Shavell's point that social and private incentives to bring suit differ. To see this, note that in the model presented here, suit is socially desirable, that is, suit should not be prohibited, if

$$pE(v) > g_s\{E_s(x) + q[1 - H(c_v)](c_o + c_v) + qE(v)\}$$
$$+ (1 - g_s)\{p[1 - H(c_v)](c_o + c_v) + pE(v)\},$$

where g_s is the probability that a potential injurer will take care under strict liability (in order to reduce expected liability),[10] and is given by

$$g_s = \int_0^{(p-q)[1-H(c_v)][E(v|v>c_v)+c_o]} dG(x),$$

---

[8] I examine the implications of this model for the optimal level of damages in Appendix B.
[9] Shavell (1982), Menell (1983), Kaplow (1986), Rose-Ackerman and Geistfeld (1987).
[10] Note that this is the probability that the cost of taking care, x, satisfies (4).

and $E_s(x)$ is the expectation of x given that the potential injurer takes care under strict liability, and

$$E_s(x) = \int_0^{(p-q)[1-H(c_v)][E(v|v>c_v)+c_o]} x \, dG(x)/g_s.$$

Thus, suit is socially desirable if

$$g_s\{(p-q)E(v) - E_s(x)\} > \{g_s q + (1-g_s)p\}[1-H(c_v)](c_o + c_v),$$

which requires that the expected net gain from taking care exceeds the expected litigation costs imposed on society. The confirmation of Shavell's result concerning the divergence between social and private incentives to sue is completed by noting that the social desirability condition is not the same as the plaintiff's incentive condition $v > c_v$.

Although Shavell's incentive divergence theorem remains valid in the model presented here, treating the typical victim's loss as random does disturb some of the results presented in the Menell, Kaplow, and Rose-Ackerman and Geistfeld papers. For in the models discussed in these papers, the injurer's expected liability (damages plus the cost of litigating) increases discontinuously at the point where the victim's loss is equal to the victim's cost of litigating. No such discontinuity is observed in a model in which the typical victim's loss (which is his anticipated recovery from bringing suit) is random. Without this discontinuity the injurer's cost-benefit analysis no longer includes the option of precluding suit altogether by exercising a level of care that makes it unprofitable for the victim to bring suit. Moreover, under the assumption that the typical victim's loss is random one can show that at the point of deciding the level of care, the injurer's cost-benefit analysis is not the same as the social cost-benefit analysis.

Because it involves a more elaborate model and the introduction of new notation, the implications of the model presented here for the Menell, Kaplow, and Rose-Ackerman and Geistfeld papers are discussed in the appendix. The appendix presents a model in which the injurer's level of caution is a continuous variable that influences the amount of the victim's damages. I demonstrate that propositions 1 and 2 remain valid in the more general model.[11]

C. Negligence

Under negligence, suit is brought when $wv > c_v$, where w = the probability that the jury will find the defendant negligent. Thus, in a negligence regime, the probability that suit will be brought after an accident has occurred is $1 - H(c_v/w)$.

Under the "Hand Formula,"[12] an actor is negligent if he fails to take care when $(p-q)E(v) > x$, which is the social desirability criterion for taking care when

[11] Rose-Ackerman and Geistfeld, on p. 488, show that, under the assumptions of their model, the injurer will produce more than the socially optimal level of output when lawsuits are permitted, provided that the injurer does not choose to produce at a level that precludes suit.

[12] I refer to the formula for negligence stated by Judge Learned Hand in *United States v. Carroll Towing Co.*, 159 F.2d 169 (2d Cir. 1947). The version presented in the text compares the marginal social cost of care to its expected marginal social benefit, ignoring litigation costs.

K. N. HYLTON 167

litigation is costless.[13] Any actor for whom $(p - q)E(v) > x$ is "potentially negligent," in the sense that he will be held negligent if his failure to take care leads to an accident which is followed by a lawsuit. It is assumed that victims correctly perceive the probability of a negligence verdict, and thus are aware of the requirements of the Hand Formula.

With perfect information, the jury will find the injurer negligent if, and only if, $(p - q)E(v) > x$ is satisfied and the injurer did not take care.

If the potential defendant could be judged negligent by a jury, because $(p - q)E(v) > x$, he will take care when

$$x < p[1 - H(c_v/w)]E(v|v > c_v/w) + (p - q)[1 - H(c_v/w)]c_o, \qquad (9)$$

where

$$E(v|v > c_v/w) = \int_{c_v/w}^{\infty} vdH(v)/[1 - H(c_v/w)]. \qquad (10)$$

Since the jury has perfect information and actors correctly perceive the likelihood of a negligence verdict, w is equal to the probability that the injurer is negligent (that is, potentially negligent and fails to take care), given that an accident has occurred. Using Bayes' Theorem, that probability is expressed as follows:[14]

$$w = p[g_n q + (1 - g_n)p]^{-1} \int_{p[1-H(c_v/w)]E(v|v>c_v/w)+(p-q)[1-H(c_v/w)]c_o}^{(p-q)E(v)} dG(x) \quad (11)$$

where g_n is the probability that a potential injurer will take care under negligence and is given by

$$g_n = \int_0^{p[1-H(c_v/w)]E(v|v>c_v/w)+(p-q)[1-H(c_v/w)]c_o} dG(x).$$

[13]This criterion minimizes the sum of expected accident losses and accident avoidance costs. Because it fails to take litigation costs into account, it is not the social desirability criterion for care in a world in which litigation is costly. However, because it is the traditional test for negligence it may be of interest to some whether actors will behave negligently, as defined by the Hand Formula, under a negligence regime or under strict liability. Whether actors behave negligently under a negligence regime is addressed briefly in this section of the text. The question whether actors behave negligently under strict liability is answered by the following result:

Under strict liability, some potential injurers will act negligently if and only if

$$\int_0^{c_v} vdH > [1 - H(c_v)]c_o.$$

If the inequality is reversed, then some potential injurers will take care even though their failure to do so would not result in a negligence verdict. If the inequality is replaced with $=$ then only those potential injurers who would be held negligent will take care.

The proof of this statement mimics that for proposition 1. The statement requires a comparison of the defendant's expected litigation cost to the expected loss suffered by non-suing victims.

[14]If victims are rational, as assumed here, they will update their forecasts of the probability of a negligence verdict using the information that an accident has occurred. Thus, the rational forecast of the probability of a negligence verdict, given that an accident has occurred, will be greater than the probability that a potential injurer will act negligently.

An equilibrium value for the probability of a negligence verdict satisfies (11). Plaintiffs will bring suit only if the probability of a negligence verdict is positive. However, (11) clearly implies that w is positive, or equivalently plaintiffs will bring suit, if and only if

$$(p - q)E(v) > p[1 - H(c_v/w)]E(v|v > c_v/w) + (p - q)[1 - H(c_v/w)]c_o. \quad (12)$$

But if (12) holds, then there will be potentially negligent injurers who fail to take care.

This confirms the fundamental result of Ordover (1978) that equilibrium in a negligence regime requires the presence of a subset of actors who refuse to obey the due care standard. The reason is the following: if under negligence, all potentially negligent actors (those for whom $(p - q)E(v) > x$) take care, then no plaintiff will expect to win a lawsuit, so suit will not be brought. But if suit is not brought, no actor will have an incentive to take care. It follows that the rational expectations equilibrium under negligence is one in which there exists a group of injurers who are potentially negligent and fail to take care.

Given an equilibrium within a negligence regime, taking care is socially desirable if, after the realization of x,

$$pE(v) + p[1 - H(c_v/w)](c_o + c_v) > x + qE(v) + q[1 - H(c_v/w)](c_o + c_v). \quad (13)$$

However, given that (12) holds in an equilibrium, the following condition must hold:

$$(p - q)E(v) + (p - q)[1 - H(c_v/w)](c_o + c_v)$$
$$> p[1 - H(c_v/w)]E(v|v > c_v/w) + (p - q)[1 - H(c_v/w)]c_o. \quad (14)$$

Thus,

Proposition 3: In equilibrium, negligence underdeters.

In other words, in an equilibrium within a negligence regime in which litigation is costly, some injurers for whom taking care is socially desirable will not take care. The reason is that a plaintiff can expect to win an award in a negligence suit only if there exists a subset of potential injurers who fail to take care and whose cost of taking care is such that $(p - q)E(v) > x$. But if an injurer's cost of taking care satisfies $(p - q)E(v) > x$, then the injurer is certainly one for whom taking care is socially desirable under the condition stated in (13). The presence of such an injurer implies that negligence underdeters.

3. CONCLUSION

This paper examines the influence of litigation costs on deterrence under strict liability and under negligence. The primary result is that private enforcement under strict liability underdeters, in the sense that not every potential injurer for whom taking care is socially desirable will take care. In addition, if an equilibrium exists in a negligence regime, negligence also underdeters. This is a natural extension of the result of Ordover (1978) that equilibrium in a negligence regime requires the existence of a subset of actors who fail to obey the due care standard.

APPENDIX A

In this section I discuss the implications of the model for the results presented in the Menell, Kaplow, and Rose-Ackerman and Geistfeld papers. Adopting notation similar to that in the Rose-Ackerman and Geistfeld paper, let

z = injurer's output, $0 \leq z < \infty$;
$P(z)$ = gross profits of injurer, $P'(0) > 0$, $P'' \leq 0$;
$D(z)$ = gross damage to victim if an accident occurs, a random variable, $D' \geq 0$, $D'' \geq 0$.

Also, assume that the probability of an accident = 1

Proposition A1: Strict liability underdeters.

Proof: The social optimum in output, z^*, maximizes the function

$$SB(z) = P(z) - \text{Prob}[D(z) > c_v]\{E[D(z)|D(z) > c_v] + c_o + c_v\}$$
$$- \text{Prob}[D(z) < c_v]E[D(z)|D(z) < c_v].$$

The injurer's net profit function, which is maximized at z^{**}, is

$$R(z) = P(z) - \text{Prob}[D(z) > c_v]\{E[D(z)|D(z) > c_v] + c_o\}.$$

This claim is proven by showing that $SB'(z) < 0$ at z^{**}. If this is so, social welfare can be increased by the injurer producing less. Substituting in the first order condition for $R(z)$, note that

$$SB'(z^{**}) = -\{(d\text{Prob}[D(z^{**}) > c_v]/dz)c_v$$
$$+ (d\text{Prob}[D(z^{**}) < c_v]/dz)E[D(z^{**})|D(z^{**}) < c_v]\}$$
$$+ \text{Prob}[D(z^{**}) < c_v](dE[D(z^{**})|D(z^{**}) < c_v]/dz)$$

Using the fact that $d\text{Prob}[D(z) > c_v]/dz = -d\text{Prob}[D(z) < c_v]/dz$, this can be rewritten

$$SB'(z^{**}) = -\{(d\text{Prob}[D(z^{**}) > c_v]/dz)(c_v - E[D(z^{**})|D(z^{**}) < c_v])$$
$$+ \text{Prob}[D(z^{**}) < c_v](dE[D(z^{**})|D(z^{**}) < c_v]/dz)\}$$

which is negative.

Proposition A2: The optimal level of care is achieved by adding to the injurer's expected litigation cost the victim's expected litigation cost plus the expected loss imposed on non-suing victims.

Proof: The social optimum in care maximizes the function

$$SB(z) = P(z) - \text{Prob}[D(z) > c_v]\{E[D(z)|D(z) > c_v] + c_o + c_v\}$$
$$- \text{Prob}[D(z) < c_v]E[D(z)|D(z) < c_v]$$

Assuming that the injurer's cost of litigating is increased by t, the injurer's net profit function is

$$R(z) = P(z) - \text{Prob}[D(z) > c_v]\{E[D(z)|D(z) > c_v] + c_o + t\}.$$

SB(z) and R(z) are equivalent if and only if

$$\text{Prob}[D(z) > c_v]t = \text{Prob}[D(z) > c_v]c_v + \text{Prob}[D(z) < c_v]E[D(z)|D(z) < c_v]$$

and the proposition follows.

APPENDIX B

In this section I examine the implications of the model presented in this paper for the optimal level of liability. Following Polinsky and Rubinfeld (1988), let Δ = the adjustment to compensatory damages. Thus, under strict liability, the victim receives $v + \Delta$ if he sues the injurer.

The optimal adjustment to compensatory damages, Δ, is chosen to maximize the net social benefit from private enforcement under strict liability, which is given by

$$NSB(\Delta) = g_s\{(p - q)E(v) - E_s(x)\} - \{g_sq + (1 - g_s)p\}[1 - H(c_v - \Delta)](c_o + c_v),$$

where

$$g_s = \int_0^{(p-q)[1-H(c_v-\Delta)][E(v|v>c_v-\Delta)+\Delta+c_o]} dG(x),$$

and where

$$E_s(x) = \int_0^{(p-q)[1-H(c_v-\Delta)][E(v|v>c_v-\Delta)+\Delta+c_o]} xdG(x)/g_s.$$

The derivative of NSB with respect to Δ is (suppressing the algebra)

$$dNSB/d\Delta = g_s(p - q)[(c_o + c_v)h + 1 - H]\{(p - q)E(v)$$
$$+ (p - q)(1 - H)(c_o + c_v)$$
$$- (p - q)(1 - H)[E(v|v > c_v - \Delta) + \Delta + c_o]\}$$
$$- [g_sq + (1 - g_s)p](c_o + c_v)h, \qquad (B1)$$

where $H = H(c_v - \Delta)$ and $h = H'$. This simplifies to

$$dNSB/d\Delta = g_s(p - q)(p - q)[(c_o + c_v)h + 1 - H][HE(v|v < c_v - \Delta)$$
$$+ (1 - H)(c_v - \Delta)] - [g_sq + (1 - g_s)p](c_o + c_v)h. \quad (B2)$$

Suppose $\Delta = c_v$. Then $h = H = 0$, so that $dNSB/d\Delta$ simplifies to $dNSB/d\Delta = g_s(p - q)(p - q)(c_v - c_v) = 0$.
Suppose $\Delta > c_v$. Then, again, $h = H = 0$, and the derivative simplifies to $dNSB/d\Delta = g_s(p - q)(p - q)(c_v - \Delta) < 0$.

Finally, suppose $\Delta < c_v$. Then the sign of the derivative is ambiguous, and depends on all of the factors summarized in the appendix of Polinsky and Rubinfeld (1988). Note that for $\Delta < c_v$, the first term in the derivative in (B2) is positive. This reflects deterrence benefits from increasing Δ: until $\Delta = c_v$, the injurer will exercise less than the socially optimal level of care. The second term in (B2) reflects the increase in litigation costs that results because with a higher level of liability more victims sue. For $\Delta < c_v$ the relevant question is whether the benefits from increasing care exceed the increased litigation costs that result from more victim suits.

Thus, as demonstrated in the Polinsky and Rubinfeld paper, the optimal adjustment to compensatory damages is generally ambiguous, because it depends on such factors as the productivity of care (in this model, the size of the difference between p and q) and the total cost of litigation. If care is sufficiently productive, the derivative with respect to Δ of NSB(Δ) will be positive for $\Delta < c_v$; thus, the adjustment which maximizes social welfare will be $\Delta^* = c_v$. However, if the derivative of NSB(Δ) is not positive for all $\Delta < c_v$ (say, because care is not "very productive"), the optimal adjustment may be at some point Δ^*, where $\Delta^* < c_v$.

One result that emerges is that the optimal adjustment to compensatory damages will *never* exceed c_v, since net social benefit declines as Δ is increased above c_v. The reason is that once $\Delta = c_v$, all victims will sue, so that all external losses are "internalized" to the injurer. Increasing Δ beyond this point has no effect on the rate at which victims sue (because all victims will sue when $\Delta = c_v$), but causes injurers to exercise care beyond the socially optimal level.

REFERENCES

Kaplow, L. "Private Versus Social Costs in Bringing Suit," *Journal of Legal Studies,* 1986, vol. 15, 371–85.

McCormick, C. T. *Handbook on the Law of Damages* (1935).

Menell, P. S. "A Note on Private versus Social Incentives to Sue in a Costly Legal System," *Journal of Legal Studies,* 1983, vol. 12, 41–52.

Ordover, J. A. "Costly Litigation in the Model of Single Activity Accidents," *Journal of Legal Studies,* 1978, vol. 7, 243–61.

Ordover, J. A. "On the Consequences of Costly Litigation in the Model of Single Activity Accidents: Some New Results," *Journal of Legal Studies,* 1981, vol. 10, 269–91.

Polinsky, A. M. and D. L. Rubinfeld, "The Welfare Implications of Costly Litigation for the Level of Liability," *Journal of Legal Studies,* 1988, vol. 17, 151–64.

Rose-Ackerman, S. and M. Geistfeld, "The Divergence Between Social and Private Incentives to Sue: A Comment on Shavell, Menell, and Kaplow," *Journal of Legal Studies,* 1987, vol. 16, 483–91.

Shavell, S. "The Social versus the Private Incentive to Bring Suit in a Costly Legal System," *Journal of Legal Studies,* 1982, vol. 11, 333–39.

[11]

Bankruptcy and care choice

T. Randolph Beard*

This article considers the care choice of a potentially bankrupt injurer when care is pecuniary and the legal system is characterized by strict liability. I show, contrary to previous results, that such an injurer may take too little or too much care, and that neither injurer care nor victim welfare is necessarily increasing in injurer wealth when injurers behave optimally. Analysis of an "expected cost function" demonstrates that injurer expected costs are a concave and increasing function of injurer assets, a result suggesting applications to the study of vertical relationships and markets for agents.

Business? It's very simple! It's other people's money.

—Dumas père

1. Introduction

■ One of the primary goals of liability law is to provide potential injurers with the proper incentives to take adequate care in their activities. In the "real world," however, circumstances can conspire against the success of this function. Of particular importance in this regard is the issue of the "judgment-proof" or "disappearing" defendant.[1] Injurers may cause accidents that have costs in excess of their resources. Under such circumstances, bankruptcy can result (with its attendant limited liability), and the injurer can escape some of the costs of its activities. The occurrence of such situations in the nuclear power, waste disposal, and transportation sectors is quite conceivable, and may present policy makers and the courts with difficult problems.

While liability systems can promote optimal behavior by causing the potential injurer to internalize relevant social costs, bankruptcy limits the ability of any liability system to actually implement the damage awards required by theory. Whenever accident costs can exceed injurer resources, it is impossible to force injurers to pay awards equal to accident costs in all cases. Injurers therefore sometimes escape the full costs of their behavior, a circumstance superficially similar to that of an externality. This divergence between social and injurer costs introduces concerns about the willingness of potentially bankrupt injurers to take adequate care in their activities.

Intuitively, the "bankruptcy as externality" view leads to two speculations. First, one might expect that potentially insolvent injurers invest suboptimally in care from the social point of view, caring as they do only about the costs they might actually have to pay. Second,

* Auburn University.

I wish to thank George Sweeney, Jennie Raymond, Jim Leitzel, John Siegfried, David Kaserman, Richard Beil, and two anonymous referees for comments on earlier drafts of this article. The usual caveat applies.

[1] These terms are introduced by Shavell (1986) and Summers (1983), respectively.

wealthier injurers may take greater care than poorer ones because they have "more to lose," and are less likely to be able to escape some costs through bankruptcy. That both these conjectures are incorrect will be shown.

The issues occasioned by judgment-proof defendants have received some treatment in the formal literatures of economics and the law. Important work includes that of Summers (1983) and Shavell (1986, 1987). Essentially, these authors lend support to the intuitive ideas given above, suggesting that the potential for insolvency causes a reduction in care levels under strict liability, an effect somewhat mitigated by increases in injurer resources.

This article takes another look at the relationship between care choice and bankruptcy and concludes that the link is not straightforward. First, I show that potentially insolvent injurers need not take too little care in their activities—they might take too much. I also demonstrate that injurer care levels are not generally increasing in injurer wealth, so that richer injurers may not take greater care than poorer ones. Then I exploit the model to produce an "expected cost function" relating injurer wealth to expected costs when injurers behave optimally, and analyze the properties of this cost function. While optimal behavior is seen to always imply that injurer welfare increases in injurer wealth, I show that victim welfare may decline in some cases as injurer assets increase. Finally, I discuss the implications of the model for the analysis of certain vertical and agency relationships. The article concludes with a summary of the results.

2. The model

■   Let us consider the case of an injurer whose activities may cause harm to victims. The actions of victims do not affect the probability or severity of accidents, so the victims will play no direct role in the analysis. The injurer can affect the probability that harm occurs by spending money on care, although, should an accident occur, the cost of the accident is random and beyond the injurer's influence.[2] Assume that, if an accident occurs, the injurer is assessed financial penalties equal to the cost of the harm, a system called strict liability. Accident costs may be so large that they exceed injurer resources. In these cases, the injurer is bankrupted and pays out all of its remaining wealth.

For purposes of what follows, it is sufficient to consider an especially simple version of the injurer's problem. In particular, I evaluate only the case of a risk-neutral injurer who can cause at most one accident, and who cannot buy liability insurance.[3]

Define the following notation:

c = injurer expenditure on care, $c \geq 0$.

W = injurer initial wealth, $W > 0$.

$\Pr(c)$ = the probability that an accident occurs, given injurer care expenditure c. Assume that $0 \leq \Pr(c) \leq 1$, and that $\Pr(c)$ is twice continuously differentiable with $\Pr'(c) < 0$ and $\Pr''(c) > 0$ for all $c \geq 0$.[4]

A = the monetary cost of an accident to victims. Assume that A is a nonnegative random variable with marginal density $f(A)$ and cumulative density $F(A)$ on the interval $[0, U]$, where $U > W$ and $f(A) > 0$ for all A in $[0, U]$.

---

[2] Hence, in the language of insurance economics, "self-protection" is possible while "self-insurance" is not. An excellent overview is in Ehrlich and Becker (1972).

[3] A risk-neutral injurer would be unwilling to buy actuarially fair insurance when bankruptcy is possible. A risk-averse injurer might buy insurance, but as this modification would add greatly to the difficulty of analysis while obscuring the main focus, we decline this complication.

[4] The assumption that $\Pr''(c) > 0$ is equivalent to the assumption that care spending is subject to diminishing returns.

$E(A)$ = the expected value of A, $E(A) = \int_0^U Af(A)dA$.

$D(W, c)$ = damages collected by victims from the injurer when an accident occurs. We have $D(W, c) = A$ if $A \leq W - c$, and $D(W, c) = W - c$ if $A > W - c$, the latter case implying bankruptcy.

Under strict liability with bankruptcy, the risk-neutral injurer's problem is to select a feasible level of care c that minimizes the expected value of the sum of victim compensation and care costs. Formally, the injurer selects a level of care c that solves

$$\min_c EC(c; W) \equiv c + \Pr(c) \cdot E(D(W, c)) \qquad (1)$$

subject to the constraint $c \geq 0$. I denote the solution to (1) by c^*.[5] Following Shavell (1986), I identify the socially optimal level of care with the solution to

$$\min_c SC(c, E(A)) \equiv c + \Pr(c) \cdot E(A) \qquad (2)$$

subject to the constraint $c \geq 0$, and denote it by $\hat{c}$.[6]

□ **Optimal care.** The potentially insolvent injurer's optimal care choice c^* is characterized by the following order conditions. If $c^* > 0$, then c^* solves

$$1 - \Pr(c)(1 - F(W - c)) = -\Pr'(c) \cdot E(D(W, c)) \qquad (3a)$$

and

$$\Pr''(c) \cdot E(D(W, c)) - 2\Pr'(c)(1 - F(W - c)) - \Pr(c)f(W - c) \geq 0. \qquad (3b)$$

Interpretation of the first-order condition (3a) in terms of costs and benefits is useful, and is motivated by the following argument. Consider the effect of a marginal increase in care spending c on injurer expected costs ($EC(c; W)$) when the probability of an accident $\Pr(c)$ is invariant to c, so that $\Pr'(c) = 0$. (In this case $c^* = 0$, of course.) Since, by assumption, care spending has no benefit, we can identify the expression $1 - \Pr(c)(1 - F(W - c))$ in (3a) with the marginal costs of care, and note that $1 - \Pr(c)(1 - F(W - c)) < 1$. Since the term $\Pr(c)(1 - F(W - c))$ is the *ex ante* probability of injurer bankruptcy given initial wealth W and care spending c, we can conclude that, when bankruptcy is possible, the expected cost of spending a dollar (on anything) is less than one dollar and is equal to the probability that bankruptcy does not occur (times one dollar). This is true because if an injurer is ultimately bankrupted, a marginal expenditure on care is irrelevant to the determination of final wealth, which is zero anyway. Hence, the possibility of bankruptcy creates a subsidy to spending, since the injurer might be, *ex post,* spending someone else's money. We thus identify the term $1 - \Pr(c)(1 - F(W - c))$ with the (expected) marginal cost of care, and the term $-\Pr'(c) \cdot E(D(W, c))$ with the (expected) marginal benefit of care, so that (3a) is interpreted as requiring equality between the marginal costs and benefits of care, a thoroughly conventional result.

If the socially optimal level of care c is positive, then $\hat{c}$ must satisfy

$$1 + \Pr'(c) \cdot E(A) = 0 \qquad (4a)$$

and

$$\Pr''(c) \cdot E(A) \geq 0. \qquad (4b)$$

The first-order condition (4a), like (3a), requires equality between the marginal costs and benefits of care, but from the social point of view.

---

[5] It is easy to show that $c^* < W$.
[6] Shavell (1986) gives a rationale for calling the solution to (2) "socially optimal."

It is useful to compare the first-order conditions for the injurer's and society's problems. Because of the payout truncation implied by a positive probability of bankruptcy, the social marginal benefit of care exceeds the injurer's private marginal benefits at all levels of care: $-\Pr'(c) \cdot E(A) > -\Pr'(c) \cdot E(D(W, c))$ at all $c \geq 0$. But it is also true that the injurer's private marginal cost of care is less than that of society $((1 - \Pr(c)(1 - F(W - c))) < 1)$, and it is this latter relationship that can overturn the intuition on the effects of potential insolvency on injurer care choice discussed in the introduction.

3. Comparison of optimal injurer and social care levels

■   The possibility of bankruptcy reduces both the injurer's costs and benefits of care relative to those of society. I shall now show that in some circumstances injurers will take too much care, while in others they will take too little.

Proposition 1. Both $\hat{c} > c^*$ and $\hat{c} < c^*$ are possible.

Proof. To see that $\hat{c} > c^*$ is possible, it is necessary only to note that $\hat{c}$ is monotone increasing in $E(A)$, and that $c^* < W$. By selecting any accident cost distribution for which $E(A)$ is large enough, and a probability function $\Pr(c)$ such that $\hat{c} > 0$, one can obtain the result that $\hat{c} \geq W$, and hence $c^* < \hat{c}$.

The proof that $c^* > \hat{c}$ is possible is based on the following idea. The reduction in the injurer's marginal benefit of care relative to that of society arises because of the payout truncation implied by bankruptcy. The difference in these marginal benefits depends on the difference between $E(A)$ and $E(D(W, c))$. The spending subsidy created by a positive probability of bankruptcy, however, depends only on the probability of bankruptcy and not on the actual frequency distribution of bankruptcy accidents. Thus, it is only necessary to find an accident cost distribution that simultaneously implies a large bankruptcy spending subsidy and a small difference between the social and (private) injurer marginal benefits of care. Let us consider such an example.

Suppose that the distribution of accident costs is given by

$$f(A) = l \quad \text{for} \quad 0 \leq A \leq W,$$

$$f(A) = h \quad \text{for} \quad W < A \leq W + \epsilon, \quad \epsilon > 0,$$

$$f(A) = 0 \quad \text{otherwise,}$$

where $0 < l < h$. This is a probability distribution whenever $l \cdot W + h \cdot \epsilon = 1$. The expected social cost of an accident, $E(A)$, is

(i) $$E(A) = \frac{W^2 l}{2} + W(1 - lW) + \frac{(1 - lW)^2}{2h}.$$

The injurer's expected accident payout, given an accident, at a care spending level of $c = 0$, $E(D(W, 0))$, is

(ii) $$E(D(W, 0)) = \frac{W^2 l}{2} + W(1 - lW).$$

Clearly, $E(D(W, 0))$ can be made arbitrarily close to $E(A)$ by making h very large (and ϵ very small so that $l \cdot W + h \cdot \epsilon = 1$ is true). The socially optimal care choice $\hat{c}$ is necessarily equal to 0 if $\partial SC(c, E(A))/\partial c > 0$ at $c = 0$, a consequence of the convexity of the program given by (2). The injurer's optimal care choice c^* is necessarily greater than 0 if $\partial EC(c; W)/\partial c < 0$ at $c = 0$. It remains only to show that there exists some convex accident probability function $\Pr(c)$ that makes both these inequalities simultaneously true.

We have

(iii) $\qquad \left. \dfrac{\partial SC(c, E(A))}{\partial c}\right|_{c=0} = 1 + \text{Pr}'(0)\left[\dfrac{W^2 l}{2} + W(1 - lW) + \dfrac{(1 - lW)^2}{2h}\right]$

and

(iv) $\qquad \left. \dfrac{\partial EC(c; W)}{\partial c}\right|_{c=0} = 1 - \text{Pr}(0)(1 - lW) + \text{Pr}'(0)\left[\dfrac{W^2 l}{2} + W(1 - lW)\right].$

By making h large (and, consequently, $\epsilon = (1 - Wl)/h$ small), $\partial SC(c, E(A))/\partial c$ at $c = 0$ can be made arbitrarily close to $1 + \text{Pr}'(0)\left[\dfrac{W^2 l}{2} + W(1 - lW)\right]$. Whenever $\text{Pr}(0) > 0$, then, there must exist a convex probability function such that $\partial SC(c, E(A))/\partial c > 0$ and $\partial EC(c; W)/\partial c < 0$ at $c = 0$. Hence, $c^* > \hat{c}\,(\approx 0)$ in these cases. (For a numerical example, let $W = .75$, $l = .1$, $h = 10$, $\epsilon = .0925$, and $\text{Pr}(c) = \exp(-.25c)$.)   Q.E.D.

Remark. The above proof establishes that there are accident cost distributions and probability functions such that $c^* > \hat{c}$ can occur. The potentially bankrupt injurer, then, does not in general spend too little on care. This reasoning can be extended to more realistic smooth accident cost distributions with little difficulty aside from technical complication. Additionally, this result is applicable to some cases in which the injurer is risk averse. In particular, an injurer that is "barely" risk averse has a utility of wealth function that is "almost" linear, and the relevant inequalities will still be sufficient.

4. The effect of changes in wealth on optimal injurer care choice

■ I consider next the effect of an increase in injurer initial wealth W on the injurer's optimal care choice. As the discussion in the last section makes clear, a wealth change will have two (contradictory) effects on this choice. An increase in injurer initial wealth, for example, raises the marginal benefit of care by increasing the expected payout to accident victims (should an accident occur) at all relevant care levels. On the other hand, increased wealth reduces the probability of bankruptcy and thus the spending subsidy that bankruptcy implies. The net effect of a wealth change on optimal care choice will depend on which of these two forces is dominant.

Performing the static analysis and assuming $c^* > 0$, the desired derivative is

$$\frac{\partial c^*}{\partial W} = \frac{1}{\lambda}[-\text{Pr}'(c^*)(1 - F(W - c^*)) - \text{Pr}(c^*)f(W - c^*)], \qquad (5)$$

where

$$\lambda = \text{Pr}''(c^*) \cdot E(D(W, c^*)) - 2\,\text{Pr}'(c^*)(1 - F(W - c^*)) - \text{Pr}(c^*)f(W - c^*).$$

The term λ is nonnegative by the second-order condition (3b), and is assumed here to be positive. Equation (5) implies, for $\lambda > 0$,

$$\frac{\partial c^*}{\partial W} > (<)\,0 \text{ iff } -\frac{\text{Pr}'(c^*)}{\text{Pr}(c^*)} - \frac{f(W - c^*)}{1 - F(W - c^*)} > (<)\,0. \qquad (6)$$

Inequality (6) suggests how an example yielding the result $\partial c^*/\partial W < 0$ can be constructed: it is necessary and sufficient that the term $-\text{Pr}'(c^*)/\text{Pr}(c^*)$ be less than the hazard rate $f(W - c^*)/(1 - F(W - c^*))$ of the accident cost distribution at $W - c^*$. Such an example is provided by the following case. Let accident costs A be uniformly distributed on the interval $[0, 1]$, and let initial wealth $W = .75$. Suppose the accident probability function is given by

$$Pr(c) = \frac{1}{2}\left(1 + \frac{.25}{.25 + c}\right).^{7}$$

With this specification, $EC(c; W)$ has a global minimum at $c^* \cong .0299$, at which point $-Pr'(c^*)/Pr(c^*)$ ($\cong 1.686$) is less than $f(W - c^*)/(1 - F(W - c^*))$ ($\cong 3.573$), so that $\partial c^*/\partial W < 0$. Cases for which $\partial c^*/\partial W > 0$ are also easily constructed.

While both $\partial c^*/\partial W < 0$ and $\partial c^*/\partial W > 0$ are possible, $\partial c^*/\partial W$ is bounded above, a consequence of the convexity of $Pr(c)$.

Proposition 2. $\partial c^*/\partial W < 1$.

Proof. We can write

$$\frac{\partial c^*}{\partial W} = \frac{a}{a + b},$$

where

$$a = -Pr'(c^*)(1 - F(W - c^*)) - Pr(c^*)f(W - c^*)$$

and

$$b = Pr''(c^*) \cdot E(D(W, c^*)) - Pr'(c^*)(1 - F(W - c^*)) > 0.$$

If $\partial c^*/\partial W \leq 0$, then $\partial c^*/\partial W < 1$. Alternatively, if $\partial c^*/\partial W > 0$, then $a > 0$ by equation (5), and $\partial c^*/\partial W < 1$.   Q.E.D.

5. A cost function for injurers

■ I consider next the specification of an "expected cost function" for the injurer that illustrates the relationship between injurer wealth and expected costs when the injurer behaves optimally.

Let $c^* > 0$ be the injurer's optimal care choice given wealth W, and denote by EC^* the injurer's corresponding expected costs.

Proposition 3. (a) EC^* is concave and monotone increasing in W.

$$(b)\, \frac{\partial EC^*}{\partial W} = Pr(c^*)(1 - F(W - c^*)).$$

Proof. (a) Concavity requires

$$\frac{\partial^2 EC^*}{\partial W^2} \leq 0.$$

Performing the necessary differentiation yields

$$\frac{\partial^2 EC^*}{\partial W^2} = \frac{\partial c^*}{\partial W}\left(Pr'(c^*)(1 - F(W - c^*)) + Pr(c^*)f(W - c^*)\right) - Pr(c^*)f(W - c^*).$$

Hence, by equation (6), $\partial^2 EC^*/\partial W^2 \leq 0$. Monotonicity is obtained immediately by differentiation.

---

[7] Note that $Pr(c)$ is strictly convex.

(b) By the Envelope Theorem,

$$\frac{\partial EC^*}{\partial W} = \Pr(c^*)[(W - c^*)f(W - c^*) + (1 - F(W - c^*)) - (W - c^*)f(W - c^*)]$$

$$= \Pr(c^*)(1 - F(W - c^*)). \qquad Q.E.D.$$

Remark. An increase in injurer initial wealth W leads, after optimal adjustment, to increased injurer expected costs, though at a less than one-for-one and decreasing rate, regardless of whether the wealth increase induces augmented or diminished care. Further, the slope of the injurer's expected cost function equals the probability of bankruptcy, so that concavity of the expected cost function implies that wealthier injurers are always less likely to be bankrupted than poorer ones, irrespective of whether the former or latter spend more on care. Additionally, increases in injurer initial wealth W always raise injurer expected final wealth; injurer expected final wealth $EF(c^*; W)$ is given by $EF(c^*; W) = W - EC(c^*; W)$, and $\partial EF(c^*; W)/\partial W = 1 - \Pr(c^*)(1 - F(W - c^*)) > 0$.

6. Victim welfare and injurer wealth

■ Victims suffer uncompensated losses only when the injurer is bankrupted. Despite the fact that the injurer's probability of bankruptcy declines in the injurer's initial wealth W, victims can be made worse off by injurer wealth increases under some circumstances. To see this, note first that the expected losses of victims $(VC(W, c))$ can be written as

$$VC(W, c) = \Pr(c)(1 - F(W - c))[E(A|A > W - c) - (W - c)], \qquad (7)$$

where $E(A|A > W - c)$ is the conditional expectation of A given $A > W - c$. Note also that

$$EC(c; W) + VC(W, c) \equiv SC(c, E(A)). \qquad (8)$$

At the injurer's optimal care choice c^*, we have

$$\frac{\partial VC(W, c^*)}{\partial W} = \frac{\partial c^*}{\partial W}(1 + \Pr'(c^*) \cdot E(A)) - \Pr(c^*)(1 - F(W - c^*)). \qquad (9)$$

Equation (9) indicates that victims are always made better off when an increase in injurer wealth W leads to increased care choice. Rearranging (9), we obtain

$$\frac{\partial VC(W, c^*)}{\partial W} = \frac{\partial c^*}{\partial W}(1 - \Pr(c^*)(1 - F(W - c^*))$$

$$+ \Pr'(c^*) \cdot E(A)) + \left(1 - \frac{\partial c^*}{\partial W}\right)(-\Pr(c^*)(1 - F(W - c^*))). \qquad (10)$$

Since $E(A) > E(D(W, c^*))$, we use equation (3a) and conclude that the term

$$1 - \Pr(c^*)(1 - F(W - c^*)) + \Pr'(c^*) \cdot E(A)$$

is negative. Since $\partial c^*/\partial W < 1$ by Proposition 2, equation (10) expresses $\partial VC(W, c^*)/\partial W$ as a weighted average of two negative values. Hence, if $\partial c^*/\partial W > 0$, then victims are made better off by the wealth increase and $\partial VC(W, c^*)/\partial W < 0$.

For an increase in injurer initial wealth to make victims worse off, it is necessary that $\partial c^*/\partial W < 0$. Referring to equation (9), it is clear that $\partial VC(W, c^*)/\partial W > 0$ when $\partial c^*/\partial W < 0$ and $E(A)$ is sufficiently large. The mean $E(A)$ can always be made large enough by making U large and shifting probability mass of the distribution $f(A)$ to the right on the interval $[W, U]$. (Perturbations of this kind have no effect on the injurer's cost minimization problem or c^*, but do increase $\hat{c}$.)

7. Applications

■ The derivative properties of the function EC^* suggest a number of applications to the study of vertical relationships and markets for agents. Suppose, for example, that a principal contemplates hiring an agent to perform some task that exposes the agent to the risk of a costly accident for which the agent is solely liable. If agents are risk-neutral, then hiring an agent requires the principal to pay compensation of at least the agent's expected costs. Since the payout truncation created by bankruptcy implies that the liability costs of the poor are less than those of the rich, poorer agents will enjoy a competitive advantage over their richer rivals, other things being equal.

To the extent that the legal system shifts liability onto downstream actors, one might expect dangerous tasks to be subcontracted by wealthy firms to judgment-proof agents. While real economies (of scope or scale) could mitigate this effect, liability costs may constitute a force for vertical disintegration in some industries. "Piercing the veil" by assigning (some) liability to the principals might make using agents as a (partial) "liability shield" more difficult, but there are circumstances in which such a policy could be hard to implement. Ringleb and Wiggins (1990), for example, discuss the problem of costly, "latent" hazards (such as arise in the environmental and product liability areas), and present empirical evidence that the structures of some industries characterized by high, long-term liability have changed in the direction of smaller (and presumably less wealthy) firms.

The issues of vertical relationships are made more complex and more interesting when the principal is inconvenienced or damaged by the agent's bankruptcy. Since agents' probabilities of bankruptcy are declining in their wealth levels, a principal who offers a low wage to agents to perform a service will attract only agents whose expected costs are low, i.e., whose initial wealth levels are low and bankruptcy probabilities high. Assuming that the principal cannot determine the financial states of agents *ex ante* and must randomly select among those agents who express interest in the principal's offer, low wage offers are more likely to result in hiring an agent who subsequently becomes bankrupt. This adverse selection phenomenon could motivate principals who suffer under agent bankruptcy to offer higher wages, thereby attracting a pool of applicants more likely on average to be solvent.[8] A mechanism similar to this was discussed by Stiglitz and Weiss (1981) in explaining some features of the credit markets.

8. Conclusion

■ This article has examined the effects of potential bankruptcy on the care choice of an injurer in an environment of strict liability. While the payout truncation implied by bankruptcy reduces the injurer's benefits of care relative to those of society, the possibility of insolvency also creates an implicit "subsidy" to care (or any other kind of) spending. This subsidy, which depends directly on the probability of bankruptcy, can be large enough to generate a number of a-intuitive results: potentially bankrupt injurers may over-invest in care relative to the social optimum, may reduce their care levels as their financial conditions improve, and may act to make victims worse off as they become wealthier.

The simple model presented in this article also may be used to define an expected cost function for injurers that relates expected injurer payouts to initial wealth when injurers behave optimally. The curvature and derivative properties of this function were examined, and applications to vertical integration and markets for agents were discussed. I have suggested that the effect of potential bankruptcy on expected liability costs could motivate

---

[8] Of course, the agent may incur costs other than potential liability, and the principal's payment to the agent affects the agent's initial wealth directly, so the issue is complex.

634 / THE RAND JOURNAL OF ECONOMICS

vertical disintegration in some industries, and might produce adverse selection phenomena in some markets for agents.

The results in this article differ from those obtained by Shavell (1986) for three reasons. First, Shavell treats care as nonpecuniary (but with a monetary equivalent), so that care does not reduce the assets available to pay damage awards, a circumstance that eliminates the subsidy effect of potential insolvency. Second, Shavell treats accidents as having a fixed rather than random cost. Finally, Shavell allows injurers to be risk averse. Unfortunately, the relationship between care choice and risk attitude is very complex.[9] One cannot conclude, for example, that more risk-averse injurers take greater care than less risk-averse injurers in the same circumstances.

For policy purposes, these results give an ambiguous message. Because of the possibility of bankruptcy, injurer financial condition does affect care choice. Because of the bankruptcy subsidy, however, injurers could spend too much on care, although the practical importance of this effect is uncertain. It is clear, however, that a better understanding of these effects could be useful in formulating regulatory policy in many areas, and that more investigation is needed.

References

BEARD, T.R. "Bankruptcy, Safety Expenditure, and Safety Regulation in the Motor Carrier Industry." Ph.D. dissertation, Vanderbilt University, August, 1988.

DIONNE, G. AND EECKHOUDT, L. "Self-Insurance, Self-Protection and Increased Risk Aversion." *Economic Letters,* Vol. 17 (1985), pp. 39–42.

EHRLICH, I. AND BECKER, G. "Market Insurance, Self-Insurance, and Self-Protection," *Journal of Political Economy,* Vol. 80 (1972), pp. 623–648.

PHLIPS, L. *The Economics of Imperfect Information.* Cambridge: The Cambridge University Press, 1988.

RINGLEB, A.H. AND WIGGINS, S.N. "Liability and Large-Scale, Long-Term Hazards." *Journal of Political Economy,* Vol. 98 (1990), pp. 574–595.

SHAVELL, S. "The Judgment Proof Problem." *International Review of Law and Economics,* Vol. 6 (1986), pp. 45–58.

———. *Economic Analysis of Accident Law.* Cambridge, Mass.: The Harvard University Press, 1987.

STIGLITZ, J. AND WEISS, A. "Credit Rationing in Markets with Imperfect Information." *American Economic Review,* Vol. 71 (1981), pp. 393–410.

SUMMERS, J. "The Case of the Disappearing Defendant: An Economic Analysis." *University of Pennsylvania Law Review,* Vol. 132 (1983), pp. 145–185.

SWEENEY, G. AND BEARD, T.R. "Self-Protection, Risk-Aversion, and 'Caution'." Mimeo, Vanderbilt University, 1990.

---

[9] See, for example, Dionne and Eeckhoudt (1985) or Sweeney and Beard (1990).

[12]

TORT LAW AS A REGULATORY REGIME FOR CATASTROPHIC PERSONAL INJURIES

WILLIAM M. LANDES and RICHARD A. POSNER*

Regulation and tort law are alternative methods (though often used in combination) for preventing accidents. The former requires a potential injurer to take measures to prevent the accident from occurring. The latter seeks to deter the accident by making the potential injurer liable for the costs of the accident should it occur. A growing literature tries to identify the relative costs and benefits of regulation versus tort law in particular accident settings.[1] Our focus is on the "catastrophic" accident. Any accident that results in death or a serious permanent injury is a catastrophe to the victim, but we shall limit our definition to accidents in which a number of victims are killed or seriously injured. Illustrations are the crash of a large passenger plane, a nuclear reactor accident in which radiation is emitted over a wide area, the sale of a drug such as DES that turns out to have adverse long-run effects on human health, and the discharge of asbestos fibers into the air in workplaces, again with such effects.

There is a widespread but uncritical belief that tort law is quite hopeless as a method of dealing with catastrophic accidents. Three points are stressed: the existence of multiple victims makes it less likely that the injurer can pay all the accident claims than is the case in a single-victim accident; the causal link to a particular victim is often unclear; and the injury may show up so many years after the accident occurred that proof of the defendant's negligence may be impossible to come by. The last two

* Landes is the Clifford R. Musser Professor of Economics at the University of Chicago Law School. Posner is a Judge of the U.S. Court of Appeals for the Seventh Circuit and a Senior Lecturer at the University of Chicago Law School.

[1] See, for example, Steven M. Shavell, A Model of the Socially Optimal Use of Liability and Regulation (April 1983) (unpublished manuscript, Harvard Law School); Donald Wittman, Prior Regulation versus Post Liability: The Choice between Input and Output Monitoring, 6 J. Legal Stud. 193 (1977).

points are frequently conjoined, since the longer the delay between the accident and the injury, the harder it is to exclude other causal factors.

We believe these points to be overstated; and to the extent we are right the argument for turning to regulation as the sole or principal means of preventing catastrophic accidents is weakened. The concern with solvency overlooks the fact that the relevant cost in considering whether a potential injurer has an incentive to take the right amount of care is not necessarily the cost of the accident if it occurs, but the cost of preventing it; if that cost is smaller than the potential injurer's wealth, he may have adequate incentives to take the right amount of care rather than let the accident happen and wipe him out completely. But, surprisingly, this is less likely to be true if the standard of liability is strict liability rather than negligence. Yet if strict liability is for this reason rejected as the standard in catastrophic accident cases, the third point in the criticism of tort law— the difficulty of proving negligence many years after the accident—is overstated. A strict liability cause of action is simpler to prove than a negligence case, and the difference is especially dramatic if there has been a long lapse of time between the accident and the full-blown injury, and hence (it is usually assumed) between the accident and trial. It is one thing to show that the defendant did something twenty years ago that causes harm today; it is another and harder thing to show that he failed to conform to the standard of care applicable to his activity twenty years ago. Tort law, however, has resources for dealing with the problem of lapse of time. If the injury on which the victim of a catastrophic accident can base a tort suit is defined not as the full-fledged illness that blooms many years after the accident but as the impact or exposure that planted the seeds of the illness, then the trial can be held soon after the accident. The victim's damages are computed under this approach in terms of reduced life expectancy, future pain and suffering, and future medical costs, rather than in terms of realized loss. This approach also solves automatically the problem of the accident known to cause injury to many people, when it is uncertain which people they are; all the potential victims can be compensated for their ex ante loss, measured at the time of suit.

These points are developed below after we first recapitulate the now-familiar economic model of accidents and tort law and extend the model to embrace the special problems presented by the catastrophic accident.

I. THE BASIC MODEL[2]

Assuming that all parties are risk neutral (so that utility equals wealth or income), that damages (*D*) (measured in dollars) are independent of the

---

[2] See William M. Landes & Richard A. Posner, The Positive Economic Theory of Tort Law, 15 Ga. L. Rev. 851, 864 (1981).

level of care taken by the parties, and that the probability of an accident (p) depends on units of care (x being the victim's and y the injurer's units), we can write the social costs of an accident as

$$L = p(x, y)D + A(x) + B(y),\qquad (1)$$

where $A(x)$ and $B(y)$ are the victim's and the injurer's costs of care, respectively. $A(x)$ and $B(y)$ increase with increases in care, while p falls with more care. We define due care as the levels of victim's and injurer's care—x^* and y^*, respectively—that minimize L. "Joint care" means that x^* and y^* are both positive, "alternative care" that one is zero and the other positive.[3]

It can be shown that both negligence and strict liability with a defense of contributory negligence create incentives for both parties to take due care in the joint-care case, while either no liability or strict liability creates incentives for due care in the alternative-care case—no liability when $y^* = 0$, strict liability when $x^* = 0$. Sometimes it is more efficient to prevent an accident by reducing the scale of the activity (either of injurer or of victim) that gives rise to the accident than by conducting the activity more carefully. An example would be running fewer trains per day, rather than installing better spark arresters, to limit crop damage from locomotive sparks. If so, this is an argument for strict liability if it is the injurer's activity that we want to reduce, and for negligence or no liability if it is the victim's.

Incentives are only one consideration in designing an optimal system of liability rules. Another is administrative cost. Negligence is, as we have noted, a more complex standard than strict liability and therefore both raises the costs of litigation and, because uncertainty leads to more litigation, increases the amount of litigation. But these effects may be dominated in particular cases by the effect of strict liability in increasing the amount of litigation by increasing the number of claims, since all accidents will give rise to prima facie liability under a strict liability regime but not under a negligence regime.

II. Extension of the Model to Catastrophic Accidents

Now let us analyze the case where there is one injurer but multiple victims. To simplify the exposition we shall assume (unless otherwise noted) that the level of victim care can have no effect on the frequency of accidents.

Let N equal the number of potential victims (for example, people living

---

[3] A final assumption is that transaction costs are so high that they prevent the parties from voluntarily negotiating the optimum level of care.

near a nuclear reactor) and assume that damages are the same for each victim if an accident occurs and that (as we have said) $x = 0$. Then

$$L = Np(y)D + B(y). \tag{2}$$

Due care is derived by multiplying the reduction in expected damages and setting it equal to the marginal cost of care. This poses no problem and is a trivial extension of the basic model. Either a negligence or a strict liability standard would provide incentives for the injurer to take due care with respect to the entire set of potential victims. But suppose the injurer's assets are insufficient to cover the damages of all victims in the event of an accident. Although this is always possible in a single-victim case, it is more likely in the multiple-victim case: if the injurer's wealth has some upper limit, W, as it must, and D is also fixed, then as N increases there will come a point where ND exceeds W. This problem is compounded by another factor. In catastrophic injury cases the amount of damages per victim is also likely to be large even though both the probability of an accident and expected damages may be small. And the likelihood that the injurer's assets will be insufficient to cover the victim's damages depends on both the damages per victim (holding expected damages per victim constant) and the number of victims.

All this, however, ignores the fact that W is likely to be positively correlated with N, because usually it takes a larger enterprise to injure more victims. The typical injurer of single victims is an automobile driver, and though the damage he can do is limited, it may exceed his ability to pay (or his insurance coverage). The typical injurer of many victims is a business firm, and the more numerous the victims the larger the firm is apt to be. The relationship between size and the number of victims is not one to one but it does raise the question whether solvency limitations are in fact a greater problem in catastrophic accident cases than in other cases. The solvency limitation would be a more important factor, however, if injurers were able to adopt strategies to reduce the amount of their wealth available for paying damages.

Assume that the solvency problem is greater in such cases, that is, $ND > W - B(y)$; let $\bar{D}$ equal the maximum amount per victim that the injurer can be made to pay ($N\bar{D} = W - B(y)$); and consider what difference it makes whether the liability standard is negligence or strict liability. Under strict liability the level of care will tend to be less than due care because the injurer will equate $-Np_y\bar{D}$ to $(1 - p)B_y$ instead of $-Np_yD$ to B_y.[4] Assuming a small probability of an accident (a proper assumption in the

---

[4] We thank Walter Oi for showing us that when there is a solvency limitation, the marginal cost of taking care is $(1 - p)B_y$, not B_y.

case of a catastrophic accident), the solvency limitation would dominate the discounting of B_y by $(1 - p)$, and the injurer will take care equal to y_1, which is less than y^*. Under negligence the injurer will either use y_1 inputs of care or bring his level of care up to the due care standard, y^*. Paradoxically, then, a negligence standard may give the injurer a greater incentive to use due care than strict liability would do. The reason is that by increasing his care from y_1 to y^*, the injurer avoids *all* liability for damages in the event of an accident, whereas under strict liability expected damages fall as care rises but the injurer still pays something; the benefits to him of additional investments in care are smaller.

Figure 1 illustrates these points. If the legal standard is strict liability, y_1 would equate the injurer's marginal benefits to his marginal costs of care given the limitation on his ability to pay full damages. From the injurer's standpoint the added cost of bringing his care up to due care (y^*) is area c + d, while the corresponding benefit to him—the reduction in expected damages—is d. From a social standpoint, however, the benefits are greater than the costs $(a + b + c + d$ exceeds $b + c + d)$. Thus, strict liability yields an efficiency loss equal to a. Under a negligence standard the injurer is faced with two choices. He can select y_1 and bear expected damages of $d + e$,[5] or he can take due care, incurring an added cost of c + d but avoiding all liability for expected damages of $d + e$. Whether the injurer uses due care (y^*) or y_1 inputs of care therefore depends on whether area e is larger or smaller than c, which depends in turn on the cost of added care, the difference between D and $\bar{D}$, and the effectiveness of added care in reducing expected damages.[6]

What if the most efficient method of accident avoidance is for the potential injurer to discontinue his activity? Whether it is or not will depend on whether

$$V \lessgtr Np(y^*)D + B(y^*), \qquad (3)$$

where V is the value of this activity relative to his next best activity (V excludes the expected damages and the costs of care). If we assume there

---

[5] At y_1, expected damages are eliminated in the amount of the area under the $-Np_y\bar{D}$ curve from 0 to y_1. Expected damages of $d + e$—the area under the $-Np_y\bar{D}$ curve to the right of y_1—still remain. Observe also that $\bar{D}$ declines as y increases because $N\bar{D} = W - B(y)$.

[6] We have shown above that strict liability leads to y_1 units of care and negligence to either y_1 or y^* units of care. However, if the legal standard of care can be varied, it is always possible to set the standard somewhere between y_1 and y^* so that the injurer under a negligence standard will choose to comply with the standard instead of using y_1. Thus, under a "second-best" standard, negligence will dominate strict liability because care between y_1 and y^* is preferable to y_1. We thank Mitch Polinsky for this insight.

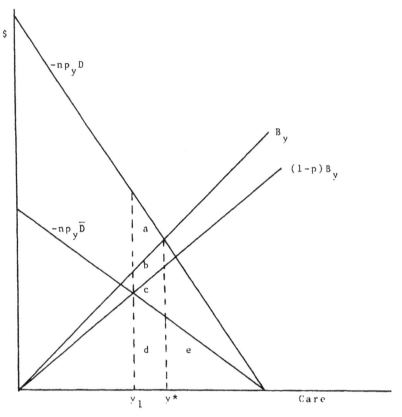

FIGURE 1

is a ceiling on the injurer's ability to pay, strict liability will generate too much activity (substitute $\bar{D}$ and y_1 above) and negligence either the same (when injurer uses y_1) or more (when injurer uses y^* to avoid paying any damages) than strict liability. This result differs from that of the usual comparison between strict liability and negligence, where a strict liability standard always induces a lower activity level by the injurer than a negligence standard.

III. Extension to Causal Uncertainty[7]

To analyze the basic problems of catastrophic accidents—causal uncertainty and the passage of time between accident and injury—we consider

---

[7] See David Kaye, The Limits of the Preponderance of the Evidence Standard; Justifiably Naked Statistical Evidence and Multiple Causation, 1982 A.B.F. Res. J. 487; Guido Cala-

a concrete example. Suppose an accident at a nuclear reactor power plant would produce an emission of radiation that might injure many persons living nearby. We shall let a equal the probability that each of N exposed persons will incur actual damages (D per person) if the accident occurs. There is also a positive probability b ($< a$) that each person will incur the same harm even if there is no accident. For example, a might be the probability that an exposed person will develop cancer given the increase in the level of radiation due to the accident, and b the probability that he will develop cancer even if there is no increase. Provisionally we assume that a and b are unaffected by either injurer or victim expenditures on care and that $p(y)$, the probability of a nuclear reactor accident, depends only on y, the injurer's inputs of care. Then we can write the loss function (including expected losses if there is no accident) as

$$L = Np(y)aD + N[1 - p(y)]bD + B(y) \tag{4a}$$

or

$$L = Np(y)(a - b)D + NbD + B(y), \tag{4b}$$

and due care as

$$- Np_y(a - b)D = B_y. \tag{5}$$

From (4b) we see that $Np(y)(a - b)D$ is the increase in expected damages due to the nuclear reactor, and NbD the expected damages in the absence of the reactor. Due care is derived by equating the expected reduction in damages to the marginal costs of care.

Notice that uncertainty over causation exists at the individual but not at the aggregate level. If, for example, $N = 1,000$, $p(y^*) = .10$, $a = .11$, and $b = .10$, a nuclear reactor accident will cause ten additional cancers ($1,000$ ($.11 - .10$)), a fact known with near certainty from the law of large numbers. Yet for each of the 110 persons in the exposed population who develops cancer, there is uncertainty over whether it was the radiation exposure or something else that caused his cancer (in the sense that if he had not been exposed, he would not have gotten cancer). Indeed, since 100 persons would have gotten cancer anyway, it is more likely than

---

bresi, Concerning Cause and the Law of Torts, 43 U. Chi. L. Rev. 69 (1975); William M. Landes & Richard A. Posner, Causation in Tort Law: An Economic Approach, 12 J. Legal Stud. 109 (1983); Glen O. Robinson, Multiple Causation in Tort Law: Reflections on the *DES* Cases, 68 Va. L. Rev. 713 (1982); Steven Shavell, An Analysis of Causation and the Scope of Liability in the Law of Torts, 9 J. Legal Stud. 463 (1980); *id.*, Uncertainty over Causation and the Determination of Civil Liability (1983) (unpublished manuscript, Harvard Law School).

not—ten times more likely, in fact—that the reactor accident did not cause any given individual's cancer.[8]

The dilemma is apparent. If none of the victims are allowed to recover damages, the defendant will pay nothing, though in fact he harmed ten people (we just do not known which ten). But if all the cancer victims are allowed to recover damages, the defendant will be forced to pay out ten times the actual damages that the accident caused. It might seem that if the first horn of the dilemma results (as it does) in underdeterrence, the second must result in overdeterrence. But whether this is true in the formal model depends on how the law defines due care and whether the legal standard is negligence or strict liability. If due care is defined with respect to the additional damages, $(a - b)D$, caused by the injurer (see equation [6]), there is no overdeterrence, so long as the standard is negligence. The injurer takes due care, y^*, and avoids any potential liability. The fact that if the accident did occur the damages would be greater than the victim's incremental loss is of purely academic interest to the potential injurer, since he will take due care and avoid paying any damages. In contrast, if negligence is defined with respect to total damages (so that due care requires a level of y that minimizes $Np(y)aD$ instead of $Np(y)(a - b)D$), the injurer must take more care than y^* to avoid liability. If the legal standard is strict liability and the injurer pays D to each cancer victim if an accident occurs, the injurer will minimize $Np(y)aD$ (instead of $Np(y)(a - b)D$), resulting always in too much care—overdeterrence.

Two further points should be mentioned. First, the formal model is incomplete, because it omits the possibility of an erroneous finding of negligence. Once that possibility is admitted, the negligence standard is likely to produce overdeterrence (even if due care is defined with respect to incremental expected damages), if the victim's damages are much greater than the increment covered by the tortfeasor and if potential defendants can reduce the likelihood of an erroneous finding of liability by talking more than due care. Second, overdeterrence may result from a reduction in the injurer's activity level (for example, substituting coal for nuclear power). This is more likely to happen if the legal standard is strict liability rather than negligence.

---

[8] Additional assumptions could of course be added to the example that might enable the law to reduce (but not eliminate) individual uncertainty. For example, people closer to the accident or receiving greater doses of radiation might have higher probabilities (higher a's) of developing cancer. Similarly, certain classes of individuals (such as nonsmokers or persons with lower incidences of cancer in their families) might have lower probabilities of developing cancer in the absence of the accident (lower b's). Thus one might be able to show that for some victims the odds that the accident caused cancer were great (a/b was high) while for others they were low (a/b was low). We ignore these complications.

We consider next whether the tort system, faced with the dilemma of too little or too much compensation, must throw up its hands and abandon the field to regulation.

IV. A New Approach to Causal Uncertainty

We think the tort law has resources for dealing with the problems identified in the preceding section. Before showing this, however, we consider from a theoretical standpoint several alternative damage rules that courts could use to deal with causal uncertainty. To simplify, we continue to use the example of the accident at the nuclear reactor facility.

1. All or Nothing

In a traditional garden variety common-law tort case, each victim, to prevail, must show that his injury would probably not have occurred but for the accident, which implies that $a - b$ is close to one (that is, a is close to one and b close to zero). Given the administrative costs of determining probabilities a and b with any exactness, such a rule tends to be efficient in a single-victim tort case.[9] In contrast, in the multiple-victim case the all-or-nothing character of the traditional approach could create a significant disincentive for the injurer to invest in safety. Since $a - b$ would be small for each plaintiff in the nuclear reactor accident example, no plaintiff would prevail. Knowing this the potential injurer would not have an incentive to take due care.

2. Compensating All Exposed Persons

If an accident occurs, each exposed person is harmed in a probabilistic sense because he faces a higher probability (a instead of b) of developing cancer in the future. In principle it should be possible to compensate potential victims appropriately for that added risk, thereby creating the right incentives for potential injurers to take care. In effect, each potential victim is compensated for his actual damages discounted by the probabil-

---

[9] The *Grimstad* case (New York Central R.R. v. Grimstad, 264 Fed. 334 (2d Cir. 1920)) is a good example of the difficulties that would arise in estimating these probabilities. The plaintiff's decedent fell from a tug and drowned. Because the tug's life preserver was not in its proper place it could not be thrown immediately to him. But it was not clear that he would have been saved had the life preserver been available, since he could not swim and drowned almost immediately. From an economic standpoint, the decision in *Grimstad* (no liability) appears to be the efficient result. The difference in conditional probabilities ($a - b$) was small, and given administrative costs a finding of no liability would not create a risk of significant underinvestment in safety. The traditional approach illustrated by *Grimstad* is discussed more fully in Landes & Posner, *supra* note 2.

ity that he would not have suffered them anyway. Thus assume from our previous example that $N = 1,000$, $a = .11$, and $b = .10$ and assume that damages are $1,000 per cancer victim. Substituting these numbers into our equation for due care (equation [5]) yields $1,000P_y(.01)(\$1,000) = B_y$. Awarding each exposed potential victim his expected incremental harm of $10 (equal to actual harm times the probability it will occur) will create an incentive for the injurer both to take due care and to select the correct activity level, since his liability is equal to the expected damages from his activity.[10] More generally, an incentive for the injurer to behave efficiently is created by awarding damages to each of the N exposed persons equal to

$$D^* = (a - b)D. \tag{6}$$

3. Compensating Victims Ex Post, Including Some Who Would Have Been Injured Anyway

This rule limits recovery to exposed persons who subsequently develop cancer. If $a = .11$ and $N = 1,000$, 110 persons will develop cancer sometime after being exposed to the radiation from the reactor accident, and they would under this rule be awarded damages. But each person's damages would be lower than the assumed harm of $1,000 per cancer, because the harm would be discounted to reflect the fact that 100 of the 110 successful plaintiffs would have gotten cancer anyway. One can show that a damage award per ex post injury equal to

$$D^{**} = \left[\frac{(a - b)}{a}\right]D, \tag{7}$$

where $(a - b)/a$ is the discount factor, would create an incentive for the injurer both to take due care and to choose the correct activity level. Since Na persons (the number who actually developed cancer) would be awarded damages of D^{**} per person, the injurer's expected liability and cost of care (assuming a strict liability standard) would equal $NapD^{**} + B(y) = Np(a - b)D + B(y)$. Minimizing this expression with respect to y yields y^*, the due care standard (see equation [5]).[11]

---

[10] Similarly, under a negligence standard the injurer will choose y^* because his expected liability plus costs of care will equal $B(y^*)$, which is less than his expected damages and costs of care for $y < y^*$.

[11] The injurer would also select y^* under a negligence standard, assuming due care is defined as the level of y that minimizes $NapD^{**} + B(y)$.

4. *Compensating Ex Post Victims Whose Injury Was Caused by the Accident*

For completeness, we consider this rule, although by assumption it cannot be used because there is no way of knowing which ten $(Na - Nb)$ of the 110 cancer victims would not have developed cancer but for the nuclear reactor accident. Under this rule each of the ten cancer victims would be fully compensated (at $1,000) and the injurer would have an incentive both to use due care and to select the correct activity level (assuming strict liability). The major advantage would be lower litigation costs because of the small number of claims, but the size of these cost savings would depend critically on being able to reduce the number of potential claimants below 110 before any lawsuits commenced—for example, by establishing that the level of exposure to radiation of 100 of the alleged victims was too slight to permit inferring a causal connection between the accident and their injury. This, however, would violate the assumption of our model that all 110 cancer victims were exposed to roughly the same amount of radiation.

We now consider the relative advantages of the second and third damage rules (the all-or-nothing rule has already been examined and the fourth rule, by assumption, cannot be used). To compare the two rules, we must bring back before the reader's attention the point made in the introduction that the problem of causal uncertainty and the problem of long delay between accident and full-blown injury are related. If, the day after the accident at Three Mile Island, three residents of Harrisburg, Pennsylvania, had suddenly lost all their hair, it would have been pretty clear in the absence of some alternative explanation that they were victims of the accident. But if twenty years after the accident there should be three excess cancer deaths in Harrisburg, it may be impossible to determine which three cancer deaths would not have occurred but for the accident. Lapse of time creates an opportunity for all sorts of other causal factors to come into play. Of course, not everything that follows closely in time upon some event is a result of that event, but it is much easier to exclude other factors when the relevant time period is short than when it is long. There is an interesting exception to this generalization, however, in the case where the accident occurs in the course of trying to save the victim from another peril. For example, Grimstad falls overboard from a boat not equipped with a life preserver, and drowns, but it is wholly uncertain whether he would have been saved if it had been so equipped.[12] Or, through medical negligence a man's lung cancer is not detected as

---

[12] See note 8 *supra*.

early as it should have been, but he probably would have died anyway if it had been detected sooner.[13] Since most people are not dying at the time they are struck down by a negligent injury, these cases are of limited practical importance; most cases of causal uncertainty involve a delayed-reaction injury, because it is only over a long period of time that the cumulative risk from other, independent causes becomes highly significant.

If we assume, as in our numerical example in the preceding section, that ordinarily the probability will be small that the delayed-reaction victim would not have fallen ill but for the defendant's act (less than 10 percent in our example), the result indicated by conventional tort thinking is no liability. But this leads, as we have said, to underdeterrence. A not very satisfactory alternative is to wait until the 110 victims develop cancer and give each victim D^{**} or 9 percent $((a - b)/a)$ of his damages. This might be too little to give the victims an adequate incentive to bring suit, in which event there would again be underdeterrence; in addition, it is an approach so at variance with traditional tort law thinking that it could not be adopted without a profound revolution in that thinking.

But there is another approach, one within the boundaries of traditional tort thinking. This is the second rule—compensating all exposed victims—examined above.[14] Consider the statutes of limitations in tort cases. The typical tort statute of limitations defines the occurrence that begins the statute's running as the "accrual" of the victim's cause of action.[15] Since there is no tort without some injury,[16] a cause of action for negligence, or for injury due to a defective product, does not accrue till there is something fairly describable as an injury. But it need not be a full-blown injury. In some states the inhalation of asbestos fibers is deemed sufficient injury to start the statute of limitations running, even though the full-blown disease (asbestosis or some other asbestos-related disease)

---

[13] As in Herskovits v. Group Health Coop., 99 Wash. 2d 609, 664 P.2d 474 (1983). Compare Kallenberg v. Beth Israel Hospital, 45 A.D.2d 177, 357 N.Y.S.2d 508 (1974); Stubbs v. City of Rochester, 226 N.Y. 516, 124 N.E. 137 (1919); and cases discussed in Landes & Posner, *supra* note 2, at 122–23; and in Wolfstone & Wolfstone, Recovery of Damages for the Loss of a Chance, 1978 Pers. Injury Ann. 744.

[14] Discussed in the context of bankrupt mass tortfeasors in Mark J. Roe, Bankruptcy and Tort: The Problem of the Mass Disaster, 84 Colum. L. Rev. (forthcoming 1984). And compare the procedure established by the Price-Anderson Act for compensating victims of nuclear reactor accident. See 42 U.S.C. §2210(o)(3); Duke Power Co. v. Carolina Environmental Study Group, Inc., 438 U.S. 59, 92 (1978).

[15] See, for example, the Minnesota statute discussed in Karjala v. Johns-Manville Products Corp., 523 F.2d 155 (8th Cir. 1975).

[16] See, for example, William L. Prosser, Handbook of the Law of Torts 4 (4th ed. 1971).

may not appear till many years later.[17] And even in states that use a "discovery" rule, thereby tolling the statute of limitations until the disease is full blown,[18] the injured party could be allowed to sue as soon as the cause of action was brought into existence by (undiagnosable) injury, even if for statute-of-limitations purposes the cause of action did not accrue till much later.[19]

If therefore the accident victim knows that he has been exposed to or has ingested a dangerous substance, traditional tort doctrine may allow him—and may even, depending on how a particular state interprets its statute of limitations, require him—to bring suit immediately, without waiting till he actually becomes ill. The computation of damages is straightforward in such a case (see D^* in equation [6]). If the victim's life expectancy has been shortened slightly as a result of an accident for which the defendant is liable under tort principles, the damages are the sum (discounted to present value) of the damages the victim's estate would have received in every future year if he had died in the accident, multiplied by the incremental probability of death associated with the accident. Suppose, for example, that if he had been killed in the twentieth year after the accident, his estate would have been entitled to $100,000. If the accident created only an additional 1 percent probability of his not surviving that long, then he would be entitled to $1,000 in damages (discounted to present value) for that year. Expected future medical expenses, future pain and suffering, future disfigurement, and so forth, can be treated similarly. Although the computation of damages in such a case would be probabilistic, in the sense that it would result in giving many accident victims a windfall, viewed ex post, the problem is no different from that which arises in computing lost future earnings, and other losses of future values, in ordinary tort cases. These computations are based on life expectancies and therefore produce windfalls for anyone who would not in fact have lived to his expected age—roughly half the plaintiffs.

This approach solves the problem presented when, after the consequences of an accident have been realized, a group of people present themselves to the court asking for full damages and it is perfectly clear

[17] See, for example, Steinhardt v. Johns-Manville Corp., 54 N.Y.2d 1008, 1010–11, 430 N.E.2d 1297, 1299, 446 N.Y.S.2d 244, 246 (1981).

[18] See, for example, Neubauer v. Owens-Corning Fiberglass Corp., 686 F.2d 570 (7th Cir. 1982); and on the varieties of accrual concepts used in asbestosis cases alone see Note, Manville: Good Faith Reorganization or "Insulated" Bankruptcy, 12 Hofstra L. Rev., 121 (1983).

[19] See Moore v. Jackson Park Hospital, 95 Ill. 2d 223, 232, 447 N.E.2d 408, 411–12 (1983). But see Morrissy v. Eli Lilly & Co., 76 Ill. App. 3d 753, 761, 394 N.E.2d 1369, 1376 (1979).

that most of them have suffered no damages as a result of the accident (90 percent in our nuclear example). Ex post only a fraction of the accident victims are losers but ex ante they all are, so the tort system should encounter no insuperable conceptual difficulties in awarding damages to all of them. There is still the problem that if the expected loss is very small on an individual basis though large in the aggregate, no individual may have an incentive to bear the costs of suit. But the class action may provide the solution to this problem. If a class action is feasible, it should not be critical how many people are exposed relative to the number who will actually suffer injury as a result of the exposure. For there will be only one suit—a class suit—regardless of the number of plaintiffs.[20] True, the more class members there are, the higher will be the costs of notice and payment in the class action; but states could choose to relax, to some extent anyway, both the requirement of individual notice to class members (as distinct from the much cheaper if much less effective method of notice by publication in a newspaper) and the requirement of individual payment; from an economic standpoint, the critical point for deterrence is that the defendant pays, not that the plaintiff receives.

Of course, the class action is no panacea, even if judicial opposition to its use in mass-tort cases can be overcome.[21] So, realistically, the lower the probability of injury (*a* in equation [4b]) and hence the larger the ratio of potential plaintiffs under the ex ante approach to potential plaintiffs under the more conventional ex post approach, the less attractive the ex ante approach is. Moreover, the ex ante approach is not feasible in a situation where people have no reason to suspect danger at the time of the accident or, what is more likely, do not have enough information to assess the magnitude of the danger. The information is required not only to motivate victims to sue but also to enable the courts to determine the magnitude of the accident costs and therefore to decide whether the defendants were negligent in failing to take precautions to avert the accident.[22] But this is not, as one might suspect, a powerful argument for regulation in lieu of tort law. After all, regulation will not work unless the government spends resources on obtaining information about the consequences of the accident in advance. And if it does obtain the information,

[20] We ignore the fact that some members of the class may decide to "opt out" and bring their own suit.

[21] See, for example, Yandle v. PPG Industries, Inc., 65 F.R.D. 566 (E.D. Tex. 1974).

[22] Observe that in determining negligence under either the ex ante or ex post approach we assume that only p, the probability of an accident, depends on the injurer's level of care. If both p and a, the probability of an injury given an accident, depended on the level of the injurer's care, the information required and hence the difficulty of determining negligence would be even greater.

all it need do is disseminate it widely, so that people have an incentive to sue and the courts have the information they need to make the negligence determination; there is no obvious reason why the government should have to embody the information in a regulatory scheme.

If the most efficient information gatherers are not government officials but potential injurers, there is an argument for combining strict liability with a discovery statute of limitations. This will allow accident victims to sue when they discover the consequences of the accident and will thereby place maximum pressure on the potential injurers to gather information about the likely consequences of their activities. At the same time it will facilitate the trial of lawsuits brought, necessarily, long after the conduct that gave rise to the suit, by removing the issue of negligence from the case.

V. THE QUESTION OF VICTIM CARE

We have assumed up to now that potential victims can do nothing to avoid or mitigate the severity of catastrophic accidents. Of course this assumption is artificial; it will now be relaxed and we shall consider how the amount of care a victim will take is affected by the various liability approaches examined above.[23]

Initially, assume that the victim's care (x) is equally productive in both the accident and no-accident states. For example, suppose that following a high-fiber diet or refraining from smoking reduces the probability of developing cancer to the same extent whether or not there is a nuclear reactor accident—that is, $a_x = b_x$. Due care for a victim is derived by first adding the total cost of victim care, $NA(x)$, to equation (4a) and then minimizing with respect of x, yielding $-b_xD = A_x$.[24] Thus x^* requires each potential victim to spend on x until the reduction in expected damages, which is independent of the likelihood of an accident, equals the marginal cost of care. Under the ex ante approach (compensating all potential victims) explored in the preceding section, a potential victim has an incentive to take due care (x^*) even if there is no defense of contribu-

---

[23] To simplify our presentation, we do not consider explicitly the effect of different damage rules on the victim's activity level, but that effect is easy to summarize. In general, a potential victim will make the correct activity choice (for example, the choice between living near a nuclear reactor plant or far away) only when he faces the full expected damages from an accident. Therefore, under strict liability victims will make incorrect activity choices but injurers will make correct ones, while under negligence victims will have incentives to make correct activity choices but injurers will not.

[24] Since we assume that all victims are identical, (4a) becomes $L = Np(y)aD + N[1 - p(y)]bD + NA(x) + B(y)$, and victim due care requires $pa_xD + (1 - p)b_xD + A_x = 0$. Assuming $a_x = b_x$, victim due care requires $b_xD + A_x = 0$.

tory negligence.[25] Since the victim is compensated ex ante for his expected incremental damages, he minimizes $bD + A(x)$. This yields x^*.[26]

Now assume that the victim's care is relatively more productive if an accident occurs—that is, that $-a_x > -b_x$. For example, suppose smoking less reduces the probability of getting cancer by a greater amount if there is a nuclear reactor accident. To simplify, let $b_x = 0$, so that taking care reduces the probability of an injury only if an accident occurs; since we have already analyzed the case where $-a_x = -b_x > 0$, our assumption that $b_x = 0$ is equivalent to analyzing the effect of additional care that is relatively more productive if an accident occurs. We assume that $a > b$ even though $-a_x > 0$ and $b_x = 0$. Two cases must be distinguished. In the first, care is undertaken prior to a possible accident (call this *prior care*). In the second care is undertaken only after the accident occurs (*after care*). The usual economic analysis of torts does not distinguish between prior and after care because the accident and injury are assumed to be simultaneous, although there is in fact a tort doctrine of "avoidable consequences" designed to induce the taking of after care.[27] For catastrophic accidents the actual injury may not show up till long after the accident, so it becomes important to distinguish between prior and after care.

For prior care, due care requires $-pa_xD = A_x$, which is obtained by discounting the expected reduction in damages $(-a_xD)$ by the probability that an accident will occur (p) and setting it equal to the marginal cost of care. Unlike our earlier case where $a_x = b_x$ (the benefits from victim care are independent of whether the accident occurs), a defense of contributory negligence is needed to insure that the victim's care level will not fall short of due care even if he is compensated immediately after the accident (what we have called the ex ante approach). Since the victim's expected compensation equals either pD^* or paD^{**}, it will offset exactly his expected incremental damages from an accident of $p(a - b)D$ (see equation [4b]). After subtracting expected compensation, his expected losses will be $bD + A(x)$. But by assumption x has no effect on b, so victim care will be zero.

---

[25] We say "even if there is no defense of contributory negligence" because in the usual analysis of strict liability (without a defense of contributory negligence) the victim takes less than due care. He is fully compensated for his injury, so taking care imposes a cost on the victim without an offsetting benefit to him. This in turn reduces his incentive to take care.

[26] The ex post approach (compensating victims when the full-blown injury occurs but discounting damages by $(a - b)/a$) also yields x^*. After the accident (but before compensation) the victim's expected damages plus costs of care equal $(a - b)D + bD + A(x)$. Subtracting his award discounted by the probability of developing cancer (aD^{**}) yields $bD + A(x)$. Minimizing the latter with respect to x yields x^*.

[27] See, for example, Prosser, *supra* note 16, at 422–23.

And yet the problem of too little victim care may not actually be a serious one in the example under consideration. Although a high-fiber diet or refraining from smoking may have a bigger impact on a than on b (the essential assumption of our analysis), still both are likely to have significant effects on reducing b.[28] When one discounts that slightly greater effect on a than b by the small probability of a nuclear reactor accident, the incremental expected benefit of additional care is likely to be negligible. So, interestingly, it may not be important to have a doctrine of contributory negligence (limited to pre-accident carelessness) in catastrophic accident cases.

Now consider victim care that is undertaken only after an accident occurs (after care), but before the consequences of the accident are felt. For example, suppose switching to a high-fiber diet or cutting out smoking reduces the probability of developing cancer only if one has been exposed to excessive radiation. From equation (4a) we know that due care requires $-a_x D = A_x$,[29] and we consider the choice between compensating all potential victims immediately after the accident by D^* per victim (see equation [6])—the ex ante approach—and compensating victims who subsequently develop cancer by D^{**} per victim (see equation [7])—the ex post approach. Under the former approach, each victim, after receiving compensation for the possibility of future harm, still faces an expected harm of $(a - b)D + bD$, and to minimize this he will set $-a_x D = A_x$, which yields the due care level, x^*. In short, having been compensated initially, the victim has the appropriate incentive to take due care, since he receives its full benefits—lower expected harm in the future. In contrast, if compensation is delayed until an exposed person develops cancer, potential victims will not have adequate incentives to take care even if we assume that their compensation is discounted by the probability that they would have developed cancer anyway. After the accident, each victim's expected compensation is aD^{**} (we multiply D^{**} by the probability of developing cancer). Deducting this expected future compensation yields $(a - b)D + bD - aD^{**} + A(x)$. Substituting for aD^{**} yields an expected loss of $bD + A(x)$, and hence the victim takes no care. (Of course, this assumes rather unrealistically that monetary compensation for a cancer injury is completely adequate.)

The economic literature on tort law contains a parallel analysis, the

---

[28] We can show this as follows. Assume $-a_x > -b_x > 0$. Due care requires (for prior care) $p(a_x - b_x)D + b_x D + A_x = 0$. Under strict liability, the victim sets $b_x D + A_x = 0$. This yields less than due care, but not much less if both p and the difference between a_x and b_x are small.

[29] We have $L = NpaD + N(1 - p)bD + NpA(x) + B(y)$, which yields $a_x D + A_x = 0$.

choice between periodic and lump-sum payments in compensation for a continuing tort such as a nuisance.[30] The argument for the lump sum is that it does not impair the victim's incentive to invest in avoiding future harm from the continuing tort. The potentially offsetting advantage of periodic payment is that it gives the injurer an incentive to develop ways of avoiding future harm. But this observation is inapplicable to the present case, because after the accident has occurred there is nothing the injurer can do to reduce its consequences as they unfold over the future; those consequences can be avoided only by the victims' investing in care, as by changing diet or quitting smoking.

VI. CONCLUSION

In view of the many criticisms that have been leveled against regulation, it would be a shame to give up on tort law as a method of regulating safety in cases of catastrophic accident without careful consideration of its actual and potential resources as a system of safety regulation. The problem of limited solvency is, we have suggested, (1) overstated and (2) perhaps a better argument for using a negligence rather than strict liability standard than for switching to regulation. The problem of causal uncertainty and long delay between accident and full-blown injury could, we have suggested, perhaps be solved by moving toward a system where the accident victim sues and obtains a judgment before his injury is full blown. This approach also has attractive properties in dealing with the serious problem of giving victims of catastrophic accidents incentives to make "life-style" changes that will reduce the severity of the delayed consequences of such accidents. Of course there are many practical problems in making such a proposal work that we have not discussed (among them the problem of causal apportionment when there are multiple injurers, which we have discussed briefly elsewhere)[31]—but regulation has its own very serious practical problems.

[30] See, for example, Richard A. Posner, Economic Analysis of Law 47–48 (2d ed. 1977).

[31] See William M. Landes & Richard A. Posner, Joint and Multiple Tortfeasors: An Economic Approach, 9 J. Legal Stud. 517, 540–41 (1980).

Part II
Applications

Conceptual Models

[13]

Journal of Real Estate Finance and Economics, 12: 37–58 (1996)
© 1996 Kluwer Academic Publishers

The Effects of Environmental Liability on Industrial Real Estate Development

JAMES BOYD
Resources for the Future, 1616 P Street, NW, Washington, DC 20036

WINSTON HARRINGTON
Resources for the Future, 1616 P Street, NW, Washington, DC 20036

MOLLY K. MACAULEY[1]
Resources for the Future, 1616 P Street, NW, Washington, DC 20036

Abstract

The paper explores the effects of current liability law on real estate transactions involving properties with potential environmental contamination. Sources of uncertainty and their likely impact on transactions are identified. Liability-driven market distortions are likely to be due less to legal uncertainty than to problems arising from asymmetric information and imperfect detection.

Key Words: liability, uncertainty, industrial redevelopment

Does the 1980 Comprehensive Environmental Response, Compensation, and Liability Act (CERCLA) inhibit the sale and redevelopment of industrial property, channeling growth away from older established urban areas ("brownfield" sites) and toward suburban or rural locations ("greenfield" sites)?[2] Many commercial real estate developers and experts believe that the effect of potential liability on property transfers is adverse and substantial. The concern has generated significant public debate, ranging from Congressional proposals to legislate the redevelopment and reuse of contaminated land, to calls by lenders and borrowers to free property transactions from onerous environmental liability provisions.[3] In a recent survey of its members, the Independent Bankers Association of America found that one out of five banks surveyed reported a mortgage loss or default due to environmental contamination, and seven out of ten indicated that there are some classes of loans their institution will not write due to environmental liability concerns.[4] Corporate financial officers and corporate managers of real estate also report that potential liability has affected their location, expansion, and other real estate decisions and has increased the amount of nonperforming contaminated property held on balance sheets.[5] The environmental concern is that a shift from brownfield redevelopment to greenfield development will contribute to urban sprawl and have a correspondingly negative impact on environmental conditions.

There is a common, but flawed, perception that development of greenfield sites necessarily enjoys a cost advantage over brownfield development. On the contrary, commercial or industrial development of greenfield sites is itself costly, as zoning laws and community opposition can often impede such development. More generally, pollution liabilities themselves do not necessarily increase the relative desirability of greenfield sites. The reason is that land prices fall to adjust for the disadvantage of owning a contaminated site, if a property is known to be polluted. In theory, the real estate market will lead current owners of polluted property to discount sales prices to account for pollution remediation or liability costs.[6] Otherwise identical properties that vary only in their level of contamination will sell for different prices. This implies that pollution *per se* does not inhibit efficient property transactions.

If pollution itself does not impede desirable trades, then what does? Even in cases where the buyer and seller both stand to gain from trade, can uncertainties associated with environmental liability reduce their willingness to engage in trade? This was the conclusion of a recent Michigan report concerning urban development and environmental liability:

> The key to encouraging reinvestment in contaminated urban properties by the private sector is through reducing uncertainty. Better information is needed by local units of government, developers, and investors on the laws establishing liability for past contamination problems and cleanup requirements.[7]

In this paper we examine whether CERCLA has the potential for distorting development decisions in this way, and the degree to which distortions reduce the efficiency of real estate markets. We develop a simple model to examine how CERCLA liability can modify the terms of trade and incentives for real estate redevelopment. We find that CERCLA-driven uncertainties do not *necessarily* reduce the likelihood of efficient property transfers and development decisions, even when sellers and buyers are risk averse. However, we show that information asymmetries between buyers and sellers and imperfections in the detection and regulation of liability likely have a more substantial negative effect on property development.

The remainder of the paper is organized as follows. Section 1 offers a context for our research by noting general trends in urban decline that predate CERCLA and the widespread imposition of environmental liability. This underscores the point that a variety of factors discourage brownfield development independent of any liability-driven distortions. This section also briefly describes CERCLA and related legislation. Section 2 presents a model of property markets in the presence of liability-generated uncertainty and risk aversion. We motivate this section through discussion of two sources of uncertainty that attend the regulation of environmental liability—uncertainty over the existence and size of liability, and uncertainty over allocation of liabilities between former and current owners. Our model shows that, contrary to many policy-makers' conventional wisdom, uncertainty alone, even in the presence of risk aversion, need not distort property markets. We note, however, that uncertainty and owner risk aversion can create distributional effects that help to explain the fervor of complaints regarding uncertainty. In this section we also discuss the beneficial role that the enforcement of indemnification contracts plays in helping to reduce uncertainty and any socially undesirable distortions that do arise. Section 3 is a brief discussion of information asymmetries between buyers and sellers and a corresponding chilling effect on property transactions. Section 4 considers imperfections in the enforcement of environmental regulation and their potential to reduce the efficiency of property markets. Section 5 offers conclusions.

1. The Economic and Legal Context of Brownfield Redevelopment

1.1. General Urban Decline

The effects of environmental legislation on real estate development must be understood in the context of the overall economic condition of urban areas. Clearly, urban decline in the United States began long before the enactment of CERCLA and related federal and state environmental legislation, and many of the conditions that appeared to be driving this decline in the recent past are still with us. The economic decline in central cities in most United States metropolitan areas results from two concurrent trends (which are not fundamentally environmentally related): (i) shifts of economic activity away from the urban areas in the Northeast and Midwest to urban areas in the South and West, and (ii) the suburbanization of population and employment in all urban areas. Both trends were underway by the end of World War II, but the interregional migration from the "rust belt" to the "sun belt" became most obvious in the 1970s.[8]

Of key importance in considering brownfield redevelopment is that both trends have also involved the shutdown of thousands of factories, warehouses, distribution centers, and retail outlets. The loss of a major employer in a region sets in motion a train of mutually reinforcing consequences—loss of other services, increased crime, increased welfare dependency and the like—that can extend blight over a much wider area. Many old industrial areas, particularly in the Northeast, are now replete with industrial sites that sit idle or are at best underutilized, and many have been abandoned altogether. These sites can be found even in cities not suffering from employment declines, where profound changes in the mix of employment have led to permanent plant shutdowns.

Numerous explanations have been put forth to explain the decline of cities, none altogether satisfactory. Inasmuch as social scientists do not have a very good theory to explain why cities are formed and why they prosper, there can be no conclusive explanation of their decline. To a considerable degree the decline has been driven by powerful and in many respects beneficial forces: rising real incomes, secular declines in transportation and energy costs, and advances in technology that make central location a less important source of competitive advantage.[9] These large-scale economic forces are largely impervious to public intervention.

The questions of why there is so much derelict industrial land in cities and why these sites are so difficult to develop are at the heart of industrial location theory. A review of that literature is outside the scope of this paper,[10] although it is relevant to note that among the conclusions in the literature, the empirical evidence of the effect of environmental regulation on land use is ambiguous.[11] Researchers in general have yet to find a systematic relationship between environmental regulation and corporate location decisions.

1.2. CERCLA and Related Statutes

The legislation that provides a mechanism for the U.S. Environmental Protection Agency (EPA) to identify and clean up sites posing imminent risks to human health or the environment includes the 1980 Comprehensive Environmental Response, Compensation and Liability

Act (CERCLA, better known as Superfund) and the 1986 Superfund Amendments and Reauthorization Act (SARA). Approximately 33,000 sites have been placed on the CERCLIS list as potentially hazardous sites (CERCLIS is the CERCLA Information System, a data base of sites which have been or need to be evaluated under Superfund). Among sites evaluated as of 1993, about 1,200 sites have been placed on the National Priorities List (NPL).[12] Properties on the NPL fall under federal EPA jurisdiction and are eligible for Superfund funding.

Under Superfund, EPA attempts to identify the Potentially Responsible Parties (PRPs) in order to extract from them the cost of remediating the contamination on a site. Ideally, PRPs fund the cleanup up-front. However, if EPA cannot initially identify PRPs or if the PRPs are recalcitrant, then the EPA may proceed with the cleanup, at federal government expense, and later sue the PRP in order to recover the costs.[13]

According to CERCLA, PRPs include past and present owners and operators of a polluted site and firms that arranged for the treatment, disposal, or transportation of hazardous substances at the site.[14] Superfund liability is strict, joint and several, and retroactive. Strict liability implies liability even if the PRP can demonstrate appropriate handling and disposal of hazardous substances. Frequently, one or more of the individuals or firms responsible for the contamination no longer exist. Joint and several liability implies that a solvent PRP can be held fully responsible for remediation costs even if it was just one of several contributors to the contamination. Retroactive liability implies PRP liability even if contamination resulted from actions that occurred prior to passage of Superfund in 1980.[15]

As will be discussed in more detail, several provisions of the law directly bear on the way transferred ownership of a site redefines the liabilities of former and current owners. In addition, while secured lenders have ownership rights when a borrowing owner defaults, CERCLA excludes from liablity "a person who, without participating in the management of a vessel or facility, holds indicia of ownership primarily to protect his security interest in the vessel or facility."[16]

Superfund is only one element of a greater patchwork of legal rules and regulations that can create uncertain liability for property owners. First, property owners who are not liable under CERCLA may nevertheless be liable under state law.[17] For example, under Pennsylvania law, if contamination is present within a 2500-foot radius of a site, it is assumed that the responsible parties for the site are liable for the contamination, even if causality or contamination pathways are uncertain.[18] In New Jersey, the Spill Compensation and Control Act allows for, among other things, treble damages in the event of noncompliance with certain regulatory orders. States are responsible for the bulk of enforcement activities (including site detection and federal notification), many have their own priority lists and cleanup funds, and most define site remediation standards for those sites pursued independently of the federal government.[19] In addition, some political subdivisions (for example, counties and municipalities) have authority to bring environmental liability actions against PRPs.[20] In general, then, many states have independent authority to force cleanups and impose liability on PRPs.

Many state programs also involve the regulation of facilities falling under subtitles C, D, and I of the Resource Conservation and Recovery Act (RCRA).[21] Liabilities may arise, for instance, based on a state's regulatory approach to leaking underground storage tanks, as allowed under RCRA. Moreover, property owners are increasingly wary of sites with possible asbestos contamination or other hazards that can prompt regulatory or third-party liability actions.[22] These risks create potentially serious, but non-CERCLA, financial liability. Thus, it is important to emphasize that Superfund is only one element of a greater patchwork of regulations and legal rules that influence incentives and govern the consequences of environmental contamination.

2. A Model of Uncertainty, Risk Aversion, and Brownfield Property Markets

If uncertainty increases the perceived costs of development, then brownfield properties that should be traded may not be traded. In turn, if the demand for brownfield properties is reduced in this way then demand for the closest substitute—greenfield properties—will increase. This section addresses the question of whether such a distortion in property markets is likely to arise given the uncertainties associated with environmental liability.

CERCLA can subject both present and past owners of real estate to potentially significant liabilities for environmental contamination. Both the size of and responsibility for these liabilities are uncertain. In this section we develop a model to describe how buyers and sellers of property respond to these possibilities. We focus on two aspects of uncertainty: uncertainty over the existence and size of liabilities, and uncertainty over the allocation of liability costs between current and former real estate holders. The model is preceded by a discussion of these sources of uncertainty.

2.1. Uncertainty Associated with the Existence and Size of Liability

This source of uncertainty is associated with the processes of site assessment, listing, and remedy selection. The environmental evaluation of a site is the first step in the process of determining whether a site is contaminated and in ranking sites on the basis of their health and ecological risks. It is therefore a key determinant of subsequent regulatory scrutiny and a signal of potential cleanup costs. The evaluation can employ either CERCLA's hazard ranking system (HRS) or state programs' ranking systems. While the quantitative standards employed by these systems provide some consistency across sites, the criteria used can differ between the federal system and state systems.[23] Moreover, there are numerous uncertainties inherent in the data and risk analysis that form the basis of these rankings. Thus, from the perspective of a current or potential property owner, the outcome of the preliminary site evaluation and listing process is highly unpredictable.

Once a site is slated for cleanup, it is still difficult to predict the cost of site remediation that will be mandated by the government. There is no consistent, objective standard for the level of risk to which a site must be returned. Also, remedial action decisions may not conform to the requirements of the law.[24] In general, individual cleanups are viewed as unique problems requiring unique solutions, there is a great deal of bureaucratic latitude in the remedy selection process, and too little attention seems paid to the development of cleanup goals and definitions. For instance, acceptable risk has many interpretations. There is also no way, even after a site remedy has been completed, to know if the cleanup is permanent because no statutory or administrative definition of a completed cleanup exists.

The unpredictability of the system is exacerbated by the fact that negotiations between potentially responsible parties and the government do not begin, nor is a site's status clarified by the government, until a property has been officially listed on the NPL. Barring a listing, there may be a realistic threat of enforcement but the costs of enforcement cannot be adequately estimated. Moreover, the regionalized management approach to Superfund means that remedies may differ significantly across regions. And again, enforcement actions brought by the states, rather than those pursued by the EPA, may imply very different remediation requirements. Thus, the assessment, listing, and remedy selection processes create significant uncertainty regarding the ultimate costs of a contaminated site.

2.2. Uncertainty Associated with the Allocation of Liability

CERCLA and state statutes have also created uncertainty regarding whether the purchaser or, alternatively, whether the seller of a property is liable for cleanup costs. While the common law typically presumes a rule of *caveat emptor*, or "buyer beware," enforcement of CERCLA allows current owners or the government to sue previous owners for cleanup costs if the condition of the property was not adequately revealed at point of sale—even when the transaction agreement explicitly transfers liability (via an "as is" clause). To quote a New Jersey Supreme Court opinion "a real estate contract that does not disclose [an] abnormally dangerous condition or activity does not shield from liability the seller who created that condition or engaged in that activity."[25] Also, a buyer beware defense will not be honored if a contaminated property was sold to a thinly capitalized firm in an attempt to have liability transferred to an enterprise that is effectively unable to pay for cleanup costs. In general, courts are not guaranteed to accept a former property owner's defense that the property was sold based on an understanding of caveat emptor.[26]

However, limiting the seller's defense of caveat emptor does not mean that the buyer is necessarily absolved of liability. Indeed, the definition of liability under CERCLA directly implies that current property owners may be liable for pollution created by previous owners. "Innocent landowner" provisions, which set forth the conditions under which a new owner will not be liable for pollution created by a previous owner are an important legal device to reduce these uncertainties. The innocent landowner defense requires that the purchaser (1) did not contribute to the contamination, (2) made all appropriate inquiry to detect the presence of contamination, (3) took due care once waste was discovered, and (4) acquired the property at a price which did not signal the presence of possible contamination.[27] While these provisions are more precisely defined than they were at CERCLA's inception, they still do not remove uncertainties associated with ownership. For instance, a landowner may not be found innocent if the property was purchased at a particularly low price. This is justifiable since a low price can be a signal of contamination to the buyer, thus making them knowledgeable of the risk. However, courts may have difficulty in objectively determining how low a low price is.[28] As another example, allowing the spread of contamination from leaking storage tanks and drums disposed of by a previous owner has been found to constitute a release under CERCLA, thus leaving the new owner liable.[29] Moreover, there is no consistent standard of qualification for having made "all appropriate inquiry" to discover contamination.[30]

Case law based on CERCLA has also expanded the conditions under which a successor corporation must bear the liabilities of firms it acquires. The traditional test held that a successor remained liable for the predecessors' liability only if the new owner represented a "mere continuation" of the former enterprise. Liability was transferred, then, only when the successor was judged to be new in name only. The new, broader test imposes liability based on whether there was a "continuation of enterprise." This judgment hinges on the degree of shareholder, officer and director continuity. It also treats as relevant whether the product being created is the same as before the takeover. As such, this new test does not require perfect continuity of corporate structure or ownership to establish successor liability.[31] Given this test, the set of parties that is potentially liable is expanded. With such an expansion, any one current or future property owner's liability contribution is made less certain.

2.3. The Model

The preceding discussion is intended in part to explain the tenor of conventional wisdom that expresses significant concern about the uncertainty associated with environmental liability statutes. The model below shows that uncertainty *per se* need not lead to inefficiency in property markets. However, market distortions can arise in the model if attitudes towards uncertainty—risk aversion—markedly differ between buyers and sellers. The model also indicates that uncertainty and risk aversion can affect the *distribution* of gains from trade— and these distributional effects, rather than market distortions, may well explain why concern over liability uncertainty figures so prominently in public debate.

Let U_i, V_i, Y_i denote respectively the utility, valuation of the property and income of individual i, $i = B, S$ (buyer and seller). $U_i = U_i(Y_i, \delta)$, where $\delta = 1$ or 0 depending on whether individual i owns ($\delta = 1$) or does not own ($\delta = 0$) the property. Let q denote the probability that the site is contaminated (or rather, that contamination at the site is discovered) and L the damages associated with a contaminated site. Assume $V_S < V_B$ so that, in the absence of contamination, trade can take place at a price p ($V_S < p < V_B$), that is beneficial to both parties. V_B and V_S at income Y are defined as follows:

$$U_B(Y, 0) = U_B(Y - V_B, 1)$$

$$U_S(Y, 1) = U_S(Y + V_S, 0) \tag{1}$$

Suppose the action takes place in three periods: In period 0 contamination may or may not have occurred. In period 1 a transaction may or may not take place, and in period 2 the benefits are enjoyed, contamination (if any) is discovered, and damages are suffered. For the trade to take place, the utilities of both the buyer and the seller must be higher after the trade than before.

If the site is contaminated, let z, $0 \leq z \leq 1$, be the probability that the seller (i.e., the original owner) is responsible for any contamination discovered subsequently. If no trade takes place, $z = 1$. Table 1 shows the gains from trade, for various outcomes, to both parties when the property is or is not traded at a price p. For ease of comparing buyer

Table 1. Distribution of gains between buyer and seller.

(a) Without Transaction:

Contamination Discovered	Seller is Liable	Probability	Seller Utility	Buyer Utility
No	—	$1 - q$	$U_S(Y_S, 1)$	$U_B(Y_B, 0)$
Yes	Yes	q	$U_S(Y_S - L, 1)$	$U_B(Y_B, 0)$

(b) With Transaction:

Contamination Discovered	Seller is Liable	Probability	Seller Utility	Buyer Utility
No	—	$1 - q$	$U_S(Y_S + p - V_S - L, 1)$	$U_B(Y_B - p + V_B, 0)$
Yes	Yes	qz	$U_S(Y_S + p - V_S - L, 1)$	$U_B(Y_B - p + V_B, 0)$
Yes	No	$q(1 - z)$	$U_S(Y_S + p - V_S, 1)$	$U_B(Y_B - p + V_B - L, 0)$

and seller utilities with and without the sale, the table makes liberal use of definition (1). For example, the seller's utility after the sale at the price p is

$$U_S(Y_S + p, 0) = U_S(Y_S + p - V_S, 1).$$

(i) *No sale.* The possible gains in terms of seller and buyer utility are shown in Table 1(a). Without a sale the prospective buyer has no expected gain and no risk. For the seller (the current owner), the expected value of retaining ownership is

$$E_{NoSale}^S = (1 - q)U_S(Y_S, 1) + qU_S(Y_S - L, 1) \tag{2}$$

Define the seller's risk aversion $\Delta_S = \Delta_S(Y_S, q, L)$ implicitly as follows:

$$U_S(Y_S - qL - \Delta_S, 1) = qU_S(Y_S - L, 1) + (1 - q)U_S(Y_S, 1) \tag{3}$$

Δ_S is the certainty equivalent of the contamination lottery; concavity of the utility function ensures that $\Delta_S > 0$. We will assume that the risk aversion Δ_S is constant with respect to income and increasing in the magnitude of loss L. Note that $\Delta_S(Y_S, 0, L) = \Delta_S(Y_S, 1, L) = 0$, as certain events generate no risk aversion, and that

$$E_{NoSale}^S = U_S(Y_S - qL - \Delta_S(Y_S, q, L), 1) \tag{4}$$

(ii) *Sale.* If the sale takes place, the possibilities are given in Table 1(b). For the seller the expected utility of getting rid of the property is

$$E_{Sale}^S = (1 - qz)U_S(Y_S + p, 0) + qzU_S(Y_S + p - L, 0)$$

$$= (1 - qz)U_S(Y_S + p - V_S, 1) + qzU_S(Y_S + p - V_S - L, 1)$$

$$= U_S(Y_S + p - V_S - qzL - \Delta_S(Y_S + p - V_S, qz, L), 1) \tag{5}$$

Comparison of (4) and (5) shows that the current owner is willing to sell if

$$p > V_S - q(1 - z)L - [\Delta_S(Y_S, q, L) - \Delta_S(Y_S + p - V_S, qz, L)] \tag{6}$$

For the buyer the expected utility of acquiring and developing the property is

$$E_S^B = (1 - q(1 - z))U_B(Y_B - p + V_B, 1) + q(1 - z)U_B(Y_B - p + V_B - L, 1)$$

$$= U_B(Y_B + V_B - p - q(1 - z)L - \Delta_B(Y_B, q(1 - z), L), 1) \tag{7}$$

It is willing to purchase if

$$p < V_B - q(1 - z)L - \Delta_B(Y_B, q(1 - z), L) \tag{8}$$

The buyer's maximum willingness to pay is clearly less than its willingness to pay (i.e., V_B) in the absence of uncertainty. The total profit from trade is the difference between the buyer's maximum willingness to pay and the seller's minimum willingness to accept, or the difference between the right-hand sides of (6) and (8). First, consider the two polar cases $z = 1$ and $z = 0$.

If the seller is liable with certainty ($z = 1$), regardless of ownership, then the trade will take place given a p such that

$$V_S - [\Delta_S(Y_S, q, L) - \Delta_S(Y_S + p, q, L)] < p < V_B \tag{9}$$

Since by assumption the risk aversion is inelastic with respect to income, (9) simplifies to $V_S < p < V_B$. Thus, the gain from trade is not reduced by the presence of the environmental risk. The reason is clear: if the liability risk resides with the current owner irrespective of whether or not they sell the property, then it is in the seller's interest to sell whenever $V_S < p$. Since the buyer will not inherit any liability risk in this scenario they will be willing to purchase at any price $p < V_B$.

If the buyer is liable with certainty ($z = 0$), the seller transfers its liability risks through sale (of course, retained ownership retains the risk). In this case, the trade will take place when

$$V_S - qL - \Delta_S(Y_S, q, L) < p < V_B - qL - \Delta_B(Y_B, q, L) \tag{10}$$

The more risk-averse is the seller, the greater the incentive to sell the property and transfer the liability risk. Whether the gains from trade are now greater or smaller than in the no-uncertainty case depends on the relative magnitudes of the buyer's and seller's risk aversion. If the magnitudes are the same ($\Delta_B = \Delta_S$), then the risk-neutral gains from trade are identical to the risk-adjusted gains from trade and there will be no distortion in the decision to transfer the property. When buyer and seller risk aversion are identical, the disutility of ownership (due to the liability risk) is independent of who owns the property and therefore the gains from trade reflect only the difference in V_B and V_S.

Now, consider the case where potential buyers are more risk-loving than sellers. Sites at risk of having liabilities, it could be argued, will tend to attract more risk-loving buyers who can profit from the seller's risk aversion.[32] In this case, liability uncertainty will not discourage a buyer who values the property more than a seller from acquiring the property. In fact, if the disparity between preferences for risk is great enough, in principle, properties may trade even if $V_B < V_S$.

Only if potential buyers are more risk averse than sellers will the costs of uncertainty keep efficient property transfers from occurring (those where $V_B > V_S$). In this case, a greenfield distortion may occur since the result is a restriction in the supply of brownfield properties. With supply restricted, developers will substitute their property acquisitions to greenfield properties. This is inefficient since there will be brownfield properties where $V_B > V_S$.

If the assignment of liability is uncertain ($0 < z < 1$), then the expression for the gains from trade is

$$V_S - [\Delta_S(Y_S + p, qz, L) - \Delta_S(Y_S, q, L)] < p < V_B - \Delta_B(Y_B, q(1 - z), L) \quad (11)$$

In this case uncertainty may increase or decrease the gains from trade, depending on the parties' relative risk aversion.

Regardless of the implications of relative risk aversion for the efficiency of the property market, risk aversion will have a distributional effect on the buyer and seller. For example, in the most plausible case where the seller is more risk averse than the buyer, the seller is penalized by its own risk aversion.[33] To see this, assume the transaction price splits the gains from trade and a risk averse seller trades with a risk-neutral buyer. Comparing (6) to the risk-neutral willingness to accept $p > V_S$ indicates that the seller's reservation price will be lower when the seller is risk averse, thus implying a distributional loss to the seller.

It is important to emphasize that the model's focus is on the efficiency of real estate transactions given liability law, and not on the law's global efficiency. For instance, the damages L imposed on the buyer or seller may not be equal to the true social loss. If so, firms' environmental safety investments and product prices may be either inefficiently high or low. But that form of inefficiency need not imply inefficient property transactions. Conversely, inefficient transactions may arise even if damages L are set optimally. Central to the efficiency of property transactions is whether liability distorts the incentive to buy and sell by creating *differential* costs or benefits to ownership. This point is underscored in the sections below.

3. Inefficiencies Due to Asymmetric Information

The analysis above assumed that potential buyers are as well informed as the seller about the environmental condition of the property. But what if, as is typically the case, the seller is better informed about the environmental quality of the parcel than potential buyers? In this section we discuss the potential for property market distortions that arise when there is an information asymmetry of this kind between the seller and possible buyers.

3.1. Adverse Selection

If liability is transferred with the property, buyers are in effect purchasing an asset of unknown quality—where quality in this sense refers to the liability it is inheriting through purchase. In this context, the information asymmetry between seller and buyers can create an adverse selection problem. As in a traditional lemons problem, buyers may discount their demand for properties based on an average expectation of liability. This discount in demand—and willingness to pay—leads high-quality property owners (those with relatively unpolluted properties) to exit the market. In turn, the buyer discount is adjusted downward to reflect the rational expectation that clean properties will not be represented in the market. The result is an adverse selection problem—in which high quality properties are not brought to market.[34]

Given this information problem alone, the inefficiency can be reduced or eliminated via contracting. An optimal contract requires that sellers provide full insurance (a warranty) against a level of product quality that is not faithfully revealed at the point of sale. With property transactions, this type of warranty can be implemented either through (1) enforcement of "duty to warn" laws, which impose liability on the original owner for misrepresentation of the environmental condition of the property or (2) an indemnity contract—as described in the previous section—that guarantees the previous owner's liability irrespective of its representations.

The effectiveness of such warranties can be limited, however. First, the original owner may have difficulty guaranteeing that it will be available to bear liabilities (and thus offer an effective warranty) in the future. If the original owner is shallow-pocketed or already insolvent it cannot be expected to meet the terms of the warranty. Indeed, a firm may actively seek to divest itself of assets after the point of sale in order to discourage the imposition of liability costs.[35] If the original owner is not able to satisfy its liabilities, the new owner may be jointly and severally liable. As a result, sellers may not be able to provide a credible warranty. Of course, a noncredible warranty fails as a signal of product quality, thus reintroducing the adverse selection problem.

3.2. Moral Hazard

In addition, warranties can introduce buyer moral hazard. Moral hazard arises if the new owner—being "insured" by the warranty—can take actions that increase the seller's expected liability. Three potential forms of moral hazard can arise in property markets. First, the new owner itself may contribute to the pollution of the site. If the environmental quality of the parcel was uncertain to begin with (the source of adverse selection) a new owner may be able to add to the site's contamination and claim that it is the previous owner's responsibility.[36] Second, if the new owner is insured against liabilities associated with the site it has an increased incentive to scrutinize the site's environmental conditions. Should any source of contamination be revealed post-sale, the new owner might draw this to the attention of regulatory authorities and seek enforcement actions against the former owner.[37] That is, the sale might increase the probability that contamination is discovered and costs are imposed on the former owner.[38]

A third source of moral hazard arises if future damages are affected by the type or extent of development. This can happen, for example, if new structures built at the site make cleanup more difficult, or if more intensive use of the site increases the number of persons exposed to contaminants. Perhaps the most problematic case occurs if contamination, severe enough to enjoin further use of the site, is discovered after nonmoveable investments at the site are made. In that case the former owner may be liable for original (predevelopment) losses plus the new owner's lost, sunk investment.[39]

3.3. An Example

To see how moral hazard leads to inefficient outcomes in this situation, suppose the prospective buyer is deciding between two types of investment in a given property, with benefits (in the absence of contamination) of V_B^1 and V_B^2, respectively. Also, suppose the current owner of the property is liable for damages of L_1 with probability q. Finally, suppose the second investment yields larger gross benefits ($V_B^2 > V_B^1$), but also larger potential losses. If the property is contaminated, we assume the first investment implies damages L_1 while the second would increase the damages to $L_2 > L_1$. The current owner's valuation of the property (without contamination) is V_S; this is the no-development value of the property.

To find the efficient outcome, we compare the expected gains under the three alternatives as shown in the second column of Table 2 (we continue to assume social risk neutrality). In particular, Investment 1 will be the efficient outcome whenever $V_B^1 > V_S$ and $V_B^1 > V_B^2 - q(L_2 - L_1)$. If the seller is liable for damages, however, there is no price at which the property will trade that will produce this result. When the sale price is p, the buyer's expected gain under the three alternative decisions is shown in the third column of Table 2.

For the buyer, investment 1 is dominated by the other two choices. If the sale price is too high, the transaction will not take place. If the transaction does take place, investment 2 will be chosen. Moral hazard thus promotes either excessive development or not enough. Since sellers are aware that once they sell the property they will have little control over decisions that can affect their liability, the latter outcome is the more likely. Moreover, seller risk aversion will exacerbate this tendency to withhold property from the market.

3.4. Indemnity

To the extent that uncertainty over the allocation of liability, combined with risk aversion, distorts property transfer decisions it is instructive to consider the role of indemnity

Table 2. Social versus private benefits of development in the presence of moral hazard.

Outcome	Expected Social Benefit	Buyer's Expected Gain
No purchase	$V_S - qL_1$	0
Investment 1	$V_B^1 - qL_1$	$V_B^1 - p$
Investment 2	$V_B^2 - qL_2$	$V_B^2 - p$

agreements in reducing such risks. At the point of transaction sellers and buyers can enter into indemnity agreements (often in the form of "hold harmless" clauses), which contractually assign liabilities to one or the other party. The advantage of such contractual arrangements is that they allow buyers and sellers to limit and insure against environmental liabilities. This in principle can reduce or eliminate uncertainty over who will be liable.[40]

The existing regulatory approach to environmental cleanup limits the effectiveness of contractual mechanisms for defining liability, however. These agreements are limited in scope relative to the numerous ways in which a property owner can be found liable under CERCLA and state statutes, and are easily contestable, both by the government and by other PRPs. The validity of indemnity contracts is largely left to state law and no uniform federal law exists, again creating jurisdictional uncertainty. This is particularly true since courts have been unclear about whether indemnity contracts are valid under CERCLA. Disagreement has surrounded section 107(e), which states that

> no indemnification, hold harmless, or similar agreement or conveyance shall be effective to transfer from the owner or operator of any vessel or facility or from any person who may be liable for a release or threat of release under this section, to any other person the liability imposed under this section.[41]

Courts also will not honor indemnity agreements made between a former owner and an undercapitalized successor since such arrangements can constitute a fraudulent attempt to escape liability.[42] Conversely, if a deep-pocketed firm purchases a property from a potentially insolvent predecessor, an indemnity agreement which absolves the buyer would not likely be honored.

It is also important to emphasize that an indemnity agreement between a buyer and seller does not prohibit liability claims brought by the government or other PRPs against the buyer. Indemnity simply allows the buyer, once the buyer has been sued and found liable, to, in turn, sue the original owner for the amount of the indemnity. As a result, indemnity agreements do not exempt any current or former property owner from the CERCLA liability process itself.[43] For these reasons, while indemnity contracts can in principle reduce liability-driven uncertainty, their practical effectiveness should not be viewed over-optimistically.[44] These forms of moral hazard impose costs on the transaction that in some cases may outweigh the benefits of a warranty to reduce the adverse selection problem. If so, the inefficiencies in the property market generated by uncertain environmental quality will not be resolved through available contractual mechanisms.[45]

4. Distortions Arising from Imperfect Detection

Risk aversion and asymmetric information are not the only potential sources of distortions in brownfields development. An additional concern arises due to the imperfect detection of pollution sources. In this section, we show that even when firms are risk neutral and buyers and sellers have perfect information, imperfect liability enforcement alone can distort property transactions.

Given limited enforcement budgets and the large costs of observing and assessing pollution risks, the government's ability to detect contaminated sites is imperfect. This, along with the fact that most formerly industrial sites are at least minimally contaminated implies a vast number of undetected properties where cleanups could be currently compelled under state and federal law. For this reason, it may be in the interest of those who currently own brownfield properties to withhold them from the market. The increased probability of detection that accompanies a sale in effect imposes a property transfer tax that can lead to deadweight losses in brownfield property markets. This distortion underlies the following type of complaint, made in arguments for a recent environmental liability reform initiative in the Pennsylvania Senate:

> Companies in Pittsburgh, Johnstown, and other communities have deliberately let industrial property stand idle indefinitely rather than even look to see what contamination might exist because they were afraid to deal with state environmental agencies.[46]

CERCLA requires that contamination be reported once discovered. However, it is unrealistic to assume that all contaminated properties have been drawn to regulators' attention.[47] First, the law does not compel the discovery of environmental risks, only that they be reported once discovered. Second, most states rely primarily on complaints, referrals, or whistleblowing to discover polluted sites. An effective means of avoiding detection and knowledge of contamination is to keep property off the real estate market.

While site assessments are costly and imperfect and regulatory intervention is uncertain even if site contamination is discovered, putting property on the market increases the probability of detection. As argued earlier, it is in a buyer's interest to undertake a site assessment, particularly when the site being purchased was formerly used for industrial purposes. In addition, it is likely that a mortgage lender will seek an assessment even if the buyer does not.[48] Moreover, the risk assessment professionals hired by the lender, buyer, or seller have an interest in faithfully representing their findings, since to fail to do so can result in their own liability.[49] These factors favor the conduct of an assessment, and the assessment in turn leads to documentation of the existing risk and the possibility of prompting scrutiny and enforcement action from the EPA or relevant state agency.[50]

Since property transfers create private incentives for detection (principally on the part of buyers and lenders), imperfect detection implies that expected liability costs increase when a property is traded. The "wedge" in the probability of detection can lead to the withdrawal of brownfield properties from the market. For several reasons, it is socially undesirable for current owners to withhold property to avoid detection. First, developers who can extract more value from the property than the current owner will not be able to purchase it and the resource will therefore be inefficiently utilized (there is a deadweight loss in the brownfield property market). Again, an efficient property market requires that property change hands if there is a potential buyer who can gain more value from utilizing the resource than the current owner (if $V_B > V_S$ it is efficient for a trade to occur). Second, the restriction in supply available to developers may lead them to develop greenfield properties as a substitute. Third, undetected pollution sources are less likely to be remediated promptly, raising the possibility that contamination will increase or be more difficult to remediate when it is detected.

Consider first an owner's decision to remediate given perfect detection. Let r denote investment in remediation that reduces an existing liability $L(r)$, where $L' < 0$, $L'' > 0$. If enforcement is perfect, the owner will pick r to minimize $L(r) + r$. This level of remediation, denoted r^*, is efficient since it minimizes the combined costs of remediation and liability. To focus on distortions due to imperfect detection, assume that liability for existing contamination resides exclusively with the current owner, unless responsibility is contractually shifted to a new owner.

If governmental detection is perfect, then liability and remediation costs do not affect the efficient transfer of the site. If the current owner retains the site, the net value of the investment is $V_S - [L(r^*) + r^*]$. If the current owner sells, it continues to bear the minimized remediation and liability cost $[L(r^*) + r^*]$ but can sell the property at some $p > V_S$ (since $V_B > V_S$). The value if it trades exceeds the value if it retains the property. Specifically.

$$p - [L(r^*) + r^*] > V_S - [L(r^*) + r^*] \tag{14}$$

Since the current owner internalizes the liability and remediation costs whether it sells or not, the transfer of the property is unaffected by liability.[51]

Now consider the case where detection is imperfect, so that a current owner expects its contamination to be discovered only with some probability $\phi < 1$. Imperfect detection reduces the expected liability costs associated with the property. If the current owner retains the property, it chooses a level of remediation to minimize $\phi L(r) + r$. This level is denoted as r^o and since $\phi < 1$, $r^o < r^*$. Note that the current owner's expected liability and remediation costs fall as a result of imperfect detection. As a result, the net value of the property to the current owner increases relative to the case where detection is perfect. Specifically,

$$V_S - (\phi L(r^o) + r^o) > V_S - (L(r^*) + r^*).[52]$$

But what if the property is traded? If a property's sale triggers increased detection efforts on the part of the government, lenders, or prospective buyers, sale leads to a greater internalization of costs by the current owner. Denote as ϕ^m the probability of detection given placement of the property on the market, where $\phi < \phi^m \leq 1$. Let r^m be the associated level of privately optimal remediation. If the property is sold, the current owner internalizes an expected cost that is greater than its expected cost if it retains the property. Formally,

$$\phi^m L(r^m) + r^m > \phi L(r^o) + r^o.$$

As a result efficient trades may not occur. To see this, note that even though $V_B > V_S$ there may not exist $p < V_B$ such that

$$p - [\phi^m L(r^m) + r^m] > V_S - [\phi L(r^o) + r^o].$$

The differential probabilities of detection create an incremental expected liability cost if the property is sold. This incremental cost in effect creates a "transfer tax" equal to

$$t = [\phi^m L(r^m) + r^m] - [\phi L(r^o) + r^o].$$

Recall that if the detection probability is one when no sale occurs, then the seller internalizes the same expected liability whether or not the property is sold.[53]

Imperfect detection is a commonly acknowledged source of inefficiency since it leads to suboptimal pollution deterrence.[54] The example illustrates an additional negative effect of imperfect detection; specifically, it reduces the supply of brownfield properties when sale of such properties increases the probability of detection. This reduction in supply implies a deadweight loss in property markets that should be included as a social cost of imperfect pollution detection.

The distortion in remediation and property transfer decisions described above can in principle be addressed by increasing the penalties levied against firms that do not voluntarily disclose pollution sources. In theory, if the probability of detection is less than one, a "damage multiplier" can be applied to the penalty levied against firms that do not disclose contamination. If the multiplier is set equal to the inverse of the probability of detection $(1/\phi)$, the firm's expected liability with imperfect detection is equal to its expected liability if the detection probability is one and damages are compensatory (equal to $L(\cdot)$).[55] Punitive damages can thereby be used to equalize the expected liability associated with retaining ownership or selling the property. This eliminates the implicit transfer tax t.

The distortion due to detection probabilities conditional on sale is similar to distortions that can arise when the buyer, seller, or both are undercapitalized relative to the scale of the liability associated with the property. As described by Segerson (1993), deep-pocketed owners may (inefficiently) choose to sell their property if sale results in a transfer of liability to a more shallow-pocketed buyer.[56] Alternatively, a shallow-pocketed owner may choose to retain ownership (inefficiently) if transfer of the property to a deeper-pocketed buyer implies that a greater level of liability cost internalization will result.[57] Recall that a solvent buyer may be found liable when a former owner is insolvent. Potential buyer or seller under-capitalizaton, like transaction-dependent detection probabilities, can create distortions in property markets because the internalized liability costs associated with the property are a function of whether or not the property is sold. Whenever this happens the transaction decision involves a weighing of private costs or benefits that is not reflected in the social value of the trade $V_B - V_S$.

5. Conclusions

There is a widespread belief that environmental liabilities arising under CERCLA and related law distort the real estate market. In particular, the concern is that potential environmental liabilities reduce the incentive to purchase and/or redevelop formerly industrial properties— properties that from a social standpoint should be redeveloped. This article evaluates that concern by exploring the incentive to buy and sell properties, given a set of legal, informational, and regulatory factors that arise when sites are potentially polluted.

THE EFFECTS OF ENVIRONMENTAL LIABILITY   53

The analysis first shows that uncertain liability costs alone do not inefficiently hamper the purchase and redevelopment of brownfield properties. While environmental liability certainly increases the costs and uncertainty of owning real estate, this need not imply less efficient use (and transfer) of industrial properties since markets capitalize into real estate prices the expected costs of liability and risk aversion. In a market with uncertainty alone, an inefficient non-transfer of brownfield properties arises only if potential buyers are more risk averse than the current owner. On a site-by-site basis this is a possibility, but economy-wide there is little reason to believe that new property developers are substantially more risk averse than current owners. The analysis suggests that relative risk aversion can affect the distribution of the gains from trade, however. In effect, the market may penalize current owners for being risk averse.

A more plausible source of land use inefficiency arises due to information asymmetries between buyers and sellers of potentially polluted property. Given that a quantification of future liability may be costly to make at the time of sale, industrial properties can suffer from adverse selection. Lacking knowledge of a site's environmental qualities, buyers may assume the worst and adjust downward their demand for industrial sites. In turn, the supply of brownfield properties may be inefficiently reduced. Contractual mechanisms, such as indemnity contracts, can in theory be used by sellers to overcome this information problem and thereby reduce adverse selection. However, such contracts often have questionable legal value and can introduce buyer moral hazard. Finally, we argue that government's imperfect ability to detect industrial pollution may itself distort real estate transfers. Since the likelihood of detection increases with a property's sale, owners of polluted property may have an incentive to withhold it from the market.

Prescriptively, the analysis suggests straightforward policy reforms such as upholding the validity of liability-shifting (risk-shifting) contracts and the imposition of punitive damages when detection probabilities are less than one. However, these prescriptions are offered with caveats and will not alleviate distortions that arise due to asymmetric information between sellers and buyers.

Notes

1. This research was largely funded under a cooperative agreement with the Environmental Protection Agency. Numerous individuals at all levels of government and in the private sector were very helpful in providing information to us. In addition, we would like to thank Mary Elizabeth Calhoon for excellent research assistance and Tom Miceli, Daniel McGrath, and Kate Probst for their useful comments on an earlier draft. Responsibility for any errors that remain lies with the authors.

2. It is important to keep in mind that the shifting of development away from brownfields and toward greenfields development is not socially undesirable per se. Substitution of greenfields for brownfields is a cause for concern only if the net social benefits of greenfield development are less than the net social benefits of redevelopment. Some previously contaminated brownfield sites should never be developed. If such sites are not cleaned up or are cleaned up inadequately, then development may increase the damages from contamination either by disturbing the site or by increasing the number of people exposed to its hazards. Greenfields may also be more efficient to develop due to, for instance, proximity to increasingly suburban labor pools and government services.

3. For example, see S. 3164 (102c Congress, 2d Session), proposed legislation "to establish a program to demonstrate the environmental, economic, and social benefits and feasibility of carrying out response actions to remediate environmental contamination and redeveloping or reusing land blighted by environmental contamination."

4. See survey results described in Hathaway (1991). Rockwell (1992) and U.S. Environmental Protection Agency (1992) also document claims that lenders are restricting capital available for property purchases due to environmental liability concerns.

5. See U.S. Environmental Protection Agency (1992).

6. This point can be made with a simple analogy. In making a choice between two homes—one with a leaking roof, the other without—the house with the leaking roof may nevertheless be more desirable if it costs less. What matters is the difference in purchase price relative to the cost of fixing the roof. In an efficient market, the house value is discounted by precisely the cost of fixing the roof. Similarly, housing rents are a function of proximity to recreation areas, mass transportation, and waste dumps. Empirical studies also have demonstrated that local tax rates—which in some ways are analogous to environmental liabilities—are capitalized into real estate values (higher tax rates imply lower rents). See e.g., Oates (1969), Hamilton (1976), and Yinger (1982).

7. Michigan House of Representatives, Special Ad Hoc Committee on Revitalizing Our Michigan Cities, Citizen Advisory Group, Findings and Recommendations State Environmental Policies, January 1993.

8. The loss of population was accompanied by a loss of employment. Jobs, especially in the Northeast, moved to the suburbs, to the American South and West, and overseas. Between 1970 and 1980 manufacturing employment declined by 9 percent in the Northeast and 3.5 percent in the Midwest, and between 1980 and 1988 the declines in these regions were 16 and 8 percent, respectively. Taken together, the two regions had two million fewer manufacturing jobs in 1988 than in 1970.

9. For example, see Bradbury, Downs, and Small (1982).

10. Two strands in the literature are particularly important—the literature on property taxation, and the related literature on property abandonment. The literature on the effects of taxation on redevelopment is complex; see, for example, Bartik (1985), Carlton (1983), Plaut and Pluta (1983), Fox (1981), McHone (1970), Charney (1983), and Oates and Schwab (1991). Among studies of abandoned industrial property are Greenberg, Popper, and West (1990), Sternlieb and Burchell (1974), and White (1986).

11. For example, see Levinson (1992), Rockwell (1992), Fournier (1992), and Lussenhop (1992).

12. Advancement to the NPL depends on a Hazardous Ranking System (HRS). After evaluating four pathways of migration—ground water, surface water, soil exposure and air migration—EPA assigns each CERCLIS site a score from 0 to 100, based on the likelihood that a hazardous substance will be released from the site, the toxicity and amount of hazardous substances at the site, and the people and sensitive environment potentially affected by contamination at the site. A score of 28.5 or greater places the site on the NPL (1992 Superfund Deskbook).

13. The total cleanup process can take up to ten years. EPA estimates that the average total cost per site is $26 million.

14. 42 U.S.C. 9607 (a).

15. For further discussion, see Probst and Portney (1992).

16. CERCLA Sec. 9601; SARA Sec. 101(b). In practice, the lender liability exemptions are not this clearcut. See discussion in Section 4.

17. See *United States v. Hooker Chemicals & Plastics Corp.*, 739 F. Supp. 125 (W.D.N.Y., 1990) or *Allied Corp. v. Frola*, 730 F. Supp. 626 (D.N.J., 1990) where recovery for surface removal was made uner CERCLA and a subsequent subsurface removal was required under state law.

18. Pennsylvania Hazardous Sites Cleanup Act (HSCA) (Act 108), 35 P.S. Sec. 6020.101, 1988.

19. As of 1990, Massachusetts had 15 (federal) NPL sites but 383 on its state priority list, with an additional 1486 on a hazardous site registry.

20. Examples of remedial actions pursued by political subdivisions can be found in Arizona, New Jersey, Pennsylvania, and Kansas. See U.S. Environmental Protection Agency (1991).

21. These subtitles regulate hazardous waste management, state and regional solid waste plans, and underground storage tanks.

22. Third party common lawsuits (actions brought by nongovernmental entities) for environmental contamination are relatively rare, but do occur. For an example see *Sterling v. Velsicol Chem. Corp.*, 855 F.2d 1188 (6th Cir., 1988) where nearby residents of a chemical plant were awarded damages due to fear of increased cancer risk and reduced property values.

23. United States Environmental Protection Agency (1991). While the HRS attempts to measure risks to human and ecological health, some observers suggest that it is an imperfect instrument for determining which sites are most deserving of enforcement activity. The Office of Technology Assessment, for example, describes a high incidence of both false positive and false negative site evaluations using the HRS. According to an

OTA report, "it is not unreasonable to assume that up to 10 percent of the sites judged as ["no further action"] ... might have made the NPL." Also the possibility of false positives is supported by discussions with state officials who admitted to questionable procedures, including repeated sampling in order to obtain a score that would allow a site to be listed (Office of Technology Assessment, 1989). A 1989 Oak Ridge National Laboratory Study found that 50% of Superfund cleanups were occurring at sites that posed no current health risk (see Doty and Travis, 1989).

24. The Office of Technology Assessment report notes that: "With too few exceptions, EPA's key remedial cleanup decisions ... are inconsistent with statutory requirements. They often are assertions or expectations instead of closely reasoned decisions supported by data and thorough analysis" (U.S. Congress, Office of Technology Assessment, 1989, p. 16).

25. *T&E Industries, Inc.* v. *Safety Light Corp.* 123 N.J. 371, 1991. Also see *International Clinical Laboratories* v. *Stevens* 710 F. Supp. 466 (E.D.N.Y., 1989) where an "as is" clause was not found to bar a claim for cleanup costs asserted by the current owner against the former.

26. See *Sunnen Prods. Co.* v. *Chemtech Indus. Inc.*, 658 F. Supp. 276, 1987 wherein "no court has accepted the defense of caveat emptor, which would improperly shift liability for environmental contamination from the responsible party to an unwitting purchaser."

27. CERCLA 42 U.S.C. Sec. 9601(35)(B), 1988.

28. In extreme cases, fraudulent transactions may be relatively easy to detect. For example, in *N.J. Department of Transportation* v. *PSC Resources, Inc.* 419 A.2d 1151 (N.J. Super. Ct. Law Div., 1980) the defendant purchased all of the predecessor's real estate and capital assets for $100. In other cases, however, the court is unlikely to have information that can conclusively demonstrate that expected contamination costs were subtracted from the purchase price.

29. *New York* v. *Shore Realty Corp.*, 759 F.2d 1032 (2d Cir., 1985).

30. Standards to fulfill the appropriate inquiry requirement have been proposed by the American Society for Testing and Materials. Adoption of the standard by the EPA is, however, viewed as unlikely (Superfund Report, VII:8, April 21, 1993).

31. See *City Environmental Inc.* v. *U.S. Chemical Co.* DC EMich., (No. 91-CV-74810-DT) 2/5/93.

32. At least two real estate investment firms have been formed recently with the sole purpose of investing in environmentally tainted property. According to the president of one, the Brookhill Group of New York, "A lot of institutions just want to unload [the sites]. They panic when they hear *environmentally distressed*. We salivate." "Toxic Sites No Longer Poison to Developers," *Wall Street Journal*, July 18, 1994, p. B-1.

33. The disutility created by risk aversion also explains why PRPs may be willing to pay a substantial premium over a "fair share" of cleanup costs in exchange for certainty about the size of their liability burden. Also, the "environmental liability insurance crisis" about which much has been written can be viewed as a symptom of significant legal and technological uncertainties (see Clarke, et al., 1988). Given wildly unpredictable liability, insurers are forced to charge premiums that are perceived as being unreasonable.

34. Akerlof (1970) is the seminal description of this problem.

35. See Ringleb and Wiggins (1990) for an empirical analysis that supports the hypothesis that U.S. firms actively seek to escape liability through the divestiture or deliberate undercapitalization of business units.

36. Clearly, this form of moral hazard can arise only if the date and source of contamination can be obfuscated by the new owner.

37. In this case, the former owner loses control over the pollution detection process and will face a higher probability of having liabilities revealed than if they retained ownership of the site. If the new owner feels that they will not be held liable, they have an incentive to remediate any pollution that does exist—since the costs of remediation will be borne by the previous owner.

38. Increasing the detection probability is desirable. However, current landowners may be disinclined to offer property for sale if it increases the probability of having liability imposed. We analyze this type of problem in more detail in Section 4.

39. It may not be clear just what the seller liability includes. In the example discussed in the text, would the seller be liable not only for the preexisting damage and the buyer's subsequent investment, but also the buyer's foregone profit? Defining liability in this way may be additional source of moral hazard (see next section), but it is the only way to provide the buyer with complete protection from liability risk.

40. Similar to indemnity agreements are covenants not to sue, where a state, or in rare cases the federal government, will agree not to pursue liability claims against the new owner of a contaminated property. Municipalities burdened with potentially contaminated properties have been urging state and federal governments to issue covenants not to sue in order to encourage urban development. Covenants not to sue provide new owners with a similar protection against uncertainty as indemnity provided by former owners.

41. A federal district court ruling in *AM International* v. *International Forging Equipment Corp.* 743 F. Supp. 525, 1990 concluded that §107(e) "disfavors (contractual) releases except under strict conditions." (Also see *International Clinical Laboratories* v. *Stevens* in footnote 19.) While this reading of section 107 has been largely discredited (Conrad, 1992), the ambiguity of CERCLA's language has undermined confidence in the use of indemnity agreements. Conditions under which indemnity is granted may also be difficult to define. See *Quadion Corp.* v. *Mache* 738 F. Supp. 270 (N.D. Il., 1990) where a property buyer was allowed to seek cleanup compensation from the former owner, despite an indemnification agreement making the buyer responsible, because the agreement used "ambiguous language" to define contamination.

42. See *United States* v. *Vertac Chem. Corp.*, 671 F. Supp. 595, 855 F.2d 856 (8th Cir., 1988) where the defendant's attempt to create a thinly capitalized subsidiary in order to acquire the parent's assets and thus avoid cleanup costs at the parent's manufacturing facility was disallowed. Also, in *Schmoll* v. *AC and S, Inc.* 703 F. Supp. 868 (D. Or., 1988) the court disregarded a sale of assets to a purportedly distinct organization on the grounds that the transaction was designed to escape asbestos liability.

43. Central to the issue of indemnity contracts and covenants not to sue is the concept of contribution. Under CERCLA, a PRP who pays to resolve its liability may in turn seek to have other PRPs "contribute" to that payment. For a site with multiple PRPs, the government, in principle, need only sue one party for the full costs of cleanup. This liable party could then seek contribution from other PRPs. Given that multiple PRPs might be involved at any site and given that the state and federal government can bring suit against any PRP, any single indemnification agreement fails to provide meaningful liability cost protection. For discussion, see Boyd and coauthors, 1993.

44. For more extensive discussion, see Boyd and coauthors, 1993.

45. There is an existing literature, primarily relating to insurance markets, on adverse selection problems in the presence of moral hazard. See Rothschild and Stiglitz (1976) or Wilson (1977). Also, see Lutz (1989) for an analysis of product warranties with consumer moral hazard. The predicted contract in these models is typically characterized by only a partial warranty.

46. "Clean Up Pollution, Protect Farmland, Create Jobs: How a Sensible Industrial Site Recycling Policy Will Benefit Pennsylvania," press release, Pennsylvania Senators Brightbill, Musto, Stewart, and Shaffer, April 1993.

47. "Any person in charge of a vessel or facility shall, as soon as he has knowledge of any release of a hazardous substance from such vessel or facility ... immediately notify the National Response Center" (42 U.S.C. Sec. 9603(a)). Similar rules apply at the state level. For instance, New Jersey's Hazardous Discharge Notice Act (N.J.S.A. Sec. 13:1k-16(a)) imposes a duty to investigate based on a "suspected discharge" and to file a report with the locality in which the property is located.

48. CERCLA includes a "secured creditor exemption" that can be read to absolve a lender of liability if a property is acquired through default. In *U.S.* v. *Fleet Factors Corp.* (901 F.2d 1550), however, a Maryland District Court made a narrow reading of the exemption, saying that "a secured creditor will be liable if its involvement with the management of the facility is sufficiently broad to support the inference that it could affect hazardous waste disposal decisions if it so chose." The EPA has subseqeuntly clarified and broadened the exemption. Nevertheless, the possibility of lender liability undoubtedly provides an incentive for risk assessment. Also, lenders have an incentive to perform due diligence even if they were to be fully exempted under CERCLA. The reason is that liabilities can lead to the bankruptcy and foreclosure of the borrower. If so, the collateral on which the loan is based is significantly devalued and, with the borrower in default, no further interest payments are collected by the lender.

49. To quote one practitioner's view of the law, "An environmental professional will be held liable for damages resulting from a negligently performed site assessment. Such liability may arise where the environmental professional ... fails to warn of the existence or extent of hazardous substances." (*Environment Reporter*, 12/4/92).

50. Moreover, several states explicitly require site assessments, governmental notification of contamination, or cleanup before properties can be transferred. Connecticut, Missouri, California, Illinois, and New Jersey all have notification-of-release requirements at the time of sale. New Jersey's Environmental Cleanup Responsibility

Act goes further, requiring cleanup (including a declaration of completion from the state) prior to sale or a consent order which requires cleanup prior to the closure of an industrial facility. Permitted hazardous waste facilities under RCRA are also subject to a notice requirement. The act requires release notification on a property's deed when a regulated facility is closed.

51. Selling the property without remediation is another alternative. Again, however, transactions will be efficient since any liability and remediation cost not borne by the current owner will be discounted in the sales price.

52. $\phi L(r^0) + r^0 < L(r^*) + r^*$ follows from a straightforward application of the envelope theorem.

53. While liability costs are internalized in this case, because the liability cost is internalized by the current owner whether or not the property is sold, there is no differential cost to transferring the property. Thus, these liability costs are akin to a lump sum, rather than a sales tax. We thank Tom Miceli for drawing this analogy to our attention.

54. For further discussion of imperfect detection, with particular reference to environmental risks, see Menell (1991).

55. If the multiplier is defined as the inverse of the detection probability a firm that withholds its property faces an expected liability of $\phi^m(1/\phi^m)L(r) = L(r)$. For the first formal articulation of the idea of damage multipliers see Becker (1968).

56. See footnote 28 for a description of legal safeguards against this type of strategy.

57. Segerson's analysis also explores the broader question of whether liability should or should not be transferred to the new owner, and the effect of the liability allocation rule on a lender's financing of the project. In a companion paper (Segerson, 1994) she explores the effect of liability extended to the buyer on remediation decisions—contingent on sale and whether or not the parties are judgment-proof (potentially insolvent).

References

Akerlof, G. "The Market for 'Lemons:' Qualitative Uncertainty and the Market Mechanism." *Quarterly Journal of Economics* 84 (1970) 488–500.

Bartik, T.J. "Business Decisions in the United States: Estimates of the Effects of Unionization, Taxes and Other Characteristics of States." *Journal of Business Economics and Statistics* 3 (1985) 14–22.

Becker, G. "Crime and Punishment: An Economic Approach." *Journal of Political Economy* 76 (1968) 169–217.

Boyd, J., W. Harrington, M. Macauley, and M. Calhoon. "The Impact of Uncertain Environmental Liability on Industrial Real Estate Development: Developing a Framework for Analysis." (Washington, D.C.: Resources for the Future) ENR 94-03 Rev1 1993.

Bradbury, K., A. Downs, and K. Small. *Urban Decline and the Future of American Cities* (Washington, D.C.: Brookings Institution), 1983.

Carlton, D.W. "The Location and Employment Choices of New Firms: An Econometric Model with Discrete and Continuous Endogenous Variables." *Review of Economics and Statistics* 65 (1983) 440–449.

Charney, A.H. "Intraurban Manufacturing Location Decisions and Local Tax Differentials." *Journal of Urban Economics*, 14 (1983) 184–205.

Clarke, R., F. Warren-Boulton, D. Smith, and M. Simon. "Sources of the Crisis in Liability Insurance: An Economic Analysis." *Yale Journal on Regulation* 5 (1988) 374–394.

Conrad, J. "CERCLA Does Not Invalidate Contractual Allocations of Liability." *Environmental Law Reporter, News and Analysis*, 22 ELR 10045, (1992).

Doty, C., and C. Travis "The Superfund Remedial Action Decision Process," ORNL/M-780, 1989.

Fox, W.F. "Local Taxes and Industrial Location." *Public Finance Quarterly* 6 (1978) 93–114.

Fournier, K. "Toledo Lucas County Urban Land/Structure Reuse: Environmental Impacts Analysis and Policy Implications." mimeo, University of Toledo, December, 1992.

Greenberg, M., F. Popper, and B. West. "The TOADS: A New American Urban Epidemic." *Urban Affairs Quarterly* 25 (1990) 435–454.

Hamilton, B. "Capitalization of Intrajurisdictional Differences in Local Tax Prices." *American Economic Review* 66 (1976) 743–753.

Hathaway, M. "Good News and Bad News." *Independent Banker*, November (1991) 24–30.

Levinson, A. "Environmental Regulations and Manufacturers' Location Choices: Evidence from the Census of Manufacturers." mimeo, Columbia University, November, 1992.

Lussenhop, J. "Union County Land Recycling Inventory." Working Paper 19, New Jersey Regional Plan Association, (1992).

Lutz, N. "Warranties as Signals Under Consumer Moral Hazard." *Rand Journal of Economics* 20 (1989) 239-255.

Menell, P. "The Limitations of Legal Institutions for Addressing Environmental Risks." *Journal of Economic Perspectives* 5 (1991) 93-113.

McHone, W. "Supply-Side Considerations in the Location of Industry in Suburban Communities: Empirical Evidence from the Philadelphia SMSA." *Land Economics* 62 (1986) 64-73.

Oates, W. "The Effects of Property Taxes and Local Spending on Property Values: An Empirical Study of Tax Capitalization and the Tiebout Hypothesis." *Journal of Political Economy* 77 (1969) 957-971.

Oates, W., and R. Schwab. "Urban Land Taxation: Fiscal Reform for the Economic Rejuvenation of Center Cities?" mimeo, University of Maryland, November, 1991.

Plaut, T., and J. Pluta. "Business Climate, Taxes and Expenditures, and State Industrial Growth in the United States." *Southern Economics Journal* 49 (1983) 99-119.

Probst, K., and P. Portney. *Assigning Liability for Superfund Cleanups: An Analysis of Policy Options*. (Washington, D.C.: Resources for the Future), 1992.

Ringleb, A., and S. Wiggins. "Liability and Large-Scale, Long-Term Hazards." *Journal of Political Economy* 98 (1990) 574-595.

Rockwell, E. "Property Transfers and Land Development: What Incentives Do Superfund Laws Create?" Preliminary Report (Boston, MA), 1992.

Rothschild, M., and J. Stiglitz "Equilibrium in Competitive Insurance Markets: An Essay in the Economics of Imperfect Information." *Quarterly Journal of Economics* 90 (1976) 629-650.

Segerson, K. "Liability Transfers: An Economic Assessment of Buyer and Lender Liability. *Journal of Environmental Economics and Management* 25 (1993) 46-63.

Segerson, K. "Property Transfers and Environmental Pollution." *Land Economics* 70 (1994) 260-272.

Sternlieb, G., and R. Burchell. *Residential Abandonment: The Tenement Landlord Revisited* (Piscataway, NJ: Rutgers University Center for Urban Policy Research), 1973.

U.S. Congress, Office of Technology Assessment. *Coming Clean: Superfund Problems Can be Solved*, OTA-ITE-433, 1989.

U.S. Environmental Protectional Agency. *An Analysis of State Superfund Programs: 50-State Study, 1990 Update*, EPA/540/8-91/002, 1991.

U.S. Environmental Protection Agency. *A Preliminary Report on the Indirect Effects of the Superfund Program*. (Washington, D.C.: U.S. EPA, Office of Policy, Planning, and Evaluation, Office of Policy Analysis, May 20), 1992.

White, M. "Property Taxes and Urban Housing Abandonment." *Journal of Urban Economics* 20 (1986) 312-330.

Wilson, C. "A Model of Insurance Markets with Incomplete Information." *Journal of Economic Theory* 16 (1977) 167-207.

Yinger, J. "Capitalization and the Theory of Local Public Finance." *Journal of Political Economy* 90 (1982) 917-943.

[14]

Economica (1996) **63**, 311–23

Lender Penalty for Environmental Damage and the Equilibrium Cost of Capital

By Anthony G. Heyes

Oxford Institute for Energy Studies and Nuffield College

Final version received 23 September 1994.

In a model of the lending relationship incorporating both adverse selection and moral hazard, we show that increasing the liability of lenders for environmental damage done by their borrowers has a qualitatively ambiguous impact upon interest rates. This calls into question the assertion of financial community representatives that such reform will necessarily drive-up interest rates and have adverse macroeconomic consequences. If it is this fear which is preventing reform then that reluctance may, in the case of many classes of pollutant, be misplaced. The implications of such reform for credit-rationing are also explored.

Introduction

There is an emerging 'conventional wisdom' that making lenders liable for all or part of any environmental damage caused by their borrowers will necessarily drive up the cost of capital and so restrain the rate of investment and growth in the economy. Segerson asserts that: '[C]learly, the interest rate that the lender charges . . . is an increasing function of the liability it will face in the event of foreclosure' (Segerson 1993: 59), whilst Thompson points out that 'it is a matter of good business sense that lenders' practices should include environmental risk considerations and that their pricing structures should be amended (i.e. interest rates raised) to reflect any new risk being carried in their books' (Thompson 1992: 30). Adherence to this view was the basis for the opposition of many to the inclusion of a clause extending lender liability in the 1993 EC Green Paper, *Remedying Environmental Damage* (Cm. (3)47), the fear raised during the consultative stages being that the result would be higher interest rates in key 'growth-engine' industries such as biotechnology, advanced chemicals and plastics. This, it was believed, would have diverse—in many cases unforeseen—knock-on effects throughout the economy.[1] In this paper I challenge the conventional wisdom that penalizing lenders for environmental damage done by their borrowers will necessarily drive up interest rates. Though the results are positive, they call into question one of the assumptions underlying recent normative critiques of this class of regulatory reform.

Civil liability is a key instrument in the environmental control of industry in most countries. Strict liability means that the injurer is required to compensate injured parties for damage done, and in the context of the environment corresponds with the 'polluter pays' principle. In the absence of market failure, a system of strict liability internalizes environmental externalities and generates the incentive for firms to take just the right amount of care in their selection of equipment, choice of scale and location and production practices (see e.g. Baumol and Oates 1988). The technological realities of many of the 'new' industries such as bioengineering and toxic waste treatment are such, however, that potential participants inevitably have assets significantly lower in value than the environmental damage that they could cause by accident. Because insolvency of the representative firm would prevent full compensation being implemented, that firm has too little incentive to prevent such accidents happening in the first place. (Shavell, 1986, refers to such firms as 'judgement proof', while Summers, 1983, talks of the parable of 'the case of the disappearing defendant'.) Furthermore, when accidents do happen, some victims will be left without the compensation to which they are entitled.

Various policy responses to the significant and growing problem of 'judgement proofness' have been suggested, one of which is the idea that banks should be penalized for the environmental damage done by those to whom they lend.[2] In the United States such provisions are already contained in the Comprehensive Environmental Response and Liability Act (CERCLA) 1980, and the associated Superfund Amendment and Reauthorisation Act (SARA) 1986. (King, 1988, provides an authoritative assessment of the extent of lender penalty under this legislation.) In the United Kingdom such provisions were contained in the Environmental Protection Act 1990 (see Thompson 1992), and the possibility of their extension was a contentious part of the government's deliberations over reform of that act (see e.g. 'Banks See Red over Green Policy', *The Observer*, 26 April 1992, p. 25). But what are the implications of such a reform for interest rates and the availability of unsecured industrial credit?

In a stylized model of the market for loanable funds, I show that introducing or extending the lender's liability for environmental damage caused by its borrowers has a qualitatively ambiguous impact upon the equilibrium cost of capital. In the model the interest rate plays two 'efficiency wage' roles simultaneously. From the lender's point of view, an increase in it is shown to mitigate (partially) a class of adverse selection problems but to exacerbate a class of moral hazard ones. (As such, our results are qualitatively distinct from those of, for example, Stiglitz and Weiss, 1982, in which an increase in the interest rate serves to mitigate *both* classes of agency problem.) This is shown to lead to a trade-off in determining how interest rates will change in response to an extension of the environmental liability of lenders. A necessary condition for the conventional wisdom (that such an extension will lead to an increase in the cost of capital) to be sustained is that the extent to which the capital market is prone to adverse selection is sufficiently significant *vis-à-vis* the extent to which it is prone to moral hazard.

Another related worry is the possibility of 'investment blight'—that extending lender liability could increase the extent to which credit is rationed (see Segerson 1993). I analyse this possibility and show that, intriguingly, an increase in the extent to which credit is rationed (in the sense of a greater proportion of prospective borrowers being excluded from attaining loans at any price) may co-exist with a decrease in the interest rates charged to those borrowers who are not excluded.

I. THE MARKET FOR UNSECURED LOANABLE FUNDS

At the start of the game, each risk-neutral firm finds itself holding the plans for a particular investment project. In order to execute the project, it must not only invest its own wealth, w, but must borrow additional funds Q from a bank.[3]

With probability $(1 - \pi)$, a project turns out successfully and yields producer surplus p, which the firm retains net of the interest r which it pays to the bank for capital services rendered.

With probability π, however, the investment project turns out to inflict large-scale environmental damage. In that event, the firm is bankrupted (i.e. its payoff is $-w$) and it defaults on the loan. The payoff to the bank will be denoted $-\mu$, where μ will be understood to be a composite variable including the value of unreturned capital, the bank's environmental liability (including any punitive sanctions) and any other costs incident upon it (such as the value of any damage to its corporate image through its involvement in the project). Policies extending lender liability will be captured by increases in μ regardless of the precise details of the liability-sharing rules devised—whether, for example, it is residual, joint, joint-and-several or, as is perhaps the most likely outcome of future legislation in the EU, it is simply a lump-sum financial penalty levied against the bank by an arbitrating court—and it is comparative statics with respect to that parameter which will occupy the analysis in later sections.

The overall probability that a given project will turn out to be damaging depends upon both the intrinsic characteristics of the plans for the project and the extent to which the safety stipulations contained in those plans are complied with during its execution.

The 'intrinsic' risk, a, is the probability that the project will turn out to be damaging if it is carried out exactly as specified in the plans. (The probability a must lie on the closed unit interval. Its value is observed privately by the prospective borrower at the start of the game: the lender knows only the distribution, $f(a)$, from which it is drawn.) Additional risk is induced, however, if in executing the project the borrower engages in 'cost-cutting'—departing covertly from the terms of the contract in such a way as to increase his return in the event that the project turns out successfully at the expense of increasing the probability that it will not. More concretely, if the borrower, during execution of the project, engages in an amount of cost-cutting b, then if the project turns out to be non-damaging his net return will be $(p-r+b)$. The overall probability that the project will result in environmental damage is assumed to be described by

(1) $\pi(a, b) = 1 - (1-a)\,e^{-b}$.

This function is illustrated in Figure 1. $\pi(a, b)$ is increasing in both of its arguments, $\pi(a, 0) = a$ while for any given value of a, $\pi \to 1$ as b is increased. (The qualitative results derived below do not depend on the particular specification adopted.)

The way in which the model is set up highlights the two distinct informational disadvantages which the borrower is likely to face *vis-à-vis* the lender in this context: (1) the prospective borrower is likely to have private information regarding the inherent characteristics of the project as proposed, and (2) the borrower, if succesful in gaining finance, is likely to be able to depart covertly from the terms of the proposal during the project's execution (e.g. 'cutting corners' in the construction, maintenance and/or operation of industrial plant). As Kraakman (1986) notes, environmental 'cowboys' are of two types: those

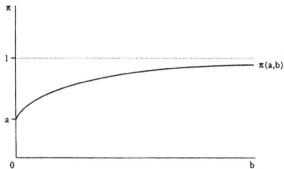

FIGURE 1. The relationship between the probability of accident (π), the intrinsic riskiness of the project (a) and the amount of cost-cutting (b).

who knowingly go ahead with projects which they know to be inherently 'bad bets' from an environmental perspective, and those who have a perfectly sound plan but seek to increase their gains by executing the project in a shoddy way. (The latter type are colloquially referred to as the 'midnight dumpers'— a stylized example being that the plans for a plant may allow for state-of-the-art disposal of waste, but the enterprising operator may elect to substitute more dangerous (but cheaper) methods of disposal when the decision arrives.) In drawing up a lending contract, then, the lender may face adverse selection and/or moral hazard.

In the simple model we develop here, the bank, having observed the assets ('wealth') of a prospective borrower, chooses whether or not to make a loan offer and, if so, at what rate of interest. The borrower decides whether or not to accept any lending contract offered and, if he does accept, how much cost-cutting to do.

The borrower's problem

The firm, knowing the 'intrinsic' riskiness of the project for which it holds plans, has to decide whether or not to apply for a loan and, if it does execute the project, how much cost-cutting to do. Solving the second-state problem first, assuming that it is going ahead with a project, the firm chooses b to maximize the expected value of its private return, denoted $F(a, b)$:

(2) $\underset{b \geq 0}{\text{Max}} \{[1 - \pi(a, b)](p - r + b) + \pi(a, b)(-w)\}.$

The first-order condition associated with an interior solution to this problem is (after substituting for π from equation (1))

(3) $F_b(a, b) = (1 - a) e^{-b^*}[1 - k - (p - r - b^*)] = 0,$

where an asterisk denotes the solution value in the usual way. (It is straightforward to verify that the second-order condition neccesarily holds.) Equation (3) says that the firm, in executing a project, will engage in covert cost-cutting up to the point at which the marginal gains from so doing (in terms of a better return in the good state) equal the marginal costs (in terms of an increased probability that the bad state will be realized).

Application of the implicit function theorem to (3) yields the two comparative statics of primary interest:

(4) $$\frac{db^*}{dr} = -\left[\frac{(1-a)\ e^{-b^*}}{F_{bb}(a, b^*)}\right] > 0$$

and

(5) $$\frac{db^*}{dw} = -\left[\frac{-(1-a)\ e^{-b^*}}{F_{bb}(a, b^*)}\right] < 0.$$

Ceteris paribus, then, the borrower will engage in less cost-cutting when the rate of interest is low and/or when its wealth is large. Both ensure that the firm has more to lose from the realization of the bad state (the former in terms of potential profit forgone, the latter in terms of own funds lost) and hence that it will be less willing to risk such a state occurring by 'cutting corners'.

Returning to the firm's initial participation decision, the firm will accept a loan offered to it if and only if it anticipates being able to make a positive (expected) return, that is iff

(6) $F(a, b^*(r, w)) = [(1 - \pi(a, b^*))(p - r + b^*) - \pi(a, b^*)w] \geq 0.$

Noting that $F(1, b^*(1, r))$ is negative and that $dF(a, b^*(a, r))/da < 0$, this amounts to a condition that the firm will apply for a loan if and only if its private information tells it that the intrinsic riskiness of the project for which it holds plans is not too great. Defining A to be that value of a that satisfies (6) with equality implies that the firm will apply for funds iff $a \leq A$, where A is characterized by

(7) $(1 - A)\ e^{-b^*}(p - r + b^*) - [1 - (1 - A)\ e^{-b^*}]w = 0.$

Implicit differentiation of (7) yields (after application of the envelope theorem in each case)

(8) $$\frac{dA}{dr} = -\left(\frac{1 - A}{p - r + b^* + w}\right)$$

and

(9) $$\frac{dA}{dw} = -\left[\frac{1 - (1 - A)\ e^{-b^*}}{(p - r + b^* + w)\ e^{-b^*}}\right].$$

Both of these are unambiguously negative. An increase in r or w, then, serves to reduce the range of projects over which the representative firm will attempt to procure a loan. Prospective borrowers 'self-select'—those who know they have intrinsically risky ideas refusing loans offered to them—with the stringency of the self-selection constraint being an increasing function of the interest rate (as well as the firm's private exposure).

The signs of the derivatives in (4) and (8) combine to give an interesting ambiguity to the effect of a change in r on the overall environmental characteristics of projects executed. An increase in r tightens the self-selection constraint (in accordance with equation (8)), causing would-be borrowers at the high-risk margin to deselect themselves. At the same time, however, that increase encourages those firms that do execute projects to do so in a less scrupulous way. In effect, the increase serves to reduce 'intrinsic' environmental risk at the expense of increasing 'induced' risk. Our analysis will show that it is the parameters of the model that, by determining the terms of this trade-off, will determine how banks will react to a change in μ.

The bank's problem

Having observed the value of an applicant's assets, w, the bank has to choose whether or not to offer to lend the required sum and, if so, on what terms. Assuming that a loan offer is made (and we will return to the related issue of credit rationing later), r will be set to maximize the expected return on the bank's capital, $R(r,A,b)$, subject to the firm's self-selection constraint (8) and reaction function (4) (i.e. the bank anticipates both the willingness of the firm to accept contracts and its propensity to cost-cut). Formally, the bank's problem is to choose r (conditional on w) to maximize $R(r, A(r, w), b(r, w))$:

$$(10) \quad \operatorname*{Max}_{r} \left\{ \int_0^{A(r,w)} [(1 - \pi(a, b^*(r, w)))r + \pi(a, b^*(r, w))(-\mu)]f(a)\, da \right\}.$$

The (interior) solution to the bank's problem, the equilibrium interest rate, will be characterized by the associated first-order condition:

$$(11) \quad \frac{dR}{dr} = \int_0^A (1 - a)\ e^{-b^*} f(a)\, da$$

$$+ \frac{dA}{dr} \{(1 - A)\ e^{-b^*} r - \mu[1 - (1 - A)\ e^{-b^*}]\}$$

$$+ \int_0^A \frac{db^*}{dr} [-(1 - a)(r + \mu)\ e^{-b^*}] f(a)\, da$$

$$= 0.$$

The first term captures the direct effect of an increase in r—that if the project goes ahead and is completed successfully the bank's share of the surplus created increases correspondingly—and is positive. The second terms captures the expected profit implications of the 'adverse selection impact' of an increase in r—that a subset of would-be borrowers at the high-risk margin are induced to reject lending contract—and is of ambiguous sign. The final term reflects the expected profit implications of the 'moral hazard impact'—that an increase in r induces those borrowers who do attain funds to engage in more 'cost-cutting' during the execution of the project—and is negative.

The impact of regulatory reform on interest rates

Of particular interest to us here are the comparative-static implications of changes in the policy parameter μ. Implicit differentiation of equation (11) yields

$$(12) \quad \frac{dr^*}{d\mu} = -\left(\left\{(dA/dr)[-(1-(1-A)\ e^{-b^*})]\right.\right.$$

$$\left.\left. + \int_0^A (db^*/dr)(-(1-a)\ e^{-b^*})f(a)\ da\right\}\Big/R_{rr}\right).$$

The denominator is negative in the vicinity of equilibrium (by the associated second-order condition) such that the sign of $dr^*/d\mu$ coincides with the sign of the numerator of the expression in braces, which is ambiguous.

Proposition. An increase in μ, the value of the penalty faced by the lender in the event that it lends to an environmentally damaging project, has a qualitatively ambiguous impact on the rate of interest charged to borrowers.

This contradicts the (apparently) universally accepted view that the impact will necessarily be positive.

When μ is increased (by legislative mandate or other means) it is unambiguous that, *ceteris paribus*, the bank will want to reduce the equilibrium riskiness of the projects it finances. The ambiguity is over the direction of the change in r needed to achieve such a reduction. Consider the numerator of the expression in braces in (12). An increase in r reduces A, implying that firms with intrinsically high-risk projects are induced to drop out of the market such that the first (composite) term is positive. This suggests that the bank will want to *raise* interest rates. Those borrowers that remain (i.e. those with private assessments of a less than A), however, are induced to engage in more post-contractual cost-cutting (db^*/dr is positive) such that the second composite term is negative, suggesting that the bank will want to *cut* interest rates. Only when the first term (that associated with the marginal impact of changes in r in reducing the adverse selection problem) is sufficiently large *vis-à-vis* the second term (which captures the analogous marginal impact on the moral hazard problem) will the expression be positive such that conventional wisdom is satisfied.

It is instructive to consider two special cases. Under pure adverse selection (which might approximate reality in those contexts where borrowers have little or no scope for covert cost-cutting during execution of the project), b is fixed (by assumption) equal to zero such that (12) becomes

$$(13) \quad \frac{dr^*}{d\mu} \approx -\left\{\frac{(dA/dr)[-(1-(1-A)\ e^{-b^*})]}{R_{rr}}\right\},$$

which is unambiguously positive: conventional wisdom is satisfied. In contrast, under pure moral hazard, with the intrinsic riskiness of all projects fixed exogeneously at some $a = a^*$, (12) becomes

$$(14) \quad \frac{dr^*}{d\mu} = -\left\{\frac{(db^*/dr)[-(1-a^*)\ e^{-b^*}]}{R_{rr}}\right\},$$

which is unambiguously negative—conventional wisdom is necessarily violated.

The result can be summarized as follows:

Proposition. The conventional wisdom that an increase in μ will induce an increase in r is satisfied when and only when the 'adverse selection impact' of a change in r outweighs the 'moral hazard impact'.

The implications of this ambiguity will be discussed in Section II.

Regulatory reform and credit-rationing

As well as the impact on r of proposals to increase μ, there is concern that such increases will lead to 'investment blight', with an increased number of prospective borrowers being unable to attain financing for investment projects on any terms (see Segerson 1993; Department of Trade and Industry 1993). The analysis in this section suggests that these predictions are well founded.

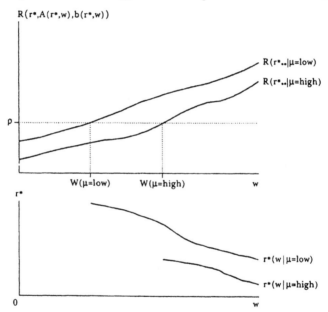

FIGURE 2. Effects of increase in μ on availability of unsecured credit and equilibrium interest rates.

Consider the upper panel in Figure 2, in which the best expected return that the bank can make *conditional on its having decided to offer a loan* (i.e. $R(r^*, A(r^*, w), b(r^*, w))$ where r^* satisfies equation (11)) is plotted against w, the wealth of the prospective borrower, for 'high' and 'low' values of μ. From the structure of the model, it is evident that $R(r^*)$ is increasing in both w and μ, as shown.

By not offering a loan at all, however, the bank can make a riskless return equal to, say, ρ. We can infer from Figure 2, then, that, unless the borrower is sinking his own assets of a value at least equal to W, the bank will be unwilling to lend money on any terms. For any borrower with wealth w less than W, the bank is unable to find any rate of interest at which its expected return on a lending contract beats the riskless return that it can get elsewhere. An increase in μ shifts this curve everywhere downwards such that this 'minimum wealth requirement' is increased and credit can be said to be more rationed in the sense that a greater proportion of would-be borrowers find themselves excluded from borrowing on any terms.

Consider, now, the lower panel in Figure 2. As drawn, it shows the case in which the expression in equation (12) is negative (the 'moral hazard impact' dominates) such that, for any given value of w, the increase in μ leads to a reduction in r^*. The two panels together illustrate an intriguing possibility: an increase in μ could lead to an increase in credit-rationing (in the sense of a greater portion of would-be borrowers being excluded from the market altogether) co-existing with a cut in the rate of interest at which the bank offers to lend money to those not excluded.

II. DISCUSSION AND CONCLUSIONS

The effect on the cost of capital of introducing/extending lender liability is, I have shown, qualitatively ambiguous. The ambiguity arises from the recognition that there are two classes of asymmetry of information regarding the environmental consequences of projects that exist between lenders and borrowers. Acceptance of the conventional wisdom that the effect will necessarily be positive requires an assumption that (at the margin) adverse selection considerations dominate moral hazard ones. There is no clear rationale for adopting such an assumption *a priori*, either in particular sectors or in aggregate. Indeed, at least in most traditional industrial contexts, the prevalent view of environmental malpractice is that of 'midnight dumping' (unscrupulous operators trying to make a 'quick buck' by cutting corners and acting irresponsibly during the project's execution), which points to moral hazard being the predominant problem (see e.g. Baumol and Oates 1988; Harford 1987 and the literature survey in Strand 1992).[4] Moreover, scepticism among lenders about how far pre-loan screening ('environmental impact assessments') can cut their exposure to environmental risk arising from default is indicative of their belief that most borrowers have considerable discretion as to how they act after a lending contract has been signed.

The model here is an application of what Kraakman (1986, 1988) has called 'gatekeeper analysis'. Kraakman defines a gatekeeper as an agent who exploits his contractual relation with another to prevent any misconduct by that other. There are two types of gatekeeper: (1) '"bouncer" . . . can disrupt misconduct by excluding wrongdoers from a particular market' and (2) a '"chaperone" . . . can disrupt misconduct in an unfolding contractual relationship' (both from Kraakman 1986, p. 63). In the context of environmental protection, one regulatory motive for the implementation of lender liability is to induce banks and other lending institutions to act as gatekeepers *vis-à-vis* industrial borrowers. Along with collateral requirements, the interest rate is likely to be the key instrument used by the bank in performing both its 'bouncing' and 'chaperoning' duties because, as we have seen, how r is set has significant implications both for what projects get financed (equation (8)) and for how carefully those that do get financed are carried out (equation (4)). The interest rate performs, in effect, a dual 'efficiency wage' function.

320   ECONOMICA   [MAY

By increasing μ, the regulator gives the bank the incentive to gatekeep more stringently—the aim being to strengthen environmental protection. Part of the bank's induced desire to be more stringent shows itself in the guise of increased credit-rationing, with an increase in the minimum wealth required by a would-be borrower in order for the lender to be willing to offer any contract at all. The other part takes the form of a change in interest rates. The existence of adverse selection means both that the bank can act as a 'bouncer' and that bouncing more stringently requires a rise in interest rates (inducing a subset of prospective borrowers at the high-risk margin to drop out of the market). By contrast, the existence of moral hazard means that at the same time the bank is a 'chaperone' and that chaperoning more stringently means cutting r (such that the incentive for the representative borrower to be careful during implementation is increased). The overall change in r is, then, ambiguous.

Intriguingly, an increase in the extent to which credit is rationed (in the sense of a greater proportion of prospective borrowers being excluded from attaining loans at any price) may co-exist with a decrease in the interest rates charged to those borrowers who are not excluded.

Stiglitz and Weiss (1982) model the lender–borrower relationship under moral hazard and adverse selection, but it is important to understand that their results and ours are not directly comparable. In their model an investment is associated with a probability distribution of returns where the borrower defaults if he is unable to pay back the promised amount (principal plus interest). The distribution of returns on a particular project is characterized by a 'riskiness' parameter ϕ, where a greater ϕ corresponds to a greater risk in the sense of Rothschild and Stiglitz (1972). When the distribution cannot be altered by the borrower (i.e. under adverse selection), the following are proved:

> *Theorem 1.* For a given interest rate there is a critical value ϕ^* such that a firm borrows from the bank if and only if $\phi > \phi^*$.

> *Theorem 2.* As the interest rate increases, the critical value of ϕ below which individuals do not apply for loans increases. (Stiglitz and Weiss 1981, p. 396)

In other words, only firms with sufficiently *risky* projects apply for loans, and an increase in r induces prospective borrowers at the *low-risk* margin to drop out. Although this appears to contradict my findings—that only those firms with projects that are sufficiently *unrisky* will wish to borrow and that an increase in r serves to exclude borrowers at the high-risk margin—the contradiction is superficial. My work is quite distinct from theirs because of the quite different concept of 'risk' being used. In their paper the financial risk faced by the lender is framed in terms of the variability of the return on an investment, with increase in risk being captured by means-preserving spreads in the distribution of those returns. Here, in contrast, 'risk' refers to the probability of an undesirable state being realized, and changes in it cannot be captured by mean-preserving spreads. Here the qualitative ambiguity of interest results from the fact that a decrease in r mitigates the moral hazard problem but exacerbates the adverse selection one. In Stiglitz and Weiss's formulation there is no such trade-off; decreases in r serve to mitigate both classes of agency problem.

The model represents the real world in a highly stylized way. The assumption, for example, that the bank chooses only whether or not to lend and at what rate of interest is a big one. The other instrument that lenders might be expected to turn to if faced by increased environmental liability would be 'environmental assessment'—screening proposals before making lending decisions. Ignoring the endogeneity of screening effort is, in practice, unlikely to be too significant in this context for two reasons. (1) There is anecdotal evidence that a great part of what we have referred to as 'intrinsic risk' would not be amenable to assessment by external screening or that, if it were, that assessment would be prohibitively expensive (Thompson 1992). This may be because screening technologies are currently underdeveloped or because there are things inherent in products and processes which can only be understood by those who have developed them and which are not amenable to 'pipe-end' assessment. (2) In most countries lenders are already required to carry out far more detailed environmental assessments than they would if left to their own devices, implying that regulatory reform (unless it were very drastic) would be unlikely to induce, at the margin, result-changing adjustments in screening intensity. Furthermore, while it might complicate analysis considerably, I believe that the qualitative results of the paper would be robust to the introduction and endogenization of environmental screening effort by the lender.[5]

Another major assumption is that the only thing the bank knows about a firm that applies for a loan is its wealth. In reality, it is likely that the greater majority of prospective borrowers would be firms with 'environmental histories' applying for expansion funds. In that case, the lender could condition current lending decisions on the particular firm's past performances. The failure of the model presented here to take account of such reputational considerations in the capital market is, I believe, its single greatest shortcoming.

The analysis presented here has been purely positive, examining what the implications of a particular class of environmental reform (introduction/extension of lender liability) for a key economic variable (interest rates) would be. No claim is made as to whether we should want higher or lower interest rates nor, analogously, as to what the welfare implications of credit rationing are in this context. By adopting a positive approach, I have side-stepped some of the most interesting questions in environmental economics, including that of how the optimal rate of environmental damage should be determined. The benefits that follow from and thus motivate the current reform programme (of which the EC Green Paper, Cm. (93)47 is a part)—an improved living environment for present and future generations—would have to be built into a much fuller model before normative conclusions could be drawn. Such normative analysis would be valuable future research. The present positive results do suggest, however, that one of the key transmission mechanisms taken for granted by such anecdotal normative analyses as currently exist—that through interest rates to investment—needs reassessment.

The longer-rung implications of the reform of environmental law also merit consideration, particularly the possibility that wholesale extension of lender liability could induce structural reorganization in the banking industry itself. An incentive would be given to banks to set up low-asset subsidiaries to specialize in lending in high-risk sectors (analogous to the type of strategic subsidiarization witnessed among borrowers in the United States when borrower liability was beefed up in the 1970s and 1980s—Ringleb and Wiggins 1990). This would raise the possibility of lender bankruptcy and—in the absence of effective regulatory response—would reduce the long-run impact of any

322   ECONOMICA   [MAY

increase in lender liability. Furthermore, in so far as offshore lenders were able to escape the liability, a switch towards them as a source of funds could be expected to occur.

It has also been assumed that ideas for projects occur to agents as 'manna from heaven'—each firm 'wakes up' one morning to find a set of project plans in its corporate pocket. In a general equilibrium model it would be interesting to endogenize the flow of ideas, with innovation the result of conscious and costly effort, and take account of the impact of the distribution of environmental liability on the number and characteristics of prospective borrowers that emerge.

Notwithstanding these shortcomings, we believe the analysis presented here is useful. We have emphasized that there are two quite distinct informational asymmetries which are likely to exist between lenders and borrowers. They are likely to be of varying degrees of importance in different industrial sectors. The analysis provides further evidence of how a particular policy package may have markedly different effects in different sectors of the economy, suggesting that it is likely to be prudent to adopt a sector-by-sector (or, possibly, hazard-by-hazard) approach to the reform of environmental liability. The European Union's current search for a general rule may, I believe, be misguided.

ACKNOWLEDGMENTS

I am grateful to Robert Cairns, David Blake, David Begg, Dennis Snower, Sandeep Kapur, Ngo van Long, two referees of this Journal and Seminar participants at Birkbeck College and University College, London, for very helpful comments on earlier drafts. Errors are mine.

NOTES

1. The author was an invited speaker at the series of consultative conferences held by the EC in Frankfurt, London and Paris in November 1993 to consider this issue. These meetings (as is usual in such cases) were held under Chatham House rules which forbid the attribution of views. See, in addition, the Advisory Committee on Business and the Environment Report (Department of Trade and Industry 1993).
2. This would be an example of what is variously referred to as vicarious, secondary or subsidiary liability, whereby legal liability is extended from the actual injurer to third parties who have some sort of relationship with the injurer (such as a bank which lends a polluter money). Thus, parents may in some circumstances be liable for the torts of their children, employers liable for those of their employees. Under British colonial law, masters were liable for the torts of their servants. (This, recall, was of some significance to the plot of the classic adventure story, *Around the World in Eighty Days* (Verne 1862), in which Phileas Fogg was detained in Hong Kong on the grounds that his manservant, Passe Partout, was suspected (falsely, as it turned out) of having stolen a pair of slippers.) See Sykes (1984) for a good general treatment of vicarious liability.
3. Note that by fixing Q we are imposing, for the sake of convenience, a particular normalization. Nothing significant rests on this.
4. For an entertaining (and insightful) review of some anecdotal evidence, see the excellent paper by Coffee (1991).
5. This is proved, in the context of a 'segmented market' (Stiglitz–Weiss) version of the current model, in Heyes (1994).

REFERENCES

BAUMOL, W. J. and OATES, W. (1988). *The Theory of Environmental Policy*, 2nd edn. Cambridge University Press.

BEARD, T. R. (1990). Bankruptcy and care choice. *Rand Journal of Economics*, **21**, 626–34.

COFFEE, J. (1991). No soul to damn, no body to kick: an unscandalised inquiry into the problem of corporate punishment. *Michigan Law Review*, **38**, 661–88.

DEPARTMENT OF TRADE AND INDUSTRY (1993). Report of the Financial Sector Working Group, February.

HARFORD, J. D. (1987). Self-reporting of pollution and the firm's behaviour under imperfectly enforceable regulations. *Journal of Environmental Economics and Management*, **14**, 293–303.

HEYES, A. G. (1994). Reform of environmental liability and the cost of venture captial: conventional wisdom reconsidered. Mimeo, Birkbeck College, University of London.

KING, S. M. (1988). Lenders liability for cleanup costs. *Environmental Law*, **18**, 241–91.

KRAAKMAN, R. H. (1986). Corporate liability strategies and the costs of legal controls. *Yale Law Journal*, **93**, 857–98.

—— (1988). Gatekeepers: the anatomy of a third-party enforcement strategy. *Journal of Law, Economics and Organisation*, **2**, 53–104.

RINGLEB, A. H. and WIGGINS, S. N. (1990). Liability and large-scale, long-term hazards. *Journal of Political Economy*, **98**, 574–95.

ROTHSCHILD, M. and STIGLITZ, J. (1970). Increasing Risk I: A Definition. *Journal of Economic Theory*, **2**, 315–29.

SCHWARTZ, A. (1985). Product liability, corporate structure and bankruptcy: toxic substances and the remote risk relationship. *Journal of Legal Studies*, **14**, 45–58.

SEGERSON, K. (1993). Liability transfers: an economics assessment of buyer and lender liability. *Journal of Environmental Economics and Management*, **25**, 46–63.

SHAVELL, S. (1986). The judgement proof problem. *International Review of Law and Economics*, **6**, 45–58.

STIGLITZ, J. E. and WEISS, A. (1982). Credit rationing in markets with imperfect information. *American Economic Review*, **71**, 393–410.

STRAND, J. (1992). Environmental accidents under moral hazard and limited firm liability. Memorandum no. 22, Department of Economics, University of Oslo.

SUMMERS, J. (1983). The case of the disappearing defendant: an economic analysis. *University of Pennsylvania Law Review*, **132**, 145–85.

SYKES, A. O. (1984). The economics of vicarious liability. *Yale Law Journal*, **93**, 1231.

THOMPSON, H. (1992). Contaminated land: the implications for property transactions and the property development industry. *National Westminster Bank Quarterly Review*, November, 20–33.

VERNE, J. (1862). *Around the World in Eighty Days*. London: Cygnet Books.

[15]

The Yale Law Journal

Volume 98, Number 5, March 1989

Sharing Damages Among Multiple Tortfeasors*

Lewis A. Kornhauser† and Richard L. Revesz††

In our society, losses are often caused by the activities of more than one actor. The apportionment of such losses among the various responsible actors raises difficult and controversial questions. Recently, courts have confronted these questions primarily when determining whether defendants held jointly and severally liable for a given harm have the right to seek contribution from other responsible parties. The availability of a right to contribution received particular attention in the early 1980s when the United States Supreme Court decided whether the right existed under antitrust law[1] and employment discrimination law.[2] More recently, the

---

* Copyright 1989 Lewis A. Kornhauser and Richard L. Revesz.

† Professor of Law, New York University.

†† Associate Professor of Law, New York University. We are grateful to Victor Goldberg, Marcel Kahan, and David Leebron for their extensive suggestions, and to the participants at faculty workshops at Columbia University, New York University, and the University of Colorado for their helpful comments. We profited from the generous financial support of the Filomen D'Agostino and Max E. Greenberg Research Fund at the New York University School of Law.

1. Texas Indus., Inc. v. Radcliff Materials, Inc., 451 U.S. 630 (1981).
2. Northwest Airlines, Inc. v. Transport Workers Union, 451 U.S. 77 (1981).

availability of contribution has been the focus of judicial attention in such dissimilar areas as securities law[3] and environmental law.[4]

Not surprisingly, these cases attracted the attention of the academic literature, in particular the law-and-economics literature, to the choice between rules of contribution and no contribution. Several commentators, most importantly William Landes and Richard Posner,[5] writing shortly before the two Supreme Court decisions,[6] asked whether apportioning a loss among the responsible parties through contribution was more desirable than the traditional common law rule that barred such contribution.[7] They concluded that as long as the relevant actors are risk-neutral,[8] no-contribution rules are efficient and provide the same incentives as rules that apportion the resulting harm.

The narrow focus of these commentators on the effects of a right to contribution obscured the most important questions raised by the apportionment of losses among responsible parties. First, because there can be no right to contribution without joint and several liability, the commentators assumed, without much discussion, that rules of joint and several lia-

---

3. Most recently, the Supreme Court granted certiorari to consider a contribution claim brought under § 12(1) of the Securities Act of 1933, 15 U.S.C. § 77(l)(1) (1982), but declined to decide whether there was a right to contribution. *See* Pinter v. Dahl, 108 S. Ct. 2063, 2070 n.9 (1988).

4. Most importantly, this question has arisen under the Comprehensive Environmental Response, Compensation and Liability Act (CERCLA), 42 U.S.C. §§ 9601-9675 (1982 & Supp. IV 1986), which imposes liability in connection with the disposal of hazardous wastes. *See, e.g.*, United States v. New Castle County, 642 F. Supp. 1258, 1269 (D. Del. 1986); Colorado v. ASARCO, Inc., 608 F. Supp. 1484, 1491 (D. Colo. 1985). Subsequent to these decisions, Congress explicitly provided a right to contribution. *See* 42 U.S.C. § 9613(f)(1) (Supp. IV 1986).

5. Landes & Posner, *Joint and Multiple Tortfeasors: An Economic Analysis*, 9 J. LEGAL STUD. 517 (1980), *revised and reprinted in* W. LANDES & R. POSNER, THE ECONOMIC STRUCTURE OF TORT LAW 190 (1987). Two subsequent articles, which focused on the right to contribution under the antitrust laws, relied heavily on the analysis of Landes and Posner. *See* Easterbrook, Landes & Posner, *Contribution Among Antitrust Defendants: A Legal and Economic Analysis*, 23 J.L. & ECON. 331 (1980); Polinsky & Shavell, *Contribution and Claim Reduction Among Antitrust Defendants: An Economic Analysis*, 33 STAN. L. REV. 447 (1981). There is also a brief, recent discussion in S. SHAVELL, ECONOMIC ANALYSIS OF ACCIDENT LAW 164-67 (1987). The classic piece on joint and several liability and contribution is Leflar, *Contribution and Indemnity Between Tortfeasors*, 81 U. PA. L. REV. 130 (1932).

One recent study of joint and several liability was published after we had completed our work on this Article. *See* Wright, *Allocating Liability Among Multiple Responsible Causes: A Principled Defense of Joint and Several Liability for Actual Harm and Joint Exposure*, 21 U.C. DAVIS L. REV. 1141 (1988). Its discussion of the efficiency considerations raised by the allocation of losses among joint tortfeasors does not expand upon the theoretical work of Landes & Posner, *supra*. *See* Wright, *supra*, at 1175-76.

6. *See supra* text accompanying notes 1-2.

7. The no-contribution rule of the common law is generally traced to Merryweather v. Nixan, 8 Term Rep. 186, 101 Eng. Rep. 1337 (K.B. 1799). Many common law courts eventually abandoned this rule. *See infra* note 48.

8. *See* Landes & Posner, *supra* note 5, at 521-24. A risk-neutral actor is indifferent between between accepting a gamble and receiving the expected payoff of that gamble. Thus, a risk-neutral actor is indifferent between receiving $10 with certainty and a 10% chance of receiving $100 (and a 90% chance of receiving nothing). In contrast, a risk-averse actor would prefer to receive the expected payoff, and a risk-preferring actor would prefer to gamble.

For discussions of whether corporations are risk-neutral, see K. ELZINGA & W. BREIT, THE ANTITRUST PENALTIES 126-29 (1976); Easterbrook, Landes & Posner, *supra* note 5, at 351-52 & n.50; Polinsky & Shavell, *supra* note 5, at 452-55.

bility would govern. In so doing, they did not consider the properties of several classes of apportionment rules not predicated on a finding of joint and several liability, and did not provide any normative guidance as to when such liability is desirable from an efficiency perspective.

Second, these commentators considered the choice between apportionment and no-contribution only under negligence, and did not examine this choice under strict liability.[9] They shed no light on the efficiency implications, in the context of multiple tortfeasors, of the shift from negligence to strict liability in many areas of accident law,[10] and of the adoption of strict liability under important federal statutes.[11]

In this Article, we show that many different classes of rules of apportionment are being applied by common law courts and advocated by commentators. The question of which rules to apply in particular situations is fraught with confusion.

We then examine the varying efficiency properties of these rules under negligence. In addition, we demonstrate that the efficiency of apportionment rules under negligence depends almost exclusively on whether the negligent actors must pay for damage caused by non-negligent actors, as they must under joint and several liability. Except where one actor's damage does not affect the extent of damage caused by another, only joint and several liability rules produce the efficient result. We use this insight to provide an economic reinterpretation of the terms "distinct," "divisible," and "indivisible" harms, which determine, both in the Restatement (Second) of Torts and in common law cases, whether joint and several liability should attach.[12]

We then consider questions of apportionment under strict liability. All the rules of apportionment currently used by the courts are inefficient. Thus, if courts were limited to a choice of traditional rules of apportionment, efficiency considerations would argue that the rule of liability should be negligence rather than strict liability.

We show, however, that there is a plausible class of apportionment rules under strict liability that produce the efficient outcome. These rules, which attach significance to whether an actor is taking the socially optimal amount of care, combine the distributional consequences of strict liability with the incentives of a negligence regime. We do not believe that

---

9. We interpret the analyses of contribution in antitrust law as ones involving negligence rules. *See* Easterbrook, Landes & Posner, *supra* note 5; Polinsky & Shavell, *supra* note 5. We do so because each conspirator could avoid liability entirely simply by refusing to join the conspiracy. Refusal to enter the conspiracy is thus equivalent to the decision to meet the standard of care.

10. *See, e.g.*, Greenman v. Yuba Power Prods., Inc., 59 Cal. 2d 57, 377 P.2d 897, 27 Cal. Rptr. 697 (1963); Henningsen v. Bloomfield Motors, Inc., 32 N.J. 358, 161 A.2d 69 (1960); RESTATEMENT (SECOND) OF TORTS § 402A (1965) [hereinafter RESTATEMENT]; Priest, *The Invention of Enterprise Liability: A Critical History of the Intellectual Foundations of Modern Tort Law*, 14 J. LEGAL STUD. 461, 505-27 (1985).

11. *See infra* note 27 (discussing CERCLA).

12. *See* RESTATEMENT, *supra* note 10, § 433A.

834   The Yale Law Journal   [Vol. 98: 831

such rules have been applied by the courts or discussed in the secondary literature. Yet, there are no logistical bars to their adoption, as they are no more cumbersome than simple rules of negligence. Under such apportionment rules, we can compensate victims fully for their losses through strict liability, without thereby creating the inefficiencies that attach under traditional strict liability rules. The choice between negligence and strict liability, therefore, need not, as it does now, give rise to a trade-off between efficiency and distributional concerns.[13]

We then consider how, given joint and several liability, contribution rules compare to no-contribution rules—the question that was the focus of attention in the early 1980s.[14] For negligence, our results are consistent with those of the prior literature.[15] For strict liability, however, no-contribution rules are generally inefficient and fail to create the same incentives as contribution rules; thus, the insights of this literature are not applicable outside of negligence.

Finally, we discuss how the various common law rules perform under negligence when courts err in defining the standard of care. Here, too, we analyze the relative merits of joint and several liability.

This Article's conclusion that several common law rules of apportionment are not efficient has more than merely descriptive significance. First, in the absence of overriding goals, the legal system should favor efficient rules; while efficiency might not be the only relevant goal, it clearly is a cognizable one.[16] Thus, the efficiency properties of joint and several liability should be considered in evaluating the recent efforts by several state legislatures to limit joint and several liability in the name of tort reform.[17] Second, the Supreme Court's current interest in economic analysis suggests that the development of the common law, or at least of the federal

---

13. Traditional strict liability rules might still be preferred over both negligence and the strict liability rules that we propose on the ground that they are easier to administer. *See infra* text accompanying note 99.

14. In the absence of joint and several liability, the question does not arise, because only an actor who has paid more than her equitable share of the liability can have a right to contribution. *See* RESTATEMENT, *supra* note 10, § 886A(2).

15. *See supra* text accompanying notes 5-8.

16. For an academic debate on the proper role of efficiency, see Easterbrook, *The Supreme Court, 1983 Term—Foreword: The Court and the Economic System*, 98 HARV. L. REV. 4 (1984) [hereinafter Easterbrook, *Foreword*]; Tribe, *Constitutional Calculus: Equal Justice or Economic Efficiency?*, 98 HARV. L. REV. 592 (1985); Easterbrook, *Method, Result, and Authority: A Reply*, 98 HARV. L. REV. 622 (1985); Fox, *The Politics of Law and Economics in Judicial Decision Making: Antitrust as a Window*, 61 N.Y.U. L. REV. 554 (1986).

17. *See, e.g.*, CAL. CIV. CODE §§ 1431-1431.5 (West Supp. 1988); COLO. REV. STAT. § 09-17-080 (Supp. 1987); UTAH CODE ANN. § 78-27-40 (1987). The California measure was recently upheld by the California Supreme Court, which rejected a challenge grounded on both the federal and state constitutions. Evangelatos v. Superior Court, 44 Cal. 3d 1188, 753 P.2d 585, 246 Cal. Rptr. 629 (1988). For surveys of recent legislative action in this area, see, e.g., Pressler & Schieffer, *Joint and Several Liability: A Case for Reform*, 64 DEN. U.L. REV. 651, 655-59 (1988); Note, *1986 Tort Reform Legislation: A Systematic Evaluation of Caps on Damages and Limitations on Joint and Several Liability*, 73 CORNELL L. REV. 628, 635-37 (1988).

common law,[18] will be affected by the efficiency properties of competing legal rules.[19]

Section I describes the model implicit in the remainder of our analysis. Section II defines the classes of apportionment rules currently employed by courts. Sections III and IV discuss the efficiency of such rules under negligence and strict liability, respectively. Section V discusses the efficiency of no-contribution rules under both negligence and strict liability, and compares it with that of rules of apportionment. Section VI analyzes the effects of departures from the social optimum in the determination of the standard of care under negligence. The Appendix provides formal proofs for various propositions.

I. DESCRIPTION OF THE MODEL

In this Section, we describe the formal model set forth in the Appendix, which provides the basis for our analysis. Because our work was initially motivated by questions raised by the Comprehensive Environmental Response, Compensation and Liability Act (CERCLA)[20] and because this Article is part of a larger work concerning the incentives generated by the statute, this description, and most of our examples, concern the disposal of hazardous wastes. The analysis, of course, applies more broadly.

Imagine a situation in which several manufacturers dump their wastes at a single landfill. The actors benefit from this dumping because the wastes are the by-product of profitable economic activity. At some time in the future, these wastes may leak into the environment and cause serious damage, including, perhaps, the contamination of groundwater supplies. For ease of exposition, we think of this damage as the cost of cleaning up the landfill and the surrounding area affected by the release.[21]

The expected damage of a release is a "social" loss because it does not fall directly on the dumpers unless there is a legal provision shifting the liability to them. Instead, it falls on the victims who would have legal

---

18. For example, questions of contribution and apportionment under CERCLA are determined by reference to the federal common law. *See, e.g.*, Colorado v. ASARCO, Inc., 608 F. Supp. 1484, 1486, 1490 (D. Colo. 1985); United States v. Chem-Dyne Corp., 572 F. Supp. 802, 809 (S.D. Ohio 1983).

19. This interest is most evident in antitrust law. *See, e.g.*, Business Elecs. Corp. v. Sharp Elecs. Corp., 108 S. Ct. 1515, 1519-23 (1988); FTC v. Indiana Fed'n of Dentists, 476 U.S. 447, 457-59 (1986). For a discussion of the use of economic analysis in other areas, see Easterbrook, *Foreword*, *supra* note 16, at 18-58. For a use of efficiency in choosing among liability rules, see United States v. Reliable Transfer Co., 421 U.S. 397, 405 n.11 (1975).

20. 42 U.S.C. §§ 9601-9675 (1982 & Supp. IV 1986).

21. We take the loss to be an impersonal or economic one: restoring the victim to his pre-accident wealth restores him to his pre-accident utility. Following the prior literature on the allocation of damages among parties, *see* sources cited *supra* note 5, we do not consider personal injuries. There is, however, a limited literature that considers such injuries in the single-actor context. *See, e.g.*, Cook & Graham, *The Demand for Insurance and Protection: The Case of Irreplaceable Commodities*, 91 Q.J. Econ. 143 (1977); Note, *An Economic Analysis of Tort Damages for Wrongful Death*, 60 N.Y.U. L. Rev. 1113 (1985).

responsibility for the cleanup, or, alternatively, who would suffer the consequences were the problem left unattended.[22] In our model, each dumper chooses the amount of waste that she will dump; a larger amount will produce a larger benefit to the actor but will also increase the social loss.[23]

The efficient amount of waste is that which maximizes the social objective function: the sum of the benefits derived by the actors minus the social loss. An economically rational dumper, however, does not make this decision based on the social objective function. Instead, she seeks to maximize her private objective function: the benefit that she derives from the activity that leads to the production of the waste minus whatever share of the social loss the legal regime allocates to her.

The share of the social loss borne by each dumper depends both on the liability rule and on the apportionment rule used to divide the social loss among the joint tortfeasors. We consider two liability rules: negligence and strict liability.[24] Negligence rules define a standard of care; if a dumper meets her standard of care, she will bear no portion of the social loss.[25] Under traditional strict liability rules, in contrast, a dumper will bear some portion of the social loss regardless of her level of care.[26] Thus, a strict liability rule can be thought of as the negligence rule that sets the standard of care at zero, so that the standard is always violated.[27]

The second factor that determines each dumper's share of the social loss is the apportionment rule. Because any portion of the social loss that is not borne by the dumpers falls on the victim, this rule determines not only how the joint tortfeasors divide the social loss among themselves but also

---

22. Under CERCLA, the victim is often the federal government, which will undertake cleanups if "there may be an imminent and substantial endangerment to the public health or welfare or the environment because of an actual or threatened release of a hazardous substance from a facility." 42 U.S.C. § 9606(a) (1982).

23. We assume that the probability of a release does not depend on the amount dumped, but that, given a release, the damage is a function of this amount.

24. To isolate the issue of apportionment among injurers, we assume that the victim cannot affect the size of that loss. Thus, we deal only with simple negligence rules (rather than negligence rules with contributory negligence) and with simple strict liability rules (rather than strict liability rules with contributory negligence or with dual contributory negligence). *See infra* note 135 (defining these rules). Our analysis, however, can easily extend to the case in which the victim's behavior affects the size of the loss. Indeed, as we note in the conclusion of this Article, the formal model of this phenomenon is similar to the model that we use.

25. In general, as the derivation of the conditions for the social optimum in the Appendix makes clear, if each actor obtains different benefits from producing the waste, each actor should also face a different standard of care. This result is consistent with Judge Learned Hand's famous formula in United States v. Carroll Towing Co., 159 F.2d 169 (2d Cir. 1947), under which actors with different costs of taking care face different standards of care. *See id.* at 173.

26. In Section IV.B., however, we propose strict liability rules under which an actor who dumps less than the socially optimal amount might not bear any portion of the loss.

27. Even though CERCLA is a strict liability statute, *see, e.g.*, New York v. Shore Realty Corp., 759 F.2d 1032, 1042 (2d Cir. 1985); City of Philadelphia v. Stepan Chem. Co., 544 F. Supp. 1135, 1140 n.4 (E.D. Pa. 1982), we analyze the effects of apportionment rules under both negligence and strict liability because there is value in thinking about whether the choice of strict liability was wise. Moreover, our model, with suitable reinterpretation for the options available to the actors, is equally applicable to the areas of law in which contribution questions are important. *See supra* text accompanying notes 1-4.

the victim's share of the damage, which is the total damage minus the sum of the shares of the total damage paid by the dumpers.

Under all eight classes of apportionment rules defined in Section II, the victim's maximum recovery is the total social loss. We exclude the possibility of punitive damages, under which a victim could recover more than the damage that he had suffered, because such damages are generally not available in the absence of intentional wrongdoing.[28]

From an efficiency perspective, the objective of the liability and apportionment rules is to induce rational actors to produce the socially efficient amount of waste.[29] Efficient apportionment rules give each private actor incentives that match those of the social objective function. This Article seeks to define the conditions under which apportionment rules will produce such a match.

II. Rules of Apportionment

We provide a taxonomy that classifies the apportionment rules commonly used by courts and advocated by commentators. The resulting categories are defined by reference to three factors: whether the rules are full liability or partial liability, unitary share or fractional share, and fixed share or proportional share. We end with a simple numerical example that illustrates the operation of the various rules.

The taxonomy that we set forth provides a framework for analyzing the efficiency properties of the various rules. It also isolates those apportionment choices open to the courts that have efficiency consequences from those that do not. Thus, it informs the discussion of the relative merits of the different rules.

A. Full Liability versus Partial Liability

In the single tortfeasor context, most of the literature assumes that the negligent actor is liable for the full loss that is caused by her actions.[30] We

---

28. *See, e.g.*, Taylor v. Superior Court, 24 Cal. 3d 890, 900, 598 P.2d 854, 859, 157 Cal. Rptr. 693, 699 (1979); Gravitt v. Newman, 114 A.D.2d 1000, 1002, 495 N.Y.S.2d 439, 441 (1985); RESTATEMENT, *supra* note 10, § 908. Recently, however, the traditional rules against punitive damages appear to have been relaxed. *See* Schwartz, *Proposals for Products Liability Reform: A Theoretical Synthesis*, 97 YALE L.J. 353, 412 (1988).

29. We assume throughout this Article that each actor has sufficient resources to bear the full social loss. In a subsequent piece, we consider how the different apportionment rules perform where there is the possibility of insolvency. *See* Kornhauser & Revesz, *Apportioning Damages Among Potentially Insolvent Actors*, 19 J. LEGAL STUD. (forthcoming 1990). For commentary on this question, see, e.g., Shavell, *The Judgment Proof Problem*, 6 INT'L REV. L. & ECON. 45 (1986); Note, *The Case of the Disappearing Defendant: An Economic Analysis*, 132 U. PA. L. REV. 145 (1983).

30. As Marcel Kahan points out, most economic models have assumed that negligent injurers are liable for all accident losses associated with their activity. Kahan, *Causation and Incentives to Take Care Under the Negligence Rule*, 18 J. LEGAL STUD. (forthcoming 1989). For examples of such works, see Brown, *Toward an Economic Theory of Liability*, 2 J. LEGAL STUD. 323, 328 (1973); Diamond, *Single Activity Accidents*, 3 J. LEGAL STUD. 107, 117 (1974); Polinsky, *Strict Liability v. Negligence in a Market Setting*, 70 AM. ECON. REV. 363, 364 (Papers & Proceedings 1980). The full

shall call such a rule a "full liability" rule. Alternatively, the negligent actor might be responsible for less than the full damage that she causes. We shall refer to such a rule as a "partial liability" rule.

Statutes that limit the liability of actors, such as the $560,000,000 limit of liability for losses from nuclear disasters,[31] or limits on malpractice liability,[32] are perhaps the simplest examples of partial liability rules.[33] Statutory caps on liability, however, create incentives analogous to those that arise when a tortfeasor is insufficiently solvent to pay for her share of the social loss; we discuss these problems in a subsequent study.[34] In this Article, instead, we consider a second class of partial liability rules, in which a negligent actor is liable only for those losses that would have been prevented through due care, or, stated differently, for the losses that are caused by the actor's negligence. The victim therefore bears the damage that would have resulted even if none of the actors had been negligent. Such a rule is consistent with certain interpretations of the common law of negligence.[35] For the remainder of this Article, our discussion of partial liability rules is restricted to rules of this type.

Consider, for example, an actor who builds a ninety-foot dam when the standard of care is one hundred feet. Under a partial liability rule, the actor is responsible only for the losses caused by those floods that would have been prevented by a hundred-foot dam; she would not have to pay for the losses caused by floods that would have occurred even if the dam had been one hundred feet high. In contrast, under a full liability rule, the actor is liable for the damages caused by all floods, even those that could not have been avoided if the dam had been a hundred feet high.[36]

---

liability nature of most economic models is analyzed extensively in Kahan, *supra*. For a discussion of how courts deal with the choice between full liability and partial liability, see *infra* text accompanying notes 38–39.

31. 42 U.S.C. § 2210(e) (1982); *see* Duke Power Co. v. Carolina Envtl. Study Group, Inc., 438 U.S. 59, 64–65 (1978).

32. *See, e.g.,* CAL. CIV. CODE § 3333.2 (West Supp. 1988); MICH. COMP. LAWS ANN. § 600.1483 (West Supp. 1988); TEX. REV. CIV. STAT. ANN. art. 4590(i), §§ 11.02-.03 (Vernon Supp. 1988); VA. CODE ANN. § 8.01-581.15 (1984 & Supp. 1988).

33. Such caps, particularly on non-economic damages, are one of the major elements of the recent tort reform movement. *See* Note, *supra* note 17, at 628, 637–38. For statutory caps on such damages, see, e.g., FLA. STAT. ANN. § 768.80 (West Supp. 1988) ($450,000); MD. CTS. & JUD. PROC. CODE ANN. § 11-108 (Supp. 1987) ($350,000); N.H. REV. STAT. ANN. § 508:4-d (Supp. 1987) ($875,000).

Several states have struck down caps on damages as inconsistent with their state constitutions. *See, e.g.,* Kansas Malpractice Victims Coalition v. Bell, 243 Kan. 333, 757 P.2d 251 (1988); Lucas v. United States, 757 S.W. 2d 687 (Tex. 1988). In other states, however, such caps have been upheld. *See, e.g.,* Fein v. Permanente Medical Group, 38 Cal. 3d 137, 157–64, 695 P.2d 665, 679–84, 211 Cal. Rptr. 368, 382–87 (1985); Johnson v. St. Vincent Hosp., 273 Ind. 374, 397–400, 404 N.E.2d 585, 600–01 (1980). For a recent overview of challenges to tort-reform laws, see Barrett, *Tort Reform Fight Shifts to State Courts,* Wall St. J., Sept. 19, 1988, at B1.

34. *See* Kornhauser & Revesz, *supra* note 29. In both cases, the tortfeasor does not "see" a portion of the social loss. For statutory caps, this portion is the amount above the cap; for insolvency, it is the amount above her solvency.

35. *See infra* text accompanying notes 38–39 (discussing whether courts use full liability or partial liability rules).

36. We assume that if a flood occurs, the level of damage is independent of the height of the dam.

Under a partial liability rule, whenever a flood occurs a court must inquire whether that flood would have occurred had the defendant not been negligent. If the flood would not have occurred, the defendant must pay the full damages caused by the flood. In contrast, if the flood would have occurred anyway, the defendant would not have to pay any damages at all.[37]

Commentators are split on whether courts apply a full liability or a partial liability rule. Mark Grady argues that, under what we call in this Article a partial liability rule, a negligent actor could advance the defense that the loss would have occurred even if she had not been negligent. He observes that this defense is quite uncommon, and therefore that courts cannot be applying a partial liability rule.[38] In contrast, Marcel Kahan

---

For similar examples, see Grady, *A New Positive Economic Theory of Negligence*, 92 YALE L.J. 799, 806-08, 822 (1983); Kahan, *supra* note 30.

37. In some contexts, one cannot determine with certainty whether the accident would have occurred without negligence. Under such stochastic conditions, the interpretation of a partial liability rule is somewhat more complex. Assume that a negligent driver has a 60% probability of hitting one pedestrian on a particular stretch of road (and a 40% probability of not hitting anyone). If he is not negligent, the driver has a 30% probability of hitting one pedestrian (and a 70% probability of not hitting anyone). The damages suffered by an injured pedestrian are $1000. When a pedestrian is hit by a negligent driver, what portion of this $1000 should be borne by the driver under a partial liability rule?

At first glance, $700 might appear to be the correct amount, since it is the full damage of $1000, discounted by the expected damage of $300 (30% of $1000) that would be caused in the absence of negligence. However, the driver's negligence cannot be said to have caused $700 in damages. The expected damage, given the driver's negligence, is $600 (60% of $1000). The negligence therefore increases the expected damage by $300 ($600 minus $300). Should the negligent driver therefore pay the victim only $300?

If under a partial liability rule the negligent driver were responsible for a damage of only $300, the driver would not pay for the full increase in expected damage caused by his negligence; if an accident occurred, the driver would pay $300, but if an accident did not occur, the driver would pay nothing. Given the 60% probability of an accident occurring when the driver is negligent, the expected cost of the driver's negligence would therefore be only $180 (as compared with an expected damage of $300). For the driver to have sufficient incentive to meet the standard of care and to avoid negligent driving, he would have to pay $500 in the event of an accident, so that his expected cost would be $300 (60% of $500).

More generally, suppose both that every accident causes a fixed loss L, and that the level of carelessness x (a higher x denotes less care) determines the probability that an accident will occur. Let c be the standard of care and suppose that the actor negligently adopts some $x > c$. We may then calculate A(x), the amount recoverable by a victim, as:

$$A(x) = [p(x) - p(c)]L/p(x), \text{ where } x > c$$
$$(A(x) = 0, \text{ where } x \leq c).$$

The desirable incentives of rules of this type are discussed in Landes & Posner, *Tort Law as a Regulatory Regime for Catastrophic Personal Injuries*, 13 J. LEGAL STUD. 417 (1984), *revised and reprinted in* W. LANDES & R. POSNER, *supra* note 5, at 256.

One reason courts might not discount the damage suffered by an injured plaintiff—to take into account the expected damage if the defendant had not been negligent—is that courts may assume that this latter amount is zero. Thus, in the example presented here, the implicit assumption might be that without negligence the probability of hitting a pedestrian would be zero, or, at most, a *de minimis* value. This type of assumption may well be inappropriate in cases involving exposure to carcinogens, which might involve significant background risk. For one approach to this problem, see Robinson, *Probabilistic Causation and Compensation for Tortious Risk*, 14 J. LEGAL STUD. 779 (1985) (courts should award damages based on probability of injury, rather than on injury itself).

38. *See* Grady, *supra* note 36, at 822. He believes, however, that courts apply, and should apply, a different causation test in which they compare the costs and benefits of untaken precautions. *See id.* at 814-17, 824-29. In an article published after their study of multiple tortfeasors, Landes and Pos-

840   The Yale Law Journal   [Vol. 98: 831

contends that the common law has, in fact, adopted a partial liability rule.[39]

But even if Grady's observation is correct, the partial liability rule still merits study because strong normative arguments have been made in its favor. Kahan argues that this rule is compelled by the requirement of causation: that an injurer's negligence, as opposed to her mere action, has caused the loss. Under the full liability rule, in contrast, the injurer is liable for losses that would have occurred even if she had not been negligent.[40]

The distinction between full liability and partial liability rules, which we have introduced for the case of a single tortfeasor, is present also for multiple tortfeasors.[41] Under a full liability rule, the maximum amount for which the negligent actors can be liable in the aggregate (and which the victim can recover) is the full social loss.[42] In contrast, under a partial liability rule, this amount is reduced to take account of the loss that would have occurred even if all of the actors had been non-negligent. While the law-and-economics literature on joint tortfeasors, including the article by Landes and Posner, has assumed the use of full liability rules, the causation rationale supporting the use of partial liability rules for single actors applies with no less force to multiple tortfeasors.[43]

The distinction between full liability rules and partial liability rules exists only under negligence. It collapses under strict liability because strict liability rules assure that the victim is compensated for his full damage.[44]

---

ner present a model in which injurers are not liable for damages that would have taken place even if they had been non-negligent. *See* Landes & Posner, *Causation in Tort Law: An Economic Approach*, 12 J. LEGAL STUD. 109, 111-14 (1983), *revised and reprinted in* W. LANDES & R. POSNER, *supra* note 5, at 228. But even in this model, once a defendant is liable, she must pay for the full damage, with no discount for the expected damage in the absence of negligence. Thus, their model does not deal with the problem of stochastic harms. *See supra* note 37.

39.   Kahan, *supra* note 30.

40.   This question is somewhat more complicated where it involves a stochastic harm. But where one cannot say with certainty whether a loss would have occurred in the absence of negligence, the question of causation needs to be reinterpreted. Suppose that a negligent driver causes an accident, and that, without negligence, the probability of this accident would have been thirty percent. In what way, then, can the negligence be said to have "caused" the loss? It did increase the probability of the accident, and therefore the expected value of the loss, but one cannot say, as one could in the dam example above, that the loss would not have occurred without the negligence.

41.   We assume here that all of the damage is caused by negligent parties. We deal below with situations in which the damage is caused both by negligent and non-negligent parties. *See infra* text accompanying notes 45-47.

42.   As we discuss below, the negligent actors will be liable for this loss under all full liability, unitary share rules. *See infra* text accompanying note 45. The negligent actors will also be liable for the full social loss under full liability, fractional share rules, provided that all actors contributing to the social loss are negligent. *See infra* text accompanying note 47.

43.   Landes and Posner assume that if one actor is negligent and the others are not, the negligent actor will pay the full damage, even if that damage, or at least part of that damage, would have occurred even had all parties been non-negligent. Landes & Posner, *supra* note 5, at 521-23.

44.   This statement holds for the type of partial liability rule that we discuss in the text, under which, for negligence, an actor is liable only for the damage in excess of that which would be caused if all actors were non-negligent. The statement does not apply to strict liability rules with caps. This

B. *Unitary Share versus Fractional Share*

The law-and-economics literature on joint tortfeasors also assumes that the negligent actors pay not only for the damages attributable to their own actions, but also for the damages attributable to the non-negligent actors.[45] Under a competing rule, the negligent actors do not pay for the damages attributable to the non-negligent actors. We refer to such a rule as a "fractional share" rule because the victim generally recovers only a fraction of the maximum damage to which he would be entitled.[46] Under a fractional share rule, the victim recovers the maximum damage only if all of the actors contributing to the harm are negligent; otherwise, he recovers less than this amount because part of the damage will be attributable to non-negligent actors. The shares of the negligent actors therefore can add up to only a fraction of the maximum damage.[47]

We refer to the rule under which the negligent actors pay for damages attributable to the non-negligent actors as a "unitary share" rule, because under it the victim recovers the maximum loss allowable whenever at least one actor is negligent, regardless of how much of the damage is caused by non-negligent actors. Thus, the shares of the negligent actors are unitary because they add up to the maximum damage recoverable by the victim.

Unitary share rules correspond to rules of joint and several liability with a right to contribution from other negligent tortfeasors,[48] whereas fractional share rules correspond to rules of non-joint (several only) liabil-

---

discussion raises the interesting question of why we should regard a rule that makes the victim bear the "excess" loss (the loss above a cap) as a strict liability rule when a rule that makes the victim bear the "basic" loss (that which ensues when all actors are non-negligent) is regarded as a negligence rule.

45. *See* Landes & Posner, *supra* note 5, at 522 ("the full loss is shifted to the negligent injurer . . . when the other injurer and the victim use due care" even though non-negligent injurer contributes to loss).

46. Under a full liability rule, this damage is the social loss; under a partial liability rule, it is the social loss minus the damage that would have resulted even if none of the actors contributing to the harm had been negligent.

47. The interpretation of fractional share rules, like the interpretation of partial liability rules, is more complex when the damages are stochastic. Assume that because of a factory's negligent treatment of toxic substances and of the background risk of cancer due to several unrelated sources, the factory's workers face a 50% probability of cancer; 20% of this probability is attributable to the background sources. Assume that without the factory's negligence the only risk of cancer to the workers would come from the background sources. The question, then, is what amount the factory must pay under a fractional share rule when a worker becomes afflicted by cancer.

As in the case of partial liability rules, *see supra* note 37, under fractional share rules, the share that should be borne by the factory is

$$[p(x) - p(b)]L/p(x),$$

where $p(b)L$ is the contribution of the background sources. In this example, the factory would pay 60% of the damage caused by each incidence of cancer ((50% - 20%)/50%).

48. Originally, no right to contribution existed under the common law. *See supra* note 7. Beginning in the late nineteenth century, however, common law courts began to recognize such a right. *See, e.g.*, Tolbert v. Gerber Indus., Inc., 255 N.W.2d 362 (Minn. 1977); Dole v. Dow Chem. Co., 30 N.Y.2d 143, 282 N.E.2d 288, 331 N.Y.S.2d 382 (1972); RESTATEMENT, *supra* note 10, § 886A comment a. Moreover, in many states, the no-contribution rule was overruled by statute. *See, e.g., id.*; UNIF. COMPARATIVE FAULT ACT § 4, 12 U.L.A. 47 (1979) (Supp. 1988) (adopted by two jurisdictions); UNIF. CONTRIBUTION AMONG TORTFEASORS ACT § 1, 12 U.L.A. 63 (1955) (adopted by 18 jurisidictions).

ity.[49] Indeed, consider the differences between joint and several liability with a right to contribution on the one hand and non-joint liability on the other. First, an actor held jointly and severally liable cannot get contribution for the portion of the damage attributable to the non-negligent actors. Second, such an actor cannot get contribution for the portion of the damage attributable to negligent actors who are insolvent. Third, such an actor must expend the transaction costs necessary to bring the contribution actions. Because in this Article we assume the absence of insolvency and transaction costs,[50] the difference between joint and non-joint liability is who pays for the share of the damage attributable to the non-negligent actors. Under joint liability, this share is borne by the negligent actors, whereas under non-joint liability it is borne by the victim. This is precisely the distinction between unitary and fractional share rules: Joint and several liability with a right to contribution therefore corresponds to a unitary share rule, whereas non-joint liability corresponds to a fractional share rule.

As with the distinction between full liability rules and partial liability rules, the distinction between unitary share and fractional share rules exists only under negligence because, again, strict liability rules compensate the victim for his full damage.

C. *Fixed Share versus Proportional Share*

The models on joint tortfeasors used in the law-and-economics literature also assume that each negligent actor pays a share of the damage that depends only on the number of actors who are negligent and is independent of the level of care taken by the negligent actors.[51] The most common rule in this family is a per capita rule, under which the amount to be paid by the negligent actors is divided equally among those actors.[52] Thus, in our hazardous waste example, two negligent actors would pay the same amount in damages even though one dumped far more than her standard of care whereas the other violated her standard only by a small margin. Commentators advocate per capita rules because they are easier to implement. Such rules are frequently used to apportion damages under the federal securities laws.[53]

---

49. For further discussion of these rules, see *infra* Section III.B.

50. *See supra* note 29. If transaction costs are positive, joint liability allocates the costs of suing additional defendants to the tortfeasors and non-joint liability allocates them to the victim. Similarly, if some wrongdoers are insolvent, under joint liability other wrongdoers must bear the unfunded portion of their allocable damages. Under non-joint liability, the victim bears this loss.

51. *See* Landes & Posner, *supra* note 5, at 522.

52. One may interpret the antitrust analyses of contribution by Easterbrook, Landes & Posner, *supra* note 5, and Polinsky & Shavell, *supra* note 5, as using the identical rule. Thus, under these models, the damages resulting from an antitrust conspiracy are divided per capita among the parties that have joined the conspiracy.

53. *See, e.g.*, Herzfeld v. Laventhol, Krekstein, Horwath & Horwath, 378 F. Supp. 112, 136 (S.D.N.Y. 1974), *aff'd in part and rev'd in part*, 540 F.2d 27 (2d Cir. 1976); Globus, Inc. v. Law

One can easily imagine a different set of rules, under which the negligent actors divide their joint liability in proportion to their levels of care. Such rules are now being applied under CERCLA, where courts will apportion liability proportionally to the amount of waste that a defendant has dumped.[54] We label such rules "proportional share" rules because they allocate damages in proportion to the waste dumped by each of the actors.[55] In contrast, we refer to rules that apportion damages among the negligent actors without regard to such considerations as "fixed share" rules.[56]

Because the literature assumed that the negligent actors would pay the portion of the loss attributable to non-negligent actors (that the rules would be unitary share rather than fractional share),[57] it did not have to allocate any amount of the damage to the non-negligent actors. Under fractional share rules, however, such an allocation is necessary and can be performed either in fixed shares or in proportional shares. Of course, under negligence rules, the non-negligent actors do not actually bear the damage attributable to them in this manner; the victim bears it instead.

The distinction between fixed share and proportional share rules holds under strict liability as well as under negligence. The only necessary reinterpretation is that under traditional strict liability rules, the damage is

---

Research Serv., Inc., 318 F. Supp. 955 (S.D.N.Y. 1970), aff'd, 442 F.2d 1346 (2d Cir.), cert. denied, 404 U.S. 941 (1971); Douglas & Bates, *The Federal Securities Act of 1933*, 43 YALE L.J. 171, 178-81 (1933). *See generally* Scott, *Resurrecting Indemnification: Contribution Clauses in Underwriting Agreements*, 61 N.Y.U. L. REV. 223, 252-59 (1986) (discussing loss apportionment under securities laws).

The per capita approach is also accepted in the UNIF. CONTRIBUTION AMONG TORTFEASORS ACT § 2, 12 U.L.A. 87 (1955), which provides that "relative degrees of fault shall not be considered," and which has been adopted by 18 jurisdictions. For applications of this rule, see, e.g., Celotex Corp. v. Campbell Roofing & Metal Works, Inc., 352 So. 2d 1316 (Miss. 1977); Commercial Union Assurance v. Western Farm Bureau Ins., 93 N.M. 507, 601 P.2d 1203 (1979).

54. *See* Colorado v. ASARCO, Inc., 608 F. Supp. 1484, 1487-88 (D. Colo. 1985). Courts can also consider other factors, such as the toxicity of the hazardous substance involved. *Id.* These factors are proxies for the risk posed by each generator. Questions of allocation under CERCLA are more complex when they involve generators on the one hand, and transporters of the hazardous wastes or owners of the waste sites on the other, *see* 42 U.S.C. § 9607(a) (Supp. IV 1986), since the risks posed by these diverse activities are more difficult to compare.

55. The proportional share approach is also accepted in UNIF. COMPARATIVE FAULT ACT § 2, 12 U.L.A. 43 (1979) (Supp. 1988), which has been adopted by two jurisdictions. For an application of this rule, see Mulinix v. Saydel Consol. School Dist., 376 N.W.2d 109 (Iowa Ct. App. 1985).

In 1975, the Supreme Court abandoned a fixed share approach to apportionment cases in admiralty, adopting a proportional share approach. *See* United States v. Reliable Transfer Co., 421 U.S. 397 (1975). Even in the securities law context, *see supra* note 53, there may be a move away from the fixed share approach. *See* McLean v. Alexander, 449 F. Supp. 1251, 1275-76 (D. Del. 1978), *rev'd on other grounds*, 599 F.2d 1190 (3d Cir. 1979).

56. The categorization scheme outlined in the text is not exhaustive. For example, a different proportional share rule would allocate the damage among the actors in proportion to the amount by which their level of waste exceeds the standard of care, rather than by reference to the actual levels of care.

In antitrust law, damages might be apportioned by market share and thus might depend upon decisions of the actors. Such damages would not depend, however, on the decision that precipitates the liability, which is the decision to conspire.

57. *See supra* text accompanying note 45.

divided among all actors who caused it, rather than simply among the negligent actors.[58]

D. *Illustrating the Effects of the Rules*

We have thus identified eight categories of apportionment rules under negligence and two categories of apportionment rules under strict liability. To illustrate further the operation of the various rules, we present a hypothetical problem. Consider, once again, the hazardous waste example, in which three waste generators, A_1, A_2, and A_3, operating under a negligence rule, dump hazardous wastes at a single site. The standard of care for each is 10 units. Assume that A_3 meets this standard of care by dumping 10 units, but that A_1 and A_2 do not, dumping 15 and 25 units, respectively; the total amount dumped is therefore 50 units. Assume that the damage resulting from this dumping in the event of a release[59] is the square of the total amount dumped—$2500 in this example.[60] Assume, also, that some time after the dumping a release occurs.

Because A_3 meets the standard of care, she will not be liable for any portion of this damage. The question is how each of the apportionment rules allocates the $2500 among A_1, A_2, and the victim, A_0, which, as the residual bearer of cleanup costs, will have to pay for the damage not covered by A_1 and A_2.

The allocations under the eight rules are indicated in the two 2x2 matrices of Figure I.[61] Under Rules 1 through 4, which are full liability rules, the negligent actors would at most pay the full damage of $2500. Under Rules 1 and 2, which are unitary share rules, A_1 and A_2 pay collectively this full amount and A_0 bears no residual damage. Rule 1 allocates the $2500 equally between A_1 and A_2; each therefore pays $1250 (1/2 of $2500); Rule 2 allocates it proportionally to the amounts dumped by A_1 and A_2; A_1 therefore pays $937 (15/40 of $2500) and A_2 pays $1563 (25/40 of $2500).

Under Rules 3 and 4, which are fractional share rules, A_1 and A_2 do not pay for the portion of the damage attributable to A_3. Rule 3 allocates equal shares to A_1, A_2, and A_3; A_1 and A_2 each therefore pays $833 (1/3 of $2500), and A_0 bears the residual damage of $833 attributable to A_3. Rule 4, instead, allocates shares in proportion to the amounts dumped by A_1, A_2, and A_3. A_1, therefore, pays $750 (15/50 of $2500); A_2 pays $1250

---

58. *See supra* text accompanying note 55.
59. *See supra* text accompanying note 21.
60. Under strict liability, A_1, A_2, and A_3 each pay $833 (1/3 of $2500) under a fixed share rule; under a proportional share rule, A_3 pays $500 (10/50 of $2500), and A_1 and A_2 pay $750 (15/50 of $2500) and $1250 (25/50 of $2500), respectively.
61. The example assumes that each fixed share rule is a per capita rule and that the proportional rule uses total waste (of the relevant group) as the denominator.

(25/50 of \$2500), and A_0 bears the residual loss of \$500 attributable to A_3.

Under Rules 5 through 8, which are partial liability rules, the maximum amount that the negligent actors would pay is \$1600: the full damage of \$2500 minus the damage that would have occurred if all the actors had been non-negligent, which is \$900 (the square of the 30 units that would have been dumped if all three actors had been non-negligent). Under Rules 5 and 6, which are unitary share rules, A_1 and A_2 pay collectively the full \$1600 and A_0 bears the residual loss of \$900. Rule 5 allocates the \$1600 equally between A_1 and A_2; each therefore pays \$800 (1/2 of \$1600). Rule 6 allocates it proportionally to the amounts dumped by A_1 and A_2; A_1 therefore pays \$600 (15/40 of \$1600) and A_2 pays \$1000 (25/40 of \$1600).

Under Rules 7 and 8, which are fractional share rules, A_1 and A_2 do not pay for the portion of the damage attributable to A_3. Rule 7 allocates equal shares of the \$1600 to A_1, A_2, and A_3;[62] A_1 and A_2 each therefore pays \$533 (1/3 of \$1600) and A_0 bears the residual loss of \$1433. Rule 8, instead, allocates shares of the \$1600 in proportion to the amounts dumped by A_1, A_2, and A_3. A_1 therefore pays \$480 (15/50 of \$1600), A_2 pays \$800 (25/50 of \$1600), and A_0 bears the residual loss of \$1220.[63]

Figure I illustrates a wide discrepancy in how the different rules allocate the damage. For example, the victim A_0 pays nothing under Rules 1 and 2, but pays more than half the damage under Rule 7. Similarly, A_2 pays almost two-thirds of the damage under Rule 2, but less than one-quarter under Rule 7. It is a powerful reflection of the common law's disarray in this area that even this very simple problem could generate such divergent results, and that each of these results would have some claim to legitimacy.[64]

---

62. The allocation of an amount of damages to A_3 is not inconsistent with a partial liability rule, which reduces the full damage award by the amount of damage that would have occurred if all actors had been non-negligent. If A_3 had not dumped at all, the total amount dumped would have been 40 units and the amount dumped if the two remaining actors had been non-negligent would have been 20 units. Under a partial liability rule, A_1 and A_2 would pay \$1200 (the square of 40 minus the square of 20). Thus, if none of the \$1600 were allocated to A_3 in our example, A_1 and A_2 would be responsible for \$400 more than the damage they would have caused if A_3 had not dumped at all. In contrast, under Rule 7, which allocates a share to A_3, A_1 and A_2 pay the total of \$1066—\$134 less than they would have paid if A_3 had not dumped at all. Under Rule 8, they pay \$1280—\$80 more than they would have paid. Thus, these two rules can be seen as moving A_1 and A_2 closer to where they would have been without A_3.

We do not argue that the only sensible rules are ones that allocate a portion of the \$1600 to A_3. Under Rules 5 and 6, for example, no such allocation is made. Rather, we make the narrower claim that there is a principled basis for allocating a portion of the \$1600 to A_3 (which will, of course, be borne by the victim A_0).

63. The purpose of this example is merely to illustrate the operation of the rules. It is a non-equilibrium example because, as we show in Section III, rational actors would not choose to be negligent under unitary share rules.

64. In fact, when we presented an earlier draft of this Article at faculty workshops, the participants suggested even more methods of apportionment. We agree that our taxonomy does not capture the full extent of plausible rules, but believe that it provides a useful way to classify the predominant

846   The Yale Law Journal   [Vol. 98: 831

FIGURE I: APPORTIONMENT UNDER NEGLIGENCE

Full Liability Rules

	Fixed Share	Proportional Share
	Rule 1	Rule 2
Unitary Share	$A_0 = 0$ $A_1 = 1250$ $A_2 = 1250$	$A_0 = 0$ $A_1 = 937$ $A_2 = 1563$
	Rule 3	Rule 4
Fractional Share	$A_0 = 833$ $A_1 = 833$ $A_2 = 833$	$A_0 = 500$ $A_1 = 750$ $A_2 = 1250$

Partial Liability Rules

	Fixed Share	Proportional Share
	Rule 5	Rule 6
Unitary Share	$A_0 = 900$ $A_1 = 800$ $A_2 = 800$	$A_0 = 900$ $A_1 = 600$ $A_2 = 1000$
	Rule 7	Rule 8
Fractional Share	$A_0 = 1433$ $A_1 = 533$ $A_2 = 533$	$A_0 = 1220$ $A_1 = 480$ $A_2 = 800$

III. APPORTIONMENT UNDER NEGLIGENCE

In this Section, we evaluate the efficiency properties under negligence of the eight classes of rules of apportionment defined above. Throughout this Section, we assume that the standards of care are set at the socially optimal level. We show that the four classes of unitary share rules are always efficient, but that the other four classes of rules generally are not. Because, as we have explained, rules of joint and several liability are unitary share rules, we then discuss the conditions under which the common law holds actors jointly and severally liable, and provide an economic reinterpretation of the legal categories that give rise to such liability.[65] Finally, we

---

common law approaches. The proofs in the Appendix cover a wider (though not exhaustive) class of rules than that described in the text.

65. *See supra* text accompanying note 12.

explain why the imposition of joint and several liability does not necessarily give rise to a trade-off between fairness and efficiency.

A. *Efficiency of the Various Rules*

In their study of joint tortfeasors, Landes and Posner considered the efficiency properties of a single rule of apportionment, which under our taxonomy would be classified as a full liability, unitary, fixed share rule (Rule 1).[66] They proved that such a rule produces the efficient outcome, but did not seek to ascertain the boundaries of the class of efficient rules or inquire whether the legal system contains rules that are not efficient.

We show that of the eight rules described in Section II, the four unitary share rules (Rules 1, 2, 5, and 6) lead to the maximization of social welfare under negligence, provided that the standards of care for each of the actors are set at the socially optimal level.[67] Thus, every full liability, unitary share rule (Rules 1 and 2) and every partial liability, unitary share rule (Rules 5 and 6) is efficient. Under such rules, the efficient outcome is attained regardless either of the benefit and loss functions or of the number of actors contributing to the damage. The class of rules examined by Landes and Posner is a special case of this general category of efficient rules.

We also show that not all of the apportionment rules currently employed by the courts are efficient. In particular, no partial liability, fractional share rule (Rules 7 and 8) ever induces efficient behavior. Moreover, the two full liability, fractional share rules (Rules 3 and 4) are inefficient for certain benefit and loss functions and number of actors contributing to the damage.

In the Appendix, we prove that for the efficient outcome to occur, the tortfeasors must, in the aggregate, be responsible at least for the increased loss resulting from departures from the standard of care, including the loss attributable to non-negligent actors. We also prove in the Appendix that as long as rules are unitary rather than fractional, it does not matter, from an efficiency perspective, whether they are full liability rules rather than partial liability rules, or fixed share rules rather than proportional share rules.

The intuition behind the result that unitary share rules will induce efficient behavior is straightforward. Consider first the case of a partial liability, unitary share rule. Under this rule, the negligent actors will be liable for the full damage caused minus the damage that results when all actors are non-negligent.

---

66. *See supra* text accompanying notes 43–45, 51.

67. For each actor, the social optimum is the level that produces the maximization of the social objective function. *See supra* text accompanying notes 22–23. We deal in Section VI with standards of care that are not set at the optimal level.

If all but one of the actors are non-negligent, it would not be rational for the remaining actor to be negligent.[68] If this actor were contemplating dumping more than the standard of care, she would face liability for the full increase in the resulting damage. If the standard of care is set at the social optimum,[69] the increased benefits that this actor would obtain through negligent conduct would be less than the increase in the damage for which she would be liable. Thus, assuming that all but one of the actors are non-negligent, the remaining actor will be non-negligent as well.

Now consider whether it would be rational for more than one actor to be negligent. A unitary share rule will assign to the negligent actors, in the aggregate, the full increase in the ensuing damage. If negligent action on the part of these actors were preferable to non-negligent action for each of them, then the total social welfare would exceed that attainable when all actors meet the standard of care, which is not possible if the standard of care is set at the social optimum.

Consider first the group of non-negligent actors; none of them either gains or loses from a change in the behavior of an actor who chooses to become negligent, because they bear none of the loss and receive none of the resulting benefits. The negligent actors, on the other hand, would capture the full additional benefits of dumping more than the standard of care, but would pay for the full additional damage. Since social welfare is maximized when all the actors meet the standard of care, the increase in damages must exceed the increase in benefits.

Thus, it would not be rational for all these actors to be negligent. However the additional damage was allocated among them, at least some of them would have to pay more than the additional benefit that they obtained by acting negligently, since the aggregate increase in benefit is less than the aggregate increase in damage. Any actors who had to pay more than their increased benefits would opt to be non-negligent. But once those actors chose to be non-negligent, the apportionment rule would allocate to other actors damages exceeding their increased benefit, since regardless of how many actors are negligent, the increase in aggregate damage caused by that negligence would continue to be greater than the increase in aggregate benefit. It is therefore not rational for more than one actor to be negligent when a partial liability unitary share rule is in force.

We have already explained that it is not rational for a single actor to be negligent either. Thus, under a partial liability, unitary share rule, all actors will be non-negligent, and the efficient result will be attained.

---

68. It would never be economically rational for an actor to dump less than the standard of care, since the actor would bear no portion of the damage even if she dumped an amount equal to the standard of care. Thus, the actor would merely forego the benefit of engaging in the economic activity that produces the wastes.

69. *See supra* text accompanying notes 22–23.

This discussion shows that any partial liability, unitary share rule is efficient, whatever additional rules are employed to apportion the damage among negligent parties. Thus, both the partial liability, unitary, fixed share rule (Rule 5) and the partial liability, unitary, proportional share rule (Rule 6) lead to the efficient outcome.

It is now easy to show that any full liability, unitary share rule (Rules 1 and 2) is efficient as well. Indeed, if the liability for the increase in damage caused by negligence, which is imposed by a partial liability rule, deters all actors from being negligent, then surely liability for the increase in damage caused by negligence *plus* liability for the damage that results when all actors are non-negligent, which is imposed by a full liability rule, would also deter all actors from being negligent. Similarly, a full liability, unitary share rule will be efficient, whatever additional rules are employed to apportion the damage among negligent parties. Thus, both the full liability, unitary, fixed share rule (Rule 1) and the full liability, unitary, proportional share rule (Rule 2) lead to the efficient outcome.[70]

In contrast to unitary share rules, fractional share rules are not generally efficient. Consider first the two partial liability, fractional share rules (Rules 7 and 8). In the Appendix, we prove that these rules always lead to an inefficient result. The intuition behind the result can be simply stated for a fixed share rule (Rule 7). Assume that all the actors are non-negligent, and that one actor contemplates dumping more than the standard of care. Because the actor would pay only a fraction of the increase in the damage, there will be a divergence between the actor's private objective function and the social objective function—she will be responsible for less than the damage that she imposes on society. Thus, the actor will have an economic incentive to dump more than the standard of care.

The two remaining rules are the two full liability, fractional share rules (Rules 3 and 4). As we show in the Appendix, whether these rules will induce the efficient result depends on the benefit and damage functions and on the number of actors. The intuition proceeds as follows for a full liability, fractional, fixed share rule (Rule 3). In the discussion of partial liability, fractional share rules, we noted that the private cost of dumping more than the standard of care is less than the social cost; thus, negligent action will result. But for full liability, fractional share rules, a negligent actor would bear not only a fraction of the increased damage that results from her negligence, but also a fraction of the damage that results when all actors are non-negligent. Whether the total private cost that an actor contemplating negligent action must face is greater than the social cost

---

70. It follows that, without uncertainty, a rule that imposed even higher damages upon the tortfeasors would also be efficient. But because punitive damages are generally unavailable, *see supra* note 28, it is important to determine which rules will provide efficient incentives in the absence of such damages. As we show, unitary share rules provide the minimum incentive necessary to induce efficient behavior.

850   The Yale Law Journal   [Vol. 98: 831

depends on the damage that results at the social optimum, which in turn depends on the benefit and damage functions and on the number of actors.

The efficiency properties of the eight rules are summarized in Figure II. All four unitary rules are efficient; the two full liability, fractional share rules are sometimes inefficient; and the two partial liability, fractional share rules are always inefficient.

While we recognize that considerations other than economic efficiency are cognizable in assessing the relative merits of the various rules, our conclusion is certainly relevant to that assessment. Proponents of inefficient apportionment rules should have the burden of explaining, on non-efficiency grounds, why such rules are preferable to efficient rules. Moreover, our conclusion that the choice of proportional share rules over fixed share rules is neither a necessary nor a sufficient condition for efficiency sheds light on the debate between these two rules,[71] a debate that has been informed, at least in part, by notions of efficiency.[72]

FIGURE II: EFFICIENCY OF THE APPORTIONMENT RULES UNDER NEGLIGENCE

Full Liability Rules

	Fixed Share	Proportional Share
Unitary Share	Rule 1 Efficient	Rule 2 Efficient
Fractional Share	Rule 3 Sometimes Inefficient	Rule 4 Sometimes Inefficient

Partial Liability Rules

	Fixed Share	Proportional Share
Unitary Share	Rule 5 Efficient	Rule 6 Efficient
Fractional Share	Rule 7 Always Inefficient	Rule 8 Always Inefficient

71. *See supra* text accompanying notes 51-56.
72. *See* United States v. Reliable Transfer, Inc., 421 U.S. 397, 405 n.11 (1975) ("A rule that divides damages by degree of fault would seem better designed to induce care than the rule of equally divided damages, because it imposes the strongest deterrent upon the wrongful behavior that is most likely to harm others.").

B. *Reconsidering Joint and Several Liability*

Our conclusion that only unitary share rules are efficient has important implications for the question of when joint and several liability is appropriate. As we have discussed, a rule of joint and several liability is a unitary share rule, since negligent actors bear damages attributable to non-negligent actors; thus, joint and several liability induces efficient outcomes.[73] In turn, a rule of non-joint (several only) liability is a fractional share rule and, in general, is not efficient.[74]

We do not mean to suggest, however, that whenever an individual is harmed by several actors, efficiency will be attained only if each negligent actor is held jointly and severally liable for the full damage. For example, if an individual has one car damaged by a negligent actor and a different car damaged by a non-negligent actor, the negligent actor need not be held jointly and severally liable for the damage to both cars. We therefore consider when joint and several liability (or a unitary share rule) is necessary to produce an efficient outcome. We also provide an economic reinterpretation of the concepts "distinct," "divisible," and "indivisible" harms,

---

73. One student commentator recently suggested that joint and several liability leads to over-deterrence. *See* Note, *supra* note 17, at 648–49. She notes that "[b]y eliminating joint and several liability, legislatures have eliminated an element of an actor's expected accident costs. An actor's expected accident costs no longer depend upon the probability that another actor who contributes to the victim's injury will be insolvent or immune from suit." *Id.* at 648. Therefore, she argues, "[j]oint and several liability sometimes forces an actor to pay for costs that do not result from his activity. These forced costs lead to a misallocation of resources because actors spend too much on safety." *Id.* at 649; *see id.* ("If the tort system holds an actor liable for costs greater than those associated with his activity, he will not engage in the most efficient level of activity—he will be too safe."). But even where there is the possibility of insolvency, which we have not explicitly addressed in this Article, *see supra* note 29, joint and several liability produces no over-deterrence under negligence, because an actor can avoid all liability by meeting the standard of care. Moreover, as we show below, *see infra* text accompanying notes 94–99, if the rule of liability is strict liability rather than negligence, there will be *under*-deterrence even if joint tortfeasors are held jointly and severally liable, because an actor thinking about departing from the social optimum does not see the full social cost of such a departure.

The student commentator also suggests that the absence of joint and several liability would be desirable from an efficiency perspective. *See* Note, *supra* note 17, at 649 ("When states limit joint and several liability, however, actors' liability corresponds more closely to activity-related costs. Thus, although limiting joint and several liability reduces the tort law's deterrent effect, it does so in a carefully tailored manner, consistent with the efficiency limitations of deterrence."). As we have indicated in the preceding section, however, rules of non-joint liability always produce under-deterrence because they do not force an actor contemplating a violation of the standard of care to "see" the full social cost of such a violation. *See supra* text accompanying notes 69–71.

For other commentaries that have supported the abolition of joint and several liability, see, e.g., Pressler & Schieffer, *supra* note 17, at 682–84; Note, *Compensation, Fairness, and the Costs of Accidents—Should Pennsylvania's Legislature Modify or Abrogate the Rule of Joint and Several Liability Among Concurrently Negligent Tortfeasors?*, 91 DICK. L. REV. 947, 974–76 (1987).

A recent article has suggested that economic theory provides no basis for determining how to allocate damages among multiple tortfeasors. *See* Wright, *supra* note 5, at 1169–79. However, under the four alternatives considered in that piece, the negligent defendants are liable, in the aggregate, for at least the full amount of the plaintiff's damage. *Id.* at 1172. Thus, this commentator does not consider situations, such as those present under partial liability rules and fractional share rules, where the plaintiff recovers less than her full damage.

74. A fractional share rule can be efficient only in the case of distinct damages, which are defined *infra* text accompanying note 82.

which are used in the Restatement and in the common law to determine when joint and several liability will attach.

The Restatement defines "distinct" harms as harms "which, by their nature, are more capable of apportionment."[75] The Restatement further classifies harms that are not distinct as either divisible or indivisible. It states: "There are other kinds of harm which, while not so clearly marked out as severable into distinct parts, are still capable of division upon a reasonable and rational basis, and of fair apportionment among the causes responsible."[76] Three categories are therefore relevant: distinct, non-distinct but divisible, and non-distinct and indivisible. Under the Restatement's approach, joint and several liability attaches only in the case of non-distinct and indivisible harms.[77]

In defining the three categories, the Restatement contemplates that a harm can be apportionable in four different senses. A distinct harm is one that is "more" capable of apportionment; a non-distinct but divisible harm is one that is somewhat less capable of apportionment; and a non-distinct and indivisible harm is presumably even less capable of apportionment. But even if a harm is non-distinct and indivisible, the defendant held jointly and severally liable may have a right to contribution, with the amount of such contribution determined by reference to the "equitable shares" of each of the defendants. This division into equitable shares is, then, another way of apportioning the damage.[78] Not surprisingly, great confusion surrounds the question of when tortfeasors should be held jointly and severally liable.[79]

We believe that the terms "distinct," "divisible," and "indivisible" should be reinterpreted in light of the efficiency properties of apportionment rules. Joint and several liability should attach, at least presumptively, when fractional rules would not guarantee an efficient outcome. As we have indicated, we recognize that tort law can serve goals other than economic efficiency.[80] However, when an inefficient rule is chosen over an efficient one, some non-efficiency justification must be provided. It is un-

---

75. RESTATEMENT, *supra* note 10, § 433A comment b.

76. *Id.* § 433A comment d.

77. *See id.* §§ 875, 881.

78. *See id.* § 886A.

79. We offer one example of the confusion. Under CERCLA, courts have held that where the harm caused by the disposal of hazardous wastes by several liable actors is indivisible, any liable actor can be held jointly and severally liable, but such an actor will be able to seek contribution. The relevant equitable shares will be determined by reference to such factors as the amount of wastes disposed by each actor and the toxicity of such wastes. *See, e.g.,* Colorado v. ASARCO, Inc., 608 F. Supp. 1484 (D. Colo. 1985); United States v. Chem-Dyne Corp., 572 F. Supp. 802, 810-11 (S.D. Ohio 1983). But in what appears to be a directly analogous situation, the Restatement adopts the opposite position. *See infra* text accompanying note 88 (discussing RESTATEMENT, *supra* note 10, § 433A comment d). In the example presented by the Restatement, unlike under CERCLA, the estimate of the quantities of pollution generated is used to defeat the plaintiff's claim of joint and several liability, rather than to calculate shares of contribution following the imposition of such liability.

80. Discussion of these issues is beyond the scope of this Article.

likely that the muddled approach of the Restatement, with different consequences attaching to the ease with which a harm is "capable of apportionment," evinces a concern for such goals.

From an efficiency perspective, there is no need to have three different
categories of harms, since there are only two possible legal consequences:
imposition or rejection of joint and several liability.[81] Because there is no
legal significance to the distinction between distinct harms on the one
hand and non-distinct but divisible harms on the other, we do not think
that it is helpful to separate harms along these lines. To the contrary, the
multiplicity of unnecessary legal categories is quite likely to breed
confusion.

Thus, we think that harms should be classified as either distinct or non-
distinct; that joint and several liability should attach only to non-distinct
harms; and that the classification should aim to isolate a category of
harms for which joint and several liability is not necessary to induce efficient outcomes.

Under these principles, a harm is distinct if the damage caused by one
actor is independent of the harm caused by other actors. In contrast,
where the damage caused by one actor increases the damage caused by
another actor, the harm is non-distinct.[82] In our hazardous waste example, the expected damage of the dumping is the square of the total amount
dumped.[83] Assume that there are two actors. If the first actor dumps five
units and the second does not dump anything, then the harm is $25. But if
the second actor were also to dump five units, the total harm would not be
$50 (twice $25) but $100 ($10 squared). Thus, the second actor can be
said to have caused a damage of $75 by dumping, even though this dam-
age would have been only $25 if the first actor had not dumped as well.

At least in part, the Restatement appears to embody a similar definition. Describing an example of distinct harms, it states:

If two defendants independently shoot the plaintiff at the same time,

---

81. We do not deal in this Article with cases in which the damages are not traceable to any one of
the several actors who might have caused a given harm. For example, in Sindell v. Abbott Laboratories, 26 Cal. 3d 588, 607 P.2d 924, 163 Cal. Rptr. 132, *cert. denied*, 449 U.S. 912 (1980), the
plaintiffs alleged that they had contracted cancer as a result of the administration of the drug DES
(diethylstilbestrol) to their mothers during their pregnancies. The plaintiffs could not identify which
manufacturers had produced the drug that their mothers had ingested. The damage was thus not
traceable. The court rejected a rule of joint and several liability, fashioning instead a "market share"
rule under which "[e]ach defendant w[ould] be held liable for the proportion of the judgment represented by its share of that market unless it demonstrates that it could not have made the product
which caused plaintiff's injuries." 26 Cal. 3d at 612, 607 P.2d at 937, 163 Cal. Rptr. at 145. Our
argument should not be interpreted as shedding light on whether this resolution was correct. For one
approach to this problem, see Shavell, *Uncertainty over Causation and the Determination of Civil
Liability*, 28 J.L. & Econ. 587 (1985).

82. As the Appendix makes clear, this result follows from the convexity of the damage function.
We do not deal here with situations in which two actors cause less damage acting in concert than they
cause acting separately.

83. *See supra* text accompanying notes 59–60.

854   The Yale Law Journal   [Vol. 98: 831

and one wounds him in the arm and the other in the leg, the ultimate result may be a badly damaged plaintiff in the hospital, but it is still possible, as a logical, reasonable, and practical matter, to regard the two wounds as separate injuries, and as distinct wrongs. The mere coincidence in time does not make the two wounds a single harm, or the conduct of the two defendants one tort.[84]

Up to this point, the example appears to be consistent with our definition of distinct harms as ones for which the damage function is separable. The damage caused by the wound in the arm would have been the same even if there had been no wound in the leg; similarly, the damage caused by the wound in the leg would have been the same even if there had been no wound in the arm.

The Restatement, however, goes on to say:

> There may be difficulty in the apportionment of some elements of damages, such as the pain and suffering resulting from the two wounds, or the medical expenses, but this does not mean that one defendant must be liable for the distinct harm inflicted by the other. It is possible to make a rough estimate which will fairly apportion such subsidiary elements of damages.[85]

While this statement is ambiguous, it can be read to suggest that the two wounds would be considered distinct even if the presence of one increased the pain and suffering or medical expenses that resulted from the other.[86] The second half of the example therefore muddles the definition and compromises an efficient outcome.[87]

The Restatement's discussion of divisible harms (for which joint and several liability does not attach) also appears to be at odds with notions of economic efficiency. It uses joint pollution to illustrate divisible harms:

> [W]here two or more factories independently pollute a stream, the interference with the plaintiff's use of water may be treated as divisible in terms of degree, and may be apportioned among the owners of the factories, on the basis of evidence of the respective quantities of pollution discharged into the stream.[88]

But it is quite unlikely that the damage function in the case of joint pollution would be linear, and therefore that the damage caused by one factory would be independent of whether another factory was also polluting. For

---

84. Restatement, *supra* note 10, § 433A comment b.
85. *Id.*
86. It may be that the Restatement refers to these as "subsidiary" damages because they involve comparatively small amounts. Certainly with respect to pain and suffering, that is no longer true.
87. Also, to the extent that a "rough estimate" has to be made, why is the harm distinct rather than non-distinct but divisible?
88. Restatement, *supra* note 10, § 433A comment d.

many pollutants, the damage function exhibits thresholds at which there are marked non-linearities. For example, as the concentration of dissolved oxygen in water decreases toward a threshold, there will be a pronounced increase in the damage caused, since the water will no longer be able to support fish.[89]

Thus, one polluter's discharge will affect the harm another causes, and the damage function will therefore not be separable. Proper attention to considerations of economic efficiency would lead to the classification of such harms as non-distinct and to the application of joint and several liability.

C. *Unitary Share Rules and Causation*

At first glance, it would appear that the requirement of causation as a predicate for tort liability argues for a fractional share rule over a unitary share rule, since negligent actors are not responsible for harms that are attributable to non-negligent actors. To the extent that considerations of fairness dictate attention to causation,[90] rules of apportionment might appear to present a trade-off between efficiency and fairness, with efficiency considerations supporting unitary share rules and fairness considerations supporting fractional share rules.

In fact, the relationship between unitary share rules and causation is not quite so straightforward. The portion of the damage that the negligent parties cause can be seen as the increase in the damage those parties produce. Admittedly, under a unitary share rule, the negligent parties pay more than this amount. But under a fractional share rule, as we have shown, they pay less than the increase in the damage attributable to them.[91] Indeed, it is precisely for this reason that fractional share rules are not generally efficient. In terms of fairness, then, fractional share rules, like unitary share rules, are problematic. There is no reason to prefer

---

89. *See* B. ACKERMAN, S. ROSE-ACKERMAN, J. SAWYER & D. HENDERSON, THE UNCERTAIN SEARCH FOR ENVIRONMENTAL QUALITY 265-67 (1974); Revesz, Book Review, 11 ECOLOGY L.Q. 451, 467 (1984).

90. For a traditional discussion of the goal of fairness in the tort system, see G. CALABRESI, THE COSTS OF ACCIDENTS 291-308 (1970). For recent moral theories of torts, see, e.g., Coleman, *Moral Theories of Torts: Their Scope and Limits: Part I*, 1 LAW & PHIL. 371 (1982); Coleman, *Moral Theories of Torts: Their Scope and Limits: Part II*, 2 LAW & PHIL. 5 (1983); Fletcher, *The Search for Synthesis in Tort Theory*, 2 LAW & PHIL. 63 (1983); Weinrib, *Toward a Moral Theory of Negligence*, 2 LAW & PHIL. 37 (1983).

91. *See supra* text accompanying notes 69-71. This point appears to be lost on some of the literature that advocates limitations on joint and several liability. For example, a student commentator notes that "[j]oint and several liability sometimes forces an actor to pay for costs that do not result from his activity. . . . When states limit joint and several liability, however, actors' liability corresponds more closely to activity-related costs." Note, *supra* note 17, at 649. She refers primarily to a solvent negligent actor's responsibility for damages attributable to a negligent actor who is insolvent, *see id.* at 648, but her argument applies with equal force to a solvent negligent actor's responsibility for damages attributable to non-negligent actors. *See also* Note, *supra* note 73, at 975-76.

charging tortfeasors less than the damage they cause to charging them more.

In particular cases, it may be that a fractional share rule slightly undercharges the negligent actors, while a unitary share rule overcharges them a great deal. For other benefit and damage functions, however, the converse will be true. Even benefit and damage functions for which fractional share rules do not significantly undercharge when the number of actors is small will undercharge more as the number of actors increases.[92] Thus, it is not possible to make a general statement about whether causation and fairness considerations recommend the use of fractional share rules rather than unitary share rules. For this reason, the choice between unitary share and fractional share rules does not give rise to a general trade-off between fairness and efficiency.

IV. APPORTIONMENT UNDER STRICT LIABILITY

In this Section, we turn to the analysis of strict liability rules. We first show that none of the apportionment rules that courts currently use and commentators advocate are efficient. We then demonstrate the possibility of plausible apportionment rules that produce the efficient outcome under strict liability. To our knowledge, the courts have not used nor have commentators advocated such rules.

A. *Existing Apportionment Rules*

Under negligence, we have seen that four classes of rules are efficient if the standards of care are set optimally. Under strict liability, in contrast, none of the classes is efficient.

Under strict liability, the range of apportionment rules is much more constrained than under negligence. As we have indicated, of the eight types of rules that we considered in the context of negligence, only two are relevant under strict liability: fixed share rules and proportional share rules.[93]

We prove in the Appendix that these apportionment rules are inefficient under strict liability. The intuition behind the result is simple for fixed share rules. Assume that all actors are dumping the optimal amount of waste and that one actor considers whether to dump more. This actor would bear not the full increase in the damage but only a portion of that increase, determined by his fixed share.[94] This creates a divergence between the actor's private objective function and the social objective func-

---

92. *See infra* Appendix, Proposition 3.
93. *See supra* text accompanying notes 44, 49–58.
94. *See* S. SHAVELL, *supra* note 5, at 164–65.

tion. This divergence will lead the actor to dump more than the social optimum.[95]

This intuition behind the reasons for the inefficiency of the existing apportionment rules under strict liability parallels the analysis that suggested the inefficiency of partial liability, fractional share rules under negligence. In both cases, an inefficient outcome results because an actor who contemplates dumping more than the socially optimal level does not bear the full increase in the damage that she imposes on society. In the case of the existing apportionment rules under strict liability, other actors must themselves bear a portion of the increase in damage caused by the actor who dumps more than the social optimum. In the example above, such actors will be liable for a fixed share of a greater damage. For partial liability, fractional share rules under negligence, the increase in damage is instead borne by the victim.[96]

The explanation for the efficiency of unitary share rules under negligence and the inefficiency of strict liability rules is that the former make an actor who departs from the optimal level of production of waste pay for the full increase in the damages she inflicts. Under strict liability, in contrast, such an actor pays for only a fraction of such damage.

This result does not depend on the discontinuity in the damage function that is presented by full liability rules under negligence, where an actor who dumps more than the socially optimal level must pay not only the

---

95. Landes and Posner use a short example to suggest that strict liability might be inefficient. *See* W. LANDES & R. POSNER, *supra* note 5, at 215; Landes & Posner, *supra* note 5, at 543. In their example, each of 10 polluters of a stream imposes costs of $1 million through his pollution. Five could avoid the pollution at a cost of $600,000 each, and the other five at a cost of $1.4 million each. Landes and Posner point out that under a negligence rule the first five would have incentives to avoid pollution, and society would therefore be wealthier by $2 million. They argue that under strict liability, however, the first five would not avoid pollution because "each will still have an expected liability of $500,000 (assuming either a no-contribution rule with each polluter equally likely to be sued for the remaining damage or a contribution rule in which damages are divided by the number of defendants)." *Id.*

They believe that if the five polluters were to eliminate their pollution they could still be held liable for a portion of the remaining damage of $5,000,000. It is certainly not clear why these polluters would be treated as joint tortfeasors, since they would not be polluting anything. If they were not treated as joint tortfeasors, then they would face the correct incentives and, in fact, would not pollute at all. Moreover, in this example, if a proportional share rule, rather than a fixed share rule, were used, strict liability would in fact produce the efficient result, since the five polluters could escape liability entirely.

What is peculiar about the Landes and Posner example is that under this example a strict liability rule *can* lead to the efficient allocation. Efficiency results in this example because under their formulation of the problem the optimal standard of care under negligence for the five polluters with lower abatement costs is zero pollution, and therefore strict liability yields the same results as negligence. Of course, in such cases, strict liability, like negligence, can lead to the efficient allocation, provided that an actor that produces no pollution is not held liable for any damage.

96. Full liability, fractional share rules are sometimes efficient because of the discontinuity that they exhibit in the damage function. An actor departing from the standard of care must pay not only her portion of the increased cost of that departure, but also the damage that is attributable to her non-negligent behavior. As we have shown, however, this discontinuity is not sufficient to guarantee efficiency. *See supra* Section III.A. (showing that full liability, fractional share rules are not always efficient).

increase in the damage caused by that departure from the optimum but also the damage that would have resulted in the absence of negligence. Indeed, partial liability rules, for which the damage function is not discontinuous, are efficient as well,[97] because they allocate the full increase in the damage to the actor who departs from the socially optimal level.

Although rules of joint and several liability are efficient under negligence, they will not produce efficient results under strict liability. In fact, assuming that all parties are solvent and that transaction costs are zero, as we have assumed for negligence rules,[98] the question of whether the harms are deemed distinct, divisible, or indivisible is of no economic consequence for strict liability rules. Under negligence, the characterization of the harm is important because it determines whether the negligent actors must pay for the damage attributable to non-negligent actors. But under strict liability, this characterization has no consequence because all of the actors violate the standard of care.

We do not present here a general argument for negligence over strict liability. Many reasons other than economic efficiency may underlie a preference for one rule over another. In particular, if the standard of care under negligence is not set at the social optimum, negligence rules will not, in general, be efficient.[99] Also, the distributional consequences of both rules are markedly different because under negligence, the victim often bears larger losses than under strict liability. Thus, in the case of joint harms, strict liability rules must be justified by reference either to the practical difficulties involved in setting the standard of care optimally, or to non-efficiency goals that are sufficiently compelling to outweigh the efficiency benefits of negligence rules.

B. *Efficient Apportionment Rules*

While the existing apportionment rules are not efficient under strict liability, we propose apportionment rules that do induce the efficient outcome. All such rules take into account whether an actor is dumping more wastes than the social optimum. In the Appendix, we formally define a class of efficient rules. Here, we suggest a simple rule in this class and show why it is efficient. Under this rule, the full damage is divided per capita among the various actors when none dump more than the socially optimal level. If some actors dump more than this level, then those actors divide the full damage among themselves per capita, and the remaining actors pay nothing.

Such a rule is efficient. If all but one of the actors meet the socially optimal level, it would not be rational for the remaining actor to dump

---

97. *See supra* text accompanying notes 68–70.
98. *See supra* text accompanying note 50.
99. *See infra* Section VI.

more than the socially optimal amount. If she were to increase her output beyond the social optimum, she would bear the full increase in the ensuing damage. In addition, she would have to pay the full damage that occurs when all actors meet the socially optimal level, rather than the per capita share of that damage, which she would pay if she did not depart from this level. In Section III, we showed in connection with partial liability, unitary share rules, that even if the only cost of departing from the social optimum was the increase in the damage, it would not be rational for an actor to dump more than that optimal level, because the additional damage for which the actor would be responsible would be greater than the additional benefit derived by such actor. Thus, when there is also another cost to departing from the social optimum, as there is here, it follows *a fortiori* that such a departure would not be rational.

Similarly, it would not be rational for a group of actors to dump more than the socially optimal level. The aggregate cost to this group of doing so is the full increase in damage resulting from such a departure, plus the portion of the damage borne by the other actors when all the actors meet the socially optimal level. We showed in Section III that even if these actors had to pay only for the increase in damage, departure from the social optimum would not be rational. Such a departure would similarly not be rational when these actors must pay not only this amount but also an additional component of damages.[100]

Under these rules of apportionment, the allocation of the loss depends to a great extent on whether the actors meet the socially optimal level. These rules, therefore, replicate for strict liability the desirable economic features of negligence rules.[101]

These efficient apportionment rules under strict liability are no more cumbersome for courts to apply than are traditional negligence rules, since both sets of rules turn on the determination of the socially optimal level. We recognize, however, that both negligence rules and the strict liability rules that we propose—unlike traditional strict liability rules—require that, for each actor, courts determine the socially optimal level of dump-

---

100. *See supra* text accompanying note 70. We prove in the Appendix that an efficient outcome would also occur if the full damage were divided proportionally among all of the actors when none dumped more than the socially optimal level, and, otherwise, proportionally among those who dump more than that level.

101. They do so by introducing what might be called "standards of apportionment" that serve the same function as standards of care under negligence. Because of this parallelism between standards of care and standards of apportionment, one could introduce classes of untraditional strict liability rules that correspond to the fractional share and unitary share rules defined under negligence. In strict liability, however, one must be careful to distinguish between rules that are unitary with respect to standards of care and rules that are unitary with respect to standards of apportionment. Every strict liability rule is unitary with respect to standards of care. *See supra* text accompanying notes 46–49. The efficient rules we propose are also unitary with respect to standards of apportionment. One can easily construct rules that are fractional with respect to standards of apportionment.

We do not pursue the analysis of unitary versus fractional share rules with respect to standards of apportionment because it would virtually duplicate that of Section III.

ing. If the costs of doing so are great, or if courts are unable to determine the social optimum,[102] traditional strict liability rules might be preferred over both negligence rules and efficient strict liability rules.

The efficient apportionment rules under strict liability that we have defined permit the disaggregation of efficiency from distributional concerns. As we have noted, under strict liability rules, by definition, the victim gets compensation for her full harm.[103] Under negligence rules, in contrast, full compensation will not be available in many instances, most notably where all the actors meet the standard of care.

Thus, under the current rules of apportionment, the choice between negligence and strict liability gives rise to a trade-off between efficiency and distributional goals. The decisionmaker (whether a court or a legislature) can achieve full compensation for the victim only at the cost of foregoing the efficiency benefits of negligence rules. In contrast, under the apportionment rules that we propose, the choice between negligence and strict liability need not present such a trade-off. To the extent that the distributional consequences of strict liability are desirable, they can be achieved without any loss in efficiency.

V. RULES OF NO CONTRIBUTION

So far, we have analyzed joint and several liability (unitary share rules) in connection with a right to contribution.[104] Here, we study rules of no contribution, which attracted the attention of the law-and-economics literature in the early 1980s. The properties of no-contribution rules shed light on the relative desirability of the contribution rules that we have discussed.

Landes and Posner make two claims about rules under which an actor who has been held jointly and severally liable cannot obtain contribution from other actors. First, they argue that rules of no contribution are efficient; and second, they argue that such rules produce incentives identical to those produced by rules of contribution.[105] Their result holds under negligence, on which they focused, but does not hold under strict liability.

A no-contribution rule is equivalent to a fixed share rule in which an actor's share is her estimate of the probability that she will be the one to be held jointly and severally liable and therefore responsible for the full damage.[106] Thus, the properties of no-contribution rules follow simply from our discussion of rules of contribution.

---

102. We address this problem in Section VI.
103. *See supra* text accompanying note 44.
104. Of course, in the absence of joint and several liability, there is no right to contribution, since such a right can be invoked only by an actor who has paid more than his equitable share of the damage. *See* RESTATEMENT, *supra* note 10, § 886A(2). Thus, for fractional rules, there can be no right to contribution.
105. *See* Landes & Posner, *supra* note 5, at 529–30.
106. Her expected damage is this probability multiplied by the cost of the full damage. The

Under negligence, we showed that apportionment rules are efficient if the sum of the shares of the negligent actors is equal to one, as it is for unitary share rules. We also showed that apportionment rules are not efficient if the sum of the shares is less than one, as it is for fractional share rules.

For a no-contribution rule to be efficient, however, the sum of probabilities that the actors attach to the risks of being held responsible for the full damage must be equal to at least one.[107] If each actor's estimate of his probability of being held liable were known to all the other actors, one would expect that the sum of probabilities would be equal to exactly one.[108] If, in contrast, the sum of these probabilities is less than one, the no-contribution rule will be equivalent to a fractional share rule, and will therefore not generally be efficient.

Under strict liability, a rule of no contribution will generally not lead to an efficient allocation. Recall from our earlier discussion that there will be a divergence between the private objective function and the social objective function, unless an actor who contemplates dumping more than the socially optimal level bears the full increase in the damage caused by such a departure. Under no-contribution rules, this result will occur only if *each* actor estimates that the probability of being responsible for the full damage is one. Thus, if the probabilities are common knowledge and therefore can be expected to *sum* to one, no-contribution rules are not efficient under strict liability.

It also follows that, under strict liability, there is little reason to suspect that a rule of no-contribution will lead to the same behavior as a rule of apportionment. Such equivalence will prevail only if each actor faces the identical incentives under both regimes. But this will happen only if each actor's share under the rule of apportionment is equal to her expected liability under the no-contribution rule. Such a coincidence seems unlikely, particularly under a proportional share rule, where an actor's share depends not only on her own decision, but also on the decisions of all the other actors.

It bears noting that while no-contribution rules will not lead to the efficient result under strict liability, rules of contribution, if properly designed, can do so, as we have explained in Section IV.B. Thus, we present an argument for allowing actors held jointly and severally liable under strict liability rules to seek contribution from other responsible actors.

---

argument that no-contribution rules are efficient assumes that all actors are risk-neutral. *See supra* note 8. We assume throughout this discussion that a single defendant will pay the full judgment.

107.   We have shown that the result will be efficient if the shares add to one. If they add to more than one, the same result will hold; with no uncertainty, there is no danger of over-deterrence because the actors can avoid all liability by meeting the standard of care.

108.   Landes and Posner assumed that the sum of the probabilities would equal one. *See* Landes & Posner, *supra* note 5, at 522.

VI. DEPARTURES FROM THE SOCIAL OPTIMUM IN THE DETERMINATION OF THE STANDARD OF CARE

To this point, we have assumed that courts can properly define the social optimum for purposes of setting the standard of care under negligence and for applying the efficient strict liability rules that we propose.[109] We have made this assumption for several reasons.

First, the traditional law-and-economics models of tort law for single injurers,[110] as well as the models for joint tortfeasors, have made the same assumption.[111] Thus, our conclusion that, under a similar assumption, certain common law rules are not efficient contradicts the central tenet of the positive economic theory of tort law.[112]

Second, under certain judicial formulations of the standard of care, such as the Hand formula,[113] courts purport to set this standard at the social optimum. Regardless of what courts actually do in practice, it is relevant to study the effects of the rules that the courts say they are applying.

Third, when analyzing a legal problem, it is important to separate it into its components. By looking initially at the effects of apportionment rules when standards of care are set at the socially optimal levels, we are able to distinguish, on the one hand, the effects that result from the "jointness" of the problem, and on the other, the effects that stem from "error" in the determination of the standard of care.

Therefore, an analysis of rules of apportionment does well to begin with the assumption that the standard of care is set at the socially optimal level. Any policy recommendation, however, must confront the reality that the standards of care governing conduct will often not be optimal.

At the outset, we must distinguish two principal ways in which the standard of care might deviate from the socially optimal level. First, courts might attempt to set the standard of care at the optimal level but might make errors in determining the social optimum.[114] Such errors might occur, for example, because courts have difficulty in ascertaining the exact benefits that dumpers receive from engaging in the activity that leads to the generation of wastes. Because the optimal standard is that which maximizes the sum of the benefits derived by the various dumpers minus the

---

109. For traditional strict liability rules, of course, there is no need to determine the social optimum.

110. *See, e.g.*, Brown, *supra* note 30.

111. *See* Easterbrook, Landes & Posner, *supra* note 5; Landes & Posner, *supra* note 5; Polinsky & Shavell, *supra* note 5.

112. The positive theory states that common law tort rules are efficient. For a comprehensive statement of the theory, see Landes & Posner, *The Positive Economic Theory of Tort Law*, 15 GA. L. REV. 851 (1981).

113. *See* United States v. Carroll Towing Co., 159 F.2d 169, 173 (2d Cir. 1947) (L. Hand, J.).

114. Similarly, courts might err in ascertaining the levels of care adopted by the actors. This problem is conceptually analogous, though not identical, to that posed when courts make errors in determining the socially optimal level.

social loss, an incorrect estimation of the benefits will lead to an incorrect standard of care.

When courts make such errors, the standard of care must be described by means of a probability distribution, rather than by a single number. We assume that the errors that a court makes in determining the social optimum are as likely to result in a standard that is too stringent as in one that is too lenient; we envision a symmetric distribution with a mean equal to the standard of care. For ease of exposition, our discussion proceeds by reference to a normal distribution.

We refer to the problem in which courts attempt to set the socially optimal standard of care but make errors in doing so as involving an optimal but uncertain standard. The standard can be said to be optimal in that its expected value is the socially optimal level.[115] The standard is uncertain, however, in that an actor who dumps at the socially optimal level might nonetheless be found to violate the standard of care because, in a given case, the court might set this standard at a level more stringent than the socially optimal level. More generally, regardless of the amount that she dumps, the dumper will not be able to determine precisely whether she will be found to have violated the standard of care.

The second type of departure from the social optimum concerns a standard of care that is set at a level different from the social optimum, either too stringently or too leniently, but which does not exhibit uncertainty. Thus, a dumper will be able to determine precisely whether her conduct will constitute a violation of the standard. We refer to this problem as involving a non-optimal but certain standard of care.[116]

A. *Optimal Standards With Uncertainty*

For single actors, the literature has extensively examined full liability rules and shown that models inducing the efficient result in the absence of uncertainty lead to inefficient results under uncertainty. In particular, uncertainty will produce over-deterrence if the standard deviation of the probability distribution is small and under-deterrence if it is large.[117]

---

115. It is true, however, that the standard announced in a particular case may well not be optimal.

116. We do not deal in this discussion with standards that are non-optimal and uncertain.

117. *See, e.g.*, S. SHAVELL, *supra* note 5, at 79-104; Craswell & Calfee, *Deterrence and Uncertain Legal Standards*, 2 J.L. ECON. & ORG. 279 (1986); Johnston, *Bayesian Fact-Finding and Efficiency: Toward an Economic Theory of Liability Under Uncertainty*, 61 S. CAL. L. REV. 137 (1987).

In each of these works, uncertainty is modelled as risk. That is, the agent knows the probability distribution from which the actual standard of care is drawn (or, equivalently, knows the probability that she will be found non-negligent given that she has adopted a specific level of care). The degree of uncertainty is then measured by the dispersion in the probability distribution. Our discussion makes a similar assumption.

These models can easily be extended to show that partial liability rules unambiguously produce under-deterrence.[118]

In the Appendix, we extend these models to multiple actors and study how four of the apportionment rules perform under uncertainty.[119] As for single actors, two opposite incentives are present under full liability, unitary share rules. First, under uncertainty, if the actor dumps more than the optimal amount, it does not necessarily follow that she will be negligent, because there is some chance that the court will set the standard of care at an even less stringent level. This effect gives her an incentive to take too little care.

But a countervailing effect is also present. In the absence of uncertainty, an actor would not take care beyond the social optimum because she could avoid all liability simply by dumping the socially optimal amount. With uncertainty, however, there is the possibility that the court will announce a standard that is too stringent. Therefore, increasing one's level of care beyond the socially optimal level reduces the probability of being held liable.

This effect gives the actor an incentive to take too much care under full liability rules. If she is found negligent, she is responsible not only for the losses that result from her departure from the standard of care, but also for the losses that would have resulted even without negligence.

In contrast, this incentive toward over-deterrence is absent under partial liability rules. Under such rules, an actor is liable only for the damage that results from her departure from the standard of care. Thus, there will never be an incentive for such an actor to take more care than the social optimum because, by definition, the decrease in benefits will be greater than the increase in resulting damage, and even under a unitary share rule the actor would not be liable for more than this latter amount. Because the incentive to undercomply is present but the incentive to overcomply is not, partial liability rules always produce under-deterrence.

It follows that partial liability, unitary share rules are always preferable to partial liability, fractional share rules because the fractional element of the rule simply exacerbates the incentive to undercomply. Thus, partial liability, fractional share rules are never preferred.

The relative desirability of the three remaining classes of rules depends on the tightness of the probability distribution that describes the uncertainty surrounding the standard of care. While we have not attempted a systematic analysis of the problem, we have the following intuitions. As in the single-actor case, for "tight" distributions (small standard deviation)

---

118. Consider, for example, the model of Craswell and Calfee. The incentives for overcompliance disappear under partial liability rules, leaving only incentives for undercompliance. *See* Craswell & Calfee, *supra* note 117, at 282.

119. In this discussion, we do not look at the difference between fixed share and proportional share rules.

the incentive to overcomply under full liability, unitary share rules is strong. This incentive, however, can be tempered in two ways: by making the rule a partial liability rule or by making it a fractional share rule. As we have stated, partial liability rules would eliminate the incentive to overcomply and would create an incentive to undercomply. Thus, when the distribution is very tight and full liability rules would produce too great an incentive to overcomply, it will be preferable to have undercompliance through a partial liability, unitary share rule.

Conversely, for distributions that are very disperse (large standard deviation), the incentive to undercomply is greater than the incentive to overcomply for all apportionment rules. Then, full liability, unitary share rules are best because they minimize the amount of undercompliance. In some intermediate range, full liability, fractional share rules are preferable because they weaken but do not eliminate the incentive to overcomply. The optimal rules derived by this analysis are shown in Figure III.

FIGURE III: PREFERRED APPORTIONMENT RULES UNDER UNCERTAINTY

	Full Liability	**Partial Liability**
Unitary Share	Disperse Distribution (high standard deviation)	Tight Distribution (low standard deviation)
Fractional Share	Intermediate Distribution (intermediate standard deviation)	Never Preferred

B. *Non-Optimal Standards Without Uncertainty*

We consider first the case of a single actor. There are two relevant possibilities: either the standard of care is more lenient than the socially optimal level (permitting the dumping of more than the socially optimal amount of waste) or it is more stringent than that level (permitting the dumping of less than the socially optimal amount of waste).

Suppose first that the standard of care is too lenient. The actor will then dump the amount permitted by the standard of care, and therefore will dump more than the socially optimal amount. Indeed, the actor would capture the increased benefits of dumping more than this amount but would not be liable for any additional damages, as she could avoid all liability by meeting the standard of care. This result holds for both full liability and partial liability rules, as in both cases excess dumping gives rise to additional benefits but no additional costs. Under both rules, the actor will dump the amount permitted by the standard of care.[120]

When the standard of care is set too stringently, the analysis is somewhat more complex. If the actor meets the standard of care, therefore dumping less than the socially optimal level, the benefits that she foregoes by not dumping at this latter level exceed the corresponding increase in damages. Under a partial liability rule, an actor dumping at the socially optimal level would be liable only for these additional damages. Thus, it would be rational for the actor to violate the standard of care and dump the socially optimal amount.[121]

Under full liability rules, in contrast, an actor dumping the socially optimal amount would be liable not only for the additional damages caused by dumping the socially optimal level rather than the amount prescribed by the standard of care, but also for the damages that result when the standard of care is met. The actor will meet the standard of care, thereby dumping less than the socially optimal amount, when the standard of care is not too much more stringent than the socially optimal amount. However, when the standard of care is far more stringent than the socially optimal amount, the actor will dump the socially optimal amount, thereby violating the standard of care.[122]

Our problem, of course, concerns multiple actors, rather than single actors. To analyze it completely, one needs to know *for each actor* whether the standard has been set too stringently or leniently.[123] While a comprehensive study of the issue is beyond the scope of this Article,[124] we can draw some conclusions from a simplified problem in which there are two actors who have identical benefit functions (and therefore identical optimal levels of care), and who face the same standard of care.

If the standard of care is set more leniently than the socially optimal level, each actor will choose a level of care equal to the standard of care for every unitary share rule, whether full liability or partial liability. No actor will dump less than the standard of care, because she can obtain additional benefits at no cost by dumping up to the level permitted by the standard of care. Nor will any actor dump more than the standard of care. If all actors are dumping at the standard of care level, an actor thinking about dumping more than the standard of care would be liable at least for

120. The concepts of unitary and fractional share have no meaning for single tortfeasors, as the question of who pays for the damages caused by non-negligent parties does not arise.

121. *See* Kahan, *supra* note 30.

122. These results are summarized in S. SHAVELL, *supra* note 5, at 83.

123. Unless each actor faces identical, linear benefit functions, a stringent standard of care for one actor does not offset a lenient standard of care for another, because the benefits foregone by the former actor are not completely recouped by the extra benefits garnered by the latter actor.

124. We hope, however, to return to this question in the future.

the full increase in the damages, which, whether a partial liability rule or a full liability rule is used, will be more than the resulting benefits.[125]

Moreover, there can be no equilibrium in which some actors dump more than the standard of care, when this standard is too lenient. As in the case of standards of care set optimally, such actors will be liable, in the aggregate, for damages greater than the ensuing benefits. Regardless of how the additional damage caused by the violation of the standard of care is apportioned among them, at least some actors would have to pay more than the additional benefit that they obtained through the violation.[126] Therefore, under both full liability, unitary share rules, and partial liability, unitary share rules, all actors will dump the amount prescribed by the standard of care when this standard is too lenient.

As is the case with single tortfeasors, the analysis is less straightforward when the standard of care is set too stringently. We first deal with partial liability, unitary share rules. Under a partial liability rule, a single tortfeasor would violate the standard of care and dump the socially optimal level. Similarly, there is no equilibrium in which any two actors would meet the standard of care because the benefits that one actor can gain by departing from the standard of care, given that the other adheres to the standard of care, are greater than the full increase in damages. Unlike the case of a single actor, however, for two actors there is no equilibrium in which the socially optimal level is met. An actor will dump at the socially optimal level only if she is liable for the full increase in damages caused by dumping more than the socially optimal level. But under a partial liability, unitary, fixed share rule, if one actor is dumping at the socially optimal level, the other actor would bear only half of the increase in damages that would result if she dumped more than the socially optimal level.[127] Thus, the actor will dump more than the social optimum.

There is another candidate for an equilibrium—the equilibrium under strict liability. Our analysis of strict liability explains that if both actors are going to be negligent, they will each dump the amount that they would have dumped under a traditional strict liability rule (we shall refer to this level as the strict liability level).[128] Once both actors have decided to be negligent, the presence of the standard of care plays no role in their decisions.

The strict liability level will be an equilibrium if the standard of care is sufficiently more stringent than the socially optimal level. Then, if one actor is dumping at the strict liability level, the other actor would not be

---

125. These damages would accrue under a partial liability rule. Under a full liability rule, the actor would also be liable for the damages that result when all actors are non-negligent.

126. *See supra* text accompanying notes 69–70.

127. This effect is also present under proportional share rules.

128. We show in the Appendix that the total amount dumped under a strict liability rule is more than the socially optimal aggregate level. Thus, when the actors are identical, each will dump more than her socially optimal level.

better off by dumping at the level prescribed by the standard of care. Indeed, the positive net benefits obtained by moving from the standard of care to the social optimum will be greater than the negative net benefits that attach to a move from the socially optimal level to the strict liability level. Thus, under this condition, there will be an equilibrium in which both actors dump at the strict liability level.

In contrast, if the standard of care is less stringent (but still more stringent than the socially optimal level), one actor will prefer to dump at the level prescribed by the standard of care, given that the other actor is dumping at the strict liability level. Because we have shown that there is no equilibrium in which both actors meet the standard of care, it follows that, in such cases, there is no equilibrium in pure strategies.[129] A full example showing these effects is presented in the Appendix.

The results are different for full liability, unitary share rules. Under such rules, an actor departing from the standard of care must bear not only the increased damages produced by this departure, but also the damages that result when both actors are non-negligent. Thus, for standards of care sufficiently close to the social optimum, there will be an equilibrium in which both actors meet the standard of care. For standards of care that are sufficiently more stringent than the social optimum, there will an equilibrium in which both actors dump at the strict liability level. The positive net benefits obtained by moving from the standard of care to the social optimum will be sufficient to counteract not only the negative net benefits that attach to a move from the socially optimal level to the strict liability level, but also the damages that result when both actors are non-negligent.

We show in the Appendix that there is an intermediate range in which the standard of care is neither sufficiently close to the socially optimal level for an equilibrium to exist in which each actor dumps the level prescribed by the standard of care, nor sufficiently far from the socially optimal level for each actor to dump at the strict liability level. In this range, there is no equilibrium in pure strategies.

The levels of care taken under full liability, unitary share rules and under partial liability, unitary share rules are set out in Figure IV for different standards of care. We denote the standard of care as c; the optimal level of care as x^*; the strict liability level of care as x_s; a_1, a_2, and a_3, are levels of care such that $0 < a_1 < a_2 < a_3 < x^*$. Figure IV shows that, when the standard of care is set at a non-optimal level, partial liability rules always produce under-deterrence (except in the range in which

---

129. Game theorists distinguish between two types of equilibria: equilibria in pure strategies and equilibria in mixed strategies. For our purposes, a pure strategy is simply the choice of a level of care. In contrast, under a mixed strategy, an actor would not pick a single level of care, but instead would pick a probability distribution over multiple levels of care. On mixed strategies, see R. LUCE & H. RAIFFA, GAMES AND DECISIONS 70-71 (1957).

there is no equilibrium in pure strategies). Full liability, unitary share rules also generally produce under-deterrence. The exception here is a range in which the standard of care is stringent but sufficiently close to the social optimum. In this case, they produce over-deterrence (for these rules too, there is a range in which there is no equilibrium in pure strategies).

It is only for full liability rules in the range of over-deterrence that fractional share rules might be preferred to unitary share rules; even there, however, they might lead to too much under-deterrence and therefore not be desirable. In all other instances, and for all partial liability rules, unitary share rules are preferable.[130]

Figure IV also reveals that setting the standard of care too stringently might lead to greater under-deterrence than setting it too leniently. Under full liability rules, if the standard of care is set in the range between 0 and a_1, the actors will choose to dump the strict liability amount, whereas if the standard of care is set between the social optimum and the strict liability level, they will dump the lesser amount prescribed by this standard of care. The same result holds, albeit in different ranges, for partial liability rules.

FIGURE IV: NON-OPTIMAL BUT CERTAIN STANDARDS OF CARE

Standard of Care		Equilibrium Levels of Care†	
		Full Liability	Partial Liability
Stringent	$0 - a_1$	x_S (u)	x_S (u)
	$a_1 - a_2$	no eq.	x_S (u)
	$a_2 - a_3$	c (o)	x_S (u)
	$a_3 - x^*$	c (o)	no eq.
Lenient	$x^* - x_S$	c (u)	c (u)
	$x_S - \infty$	c (u)	c (u)

† "u" denotes under-deterrence; "o" denotes over-deterrence; "no eq." denotes no equilibrium in pure strategies.

130. Our analysis of optimal standards with uncertainty and non-optimal standards without uncertainty, which we have applied primarily to negligence rules, applies also to the efficient strict liability rules that we propose in this Article.

In conclusion, we return to the question of when joint and several liability is desirable, from an efficiency perspective, under negligence rules.[131] We showed in Section III that, when the standard of care is set optimally without uncertainty, joint and several liability is necessary to induce the efficient outcome. We show in this Section that joint and several liability is preferable to non-joint (several only) liability except in two special circumstances. Opponents of joint and several liability must defend the existence of optimal but uncertain standards and argue that the probability distribution that describes the standard of care is neither tight enough to recommend the use of partial liability, unitary share rules nor disperse enough to call for full liability, unitary share rules. Alternatively, they must point to non-optimal but certain standards under full liability rules, and argue that the standard of care is too stringent but not so stringent as to preclude an equilibrium in which actors meet the standard of care, and that the under-deterrence that might be caused by non-joint liability is no more undesirable than the over-deterrence of joint and several liability. The opponents of joint and several liability within the tort reform movement have not met this burden.[132]

CONCLUSION

Our analysis has two principal conclusions. First, we study negligence rules with the standards of care set at the socially optimal levels and show that any unitary share rule will be efficient, but that other rules will not. Second, we study strict liability and show that none of the existing rules of apportionment are efficient, but that one can design efficient apportionment rules.

These results are analogous to those reached in the economic literature on the apportionment of losses between an "injurer" and a "victim," each of whose actions influence the expected cost of an accident.[133] In this literature, the legal rule assigns the loss to one party or the other, just as the rule of apportionment does for multiple tortfeasors. In the injurer/victim context, a rule of comparative negligence provides the closest analogy to a rule of apportionment under negligence for multiple injurers.

Recent studies of comparative negligence have shown that when the standards of care are set optimally, both victim and injurer will adopt the socially optimal levels of care.[134] This argument parallels the argument

---

131. We have indicated that, for traditional strict liability rules, given the assumptions of this Article (in particular, the lack of insolvency), the choice between joint and several liability on the one hand and non-joint (several only) liability on the other has no efficiency consequences. *See supra* text accompanying notes 98–99.

132. *See supra* note 73.

133. In contrast, under the model that we use to study the problem of joint tortfeasors, the cost of the accident is independent of the victim's actions.

134. Both Cooter & Ulen, *The Economic Case for Comparative Negligence*, 61 N.Y.U. L. Rev. 1067 (1986), and Haddock & Curran, *An Economic Theory of Comparative Negligence*, 14 J. LEGAL

that establishes an identical result for the rules of pure negligence, negligence with contributory negligence, strict liability with contributory negligence, and strict liability with dual contributory negligence.[135] The structure of each of these rules identifies a "default" bearer of liability and gives the other actor an opportunity to avoid all liability by meeting her standard of care. In equilibrium, the injurer as well as the victim "sees" the full social cost of her decision. The default bearer of liability sees it because, in equilibrium, she in fact bears the loss. The other actor sees the full social cost of her decision because, in equilibrium, a marginal decrease in her level of care would make her negligent and shift the entire loss to her.

Under negligence, unitary share rules of apportionment function identically. The victim serves as the default bearer of liability. The negligence rule assures that any injurer can avoid all liability by meeting the standard of care. A unitary share rule assures that, if a single injurer deviates from her standard of care (while all others meet theirs), then a cost at least equal to the full increase in the loss will fall on her alone.[136] Thus, all injurers "see" the full loss in equilibrium.

Similarly, under the apportionment rules that we propose, in the strict liability context, if all actors are at the optimum, an actor contemplating a departure from the optimum faces a cost that is greater than the full increase in the loss. This actor therefore also "sees" the full loss in equilibrium.

Conversely, the existing apportionment rules under strict liability are inefficient for the same reason that strict liability is inefficient in the standard victim/injurer context.[137] As losses are purely economic,[138] the victim

---

STUD. 49, 68-71 (1985), show that, if the standards of care are set "optimally," both injurer and victim will adhere to their standards of care; hence, the victim will bear the entire loss. ("Optimality" refers to the levels of care that minimize the sum of accident prevention costs and expected losses from the accident.)

Neither article analyzes cases in which the standard of care is set non-optimally and without uncertainty. These cases are more complex. First, fix the victim's standard of care at the optimal level. Now increase the injurer's standard of care above the optimal level for the injurer. The injurer's optimal response, given that the victim continues to meet his standard of care, is, over some range of values, to set her level of care at the optimal level. The victim's optimal response to this decision, however, is to set his level of care at less than the optimal level. Faced with this decision, the injurer might well choose a level of care higher than the optimum, in which case the victim might best respond with a different level of care. Hence, no equilibrium in pure strategies may exist.

135. Under a scheme of pure negligence, the injurer is liable if she violates her standard of care, regardless of the victim's level of care. For negligence with contributory negligence, the injurer is liable if she violates her standard of care, except when the victim violates his standard of care. Under strict liability with contributory negligence, the injurer is liable regardless of her level of care unless the victim violates his standard of care. Finally, for strict liability with dual contributory negligence, the injurer is liable, except when the victim violates his standard of care and the injurer does not violate her standard of care. Mathematical descriptions of these rules are provided in Brown, *supra* note 30.

136. Under partial liability rules, the actor will have to bear the full increase in the loss. Under full liability rules, she will have to bear this increase plus the loss that results when the standard of care is met.

has no incentive to take care and hence too many accidents will occur. In the multiple actor context, each injurer under strict liability bears some, but not all, of the loss. At the socially optimal level of care, the marginal benefit of expected loss reduction exceeds the costs of producing that reduction. Consequently, each injurer takes too little care (or, in our model, dumps too much waste). Thus, the analogies that we present in this conclusion serve to explain the connection between what are, in fact, closely related areas of tort law.[139]

---

137. *See* S. SHAVELL, *supra* note 5, at 11. Fractional share rules under negligence fail for the same reason.

138. *See supra* note 21.

Appendix

We now define our model more formally, and set forth the notation that we will use. Suppose that there is a set N of actors engaging in an activity. Each actor i ϵ N adopts a *level of care* x_i ϵ (0,∞). We employ the convention that a higher x_i represents *less* care (or more carelessness).

Each actor i derives a *benefit*, $B_i(x_i)$, from choosing to engage in the activity with the level of care x_i. We assume that each benefit function is concave. The actors' choices x_i cause a *social loss*, L(x), where x is the vector whose ith component is x_i. We assume that L(x) is convex, with L(0) $\geq$ 0 and $\partial L(x)/\partial x_i$ > 0 for i ϵ N. We also assume that each actor has sufficient assets to bear the full liability for the social loss, thus avoiding the complicated analysis of the effect of insolvency on rules of contribution. Moreover, we follow the prior literature in considering solely an impersonal or economic social loss and in excluding personal injuries from the analysis.

The *social objective function*, W(x), is defined by W(x) = $\Sigma B_i(x_i)$ - L(x).[140] It is the sum of benefits that the actors derive from the activity minus the social loss that they cause. Let x* be the vector that maximizes the social objective function. To insure a unique interior maximum, we require that the B_i be strictly concave, that L be strictly convex, and that $B_i'(0)$ > $\partial L(0)/\partial x_i$, where $\partial L(0)/\partial x_i$ denotes the partial derivative of L(x) evaluated at x = 0.[141]

A *rule of negligence* is defined as a vector c, where the ith component, c_i, of the vector is the standard of care for actor i. To meet the standard of care actor i must set $x_i \leq c_i$; if she does so, under a negligence rule, she will bear no portion of the social loss. Let M = { i | x_i > c_i } be the set of negligent actors. Under this formulation, a *strict liability* rule is simply a special case of a negligence rule with c = 0.

A *rule of apportionment* consists of a vector of *share functions*, f(x,c), with 0 $\leq$ $f_i(x,c)$ $\leq$ 1, and an *allocation function*, A(x,c), such that for each actor i, $f_i(x,c)$ is the actor's fractional share of the total amount of damage allocated to injurers; we also define actor i's share of liability as the product $f_i(x,c)A(x,c)$ of the actor's share function and the allocation function. We consider only allocation functions of the form A(x,c) = L(x) - K(c), where K(c) is constant in x and depends only on c. Since c affects

---

140. Where the limits of summation are not indicated, the summation is over the set i ϵ N. *See infra* note 144.

141. Our social objective function is equivalent to that used by Landes and Posner. *See* Landes & Posner, *supra* note 5, at 521-22. Their function minimizes costs rather than maximizes benefits. Consequently, they interpret x_i as an actor's level of care (with higher levels of x_i leading to smaller losses), whereas we interpret it as an actor's level of carelessness (so that lower levels of x_i lead to smaller losses). Higher levels of care, in Landes and Posner's model, carry with them higher costs (or negative benefits).

$A(\mathbf{x},\mathbf{c})$ only through this constant term, we shall suppress the dependence of $A(\mathbf{x},\mathbf{c})$ on $\mathbf{c}$ and write the allocation function simply as $A(\mathbf{x})$. Accordingly, we may define the five main types of liability rules.

Definition: A rule of apportionment is a *full liability rule* if and only if $A(\mathbf{x}) = L(\mathbf{x})$.

Definition: A rule of apportionment is a *partial liability rule* if and only if $A(\mathbf{x}) \leq L(\mathbf{x})$ for all $\mathbf{x}$, with strict inequality for some $\mathbf{x}$.[142]

Definition: A rule of apportionment is a *(common law) partial liability rule* if and only if $A(\mathbf{x}) = \max \{ L(\mathbf{x}) - L(\mathbf{c}), 0 \}$.[143]

Definition: A rule of apportionment is a *unitary share rule* if and only if for all $\mathbf{x}$ and $\mathbf{c}$, $\Sigma_M f_i(\mathbf{x},\mathbf{c}) = 1$ if M is non-empty.[144]

Definition: A rule of apportionment is a *fractional share rule* if and only if for all $\mathbf{x}$ and $\mathbf{c}$, $\Sigma_M f_i(\mathbf{x},\mathbf{c}) < 1$ for some M (and equal to 1 otherwise). The text (and the figures in the text) require a strict inequality for all M different from N.

Consider a negligence rule with standard of care $\mathbf{c}$ and a rule of apportionment that assigns $f_i(\mathbf{x},\mathbf{c})A(\mathbf{x})$ to actor i. The ith *payoff function* is defined by

$$V_i(\mathbf{x},\mathbf{c}) = \begin{cases} B_i(x_i) - f_i(\mathbf{x},\mathbf{c})A(\mathbf{x}) & \text{for } x_i > c_i \\\\ B_i(x_i) & \text{otherwise} \end{cases}$$

The n payoff functions and n strategy spaces $(0,\infty)$ define a game, the Nash equilibrium of which we study. A vector $\mathbf{y}^*$ is a *Nash equilibrium* of the game if and only if for each i, $V_i(y_i, y_{-i}^*) \leq V_i(\mathbf{y}^*)$, where (y_i, y_{-i}^*) is the n-vector for which the ith component is y_i and the jth component is y_j^* for $j \neq i$.

With this background, we may consider the following propositions.

Proposition 1: Consider a negligence rule in which the standard of care for each i is set at x_i^*. Let $\{ f(\mathbf{x},\mathbf{x}^*), A(\mathbf{x}) \}$ be a rule of apportionment that satisfies

(a) $A(\mathbf{x}) \leq L(\mathbf{x})$;

(b) $\partial A(\mathbf{x})/\partial x_i = \partial L(\mathbf{x})/\partial x_i$ for each i; and

---

142. Because we deal with risk-neutral actors (and ignore insolvency), we have elided distinctions between ex ante and ex post losses. Our loss function $L(\mathbf{x})$ is actually an ex ante loss function. More generally, $L(\mathbf{x}) = p(\mathbf{x})D(\mathbf{x})$, where $p(\mathbf{x})$ is the probability of the loss occurring given choice $\mathbf{x}$, and $D(\mathbf{x})$ is the ex post loss suffered (in the event of an accident) given $\mathbf{x}$. To pursue the ex ante/ex post distinction, we should write $A(\mathbf{x}) = p(\mathbf{x})C(\mathbf{x})$, where the actor pays $C(\mathbf{x})$ in the event of an accident. The "no-punitive-damages" condition of the text would then require $C(\mathbf{x}) \leq D(\mathbf{x})$.

143. Full liability and partial liability rules do not exhaust the class of possible rules. There are also *punitive liability rules* in which $A(\mathbf{x}) \geq L(\mathbf{x})$ with strict inequality for some $\mathbf{x}$. We do not consider punitive liability either in the text or in this Appendix. Similarly, there are many partial liability rules with $A(\mathbf{x},\mathbf{c}) \leq L(\mathbf{x})$ for all $\mathbf{x}$ and $\mathbf{c}$ that have more complex dependence on $\mathbf{c}$ than the (common law) partial liability rules considered in the rest of the Appendix and throughout the text.

144. A summation over the set $i \in M$ is indicated as Σ_M; the same convention is used for summations over other sets, except as indicated *supra* note 140.

(c) $\Sigma_M f_i(\mathbf{x},\mathbf{x}^*) = 1$ where M is non-empty.
Then $\mathbf{x}^*$ is the unique Nash equilibrium.

Note that condition (b) is satisfied by any full liability rule and, for the purposes of the proof, any (common law) partial liability rule. The (common law) partial liability rules discussed in the text set $K(c) = L(\mathbf{x}^*)$ when the standard of care is set optimally. Condition (c) requires that the rule be unitary. Proposition 1 therefore states that any unitary rule that sets the standard of care optimally induces efficiency.

Proof: Optimality of $\mathbf{x}^*$ implies that for each i, x_i^* satisfies $B_i'(x_i) - \partial L(\mathbf{x})/\partial x_i = 0$. Given condition (b), $\mathbf{x}^*$ also maximizes $\Sigma B_i(x_i) - A(\mathbf{x})$. It is therefore clear that $\mathbf{x}^*$ is a Nash equilibrium. For suppose that all actors except i have chosen $x_j = x_j^*$. Then i, who must bear the entire loss $A(\mathbf{x})$, chooses x_i to maximize

$$V_i((x_i,\mathbf{x}_{-i}^*),\mathbf{x}^*) = \begin{cases} B_i(x_i) - A(x_i,\mathbf{x}_{-i}^*) & \text{for } x_i > x_i^* \\ \\ B_i(x_i) & \text{otherwise} \end{cases}$$

By definition of the optimum, x_i^* maximizes

$$B_i(x_i) - A(x_i,\mathbf{x}_{-i}^*)$$

Thus i will choose $x_i = x_i^*$.

Suppose another Nash equilibrium $\mathbf{x}'$ exists; given the above, at $\mathbf{x}'$, m actors (with $m > 1$) must be negligent and (n-m) non-negligent. Thus for j in N-M, $x_j' = x_j^*$, and for j in M, x_j' maximizes

$$V_j((x_j,\mathbf{x}_{-j}'),\mathbf{x}^*) = B_j(x_j) - f_j((x_j,\mathbf{x}_{-j}'),\mathbf{x}^*)A(x_j,\mathbf{x}_{-j}')$$

with $V_j(\mathbf{x}',\mathbf{x}^*) \geq B_j(x_j^*)$. Thus

$$V(\mathbf{x}',\mathbf{x}^*) = \Sigma_N V_j(\mathbf{x}') = \Sigma_M B_j(x_j') + \Sigma_{N-M} B_j(x_j^*) - A(\mathbf{x}')$$
$$\geq \Sigma_N B_j(x_j^*)$$
$$> \Sigma_N B_j(x_j^*) - L(\mathbf{x}^*)$$

which violates the optimality of $\mathbf{x}^*$.[145] Q.E.D.

Corollary 1: Consider a rule of no-contribution under which each actor's expected share is common knowledge in that such shares are publicly known. If the legal rule sets each actor's standard of care at x_i^*, then the unique Nash equilibrium has $x_i = x_i^*$ for all i.

Proof: If expected shares are common knowledge, then the negligent actors know that they will bear the entire loss; thus each believes that she faces the maximization problem described in the proposition. Q.E.D.

The common knowledge assumption of the corollary states that the sum of the parties' expected shares of the loss is 1. Of course, if the sum of

---

145. The structure of this proof of uniqueness appears in Landes & Posner, *supra* note 5, at 523-24, as a proof of existence.

expected shares exceeds 1, then the unique Nash equilibrium remains x_i = x_i^* for all i; indeed, no actor will choose a level of care more stringent than the standard of care because doing so would entail foregoing benefits with no compensating decrease in liability.

* * * *

For a wide class of (common law) partial liability, fractional share rules, efficiency never results. That is,

Proposition 2: Suppose a rule of negligence with standards of care set at the social optimum $\mathbf{x}^*$ prevails. Let $\{ f(\mathbf{x},\mathbf{x}^*), A(\mathbf{x}) \}$ be a rule of apportionment that satisfies

(a) $\Sigma_M f_i(\mathbf{x},\mathbf{x}^*) < 1$ for every set M (different than N) of negligent actors; and

(b) $A(\mathbf{x}) = L(\mathbf{x}) - L(\mathbf{x}^*)$.

Then,

(1) $\mathbf{x}^*$ is not a Nash equilibrium;

(2) Let $\mathbf{y}$ be a Nash equilibrium in pure or mixed strategies; actor i's strategy y_i is described by a probability distribution function $G_i(x_i)$ on the interval $(0,\infty)$. For every i, $G_i(x_i) = 0$ for $x_i < x_i^*$, and there exists at least one actor k for which $G_k(x_k^*) < 1$.

Condition (a) conforms to the definition of fractional share rules used in the text. Condition (b) identifies a (common law) partial liability rule.

Proof: Consider actor i's payoff function when all other actors j choose x_j^*:

$$V_i((x_i,\mathbf{x}_{-i}^*),\mathbf{x}^*) \quad = \quad \begin{cases} B_i(x_i) - f_i((x_i,\mathbf{x}_{-i}^*),\mathbf{x}^*)A(x_i,\mathbf{x}_{-i}^*) & \text{for } x_i > x_i^* \\ \\ B_i(x_i) & \text{otherwise} \end{cases}$$

The first-order condition, conditional on being negligent, is

$$f_i \, \frac{\partial A(x_i,\mathbf{x}_{-i}^*)}{\partial x_i} \; + \; A(x_i,\mathbf{x}_{-i}^*) \, \frac{\partial f_i}{\partial x_i} \; = \; B_i'(x_i)$$

Evaluating the left hand side at x_i^* yields

$$f_i \, \frac{\partial A(\mathbf{x}^*)}{\partial x_i} \; + \; A(\mathbf{x}^*) \, \frac{\partial f_i}{\partial x_i}$$

But condition (a) states that $f_i < 1$, and condition (b) implies that $A(\mathbf{x}^*) = 0$. Thus

$$f_i \, \frac{\partial A(\mathbf{x}^*)}{\partial x_i} \; + \; A(\mathbf{x}^*) \, \frac{\partial f_i}{\partial x_i} \; < \; \frac{\partial A(\mathbf{x}^*)}{\partial x_i} \; = \; B_i'(x_i^*)$$

It follows that x_i^* does not satisfy the first-order condition for actor i. This proves part (1). Part (2) follows from the fact that, in equilibrium, no actor will ever choose $x_i < x_i^*$ because doing so would entail foregoing benefits with no compensating decrease in liability. Q.E.D.

Note that condition (a) is not necessary for the proof in that it requires that the negligent parties (in the set M) *never* bear the entire loss $A(x)$ unless $M = N$. To show that x^* is not an equilibrium we required only that $f_i < 1$ for the set $M = \{i\}$ for *some* i, not for every i. That assumption is necessary and sufficient to insure that x^* is not a Nash equilibrium.

* * * *

Whether full liability, fractional share rules induce the efficient result depends on the benefit and loss functions and on the number of actors. That is,

Proposition 3: Suppose a rule of negligence with standards of care set at the social optimum x^* prevails. Let $\{f(x,x^*), A(x)\}$ be a rule of apportionment that satisfies

(a) $\Sigma_M f_i(x,x^*) < 1$ for every set M (different than N) of negligent actors; and

(b) $A(x) = L(x)$.

Then whether x^* is a Nash equilibrium depends on $B_i(x_i)$, $L(x)$, and n.

Proof: We prove this proposition by providing an example in which x^* is a Nash equilibrium and a counterexample in which it is not. Consider a full liability, fractional, fixed share (per capita) rule (Rule 3). Let there be n actors; $L(x) = X^r$, where $X = \Sigma x_i$; and for each actor i, let $B_i(x_i) = x_i$. Then the optimum total production $X^* = (1/r)^{1/(r-1)}$, and the standard of care can be set at $x_i^* = (1/n)X^*$ for all i.[146] Suppose that (n-1) actors meet the standard of care; the question then is whether it would be rational for the remaining actor, actor i, to be negligent. If actor i meets the standard of care, she will not be liable for any of the damage. If, in contrast, she is negligent, she will be liable for 1/n of the total damage. Actor i's payoff function is given by

$$V_i((x_i,x_{-i}^*),x^*) = \begin{cases} x_i - (1/n)\left\{ x_i + [(n-1)/n](1/r)^{1/(r-1)} \right\}^r & \text{for } x_i > x_i^* \\ \\ x_i & \text{otherwise} \end{cases}$$

The first-order condition for i's maximization problem, conditional on her being negligent, is

---

146. Since the benefit functions are identical and linear, it does not matter how X^* is divided among the actors.

878   The Yale Law Journal   [Vol. 98: 831

$$1 - (r/n)\left\{ x_i + [(n-1)/n](1/r)^{1/(r-1)} \right\}^{r-1} = 0$$

Solving for x_i we have

$$x_i = (n/r)^{1/(r-1)} - [(n-1)/n](1/r)^{1/(r-1)}$$

It follows that x^* is not a Nash equilibrium if i's payoff from being negligent is greater than her payoff from being non-negligent, that is, if

$$(n/r)^{1/(r-1)} - [(n-1)/n](1/r)^{1/(r-1)} - (1/n)(n/r)^{r/(r-1)} - (1/n)(1/r)^{1/(r-1)} > 0$$

which is equivalent to

$$(n/r)^{1/(r-1)} - (1/r)^{1/(r-1)} - (1/n)(n/r)^{r/(r-1)} > 0$$

which holds if and only if

$$(1/r)^{1/(r-1)}\left\{ n^{1/(r-1)}[1 - 1/r] - 1 \right\} > 0$$

which reduces to

$$n^{1/(r-1)}[1 - 1/r] > 1$$

For $n = 2$, this expression holds for $1 < r < 2$; for larger n, it holds for all $r > 1$ Q.E.D.

* * * *

Recall that we may write strict liability as a negligence rule which sets the standard of care at 0 for each i.

Proposition 4: Suppose a rule of strict liability governs. Let $\{ f(x,0), A(x) \}$ be a rule of apportionment that satisfies
(a) all $f_i(x,0) = q_i$, or all $f_i(x,0) = x_i/X$, where $X = \Sigma x_i$;
(b) $A(x) = L(x)$; and
(c) $\Sigma f_i(x,0) = 1$.
Then, (1) x^* is not a Nash equilibrium; and (2) if $A(x) = \alpha(X)$ for some function α,[147] then any Nash equilibrium x' has the property $X' > X^*$.

Proof: Consider actor i's payoff function when all other actors j choose x_j^*:

$$V_i((x_i, x_{-i}^*), 0) = B_i(x_i) - f_i((x_i, x_{-i}^*), 0)A(x_i, x_{-i}^*)$$

The first-order condition is

$$f_i \frac{\partial A(x_i, x_{-i}^*)}{\partial x_i} + A(x_i, x_{-i}^*) \frac{\partial f_i}{\partial x_i} = B_i'(x_i)$$

---

147. That is, $A(x)$ depends only on Σx_i.

For $f_i = q_i$ this becomes

$$q_i \frac{\partial A(x_i, \mathbf{x}_{-i}{}^*)}{\partial x_i} = B_i{}'(x_i)$$

Evaluating the left-hand side at $x_i{}^*$ yields

$$q_i \frac{\partial A(\mathbf{x}^*)}{\partial x_i}$$

Condition (c) implies that there is at least one i, say k, such that $q_k < 1$. For actor k, $x_k{}^*$ does not satisfy the first-order condition as

$$q_k \frac{\partial A(\mathbf{x}^*)}{\partial x_k} < \frac{\partial A(\mathbf{x}^*)}{\partial x_k} = B_k{}'(x_k{}^*)$$

This proves part (1) for $f_i = q_i$.

For $f_i = x_i/X$, the first-order condition is

$$[x_i/(x_i + \Sigma_{j \neq i} x_j{}^*)] \frac{\partial A(x_i, \mathbf{x}_{-i}{}^*)}{\partial x_i} +$$

$$A(x_i, \mathbf{x}_{-i}{}^*) (\Sigma_{j \neq i} x_j{}^*)/(x_i + \Sigma_{j \neq i} x_j{}^*)^2 = B_i{}'(x_i)$$

Evaluating the left-hand side at $x_i{}^*$ yields

$$(x_i{}^*/X^*) \frac{\partial A(\mathbf{x}^*)}{\partial x_i} + A(\mathbf{x}^*) (\Sigma_{j \neq i} x_j{}^*)/X^{*2}$$

But given the strict convexity of $A(\mathbf{x})$, $A(\mathbf{x}^*)/X^* < \partial A(\mathbf{x}^*)/\partial x_i$. Thus

$$(x_i{}^*/X^*) \frac{\partial A(\mathbf{x}^*)}{\partial x_i} + A(\mathbf{x}^*)(\Sigma_{j \neq i} x_j{}^*)/X^{*2} < \frac{\partial A(\mathbf{x}^*)}{\partial x_i} = B_i{}'(x_i{}^*)$$

It therefore follows that $x_i{}^*$ does not satisfy the first-order condition. This proves part (1) for $f_i = x_i/X$.

Assume that, for $f_i = q_i$, there is an equilibrium $\mathbf{x}'$ for which $X' \leq X^*$. Given the first-order condition,

$$q_i \alpha'(X') = B_i{}'(x_i')$$

But given the convexity of $A(\mathbf{x})$,

$$B_i{}'(x_i') = q_i \alpha'(X') \leq q_i \alpha'(X^*) \leq \alpha'(X^*) = B_i{}'(x_i{}^*)$$

Since $B_i(x_i)$ is strictly concave, it follows that $x_i' \geq x_i{}^*$ for all i. Moreover, for some k, $q_k < 1$, from which it follows that $x_k' > x_k{}^*$. These inequalities contradict the assumption that $X' \leq X^*$. This proves part (2) for $f_i = q_i$. There is a similar proof for $f_i = x_i/X$. Q.E.D.

Corollary 1: $\mathbf{x}^*$ is not a Nash equilibrium under a rule of strict liability and a no-contribution rule.

Proof: A no-contribution rule is simply a fixed share rule. Q.E.D.

Corollary 2: A rule of apportionment and a rule of no-contribution will be equivalent under strict liability if and only if f_i equals i's expected share of liability under no-contribution.

Proof: Each actor's maximization problem is a function of f_i. Q.E.D.

* * * *

One can design a rule of apportionment that induces efficiency even under strict liability. Proposition 1 strongly suggests the form that rule of apportionment should have. Strict liability requires that the actors bear the entire loss $L(\mathbf{x})$ but the rule of apportionment permits us to make the assignment of the loss depend on meeting "standards of apportionment." That is, we may essentially use the rule of apportionment to replicate, under strict liability, the incentive scheme generated by a negligence regime.

The statement and proof of Proposition 5 require some additional notation. Let $M^* = \{ i \mid x_i > x_i^* \}$ where x_i^*, as before, indicates the choice of x_i that maximizes social welfare. With this definition, we may state and prove the following.

Proposition 5: Suppose strict liability governs the actors' actions. Let $\{ f(\mathbf{x},0), A(\mathbf{x}) \}$ be a rule of apportionment that satisfies

(a) $A(\mathbf{x}) = L(\mathbf{x})$;

(b) for all $\mathbf{x}$ such that M^* is empty,

   (i) $\Sigma f_i(\mathbf{x},0) = 1$;

   (ii) for each i, on the interval $(0,x_i^*]$, x_i^* maximizes

$$B_i(x_i) - f_i(\mathbf{x},0)A(\mathbf{x}); \text{ and}$$

(c) for all $\mathbf{x}$ such that M^* is non-empty, $\Sigma_{M^*} f_i(\mathbf{x},0) = 1$.

Then $\mathbf{x}^*$ is the unique Nash equilibrium.

Proof: We first show that $\mathbf{x}^*$ is an equilibrium. So suppose that all actors except i have chosen $x_j = x_j^*$. Then by condition (c), if i is negligent, she will bear the entire loss $A(x_i, \mathbf{x}_{-i}^*)$. Thus she would choose x_i to maximize

$$B_i(x_i) - A(x_i, \mathbf{x}_{-i}^*)$$

But x_i^* maximizes this expression; i would thus adopt x_i^*. The proof of uniqueness is essentially the same as that given in Proposition 1. Q.E.D.

Note that condition (c) creates discontinuities at $\mathbf{x}^*$ that replicate, through the rule of apportionment, the incentives generated by a full liability, unitary share rule under negligence with the standards of care set optimally. In turn, condition (b)(ii) insures that x^* is the unique equilibrium with M^* empty.[148]

Proposition 5 does not necessarily capture all the rules of apportionment that induce efficiency under strict liability. Appropriate incentives require only that the change in f_i at x^* be sufficiently dramatic to induce the choice of x_i^*. Thus some continuous and perhaps even differentiable set of f_i might induce efficiency.

* * * *

We now turn to the case of uncertainty.

Proposition 6: Suppose there are two actors. Consider a negligence rule with the standard of care for actor 1 drawn from a probability distribution with mean x^* and the standard of care for actor 2 drawn from a probability distribution with mean y^*. Let the rule of apportionment be $A(x,y) = L(x,y) - L(x^*,y^*)$. Then,

(a) the partial liability rule $A(x,y)$ always yields under-deterrence; and

(b) a partial liability, fractional share rule under-deters more than a partial liability, unitary share rule.

Proof: The logic of the proof follows that used by Craswell and Calfee in their analysis of the single actor case.[149]

Let $\Pi(x \mid y^*)$ be one actor's expected profit given that the other actor is operating at the social optimum. Let $F(x)$ be the probability that this actor is held liable given that she has adopted level of care x, and let $G(y)$ be the probability that the other actor is held liable given that she has adopted level of care y.[150] For a unitary, fixed share (per capita) rule,

---

148. In the absence of condition (b)(ii), the f_i might be such that a set of discontinuities occurs at some point $x' < x^*$; that is, at a point x' each of whose components is less than the corresponding component of x^*. These f_i would reproduce a full liability, unitary share rule under negligence with the standards of care set non-optimally; as shown below, such a rule need not induce efficiency.

Also suppose that the f_i have discontinuities at both x' and x^*. Under negligence, there would be no multiplicity of equilibria because, for $x' < x^*$, the injurers bear none of the liability. Under strict liability, in contrast, there could be multiple equilibria because the injurers bear all the liability.

Note that the possibility of multiple equilibria is not ruled out simply by requiring that f_i be continuous, as there may be such multiple equilibria with continuous functions if f_i is rising sufficiently rapidly. Both fixed share rules and proportional share rules satisfy condition (b)(ii).

149. Craswell & Calfee, *supra* note 117.

150. The probability distribution functions F and G are derived from the respective distributions over the standards of care.

$$\Pi(x\,|\,y^*) = B(x) - F(x)\,\{\,[1 - G(y^*)]A(x,y^*) + G(y^*)A(x,y^*)/2\,\}$$
$$= B(x) - F(x)A(x,y^*)[1 - G(y^*)/2]$$

Then

$$\frac{\partial\Pi(x^*\,|\,y^*)}{\partial x} =$$

$$B'(x^*) - [1 - G(y^*)/2]\,\{\,F(x^*)\,\frac{\partial A(x^*,y^*)}{\partial x} + F'(x^*)A(x^*,y^*)\,\}$$

But $B'(x^*) = \partial A(x^*,y^*)/\partial x$. Thus

$$\frac{\partial\Pi(x^*\,|\,y^*)}{\partial x} = \{\,1 - [1 - G(y^*)/2]\,\}\,F(x^*)\,\frac{\partial A(x^*,y^*)}{\partial x}$$
$$- [1 - G(y^*)/2]F'(x^*)A(x^*,y^*)$$

If $A(x^*,y^*) = 0$, as it is for a (common law) partial liability rule,[151] then the second term is zero, the first term is positive, and there are incentives to undercomply.

For a fractional, fixed share (per capita) rule,

$$\Pi(x\,|\,y^*) = B(x) - F(x)A(x,y^*)/2$$

Then

$$\frac{\partial\Pi(x^*\,|\,y^*)}{\partial x} = [1 - F(x^*)/2]\frac{\partial A(x^*,y^*)}{\partial x} - F'(x^*)A(x^*,y^*)/2$$

If $A(x^*,y^*) = 0$, as it is for a (common law) partial liability rule, then the second term is zero, the first term is positive, and there are incentives to undercomply. Comparing the expressions for the unitary and fractional rules, the incentive to undercomply is smaller for unitary share rules than for fractional share rules. Q.E.D.

* * * *

Finally, we present an example that illustrates the responses of two identical actors, to standards of care that are certain but are set too stringently. We perform the analysis for unitary, fixed share (per capita) rules.

151. Our formulation of the model is better suited to an interpretation in which the standard of care is known for certain but the court makes errors of fact-finding. Under the interpretation in the text, where $E(c_1) = x^*$ and $E(c_2) = y^*$, it would seem more appropriate to define the partial liability rule as a function not of the *mean* standard of care but of the *realized* standard of care (that is, to set $A(x,y,c_1,c_2) = L(x,y) - L(c_1,c_2)$ where c_1 is the standard of care imposed on actor 1 and c_2 the standard of care imposed on actor 2). The analysis of this model is more complex as actor 1 is concerned with $E[A(x,y)] = L(x,y) - E[L(c_1,c_2)]$. Each actor thus apparently faces an additional incentive to undercomply as, by the strict convexity of L and Jensen's inequality, $E[L(c_1,c_2)] \geq L(x^*,y^*)$ and therefore $E[A(x,y)] < L(x,y) - L(x^*,y^*)$. On Jensen's inequality, see M.H. DEGROOT, OPTIMAL STATISTICAL DECISIONS 97 (1970).

Let $L(\mathbf{x}) = X^r$, where $r > 1$; and let $B_i(x_i) = x_i$. Recall that $X = \Sigma x_i$. The optimum total production $X^* = (1/r)^{1/(r-1)}$, and the optimal standard of care can be set at $x_i^* = x^* = \frac{1}{2}(1/r)^{1/(r-1)}$. Throughout this example, both actors face the same standard of care.[152]

For ease of exposition, we define the equilibrium level of care under a strict liability, fixed share (per capita) rule. Under such a rule, each actor would maximize

$$x_i - \frac{1}{2}X^r$$

Let (x_s, x_s) be the equilibrium level of care. Then $x_s = \frac{1}{2}(2/r)^{1/(r-1)}$. Even though in this example we are studying the behavior of negligence rules, we define the equilibrium under strict liability because if both actors decide to violate the standard of care, they will behave as if they were governed by a strict liability rule.

We consider first how a full liability rule under negligence performs under standards of care that are more stringent than the social optimum. There is an equilibrium at (x_s, x_s) where the standard of care is set in the range $0 \le c \le a_1$, where a_1 is defined by

$$a_1 = x_s - \frac{1}{2}(2x_s)^r$$

The value a_1 is the highest level of the standard of care for which, given that one actor is operating at x_s, the other actor will also choose x_s rather than meet the standard of care. The left hand side of the equation gives one actor's benefit from meeting the standard of care set at a_1, and the right hand side is the benefit to that actor from operating at x_s, given that the other actor is also operating at x_s. Substituting for x_s in the preceding equation we obtain

$$a_1 = (2/r)^{1/(r-1)}(r - 2)/(2r)$$

Note that $a_1 > 0$ for all $r > 2$, and that $a_1/x^* = (2)^{1/(r-1)}(1 - 2/r) < 1$ for all r. Thus $a_1 < x^*$. It follows that if the standard of care is set sufficiently below x^*, a negligence rule behaves like a strict liability rule.

There is an equilibrium at (c,c) where the standard of care is set in the range $a_2 \le c \le x^*$ for $a_2 = a_m - (a_m + a_2)^r \ge 0$, where $a_m = \text{argmax} [x - (x + a_2)^r]$. The value a_2 is the lowest level of the standard of care for which, given that one actor is meeting the standard of care, the other actor will also meet the standard of care. The value a_m is the optimal level of care for an actor who has chosen to violate the standard of care set at a_2, given that the other actor has chosen to meet that standard. Solving first for a_m we obtain

---

152. *See supra* note 146.

$$1 = r(a_m + a_2)^{r-1}$$
$$a_m = (1/r)^{1/(r-1)} - a_2$$

It follows that

$$a_2 = (1/r)^{1/(r-1)} - a_2 - (1/r)^{r/(r-1)}$$
$$a_2 = (1/r)^{1/(r-1)}(r - 1)/(2r)$$

Note that $a_2 > 0$ for all $r > 1$. Note also that $a_1 < a_2 < x^*$ for all r. Thus if the standard of care is sufficiently close to x^*, the actors will meet the standard of care. Finally, note that where the standard of care is set in the range $a_1 < c < a_2$, there is no equilibrium in pure strategies. Where the standard of care is in this range, it is neither sufficiently close to the socially optimal level for an equilibrium to exist in which each actor meets the standard of care, nor sufficiently far from the socially optimal level for an equilibrium to exist in which each actor operates at the strict liability level.

We now turn to the examination of (common law) partial liability rules. There is an equilibrium at (x_s, x_s) where the standard of care is set in the range $0 \leq c \leq a_3$, where a_3 is defined by

$$a_3 = x_s - [(2x_s)^r - (2a_3)^r]/2$$
$$a_3 - \tfrac{1}{2}(2a_3)^r = x_s - \tfrac{1}{2}(2x_s)^r$$

The value a_3 is the highest level of the standard of care for which, given that one actor is operating at x_s, the other actor will also choose x_s rather than meet the standard of care. As in the case of full liability rules, a negligence rule behaves like a strict liability rule if the standard of care is set too stringently. Note that where the standard of care is set in the range $a_3 < c < x^*$, there is no equilibrium in pure strategies.[153]

Finally, to compare full liability and (common law) partial liability rules, we need to determine the relationship between a_2 and a_3. Substituting for a_2 and x_s, it follows that

$$a_2 < x_s - [(2x_s)^r - (2a_2)^r] \text{ for all } r > 2$$

Thus $a_2 < a_3$ for all $r > 2$. As a result, where the standard of care is set in the range $a_2 < c < a_3$, a (common law) partial liability rule produces an equilibrium at (x_s, x_s), causing under-deterrence, whereas a full liability rule produces an equilibrium at (c,c), causing over-deterrence.

---

153. *See supra* text accompanying notes 126–29. For both full liability and partial liability rules, to show the non-existence of an equilibrium in pure strategies, one must also show, as one can, that there is no asymmetric equilibrium in which one actor meets the standard of care and the other does not.

[16]

Indivisible Toxic Torts:
The Economics of Joint and Several Liability

Tom H. Tietenberg

The economics literature concerned with cost-effective or efficient pollution control has traditionally devoted most of its attention to analyzing the effects of legislative or regulatory policy instruments, such as emission taxes or marketable emission permits.[1] Recent contributions have expanded this focus to include the effects of monitoring and enforcement policies.[2] With a few noteworthy exceptions,[3] however, the role of the court system in general and liability law in particular have not received analytical attention among environmental economists in proportion to their importance in resource allocation.

In certain situations liability law can be a valuable weapon in the arsenal of policy responses to pollution problems. By creating legal precedents which assure that pollution damages inflicted on some other party will be borne by the polluter, liability law can create incentives for polluters to take efficient levels of precaution. By providing an alternative means of internalizing externalities, judicial remedies can complement legislative and administrative remedies. At the same time damage payments can compensate directly those victims of pollution who are parties to the suit, an attribute not shared by traditional regulatory approaches.

Although court decisions have the capability in principle to sustain efficient resource allocations, by no means are efficient allocations preordained. The desirability of judicial outcomes depends crucially on such factors as the information available to the court at the time the decision is rendered, the ability of the polluter to pay damage awards and the legal doctrine on which the court bases its decision. Not all legal doctrines are equally efficient.

In this paper the use of the "joint and several liability" doctrine as a means of financing the restoration of contaminated waste sites is analyzed.[4] Long used in the common law in a variety of contexts, this doctrine has begun to play an important role in the control of toxic substances. In interpreting the Comprehensive Environmental Response, Compensation, and Liability Act (known popularly as the "Superfund" Act), the courts have allowed the government to sue "potentially responsible parties" (i.e., disposal site owners and operators, waste generators and transporters) for damages and site recovery costs under the joint and several liability concept.[5] By

Tietenberg is professor, Department of Economics, Colby College, Waterville, Maine.

The author gratefully acknowledges the helpful comments received from James Meehan, Randy Nelson, the members of the Colby-Bates-Bowdoin Seminar Series, and two anonymous referees.

[1] For a comprehensive review of this literature see Bohm and Russell (1985).

[2] For a review of this literature, as well as some significant contributions, see Russell, Harrington, and Vaughan (1986).

[3] See Bromley (1978), Opaluch (1984), Opaluch and Grigalunas (1984), Johnson and Ulen (1986), Segerson (1986), Sullivan (1986), Cichetti and Haveman (1988), Dechert and Smith (1988), Grigalunas and Opaluch (1988), and Segerson and Micelli (1988).

[4] The two economic analyses of the multiple tortfeasors case of which the author is aware are Landes and Posner (1980) and Segerson and Micelli (1988). The focus of those articles is very different in that they examine the effects of the doctrine in a common law setting rather than the legislatively-triggered toxic substance control setting considered here. In particular this article delves into the effects on incentives created by government litigation strategies, a subject not covered by either of the other papers.

[5] See, for example, United States v. Conservation Chemical Company, 589 F. Supp. 59 (1984) and United States v. Chem-Dyne Corp., 572 F. Supp. 802 (1983) and the cases cited therein.

Land Economics Vol. 65. No. 4, November 1989

establishing precedents that will govern the liability of those currently involved with active toxic waste sites, these doctrines can create incentives to take precaution as well as create opportunities for the government to enlist private revenue sources in the effort to clean up the hundreds of toxic waste sites. As this paper demonstrates, both the revenue-raising capabilities and the incentive effects of the current policy are sensitive to the legal context of the suit and the litigation strategy chosen by the government.

The paper opens by defining the joint and several liability doctrine, elaborating the conditions under which it can be used, and describing the recent history of its use in toxic substance control. It then investigates the extent to which this approach encourages efficient precautionary behavior by analyzing the incentives created by the precedents flowing from the court decisions. A noncooperative game theory model is used to characterize the Nash equilibria resulting from the interdependence of actions by the government litigation team and the set of potentially responsible parties. Specifically examined legal regimes are joint and several liability with and without the right of contribution in both a negligence context and a strict liability context. The various Nash equilibria are compared to each other and to the efficient allocation. Since the joint and several liability doctrine is typically applied in those cases where it is difficult or impossible to apportion the responsibility among the potentially responsible parties (PRPs) on anything but an arbitrary basis, indivisibility is a key aspect of the economic model. The final section draws out the policy implications of the analysis.

I. THE JOINT AND SEVERAL LIABILITY DOCTRINE

Reduced to its essence, the joint and several liability doctrine makes each successfully sued defendant potentially liable for an amount up to the entire damage caused, regardless of the magnitude of its individual contribution. This doctrine has a long history in the common law, but its use has changed rather dramatically over the years. In English common law, the historical foundation for our own common law, tortfeasors were and are jointly and severally liable only when they have acted in concert to produce a harm; in the United States, however, joint and several liability can now be found where the independent acts of two parties have concurred to produce a single and indivisible result.[6] Over time the definition of what is truly indivisible has also been expanded rather dramatically.[7]

The use of the joint and several liability doctrine in toxic substance control was triggered by the passage of the Superfund Act in 1980[8] and buttressed by the passage of the Superfund Amendments and Reauthorization Act of 1986.[9] Although neither act specifically calls for the imposition of joint and several liability the government has used that theory in pursuing defendants, and this litigation strategy has been upheld by the courts. In the key case, United States v. Chem-Dyne Corp, Judge Rubin stated that the imposition of the doctrine of joint and several liability was possible if the harm was caused by two or more parties and if their respective contributions were indivisible. Indivisibility in this context means that it is difficult or impossible to apportion the responsibility among the respective parties on anything but an arbitrary basis. That condition is commonly met in toxic substance control.[10]

---

[6] 74 Am Jur 2d §61:671.

[7] Consider, for example, Summers v. Tice, 33 Cal 2d 80, in which two careless pheasant hunters fired in the direction of the plaintiff, wounding him. Because the court could not determine which hunter had fired the bullet that inflicted the wound they were held to be jointly and severally liable.

[8] 42 U.S.C. §9601–9657.

[9] 100 Stat 1613.

[10] Such obvious devices as apportioning responsibility on the basis of volume of waste contributed have normally been rejected by the courts, because volume is typically only one of several significant factors that determine responsibility. Examples of other determining factors include the toxicity of the substance, the amount of disposal precaution taken, and the proper apportionment for the site managers and/or owners, for whom volume would be a completely inadequate indicator of their responsibility.

The Superfund Amendments and Reauthorization Act of 1986 left the joint and several liability doctrine intact, though some modifications were introduced. In particular, while U.S. common law historically has not granted the right of contribution to those held liable under the joint and several liability doctrine, the Superfund Amendments and Reauthorization Acts created a statutory right of contribution.[11] The right of contribution allows parties that have made payments (either by settling out of court or in response to a court decision) to seek reimbursement from other potentially responsible parties that have not. This right of contribution can be exercised by those settling out of court as well as those assessed damages following a trial. Once a party signs a consent decree of either type, however, they cannot be sued for contribution by other parties.[12]

The government enforces this act by encouraging PRPs to clean up the site on their own, but it is prepared to investigate and even to clean up identified hazardous waste sites if necessary and to finance the effort from the several billion dollar Hazardous Substance Response Trust Fund created by the Act. It then seeks reimbursement from parties who are potentially responsible for the conditions at each particular site. The potentially responsible parties are liable for any costs of restoring the site to a safe status as well as "damages for injury to, destruction of, or loss of natural resources, including the reasonable costs of assessing such injury, destruction, or loss resulting from such a release."[13] If any liable party "fails without sufficient cause to properly provide removal or remedial action," they may be assessed punitive damages of "three times the amount of any costs incurred by the Fund as a result of such failure to take proper action."[14]

The thrust of this modern statutory view is that joint and several liability becomes the presumed doctrine unless the defendants can bear the far-from-trivial apportionment burden. From the point of view of the government this modern view has some attractive features. It provides a basis for recovering all site restoration costs and damages even when one or more contributors to the problem are judgment proof, such as when a PRP cannot be identified or is insolvent. With proportional apportionment, the share of financial responsibility that would have been borne by judgment proof PRPs remains unrecovered, and the taxpayers must foot the bill. This doctrine also lowers the government's burden of proof. If in proving the liability of each party the government were forced to defend a particular apportionment of responsibility, failure to provide adequate support for the chosen apportionment scheme could result in a victory for the defendants and a failure to recover any revenue. With indivisibility any such apportionment is necessarily arbitrary. Under joint and several liability the government has only to prove that the PRP bore some causal responsibility. The fact that the degree of culpability is uncertain would not bar recovery.

Criticisms of the joint and several liability doctrine typically are based upon its perceived lack of fairness. Defendants who are sued successfully under this doctrine can end up paying the entire liability for a toxic chemical incident even if they were only responsible for a small percentage of the damage. That allocation of liability is widely viewed as inequitable.[15] Allowing the right of contribution is one way Congress has tried to deal with this perceived inequity. Aggrieved parties can seek reimbursement from those deemed to have failed to bear their fair share of the burden.

---

[11] Allowing the right of contribution in joint and several liability cases is now granted in the overwhelming majority of states as well. See Pressler and Schieffer (1988, 662).

[12] See May (1987).

[13] 42 U.S.C. §9607c.

[14] 42 U.S.C. §9607c3. Presumably this provision implies that the treble damages apply only to the incremental costs caused by inaction or negligent action following the government's notice that recovery was to occur, not to actions taken prior to that notice. For our purposes the important point is that negligent action per se does not trigger treble damages.

[15] As an example of this view see Dubuc and Evans Jr. (1987).

II. AN ECONOMIC MODEL OF JOINT AND SEVERAL LIABILITY

In the traditional model used to examine the large number of doctrines that comprise tort law (the civil, as opposed to criminal, body of law dealing with wrongs inflicted on another party) the parties to an incident are said to be acting efficiently if they individually choose a level of precaution that minimizes the total sum of precaution costs and expected damages for society as a whole.[16] Symbolically, let

J = the total number of PRPs associated with the contaminated site of interest;

x_j = the level of precaution taken by the jth PRP (e.g., a waste generator, disposal site owner, manager or transporter);

x = a set containing the J x_j's;

$w_j(x_j)$ = a function relating total precautionary costs to the level of precaution taken by the jth PRP;

$p(x)$ = a function mapping the J elements of the set x into the ex ante probability of an incident; and

A = a scalar representing the cost of restoring the site and compensating for the level of damage caused by the incident.

The value of $p(x)$, the likelihood of an incident, is assumed to be jointly determined by the actions of all PRPs, a specification which captures the indivisibility nature of this kind of tort; the marginal expected damages of any unit of precaution taken by any PRP depends on the actions taken by the others. It is further assumed that

$$\frac{\partial w_j(x_j)}{\partial x_j} > 0 \text{ and } \frac{\partial p(x)}{\partial x_j} < 0. \qquad [1]$$

Assuming risk neutrality, in this framework the set of efficient precaution levels (x^*) is the set which minimizes:

$$\sum_{j=1}^{J} w_j(x_j) + p(x)A. \qquad [2]$$

Assuming the second-order conditions hold, each element of the set of efficient levels of precaution must satisfy:

$$\frac{\partial w_j(x_j)}{\partial x_j} + \frac{\partial p(x)}{\partial x_j} A = 0 \qquad j = 1, \ldots, J. \quad [3]$$

Verbally, this result implies that each party to the incident should take additional precaution until the marginal cost of the additional precaution is equal to the marginal reduction in expected damage.[17]

The nature of the incentives for precautionary behavior depends crucially on whether the parties to the incident are held strictly liable for their actions or judged by a negligence test. In the common law the joint and several liability doctrine has been applied in both contexts; whether negligence or strict liability is applied is determined by the circumstances. Under strict liability any subset of potentially responsible parties could be held liable for the amount necessary to compensate the victim, regardless of any precautions they may have undertaken, while under negligence they are held liable only if their behavior violated some prescribed standard of care.

Negligence

Under a negligence doctrine potentially responsible parties would be held liable if they failed to meet a court imposed standard of care (i.e., the party is declared negligent). Let $\hat{x}_j$ be the legally established

---

[16] I first became aware of this model in Brown (1973). A large number of applications of this model can be found in Cootner and Ulen (1988). The application in this paper differs from the traditional model primarily in that two parties are jointly responsible for the damage (rather than the more traditional single party focus), and the victim's role is eliminated. In this case since the suits are by the government rather than victims, focusing on the behavior of the potentially responsible parties is appropriate.

[17] This solution is strictly correct only for interior solutions. In the case of corner solutions this expression could be positive as long as the corresponding level of precaution were zero. This would be the case, for example, if the marginal cost of the first unit of precaution exceeded the marginal benefit of the associated reduction in expected damages.

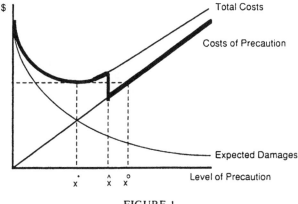

FIGURE 1

standard of care for the *j*th potentially responsible party. If $x_j < \hat{x}_j$ then that party would be liable for assessed damages, whereas if $x_j \geq \hat{x}_j$ it would escape any liability. The cost function faced by a typical party under the negligence doctrine is illustrated in Figure 1.

Since the level of expected damage is assumed to decline with the level of precaution, the PRP would attempt to choose that positive level of precaution which would minimize the sum of its costs of precaution and expected damages. For all $x_j < \hat{x}_j$ the party would bear both the cost of any precautions taken as well as any remaining damage. For all $x_j \geq \hat{x}_j$ the party would bear only the costs of further precaution; it would have been relieved of the obligation to compensate for any damages caused by behaving non-negligently.

The outcomes resulting from the application of liability doctrines in this toxic tort setting can be modeled as a noncooperative game. The players are the set of PRPs and the government. The government's strategic choice involves selecting which PRPs to sue, using the predetermined standard of care as established by precedent, while each PRP's strategic choice involves selecting its level of precaution. All parties are presumed to know the predetermined standard of care that would be applied to each PRP.

The government's objective in this game is specified as maximizing its net litigation benefits subject to its budget constraint. Net litigation benefits are defined as the level of damages recovered from the litigants minus the cost to the government of litigation. Litigation costs are assumed to increase with the number of parties being sued.

Each PRP's objective is to minimize its total costs, considering both its costs of precaution and its expected liability payments. Selecting noncooperative game theory to model government and PRP choices is dictated by the interdependence between the government's strategy and the strategies chosen by the PRPs as well as the interdependence among the choices of the PRPs. While any PRP's precautionary costs are independent of the actions taken by the other players, the expected liability that it would bear for any chosen level of precaution would in general depend on the level of precaution taken by the other PRPs and the targeting strategy implemented by the government.

The solution concept employed in this analysis is the *Nash equilibrium*. A set of strategies is said to represent a Nash equilibrium if, given the choices of all other players, no player could improve his/her situation by choosing another feasible strategy.

The rules of the game dictate a clear government strategy. The government would want to target only negligent parties for litigation; targeting those who had met the standard of care would raise litigation expenses without raising any additional revenue.[18]

Given the government's strategy, PRP behavior can be modeled. Forcing PRPs to face a negligence test creates a discontinuous cost function (highlighted in Figure 1) for the potentially responsible parties. It would never be optimal for a potentially responsible party to choose a level of precaution greater than $\hat{x}_j$ since further precautionary expenditures would raise costs without producing any reduction in the amount paid in compensation. Furthermore, although the sum of expected damage costs and precautionary expenditures could reach its minimum at a point to the left of $\hat{x}_j$ if the court imposed an excessively stringent standard of care, the party would normally still choose $\hat{x}_j$ as long as it was cheaper to bear only precaution costs at $\hat{x}_j$ than to bear the total of precaution costs and expected damages at the efficient standard of care. (In Figure 1 the PRP would choose $\hat{x}$ unless the standard of care were to the right of x^0; if it were to the right of x^0 the PRP would choose x^*.)

The conclusion that PRPs would choose the standard of care prescribed by precedent is very robust to errors by the court both in setting that precedent and in the level of damages assigned. If the court were to err by establishing an inefficiently low standard of care, the PRP would always prefer to meet the lower court-prescribed standard of care than to select the efficient level of care because it would result in lower costs to that PRP. If the court erred by choosing an inefficiently high standard of care, the error would have to be very large before the PRP would prefer the efficient standard of care to that established by precedent. An error this large is an especially remote possibility given that the courts use an explicitly economic rationale in establishing standard of care precedents.[19] Therefore, in what follows we shall assume $\hat{x} < x^0$. With this assumption, the Nash equilibrium strategy for all PRPs

would be to meet the known standard of care whether or not it was efficient.

In a negligence context the main effect of authorizing the joint and several liability doctrine is to change the expected damages faced by negligent PRPs. In essence, authorizing the joint and several liability doctrine raises the cost of being found negligent by increasing the expected damages. In the absence of joint and several liability negligent parties would bear only their proportional responsibility for the damage; the sum of the payments received from all negligent parties would be less than the actual damages unless, of course, all PRPs were declared negligent. No payments would be extracted from non-negligent parties, and the damages attributed to them would go uncompensated. In contrast, under joint and several liability negligent parties would be assessed the entire damage; they would be required to absorb not only that portion of the damage that would have been attributed to them in the absence of joint and several liability, but they must also pick up some pro rata share of the damage caused by non-negligent and non-sued parties.

What effect would this rise in expected damages have on the equilibrium behavior of the PRPs? Within the negligence framework the typical PRP would take no more precaution with joint and several liability imposed than it would with proportional liability. This perhaps surprising result is, of course, due to the discontinuity in the cost function associated with the negligence approach. Since the PRP minimizes its ex-

---

[18] The significant issue of whether the government litigation team would target all negligent parties, or only some of them, is covered below once PRP behavior is clarified.

[19] Though further treatment of this issue is beyond the scope of this paper, an excellent statement of the information that the court must have before it and the precise way it must be used in order to establish an efficient standard of care can be found in Brown (1973). It turns out that expecting the court to formulate an economic definition of the standard of care is not an unreasonable expectation. See the United States v. Carroll Towing Co., 159 F.2d 169 (1947) for the initial formulation of the now famous Learned Hand rule.

pected costs by simply meeting the standard of care established by the court, that level of care minimizes its costs with or without joint and several liability. The fact that a PRP would be forced to pay higher levels of compensation with joint and several liability if it failed to meet the court-established standard of care is immaterial, since it can avoid these additional expenditures by simply choosing $x_j = \hat{x}_j$, a strategy that continues to be in its self-interest with or without joint and several liability.

Would authorizing the joint and several liability doctrine affect the government's optimal litigation strategy? It certainly doesn't change the desirability of targeting only negligent parties, but it does introduce the possibility of suing fewer than the total number of negligent parties if more than one party were negligent. Since in the Nash equilibrium all PRPs minimize their costs by meeting the standard of care the government would have no opportunity to take advantage of the flexibility offered by the joint and several liability doctrine; there would be no negligent parties to sue.[20]

Would authorizing the right of contribution change the Nash equilibrium? Because all PRPs would find it in their interest to meet the standard of care, they would not pay any damages. Though the right of contribution would lower the effective expected damages by allowing negligent parties to seek partial reimbursement from other negligent parties, as long as $\hat{x} < x^0$ PRPs would not be induced to act negligently by the introduction of the right of contribution. The Nash equilibrium would be the same with or without the right of contribution.

Several implications emerge from this analysis of behavior in a negligence context. In a Nash equilibrium the government would target only negligent parties for litigation and, in response, PRPs would meet the court-dictated standard of care. This outcome is independent of the joint and several liability doctrine and also the right of contribution. The resulting expected damages would not normally be efficient unless the court were to choose an efficient

standard of care. Whether the expected damages were too high or too low would depend directly on whether the court dictated standard of care were correspondingly too high or too low. An excessively harsh standard of care would imply inefficiently low expected damages, while an inefficiently lax standard would imply excessive expected damages.

Paradoxically, the amount of expected revenue recovered under negligence would be zero regardless of whether joint and several liability or the right of contribution were authorized. Under the assumptions we have specified, it would always pay targeted PRPs to choose the court-prescribed standard of care, thereby relieving themselves of the obligation to contribute to site clean-up. Government litigation expenditures would also be zero, because there would be no point in suing parties that were not negligent.

Strict Liability

The liability approach prescribed by the Act was strict liability.[21] Under strict liability the government does not have to prove that a PRP violated its standard of care; conversely the PRPs cannot use the level of precautions undertaken as a defense, regardless of how extraordinary those precautions may have been. The main burden of proof the government faces is in showing that the PRP in some sense caused, or at least partially caused, the damage.

Consider first the nature of the Nash equilibrium if the legal regime were strict liability but neither joint and several liabil-

---

[20] This conclusion is, of course, sensitive to the specification of the model. If the standard of care were not known by all parties, for example, some could inadvertently violate the standard, making them vulnerable to a suit.

[21] The act did this not by mandating strict liability, but rather by limiting the defenses any defendant could offer. Exercising due care is specifically omitted as an allowable defense except when the contamination is caused by a third party with whom the defendant had no contractual relationship. See 42 U.S.C. §9607b.

ity nor the right of contribution were authorized. For ease of reference we refer to this case as pure strict liability. We then sequentially add joint and several liability and right of contribution to the model and derive their incremental effects.

In pure strict liability the government's Nash equilibrium strategy would be to target all PRPs for litigation that passed a positive net benefits test. If the amount of money recovered from a particular PRP would be less than the government's costs of litigating, that PRP would fail the net benefits test (e.g., those PRPs expected to bear a very small share of the damages). Given the lower litigation costs for both parties for an out of court settlement and the relative ease of establishing some degree of causal responsibility, it is likely that the net benefits of an out of court settlement would be positive, even for these PRPs. In general, therefore, all parties could be expected to be held accountable for their share of the damages either by trial or out of court settlement.[22]

With strict liability the absence of a negligence test means that each party must directly trade off extra precautions with resulting reductions in expected damage. Whereas the level of damage assessment was not a significant factor in determining the Nash equilibrium under negligence it becomes very important under strict liability. Let s_j be the known share of the constant damage assigned to the jth PRP in a pure strict liability settlement. The jth PRP therefore would want to minimize:

$$w_j(x_j) + p(x)s_jA. \qquad [4]$$

Current rules of apportioning damage require that the total collections from the PRPs not exceed the amount of the damage. This implies that $\Sigma s_j = 1.0$ over the set of J PRPs. The first order conditions characterizing the Nash equilibrium for this PRP would be

$$\frac{\partial w_j(x_j)}{\partial x_j} + \frac{\partial p(x|\bar{x})}{\partial x_j} s_jA = 0, \qquad [5]$$

where the $x|\bar{x}$ notation captures the fact that the PRP would be minimizing its costs given the fixed precaution levels by the other PRPs.

Is the efficient allocation a Nash equilibrium? In general it is not. Referring back to equation set [3], which characterizes the efficient allocation, it is clear that as long as $s_j < 1.0$, as it would be unless there were only one PRP, the jth PRP would take less than the efficient level of precaution even if every other PRP were taking its efficient level of precaution; the marginal expected damages are too low with this type of apportionment rule to support efficient precautionary behavior.[23] What is true for the jth PRP would also be true for the others. In general, the Nash equilibrium solution for pure strict liability would involve too little precaution, and the expected damages would be too high relative to an efficient allocation.

What is the effect of authorizing joint and several liability without contribution? Armed with the joint and several liability doctrine the government litigation team could recover the entire amount of damages from any single party. Suing more parties than necessary to secure the full amount of damages would raise litigation costs with no commensurate benefit.[24] The government's Nash equilibrium strategy, there-

---

[22] EPA in fact routinely settles out of court with small PRPs. See U.S. General Accounting Office (1988).

[23] This result is consistent with earlier work. See Green (1976) and White and Wittman (1979). A similar result was independently derived using a slightly different model in Segerson and Micelli (1988).

[24] Any party that negligently ignored an administrative order that restoration should begin would be subject to treble damages, a clear exception to the normal limit on damages. Note, however, that this only applies to those PRPs who are negligent after the order is issued. Firms that may have been negligent before the administrative order, but which comply fully with the order, would not face treble damages. Those firms that engaged in negligent behavior after notification, if any, would also clearly be targeted for litigation, although our model implies that no firm would violate the order because of the drastic financial consequences of doing so.

fore, would be to sue the smallest number of PRPs possible and still receive the full damages.[25]

How would the government select those PRPs to target for litigation? Since the burden of proof typically would not vary widely among the PRPs, the government would target the wealthiest PRPs to assure that the damages could, and would, be paid.

Wealth targeting has a very important consequence for modeling PRP reactions to this known litigation strategy. PRPs would be able to determine in advance whether they would be targeted for litigation. Large, wealthy corporations would be targeted; smaller operations would not. In essence, this targeting strategy partitions the set of PRPs into two categories—those who would expect to be sued and those who would not expect to be sued.

Given the government's Nash equilibrium targeting strategy, it is possible to derive the PRP strategies and subsequently to characterize the resulting equilibrium. Consider first the behavior of those PRPs that know they would not be targeted for litigation. Since the nontargeted parties would be immune from suits, their expected share of the damages would be zero. Taking precautions would not reduce expected compensation payments, but it would raise precautionary expenditures. It immediately follows that the Nash equilibrium strategy for this group would be to take no precautions at all.

In response the targeted parties would undertake a higher degree of precaution than would have been the case if the nontargeted parties were taking precautions as well. As a result of the anticipated failure of the nontargeted parties to take precautions the marginal expected damage function facing each targeted PRP would shift upward. Facing higher expected damages, the targeted firms could minimize costs by taking more precautions when joint and several liability is authorized than when it is not; this additional precaution is a partial offset for the reduced precautions taken by nontargeted PRPs. Because this substitution of in-

creased targeted PRP precaution for reduced precaution by nontargeted PRPs will typically reduce the likelihood of a contamination incident at a higher cost than would be possible if the same reductions were achieved by a cost-effective allocation of responsibility among the two types of PRPs, the Nash equilibrium expected damages would be higher with joint and several liability than without. This follows directly from the higher likelihood of an incident.

A second factor reinforces the tendency of targeted PRPs to take more precautions with joint and several liability than they would have with pure strict liability: the targeted firms face a higher expected share of the damages when joint and several liability is authorized than when it is not. This follows directly from the fact that the set of targeted PRPs would be assessed 100 percent of the damage under joint and several liability even though they may have contributed significantly less than 100 percent of the damage. Under pure strict liability the responsibility for "orphan" shares, those not paid for one reason or another, are not shifted to the remaining PRPs. Thus, in addition to the higher marginal expected damages resulting from nontargeted PRP failure to take precaution, the targeted PRPs are also faced with paying a larger share of the resulting damages. Both of these effects induce cost-minimizing targeted PRPs to take more precautions in this Nash equilibrium than they would have if joint and several liability were not authorized.

What is the effect of adding the right of contribution to the joint and several liability doctrine? With the right of contribution targeted firms can seek partial reimbursement for the damages they were assessed. This should not have any direct effect on

---

[25] If the government was assured it could recover the entire amount of damages from a single party, according to our model it would sue only that party. As a practical matter the government may need to sue more than one if for no other reason than the court's reluctance, on fairness grounds, to pin all the financial responsibility on a single defendant.

the government's Nash equilibrium strategy. Neither its ability to secure damages from the targeted PRPs nor its litigation costs would be affected.[26]

PRP behavior would be affected, however. Consider first the nontargeted PRPs. With the right of contribution authorized they would face the possibility of paying some expected damages. If we express the ex ante probability that a reimbursement suit against the jth nontargeted PRP would be successful as t_j, and the share of the damages it would bear in the event of a successful suit as r_j, then the objective function of the jth nontargeted PRP can be expressed as

$$w_j(x_j) + t_j r_j p(x|\bar{x})A. \qquad [6]$$

The first order conditions for its Nash equilibrium would be

$$\frac{\partial w_j(x_j)}{\partial x_j} + t_j r_j \frac{\partial p(x|\bar{x})}{\partial x_j} A = 0$$
$$j = 1, \ldots, J. \quad [7]$$

Several implications follow immediately. With the right of contribution authorized nontargeted firms would have an incentive to take some precaution; expected damages would no longer be zero. In general, however, the precautions they would take would normally be less than would be the case with pure strict liability. This result follows from the presumption that normally r_j, the share it would be required to pay if it lost a contribution suit, would be less than or equal to q_j, the share it would be required to pay under pure, strict liability. This presumption seems reasonable because the court would be unlikely to sanction assessing the nontargeted firm with a larger share of the damages than justified by its overall share of the responsibility. Unless the PRP believes that a reimbursement suit would always be successful (i.e., $t_j = 1.0$), $t_j r_j$ will be less than q_j, implying that the nontargeted PRP would take less precaution than it would under pure strict liability but more than it would if joint and several liability were authorized without the right of contribution.

Targeted PRP behavior would also be affected by authorizing the right of contribution. If we denote its pre-contribution suit share of the damages as $\hat{q}_j$, its objective function would become

$$w_j(x_j) + t_j(\hat{q}_j - r_j)p(x|\bar{x})A$$
$$+ (1 - t_j)(\hat{q}_j)p(x|\bar{x})A, \quad [8]$$

where t_j is the probability of winning a contribution suit and r_j is the share of damages borne by the other party in the event of a successful suit. The first order conditions for the Nash equilibrium would be

$$\frac{\partial w_j(x_j)}{\partial x_j} + t_j(\hat{q}_j - r_j) \frac{\partial p(x|\bar{x})}{\partial x_j} A$$
$$+ (1 - t_j)(\hat{q}_j) \frac{\partial p(x|\bar{x})}{\partial x_j} A = 0. \quad [9]$$

If r_j is less than or equal to $\hat{q}_j$ and t_j is less than or equal to 1.0 then it immediately follows that the targeted firm would take no more (and would normally take less) precaution than it would if the right of contribution were not authorized. If we further accept the plausible assumption that after a successful contribution suit the targeted PRP would end up with the share of damages it would have borne with pure strict liability (i.e., $q_j = \hat{q}_j - r_j$), then it follows that the targeted PRP would take more precautions than it would had the prevailing doctrine been pure strict liability. Not only would it have to compensate for the lack of precaution by the nontargeted PRPs and to bear a share of the resulting damages that was at least as large as that borne under pure strict liability, but the probability of winning its reimbursement suit would typically be less than 1.0.

---

[26]There may be some indirect effects. For example, the courts may be more willing to impose the full damages on a small set of PRPs if those PRPs have the right of contribution. If valid, this point would imply that the government litigation team could sue even fewer PRPs when the right of contribution is authorized, because it would be easier to overcome the court's fairness concerns.

It is now possible to summarize the strict liability analysis by comparing the Nash equilibria. Relative to pure strict liability, incorporating the joint and several liability doctrine without the right of contribution would increase expected damages from toxic incidents, but it would also increase the amount of precautions taken by the reduced set of those PRPs targeted for litigation. The increased likelihood of an incident results from the government litigation team's incentive to sue fewer parties under joint and several liability. This altered behavior by the government translates into altered behavior by the PRPs.

The loss of incentive to take precautions by those who can expect to escape government litigation under joint and several liability but would face litigation under pure strict liability is one source of the increased likelihood of a toxic site incident; another is the less than perfect substitutability of precaution possibilities among the two types of PRPs. Although those targeted for litigation when joint and several liability is authorized but the right of contribution is not have an incentive to take increased precautions, these extra precautions are necessarily less cost effective than those that would have been taken by the nontargeted parties, so their impact on the probability of an incident is smaller. In the Nash equilibrium, therefore, expected damages increase.

Authorizing the right of contribution as a complement to the joint and several liability doctrine tends to increase the precautions of nontargeted firms while decreasing the precautions taken by targeted firms. If we ignore the extra litigation costs borne by the targeted firms as they seek contribution, unless all contribution suits were expected to be successful joint and several liability accompanied by a right of contribution would normally lead to higher expected damages than would be the case with pure strict liability. However, the expected damages would not be as high as they would if joint and several liability were authorized but the right of contribution were not. In this sense, the right of contribution represents an adjustment toward efficiency.

Joint and several liability in a strict liability framework is a much more reliable revenue raiser than pure strict liability. Parties that cannot be sued because they are judgement proof leave uncollectable shares of the financial responsibility. Only joint and several liability in a strict liability framework offers a realistic prospect of 100 percent recovery of the costs of toxic site restoration and damages; any party contributing to an indivisible damage against whom causation is proved could be assessed the entire cost.

III. POLICY IMPLICATIONS

The framers of the 1986 amendments to the Superfund bill were faced with the need to finance the clean up of a large number of existing toxic waste sites. While public funds were needed to initiate the cleanup effort it was necessary and desirable to involve private funds in the effort, both to increase the possible scale of the cleanup effort and to motivate those engaged in the business of using, transporting, storing, and disposing of toxic wastes to exercise efficient precaution. The route they chose was to allow the government not only to hold potentially responsible parties strictly liable for toxic waste incidents but also to seek recovery of site cleanup costs under the joint and several liability doctrine.

The analysis in this paper relies on an admittedly stylized model, yet it does offer some insight into the effects of these doctrines. Using the liability system to raise revenue has the distinct advantage that it retains a direct link between the causal responsibility for the incident and the financial responsibility for restoring it to a safe condition. Contrast this, for example, with the rather general tax used to create the Hazardous Substance Response Trust Fund, the "seed capital" pool of money used by the government to initiate restoration. With a general tax on production the level of precautionary behavior undertaken by a taxpaying firm has absolutely no effect on the tax bill. Revenue is collected, but this method of collection fails to provide any incentives for reducing the expected costs of toxic incidents. Coupling strict liability with the joint and several liability doctrine has strengthened the government's ability to fund restoration efforts with privately raised revenues.

These advantages, however, have been achieved at some cost. The precautionary incentives created are not sufficient to support an efficient outcome. Because the joint and several liability doctrine creates an incentive for the government to economize on litigation outlays, fewer plaintiffs are brought before the court than might have reasonably borne some responsibility for the incident.[27] When it is possible for the nontargeted PRPs to recognize in advance that they are not likely to be the targets of government litigation their incentive to take precautions is lost. While targeted parties have an incentive to compensate for these lost precaution opportunities by undertaking more precaution themselves, this compensating precaution is insufficient to reduce damages to the efficient level and is excessively expensive for targeted PRPs. The total PRP precautionary expenditures with this compensating precaution would normally exceed those that could have produced the same likelihood of an incident had the nontargeted parties taken the efficient level of precautions available to them.

The analysis also identifies how EPA litigation strategy could have a major effect on the size of these inefficiencies. The deficient precautionary incentives caused by the government's temptation to pursue fewer plaintiffs are exacerbated when "wealth targeting" rather than "precaution targeting" is used by EPA to choose which PRPs will be brought before the court. Wealth targeting implies choosing those defendants that can most easily afford to cover the costs whether or not they have the capability to reduce significantly the likelihood of this type of incident. Wealth targeting is attractive to the government because a few wealthy PRPs could, with joint and several liability, be tapped for the entire cost. Yet, to the extent the parties whose precautionary expenditures could have made a large difference in the likelihood of an incident are not targeted for litigation, damages would be higher, perhaps substantially higher, than necessary. In essence, the strategy which minimizes litigation costs is not necessarily the strategy that minimizes society's expected costs from toxic incidents. Some observers believe wealth targeting is the dominant current strategy.[28]

The 1986 Superfund amendments included a right of contribution provision which may diminish, but probably not eliminate, this inefficiency. By authorizing the right of contribution for settling PRPs,[29] Congress has allowed any party that has paid or agreed to pay to seek contributions from noncontributing but culpable PRPs. Although pursuing the right of contribution clearly involves extra legal costs (as compared to a situation in which the party from whom they are seeking contribution was directly targeted by the EPA),[30] the possibility that nontargeted PRPs could ultimately be sued by targeted PRPs should restore some of the incentive of nontargeted PRPs to take precautions.

The practice of imposing a disproportionate share of the liability on a few parties could conceivably distort the competitiveness of targeted waste generators with a consequent loss of efficiency. The cost functions of targeted firms would necessarily shift up more than efficiency would dictate, potentially placing them at a competitive disadvantage. Whether this is a signifi-

---

[27] In United States v. Conservation Chemical Co. (1984), for example, the government chose to sue five parties: Conservation Chemical Co., the owner of the disposal site, and four corporations (Armco, FMC, IBM and Western Electric) which had disposed of chemicals at the site. A motion by two of the defendants to dismiss the suit because the government failed to join 46 other contributing generators was denied. 14 ELR 20207 at 20209.

[28] See Dubuc and Evans (1987, 10199).

[29] Section 122(a) of the Superfund Amendments and Reauthorization Act of 1986.

[30] In essence the EPA is shifting the legal costs it would otherwise incur for recovering from the other parties to the targeted parties. Because there are fixed costs associated with trials, it seems likely that this approach has the effect of raising the total transactions costs associated with defining the ultimate allocation of financial responsibility.

cant aspect of the problem must await empirical analysis.

One other source of inefficiency results from the lack of incentive for EPA to select cost effective clean-up technologies. The selection of these technologies is typically controlled by EPA. With the joint and several liability doctrine EPA has a significantly easier time recovering site restoration costs than would be possible without the doctrine. It seems plausible, therefore, that it also has less incentive to assure that the chosen technologies are cost effective. The PRPs, who would have a large financial stake in choosing cost effective technologies, are forced to foot the bill without having much, if any, say in the means by which the site is cleaned up. The implication is that more dollars than necessary are probably being spent to achieve the attained level of site restoration or, equivalently, much more site restoration could have taken place with the same level of expenditures.[31]

A final source of inefficiency plagues any ex post judicial remedy. Judgement-proof parties would have no incentive to take precautions under any of the legal approaches discussed in this paper. "Judgement-proof" is an attribute inherent in the nature of the party; it does not emanate from any litigation strategy. If a firm is bankrupt, cannot be identified, or has gone out of business, it can escape financial responsibility and EPA can do little about it. This is one of the reasons why judicial remedies frequently represent an incomplete approach to environmental incidents and must therefore be complemented by ex ante regulatory strategies.

APPENDIX
A SIMPLE NUMERICAL EXAMPLE

The purpose of this appendix is to illustrate some of the principles discussed in the body of the paper. Consider applying a numerical version of the model in the strict liability context. Assume that there are two PRPs and that the following parameters and functional forms apply:

$$w_x(x) = 4x$$

$$w_y(y) = 2y$$

$$p(x, y) = \frac{1}{(x + 1)(y + 1)}$$

$$A = \$1000.$$

The efficiency conditions are

$$\frac{\partial w_x(x)}{\partial x} + \frac{\partial p(x, y)}{\partial x} A = 0$$

$$\frac{\partial w_y(y)}{\partial y} + \frac{\partial p(x, y)}{\partial y} A = 0.$$

Substituting the above values into these equations we obtain

$$4 - \frac{(y + 1)}{[(x + 1)(y + 1)]^2} (1000) = 0$$

$$2 - \frac{(x + 1)}{[(x + 1)(y + 1)]^2} (1000) = 0.$$

It can easily be verified that $x = 4$ and $y = 9$ satisfies these conditions. These values also imply

$$p(x, y) = \frac{1}{(x + 1)(y + 1)} = .02.$$

The implied expected damages are therefore $20. The first party would spend $16 on precautions while the second would spend $18.

If each party knows in advance that it will bear half of the actual cost of damages then the Nash equilibrium conditions would be

$$4 - \frac{(y + 1)}{[(x + 1)(y + 1)]^2} (500) = 0$$

$$2 - \frac{(x + 1)}{[(x + 1)(y + 1)]^2} (500) = 0.$$

The solution (accurate to the second decimal place) is $x = 2.97$ and $y = 6.94$. The resulting likelihood of an expected accident would be .032, and the expected damages would be $32. The Nash equilibrium would not be efficient.

Suppose now that the second party knows

---

[31] There is some evidence that this problem is already beginning to surface. See Naj (1988).

that, due to the government's litigation strategy, it would never be sued. Substituting $A = 0$ into its Nash equilibrium equation immediately implies $y = 0$. (In this corner solution the stated Nash equilibrium condition holds as an inequality, so the value of y must be equal to zero.) To find the resulting Nash equilibrium for the first firm substitute $y = 0$ into its equation and solve:

$$4 - \frac{(0 + 1)}{[(x + 1)(0 + 1)]^2} (1000) = 0$$

or $x = 15.8$.

Notice that this implies that it is now in the first PRP's interest to take extra precautions, but that, despite this, expected damages rise from $20 to $59.50.

$$p(x, 0) = \frac{1}{(16.8)(1 + 0)} = .0595.$$

If the first party had not increased precaution his or her expected damages would have been higher,

$$p(x^*, 0) = \frac{1}{5} = .20$$

Expected Damages = $200,

as would total costs. They would equal $(4)(4) + \$200 = \$216$ without compensating precaution and $(15.8)(4) + 59.50 = \$122.70$ with compensating precaution.

References

Bohm, Peter, and Clifford S. Russell. 1985. "Comparative Analysis of Alternative Policy Instruments." In *Handbook of Natural Resource and Energy Economics: Volume 1.* eds. Allen V. Kneese and James L. Sweeney. Amsterdam: North-Holland.

Bromley, Daniel W. 1978. "Property Rules, Liability Rules and Environmental Economics." *Journal of Economic Issues* 12 (March):43–60.

Brown, John P. 1973. "Toward an Economic Theory of Liability." *Journal of Legal Studies* 2 (June):323–49.

Cicchetti, Charles J., and Robert H. Haveman. 1988. "Environmental Litigation and Economic Efficiency: Two Case Studies." In *Environmental Resources and Applied Welfare Economics: Essays in Honor of John V. Krutilla,* ed. V. Kerry Smith. Washington, D.C.: Resources for the Future, Inc.

Cootner, Robert, and Thomas Ulen. 1988. *Law and Economics.* Glenview, IL: Scott, Foresman and Company.

Dechert, W. Davis, and James L. Smith. 1988. "Environmental Liability and Economic Incentives for Hazardous Waste Management." *Houston Law Review* 25:935–42.

Dubuc, Carroll E., and William D. Evans, Jr. 1987. "Recent Developments under CERCLA: Toward a More Equitable Distribution of Liability." *Environmental Law Reporter* 17 (June):10197–204.

Green, Jerry. 1976. "On the Optimal Structure of Liability Laws." *The Bell Journal of Economics* 7 (Autumn):553–74.

Grigalunas, Thomas A., and James J. Opaluch. 1988. "Assessing Liability for Damages under CERCLA: A New Approach for Providing Incentives for Pollution Avoidance." *Natural Resource Journal* 28 (Summer):509–33.

Johnson, Gary V., and Thomas S. Ulen. 1986. "Designing Public Policy toward Hazardous Wastes: The Role of Administrative Regulations and Legal Liability Rules." *American Journal of Agricultural Economics* 68 (Dec.):1266–71.

Landes, William M., and Richard A. Posner. 1980. "Joint and Multiple Tortfeasors: An Economic Analysis." *Journal of Legal Studies* 9 (June):517–55.

Mays, Richard H. 1987. "Settlements with SARA: A Comprehensive Review of Settlement Procedures under the Superfund Amendments and Reauthorization Act." *Environmental Law Reporter: News and Analysis* (April):10101–13.

Naj, Amal Kumar. 1988. "How to Clean Up Superfund's Act." *The Wall Street Journal,* 15 Sept.

Opaluch, James J. 1984. "The Use of Liability Rules in Controlling Hazardous Waste Accidents: Theory and Practice." *Northeastern Journal of Agricultural Economics and Resource Economics* 13 (Oct.):210–17.

Opaluch, James J., and Thomas A. Grigalunas. 1984. "Controlling Stochastic Pollution Events with Liability Rules: Some Evidence from OCS Leasing." *Rand Journal of Economics* 15 (Spring):142–51.

Presler, Larry, and Kevin V. Schieffer. 1988. "Joint and Several Liability: A Case for Reform." *University of Denver Law Review* 64:651–84.

Russell, Clifford S., Winston Harrington, and William J. Vaughan. 1986. *Enforcing Pollution Control Laws*. Washington, D.C.: Resources for the Future, Inc.

Segerson, Kathleen. 1986. "Risk Sharing in the Design of Environmental Policy." *American Journal of Agricultural Economics* 68 (Dec.):1261–65.

Segerson, Kathleen, and Thomas J. Micelli. 1988. "Joint Liability in Torts: Long-Run and Short-Run Efficiency Effects." University of Connecticut Working Paper.

Sullivan, Arthur M. 1986. "Liability Rules for Toxics Cleanup." *Journal of Urban Economics* 20 (Sept.):191–204.

U.S. General Accounting Office. 1988. *Superfund: Assessment of EPA's Enforcement Program* (October) GAO/RCED-89-40BR.

White, Michelle, and Donald Wittman. 1979. "Long-run Versus Short-run Remedies for Spatial Externalities: Liability Rules, Pollution Taxes and Zoning." In *Essays on the Law and Economics of Local Government*, ed. Daniel Rubinfeld. Washington, D.C.: Urban Institute.

[17]

Liability for Groundwater Contamination from Pesticides

KATHLEEN SEGERSON[1]

Box U-63 Department of Economics, University of Connecticut, Storrs, Connecticut 06269-1063

Received September 11, 1989; revised December 21, 1989

This paper considers the extent to which farmers should be held liable for groundwater contamination from agricultural pesticides. The problem is first viewed as a standard tort and then as a case of product liability, where the question of shifting liability to the manufacturer of the pesticide is considered. The results suggest that, when the problem is viewed as a case of product liability, farmer exemptions from liability can still lead to efficient levels of pesticide use, provided appropriate application methods keyed to site characteristics can be ensured through regulation or other means. © 1990 Academic Press, Inc.

I. INTRODUCTION

Although agricultural pesticides have been used for many years, it is only recently that widespread attention has focused on their potential environmental effects. This is due in a large part to recent publicity surrounding the discovery of pesticides in some wells that provide drinking water to households. In addition to actual discoveries of groundwater contaminated by pesticides, Nielsen and Lee [12] have concluded that the potential for pesticide contamination of aquifers is large in certain regions of the country.[2]

Given both the actual and the potential contamination problems that exist, an important issue is who should be liable for the costs of cleaning up the contaminated resource or providing alternative sources of drinking water. In particular, to what extent should farmers be held liable for these costs?

The question of liability for groundwater contamination from pesticide use is of interest at both the federal and the state level. For example, in a recent study [21] the U.S. Environmental Protection Agency stated that

> When contamination of ground water appears to be a result of registered use, and that use was based on sound data and reasonable efforts to predict the potential for contamination, it is not clear who should be considered the responsible party. In this situation, several parties have some involvement, including the user who applied the pesticide, the registrant who brought the pesticide to market, and EPA and state agencies who registered the product.

However, the Comprehensive Environmental Response, Compensation and Liabil-

---

[1] The author acknowledges the research assistance of Donald Vandegrift, the useful comments of Tom Miceli and three anonymous reviewers, and the financial support of the Institute of Water Resources at the University of Connecticut under a grant from the U.S. Department of Interior, U.S. Geological Survey.
[2] Groundwater contamination is only one of several environmental hazards posed by the use of agricultural chemicals. Other potential damages can result from direct exposure of farm workers, drifting during aerial spraying, runoff to surface water, and residues on food products. Concern about some of these hazards has existed for some time. See Hall *et al.* [7] for an overview.

ity Act (CERCLA), Section 107(i), currently restricts farmer liability for contamination from application of a registered pesticide product. Other federal restrictions have been considered.

At the state level, Connecticut recently enacted similar limits on farmer liability.[3] Concerns over groundwater contamination from pesticides heightened when ethylene dibromide (EDB) was discovered in wells in the northcentral part of the state. Although legislation was in place to govern the State's response to groundwater contamination, the legislation had not originally been designed with agricultural sources of contamination in mind. In particular, the liability for providing potable water that was statutorily imposed on "responsible parties" had never been applied to farmers before. Questions arose about the appropriateness of holding farmers liable for damages resulting from the use of pesticides when that use had been in accordance with accepted and approved application procedures. A settlement was finally reached that divided the costs of providing potable water between the farmers and the manufacturers of the pesticide, with the manufacturers paying a much larger share. In addition, farmers were given some relief from liability for future pesticide contamination problems, provided that they comply with certain requirements specified in the statutory exemption that they were granted.

The purpose of this paper is twofold: (1) to examine from an economic perspective the general question of the extent to which farmers should be held liable for damages due to groundwater contamination from pesticide use and (2) to evaluate exemptions from liability for groundwater contamination from pesticides. The paper is organized as follows. The next section considers the general question of farmer liability for groundwater contamination from pesticides when viewed as an example of a tort. In this case, the only potentially responsible party is the farmer since it is the farmer's action (use of the pesticide) that causes the damages. Section III views liability for groundwater contamination from pesticide use as an example of product liability and asks to what extent, if any, liability for contamination should be shifted from the farmer to the manufacturer of the pesticide. The final section uses the general results from Sections II and III to evaluate farmer exemptions from liability.

II. CONTAMINATION AS A GENERAL TORT

"Tort" is the legal term for an action by one party that harms another party, or in economic terms, a negative externality. Pollution that is generated by one party and harms the well-being or the property of a neighboring party is thus an example of a tort. For example, if runoff from a farmer's manure storage pile seeps into a neighbor's basement, the neighbor can seek legal relief (damages and/or an injunction) under the law of torts. The farmer is likely to be held accountable for harms caused by his "actions," where here his action is the storage of manure

The application of pesticides is similar to the storage of manure in that it is a normal part of the farm's production process that has the potential to cause harm to neighboring parties. In this sense, groundwater contamination from pesticide

---

[3]For a discussion of other state-level groundwater exemption legislation, see Centner [5]. The Connecticut case appears to be unique in that the exemption was precipitated by the ethylene dibromide case, where some farmers were actually held liable for the costs of providing bottled water. In other states, the threat of liability rather than its imposition led to passage of the exemptions.

use should simply be viewed as another example of a tort, where the actions of the farmer harm households that rely on the groundwater for drinking water.[4] If groundwater contamination from pesticide use is viewed in this way, the standard economic models of tort law can be applied to determine the efficient assignment of liability.

Consider first the case of a unilateral tort, where the expected damages depend only on the actions of the injurer and not on the actions of the victim.[5] In the pesticide case, this means that only the farmer is able to prevent or reduce groundwater contamination. The affected household is unable to take any preventive actions. In general, preventive actions by the injurer (farmer) can take either or both of two forms: (1) the exercise of care or precautionary behavior (for example, taking extra care in the timing and the method of pesticide application) and (2) changes in the level of the injury-causing activity (reductions in the amount of pesticide applied).

Brown [3] has shown that for unilateral torts where expected damages are affected only by the level of care (and not by the injurer's activity level) in the short run economic efficiency can be attained by either (1) making the injurer strictly liable (i.e., liable regardless of the amount of care exercised) for all damages, or (2) imposing a negligence rule under which the injurer would be liable for damages that occurred only if he had not met the standard of "due care." The negligence rule is efficient provided that the standard of due care set by the court is the efficient level of care.[6]

In the case of pesticide application, due care might be considered to be application in compliance with all approved standards and instructions. This suggests that, if farmers have no flexibility in the amount of pesticide applied and can only reduce the possibility of contamination through changes in application procedures, then either strict liability or a negligence rule would lead to short-run efficiency.[7]

This symmetry between strict liability and negligence does not hold when the injurer can also alter his activity level in a way that can affect expected damages. In many cases, farmers will be able to alter the level of pesticide use. In this case, Shavell's [17] results imply that the negligence rule will not lead to an efficient outcome even in the short run if the due standard of care to which the injurer is held is defined only in terms of care and not in terms of the injurer's activity level. For example, if farmers are considered to be non-negligent for purposes of liability as long as they have complied with approved application procedures, then the negligence rule would induce an efficient amount of care, but it would not provide any incentive for a reduction in pesticide use. Strict liability, on the other hand,

[4] This is the approach taken by Centner [4].

[5] This means that neither the probability of damages occurring nor the magnitude of those damages should they occur depends on any actions that could be taken by the victim.

[6] These efficiency results presume that if a firm is found to be liable, it will pay the full amount of damages. If the firm's assets are less than the potential damages or if it can reduce or escape payment through reorganization, then the incentive effects of liability are diluted and the result is no longer efficient. In addition, efficiency does not result if the probability that a responsible party will be successfully sued is less than one because of information or transaction costs. See Hall *et al.* [7] for a general discussion of these issues and Shavell [19] for a model of liability that incorporates them. We abstract from these problems throughout the analysis presented here.

[7] Polinsky [14] has shown that strict liability is preferred to a negligence rule in the long run when the number of injuring firms is allowed to vary.

would provide an incentive for both increased care and decreased use, since either of these would reduce expected damages and thereby reduce expected liability. Thus, if farmers are able to adjust their levels of pesticide use, to hold them strictly liable for any resulting groundwater contamination would lead to a more efficient outcome than if they were allowed to be relieved of liability if they had complied with approved application procedures.

The above arguments for injurer liability assume that the actions of the injured party or "victim" do not affect expected damages. In the case of groundwater contamination, there is little that affected households can do to prevent the contamination of an aquifer. However, if the tort is viewed not as contamination of the aquifer but rather as damages from consuming contaminated drinking water, then households can take some action to prevent these damages. For example, they can install filtration units to remove contaminants before drinking the water or seek alternative sources of drinking water (e.g., bottled water). In fact, Raucher [15] has suggested that in some cases this may be a more cost-effective approach to groundwater contamination than either cleanup or prevention.

Shavell [17] has shown that, in general, strict liability does not lead to an efficient outcome when the actions of both the injurer and the victim can affect expected damages, because it does not provide the proper incentives to the victim. However, this result implicitly assumes that the preventive actions that could be undertaken by the victim are distinct from those that could be undertaken by the injurer. In the case of groundwater contamination, filtration units or bottled water could also be provided by the farmer rather than by the household.[8] If these approaches are the least-cost options, then under a strict liability rule they would be chosen by an economically rational farmer. In other words, given the choice among (i) taking preventive actions to reduce contamination (and thus reduce liability), (ii) compensating victims by cleaning up the resource once contamination has occurred, and (iii) compensating victims for contamination by providing filters or bottled water, the farmer would choose the least costly alternative. If (iii) is the most efficient (least cost) alternative, it is the one that would be chosen by the farmer under a strict liability rule. Thus, in this case, strict liability would still lead to efficiency even if contamination is viewed as a bilateral tort.[9, 10]

In summary, when groundwater contamination from agricultural pesticides is viewed as a general tort, imposing strict liability on farmers for contamination will be efficient. The negligence approach, however, will not be efficient if efficiency

---

[8] Farmer "provision" of bottled water or filtration devices does not necessarily require that farmers physically supply these goods, but simply that the costs of these goods be borne by the farmer.

[9] This result assumes that the farmer knows ex ante the efficient amount of bottled water or filtration that would have to be provided to households with contaminated wells. Such information may be available from previous cases of third party provision. In addition, it assumes that the administrative costs associated with farmer provision are not significantly higher than those associated with self-provision. The magnitude of these administrative costs will depend upon the specific arrangements made for provision or payment.

[10] This result will hold in the short run where the number of farmers and victims is fixed. In the long run, strict liability will provide the correct incentives for farmers but not for victims. If victims are guaranteed compensation for damages, there will be excessive entry by victims since they will have no incentive to avoid potential contamination areas when making location decisions. I am indebted to an anonymous reviewer for emphasizing this point. One way to reduce entry incentives is to deny victims recovery if they are deemed to have "come to the nuisance." This approach has been used in "Right to Farm" legislation. See also footnote 21.

requires a change in pesticide use and the due standard of care is defined solely in terms of application procedures, since it will not provide an incentive for reduced use. Thus, strict liability is preferred on efficiency grounds.

III. CONTAMINATION AS A CASE OF PRODUCT LIABILITY

The tort approach discussed above treated groundwater contamination from pesticide use as though it were no different from contamination from manure storage or any other action of the farmer. Under this approach, there is no apparent reason to shift liability from the farmer, since it is clearly the farmer's action (use of the pesticide) that generates the negative externality. Unlike manure, however, pesticides are purchased products. They have been produced and sold to the farmer by a separate firm, the manufacturer. This raises the possibility of viewing contamination from pesticides as a case of product liability and shifting some or all of the farmer's liability to the manufacturer, thus holding the manufacturer liable for some or all of the damages caused by its product. In this section we view pesticide contamination as a case of product liability and consider the extent (if any) to which the manufacturer should be held liable for damages.

III.1. The Nature of Product Liability

Historically, product liability cases were governed by the doctrine of "privity," which held that the only person who could recover damages from the manufacturer of a (defective) product was the immediate purchaser [6]. Product liability was based on implied warranty concepts and only the immediate purchaser was viewed as having received an implied warranty from the seller. Recently, however, liability for damages from defective products has been extended to ultimate users or consumers of the product and to "bystanders" injured by the product.

Several reasons have been given for the extension of liability to cover damages to non-users or bystanders. (See, for example, [13] and [21].) First, when liability was extended to injuries to ultimate users or consumers, the implied warranty or contractual principles upon which product liability had been based were eroded. They were replaced by principles of strict liability under the general law of torts. Given this shift, there was no logical reason to exclude bystanders from protection by product liability laws. In fact, the argument for protection of bystanders is viewed by some as being even stronger than that in favor of users since bystanders do not have an opportunity to inspect the product for defects and to purchase only from reputable manufacturers [13]. In addition, bystanders cannot be viewed as voluntarily "assuming the risk" associated with use of the product [6]. Finally, the manufacturer is generally in a better position to exercise care to reduce the possibility or the magnitude of damages than the bystander and can generally spread the risk resulting from liability more easily.

Most cases of product liability involve products that are "defective," either in terms of construction or design. Some, however, have involved products that are unavoidably or inherently dangerous. The manufacturer cannot make the product safer without also reducing its beneficial properties and the dangers are present in every batch of the product produced. Examples include industrial chemicals and vaccines. Pesticides can also be viewed as inherently dangerous products since their beneficial properties cannot be divorced from those that can cause harm if found in groundwater.

Groundwater contamination from pesticides is thus an example of an inherently dangerous product injuring a bystander. Unfortunately, the existing literature on product liability does not seem to address such cases. The discussion of inherently dangerous products is primarily in the context of injuries to users of the product (e.g., cigarettes or vaccines). The discussion of cases of bystander injuries focus on defective products (e.g., exploding shotgun shells or defective brakes), where it is clearly the production of the good rather than its use that was at fault. In both of these discussions, any liability that is assigned naturally falls on the manufacturer of the product. There is no question of allocating liability between two potentially responsible parties, the manufacturer and the user of the product, or holding both of them responsible for compensation to a third party, the injured bystander. Thus, the literature provides no direct analogue to the groundwater contamination problem of interest here. Some of the principles that have been used in the economic analysis of product liability (e.g., [10]) can, however, be adapted to this problem to provide some insight into the efficiency aspects of alternative allocations of liability between farmers and manufacturers.

III.2. Controlling the Level of Use

Consider first the case where (i) both farmers and manufacturers are risk neutral, (ii) all farmers are identical, and (iii) expected damages due to contamination depend only on the quantity of pesticides used. (The implications of relaxing these assumptions are considered below.) In this case it can be shown that a strict liability rule that holds the farmer and the manufacturer jointly and severally liable for damages would be efficient.

This result can be demonstrated using a simple partial equilibrium model.[11] Net private benefits from the production of pesticides are given by

$$P_x x - C(x),$$

where P_x is the per unit price of the pesticide, x is the quantity produced/consumed, and $C(x)$ is the private cost of production. Net private benefits from the production of agricultural goods using pesticides and other inputs (L) are

$$P_a F(x, L) - P_x x - wL,$$

where P_a is the price of the agricultural good, $F(x, L)$ is the production function for agricultural output, and w is the price of the other input.[12] It is assumed that the use of pesticides generates expected damages $D(x)$ that depend on pesticide

---

[11] I am indebted to Tom Miceli for pointing out this simple framework for demonstrating the result. A proof using a general equilibrium model and the concept of pareto efficiency (analogous to the approach used in Baumol and Oates [2], Chap. 4) is available from the author upon request.

[12] Both agricultural producers and pesticide manufacturers are assumed to be price-taking profit-maximizers. Although a given pesticide may be produced and sold by only a small number of firms, the existence of close substitute products should limit the exploitation of market power. If the pesticide industry were modeled as a monopoly or oligopoly, then the efficiency analysis presented in this paper would have to be modified to reflect second best considerations. Of course, other market imperfections, such as the other environmental hazards posed by the use of agricultural chemicals (see footnote 2), would raise second best questions as well.

LIABILITY FOR CONTAMINATION 233

use.[13] Net social benefits from the joint production and use of pesticides in the agricultural sector are thus[14]

$$B = P_a F(x, L) - C(x) - wL - D(x). \tag{1}$$

The socially efficient level of x is the level that maximizes B, or equivalently the level that solves the first-order condition

$$B_x = P_a F_x - C'(x) - D'(x) = 0, \tag{2}$$

where subscripts on functions denote partial derivatives.[15] Under a strict liability rule with joint and several liability, the manufacturer expects to pay some fraction s_1 ($0 \leq s_1 \leq 1$) of any damages that occur. He thus chooses his levels of production to maximize expected profit, $P_x x - C(x) - s_1 D(x)$. The profit-maximizing level satisfies the first-order condition

$$P_x - C'(x) - s_1 D'(x) = 0. \tag{3}$$

Likewise, the farmer expects to pay a fraction s_2 ($0 \leq s_2 \leq 1$) of the damages that occur.[16] He chooses his use of pesticides to maximize expected profits from agricultural production, $P_a F(x, L) - P_x x - wL - s_2 D(x)$. His choice of x thus satisfies the first-order condition

$$P_a F_x - P_x - s_2 D'(x) = 0. \tag{4}$$

By substituting (3) and (4), it is clear that the equilibrium level of x will satisfy

$$P_a F_x - C'(x) - (s_1 + s_2) D'(x) = 0. \tag{5}$$

Comparing (5) to (2) shows that the equilibrium level of x will also be efficient as long as $s_1 + s_2 = 1$, i.e., as long as the manufacturer and the farmer expect their total contributions to just equal actual damages, as would be expected under joint and several liability. Thus, a rule of strict liability with joint and several liability would lead to an efficient level of pesticide use regardless of the expected allocation of damages between the manufacturer and the farmer.

Although the above model was used to show that a rule of joint and several liability is efficient, it should also be clear that efficiency can be attained either by holding the farmer entirely responsible for the expected damages with no shifting to the manufacturer ($s_1 = 0$ and $s_2 = 1$) or by treating the problem exclusively as a

[13]Note that D would reflect the expected cost of providing bottled water or filtration units if these were the least cost responses.

[14]This formulation of social benefits ignores any enforcement or administrative costs that would be associated with policies to reduce damages. For example, it ignores the litigation costs that accompany the use of liability rules. For a discussion of the effect of litigation costs on efficiency, see Shavell [18].

[15]We assume throughout that all solutions are interior and that all second-order conditions are satisfied.

[16]It is assumed here and throughout the paper that there is a single farmer responsible for damages and that the responsible farmer can be identified. Thus, we ignore the difficulties of uncertainty regarding the source of contamination and the allocation of damages when there are multiple farmers who contaminate a single well. For a discussion of these issues in a more general context, see Shavell [20], Kornhauser and Revesz [9], and Miceli and Segerson [11].

case of product liability and holding the manufacturer responsible for all damages that result from the use of his product ($s_1 = 1$ and $s_2 = 0$).

The intuition behind this result is the same as that underlying the well-known result from public finance that an excise tax placed on a producer is equivalent to an equal tax placed on the consumer. Because the expected liability can be shifted forward or backward through changes in the equilibrium price of pesticides, the equilibrium output level is the same regardless of which party is nominally liable for damages. This suggests that the allocation of expected damages between the farmer and the manufacturer does not have any efficiency effects.

The above result depends crucially on the assumptions made initially, namely, risk neutrality for all parties, identical farmers, and expected damages that depend only on the level of use. In most discussions of product liability, risk aversion/loss spreading and incentives to take care (as opposed to just decrease use) are important issues. We consider next the importance of these issues for the case of groundwater contamination from pesticides.

III.3. Care by the Farmer

Suppose that farmers could change the expected damages from pesticide use by changing their application procedures. Using procedures that lead to lower expected damages might then be viewed as "taking care." Application procedures could be (and are) regulated, and compliance with these regulations could ensure proper care, provided that the type of care needed to reduce the possibility of contamination is not too site-specific. If regulation can be used to ensure proper care, then the above result, given only concern with the level of use, would still hold.

However, if a regulatory approach is not sufficient to ensure proper care (because either the regulations cannot be adequately enforced or the proper care is too site-specific), then the design of the liability rule must consider incentives to take efficient care. In this case holding farmers fully liable, i.e., no shifting of liability to manufacturers, under a strict liability rule would provide the proper incentives for farmers both to decrease use and to take care, as noted in the discussion of contamination as a tort. On the other hand, dividing liability between the farmer and the manufacturer or holding the manufacturer fully liable would provide the proper incentive to reduce use, but it would not provide the correct incentive to the farmer to take care.[17] However, allowing partial or full shifting of liability to the manufacturer only when the farmer exercises due care, i.e., applying a negligence rule to the farmer, would still lead to an efficient outcome.[18]

These results can be illustrated by extending the simple model outlined in the previous subsection to include care. Let y be the care level of the farmer and let $V(y)$ be the cost of care. Expected damages from pesticide use are then given by $D(x, y)$ rather than simply by $D(x)$. In addition, y could enter the farm's produc-

---

[17]This assumes that the manufacturer is not able to observe the care level of any individual farmer and tailor the price of pesticides to that level of care.

[18]The efficient use of a negligence rule requires, however, that the court be able to determine the level of care exercised by the farmer and to compare it to a due standard of care. If the associated information costs are prohibitively high (as might be expected when the proper care is very site-specific), then the negligence rule applied to the farmer will not ensure efficient care. In this case, use of a comparative negligence rule could improve efficiency [16]. See Section III.6 for related discussion.

tion function, which would become $F(x, L, y)$. If increased care involves the use of application procedures that keep pesticides in place and reduce leaching, then increased care could increase efficacy and thus output. Note that this formulation allows substitutability between the quantity of pesticides applied and the application procedures used in the production of output. The same level of output can be produced with fewer pesticides if they are applied more carefully.

Given the possibility of taking care, under a strict liability rule the farmer now chooses the levels of pesticide use and care to maximize

$$P_a F(x, L, y) - P_x x - wL - s_2 D(x, y) - V(y).$$

The first-order conditions for these choices are

$$P_a F_x - P_x - s_2 D_x = 0 \tag{6}$$

and

$$P_a F_y - s_2 D_y - V'(y) = 0. \tag{7}$$

The first-order condition for the optimal production of x by the manufacturer continues to be Eq. (3), with $D'(x)$ replaced by D_x. Social net benefits from the production and use of pesticides are now given by

$$B = P_a F(x, L, y) - C(x) - wL - D(x, y) - V(y).$$

The first-order conditions for the socially efficient levels of pesticide use and care are thus

$$P_a F_x - C'(x) - D_x = 0 \tag{8}$$

and

$$P_a F_y - D_y - V'(y) = 0. \tag{9}$$

When one compares (8) and (9) to (6) and (7) (making use of (3)), it is clear that under strict liability the outcome will be efficient if and only if $s_1 = 0$ and $s_2 = 1$, i.e., if and only if the farmer is held strictly liable for all damages.

Alternatively, the efficient outcome could be attained with the rule

$$
\begin{array}{ll}
s_1 = 0 \text{ and } s_2 = 1 & \text{if } y < y^* \\
s_2 = 1 - s_1 \text{ for any } 0 \le s_1 \le 1 & \text{if } y \ge y^*,
\end{array} \tag{10}
$$

where y^* is the efficient level of care.[19] This rule essentially applies a form of a negligence rule to the farmer, under which the farmer is fully liable if found negligent but otherwise pays only a share (or none) of the damages. If $s_2 = 0$ (i.e., $s_1 = 1$) when $y \ge y^*$, then the farmer is subject to a standard negligence rule, where compliance with the due standard of care absolves him of all liability.

---

[19]That is, y^* is the solution to (9) given that x and L are also at their socially efficient levels. See the Appendix for more detail.

Under the above negligence rule, the farmer's choice problem becomes

$$\text{Maximize} \left\{ \max_{x, L, y < y^*} \pi(x, L, y) - D(x, y), \max_{x, L, y \geq y^*} \pi(x, L, y) - s_2 D(x, y) \right\},$$

$$\underset{x, L, y}{}$$

$$(11)$$

where $\pi(x, L, y) = P_a F(x, L, y) - P_x x - wL - V(y)$. A proof that this rule leads the farmer to choose y^* is given in the Appendix.

Note that in the case of pesticide use, a negligence rule for the farmer results in efficiency despite the fact that the standard of care is defined only in terms of the amount of care. This result is in direct contrast to the effect of a negligence rule for a standard tort. As discussed in Section II, the negligence rule for torts does not result in efficiency when damages are affected by the activity level because it does not induce an efficient activity level. In the case of interest here, however, this inefficiency is eliminated if the liability is shifted to the manufacturer, since the manufacturer in turn shifts it back to the farmer through an increase in the price of pesticides. The shifting ensures that the price of pesticides reflects both marginal production costs and marginal external damages from pesticide use, regardless of whether the farmer or the manufacturer is legally liable for damages (see Section III.2).

Finally, it can easily be shown that, in the long run, the negligence rule is equivalent to a strict liability rule. Again the explanation lies in shifting. In long-run equilibrium, revenue from the sale of pesticides must equal total costs, including both production costs and expected liability payments by pesticide manufacturers. Thus, $P_x x = C(x) + s_1 D(x, y)$ if $y \geq y^*$, and $P_x x = C(x)$ if $y < y^*$. Given this, the farmer's problem reduces to

$$\underset{x, L, y}{\text{Maximize}} \ P_a F(x, L, y) - C(x) - wL - V(y) - D(x, y), \qquad (12)$$

which is equivalent to the choice problem under strict liability for the farmer. In other words, the farmer ultimately pays the full amount of damages, either directly if he is negligent or indirectly (through the increased pesticide price) if he is not.[20]

III.4. Care by the Manufacturer

Since pesticides are inherently dangerous (rather than defective) products, the manufacturer is not able to produce them in such a way that the potential dangers from their use are reduced without simultaneously destroying their beneficial properties. In this sense, the manufacturer is not able to exercise greater care in the construction or the design of the product. He may, however, be able to conduct research on the risks associated with use of the pesticide and use the results of that research to develop warnings or application procedures to reduce those risks. Conducting the proper amount of research and development could then be viewed as exercising "care".

---

[20]Shavell [17] reaches a similar conclusion regarding the use of negligence to govern accidents between sellers and customers when customers correctly perceive risks. In his model, the zero profit constraint stems from the linearity assumptions that are imposed.

Theoretically, the proper amount of R & D related to pesticide risks can be ensured through regulations, such as those governing the registration of a pesticide for sale. In this case, the liability rule would not have to be used as a way to ensure sufficient care by the manufacturer, and the results derived above for the case where care by the manufacturer was not a determinant of expected damages would continue to hold. In practice, however, ensuring proper R & D through regulation is difficult because of information costs. Thus, the indirect effect of the liability rule on the incentives for the manufacturer to engage in risk-reducing R & D should be considered when choosing among alternative rules.

The possibility of care by the manufacturer can be incorporated into the above model by simply expressing expected damages as $D(x, y, z)$, where z is the amount of care or R & D undertaken by the manufacturer. In this case, it can easily be shown that, if the farmer's care level must be controlled through liability (rather than regulation), then a liability rule that shifts the full amount of damages to the manufacturer if the farmer exercises efficient care (i.e. $y \geq y^*$) will result in efficient care by both the farmer and the manufacturer and an efficient level of pesticide use. The negligence rule applied to the farmer will induce the farmer to undertake efficient care. Given this, the manufacturer will be held liable for all damages and thus will be induced to exercise efficient care and efficient production. Note that in this case an allocation of damages between the farmer and the manufacturer would not yield efficiency, because the manufacturer would not face the incentives necessary to ensure an efficient amount of care or R & D. The same logic can be used to show that efficiency would also result from a rule that holds the farmer strictly liable for all damages if the manufacturer exercises the efficient amount of care.

In summary, if regulations regarding pesticide application procedures and registration can be used to ensure efficient care by both the farmer and the manufacturer, then the results derived under the assumption that only the level of use affected expected damages in the previous section continue to hold; i.e., the allocation of liability between the farmer and the manufacturer has no efficiency effects. In particular, holding either the farmer or the manufacturer strictly liable for all damages or holding them jointly and severally liable will lead to efficiency. Alternatively, if sufficient care for both must be ensured indirectly through the choice of a liability rule, then a rule that holds the manufacturer strictly liable for the full amount of damages if the farmer is not negligent (in the sense of exercising efficient care) will be efficient. However, the opposite rule, which holds the farmer strictly liable for all damages if the manufacturer is not negligent, would also be efficient.

III.5. The Role of Risk Aversion

As noted above, one argument that has been used in favor of product liability is that manufacturers are better able to bear the risks of injury or damage. Since the manufacturer is in most cases a large firm that produces many products and sells to many buyers, it might be able to spread risks either through the purchase of insurance or through self-insurance. If its risks can be sufficiently spread, then the manufacturer can be treated as risk neutral. The farmer, on the other hand, is likely to be risk averse since his operation will generally be much smaller and offer few possibilities for risk spreading.

If the manufacturer is risk neutral and the farmer is risk averse, then the well-known results regarding risk sharing (e.g., [8]) suggest that the allocation of liability between the two will have efficiency effects. In particular, if expected damages are affected only by the level of pesticide use, efficiency is achieved by making the manufacturer strictly liable for the full amount of damages. The manufacturer would thus bear all of the risks of contamination. The farmer would bear no risks since he would not be directly liable for any damages. The correct ex ante incentives would be maintained, however, since pesticide prices would reflect marginal expected damages.

If liability insurance is not available to the manufacturer or he is not otherwise able to spread risks, then it is possible that both the farmer and the manufacturer should be viewed as risk averse. In this case, the risk associated with liability would impose a cost on either party. However, if society as a whole is risk neutral (see Arrow and Lind [1] for arguments in support of this assumption), then a first best outcome is still possible. Liability works as an incentive for decreased use through ex ante increases in the price of pesticides that reflect expected ex post liability. Similar incentive effects can be achieved, however, through a per unit tax on pesticides. If the level of the tax is set so that marginal tax payments equal marginal expected damages, then ex ante the tax will have the same marginal effect on behavior as liability. In particular, imposing the tax on either the purchaser (farmer) or the seller (manufacturer) will lead to an efficient level of use. Payment of the tax would be in lieu of liability for either the farmer or the manufacturer. If the fund is set up so that any deviation of actual compensation payments (damages) from fund contributions by pesticide user/producers comes from or goes into general tax revenues, then the uncertainty associated with damages from contamination are borne by society as a whole rather than by the fund's contributors. If society is risk neutral, this results in a first best outcome in terms of both incentives for decreased use and allocation of risk.

A tax based solely on pesticide use can be used to ensure an efficient reduction in the level of use, but it cannot ensure sufficient care in the use of pesticides by the farmer or in risk-reducing R & D by the manufacturer. If sufficient care cannot be ensured through regulation, then a pure tax approach will not be efficient. However, if tax payments absolve the farmer and the manufacturer of liability only if they engage in efficient care, then the outcome will still be efficient. If each expects to be fully liable if he does not exercise due care, each will face the proper incentives regarding care. Thus, the negligence provision of the policy will ensure efficient care while the tax will ensure an efficient level of use.[21]

III.6. The Role of Heterogeneity

Thus far, farmers have been assumed to be identical, in terms of both production costs and, more importantly, expected groundwater contamination from pesticide use. This may be an appropriate assumption for specialized pesticides used on crops that require certain soil characteristics with relatively uniform leaching properties (such as sandy soils). In most cases, however, the potential for

---

[21]As noted by Shavell [17], use of a negligence rule plus a tax can also lead to a first best outcome when victim incentives are important. If the tax revenue is not used for victim compensation, then victims will bear the full cost of damages and thus be induced to behave efficiently in both the short run and the long run.

contamination from use of a particular pesticide will vary widely across farms, depending upon site-specific characteristics. We consider briefly the implications of this for the results discussed above.

Even with heterogeneity across users, the above results regarding the efficiency of different rules would continue to hold if a manufacturer could charge each farmer a different price for its product to reflect its different expected liability payment from that farmer's use of the product. In this case, the increased price paid by the farmer would reflect his site-specific pollution potential. In practice, however, such individualized prices cannot be set. Instead, the manufacturer must charge a single price, on the basis of the average expected liability across farms. This price will be too high for farmers with low contamination potential and too low for those with high contamination potential. Thus, any liability borne by the manufacturer will not be shifted to farmers efficiently.

Without individualized prices, efficiency may be possible under a negligence rule if the due standard of care is defined in terms of both care and site-specific use. For example, even if he exercised sufficient care, the farmer could be deemed negligent if he used a certain pesticide in an area where contamination was likely (e.g., using aldicarb on sandy soils). Alternatively, efficiency could be achieved if regulations regarding use of the product could be tailored to site characteristics (such as banning use in certain areas). In this case, heterogeneity would be dealt with through regulation.

If regulation is insufficient or negligence cannot be adequately defined in terms of use, then efficient farmer choices require that farmers face full liability directly. Although this implies that a negligence rule for the farmer would not be efficient,[22] efficiency could still be attained with a standard negligence rule applied to the manufacturer. If the manufacturer is absolved of all liability if he complies with the due standard of care in testing and marketing his product, he will be induced to undertake the efficient amount of care. Given this, the farmer will be held liable for all damages, and thereby be induced to act efficiently as well.

IV. EVALUATION OF FARMER EXEMPTIONS

Table I provides a summary of efficient liability rules under the various cases considered above. These results can be used to evaluate the efficiency implications of exempting farmers from liability for groundwater contamination from agricultural pesticides. In particular, the results imply that farmer exemptions can still lead to efficiency, provided that the following conditions are met:

(i) the exemption is conditional on efficient care by the farmer, i.e., on non-negligent farmer behavior;

(ii) the exemption is restricted to contamination from the use of purchased products;

(iii) the liability is then borne by the manufacturer of the product; and

(iv) manufacturers are risk neutral.

Under these conditions, efficiency is still possible even though farmers bear no direct liability, since they will indirectly pay for expected damages through in-

---

[22]Rubinfeld [16] considers the case of heterogeneous injurers and shows that use of a comparative negligence rule reduces the efficiency loss from the level that would exist under the standard negligence rule.

creased product prices. Thus, the correct incentives regarding pesticide use will be maintained. In addition, the allocation of risk will be efficient, since a risk neutral party (manufacturers) will bear all of the risk.

Of these four conditions, (i) is likely to be the most difficult to implement in practice. In general, site-specific farm characteristics lead to differing contamination potentials from pesticide use. This suggests that efficient care will vary across farmers. If a farmer exemption is to be used, this heterogeneity must be dealt with in some other way. As noted above, one possibility is the regulation of pesticide use on the basis of site-specific characteristics. If these regulations could be adequately enforced, they would lead to efficient levels of farmer care. Alternatively, in the absence of regulation, the due standard of care could be defined in terms of both care and use. For example, use of the pesticide under certain conditions or in certain areas could be considered negligent behavior de facto. However, if such approaches cannot adequately address farmer heterogeneity, then farmer exemptions will lead to inefficient use of pesticides.

APPENDIX

This appendix proves the efficiency of the negligence rule in (10).

Let (x^*, L^*, y^*) denote the socially efficient outcome, i.e., the simultaneous solution of (8), (9), and $P_a F_L - w = 0$.

If the farmer bears a share s_2 ($0 \le s_2 \le 1$) of the damages, then given a level of y, he will choose x and L to maximize $\pi(x, L, y) - s_2 D(x, y)$. The corresponding first-order conditions are

$$P_a F_x - P_x - s_2 D_x = 0 \tag{A1}$$

$$P_a F_L - w = 0. \tag{A2}$$

If the manufacturer bears $s_1 = 1 - s_2$ of the damages, his first-order condition is given by (3). Substituting (3) into (A1) implies that in equilibrium

$$P_a F_x - C'(x) - D_x = 0. \tag{A3}$$

Denote the simultaneous solutions to (A2) and (A3) by $\tilde{x}(y)$ and $\tilde{L}(y)$. Note that $\tilde{x}(y^*) = x^*$ and $\tilde{L}(y^*) = L^*$.

Next define $\tilde{y}(s_2)$ to be the solution to

$$\max_y \pi(\tilde{x}(y), \tilde{L}(y), y) - s_2 D(\tilde{x}(y), y). \tag{A4}$$

After simplification (using (A2), (3), and (A3)), the first-order condition for (A4) becomes

$$\pi_y - s_2 D_y = 0. \tag{A5}$$

Clearly, $\tilde{y}(1) = y^*$. In addition, $d\tilde{y}/ds_2 > 0$. Thus, for all $0 \le s_2 < 1$,

$$\tilde{y}(s_2) < \tilde{y}(1) = y^*. \tag{A6}$$

TABLE I
Summary of Efficient Rules

Farmer heterogeneity	Risk preferences of farmers	Risk preferences of manufacturer	Relevant control variables[a]	Efficient rule(s)
			Viewed as tort	
NA	Neutral	NA	F-care	(1) Strict liability for farmer, or (2) Negligence rule for farmer
NA	Neutral	NA	Use, F-care	Strict liability for farmer
			Viewed as product liability	
No	Neutral	Neutral	Use	(1) Joint and several strict liability, or (2) Strict liability for farmer, or (3) Strict liability for manufacturer
No	Neutral	Neutral	Use, F-care	(1) Strict liability for farmer, or (2) Negligence rule for farmer
No	Neutral	Neutral	Use, F-care, M-care	(1) Negligence rule for farmer, or (2) Negligence rule for manufacturer
Yes	Neutral	Neutral	Use, F-care, M-care	Negligence rule for manufacturer
No	Averse	Neutral	Use, F-care, M-care	Negligence rule for farmer
No	Averse	Averse	Use, F-care, M-care	Negligence rule for both farmer and manufacturer plus pesticide tax, provided society can spread risks

[a]Variables that affect expected damages and can be varied by farmer or manufacturer. Use = level of production/ consumption of pesticides, F-care = care by farmer, M-care = care by manufacturer.

242 KATHLEEN SEGERSON

Given these definitions, the farmer's problem under the negligence rule given in (10) can be written as

$$\max_y \left\{ \max_{y<y^*} \pi(\bar{x}(y), \bar{L}(y), y) - D(\bar{x}(y), y), \right.$$

$$\left. \max_{y\geq y^*} \pi(\bar{x}(y), \bar{L}(y), y) - s_2 D(\bar{x}(y), y) \right\}. \tag{A7}$$

The solution to the second problem in brackets (for $y \geq y^*$) is clearly a corner solution (y^*) since by (A6) the unconstrained solution $\bar{y}(s_2)$ is less than y^* for all $0 \leq s_1 < 1$. Furthermore,

$$\pi(x^*, L^*, y^*) - s_2 D(x^*, y^*) > \pi(x^*, L^*, y^*) - D(x^*, y^*)$$

for all $0 \leq s_2 < 1$, and by definition of (x^*, L^*, y^*)

$$\pi(x^*, L^*, y^*) - D(x^*, y^*) \geq \pi(\bar{x}(y), \bar{L}(y), y) - D(\bar{x}(y), y)$$

for all y (and thus for all $y < y^*$). This implies that the maximum value of the objective function in the second problem of (A7) must exceed the maximum value of the objective function in the first problem. Thus, the farmer chooses y^*, $\bar{x}(y^*) = x^*$, and $\bar{L}(y^*) = L^*$. Q.E.D

REFERENCES

1. K. J. Arrow and R. C. Lind, Uncertainty and the evaluation of public investment decisions, *Amer. Econom. Rev.* **60**, 364–378 (1970).
2. W. J. Baumol and W. E. Oates, "The Theory of Environmental Policy," Cambridge Univ. Press, New York (1988).
3. J. Brown, Toward an economic theory of liability, *J. Legal Stud.* **2**, 323–350 (1973).
4. T. J. Centner, Liability rules for groundwater pesticide contamination, *in* "Proc. Conference on Pesticides in Aquatic and Terrestrial Environments," Virginia Water Resources Research Center, Virginia Polytechnic Institute and State University, Blacksburg, Virginia, in press.
5. T. J. Centner, Blameless contamination: New state legislation regulating liability for agricultural chemicals in groundwater, unpublished manuscript, Department of Agricultural Economics, University of Georgia (1989).
6. R. Epstein, "Modern Products Liability Law," Quorum Books, Westport, CT (1980).
7. D. C. Hall, B. P. Baker, J. Franco, and D. A. Jolly, Organic food and sustainable agriculture, *Contemp. Policy Issues* **7**, 47–72 (1989).
8. B. Holmstrom, Moral hazard and observability, *Bell J. Econom.* **10**, 74–91 (1979).
9. L. A. Kornhauser and R. Revesz, Sharing damages among multiple tortfeasors, *Yale Law J.* **98**, 831–884 (1989).
10. W. M. Landes and R. A. Posner, A positive economic analysis of products liability, *J. Legal Stud.* **14**, 535–583 (1985).
11. T. J. Miceli and K. Segerson, Joint liability in torts: Marginal vs. non-marginal incentive effects, *Internat. Rev. Law Econ.*, in press.
12. E. Nielsen and L. Lee, "The Magnitude and Costs of Groundwater Contamination from Agricultural Chemicals: A National Perspective," AER 576, US Department of Agriculture, Economic Research Service, Washington, DC (1987).
13. D. W. Noel, Defective products: Extension of strict liability to bystanders, *Tenn. Law Rev.* **38**, 1–13 (1970).
14. A. M. Polinsky, Strict liability vs. negligence in a market setting, *Amer. Econom. Rev.* **70**, 363–367 (1980).

15. R. L. Raucher, The benefits and costs of policies related to groundwater contamination, *Land Econom.* **62**, 33–45 (1986).
16. D. L. Rubinfeld, The efficiency of comparative negligence, *J. Legal Stud.* **16**, 375–394 (1987).
17. S. Shavell, Strict liability versus negligence, *J. Legal Stud.* **9**, 1–25 (1980).
18. S. Shavell, The social versus private incentive to bring suit in a costly legal system, *J. Legal Stud.* **11**, 333–339 (1982).
19. S. Shavell, A model of the optimal use of liability and safety regulation, *Rand J. Econom.* **15**, 271–280 (1984).
20. S. Shavell, Uncertainty over causation and the determination of civil liability, *J. Law Econom.* **28**, 587–609 (1985).
21. "University of Chicago Law Review," Vol. 38, "Strict Products Liability to the Bystander: A Study in Common Law Determinism," pp. 625–646 (1971).
22. US Environmental Protection Agency, "Agricultural Chemicals in Ground Water: Proposed Pesticide Strategy," Office of Pesticides and Toxic Substances, Washington, DC (1987).

[18]

The Structure of Penalties in Environmental Enforcement: An Economic Analysis

KATHLEEN SEGERSON

Department of Economics, Box U-63, Room 330, The University of Connecticut, Storrs, Connecticut 06269

AND

TOM TIETENBERG*

Department of Economics, Miller Library 234, Colby College, Waterville, Maine 04901

Received August 1, 1991; revised November 4, 1991

I. INTRODUCTION

The enforcement of environmental laws has undergone some rather dramatic changes over the last decade. Civil and criminal monetary penalties have been imposed more frequently on violators and the size of the penalties has increased.[1] Individuals, both corporate employees and officers, have become more common targets for penalties.[2] Finally, incarceration has not only become a more commonly imposed sanction,[3] but the resulting jail sentences are longer.[4]

Despite this trend toward increased use of individual sanctions in the form of fines or incarceration, the efficiency implications of this trend have received little attention. The related work that has been published falls into two categories. The first considers the relative impacts or merits of holding firms liable for the actions of their employees, a principle known as "vicarious liability" [31, 32, 11, 29, 15]. Arguments in favor of vicarious liability presume that the firm can sanction employee malfeasance internally through compensation schemes that are tied to

*Tom Tietenberg's participation in this research project was funded by sabbatical research grants from Colby College and Resources for the Future, Inc., and a senior research fellowship from Woods Hole Oceanographic Institution. This financial support is gratefully acknowledged. The authors also thank Tom Miceli, Mark Cohen, and three anonymous reviewers for their contributions to the paper.

[1] From its creation through fiscal year 1989 the United States Environmental Protection Agency has imposed $185.9 million in civil penalties. In FY 1989, $34.9 million in civil penalties were assessed, $21.3 million in civil judicial penalties (the second highest in agency history) and $13.6 million in administrative penalties (an all-time record). See [17].

[2] For an examination of how courts have begun to expand individual liability for corporate environmental violations, see [5].

[3] The number of criminal cases referred to the Department of Justice by EPA rose from 0 in fiscal year 1981 to 60 in fiscal year 1989 [17].

[4] For a discussion of this and related issues see [30].

179

workers' actions. However, in many cases involving environmental risks, internal sanctioning may not be possible. In addition, whenever those risks result from a combination of decisions made by both employees and executive officers or other managers of the firm, the appropriate allocation of liability among the responsible parties may be difficult to determine.

The second strand of related literature addresses the question of whether individual sanctions, if imposed, should take the form of fines or incarceration. Following the seminal article by Becker [1], this literature concludes that, if possible, fines should be used rather than incarceration, since the social costs associated with incarceration are so much higher. These increased costs include both the actual costs of incarceration (such as the costs of prisons and the opportunity cost of the individual's time) and increased transactions costs associated with the use of incarceration as a sanction.[5] However, when an individual's assets limit the incentive effects of a fine or fines are too low (due, for example, to binding statutory limits), then incarceration may be a second best alternative. If incarceration is to be used as an alternative to fines when fines provide insufficient incentives, what form should the incarceration rule take? Should all individual actions that result in environmental damages be subject to incarceration or should the incarceration option be reserved for certain types of actions?

In this paper we consider the design of efficient sanctions in the context of actions by employees and firms that lead to environmental risks. We address first the choice between imposing fines on the firm itself or imposing them directly on the employees whose decisions can affect those risks. Having derived conditions under which these two distinct approaches will yield the same outcome, we then consider the conditions under which one approach or the other may dominate or when some combination of the two should be used. We then turn to the question of whether incarceration is a possible instrument for inducing efficient behavior when fines provide inadequate incentives, and, if so, what form the incarceration rule should take.

In our examination of both fines and incarceration, we focus on the contractual relationship between an employer (the firm) and its employee (e.g., an environmental risk manager) and the role that this relationship plays in determining the design of efficient sanctions. In particular, we use a principal–agent model to examine the effect of corporate and individual sanctions on compliance incentives in the environmental context, including for individuals the effects of both monetary sanctions and incarceration. Our conclusions suggest that, while the traditional use of corporate penalties for enforcement is still justified in many cases, there are circumstances under which the use of individual fines or incarceration may improve efficiency.

---

[5]For example, incarceration is normally possible only with a criminal conviction, and criminal convictions require a more stringent standard of proof than do civil convictions [16]. In some cases, however, environmental enforcers have discovered ways of lowering this prosecutorial burden. For example, the Chicago office of the EPA has moved toward using consent decrees signed between a Federal judge and the polluter (typically local governments in this instance). The effect of such action is that after the consent decree is in force non-compliance is considered a violation of the consent decree which results in a contempt of court citation, substantially increasing the likelihood of incarceration without increasing the burden of proof. We are indebted to an anonymous referee for pointing this out to us.

II. THE DESIGN OF EFFICIENT FINES

The efficiency of alternative liability rules designed to induce individuals to take efficient precautions in preventing injuries to others is the subject of a large and growing body of literature.[6] In cases of "unilateral" care, where the injured party (victim) is unable to affect the probability or magnitude of damages, this literature suggests that the injurer will face efficient incentives when subject to a strict liability rule which holds him accountable for any damages resulting from his actions.[7] The same efficient incentives would be created by an equivalent fine that is paid to a third party (such as the government) rather than to the victim.[8] These results suggest that, in order to ensure efficient incentives, liability or a fine should be imposed on each party in an amount equal to the damages that result from its actions. If the actions of more than one party combine to determine damages, then each party should be liable for its incremental contribution to damages [33, 14].

Environmental risks are often the product of combined actions of multiple parties. For example, an environmental risk manager makes day-to-day decisions about the operations of plant and equipment, while higher level managers or corporate executives make overriding safety-related policy decisions, as well as decisions affecting the scale of operations. Both types of decisions can affect the probability and/or magnitude of environmental damages. Thus, environmental risks are often the result of multiple decisions by multiple parties.

The standard results (discussed above) that suggest that each party should be liable for his/her incremental contribution do not necessarily hold in this context. Unlike standard "accidents" where the parties involved are unrelated, here the firm and its employees (in particular the environmental risk manager) have a contractual relationship. The wage contract provides a potential mechanism through which one party can influence the incentives faced by the other party.

In essence the incentive problem associated with managing environmental risk can be characterized as a type of principal–agent problem.[9] Different remedies trigger different consequences for the firm (principal), and as a result of both the nature of the remedy and the response of upper-level managers, different conse-

---

[6]See [29] for an excellent overview.

[7]Efficiency can also result from the use of a negligence standard, under which the injurer is liable only if he failed to exercise "due care." See [29] for a discussion of this result and [18] for conditions under which it would not hold.

[8]Of course the goal of victim compensation is not ensured if fines are used instead of direct liability to the injured party. However, fines are often used in cases where the victim is not a single identifiable individual (such as an accident victim) but rather a group of (possibly unidentified) individuals (such as "society at large"). This is particularly likely in the context of environmental damages, where the specific individuals suffering from environmental damage (e.g., decreased air quality) are not easily identified. Fines can also dominate direct liability in cases of bilateral care where victim compensation can reduce a potential victim's incentives to avoid damages.

[9]The safety impacts of the agency relationship between firms and employees have been examined by others, including [11, 31, 32, 15]. Both [11] and [15] present formal (mathematical) principal–agent models. However, they both focus on the case where contingent contracts are possible, i.e., where the wage depends on whether or not an accident occurs. In addition, in [15] expected damages depend only on the actions of the worker. While [11] considers the case where the employer's actions can also affect damages, his use of a contingent contract implies that wages can be made to depend on the employer's choice of care. We consider situations in which this is not possible. Our analysis also differs in its focus on efficiency analysis.

182   SEGERSON AND TIETENBERG

quences for the environmental manger (agent). Under what conditions can each of
the remedies achieve efficiency? Does any one remedy dominate?

Characterizing an Efficient Outcome under a System of Fines

Imagine that an environmental manager (worker) is responsible for some particular risk (such as waste disposal). Assume for simplicity that the probability of an
accident is fixed, but if an accident occurs, the level of damages depends on the
amount of "care" exercised by the worker and the decisions (safety expenditures
and/or output level) of the firm.[10] All parties are assumed to be risk neutral[11] and
all costs (including the various psychic costs associated with incarceration) can be
converted into monetary equivalents.[12] Finally, we assume that enforcement
through fines (although not through incarceration) is costless.[13]

These assumptions and their implications can be formalized as follows:
Let a = the actions (level of care) taken by the employee,

x = the firm's production level,[14]

$B(x)$ = benefits (revenue) from production, $B'(x) > 0$,

$C(x)$ = the total cost of production,[15] $C'(x) > 0$,

W = direct payment from the firm to the worker (wage or salary),

$D(x, a)$ = environmental damage if an accident occurs,[16] $D_x > 0$, $D_a < 0$,

---

[10] In reality, both the probability of an accident and the level of damages could depend on care and
output. It would be conceptually easy, but expositionally cumbersome, to include both effects in the
model. Since our results do not depend on this distinction, we opt here for simplicity. Note that
simplicity could also have been attained by assuming that only the probability of an accident varies with
behavior, i.e., that damages are fixed.

[11] For related models that incorporate risk aversion, see [19] and [15]. In general penalty structures
will affect not only the incentives faced by two parties, but also the allocation of risk between them.
When one of the parties is risk averse, then efficient risk-sharing implies that all of the risk should be
placed on the risk-neutral party. While we do not consider risk-aversion (and thus risk-sharing) here,
some of its implications for our analysis are immediate. For example, even when the incentive effects of
corporate and individual fines are identical (see below), they would not necessarily be perfect
substitutes. In particular, if firms are risk-neutral and workers are risk-averse, corporate fines would be
preferred because they yield a more efficient allocation of risk. Likewise, when the incentive effects of
the two types of fines are not identical, a trade-off between efficient incentives and efficient risk-sharing might exist. Such a trade-off would affect the design of an efficient policy.

[12] This is a standard assumption in economic models of agency theory (e.g. [8, 24, 15]) and crime
(e.g. [20, 28]).

[13] In particular, in order to focus on the incentives of the firm and the worker, we ignore the cost of
detecting violations and imposing fines, thereby implicitly assuming that the probability of detection is
one. (The implications of relaxing this assumption are discussed below.) Thus, we abstract from issues
relating to the optimal tradeoff between the probability of detection and the magnitude of the fine that
arise in the context of costly enforcement. See Polinsky and Shavell [19] for a discussion of these issues.

[14] Alternatively, x could represent the firm's investment in safety (e.g., expenditures on safety
equipment, training, etc.). Our results would apply under this interpretation of x as well. (Note that in
this case, $B(x) = 0$, $C(x) = x$, $D_x \leq 0$ (see definitions below) and (1) reduces to a cost-minimization
problem.)

[15] For simplicity we assume that production costs do not depend on care, an assumption that is also
made by [15]. Our results would also apply, however, to the case where C depends on a, i.e.,
$C = C(x, a)$.

[16] We measure these damages net of any private internal damages that might result from an
accident. Thus, D should be interpreted as third party damages. In addition, while we use the term

p = probability of an accident,

$V(a)$ = the dollar equivalent to the employee of the disutility of exercising care,[17] $V'(a) > 0$, and

U^0 = the employee's opportunity cost of working for the firm.

(Subscripts on functions denote partial derivatives.) Note that we allow damages to depend on both a and x, since, for example, the size of the potential injury caused by an operation could depend on both the size of the operation (x) and how carefully it is conducted (a).

The socially efficient choice involves selecting those values of x and a (denoted x^* and a^*) that maximize[18]

$$B(x) - C(x) - V(a) - pD(x, a). \qquad (1)$$

The corresponding first order conditions are

$$B'(x^*) - C'(x^*) - pD_x(x^*, a^*) = 0 \qquad (2)$$

$$V'(a^*) + pD_a(x^*, a^*) = 0. \qquad (3)$$

These conditions imply that the production level should be increased until the marginal benefit equals the marginal cost (including any increase in expected damage due to the expanded production) and the level of precautionary actions should be increased until the marginal cost of additional precaution equals the marginal reduction in expected damage.[19]

Our interest is in determining whether a system of penalties can be designed to ensure that the private choice of x and a are socially efficient. We focus initially on the case where the penalties take the form of fines (rather than incarceration) and consider two types of fines: (i) a fine, F, that could be levied against the corporation in the event of an accident, and (ii) a fine, G, that could be levied against the environmental risk manager. Since in practice fines on firms and individuals can be used individually or in combination, we allow for both types of fines and let the model determine the efficient combination of the two. In addition we allow the magnitudes of the fines to vary with damages, i.e., $F = F(D)$ and $G = G(D)$, which assumes that damages can be measured *ex post* with certainty.

"accident," this should be broadly interpreted to include both sudden releases or exposure where the damages are immediately apparent and gradual or long term releases or exposure where damages are not apparent for some time.

[17]This assumes that the worker's utility function is separable in money and care, an assumption that is standard in agency models [e.g. 8, 24, 15].

[18]In the literature on the economics of crime, there has been a debate about whether the benefits of a criminal activity to the criminal himself should be included in the measure of social benefits. A useful survey of the issues is provided in Lewin and Trumbull [13]. They argue that the benefits of truly criminal activities (such as murder, rape and theft) should not be included while the benefits of activities that more closely resemble civil violations (such as regulatory offenses) should be included. In our case, since the purpose of the worker's actions is not to inflict harm and thus we would not generally view the worker's disutility from undertaking care as "reprehensible," it seems appropriate to include it in the measure of social benefits.

[19]If x is interpreted as the firm's investment in safety (see Footnote 14), then this latter condition applies to x as well.

Allowing the fines to vary with D does not, however, rule out *a priori* the possibility that the efficient fine will be unrelated to damages, i.e., that under the efficient set of fines $F'(D)$ and/or $G'(D)$ will be zero. Thus, whether the efficient fine is related to damages or not will be determined by the model.

Consistent with previous models of optimal fines e.g., [19, 20], our model does not explicitly distinguish between criminal and civil penalties *per se*. There are two ways that one might try to distinguish between the two types of penalties in a formal economic model.[20] First, one could easily distinguish between the probability of conviction under the two types of penalties, reflecting the higher standard of proof required for criminal fines. However, since this would complicate the model without adding additional insight, we have chosen to abstract from the enforcement/conviction aspect of the problem and assume that the probability of conviction is one. (The implications of relaxing this are noted below.) Secondly, one could try to distinguish between criminal and civil penalties by equating them with intentional and unintentional violations, where an intentional violation would correspond to "knowingly" inflicting damages and thus be subject to criminal fines. Landes and Posner [12, Chap. 6] develop an economic model of "intentional" torts, which they define as torts that yield benefits for the injurer only when damages are inflicted on the victim (the injurer deliberately inflicts a wrongful injury). This approach seems inappropriate in our context, since, even if the worker knew that his actions were endangering someone, the main purpose of those actions is not to inflict injury.[21]

Since damages depend on the actions of two parties, the worker (who chooses a) and the firm (or its production manager, who chooses x), our problem is similar to the case of "joint torts" considered in [33] and [14]. However, unlike the joint tort cases in which the actions of two independent parties combine to cause damages, the parties whose actions jointly affect D in our analysis are governed by contractual relationships. As noted by [25] and [22], the existence of a contractual relationship provides a mechanism by which one party can shift some of its liability or costs onto the other party to the contract. However, in order to shift costs efficiently, the relationship between the two parties must provide a mechanism for fully internalizing any costs that one party's actions can impose on the other party. The existence of such a mechanism depends on the ability to observe or monitor certain actions.

In our context, the firm and the employee have a contractual relationship through the employment contract, and the wage rate provides a possible mechanism for shifting costs forward (from worker to firm) or backwards (from firm to worker). For simplicity, we assume that the employee has a fixed opportunity cost

[20]To the extent that the distinction between the two rests primarily on moral bases (see, for example, [13]), then little can be done in a formal economic model to capture this distinction.

[21]Thus, his actions would fall instead under Landes and Posner's [12] category 1 (undertaking an activity with a high probability of causing an injury but not desiring or benefiting from the occurrence of the injury), which they argue is an inappropriate economic definition of "intentional" tort. If intentional is simply defined as knowing that an injury is possible (or even likely), then the actions in our model are all intentional since we assume that all parties make choices voluntarily with full information about all of the relevant functions and parameters. Under this definition, modeling unintentional behavior would require incorporating imperfect information about the relevant relationships, which would cause the perceived distribution of outcomes to differ from the actual distribution. We are unaware of any previous models of criminal activity that have explicitly distinguished between intentional and unintentional effects in this way.

of working for the firm (denoted U^0) and that the firm captures all of the potential rent.[22] Thus, the firm chooses the wage (or, equivalently, salary) of the employee, subject to the constraint that the employee's monetary return from this employment just equals his opportunity cost.[23] In the following sections we ask whether corporate or individual penalties can be designed to ensure that efficient levels of x and a are chosen.

A First-Best Solution with F and G Perfectly Substitutable: $W = W(a, x)$

Consider first the case where the actions of the employee are observable or can be monitored with perfect certainty, so that wages can vary with the choice of a. Assume, furthermore, that wages can be made contingent on the performance of the firm $(B(x) - C(x))$, and thereby contingent on x. Thus, the employment contract takes the form $W = W(a, x)$. Note that, while the level of the wage depends on the levels of a and x, it does not depend on whether an accident occurs. Thus, it is not a contingent contract in the sense considered by Newman and Wright [15]. Faced with a fine F for any accident, the firm chooses x and W to maximize its net benefits:

$$B(x) - C(x) - W(a, x) - pF(D(x, a)) \qquad (4)$$

subject to a being chosen by the employee to maximize

$$W(a, x) - V(a) - pG(D(x, a)), \qquad \text{and} \qquad (5)$$

$$W(a, x) - V(a) - pG(D(x, a)) = U^0. \qquad (6)$$

The constraint in (6) ensures that the worker's expected return from the job, given his choice of a and his wage contract, just equals his opportunity cost.[24]

Consider first the firm's choice of W. Clearly, for any level of x, the firm wants to minimize $W(a, x) + pF(D(x, a))$, i.e., it wants the worker to choose a level of a that minimizes the wages it pays plus its expected fine. Adding $pF(D(x, a))$ to both sides of (6) and rearranging terms yields[25]

$$W(a, x) + pF(D(x, a)) = U^0 + V(a) + pG(D(x, a)) + pF(D(x, a)). \quad (7)$$

Minimizing this expression yields the first-order condition for the level of a that minimizes the firm's costs, i.e., the level that the firm would like to see the

---

[22] This is a standard assumption in agency models (e.g. [8, 24, 15]). The implications of relaxing it are noted below.

[23] Since we are interested in incentives regarding environmental risks rather than labor supply decisions, we abstract from the employee's choice of the number of hours worked and instead assume that, if he works for the firm, he works for a fixed number of hours.

[24] Note that, if all of the rent from the wage contract is not captured by the firm, then (6) would be specified as an inequality rather than an equality constraint. Furthermore, this specification of the firm's choice problem presumes that there exists a combination of x, a and $W(a, x)$ satisfying (5) and (6) that yields net benefits in excess of $\text{Max}\{B(x) - C(x) - pF(D(x, 0))\}$, i.e., that it is "worth it" for the firm to hire the environmental risk manager provided a is chosen to satisfy (5).

[25] Note that such a substitution would not be possible if the worker were risk-averse, since (6) would depend on expected utility rather than expected wages, as in [15]. In the case of risk-neutrality, however, (6) implies that the firm is actually indifferent to the actual wage contract as long as it induces the level of a that minimizes overall costs for the firm.

employee choose:[26]

$$V'(a) + p\{G'(D)D_a(x,a) + F'(D)D_a(x,a)\} = 0. \tag{8}$$

Given $W(a, x)$, the employee will in fact choose a to maximize his return from employment, $W(a, x) - V(a) - pG(D(x, a))$. The corresponding first-order condition is

$$W_a(a, x) - V'(a) - p\{G'(D)D_a(x,a)\} = 0. \tag{9}$$

From (8) and (9), it is clear that, if the firm wants the employee to choose the level of a that minimizes (7), it can choose the wage function such that

$$W_a(a, x) = -pF'(D)D_a(x,a).$$

This implies that the wage function takes the form

$$W(a, x) = k(x) - pF(D(x, a)), \tag{10}$$

where $k(x)$ is independent of the worker's choice of a.[27] Faced with this wage function the worker's choice of a to maximize his return would simultaneously minimize the firm's costs for any given x. Furthermore, the equilibrium level of k can be determined from (6) and (10), which imply that

$$k(x) = U^0 + V(a_e) + p(G(D(x,a_e)) + F(D(x,a_e))), \tag{11}$$

where a_e is the equilibrium choice of a.

Consider next the firm's choice of x. Given (10) and (11), the firm's choice problem can be rewritten as:

$$\text{maximize } B(x) - C(x) - U^0 - V(a_e) - p(G(D(x,a_e)) + F(D(x,a_e)))$$
$$\tag{12}$$

subject to (5) and (6).[28] The corresponding first-order condition for x is

$$B'(x) - C'(x) - p[G'(D)D_x(x,a_e) + F'(D)D_x(x,a_e)] = 0. \tag{13}$$

Note that, in choosing x, the firm considers the impact of that choice on the wages that it must pay. In other words, higher levels of x *ceteris paribus* imply higher levels of damages, which in turn imply higher possible fines on both the firm and the employee. As compensation for his higher fines, the employee requires a

---

[26] Here and throughout the paper we assume that the solutions to first-order conditions are unique and that the corresponding sufficient second-order conditions are met. For a discussion of how to formulate a principal–agent problem without these assumptions, see [6].

[27] This wage function is not unique. For example, if utility were normalized so that $V(a) = a$ and $G = 0$, then the firm can induce any given level of a (say a') through a wage function of the form $W(a, x) = k(x) + pF(D(a, x))/F'(D)(D_a(a', x))$. It could thus induce its most preferred level by setting a' equal to that level. This is similar to the wage function used in [15].

[28] Note that, given (10) and (11), the firm's objective function is independent of the actual choice of a.

higher wage to induce him to work for the firm. Thus, through the wage contract, fines imposed on the worker can affect the net return of the firm.

Likewise, the wage contract provides a mechanism for shifting the firm's fines onto the worker. Given (10), the first-order condition for (5) becomes

$$V'(a) + p[G'(D)D_a(x,a) + F'(D)D_a(x,a)] = 0. \tag{14}$$

Thus, the worker considers the effect of his choice of a on the firm's expected fine. The higher the expected fine the firm has to pay, the lower the wage it will pay to its worker.

Having defined the conditions for the equilibrium choices of x and a, we can now determine whether corporate or individual fines can ensure that those choices are efficient. Comparing (13) and (14) to (2) and (3), it is clear that the private outcome will be socially efficient if

$$F = D(x,a) \quad \text{and} \quad G = 0 \quad \text{or} \tag{15}$$

$$F = 0 \quad \text{and} \quad G = D(x,a). \tag{16}$$

This result suggests that efficiency can be achieved with either (i) a monetary penalty placed on the corporation alone, without any penalty on the worker, or (ii) a penalty on the responsible individual, without any corresponding penalty on the firm.[29] In other words, with $W = W(a,x)$ given by (10) and (11), F and G (appropriately set) are perfect substitutes.

The efficiency of using F alone is consistent with the standard results of principal–agent models, e.g. [24, 8], where under risk neutrality efficient incentives result from a payoff scheme that transfers the full payoff of the principal to the agent, plus or minus a constant take for the principal (as in (10)).

The second case (a penalty on the worker only) has no analogy in the standard principal–agent models, since those models assume that the payoff/penalty is only realized directly by the principal. Here, the ability to penalize the worker directly through individual fines provides an extra mechanism for inducing efficient incentives. It is interesting to note that the use of individual penalties alone leads not only to the efficient level of a, but also to the efficient level of x. Forward shifting of the costs borne by the worker through demands for higher wages provides the link. Since increases in x lead to higher expected damages, which in turn imply higher penalties for the worker, the worker will demand (through (6)) a compensating increase in wages. Thus, the worker is able to shift his penalty onto the firm, thereby internalizing the effect of x on damages and inducing the firm to choose an efficient level of x.[30]

---

[29]Other combinations could lead to efficiency as well. In particular, any fine structure of the form $F(D) = sD + k_F$ and $G(D) = (1 - s)D + k_G$ would be efficient as well, where $0 \le s \le 1$ and k_F and k_G are constants. With $0 < s < 1$, a total fine equal to damages would be apportioned between the worker and the firm. With k_F and $k_G > 0$, each would in addition pay a fixed penalty every time an accident occurred. Note, however, that such "lump sum" penalties would have no effect on our results. The lump-sum component for the wage rate (as determined by (6)) would simply adjust to reflect $k_G > 0$. In addition, $k_F > 0$ would not affect the firm's marginal incentives regarding the choice of x. While it could affect a firm's entry/exit decision (i.e., the decision about whether to produce at all), such non-marginal incentives are not considered here. (See [14]). For these reasons, we assume here and throughout the paper that arbitrary lump-sum fines are not used (i.e., that $k_F = k_G = 0$).

[30]In standard principal–agent models, the principal cannot influence the outcome directly, and thus there is no need to ensure efficient incentives for the principal.

188   SEGERSON AND TIETENBERG

Finally, the above result is consistent with previous work showing that, when two parties have a contractual relationship, then the efficient outcome can be achieved by placing liability on either of the two, since through forward or backward shifting one party can always transfer costs to the other e.g. [25, 22]. Note, though, that it would not be efficient to fine *both* the worker and the firm for the full amount of the damages. Unlike the cases of joint torts considered in [33] and [14], here requiring both parties to be fully liable for damages (even at the margin) would lead to excessive levels of precaution.

While we have developed the substitutability between corporate and individual penalties under the assumption that the worker's actions are observable (so that wages can vary with a), it should be clear from (10) that the results would continue to hold if the firm instead based wages directly on the extent of the fines that were actually incurred by the firm. For example, the firm could base much of the worker's salary on end-of-year bonuses that were dependent on the firm's performance and its safety or environmental record. In this case, (10) becomes

$$W(x, F) = k(x) - pF. \tag{10}'$$

Clearly, either (15) or (16) yield efficiency in this case as well.[31]

While the case where wages can vary directly with both x and a may be very optimistic (in terms of the amount of flexibility available), considering it performs two functions. First it suggests that when the necessary conditions are present, either corporate or individual monetary penalties are sufficient to produce the appropriate incentives. This is a powerful conclusion which supports both the traditional economic model of corporate harm and a good deal of current practice.[32]

Perhaps more importantly, however, the model allows us to isolate the conditions that would ensure that corporate and individual penalties are perfect substitutes. In particular, perfect substitutability is ensured if: (1) in the absence of contingent contracts, the actions of the employee are observable so that wage structures can be used to penalize inefficient behavior and reward efficient behavior;[33] (2) wages can vary with the performance of the firm so that firms will be induced to make efficient decisions; (3) principals have the ability to manipulate wages sufficiently that the proper correspondence with actions can be established;[34] (4) the penalty or fine is set at the correct level; and (5) both the corporation and the worker have sufficient assets to be able to pay the penalties that are imposed on them.

Violating any one of these conditions can destroy the perfect substitutability of individual and corporate sanctions. We believe that a violation of each of these circumstances is present to some degree in various types of environmental problems. To trace out the implications we consider the effect of relaxing each of these conditions.

---

[31] In fact, this is similar to the contingent contract that would be implied by the standard principal–agent model under risk neutrality, where outputs are observable but inputs are not. In the standard model, however, since payoffs do not depend on x, k would not have to depend on the decisions of the firm.

[32] For firms receiving criminal fines between 1984 and September 1990 for environmental crimes, slightly less than one half involved penalties levied only against the organization. See [4].

[33] For evidence that compensation systems can be (and have been) devised to encourage managers to act in accordance with the long range interests of their employer, see [7].

[34] Corporations are clearly attempting to do this. See the discussion of DuPont's strategy in [9].

Imperfect shifting. The above model assumes that costs can be shifted perfectly between the worker and the firm through the wage contract. Perfect shifting requires that (i) wages can be based on inputs or outputs (a or F) and the firm's decisions (x), and (ii) the wage is determined by the opportunity cost of the worker's employment with the firm (Eq. (6)). However, in many situations posing environmental risk these conditions are unlikely to hold. For example, in many cases it will not be possible for upper-level managers (those who determine wages) to monitor continually the day-to-day operations of the firm; workers whose actions can affect environmental risks can engage in behavior that avoids detection. Likewise, it will very often not be possible to base wages on the environmental performance of the firm. For many environmental risks the consequences of employee actions may not become apparent until some time in the future (if ever), possibly after the worker has left the firm. Thus, even if a can be inferred *ex post* (from the observed values of D and x), it may not be possible to adjust the worker's wage accordingly. In addition, it may not always be possible to trace the cause of an accident (such as a spill) back to the actions of a specific employee.[35] Alternatively wages may be governed by contracts such as union or civil service contracts. For all of these reasons firms may not be able to vary wages either directly or indirectly with the actions of the employee or the size and frequency of the penalties it faces. Thus, backward shifting may not always be possible.

The possibilities for forward shifting may similarly be limited. As long as wages are set by contract, at least in the short run workers will not be able to secure increased compensation for firm-level decisions that expose them to higher penalties.[36] Likewise, workers may lack the individual bargaining power necessary to secure demands for compensating wage increases, due, for example, to limited mobility. In such cases, they will not be able to shift the incidence of the penalties forward to the firm. In this subsection, we consider the implications of imperfect shifting for the design of efficient fines.

Suppose first that wages cannot be based upon either the worker's input (a) or the outcome (F), i.e., W is independent of both a and F. It is thus determined solely by (6)

$$W(x) = k(x) = U^0 - V(a_e) - pG(D(x, a_e)),\qquad(17)$$

where a_e is the new equilibrium level of a that maximizes the worker's full return from employment. Given that the worker views W as constant, he chooses a to satisfy

$$V'(a) + p[G'(D)D_a(x, a)] = 0.\qquad(18)$$

Given the worker's choice of a, the firm in turn chooses the level of x (denoted x_e) to

$$\text{maximize } B(x) - C(x) - U^0 - V(a_e) - p[G(D(x, a_e)) + F(D(x, a_e))]\qquad(19)$$

---

[35] In some cases it may not even be possible to trace the cause to a particular firm. See [26] for a discussion of issues related to uncertainty over causation.

[36] In the long run, as contracts are renegotiated, the exposure of individuals to penalties may be a bargaining issue that affects subsequent wages.

or, equivalently the level of x that satisfies

$$B'(x) - C'(x) - p[G'(D)D_x(x, a_e) + F'(D)D_x(x, a_e)] = 0. \qquad (20)$$

Comparing (18) and (20) to (2) and (3), it is clear that the use of individual penalties alone in this case would lead to efficiency (i.e., $a_e = a^*$ and $x_e = x^*$), while penalties on the corporation alone would not. In other words, $F = 0$ and $G = D$ yields an efficient outcome, while $F = D$ and $G = 0$ does not. Imposing a penalty on the individual induces the worker to take an efficient amount of care. In addition, since the worker's wage varies with x, through forward shifting he can induce the firm to choose an optimal level of x. Thus, efficiency of both a and x are ensured with individual penalties. The same is not true, however, with corporate penalties. Since the wage is independent of the worker's actual actions, the firm has no means of shifting the cost of penalties back to the worker. While corporate penalties can be used to induce an efficient choice of x (given a), they will not induce the worker to choose a efficiently. Thus, when wages cannot be based on the actions of the worker or the resulting fines, then the use of individual penalties is preferred to the use of corporate penalties.

Efficiency of individual penalties in the case where a is not observable requires that the wage in (17) be allowed to vary with the firm's choice of x, i.e., that the worker be able to demand higher wages from firms with more output (or lower safety expenditures) and therefore higher expected environmental damages. It should be clear that if wages were allowed to vary with a but not with x, then the opposite results would be obtained. In other words, with a wage function $W(a)$ that depends on a but is independent of x, corporate penalties lead to efficiency while individual penalties do not. Here, basing wages on the worker's actions allows the firm to shift its expected penalties back to the worker so that the effects of the worker's actions will be internalized. However, if wages are independent of x, the worker has no means of shifting the marginal external effects of x back to the firm. Thus, the wage contract can be a substitute for direct penalties on the worker but not for direct penalties on the firm.

Consider finally the case where the wage is independent of both a and x, i.e.,

$$W = U^0 + V(a_e) + pG(D(x_e, a_e)), \qquad (21)$$

where a_e and x_e are the equilibrium choices of a and x under a fixed wage. Since the worker views W as fixed, its choice of a (a_e) satisfies

$$V'(a) + [pG'(D)D_a(x, a)] = 0. \qquad (22)$$

Likewise, the firm's choice of x (x_e) satisfies

$$B'(x) - C'(x) - pF'(D)D_x(x, a) = 0. \qquad (23)$$

Comparing (22) and (23) to (3), it is clear that with a fixed wage efficiency (i.e., $a_e = a^*$ and $x_e = x^*$) requires that *both* corporate and individual penalties be used simultaneously. Neither can achieve an efficient choice of both x and a by itself. With W independent of both x and a, neither forward nor backward shifting will internalize costs. Thus, the contractual relationship between the worker and the firm is unrelated to the externality and the problem reduces to the standard case of a joint tort where no contractual relationship exists. For such cases, efficiency requires that each party must bear its costs directly at the margin, e.g. [33, 14]. In our context, this implies that corporate and individual penalties should be used *simultaneously*.[37] Note that this result would continue to hold if wages were determined by bargaining rather than by (6) (so that workers and employers share the employment rent), as long as the bargained wage is independent of the actual choices of x and a.

Other limitations. To achieve efficiency with the use of individual or corporate penalties alone, our model suggests that the penalty (either F or G) should be set equal to the actual level of damages. This result assumed that enforcement is perfect, i.e., that the probability of detecting damages and imposing the associated fine is one. In practice, damages can go undetected and, even when damages are detected, fines may not always be imposed. In this case, the expected fine will equal pqF (or pqG), where q is the conditional probability that the fine will be imposed, conditional on damages having occurred.[38] Clearly, with $q < 1$, the efficient fine will equal D/q, which exceeds D. In addition, the lower the probability of enforcement, the higher the efficient fine will be.

Cohen [3] compared the level of monetary sanctions with the amount of harm caused and found that the sanctions were on average about equal to the harm for large harms and greater than the harm for small harms.[39] This implies that the monetary sanctions are too low to ensure efficient incentives unless the probability of a sanction being imposed for every violation is 1.0 or private settlements, reputational losses and other associated costs are sufficiently large to offset the difference.[40] Inefficiently low penalties can result either from penalty determination procedures (a reluctance of courts to impose penalties that exceed damages and could trigger bankruptcy) or from statutory limits.[41] In addition, problems in measuring the full amount of social damages and assigning the liability to responsible parties can lead to inefficiently low penalties as well.

A second limitation to the use of either individual or corporate fines is the problem of insufficient assets to pay the imposed fines. Though long recognized as a source of inefficiency in tort law remedies, e.g. [27, 28], insufficient assets can

---

[37] In [14] it is demonstrated that to achieve efficient non-marginal (entry/exit) incentives, each party's liability must be adjusted by a constant to ensure that each pays only his incremental contribution to damages. Here, such an adjustment could be achieved through a change in the fixed (constant) wage.

[38] Note that q could depend on the level of damages, with an increase in the level of damages leading to an increase in the probability of detection.

[39] In [3] total sanctions are defined as including all government imposed sanctions including federal fines, restitution, administrative penalties, state fines, voluntary restitution, and court-ordered payments to victims. This definition does not include nonmonetary sanctions, losses to reputation or private settlements.

[40] In general the total sanction should be a multiple of the harm where the multiple is equal to the inverse of the likelihood that a violation will result in a monetary sanction. See [19].

[41] See [23] for a more detailed discussion of this point.

192   SEGERSON AND TIETENBERG

undermine the efficiency of the use of financial penalties in enforcement as well. Furthermore, introducing individual penalties provides a new source of concern about the problem of insufficient assets since individuals typically have fewer assets than the organizations that employ them. Insufficient assets change the nature of taking environmental risks by curtailing the size of the penalty that would have to be paid.[42] When firms have insufficient assets to pay the fine, their downside risk is truncated.[43] Thus, even if the courts were routinely imposing an efficient level of monetary sanctions, the polluter with insufficient assets to pay the mandated fines would face insufficient incentives.[44]

III. THE CRIMINAL SANCTIONS ALTERNATIVE

When a firm's or an individual's assets are insufficient to cover the efficient penalties that would be levied on them or when the actual penalties are below the efficient levels, then incarceration might be used either as a substitute penalty or as an addition to the monetary penalty to promote efficiency.[45] With the use of incarceration, two extra social costs are introduced: (i) the dollar equivalent of the direct disutility (or lost income) from a jail sentence for the worker (J), which is a monotonically increasing function of the number of years spent in jail, and (ii) the social costs of incarceration (S), including the costs of providing capital (prisons), labor (guards and support personnel) and raw materials and services (uniforms), which also increase with the length of the sentence. Neither of these costs exist with a fine. Therefore as long as any specific level of deterrence achieved by incarceration could also be achieved by a fine, fines dominate [20]. However, in a second-best world (where efficient fines cannot be levied for one reason or another) incarceration may have some role to play. We consider here the limiting case where fines cannot be used at all and therefore the only instrument available is incarceration. While we focus on incarceration of the worker only, the corresponding results for incarceration of corporate executives or managers (i.e., those individuals who chose x) should be apparent.

In previous economic analyses of incarceration [20, 28], the "criminal" activity is modeled as a discrete choice; the individual either engages in the activity or does not. In our context, however, the activity (care) is a continuous choice. Having a continuous choice variable forces us to confront the issue of how to define the

---

[42] In some ways the problem of insufficient assets might be even more severe in enforcement than in tort law. Most tort law damages paid to individuals and costs incurred in cleaning up sites are insurable, providing another source of assets to be tapped. Fines, however, are typically not insurable, particularly criminal fines which fulfill the *scienter* requirement.

[43] This could create an incentive to set up underfunded subsidiaries for the sole purpose of keeping environmental risks away from the parent corporation. This has apparently happened in the United States according to evidence presented in [21].

[44] This problem could be reduced somewhat by using a "negligence" approach to fines, i.e., imposing the fine only if the party failed to comply with a due standard of conduct. See [2] for a discussion of this approach.

[45] An alternative to incarceration is community service requirements. As with incarceration, community service imposes time costs on the individual as a substitute for monetary costs. However, those time costs generate positive benefits for society in a way that they might not in the case of incarceration. In addition, community service avoids the social costs of incarceration (see below).

point at which the possibility of incarceration should be triggered. Should an individual who undertakes a great deal of care still be subject to incarceration if an accident occurs? Or should the possibility of incarceration be reserved for cases where the level of care was "criminally" low? This distinction is similar to the distinction in tort law between the use of a strict liability rule (liability regardless of the level of care) and a negligence rule (liability only for failure to exercise "due" care). While such a distinction has not been made in previous economic analyses of incarceration, it is crucial in analyzing the role of incarceration in ensuring efficient incentives. In particular, we show below that an incarceration rule based on strict liability principles will not generally yield efficient care, while a rule based upon negligence principles can.[46]

Since it is most closely linked to the analyses of fines above, we consider first an incarceration rule based on strict liability principles. In other words, we assume that if an accident occurs, a jail sentence will be imposed with the length of the jail sentence determined by the level of damages. Since both the disutility of the jail sentence and the cost of incarceration are monotonically increasing in the number of years spent in jail, we can specify the model in terms of J rather than the number of years. Thus, $J = J(D)$ and $S = S(J)$. In addition, we allow for the possibility that the jail sentence will result in reputational losses that exceed the direct disutility of jail. Thus, the total cost of a jail sentence to the worker is $(1 + \phi)J$, where $\phi J \geqslant 0$ equals reputational costs, which are assumed to be proportional to the severity of the jail sentence.

With incarceration the socially optimal choices of a and x will solve

$$\text{maximize } B(x) - C(x) - V(a)$$

$$- p\{D(x,a) + J(D(x,a)) + S(J(D(x,a)))\}, \qquad (24)$$

which yields the following first-order conditions:

$$B'(x) - C'(x) - p\{1 + J' + S'J'\}D_x(x,a) = 0, \qquad \text{and} \qquad (25)$$

$$V'(a) + p\{1 + J' + S'J'\}D_a(x,a) = 0. \qquad (26)$$

Note that in this formulation we assume that possible reputational losses to the worker from incarceration are not viewed as social losses.[47] While this violates a strict utilitarian approach to defining social welfare, it is consistent with the belief by some that certain private costs resulting from criminal activity should not be

---

[46]This is in direct contrast to the standard results from the economic analysis of torts. It is well-known that in unilateral care cases efficient care by an individual can be induced through either strict liability or negligence. Even in the standard analysis of bilateral care, strict liability imposed on one party will lead to efficient care by that party, conditional on the care levels of others (which may not be efficient). Thus, while the overall outcome may not be efficient, the incentives of the party facing strict liability will be correct. (See, for example, [25]). This result does not hold in the case considered here, however.

[47]Reputational losses may result in social losses if they prevent the worker from being employed to his fullest potential. We ignore this possibility here.

included in measures of social costs (e.g. [13]). The implications of relaxing this are noted below.

Likewise, with incarceration of individuals but no fines, the firm chooses x to

$$\text{maximize } B(x) - C(x) - W \tag{27}$$

subject to the employee choosing a so as to

$$\text{maximize } W - V(a) - p(1 + \phi)J(D) \text{ and} \tag{28}$$

$$W - V(a) - p(1 + \phi)J(D) = U^0. \tag{29}$$

Note that this problem has the same form as (4)–(6), with $F = 0$ and $G = (1 + \phi)J$. Thus, the analysis of the private decisions in the case of fines can be used to infer behavior when incarceration is used instead.

Consider the case where wages can vary with both x and a, i.e., $W = W(a, x)$.[48] Letting $F = 0$ in (10), the firm chooses a wage contract of the form

$$W(a, x) = k(x) = U^0 + V(a_e) + p(1 + \phi)J(D(x, a_e)), \tag{30}$$

where a_e is the new equilibrium choice of a. Note that this wage function is independent of the actual choice of a. Given this function, the worker chooses a to satisfy the following first-order condition:

$$V'(a) + p(1 + \phi)J'D_a(x, a) = 0. \tag{31}$$

Likewise, the firm's choice of x is given by

$$B'(x) - C'(x) - p(1 + \phi)J'D_x(x, a_e) = 0. \tag{32}$$

Comparing (25) and (26) to (31) and (32) implies that, to ensure efficient choices of x and a through incarceration, the following condition must hold:

$$p(1 + \phi)J' = p(1 + J' + J'S'), \tag{33}$$

or, equivalently,

$$J' = 1/(\phi - S'). \tag{33'}$$

From (31) it is clear that, in order to achieve efficiency, J' must be strictly positive.[49] Clearly this requires that $\phi > S'$, i.e., that marginal reputational costs exceed the marginal costs of incarceration. If the marginal reputational costs are small relative to incarceration costs, then efficiency cannot be achieved through incarceration. The inability to ensure efficiency through incarceration when repu-

---

[48]The results for the other forms of W are similar. For example, if W is independent of x, then the same issues arise in ensuring an efficient choice of a. The only difference is that, since backward shifting is not possible, there is no way to ensure an efficient choice of x.

[49]Since $V' > 0$ and $D_a < 0$, if $J' \leq 0$, then the agent would choose a equal to zero, which is assumed to be inefficient.

tation costs are "small" can be explained as follows. Suppose reputational costs are zero. Then the private costs of incarceration are only the opportunity costs of the worker, J. The social costs, on the other hand, are the opportunity costs, plus the damages, plus the costs of incarceration, $D + J + S$. Thus, regardless of the form of J, private costs are less than social costs and incarceration cannot induce efficiency.[50] Contrary to what has been thought, however, the inefficiency of incarceration here does not stem from the mere existence of incarceration costs. It should be clear from the above model that, even with $S = 0$, the problem remains. As long as the opportunity cost of the time spent in jail is included in the measure of social losses, as is typical in models of incarceration [20, 28], the private costs (J) will still be less than the social costs ($D + J$) and J cannot be set so that private and social costs are equal even at the margin.[51] As a result, the worker will choose a level of a that is less than the efficient level. A similar result holds for the firm's choice of x. This inefficiency can only be offset by sufficiently high reputational costs.

Note, also, that the potential inefficiency of incarceration cannot be eliminated by coupling incarceration with fines. If the worker's assets are insufficient or the efficient fine would exceed a statutory limit, then in the relevant range the worker will view the fine as fixed at its maximum level (equal to his assets or the legal limit).[52] The existence of the fine will then have no effect on the worker's marginal incentives. Thus, in the absence of sufficient reputational costs, marginal social costs will continue to exceed marginal private costs and an inefficient amount of care will be chosen.

These conclusions regarding the inefficiency of incarceration hinge on the strict liability form of the incarceration rule that is considered above. In contrast, it is possible to base an incarceration rule on negligence principles, where a jail sentence would only be imposed if the level of care were less than some standard. We consider a negligence-based approach next and show that such a policy could induce efficient care.

Suppose, for example, that a jail sentence with disutility J is imposed if an accident occurs and care was less than the due standard. (No sentence is imposed if the worker took sufficient care.) Assume that the due standard of care is set equal to the socially efficient level of a (a^*) which solves (1).[53] For simplicity, we consider only the case where W is independent of x and a.[54] In this case, the

---

[50]A similar conclusion would hold if reputation costs are positive but are included in the measure of social cost.

[51]Note that this inefficiency does not arise in the models used in [20] and [28] since they consider only discrete choices problems (whether to undertake the activity or not) where marginal incentives are not an issue.

[52]If the level of damages at the efficient choice of a is below the worker's assets, then efficient care can be induced through the use of a fine alone (see analysis of fines above) and incarceration is unnecessary.

[53]This is a standard assumption in economic analyses of negligence rules (e.g. [25]). In practice, however, the actual standard of care applied may differ from the efficient level. See [10] for a discussion of related issues.

[54]This assumption simplifies the analysis by allowing the decisions of the worker and the firm to be considered separately. It implies, however, that penalties imposed on the worker cannot be shifted to the firm, so that, in the absence of direct penalties on the firm, an efficient level of x will not be chosen. Here our interest is simply in the effects of incarceration on incentives of the individual on whom it is imposed rather than the possibility for shifting costs between parties.

196   SEGERSON AND TIETENBERG

worker will choose to maximize his net return, given by

$$W - V(a) - pJ(1 + \phi) \qquad \text{if } a < a^*, \text{ and} \qquad (i)$$

$$W - V(a) \qquad\qquad\qquad \text{if } a \geq a^*. \qquad\qquad (ii)$$

Let a' denote the level of a that maximizes (i).[55] Since $V' > 0$, the level of a that maximizes (ii) (given $a \geq a^*$) is clearly a^*. Thus, the worker will choose a^* if and only if

$$W - V(a') - pJ(1 + \phi) \leq W - V(a^*). \qquad (34)$$

(We assume that when the two returns are equal, the worker chooses a^*.) Thus, if the social planner wants to ensure an efficient choice of a, he should set the jail sentence to satisfy

$$J \geq \{V(a^*) - V(a')\}/p(1 + \phi) > 0. \qquad (35)$$

In other words, if a jail sentence with disutility exceeding $\{V(a^*) - V(a')\}/p(1 + \phi)$ is imposed when an accident occurs if and only if the worker's choice of a was less than a^*, the worker will be induced to choose the first best level of care a^*. Note that, in this case, no jail sentences would ever actually be imposed (if the rule works perfectly) so that the costs of incarceration would never be incurred.

Condition (35) suggests that the efficient penalty is independent of the level of damages. Instead, it is determined by the size of the penalty necessary to deter inappropriate behavior (defined to be $a < a^*$). Clearly, the greater the private benefit of inappropriate behavior ($V(a^*) - V(a')$), the larger the jail sentence must be to deter it. Likewise, the smaller the probability that it will be imposed, the larger the necessary penalty.[56] Positive reputational costs also reduce the required sentence.

Finally, consider the impacts of fines in this context. If the maximum fine is imposed when an accident occurs regardless of the level of a, then condition (35) will still determine the efficient jail sentence since the worker would incur the penalty regardless of his choice of a, i.e., the penalty will enter both sides of (34). However, if the fine is imposed along with the jail sentence only when a is less than the standard, then clearly the level of J necessary to induce deterrence will be smaller. Note that, to the extent that in practice the system is imperfect and jail sentences are actually imposed, smaller jail sentences would result in lower social costs. Thus, coupling incarceration with a fine imposed only if the level of care falls below the standard would be preferable to the use of incarceration alone.

Although a negligence standard for criminal penalties no doubt sounds like an unrealistic proposal to those familiar with the use of criminal penalties in nonenvironmental settings, this concept has recently been applied.[57] According to Section 1319(c)(1) of Title 33 of the U.S. Code, negligent violations of Clean Water Act

---

[55]Note that, if J is independent of damages, then $a' = 0$.

[56]These results are consistent with the results obtained in [28].

[57]Negligence standards are not entirely uncommon in other areas of criminal law. For example, individuals who have engaged in reckless driving could well be charged with negligent homicide. We are indebted to a reviewer for noting this parallel.

provisions can now trigger criminal penalties. Fines of up to $25,000 per day and 1 year in prison are authorized for a first offense with higher penalties authorized for repeat offenders. Our model suggests that this novel approach to enforcement may be filling an important niche.

IV. SUMMARY AND CONCLUSIONS

The traditional penalty structure for managing environmental risks involves administrative or civil financial penalties imposed on organizations rather than penalties or jail sentences imposed on individuals.[58] Targeting firms rather than individuals involves lower transactions costs and is less likely to create serious financial disruptions.[59] The perceived effectiveness of this approach in creating appropriate incentives for workers hinges on the firm's ability to sanction its employees internally for actions that contribute to environmental risks.

In practice, the efficient management of environmental risks is often more complicated than implied by this simple rationale. Risks can results from a combination of actions by workers and management. While workers may control day-to-day decisions that affect the level of risk, managers set overall safety policies and make decisions about safety investments and expansion of the firm's operations, which may also affect the magnitude of the associated risks. In such cases the enforcement approach must be structured to ensure that both parties face efficient incentives to reduce these risks.

In this paper we have examined the efficiency of alternative penalty structures, including both corporate and individual fines as well as incarceration, in the context of this more realistic setting. In particular, we compare alternative approaches, recognizing the role that both workers and management play in determining the ultimate level of environmental risks and the contractual relationships that allow workers and management to shift the ultimate incidence of any imposed penalty.

Using a simple principal–agent model, we have derived conditions for the traditional approach of using corporate penalties to be justified on efficiency grounds. Corporate penalties can be fully efficient if the firm can adequately monitor the employee's activities and base his/her wages on the environmental consequences of those activities. With full observability and completely flexible compensation schemes, the firm is able to shift the corporate penalty onto the worker through a compensating wage reduction. This shifting induces efficient care by the workers, even if they face no direct penalties themselves. If, in addition, the worker has an exogenous reservation level of utility that dictates an "acceptable" wage level and the wage demand can vary with the risk-related decisions of the firm, then any wage reduction will, in turn, be shifted back to the firm. Our model

---

[58]See [17] for a breakdown of the EPA's enforcement actions. This report shows that about 90% of federal enforcement actions take the form of administrative proceedings.

[59]The difference in transactions costs between individual and corporate penalties, however, seems to be getting smaller over time. Officers and directors of corporations have traditionally been protected from liability for wrongs normally attributable to the organization. Increasingly these traditional protections are being eroded in both the common law and the statutory law, thereby reducing the traditional burden of proof faced by government enforcers. See [5] for a discussion of this trend in environmental law.

suggests that under these conditions efficient incentives could also have been achieved with a penalty on the individual worker without any penalty on the firm.

Under the full observability and wage flexibility assumptions the combined effect of forward and backward shifting of corporate penalties assures efficient incentives for both the worker and the firm; corporate and individual sanctions are perfect substitutes in terms of their incentive effects. Such a result is consistent with previous work showing that, when two parties have a contractual relationship, the efficient outcome can be achieved by placing the penalty on either party. Our analysis also makes clear, however, that it would not be efficient to fine *both* the worker and the firm for the full amount of damages. Given their lower transaction costs, corporate penalties would be preferred.

In practice fulfilling these conditions for perfect substitutability between corporate and individual penalties may not be possible. Long lag times in discovering the environmental effects of a worker's actions may prevent shifting the incidence of corporate penalties to responsible employees. Whenever wages are dictated by inflexible contracts established by bargaining that focuses on other issues, the necessary backward and forward shifting cannot occur. Finally corporate penalties that are large in comparison to the earnings of environmental risk managers cannot, as a practical matter, be recovered from compensating reductions in wages.

Without such backward and forward shifting the two penalty types are not necessarily perfect substitutes. One penalty or the other (or even some combination of the two) may be preferred. According to our analysis individual penalties may be preferred if wages cannot be based on the worker's day-to-day decisions, but workers can demand higher compensation from firms forcing them to face higher potential penalties. Likewise if wages are unrelated to the safety decisions of either the worker or the firm, then the problem reduces to one of "joint torts" and penalties on both the worker and the firm would be necessary to induce efficient incentives.

Neither type of financial penalty, either separately or in combination, can produce efficient behavior when the penalties are set incorrectly (as a result, for example, of institutional or statutory constraints) or whenever the parties involved have insufficient assets to pay the penalty. In such cases incarceration may promote efficiency when used either as a substitute for or in combination with financial penalties.

To consider the potential role for incarceration in this "second-best" world, we examined the incentive effects of two alternative sentencing or incarceration rules, one based upon strict liability principles and the other based upon negligence principles. Our results suggest that sentencing practices based upon strict liability principles can produce an efficient outcome if and only if reputational costs are large enough. Marginal reputational costs must exceed the marginal costs of incarceration. If the marginal reputational costs are small relative to incarceration costs, efficiency cannot be achieved through a strict liability incarceration rule. If reputational costs are zero, regardless of the form of J, private costs would be less than social costs and incarceration could not induce efficiency.

When a jail sentence is based on negligence principles (imposed only when employee actions fall below some established threshold), our analysis indicates that efficient incentives can be preserved even in the absence of reputational costs. In this case the efficient penalty would be independent of the level of damages. Instead, it would be determined by its effectiveness in deterring inappropriate behavior. The greater the private benefit of inappropriate behavior, the larger the jail sentence must be to deter it. Likewise, the smaller the probability that the sentence would be imposed, the larger the necessary sentence. Positive reputational costs also reduce the required sentence. To the extent that in practice the system is imperfect (implying that fines by themselves are insufficient), smaller jail sentences coupled with fines imposed only if the level of care falls below the efficient level would be preferable to the use of incarceration alone.

REFERENCES

1. G. Becker, Crime and punishment: An economic approach, *J. Polit. Econom.* **78**, 169–217 (1968).
2. M. A. Cohen, Optimal enforcement strategy to prevent oil spills: An application of a principal–agent model with moral hazard, *J. Law Econom.* **30**, 23–51 (1987).
3. M. A. Cohen, Corporate crime and punishment: An update on sentencing practice in the federal courts, 1988–1990. *Boston Univ. Law Rev.* **71**, 247–280 (1991).
4. M. A. Cohen, Criminal penalties, *in* "Innovation in Environmental Policy: Economic and Legal Aspects of Recent Developments in Liability and Enforcement" (T. H. Tietenberg, Ed.), Edward Elgar Publishing, Cheltingham, England, (1992).
5. D. M. Cordiano and D. J. Blood, Individual liability for environmental law violations, *Conn. Bar J.* **64**, 214–236 (1990).
6. S. J. Grossman and O. D. Hart, An analysis of the principal–agent problem, *Econometrica* **51**, 7–45 (1983).
7. K. Hagerty, A. Ofer, and D. Siegel, "Managerial Compensation and Incentives to Engage in Far-Sighted Behavior," delivered at the Allied Social Science Convention, Washington, DC (December 29, 1990).
8. B. Holmstrom, Moral hazard and observability, *Bell J. Econom.* **10**, 74–91 (1979).
9. D. Kirkpatrick, Environmentalism: The new crusade, *Fortune* **121**, 44–50, 54–55 (February 12, 1990).
10. C. D. Kolstad, T. S. Ulen, and G. V. Johnson, *Ex post* liability for harm vs. *ex ante* safety regulation: Substitutes or complements?, *Amer. Econom. Rev.* **80**, 888–901 (1990).
11. L. A. Kornhauser, An economic analysis of the choice between enterprise and personal liability for accidents, *Cal. Law Rev.* **70**, 1345–1392 (1982).
12. W. M. Landes and R. A. Posner, "The Economic Structure of Tort Law," Harvard Univ. Press, Cambridge, MA (1987).
13. J. L. Lewin and W. N. Trumbull, The social value of crime, *Internat. Rev. Law. Econom.* **10**, 271–284 (1990).
14. T. Miceli, and K. Segerson, Joint liability in torts: Marginal and infra-marginal efficiency, *Internat. Rev. Law Econom.* **11**, 235–249 (1991).
15. H. A. Newman and D. W. Wright, Strict liability in a principal–agent model, *Internat. Rev. Law Econom.* **10**, 219–231 (1990).
16. Office of Enforcement and Compliance Monitoring, United States Environmental Protection Agency, "Fundamentals of Environmental Compliance Inspections," Government Institutes, Inc., Rockville, MD (1989).
17. Office of Enforcement, "Enforcement Accomplishments: FY 1989," United States Environmental Protection Agency, Washington, DC (1990).
18. A. M. Polinsky, Strict liability vs. negligence in a market setting, *Amer. Econom. Rev.* **70**, 363–367 (1980).
19. A. M. Polinsky and S. Shavell, The optimal tradeoff between the probability and magnitude of fines, *Amer. Econom. Rev.* **69**, 880–891 (1979).
20. A. M. Polinsky and S. Shavell, The optimal use of fines and imprisonment, *J. Public Econom.* **24**, 89–99 (1984).
21. A. H. Ringleb and S. N. Wiggins, Liability and large-scale, long-term hazards, *J. Polit. Econom.* **98**, 574–595 (1990).
22. K. Segerson, Liability for groundwater contamination from pesticides, *J. Environ. Econom. Management* **19**, 227–243 (1990).

23. K. Segerson and T. Tietenberg, Defining Efficient Sanctions, *in* "Innovation in Environmental Policy: Economic and Legal Aspects of Recent Developments in Liability and Enforcement" (T. H. Tietenberg, Ed.), Edward Elgar Publishing, Cheltingham, England, (1992).

24. S. Shavell, Risk-sharing and incentives in the principal-agent relationship, *Bell J. Econom.* **10**, 55–73 (1979).

25. S. Shavell, Strict Liability versus negligence, *J. Legal Stud.* **9**, 1–25 (1980).

26. S. Shavell, Uncertainty over causation and the determination of civil liability, *J. Law Econom.* **28**, 587–609 (1985).

27. S. Shavell, The judgment proof problem, *Internat. Rev. Law Econom.* **6**, 45–58 (1986).

28. S. Shavell, The optimal use of nonmonetary sanctions as a deterrent, *Amer. Econom. Rev.* **77**, 584–592 (1987).

29. S. Shavell, "Economic Analysis of Accident Law," Harvard Univ. Press, Cambridge, MA (1987).

30. J. W. Starr and T. J. Kelly Jr., Environmental crimes and the sentencing guidelines: The time has come ... and it is hard time, *Environ. Law Rep.* **20**, 10096–10104 (1990).

31. A. O. Sykes, An efficiency analysis of vicarious liability under the law of agency, *Yale Law J.* **91**, 169–206 (1981).

32. A. O. Sykes, The economics of vicarious liability, *Yale Law J.* **93**, 1231–1280 (1984).

33. T. H. Tietenberg, Indivisible toxic torts: The economics of joint and several liability, *Land Econom.* **65**, 305–319 (1989).

Empirical Models

[19]

Controlling stochastic pollution events through liability rules: some evidence from OCS leasing

James J. Opaluch*

and

Thomas A. Grigalunas*

Under the OCS Lands Act, firms are strictly liable for damages from oil spills. To the extent that this liability rule causes firms to internalize environmental risks, incentives for damage avoidance behavior are provided. Using data from the 1979 Georges Bank lease sale, we use a robust estimation technique to test the hypothesis that potential environmental costs are reflected in bids for OCS leases. The results indicate a substantial response to environmental risks. Recognizing reduced rents, we estimate that total high bids have declined by 20% because of firms' perceptions of environmental risks. The results suggest that liability rules have considerable potential in controlling stochastic pollution events.

1. Introduction

■ The Outer Continental Shelf (OCS) is a major potential source of domestic energy supplies (U.S. Department of Interior, 1981). Exploiting these reserves can lead, however, to substantial damages to the environment and to fisheries through accidental oil spills and chronic low-level pollution.[1] In recognition of this social tradeoff, Congress enacted the Outer Continental Shelf Lands Act of 1978 (OCSLA), (P.L. 95-372). This legislation requires offshore oil and gas operators to use the best available and safest technology (BAST) when economically feasible (Sec. 21). In addition, firms responsible for any offshore oil-related spill are held strictly liable for the damages of the spill (Sec. 303).[2]

While the purpose of strict liability in the OCSLA is to compensate damaged parties, this liability can be viewed as a tax on external costs (Just and Zilberman, 1979), which should cause firms to internalize the expected environmental costs of developing reserves. Thus, the OCSLA provides firms with economic incentives to control for environmental risks through investing in safe technology, altering production rates, and avoiding environmentally sensitive areas (Conrad, 1980). But public debate has paid scant attention to the role of economic incentives as a policy instrument for controlling the environmental risks of OCS development. To date, most of the discussion of managing environmental risk has focused on detailed regulations and technological requirements.

* University of Rhode Island.

We wish to acknowledge research assistance of John Mackenzie, as well as useful comments by an anonymous referee and the Editorial Board. Any remaining errors are the sole responsibility of the authors. Financial support from the Rhode Island Agricultural Experiment Station is gratefully acknowledged (AES Contribution No. 2178).

[1] Reviews of the possible environmental risks of offshore oil and gas development can be found in U.S. Council on Environmental Quality (1974), U.S. Department of Interior (1981), and National Academy of Sciences (1981).

[2] Strict liability under the OCSLA provides that a polluter will be held liable for damages with a probability of one, with limited defenses for acts of war or related hostilities, negligence by third parties, or grave unanticipated natural disasters (Sec. 304). In contrast, without strict liability, the determination of whether a polluter is liable for damages is based on the common law doctrine of negligence. Since negligence is difficult to ascertain and costly to prove, the probability of a polluter's being held liable for damages may be considerably less than one.

Given the incentives provided by strict liability, one might argue that requiring the use of BAST is at best redundant and possibly a source of inefficiency. This argument, however, involves some fairly strong assumptions. In particular, the firms' perceptions of environmental risks must be consonant with the perceptions of society at large. Firms' evaluations may diverge from social perceptions for several reasons, including:

(1) Serious empirical difficulties may lead to vastly differing estimates of the probability of a spill or the damages resulting from a spill (Grigalunas *et al.*, 1983).

(2) Liability limits under the OCSLA may lead to incomplete internalization, although these limits would not prove binding for the vast majority of spills.[3]

(3) Firms may face additional costs, other than liability for damages, because of adverse publicity following a spill or because of governmentally imposed delays in leasing or exploiting tracts in environmentally sensitive OCS areas.[4]

Nevertheless, if future environmental policy is to be based on providing incentives for actions by firms, as economists usually argue, then an important issue concerns the perceptions of environmental risk by industry and the extent to which firms respond to liability for these risks.

This article examines some available evidence on firms' perceptions of potential liability for environmental damages from stochastic pollution events. OCS bidding provides a perhaps unique opportunity to examine this issue because strict liability laws have recently been put in place, and the bidding system for auctioning leases provides a vehicle for assessing firms' evaluations of environmental risk at a single point in time, on the day of the lease sale. Although, strictly speaking, the results apply only to the case considered here, we view this article as a first step toward determining the effectiveness of liability for stochastic environmental damages as a policy tool for eliciting optimal precautionary behavior by firms.

Section 2 reviews the pertinent literature and relates the model employed in this study to previous work. Section 3 describes the empirical model, the data sources, and the results. The conclusions of the study and suggestions for further research are given in Section 4.

2. The framework for estimating perceptions of environmental risks

■ Leases for OCS oil and gas development are sold on the basis of a first-price, sealed bid auction, in which the firm submitting the highest bid on a particular tract wins the right to develop the tract and pays an amount equal to the bid.[5] A considerable literature has examined such auctions, and several important results have been derived concerning

---

[3] Under the OCSLA firms are held strictly liable for damages up to a stated maximum. In the case of a tanker spill, liability is limited to $250 thousand or $300 per gross ton, whichever is greater. For spills from an offshore facility, firms are liable for all removal costs plus up to $35 million per incident for damages to, or loss of use of, real or personal property, damages to natural resources, loss of profits or earnings, and loss of tax revenue for up to a period of one year (Sec. 303). To place these figures into perspective, the highly publicized 1969 Santa Barbara Channel oil spill caused estimated social costs of $28.8 million (in 1978 dollars), a large share of which comprised well-control costs and the value of lost oil, costs to which the limits on strict liability set by the OCSLA do not apply. When negligence can be proved, there is no upper limit to the operator's liability for a spill (Sec. 304).

[4] Because we are considering low probability events with potentially large economic consequences, risk aversion may be an important issue. As argued by Conrad, however, the degree of risk aversion may be reduced because of the spreading of risk over large numbers of projects, in addition to spreading variability of profits over large numbers of shareholders in the company. Hence, the importance of risk aversion in this context is not altogether clear.

[5] The OCSLA also provides for leasing tracts with net profit share, royalty rate, or work commitment as the bid variable (Sec. 205). In the sale considered below, all tracts were sold by cash bonus bid with either fixed or variable rate royalty.

firms' bidding behavior. In particular, it has been emphasized that when bidding under incomplete information, each participant must account for the fact that other information may be available to its competitors.

All else equal, the firm with the highest estimate of tract value will submit the highest bid. This implies that a firm will tend to overestimate the value of tracts that it eventually wins, even if all firms have unbiased estimates of the value of each tract (Rothkopf, 1969; Capen, Clapp, and Campbell, 1971; Milgrom and Weber, 1982). Hence, a firm's expectation of rents, conditional on its winning the auction, will be less than its unconditional expectation. The more firms that bid for a particular tract, the more each one's conditional expectation should be adjusted downward. Thus, a firm's optimal bidding strategy involves submitting lower bids on tracts with more competing firms, all else being equal (Rothkopf, 1969; Wilson, 1977). Gilley and Karels (1981) provide empirical validation for this conceptual argument.

Although bids by individual firms are inversely related to the number of bidders, the same analyses show that the winning bid is positively related to the number of bidders (Rothkopf, 1969; Wilson, 1977; Reece, 1978). An extensive applied study by Mead, Sorensen *et al.* (1980) provides strong empirical support for the hypothesis that the high bid increases with the number of bidders for a tract, other things being equal. Under appropriate assumptions, the equilibrium price resulting from a first-price, sealed bid auction can be shown to be a consistent estimate of tract value, even when no individual firm knows the value with certainty (Wilson, 1977; Milgrom, 1979).

The results of Reece (1978) are the most pertinent for this study, and they will be discussed in some detail. Reece examines the distribution of rents from OCS leasing under the assumption that auction participants choose the bidding strategy that maximizes expected net revenues. Since the problem is sufficiently complex that analytic results cannot be obtained, Reece uses a simulation model to generate the proportion of rent captured by the government through the bidding process (i.e., the ratio of the winning bid to the expected rent), the proportion captured by the firm, and the proportion captured by society as a whole. These proportionality factors are generated for a variety of values of the number of participants and the variability of expected rents. Reece's work implies a model with the maximum bid determined by

$$B_j = P(N_j, \sigma_j^2)E(R_j),$$

where B_j is the high bid for the jth tract and $P(\cdot)$ is the proportionality factor. The factor $P(\cdot)$ is a function of N_j, the number of participants in the auction of the jth tract, and of σ_j^2, the variability of the estimated tract value around its true value.

The expected rent is defined as

$$E(R_j) = \int_0^\infty \int_0^\infty (V_j - C_j - e_j)f(V_j, e_j)dV_j de_j,$$

where V_j is the present value of the jth tract, net of variable costs; C_j represents the fixed costs associated with exploring and developing the tract; e_j represents the environmental costs to the firm due to liability for damages from an oil spill from tract j; and $f(\cdot)$ represents the joint density function for tract value and environmental risk. Thus, the winning bid on each tract should be proportional to the expected rent from developing the tract, net of expected environmental risks as perceived by the firm through the liability for damages.

A central issue that arises in using OCS bidding to attempt to assess the effectiveness of liability laws in controlling stochastic pollution events is whether the analysis should focus on high bids or on all bids submitted for individual tracts. Industry decisions concerning the actual development of tracts are made by the firm that wins the auction. If, for example, winning bids are typically submitted by firms that underestimate the expected environmental costs of development, and hence overestimate the expected rent, then using all bids to estimate the response to environmental sensitivity overstates the degree of environmental protection provided by liability rules. Therefore, the analysis of the effectiveness of strict liability should focus on high bids. Given a cross section of winning bids on tracts, where environmental risk varies over tracts, one should be able to estimate the extent to which the high bid on each tract reflects the environmental risk associated with the tract.

3. Application of the model

■ **Model specification and data.** The model described in the previous section was applied to the December 1979 lease sale #42 in the North Atlantic (Georges Bank). This OCS lease sale is a particularly appropriate application because of the importance of Georges Bank's commercial fisheries, because of the relative proximity of the sale area to intensively used coastal beaches, and because of the extent to which the area has been the subject of study. The highly contentious nature of environmental concerns for Georges Bank is underscored by several delays in the lease sale date, by the litigation preceding the sale, and by the deletion of 28 tracts from the sale, all for environmental reasons.[6] Further, the fact that sale #42 was the first lease sale in the Georges Bank area avoids the potential difficulty of informational asymmetries, whereby firms' bidding behavior could be influenced by information acquired as a consequence of a prior sale (Hughart, 1975; Mead, Sorensen, and Moseidjord, 1982).

As described in the previous section, the model employed in this study yields the following equation for the maximum bid:

$$B_j = P(N_j, \sigma_j^2)E(R_j(V_j, C_j, e_j)),$$

where all variables are as defined above. Thus, the high bid is proportional to the expected rent, where the proportionality factor depends upon the number of auction participants and the variability of tract value. For the purpose of this study, this proportionality factor is assumed to be of the form

$$P(N_j, \sigma^2) = 1 - \frac{1}{aN^b + c},$$

where a, b, and c are parameters which depend upon the uncertainty concerning tract value.

This specification represents a generalization of the multiplicative bidding strategy studied by Rothkopf (1969), whereby firms submit bids that are proportional to the expected rent. Rothkopf demonstrates that if all firms employ a multiplicative strategy, then the high bid is of the form

$$B_j = \left[1 - \frac{1}{NM - (M + 1)}\right]E(R_j),$$

where M is an inverse measure of the spread or uncertainty concerning tract value.[7] Hence, the formulation employed in this study includes the multiplicative bidding strategy as a special case with

$$b = 1$$

$$a = -(c + 1) = M.$$

---

[6] A summary of the environmental actions and debate concerning the first Georges Bank lease sale can be found in Robadue and Tippie (1980).
[7] Rothkopf assumes that value estimates are distributed as the two-parameter Weibull distribution, where M, the spread parameter, is related to the variance according to the relationship,

$$1/\sigma = \Gamma(1 + 1/M)[\Gamma(1 + 2/M) - \Gamma^2(1 + 1/M)]^{-1/2},$$

where $\Gamma(\cdot)$ is the gamma function. (See, for example, Gumbel (1958).) As stated by Rothkopf, M varies smoothly from 1 to 10 to 100 to ∞ as b_{ij}/σ goes from 1 to 8.3 to 78.5 to ∞, when employing the notation used in this article.

Under the assumption that bidders maximize expected profit, Reece generates values of the proportionality factor for a number of levels of N and σ^2. Capen, Clapp, and Campbell (1971) state that the appropriate (standardized) value for σ^2 in a previously unexplored region is 1.2. Hence, the results of Reece were used to calibrate the function $P(N, \sigma^2)$ for $\sigma^2 = 1.2$.[8]

Following Reece, the proportionality factor is assumed to be a nonstochastic function. Given the number of auction participants and the uncertainty concerning tract value, a model of the following form was constructed:

$$\frac{B_j}{P(N_j, \sigma^2)} = E(R_j(V_j, C_j, e_j)).$$

The dependent variable was determined by dividing the high bid on each tract by the proportionality factor constructed from the results of Reece. The high bid for each tract was identified from information on bids by the 31 participating companies, which was obtained from published sources (U.S. Department of Interior, 1980a). High bids on individual tracts ranged from $200 thousand to $80.3 million. The total high bids submitted for the 73 tracts bid upon amounted to $827.8 million, of which $813 million was accepted by the Department of the Interior for the 64 tracts actually sold (U.S. Department of Interior, 1980b).[9]

The unpublished USGS estimate of the expected net value of each tract is used as a measure of tract value[10] and is denoted as *VALUE* in the regression model. These estimates are derived by the USGS through the use of a Monte Carlo simulation model, which estimates the expected discounted value, given distributions on economically recoverable resources, recovery factors, and production profiles, as well as exploration, development, and operating costs. Royalties and corporate taxes also are included in the USGS model to determine net returns, but tract-specific estimates of possible environmental costs are not included.

The variable measuring environmental sensitivity was constructed from information in the Environmental Impact Statement (EIS) for lease sale #42 (U.S. Department of Interior, 1977). This variable measures the potential threat to major resources in the area. In terms of fisheries, the EIS considered the threat to cod and haddock spawning areas and to shellfish grounds on Georges Bank. In 1980 the value of landings from these three fisheries amounted to $77 million, about two-thirds of the value of all domestic landings from Georges Bank. The variable also includes the threat to surrounding shorelines. This category of risk is particularly important because of possible compensable losses incurred by coastal residents and recreational businesses as a result of a spill. In addition, the cost of cleaning up oil that comes ashore can represent one of the largest costs of a spill (Anderson *et al.*, 1983; Grigalunas *et al.*, 1983; Organization for Economic Cooperation and Development, 1982a, 1982b).

The specific measure of environmental risk is the probability that the trajectory of a spill would intersect fishing areas mentioned above or would strike shore. These probabilities are given in the EIS for eleven hypothetical, geographically dispersed launch sites throughout the lease area, and six of the sites are contained in the area sold. The probability estimates contained in the EIS were derived from the initial oil spill trajectory modelling work by the Offshore Oil Task Group (1973), which was refined by Smith, Slack, and Davis (1976).

The variable measuring environmental sensitivity, denoted *ENVIRON*, is equal to the sum of the probabilities of coming ashore, striking shellfish areas, and striking cod and haddock spawning grounds,[11] scaled by a factor of 100. This measure of environmental sensitivity varies from 15 for the least sensitive tracts to 34 for the most sensitive (i.e., the sum of the probabilities varies from .15 to .34).

The model also includes a variable to measure scale economies and information externalities which can be realized by a firm that develops adjacent tracts. This variable, denoted as *ADJ*, is the number of tracts adjacent to the tract of interest that were won by the same firm.

A single consortium placed (apparently) extraordinarily high bids on the three adjoining tracts in the sale, and in industry parlance, it left roughly $235 million on the table.[12] The high bids on these tracts were $75.2, $79.2, and $80.3 million, while the second highest bids were $3.1, $13.2, and $12.1 million, respectively. The corresponding USGS-based estimates of value were $424, $71, and $7.8 thousand. To account for the extreme variation resulting from these three observations, a dummy variable, denoted *D3*, was introduced which equals 1 for these three tracts and zero otherwise. Without this dummy variable, however, qualitatively similar results are obtained, as will be discussed below.

Several statistical difficulties arise in a regression analysis of OCS bidding behavior. The first difficulty concerns sample selection bias, which results because observations are only available in cases where firms submit positive bids and tracts are actually sold. Since the present analysis concerns high bids, this form of bias occurs because there are cases where no bids are submitted in excess of the government's reservation price for a particular tract (see footnote 9 above). Of the 116 tracts offered for sale, bids were submitted for 73. The high bid exceeded the reservation price in 64 cases, and these tracts were sold. Gilley and Karels (1981) address this sample selection difficulty by using a two-step procedure developed by Heckman (1976, 1979). Unfortunately, presale value estimates are not available for unsold tracts in our study, and hence Heckman's procedure cannot be employed here.

Under special circumstances, however, the direction of the sample-selection bias can be determined. It can be shown that in an ordinary least squares regression, the sample-selection problem causes the coefficients to be biased downward in absolute value when the variables in the regression are normally distributed (Olsen, 1980; Goldberger, 1981). As shown by Poirer and Melino (1978), these results can be extended to the lognormal distribution under quite general conditions. This implies that in the results given below, the estimated coefficient on *ENVIRON* is biased towards zero, and hence represents a conservative estimate of firms' response to environmental risk.

The second statistical difficulty results from the nonnormality inherent in the problem being addressed. Empirical evidence indicates that the distribution of the size of petroleum deposits closely approximates the lognormal distribution (Uhler and Bradley, 1970; Kaufman, 1963) as does the distribution of bids on individual tracts (Arps, 1965; Brown, 1969). Because the lognormal distribution has a "thick" tail to the right as compared with the normal distribution, the ordinary least squares (OLS) estimator may have poor properties owing to excessive weight's being placed on outlying observations. To cope with this difficulty we used a robust estimation technique whereby outlying observations are given less weight (Bickel, 1975; Huber, 1977). In its general form, the estimator can be described as

$$\min_{\hat{B}} \phi(Y - X\hat{B}).$$

---

[11] An analysis of the initial regression results revealed a high degree of multicollinearity among the three environmental variables. In the final model, the *ENVIRON* variable is the sum of the probabilities for each of the indicated categories of environmental risk. As a result of this aggregation, of course, it is not possible to ascribe firms' perceptions of environmental risk to any one of the environmental factors included.

[12] As of May, 1983, eight wildcat wells, all dry holes, have been drilled on Georges Bank, and it thus remains to be seen whether any commercially recoverable oil and gas will be found in this OCS region.

The OLS estimator is defined as $\phi(Z) = Z^2$. For the results given below we used the function

$$\phi(Z) = \begin{cases} Z^2 & \text{if} & |Z| < \alpha s \\ 0 & \text{otherwise,} \end{cases}$$

where s represents the estimated standard deviation of the disturbance term. A number of alternative values for α were tested, and it was found that the estimator quickly converged. Identical qualitative results were obtained for α within the range of .5 to 6, as will be presented below.

□ **Results.** The results are presented in Table 1, with the robust estimator given for $\alpha = 2$. As can be seen from the table, the qualitative results of the two models are identical. In both cases all coefficients are of the expected sign and are statistically significant at the 95% level. Moving from OLS to robust estimation, the coefficient on *VALUE* increases by a factor of almost two, from .76 to 1.43, while the coefficients on *ENVIRON* and *ADJ* each decrease in absolute value by a similar factor.

Examining the data *ex post* revealed that in ten cases the actual high bid exceeded the predicted high bid by several orders of magnitude. Of these ten outliers, eight occurred in areas of low environmental risk. Clearly, these outliers reflect widely divergent estimates of the value of the tracts and not the internalization of environmental costs. It is important to filter out these extreme variations to capture the response to environmental risk. The robust estimation technique described above was used to filter this information.

As shown in Table 2, the coefficients undergo an abrupt change when α is reduced from ∞ (the OLS estimator with no dummy) to 6. Further reduction in α results in purely random variation in all three parameters, and the ranges lie essentially within one standard error of the estimates for $\alpha = 2$. Hence, eliminating the influence of a small number of outlying observations has a considerable quantitative impact on the parameter estimates, while further experimentation with different values of α indicates that the estimates quickly become quite stable.

These results indicate a statistically significant and quantitatively large response of bids to environmental risks. Using the results of the robust estimator for $\alpha = 2$ suggests that high bids on individual tracts are predicted to be between \$1.67 million (with one bidder) and \$4.33 million (with seven bidders) lower for the most environmentally sensitive tracts as compared with the least environmentally sensitive tracts, all else equal. In the aggregate, we estimate that if all tracts had zero environmental risk, total high bids would be increased by \$236.7 million above what they were, given the actual environmental

TABLE 1	Estimation Results (*t*-statistics in parentheses)	
	OLS	Robust Estimator ($\alpha = 2$)
VALUE	.76 (2.07)	1.43 (12.93)
ENVIRON	−.89 (2.01)	−.40 (2.97)
ADJ	3.91 (1.96)	1.68 (2.74)
D3	140.34 (9.72)	—
Intercept	13.04 (3.19)	5.01 (4.18)
R^2	.69	.84
Number of Observations with Nonzero Weights	64	49

TABLE 2 **Estimation Results with Alternative Values of α (t-statistics in parentheses)**

	α						
	∞	6	3	2	1.5	1	.5
VALUE	.20	1.17	1.28	1.43	1.37	1.42	1.36
	(.34)	(6.80)	(11.24)	(12.93)	(13.33)	(16.83)	(22.29)
ENVIRON	−1.54	−.47	−.43	−.40	−.46	−.34	−.54
	(2.20)	(2.12)	(2.93)	(2.98)	(3.70)	(3.39)	(7.07)
ADJ	9.33	2.37	1.97	1.68	1.92	1.40	1.25
	(3.05)	(2.46)	(2.90)	(2.74)	(3.51)	(2.50)	(2.79)
Intercept	12.76	6.91	5.10	5.01	4.43	3.76	5.87
	(1.95)	(3.50)	(3.81)	(4.18)	(3.98)	(4.45)	(7.57)
R^2	.21	.60	.80	.84	.87	.93	.99
Number of Observations with Nonzero Weights	64	54	51	49	45	36	15

risks.[13] This represents quite a substantial response, greater than we expected *a priori*. To place this figure in perspective, the expected environmental damages that can be viewed as potentially compensable under the OCSLA from developing the Georges Bank lease area could total $101 million (U.S. Department of Interior, 1979a).

Several factors may explain this apparent discrepancy. First, damage estimates by the Department of Interior do not include removal costs, nor do they allow for monetized estimates of damages to noncommercial natural resources, both of which are compensable under OCSLA. Secondly, part of the differential may be attributed to company concerns about potential legal actions delaying development in environmentally sensitive areas, or the difference may reflect company concerns about adverse publicity that would inevitably accompany a large oil spill on Georges Bank, particularly should the spill come ashore. Finally, risk aversion on the part of firms may lead to a response in excess of the expected monetary value of damages for which the company would be held liable. This may be particularly important in view of the regulatory uncertainty resulting from a lack of experience with the administrative determination of damages under the OCSLA.

4. Conclusions

■ In this article we attempted to determine whether firms consider environmental risk when bidding for the right to explore and develop offshore oil tracts. Economic theory suggests that firms should internalize environmental costs, since they are held strictly liable for damages from oil spills under the OCSLA. If these costs are internalized, then strict liability has considerable potential as a policy tool for controlling environment risks.

[13] This calculation assumes that the number of auction participants is independent of the environmental sensitivity. Thus, predicted high bids are calculated as $B_j = P(N_j, \sigma^2)E\,(R_j|e = 0)$. If lower environmental risk increases the number of bidders, then predicted high bids would be increased further through the proportionality factor, $P(N_j, \sigma)$. But potential bidders who submit zero bids because of environmental risk cannot be assumed to be a random sample of all potential bidders. Instead, the firms for whom environmental sensitivity overrides the estimated tract value will typically have lower value estimates, and hence are unlikely to have submitted the high bid had environmental risk been zero. The results given in the text are based on the assumption that these firms would never submit the high bid on that particular tract, and hence do not affect estimates of high bids with zero environmental risk. The alternative polar assumption is that these firms are randomly selected from potential bidders. The analysis can be done under this assumption by viewing N_j as endogenous and by performing the calculation with predicted values for N_j in the proportionality factor. Under this assumption, total high bids are predicted to be reduced by $328.2 million. The results of the article are based, however, on the assumption of no effect on high bids, rather than the random selection assumption, both because it appears more realistic and because it maintains the conservative estimate of response to environmental risk.

The results indicate that environmental risk is an important factor in determining high bids on tracts. Employing a robust estimation technique to allow for nonnormality inherent in data on petroleum structures, we predict that high bids are between $1.67 million and $4.33 million lower for the most environmentally sensitive tracts as compared with the least sensitive tracts, other things being equal. Total high bids are estimated to have been reduced by $236.7 million because of industry perceptions of environmental risks from oil spills on Georges Bank. This figure is in excess of 25% of the total high bids actually submitted, and is more than twice the expected environmental damages of $101 million potentially compensable under the OCSLA, as estimated by the U.S. Department of Interior (1979a). Several factors were identified which may explain this discrepancy, including underestimation of damages by the Department of Interior, the costs of adverse publicity resulting from a spill, and risk aversion on the part of firms.

Further evidence, and perhaps more refined estimates, can be provided by extending this analysis to other OCS sales and regions. It may also be of interest to disaggregate environmental risks to individual resources. Owing to high collinearity, it was not possible to disaggregate the environmental risk variable by resource in this article. It would perhaps be of greater potential interest to extend the model presented here to analyze the effect of changes in liability rules by examining OCS regions where lease sales occurred before and after enactment of the OCSLA.

It is not possible to judge with any degree of confidence the extent to which the damage-avoidance behavior revealed in this article is "optimal," since we do not now, nor likely shall we ever, understand the complex effects of oil in the environment to a sufficient degree to determine precise measures of social damage resulting from an oil spill.[14] Nevertheless, the results of this study do indicate that there is a substantial industry response to environmental sensitivity. This suggests that liability for damages has considerable promise as a policy tool for encouraging damage-avoidance behavior.

References

ANDERSON, R.C., CONGAR, R., AND MEADE, N.F. "Emergency Response, Cleanup, and Restoration." *Assessing the Social Costs of Oil Spills: The AMOCO CADIZ Case Study.* Washington, D.C.: U.S. Department of Commerce, N.O.A.A., 1983, pp. 37–56.

ARPS, J.J. "A Strategy for Sealed Bidding." Paper presented at Society of Petroleum Engineers Economics and Evaluation Symposium, Dallas, March 4–5, 1965. Reprinted in Society of Petroleum Engineers Reprint Series, No. 3: *Oil and Gas Property Evaluation and Reserve Estimates,* 1970 ed.

BICKEL, P.J. "One-Step Huber Estimates in the Linear Model." *Journal of the American Statistical Association,* Vol. 70, No. 350 (June 1975), pp. 428–434.

BRADLEY, P.G. "Marine Oil Spills: A Problem in Environmental Management." *Natural Resources Journal,* Vol. 14 (July 1974), pp. 337–359.

BROWN, K.C. *Bidding for Offshore Oil: Toward an Optimal Strategy.* Dallas: Southern Methodist University Press, 1969.

CAPEN, E.C., CLAPP, R.V., AND CAMPBELL, W.M. "Competitive Bidding in High Risk Situations." *Journal of Petroleum Technology* (June 1971), pp. 641–651.

CONRAD, J.M. "Oil Spills: Policies for Prevention, Recovery, and Compensation." *Public Policy,* Vol. 28, No. 2 (Spring 1980), pp. 143–170.

COUNCIL ON ENVIRONMENTAL QUALITY. *OCS Oil and Gas—An Environmental Assessment.* Washington, D.C.: U.S. Government Printing Office, April 1974.

GILLEY, O.W. AND KARELS, G.V. "The Competitive Effect in Bonus Bidding: New Evidence." *Bell Journal of Economics,* Vol. 12, No. 2 (Autumn 1981), pp. 637–648.

GOLDBERGER, A. "Linear Regression after Selection." *Journal of Econometrics* Vol. 15, No. 3 (August 1981), pp. 357–366.

GRIGALUNAS, T.A., ANDERSON, R.C., BROWN, G.M., JR., CONGAR, R., MEADE, N.F., AND SORENSEN, P.E. "The Economic Costs of Oil Spills: Lessons from the AMOCO CADIZ Incident." University of Rhode Island, Department of Resource Economics Staff Paper #83-13, 1983.

---

[14] There are other complications. The Oil Spill Pollution Fund of the OCSLA provides for compensation for transfers and pecuniary effects in addition to social costs. Thus, there is the potential for firms to be held liable for damages that exceed the amount necessary to induce optimal behavior, although there has not been sufficient experience with the administration of the oil spill fund to judge whether this will in fact be the case. For further discussion of the problems involved in quantifying economic damages from oil spills, see Grigalunas et al. (1983).

GUMBEL, E.J. *Statistics of Extremes.* New York: Columbia University Press, 1958.

HECKMAN, J.J. "The Common Structure of Statistical Models of Truncation, Sample Selection and Limited Dependent Variables and a Simple Estimator for Such Models." *Annals of Economic and Social Measurement,* Vol. 5, No. 4 (Fall 1976), pp. 475–492.

————. "Sample Selection Bias as a Specification Error." *Econometrica,* Vol. 47, No. 1 (January 1979), pp. 153–161.

HUBER, P.J. *Robust Statistical Procedures.* Philadelphia: Society for Industrial and Applied Mathematics, 1977.

HUGHART, D. "Informational Asymmetry, Bidding Strategies, and the Marketing of Offshore Petroleum Leases." *Journal of Political Economy,* Vol. 83 (1975), pp. 969–985.

JUST, R.E. AND ZILBERMAN, D. "Asymmetry of Taxes and Subsidies in Regulating Stochastic Mishap." *Quarterly Journal of Economics,* Vol. 93, No. 1 (January 1979), pp. 139–148.

KAUFMAN, G.M. *Statistical Decisions and Related Techniques in Oil and Gas Exploration.* Englewood Cliffs, N.J.: Prentice-Hall, 1963.

MEAD, W.J., SORENSEN, P.E., AND MOSEIDJORD, A. *Competitive Bidding under Asymmetric Information.* Community and Organization Research Institute, University of California, Santa Barbara, 1982.

————, ———— with JONES, R.O. AND MOSEIDJORD, A. *Competition and Performance in OCS Oil and Gas Lease Sales and Lease Development, 1954–1969.* Final Report USGS Contract No. 14-08-0001-16552, Reston, Va.: March 1980.

MILGROM, P.R. "A Convergence Theorem for Competitive Bidding with Differential Information." *Econometrica,* Vol. 47, No. 3 (May 1979).

———— AND WEBER, R.J. "A Theory of Auctions and Competitive Bidding." *Econometrica,* Vol. 50, No. 5 (September 1982).

NATIONAL ACADEMY OF SCIENCES. *Safety and Offshore Oil.* Report by the Committee on Assessment of Safety of OCS Activities, Marine Board, National Research Council. Washington, D.C.: National Academy Press, 1981.

OFFSHORE OIL TASK GROUP. *The Georges Bank Petroleum Study,* Vol. 2. Cambridge: Massachusetts Institute of Technology, 1973.

OLSEN, R.J. "Approximating a Truncated Normal Regression with the Method of Moments." *Econometrica,* Vol. 48, No. 5 (July 1980), pp. 1099–1105.

ORGANIZATION FOR ECONOMIC COOPERATION AND DEVELOPMENT. *The Cost of Oil Spills.* Paris: 1982a.

————. *Combatting Oil Spills: Some Economic Aspects.* Paris: 1982b.

POIRIER, D.J. AND MELINO, A. "A Note on the Interpretation of Regression Coefficients within a Class of Truncated Distributions." *Econometrica,* Vol. 46, No. 5 (September 1978), pp. 1207–1210.

REECE, D. "Competitive Bidding for Offshore Petroleum Leases." *Bell Journal of Economics,* Vol. 9, No. 2 (Autumn 1978), pp. 369–384.

ROBADUE, D.D., JR. AND TIPPIE, V.K. "Public Involvement in Offshore Oil Development: Lessons from New England." *Coastal Zone Management Journal,* Vol. 7 (Fall 1980), pp. 237–270.

ROTHKOPF, M.H. "A Model of Rational Competitive Bidding." *Management Science,* Vol. 15, No. 7 (March 1969), pp. 362–373.

SMITH, R.A., SLACK, J.R., AND DAVIS, R.K. *An Oil Spill Risk Analysis for the North Atlantic Outer Continental Shelf Lease Area.* U.S. Geological Survey Open-File Report 76-620. Reston, Va.: U.S. Geological Survey, 1976.

UHLER, R.S. AND BRADLEY, P.G. "A Stochastic Model for Determining the Economic Prospects of Petroleum Exploration over Large Regions." *Journal of the American Statistical Association,* Vol. 65, No. 330 (June 1970), pp. 623–630.

UNITED STATES CONGRESS. *Outer Continental Shelf Lands Act Amendments of 1978.* Pub. L. 95-372, 95th Congress.

U.S. COUNCIL ON ENVIRONMENTAL QUALITY. *OCS Oil and Gas—an Environmental Assessment,* 5 Vols., 1974.

U.S. DEPARTMENT OF INTERIOR, BUREAU OF LAND MANAGEMENT. *Final Environmental Statement,* OCS Sale No. 42, 5 Vols., 1977.

————. "Secretarial Issues Document, OCS Sale No. 42." Washington, D.C.: June 1979a.

————. "USGS Presale Resource Estimates for Successfully Bid Tracts, North Atlantic Sale 42 (December 1979)." 1979b.

————, BUREAU OF LAND MANAGEMENT, NEW YORK OCS OFFICE. "OCS Sale #042 Condensed Bid Recap by Tract." Mimeo, 1980a.

————. "Interior Accepts High Bids of $816,616,546 from Georges Bank Lease Sale." Mimeo, January 15, 1980b.

————. *Final Environmental Impact Statement, Proposed Five-Year OCS Oil and Gas Lease Sale Schedule, January, 1982–December, 1986.* Washington, D.C.: 1981.

————, MINERALS MANAGEMENT SERVICE. "Description of MMS Resource Economic Evaluation Model." Unpublished manuscript by Gary Lore, 1982a.

————. "Estimated Risked Expected Net Present Worth of Tracts Sold at Lease Sale #42." John Lee, personal communication, 1982b.

WILSON, R.B. "A Bidding Model of Perfect Competition." *Review of Economic Studies,* Vol. 44, No. 3 (October 1977), pp. 511–518.

[20]

Risk Premiums for Environmental Liability: Does Superfund Increase the Cost of Capital?[1]

Steven Garber*

RAND, 1700 Main St., Santa Monica, California 90407

and

James K. Hammitt[†]

Harvard University, School of Public Health, 718 Huntington Ave., Boston, Massachusetts 02115

Received August 26, 1997; revised July 1998

Superfund liability may impose financial risk on investors and thereby increase firms' costs of capital. We analyze monthly stock returns for 73 chemical companies using several measures of Superfund exposure. Additional exposure appears to increase costs of capital for larger firms, but perhaps not for smaller firms. From 1988 to 1992, we estimate an average increase in cost of capital for 23 larger firms of between 0.25 to 0.40 percentage points per year. The social cost of Superfund-related financial risk in the chemical industry may be as high as $800 million annually or enough to clean up about 20 sites. © 1998 Academic Press

1. INTRODUCTION

The federal "Superfund" law, enacted in December 1980, imposes liability on firms, municipalities, and other "potentially responsible parties" (PRPs) for cleaning up contaminated sites selected by the U.S. Environmental Protection Agency (EPA). The effects of the program have received considerable attention from researchers. Costs to PRPs are expected to be substantial. Future (undiscounted) Superfund cleanup costs have been estimated as $100–$300 billion over 30 years [40]. CBO [43] estimates a present value of total cleanup costs of $42–$120 billion (using a 7% discount rate), of which an estimated 58% will be paid directly by PRPs. Although the value of environmental and health benefits is difficult to estimate, there is considerable reason to believe that—for at least some Superfund sites—federal standards push cleanup well beyond the point where incremental

[1]This work was supported by the U.S. Environmental Protection Agency through a cooperative agreement with RAND and by the Institute for Civil Justice at RAND. We thank an associate editor and two very constructive referees, John Adams, Lloyd Dixon, Suzanne Giannini-Spohn, Ed Keating, Richard Morgenstern, Dan Relles, Roland Sturm, Mark Weinstein, Martin Weitzman, and seminar participants at Harvard University and the AERE annual meeting for helpful discussion and comments; Perry Beider, Tom Gillis, and Katherine Probst for generously providing information; Susan McGlamery and Roberta Shanman for extensive help in locating information; and Sung-Ho Ahn for capable and tireless programming assistance. Opinions are those of the authors and do not necessarily reflect the views of RAND or its research sponsors.

* E-mail address: Steven_Garber@rand.org.
† E-mail address: jkh@hsph.harvard.edu.

benefits exceed incremental costs [23, 24, 42]. In addition, PRPs bear litigation and other transaction costs in determining how a site will be cleaned up and how costs will be shared. Transaction costs have been estimated as 10-40% of PRP cleanup costs [2, 14].

Even though liability for *past* waste disposal practices appears unavoidable (sunk), Superfund may also affect business behavior and resource allocation outside the environmental sphere by raising a firm's cost of capital. According to standard reasoning in finance, investors require higher expected returns on securities they perceive to be riskier. Whether Superfund liability—which is hard to predict—makes holding a firm's securities riskier to investors depends on whether they can diversify the associated variability in the firm's returns.

We examine whether Superfund liability increases the cost of capital, focusing on the chemical industry, which is expected to bear a larger share of Superfund costs than any other industry. Potential Superfund costs in this industry appear large enough relative to profits for cost-of-capital effects to be plausible. Probst *et al.* [37] estimate that the chemical industry will bear 25% of total Superfund costs, suggesting industry costs on the order of $1 billion per year. The (almost 50) Fortune 500 chemical companies had profits of about $6 billion in 1991 and losses of about $4 billion in 1992, the last 2 years of our sample period [17, 18].

We are aware of only one econometric study examining effects of Superfund on financial risks of any kind.[2] Dalton, Riggs, and Yandle [11] examine stocks of 23 petroleum and 19 chemical companies and estimate risk effects during periods of roughly two weeks surrounding each of eight Superfund-related events between August 1978 and December 1980. That study provides little information on costs of capital, as it considers only a short period (before Superfund was implemented) and does not consider differences between firms in exposure to liability.

In contrast—and consistent with the finance literature—we define cost-of-capital effects (if any) to be long-lived. We view differences in potential liability across companies as the key to estimating such effects. More specifically, we analyze returns to common stocks of individual chemical companies traded on the New York or American stock exchanges during the period 1976–1992. We analyze how monthly returns since December 1980 (when Superfund was enacted) vary among firms according to their differing levels of exposure to potential Superfund-related cleanup and litigation costs.

Cost-of-capital effects may differ among firms of very different sizes for several reasons, and our estimates suggest a difference. Among the largest chemical companies in our sample, costs of capital appear to increase with potential Superfund costs, but there is no consistent evidence of such an effect among the smallest companies. The lack of consistent evidence for smaller firms may be due to investors having little information about relative Superfund exposure of smaller firms or forming divergent assessments of relative exposure. The results for large chemical companies suggest that (a) investors are aware of differences in potential financial liabilities among these firms, and (b) capital markets penalize large firms for past waste-disposal activities not only at the time that such liabilities come to light, but also during the protracted period while liabilities are resolved and actual costs are determined. Increases in the cost of capital represent social costs of

---

[2]Sohl and Wetzel [41] present survey evidence suggesting that Superfund liability increases costs of capital for very small firms.

bearing financial risk. We estimate that, for the chemical industry, this cost is several hundred million dollars per year, of the order of half as large as the industry's annual cleanup cost.

Section 2 provides background on aspects of the Superfund program. Section 3 describes our methods. Results are presented in Sections 4 and 5, and our conclusions are in Section 6.

2. THE SUPERFUND PROGRAM

The Superfund program was established under the Comprehensive Environmental Response, Compensation, and Liability Act of 1980 (CERCLA). The final form of CERCLA—or passage of any legislation in 1980 addressing inactive toxic waste sites—could not have been confidently predicted before the Presidential election in November [19]. CERCLA was amended by the 1986 Superfund Amendments and Reauthorization Act (SARA) after 3 years of Congressional activity and a House–Senate conference that reconciled two very different bills between February and October 1986 [3]. Since 1986, Superfund has been reauthorized but not amended.

PRP liability is very broad. It is "retroactive, strict, and joint and several," meaning that a single firm may be held liable for all remediation costs at a site even if the firm contributed only a small proportion of the hazardous materials and acted in accordance with established, legal practice of the time.

The federal Superfund program involves sites judged to present particularly serious environmental and public-health risks. Such sites are formally "listed" by the EPA on the National Priorities List (NPL). For a site on the NPL, the EPA informs parties it identifies of their status as PRPs. Other parties may become involved when they are identified and sued by PRPs for "contribution" (i.e., to share the cost).

As of May 1996, the NPL contained 1073 sites, excluding federal facilities [48]. The eventual number of NPL sites may be as low as 2000 [37, p. 20] or as high as 7800 [43]. The eventual number of sites cleaned up under state programs similar to the federal program may far exceed the number under the federal program.[3] The average state site is believed to be much less costly to clean up than the average NPL site, however, and the total cost of cleaning up state sites may turn out to be much less than the total cost of cleaning up the NPL sites.[4]

The prototypical Superfund process at a site involves substantial time, money, and uncertainty for PRPs. Cleanup proceeds through a number of lengthy, formalized stages that determine the magnitude and timing of costs [1]. The typical time from listing to completing construction of the remedy is a decade or longer [1, 44]. There are few accepted principles for allocating responsibility and negotiations can be protracted. The allocation may be based on the volume and the toxicity of the materials each PRP contributed to the site, but such information is often unavailable.

---

[3]As of 1993, the number of "known and suspected non-NPL sites" was more than 100,000 with more than 40,000 of them having been "identified by States as needing attention." [46, p. 61].

[4]The cost of cleaning up the state sites is estimated to be about 20% of the cost of cleaning up the NPL sites [40].

In addition to uncertainty about site-level costs and their allocation, the future of the entire program has been a source of substantial uncertainty about eventual costs to PRPs. The constitutionality of many of the key liability provisions were challenged in court, and eventually upheld [4, 30]. The extent of coverage provided to PRPs via commercial liability insurance has been extensively litigated in the state courts. The administration of the program has also undergone occasional review and revision (e.g., [38]).

3. THEORY AND METHODS

Basic Financial Theory

A firm's cost of capital is determined by the expected rate of return investors require to hold the firm's securities (e.g., stocks and bonds). It is widely accepted in the finance literature that: (a) investors require a higher expected return on a security the more risky it is for them to hold that security; and (b) the riskiness of a security to investors depends on the extent to which they can offset the variability in its future returns by incorporating the security in a portfolio. A key implication is that a firm's cost of capital is higher the greater is the undiversifiable or systematic risk of its securities.

As in the empirical finance literature, our econometric work focuses on returns to common stocks (equity). Greater exposure to Superfund liability should decrease the value of a company's stock—by increasing investors' expectations of future costs—and may also affect the cost of capital by increasing systematic risk. Figure 1 illustrates this distinction.

In the figure, $\ln V$ is the logarithm of the value of a company's stock, which is plotted against time. Before date τ, the rate of return on the stock (the slope of the line segment AB) is higher the greater is the systematic risk of holding the asset during this period, as assessed by investors. At time τ, assume that investors suddenly become aware that the company may be held liable for (additional) Superfund costs. Suppose first that this news has no effect on investor assessments of systematic risk. Then the value of the company's stock will decrease from its value at B to its value at C to reflect the present value of expected (additional) Superfund costs, but the expected rate of return on the stock after τ will be the same as before τ (CD is parallel to AB). In this case there is a *wealth* effect of Superfund, but no effect on the cost of capital. Alternatively, suppose that investors perceive an increase in systematic risk along with the (additional) Superfund costs. Then the expected rate of return of the stock starting at τ will be higher (EF is steeper than AB)—as it must be to compensate investors for the increased risk—and the wealth effect will be larger (from B to E). Note that wealth effects occur immediately[5] but cost-of-capital effects would persist until the additional systematic risk is resolved.

The extent to which firm-level risks can be diversified by investors is often unclear *a priori*, as is the case with the risks of interest here. Some risks associated with exposure to Superfund liability are related to factors specific to individual

---

[5]Wealth effects of selected Superfund developments are estimated using "event study" methods by [5, 11, 26].

SUPERFUND AND THE COST OF CAPITAL 271

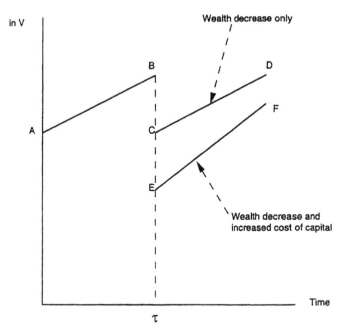

FIG. 1. Wealth and cost of capital effects of an increase in Superfund exposure at date τ.

sites (e.g., the extent of contamination, costs and effectiveness of selected remedies, outcomes of lawsuits) and are likely to be diversifiable. Other risks involve
more general—and less diversifiable—determinants of future Superfund costs
(e.g., total number of sites to be cleaned up, cleanup standards, innovation in
treatment technologies) as well as non-Superfund factors that may be correlated
with Superfund costs such as the future stringency of other environmental regulations and liability. In short, the degree to which Superfund risks are diversifiable is
an empirical question.

Using the Capital Asset Pricing Model to Estimate Superfund Effects

The asset-pricing theories most commonly used in empirical work are the capital
asset pricing model (CAPM) and the arbitrage pricing theory (APT). We report
estimates based on CAPM, which is simpler and more often used. We obtained
similar results using APT.[6]

According to CAPM, the systematic risk of a security depends on the correlation
between its return and the return on a market portfolio of securities. The larger
the correlation, the less the variability in a security's return can be diversified by
combining it with the market portfolio.

We estimate effects of Superfund by augmenting a standard CAPM specification. In a standard specification, one might estimate the systematic risk of the stock

---

[6]Details are contained in an Appendix available from the authors.

of company i by regressing r_{it}, its return during time period t, on RM_t, the contemporaneous return on a broad portfolio of stocks (where both returns are expressed as deviations from the return on a risk-free security),

$$r_{it} = \alpha + \beta_i RM_t + \varepsilon_{it}. \tag{1}$$

The regression coefficient in (1), $\beta_i = \partial E(r_{it})/\partial RM_t$, is commonly called firm i's *equity beta*. It measures the sensitivity of the return on the stock to fluctuations in the return on the market portfolio (generally called the "market return").

We analyze potential effects of Superfund on costs of capital by first analyzing econometrically whether firms' equity betas vary—other things equal—in accordance with their relative levels of exposure to Superfund liability.[7] Specifically, we analyze a generalization of (1) in which firms' equity betas are assumed to be determined as

$$\beta_i = \theta_i + \gamma X_{it}, \tag{2}$$

where X_{it} is a measure of firm i's exposure to Superfund liability at time t (as perceived by investors) and θ_i is a firm-specific baseline β for firm i (i.e., β_i in the absence of Superfund liability). The goal is to estimate $\gamma = \partial \beta_i / \partial X_{it}$, which measures the sensitivity of investor risk to (perceived) Superfund exposure.

We also add variables to improve efficiency and to guard against bias in estimating γ. Combining (1) and (2), pooling firms, and including X_{it} and $CHMSHK_{it}$ yields the estimating equation,

$$r_{it} = \alpha + \theta_i D_i RM_t + \gamma X_{it} RM_t + \delta X_{it} + \rho CHMSHK_{it} + \varepsilon_{it}, \tag{3}$$

where the D_i are dummy variables distinguishing firms. The dependent variable in (3) is defined as the return on the stock of company i in month t in excess of the return on 30-day U.S. Treasury bills (a common choice for a risk-free security).[8] Our measure of the market return RM_t is the return in month t on a value-weighted portfolio of all stocks traded on the New York and American exchanges (NYSE and AMEX), also expressed as a deviation from the return on 30-day Treasury bills.

The exposure measure X_{it} is included because many Superfund-related shocks (for example, court rulings that were not entirely anticipated) should affect firms' values in proportion to their exposure.[9] The variable $CHMSHK_{it}$ is an index of returns to the sample firms *other than firm i* in month t—constructed by weighting

---

[7] Firm-specific equity betas have been used to study the effects of rate-of-return regulation [36] and adoption of nuclear power [16] on electric utilities' cost of equity capital.

[8] Table I collects names and descriptions of all variables and details data sources.

[9] We also exclude from estimation data for 12 months during which we expect particularly important unanticipated Superfund events: November and December of 1980 (the months during which the final CERCLA took shape and was signed into law) and January–October 1986 (the last 10 months of the protracted Congressional activity that produced SARA). We searched several commentaries on the case law for landmark court rulings that might have had major impacts on chemical companies, but none was apparent. Broadly stated, (federal) court rulings on challenges to the major aspects of the CERCLA liability standards (i.e., strict, joint and several, and retroactive) were a series of district court rulings upholding the standards and subsequent circuit court rulings upholding the district court rulings. Individual rulings in state courts on the exclusion of insurance coverage did not seem sufficiently discrete and important to warrant deletion of sample months.

returns by market equities in the previous month—minus RM_t.[10] It is included to control jointly for industry-wide shocks unrelated to Superfund and Superfund-related shocks whose effects are not proportional to exposure. To examine specification sensitivity, we also estimate equations without $CHMSHK_{it}$.

Finally, ε_{it} is a stochastic disturbance with mean zero. To allow for shocks that are common to the chemical industry but not captured by our independent variables, we use standard random-effects (or error-components) specifications. In particular, we assume that

$$\varepsilon_{it} = v_t + e_{it},$$

where e_{it} is assumed i.i.d. with variance Var(e) and the monthly random effects v_t are assumed uncorrelated across months and to have constant variance Var(v).

Equations are estimated by OLS and GLS (the latter allowing for the random, monthly effects). If Var(v) = 0, then Eq. (3) is classical and OLS estimation is appropriate. If Var(v) > 0, then the regression disturbances are correlated across companies in each month and GLS estimation is appropriate. We report a Lagrange-multiplier statistic—based on Breusch and Pagan [8]—for the presence of the monthly random component.[11] Its distribution is χ^2 with 1 degree of freedom under the null hypothesis that Var(v) = 0. Relatively large values of the statistic favor rejection and GLS estimation.

The random monthly components represent industry-wide shocks in a less restrictive way than captured by *CHMSHK*. We view these components as a complement to *CHMSHK* when it is included in tne regression and as a substitute for *CHMSHK* when it is excluded from the regression. However, because we are not conditioning on these components, the random-effects specification yields inconsistent estimates if the random effects are correlated with the regressors.[12] Thus, we view the equations including *CHMSHK* as more reliable, and we highlight them in the text, because they control explicitly for (some) industry-wide shocks.[13]

Effects on Equity Betas and Effects on Costs of Capital

Estimation of (3) allows us to examine whether more Superfund exposure makes it riskier to hold a firm's stocks, and therefore increases its cost of *equity* capital. A firm's overall cost of capital—which is the object of study—depends on the cost of equity capital, cost of debt (i.e., required returns on bonds) and the firm's financial leverage. Wealth effects of Superfund, by reducing the value of a firm's equity, would increase financial leverage and the riskiness of the firm's stock even if Superfund does not increase the firm's overall cost of capital. Translating estimates of effects on firm equity betas into effects on overall costs of capital (if any) involves the following considerations.

---

[10] The exclusion of the return of firm i and the use of lagged weights are to avoid simultaneity with r_{it}.

[11] See, for example, Greene [22, pp. 491–492] or Judge *et al.* [31, p. 526].

[12] See, for example, Greene [22, pp. 494–495] or Judge *et al.* [31, p. 537].

[13] Fixed-effects estimation—i.e., including a dummy variable for each sample month, thereby conditioning on the monthly effects—would produce perfect colinearity because RM_t is constant across firms in each month. Thus we cannot perform a specification test for the consistency of the random-effects specification [25]. See, for example, Greene [22, p. 495] or Judge *et al.* [31, p. 537].

Following standard analyses in finance (e.g., [39, Chap. 12]), a firm's overall cost of capital is a weighted average of its costs of equity and debt,

$$r = \left(\frac{E}{E + D}\right) r_E + \left(\frac{D}{E + D}\right) r_D, \tag{4}$$

where:

r = the firm's (overall) cost of capital (percent per month),
r_E = the firm's cost of equity capital (percent per month),
r_D = the firm's cost of debt (percent per month),
E = market value of the firm's equity (stocks), and
D = market value of the firm's debt (bonds).

The cost of equity capital is

$$r_E = R_F + \beta RM, \tag{5}$$

where β is the beta for the firm's stock, R_F is the risk-free rate of return, and RM is the rate of return on the market portfolio in excess of risk-free rate. With the standard assumption that $r_D = R_F$ (i.e., ignoring any systematic risk on debt), combining (4) and (5) yields

$$r = R_F + \left(\frac{E}{E + D}\right) \beta RM. \tag{6}$$

Finally, because Superfund (potentially) increases β and decreases E (through the wealth effect), but does not affect R_F or RM, the change in a firm's overall cost of capital due to Superfund is

$$\Delta r = \left[\left(\frac{E}{E + D}\right)(\beta + \Delta\beta) - \left(\frac{E + \Delta E}{E + \Delta E + D}\right)\beta\right] RM, \tag{7}$$

where β is the equity β without Superfund, $\Delta\beta$ is the increase under Superfund, E is firm equity with Superfund, and $\Delta E > 0$ is the wealth effect; i.e., the equity lost due to Superfund liability. Estimates of γ from (3) tell us only about changes in β. Superfund would be inferred to increase overall costs of capital only if estimated percentage increases in β exceed percentage decreases in $E/(E + D)$ due to wealth effects.

Data

We focus on a single industry for three reasons. First, links from feasible measures of Superfund exposure to potential changes in systematic risk may differ across industries. Second, costs of capital may be sensitive to (unmeasured) contemporaneous exposure to environmental regulations or forms of environmental liability other than Superfund (e.g., tort for personal injury or natural-resource damages). We expect that correlations between Superfund exposure and other regulatory and liability exposure is greater between industries than within them, so that restricting attention to a single industry guards against bias due to such unmeasured factors. Finally, focusing on a single industry reduces potential confounding by still other factors that may differentially affect returns across industries.

Because cost-of-capital effects, if any, could be subtle, it seems sensible to look first where they are most likely to exist. We focus, then, on chemical manufacturing—an industry in which companies are especially heavily exposed to Superfund liability.

We estimate models over the period January 1976 through December 1992. Data on monthly stock returns (adjusted for dividends and splits) are from the Center for Research on Securities Prices (CRSP). Our sample includes 73 firms with stock traded for at least 24 months after December 1980 on either the NYSE or AMEX, and for which the primary three-digit SIC code (as reported by CRSP) during any month after the passage of CERCLA was 281 (industrial inorganic chemicals), 282 (plastics), 285 (paints), 286 (industrial organic chemicals), or 289 (miscellaneous chemical products).[14]

We estimate cost of capital effects using all available observations. We also estimate using subsets of observations selected by real market equity (ME). This allows us to examine separately the experience of relatively large and small firms, which is of interest for reasons discussed presently. Rather than assigning *firms* to groups, we defined our subsamples using post-CERCLA *firm-month pairs* to avoid eliminating firms that grew or shrank rapidly during the post-CERCLA period.[15]

Our definitions of relatively large and small firms were based on three objectives: (a) providing meaningful separation between the two groups; (b) having sufficient sample variation in Superfund exposure to allow usefully precise estimation;[16] and (c) using round numbers as cutoffs. The "high-ME sample" and the "low-ME sample" include, respectively, observations for the 23 firms having real market equity over $1 billion and the 54 firms having real market equity under $500 million for at least 24 months post-CERCLA (December 1979 dollars).[17] Each estimation sample includes *all* pre-CERCLA observations for all firms that contribute post-CERCLA observations to that sample and all post-CERCLA observations meeting the relevant market equity criterion. The number of post-CERCLA observations for the low-ME sample (4356) is considerably larger than the corresponding number for the high-ME sample (1871).[18] Tables A.I and A.II (in the Appendix) list the sample companies and describe the composition of the samples in some detail.

[14] The excluded three-digit industries from the (two-digit) chemicals major industry group include pharmaceuticals, soaps and detergents, and agricultural chemicals.

[15] For example, if CERCLA had major financial impacts on some firms that were relatively large before 1980, eliminating them from consideration could mask the effects under study. In an earlier version of this article, however, we assigned firms to groups and obtained similar results to those reported here.

[16] In choosing the cutoffs defining the two samples, we attempted to achieve some balance in the total sums of squares of the number of sites at which firms were named (around the respective group means).

[17] Throughout, nominal market equity is deflated using a monthly price index (December 1979 = 1.0) constructed from smoothed quarterly values of the implicit price deflator for gross domestic product.

[18] For the full period, total observations in the low-ME and high-ME samples are 3089 and 6456, respectively. The unequal sample sizes resulted from our effort to balance the amount of sample information available to estimate cost-of-capital effects. Despite the larger post-CERCLA sample size for the low-ME group, the post-CERCLA total sum of squared deviations for the number of NPL sites at which firms are named is considerably larger for the high-ME sample (roughly 535,000 as compared with 180,000).

We consider separately sets of observations grouped by firm size because effects of differences in levels of Superfund liability could differ between very large and much smaller firms. The market equities of the sample firms during the post-CERCLA period range over 4 orders of magnitude, but the numbers of sites at which firms are named do not vary nearly in proportion (see Table A.I). This suggests that relative Superfund liability may be a more important factor among smaller firms. Potentially offsetting this effect, however, investors may expect larger firms to bear a disproportionate share of Superfund costs because they have deeper pockets or because smaller firms may more readily escape government attention and suits for contribution by other PRPs. Perhaps more importantly, there is considerable evidence (discussed in the following text) that investors were less well informed about the relative Superfund exposure of smaller companies.[19]

Superfund Exposure Measures

Conceptually, the Superfund exposure variable (X_{it}) represents investors' assessments in month t about firm i's future Superfund costs, including those associated with future NPL and state sites. Because it is impossible to reconstruct investor perceptions, we employ six alternative measures based on different assumptions about what investors knew and when.

Investors appear to have been poorly informed about potential Superfund liabilities. Firms did not typically disclose information about Superfund exposure in financial reports to investors and the Securities and Exchange Commission (SEC), at least up through 1992, the last year in our data. According to legal guidelines, firms are required to disclose Superfund liabilities only if they are "material."[20] On May 11, 1988 a front-page story in the *Wall Street Journal*—with the headline: "See No Evil: Can $100 Billion Have 'No Material Effect' On Balance Sheets?" [35]—reported that few companies had been providing quantitative information about future liabilities for toxic waste cleanups and that "Wall Street has yet to confront the potential [financial] damage [of Superfund]."[21]

Investors may, of course, know more about potential Superfund liabilities than companies report. For example, the EPA maintains a publicly available database (SETS), which lists by NPL site the PRPs notified by EPA. It seems, however, that this information was barely used by the investment community. An electronic search of investment-bank research reports turned up only one report providing quantitative information about Superfund exposure of individual firms.[22] That report [32] describes a Kidder, Peabody & Co. database claimed to provide the only

[19] Separate estimation for firm size classes also may be warranted because the structure of returns may differ by firm size [9, 10, 15].

[20] Material information is "information that a reasonable investor would consider significant in making an investment decision" [27, p. 84].

[21] Moody's Investor's Services is reported to have started requiring "companies to provide financial data about environmental liabilities" in 1988 [33]. Geltman [20, pp. 130–131] reports that SEC enforcement was stepped up "[p]artially in response to" the 1988 *Wall Street Journal* article [35]. Even after our sample period, many companies were failing to report material environmental liabilities, and it was predicted that the SEC would soon crack down [21].

[22] We searched the Investext database for the period 1985–1992 using the keywords "Superfund," "CERCLA," and "hazardous waste." The database is described as "the world's largest database of company, topical, and geographic analysis ... comprised of more than 320,000 full-text reports written by analysts at 180 prestigious investment banks and research firms worldwide" [12].

then-existing capability (government or private) to link sites to PRPs and to count the sites at which a company or one of its subsidiaries is named. In 1992, the Investor Responsibility Research Center began reporting to its subscribers the number of NPL sites at which each Standard and Poors (S & P) 500 firm or any of its subsidiaries is listed as a PRP [29].

At least through 1992 (the end of our sample period), investors' information about Superfund exposure of individual firms may have been restricted almost entirely to NPL sites listed by that time, and information about even those sites may have been quite sketchy. Information appears to have been even more limited for smaller firms. For example, IRRC [29] covers only companies in the S & P 500, and econometric evidence suggests that (other factors held constant) larger firms tend to disclose more about environmental liabilities [6, 34].

We construct alternative exposure variables based on different assumptions about the amount and timing of information possessed by investors. A central component of each is the set of NPL sites at which a firm (or any of its subsidiaries) is named as a PRP. (We count each site only once, even if multiple subsidiaries are named.)[23] Our counts of the number of sites at which each sample firm is named in SETS by December 1992 are reported in Table A.I.[24]

All exposure measures are defined to equal zero prior to passage of CERCLA. Our six alternative measures (detailed in Table I) result from combining an assumption about when investors become aware of a firm's exposure at a particular site with an assumption about investors' beliefs about the cost of being exposed at a site. The two assumptions about when investors become aware of a site are:

• "Farsighted versions" (for which the variable name begins with F) assume investors foresee the sites at which each firm would be named through December 1992 as soon as any site where the firm is named is proposed for listing on the NPL.[25]

• "Myopic versions" (for which the variable name begins with M) assume investors become aware of a firm's PRP status at each site only when the site is proposed for listing on the NPL.

The three assumptions about investor assessments of costs to a firm of being named as a PRP at an individual site are (in increasing order of information used

---

[23] We used Disclosure Information Service [13] to identify—from 10-K forms filed for 1992 with the SEC—subsidiaries of the chemical firms in our sample, and we searched the December 15, 1992 version of SETS [45] for the names of these parents and subsidiaries. The process of matching names was laborious because of the use of various forms for a firm name and abbreviations and misspellings in SETS (which includes roughly 20,700 distinct PRP names). All matches made by computer were manually verified, and all PRP names that appeared more than once in SETS but did not produce a match were checked to verify that they were not one of our 73 companies or any of the subsidiaries identified.

[24] We found 212 NPL sites at which one or more of our sample firms was named.

[25] Almost all sites that are proposed for the NPL are eventually listed: as of May 1996, of the 1462 sites that had ever been proposed for listing, 1335 (91%) had been listed, 75 (5%) had been dropped without listing, and 52 (4%) remained pending [48]. Consistent with the view that the news is in the proposal rather than in the official listing, an electronic search of the *Wall Street Journal* uncovered five stories during our sample period (December 21, 1982; September 2, 1983; October 3, 1984; September 6, 1985; July 14, 1989) reporting on EPA proposals to expand the NPL and none reporting official listings of sites.

TABLE I

Variable Names, Descriptions, and Data Sources

Name	Description	Data sources
D_i	= 1 for company i, zero otherwise	
	Financial variables	
r_{it}	Return on stock of company i in month t minus return in month t on 30-day Treasury bills ($\times 10^3$)	Stock returns: CRSP Treasury bill returns: Ibbotson Associates (1993, Table A-14) Market index: CRSP (NYSE and AMEX combined)
RM_t	Excess (over 30-day T-bill) return on value-weighted market index in month t ($\times 10^3$)	
ME_{it}	Real market equity of firm i in month t (in millions of December 1979 dollars)	Nominal market equities: CRSP; GDP deflator: Economic Reports of the President
$CHMSHK_{it}$	Return in t for sample chemical companies other than i (weighted by market equities in $t-1$) ($\times 10^3$) minus RM_t	
	Superfund exposure: All equal zero before CERCLA and otherwise equal	
$F\#SITES_{it}$	Number of NPL sites at which company i is named through December 15, 1992 (equals zero until first month company is named at any site)	Subsidiaries of chemical companies: Disclosure (1993) Sites identified from EPA (1992)
$M\#SITES_{it}$	Number of sites proposed for NPL by month t at which company i is named through December 15, 1992	Site proposal dates: EPA (1994)
$F\#/OWNEQ_{it}$ $M\#/OWNEQ_{it}$ $FEQSHR_{it}$	$F\#SITES_{it}$ divided by ME_{it} ($\times 10^8$) $M\#SITES_{it}$ divided by ME_{it} ($\times 10^8$) Sum over sites (included in $F\#SITES$) of company i's share of combined (month t) market equity of large PRPs at site, divided by ME_{it} ($\times 10^{16}$)	Market equities: CRSP S & P 500 PRPs: IRRC (1992) Market equities: CRSP for NYSE and AMEX companies, COMPUSTAT for others
$MEQSHR_{it}$	Sum over sites (included in $M\#SITES$) of company i's share of combined (month t) market equity of large PRPs at site, divided by ME_{it} ($\times 10^{16}$)	
$SITES88_{it}$ $OWNEQ88_{it}$ $EQSHR88_{it}$	Equals zero before May 1988 and $F\#SITES_{it}$ otherwise Equals zero before May 1988 and $F\#/OWNEQ_{it}$ otherwise Equals zero before May 1988 and $FEQSHR_{it}$ otherwise	

by investors):

- Investors assess exposure in proportion to a count of sites at which a firm is named. Variables based on this assumption have *#SITES* in their name.

- Exposure is proportional to the number of sites at which a firm is named relative to the real market equity of the firm. These variables have *#/OWNEQ* (*own equity*) in their names.

- Exposure of firm *i* at each site is proportional to its share of real market equity among S & P 500 PRPs and other sample chemical companies—which we refer to jointly as "large PRPs"—also named at that site. These exposure variables have *EQSHR* (*equity share*) in their names.

Exposure measures *F#SITES* and *M#SITES* may seem naive because they are not scaled relative to the size of the company and the dependent variable is a rate of return. Exposure measures *F#/OWNEQ* and *M#/OWNEQ* do explicitly express exposure relative to the size of the firm, but are not sensitive to what other companies are named as PRPs along with company *i*. These measures might be interpreted as pessimistic in that each PRP is assumed to be liable for the entire cost of a site. Finally, measures *FEQSHR* and *MEQSHR*—which explicitly account for other large PRPs and their relative sizes—are motivated by the possibility that costs will be allocated in proportion to the respective depths of the PRPs' pockets. The exposure measures do not involve variation across sites in expected cleanup costs or litigation expenses because there was no reliable source of such information—at least during our sample period—for investors or researchers.[26]

Table II presents correlation matrices for the complete sample and the high- and low-ME samples computed without months prior to January 1981 (for which all exposure measures are zero). For the full sample, the correlations between pairs of exposure measures range from virtually 0 up to about 0.96. Within the high-ME sample, all of the correlations are substantial, ranging from 0.33 to 0.91. For the low-ME sample, the correlations are sometimes smaller and sometimes larger than those for the high-ME sample and range more widely. There is, then, econometric and substantive relevance to considering various measures of investor assessments of relative Superfund exposure.

Examining sensitivity of inferences to the use of alternative exposure measures not only allows us to gauge the extent to which our inferences may require reliance on a particular measure; it also provides information concerning the extent to which our estimates of cost-of-capital effects are attributable to Superfund rather than to environmental costs or liabilities more generally. Specifically, the six alternative exposure measures incorporate different pieces of Superfund-specific information; such details seem unlikely to be highly correlated with other environmental liabilities.[27]

---

[26] For example, even an EPA database compiled by surveying Superfund site managers in 1992—"U.S. EPA Superfund Program Survey for GAO/CBO/RFF"—contained expected cost information for only about half of NPL sites. (Tabulations from data provided in May 1993 by Perry Beider of CBO.)

[27] We expect that our measures and estimates reflect to some extent investor assessments of exposure at future NPL sites and state sites because exposure at current NPL sites may be used to assess those other liabilities.

GARBER AND HAMMITT

TABLE II

Correlations among Exposure Measures: Post-CERCLA Observations (1981–1992)

	F#SITES	F#/OWNEQ	FEQSHR	M#SITES	M#/OWNEQ	MEQSHR
			Full sample, 7624 observations			
F#SITES	1					
F#/OWNEQ	−0.007	1				
FEQSHR	−0.072	0.725	1			
M#SITES	0.942	−0.017	−0.069	1		
M#/OWNEQ	−0.018	0.961	0.753	−0.002	1	
MEQSHR	−0.056	0.824	0.884	−0.050	0.859	1
			High market equity sample, 1871 observations			
F#SITES	1					
F#/OWNEQ	0.472	1				
FEQSHR	0.490	0.667	1			
M#SITES	0.908	0.414	0.329	1		
M#/OWNEQ	0.405	0.909	0.504	0.500	1	
MEQSHR	0.511	0.707	0.644	0.601	0.800	1
			Low market equity sample, 4356 observations			
F#SITES	1					
F#/OWNEQ	0.182	1				
FEQSHR	−0.061	0.722	1			
M#SITES	0.923	0.158	−0.060	1		
M#/OWNEQ	0.136	0.959	0.750	0.166	1	
MEQSHR	−0.044	0.827	0.883	−0.035	0.861	1

Finally, effects of across-firm differences in Superfund exposure may have increased as information improved during the later part of the sample period. Accordingly, we consider supplementary specifications allowing shifts in the regression relationships in May 1988, when the *Wall Street Journal* called attention to financial disclosure of Superfund liabilities and triggered additional attention by the SEC [35].

4. ESTIMATED EFFECTS ON EQUITY BETAS

Equation (3) is estimated for all 73 sample firms (Table III) and separately for the high- and low-ME samples (Tables IV and V).[28] For each sample, we considered twelve specifications alternatively representing Superfund exposure (X_{it}) by each of six measures and including or excluding *CHMSHK*.

Each specification is estimated by OLS and GLS. Tables III and V report GLS estimates because the data indicate a monthly error component for the full and low-ME samples. In Table IV we report OLS estimates because for the high-ME sample the first step of the GLS estimator produced negative—albeit very small—values for the variance of the monthly component,[29] from which we infer

---

[28] Descriptive statistics for the three samples are presented in Table A.II.

[29] The values are less than 1% of the estimated variance of the error term.

SUPERFUND AND THE COST OF CAPITAL   281

TABLE III

Regression Estimates for Full Sample (73 Firms)
(GLS estimates with monthly random effects)
(asymptotic t-statistic)

	F#SITES	F#/OWNEQ	FEQSHR	M#SITES	M#/OWNEQ	MEQSHR
			Exposure measure (X)			
X-RM (γ)	8.30E-03	−2.42E-03	−5.87E-05	8.27E-03	−1.72E-03	−5.37E-05
	(2.71)	(−1.31)	(−1.42)	(2.40)	(−0.90)	(−1.38)
CHMSHK (ρ)	−8.15E-02	−8.04E-02	−7.93E-02	−7.96E-02	−8.01E-02	−8.05E-02
	(−1.03)	(−1.01)	(−1.00)	(−1.00)	(−1.01)	(−1.01)
X (δ)	1.72E-02	1.25E-01	−3.75E-04	1.24E-02	5.25E-02	7.56E-05
	(0.21)	(1.37)	(−0.22)	(0.13)	(0.52)	(0.04)
Constant	1.687	1.566	1.913	1.754	1.780	1.884
	(0.81)	(0.77)	(0.95)	(0.84)	(0.88)	(0.94)
Average (θ)	1.179	1.228	1.228	1.189	1.226	1.226
Std. dev. (θ)	0.427	0.409	0.405	0.425	0.410	0.406
Var[e_{it}]	8,437	8,443	8,444	8,439	8,445	8,444
Var[v_t]	885	861	859	878	861	861
Adjusted R^2	0.23	0.23	0.23	0.23	0.23	0.23
Lagrange	345	346	345	344	345	347
Sample size	10,710	10,710	10,710	10,710	10,710	10,710

Notes. Estimates reflect scaling of variables detailed in Table I. Lagrange-multiplier statistic distributed $\chi^2(1)$ under null hypothesis Var[v_t] = 0.

TABLE IV

Regression Estimates for High Market Equity Sample (23 Firms)
(OLS estimates)
(t-statistic)

	F#SITES	F#/OWNEQ	FEQSHR	M#SITES	M#/OWNEQ	MEQSHR
			Exposure measure (X)			
X-RM (γ)	5.06E-03	1.25E-01	5.52E-03	5.65E-03	1.56E-01	1.20E-02
	(2.75)	(3.02)	(1.80)	(2.72)	(3.17)	(2.62)
CHMSHK (ρ)	0.486	0.484	0.487	0.487	0.486	0.488
	(11.33)	(11.31)	(11.36)	(11.37)	(11.34)	(11.39)
X (δ)	0.011	1.177	0.058	0.014	1.498	0.053
	(0.17)	(0.77)	(0.53)	(0.19)	(0.84)	(0.33)
Constant	−0.038	−0.588	−0.280	−0.049	−0.640	−0.216
	(−0.03)	(−0.43)	(−0.21)	(−0.04)	(−0.48)	(−0.16)
Average (θ)	1.077	1.073	1.097	1.081	1.070	1.084
Std. dev. (θ)	0.254	0.246	0.243	0.252	0.247	0.243
Adjusted R^2	0.460	0.461	0.460	0.460	0.461	0.460
Sample size	3,089	3,089	3,089	3,089	3,089	3,089

Note: Estimates reflect scaling of variables detailed in Table I.

282   GARBER AND HAMMITT

TABLE V

Regression Estimates for Low Market Equity Sample (54 Firms)
(GLS estimates with monthly random effects)
(asymptotic t-statistic)

	F#SITES	F#/OWNEQ	FEQSHR	M#SITES	M#/OWNEQ	MEQSHR
			Exposure measure (X)			
X-RM (γ)	6.74E-03	−1.94E-03	−5.04E-05	7.17E-03	−1.24E-03	−4.92E-05
	(0.83)	(−0.90)	(−1.06)	(0.71)	(−0.56)	(−1.09)
$CHMSHK$ (ρ)	0.108	0.109	0.110	0.108	0.109	0.109
	(0.93)	(0.93)	(0.94)	(0.93)	(0.94)	(0.94)
X (δ)	0.315	0.115	−0.001	0.379	0.050	0.000
	(1.26)	(1.07)	(−0.27)	(1.23)	(0.42)	(0.03)
Constant	3.147	3.734	4.250	3.174	4.031	4.189
	(1.05)	(1.27)	(1.46)	(1.06)	(1.38)	(1.44)
Average (θ)	1.244	1.270	1.269	1.248	1.266	1.268
Std. dev. (θ)	0.553	0.544	0.540	0.554	0.545	0.540
Var[e_{it}]	11,288	11,293	11,295	11,289	11,296	11,295
Var[v_t]	1,290	1,264	1,260	1,288	1,263	1,262
Adjusted R^2	0.193	0.194	0.194	0.193	0.194	0.194
Lagrange	417	425	425	418	424	427
Sample size	6,456	6,456	6,456	6,456	6,456	6,456

Notes. Estimates reflect scaling of variables detailed in Table I. Lagrange-multiplier statistic distributed $\chi^2(1)$ under null hypothesis Var[v_t] = 0.

that (when *CHMSHK* is included) no monthly error component is present for the high-ME sample.[30]

Within Tables III–V, individual columns report estimates for regressions that differ only by the exposure measure used. To conserve space, we report only the means and standard deviations of the estimates of the θ_i in Eq. (3).

Estimates for the Full Sample

First consider Table III. Before examining the estimates of γ, we consider estimates of interest primarily for diagnostic purposes. The estimates of the coefficient of *CHMSHK* are negative but are very small in absolute value and are not statistically significant. Five of the six estimated coefficients of the exposure measures (the δs) are positive but are not statistically significant, which suggests that monthly data, our measures, or both are too crude to provide reliable estimates of any wealth effects of Superfund that occur as investors revise their beliefs about Superfund exposure. The average of the 73 estimates of baseline firm betas (i.e., the θ_i) ranges from about 1.18 to 1.23, with standard deviations a bit above 0.40. The adjusted R^2s are almost completely insensitive to the choice of exposure measure, rounding to 0.23. The variance of the monthly component of the disturbance (Var[v_t]) is in all cases estimated to be a bit more than 10% of the

---

[30] The sensitivity of our quantitative conclusions to the use of OLS or GLS and to inclusion of *CHMSHK* is examined in detail (see Table VII and its discussion). The corresponding estimates of γ are reported in an Appendix available from the authors.

variance of the classical component (Var[e_{it}]), and the Lagrange-multiplier statistics (roughly 350) all allow confident rejection of the hypothesis that no monthly component is present,[31] which explains why we focus on GLS estimates for the full sample.

The estimates of γ do not provide robust evidence of a monotonic relationship between Superfund exposure and firm betas across the firms in the full sample. The estimates of γ are positive and are statistically significant for the two exposure measures involving only counts of sites, but are negative and insignificant for the four others. One interpretation is that within this sample the equity betas do increase with Superfund exposure, but that only our simplest exposure measures reflect the information available to investors for all sample firms. Alternatively, differences in Superfund exposure may have no monotonic effect on costs of capital, as suggested by the estimates based on the other exposure measures. However, as it happens, pooling companies of such disparate sizes appears responsible for much of the ambiguity suggested by the estimates in Table III.

Estimates for Subsamples Based on Firm Size

The estimates reported in Table IV suggest a much more robust set of conclusions about the effects of differences in Superfund exposure on equity betas within the high-ME sample. The estimates of γ are positive and are statistically significant—with t-ratios ranging upward from 1.80—for all six exposure measures. Qualitatively, this suggests that among especially large chemical companies increases in Superfund exposure increase costs of equity capital. Other estimates in Table IV—of interest for diagnostic purposes—are largely consistent with those for the full sample. The most notable differences from the estimates for the full sample are that: (a) on average, large firms' monthly returns are a bit less sensitive to market returns, and this sensitivity varies somewhat less than within the full sample (i.e., the average estimates of θ_i are smaller and their standard deviations are quite a bit smaller); (b) firm returns within the high-ME sample move systematically with our index of chemical company returns, and are about half as sensitive to CHMSHK as to the market return; and (c) the equation fits considerably better for the large firms, with adjusted R^2 statistics all rounding to 0.46. In sum, in addition to providing very different indications about the determinants of equity betas, the econometric specification performs substantially better for the high-ME sample than it performs for the full sample.

The estimates in Table V suggest very different conclusions for small firms. Here the estimates of γ have the same sign pattern as for the full sample, but in no case is an associated t-ratio larger than 1.1 in absolute value. Comparison of Tables IV and V indicates that point estimates of γ based on *F#SITES* and *M#SITES* are a bit larger for the low-ME firms than for the high-ME firms, but that the standard errors are about four times as large for the low-ME sample. Estimates based on the other four exposure measures are much smaller in absolute value for the low-ME than for the high-ME sample, and the standard errors are much smaller as well. Thus, the differences between the high- and low-ME samples for the four more complicated exposure measures are not attributable to imprecise estimation of γ in the low-ME sample.

---

[31] The 1% critical value of a $\chi^2(1)$ is 6.66.

284   GARBER AND HAMMITT

Estimates Allowing for a Shift in 1988

The estimates in Table VI examine whether there was a change in the regression relationship between the early and later parts of the post-CERCLA period. As a dividing point, we use May 1988 when the *Wall Street Journal* published the article that drew widespread attention to undisclosed Superfund liabilities.

The specifications here augment those in the first three columns of Tables IV and V by adding the variables *#SITES*88, *#/OWNEQ*88, and *EQSHR*88 (referred to in the table as "*X* post 1988") and their interactions with *RM* ("*X* post 1988-*RM*"). The variables *#SITES*88, *#/OWNEQ*88, and *EQSHR*88 are equal to *F#SITES*, *F#/OWNEQ*, and *FEQSHR*, respectively, beginning in May 1988, and zero before May 1988. The coefficients of the interaction variables are increments to the effects of Superfund exposure on equity betas for all sample months beginning with May 1988. These coefficients would be positive if after that month investors were better informed about relative Superfund exposure of different firms, they perceived more systematic Superfund risk generally, or both.

The estimates in Table VI for the high-ME sample provide considerable support for this possibility. Specifically, for that sample: (a) all three coefficients of the interactions of RM_t with a post-May 1988 exposure measure are positive, larger than the corresponding coefficients of *X-RM*, and statistically significant; and (b)

TABLE VI

Regression Estimates Allowing for Shift in 1988 (t-statistic)

	High market equity sample (OLS) Exposure measure (X)			Low market equity sample (GLS) Exposure measure (X)		
	F#SITES	*F#/OWNEQ*	*FEQSHR*	*F#SITES*	*F#/OWNEQ*	*FEQSHR*
X-RM	3.75E-03	9.07E-02	3.51E-03	1.08E-02	−1.31E-03	−2.71E-05
	(1.89)	(2.01)	(1.09)	(1.26)	(−0.60)	(−0.56)
X post 1988-*RM*	4.20E-03	1.14E-01	9.65E-03	−1.98E-02	−1.95E-02	−4.99E-04
	(1.80)	(1.95)	(2.12)	(−1.47)	(−1.93)	(−2.30)
CHMSHK (ρ)	0.489	0.489	0.491	0.103	0.103	0.104
	(11.40)	(11.41)	(11.43)	(0.89)	(0.88)	(0.89)
X (δ)	−0.010	0.252	0.040	0.430	0.131	−0.000
	(−0.13)	(0.14)	(0.33)	(1.43)	(1.14)	(−0.22)
X post 1988	0.038	2.113	0.023	−0.292	−0.020	0.002
	(0.38)	(0.86)	(0.13)	(−0.56)	(−0.06)	(0.38)
Constant	−0.044	−0.631	−0.296	3.199	3.780	4.210
	(−0.03)	(−0.47)	(−0.22)	(1.06)	(1.28)	(1.44)
Average (θ)	1.076	1.071	1.092	1.239	1.286	1.290
Std. dev. (θ)	0.254	0.246	0.243	0.541	0.539	0.525
Var[e_{it}]				11,290	11,293	11,291
Var[v_t]				1,293	1,267	1,277
Adjusted R^2	0.461	0.461	0.460	0.194	0.195	0.195
Lagrange				406	411	421
Sample size	3,089	3,089	3,089	6,456	6,456	6,456

Notes. Estimates reflect scaling of variables detailed in Table I. Lagrange-multiplier statistic distributed $\chi^2(1)$ under null hypothesis Var[v_t] = 0.

the coefficients of *X-RM*, which represent cost-of-capital effects before May 1988, are about 30% smaller than in Table IV, and two of three remain statistically significant. Taken together, the estimates suggest that the effect of an increment of measured Superfund exposure was more than twice as large during the later part of the period as the average effect during the full period.

Estimates in Table VI for the low-ME sample are again sensitive to the choice of exposure measure. Moreover, the estimates suggest a decrease in the effect of Superfund during the later part of the sample period.

Summary

Qualitatively, the estimates in Tables III–VI suggest that: (a) higher Superfund exposure leads to higher equity betas among the relatively large chemical companies; (b) the effects among these companies were about twice as large after mid-1988 as the average effect from 1981 through 1992; and (c) if there are cost-of-capital effects for smaller firms, either investors used site counts to assess exposure or the effects do not vary with relative exposure.

5. COSTS OF CAPITAL AND SOCIAL RISK BEARING

Effects of differences in exposure to Superfund liability on the costs of *equity* capital can be derived using Eqs. (2) and (5) and estimates of γ. Predicted effects on monthly costs of equity capital of being named at an additional 10 NPL sites are presented in Table VII, which also examines the sensitivity of the predictions to choice of exposure measure, estimation technique, and inclusion of *CHMSHK*.[32]

In view of the considerable diversity among the six exposure measures, the predictions for the high-ME sample are surprisingly robust. All but one of the 18 estimates of γ suggest that being named as a PRP at 10 additional sites—about $\frac{1}{5}$ the sample range—would increase costs of equity capital by 0.01–0.028% per month or roughly 0.1–0.3% per *year*.

For the low-ME sample, GLS estimation using the exposure measures involving only site counts leads to predicted cost-of-capital effects larger than any estimated for the high-ME sample, although none is statistically significant. The predicted decreases in cost of equity capital for the other four exposure measures are much smaller in absolute value and also are statistically insignificant.

An increase in the cost of *equity* capital need not imply an increase in the overall cost of capital if it reflects only increased financial leverage due to a wealth effect. To consider changes in overall cost of capital due to Superfund liability, we use Eq. (7) and we focus on the firms in the high-ME sample and the simplest exposure measure: *F#SITES*.[33] To apply Eq. (7), we need to quantify equity β, the ratio

---

[32] The predicted effects are the product of: (a) the increase in the relevant exposure measure associated with a 10-site increase calculated using the post-1980 mean market equity, equity share, and (for the myopic exposure measures) mean site proposal date, for the appropriate sample; (b) the mean excess market return of 0.5077% per month for the post-CERCLA sample period; and (c) the relevant estimate of γ. Because the predicted effects are proportional to the number of additional sites, predictions for different numbers of additional sites can be easily computed.

[33] In view of Table VII, estimates presented in the following text would be similar for other exposure measures. The more complicated exposure measures suggest effects roughly $\frac{1}{3}$ smaller.

286   GARBER AND HAMMITT

TABLE VII

Predicted Changes in Costs of Equity Capital (0.1%/month) for 10-Site Increase in Exposure
(standard error)

	Exposure measure (X)					
	F#SITES	F#/OWNEQ	FEQSHR	M#SITES	M#/OWNEQ	MEQSHR
High market equity sample						
OLS with	0.257	0.176	0.109	0.238	0.181	0.197
CHMSHK	(0.094)	(0.058)	(0.061)	(0.088)	(0.057)	(0.075)
OLS without	0.276	0.186	0.102	0.243	0.184	0.191
CHMSHK	(0.096)	(0.059)	(0.062)	(0.089)	(0.058)	(0.077)
GLS without	0.255	0.183	0.076	0.236	0.191	0.176
CHMSHK	(0.118)	(0.073)	(0.076)	(0.111)	(0.071)	(0.091)
Low market equity sample						
GLS with	0.342	−0.069	−0.048	0.295	−0.036	−0.038
CHMSHK	(0.410)	(0.076)	(0.046)	(0.417)	(0.064)	(0.035)
GLS without	0.357	−0.068	−0.048	0.307	−0.035	−0.038
CHMSHK	(0.411)	(0.076)	(0.046)	(0.417)	(0.064)	(0.035)
OLS with	−0.429	−0.115	−0.065	−0.413	−0.066	−0.042
CHMSHK	(0.358)	(0.078)	(0.047)	(0.362)	(0.065)	(0.036)
OLS without	−0.393	−0.112	−0.064	−0.398	−0.065	−0.041
CHMSHK	(0.358)	(0.078)	(0.047)	(0.362)	(0.066)	(0.036)

$E/(E + D)$, and the changes in β and in market equity for the sample firms
assuming alternatively that $F\#SITES = 0$ (to represent no Superfund liability) and
that $F\#SITES$ equals its actual (firm-specific) value. Separate estimates are
presented for the entire post-CERCLA sample period (1981–1992) and the period
1988–1992.

For β in the absence of exposure we use 1.077, the average estimated baseline
beta for the large firms (from Table IV, column 1). To represent effects of
Superfund exposure we add $\Delta\beta = \hat{\gamma} \times (F\#SITES)$ where $F\#SITES$ varies by
firm, $\hat{\gamma} = 0.00506$ for the 1981–1992 period (from the first column of Table IV),
and $\hat{\gamma} = 0.00795$ for the 1988–1992 period (i.e., $\hat{\gamma} = 0.00375 + 0.00420$ from the
first column of Table VI).

We use observed values of $E/(E + D)$ to represent this ratio in the presence of
Superfund.[34] We assume that Superfund has no effect on D, and we focus on the
wealth effects ΔE.[35]

Conceptually, wealth effects are the present value of expected future
Superfund-related costs as assessed by investors. These costs include site assessment, cleanup, operation and maintenance, and transaction costs for NPL and
state sites anticipated by investors (during the respective time periods). There is

[34] Specifically, we use the average real values of E (market equity) and D (total liabilities) for
1981–1992 and for 1988–1992; nominal end-of-fiscal-year values of E and D were obtained from
Compustat. The ratio $E/(E + D)$ averages 0.557 across the high-ME firms for the 1981–1992 period.
[35] Using an event-study approach would be expected to greatly underestimate total wealth effects of
Superfund—and to understate the discrepancy between changes in costs of equity capital and changes
in overall costs of capital—because the timing of many changes in investor information cannot be
determined. See, for example, Binder [7] in the context of regulatory events more generally.

substantial uncertainty about investor assessments of these costs. We develop a range of estimates to span the plausible range.

Based on Probst *et al.* [37], we assume that for each site at which a firm is named a PRP, total costs of site assessment, cleanup, and operations and maintenance are $41.1 million,[36] and that transactions costs involve an additional 20%.[37] We further assume that a firm's share of the total costs at each site will equal its share of the total market equity among large PRPs named at the site. These assumptions allow calculation of expected cleanup costs for our sample firms at the 1150 NPL sites proposed by May 1992, and hence represented in our data.[38] To account for future NPL sites, we assume they involve the same per-site costs[39] and we consider a range for the cumulative total of NPL sites of 2000–7800.[40] We add 20% to account for costs at state sites [40]. The proportionate change in the ratio $E/(E + D)$ due to the estimated wealth effects is fairly small for all cases examined in the following text. For the case with the smallest wealth effects, it averages 0.020 across firms (with a maximum of 0.064); for the case with the largest wealth effects, it averages 0.059 (with a maximum of 0.17).

Table VIII reports estimates of changes in overall cost of capital averaged for the 23 firms in the high-ME sample under various assumptions about the eventual number of NPL sites and the number of sites cleaned up per year.[41] In all cases, we assume that future costs are spread evenly over time, and present values are calculated using an annual (real) discount rate of 5%.[42] Estimated effects of Superfund liability on overall cost of capital range from 0.006 to 0.034% per month. Thus, even using a broad range of assumptions to account for changes in financial leverage we conclude that among our high-ME firms additional Superfund exposure increases overall costs of capital.

Increases in costs of capital may affect the investment behavior of firms.[43] Moreover, they reflect disutility—and hence social costs—of additional risk bearing by investors holding the securities of the high-ME firms.[44] Also reported in

[36] This figure represents total undiscounted costs of site assessment, cleanup, and operations and maintenance for sites associated with chemical manufacturing (see [37, Table 3-1, pp. 36–37; pp. 129–133].)

[37] The 20% increment corresponds to a transaction cost share of 25% [14].

[38] EPA reports that, as of December 1992, the NPL included 1085 nonfederal sites. An additional 40 sites had been removed from the NPL after cleanup and 25 sites had been proposed but not yet formally listed [47].

[39] This assumption tends to overstate actual costs and wealth effects—and to reduce estimated effects on costs of capital—because future sites are likely to be less contaminated and to involve lower costs, on average, because EPA has attempted to list the most hazardous sites first.

[40] CBO [43] estimate the eventual cumulative total of NPL sites as 2300 to 7800 and Probst *et al.* [37, p. 20] estimate 2000 to 3000.

[41] Based on the historical pace of cleanup, we view 100 sites per year as optimistic and 300 per year as implausibly so. However, as becomes clear presently, the calculations are not very sensitive to the assumed pace of cleanup, and assuming a faster pace tends to increase estimated wealth effects and as a result decrease estimated cost-of-capital effects.

[42] This rate is conservative—i.e., it tends to overstate wealth effects. It is approximately the excess (above Treasury-bill) cost of equity capital for the high-ME sample during the post-CERCLA period.

[43] When evaluating a project, firms should, in principle, use a cost of capital adjusted for the riskiness of the project [39, Chap. 12]. In practice, such adjustment is difficult and firm-level costs of capital carry substantial weight.

[44] The compensation investors receive for bearing these risks is a transfer but this does not imply that bearing the risk is socially costless. To the extent that Superfund liability provides incentives for appropriate waste-handling procedures, the increase in cost of capital may improve allocative efficiency.

GARBER AND HAMMITT

TABLE VIII

Estimated Changes in Cost of Capital and Social Cost of Risk Bearing
for 23 Firms in High-ME Sample
(5% annual discount rate)

	100 sites/year		300 sites/year	
Total NPL sites	Overall cost of capital increase (0.1%/month)[a]	Annual risk-bearing cost (million 1993 $)	Overall cost of capital increase (0.1%/month)[a]	Annual risk-bearing cost (million 1993 $)
	1981–1992 Regression estimates:			
2000	0.190	343	0.171	322
3000	0.177	329	0.142	292
7800	0.158	309	0.061	205
	1988–1992 Regression estimates:			
2000	0.342	821	0.325	802
3000	0.330	808	0.298	772
7800	0.313	788	0.225	685

[a] Average across 23 firms.

Table VIII are estimates of the annual social cost of bearing this risk. These are obtained by multiplying for each firm its incremental cost of capital by its average ME expressed in 1993 dollars and summed over firms. The costs range from about $200 to $350 million annually using the 1981–1992 estimates and $685 to $820 million using the 1988–1992 estimates.[45] These costs are a substantial fraction of the annual chemical industry cleanup cost, estimated at around $1 billion [37, 43].

6. CONCLUSIONS

Superfund imposes liability and costs on industrial companies for past waste disposal practices. We consider empirically one mechanism through which such sunk or unavoidable costs could affect future company decisions: effects of Superfund liability on costs of capital. We also estimate social costs of bearing financial risk associated with Superfund liability.

Among large chemical companies, we find robust evidence that additional Superfund exposure increases costs of capital. Estimates using different exposure measures and regression specifications[46] indicate that being named at 10 additional sites on the National Priorities List—about $\frac{1}{5}$ of the sample range—would raise the real cost of *equity* capital for a large chemical company by between 0.010 and 0.028% per month.[47] Averaged over the 23 firms in our sample, observed levels

[45] This range may approximate the cost for the chemical industry. Costs of bearing risk associated with smaller companies are not likely to alter these estimates substantially because the high-ME firms account for 95% of the 73-firm total of ME-weighted numbers of NPL sites at which firms are named. Recall, however, that our sample does not include firms classified as pharmaceutical or agricultural chemical manufacturers.

[46] Similar results are also obtained from regressions based on the arbitrage pricing theory. See the Appendix available from the authors.

[47] See the top panel of Table VII.

of exposure and our regression estimates imply increases in overall costs of capital (after accounting for increases in financial leverage) between 0.006 and 0.019% per month for the 1981–1992 period. Moreover, our estimates distinguishing the earlier and the later parts of the 1981 to 1992 period (Table VI) suggest that current effects are even larger. Effects on economic behavior have not been studied. Substantial increases in costs of capital, however, would be expected to affect investment decisions.

In contrast to the larger firms, we find no consistent evidence across our exposure measures of cost-of-capital effects related to relative Superfund exposure among smaller chemical companies. Given the evidence that larger firms pay cost-of-capital penalties for Superfund exposure, it may seem surprising if smaller firms do not. Our evidence is consistent with both the existence and the absence of cost-of-capital effects for smaller firms. Consider each possibility in turn.

Smaller firms could escape cost-of-capital penalties related to relative exposure if: (a) investors are largely unaware of their exposure, as some direct evidence reviewed previously indicates; (b) investors believe that Superfund costs of smaller firms are largely predictable; (c) unpredictable components of Superfund costs for smaller companies are largely diversifiable; or (d) investors disagree sufficiently about relative exposure among smaller companies.[48] None of these possibilities seems entirely implausible.

Nonetheless, smaller firms may pay cost-of-capital penalties. First, smaller firms may pay penalties according to relative exposure with investors using site counts to assess exposure (i.e., the more sophisticated exposure measures are not relevant for the smaller firms). Second, smaller firms may pay cost-of-capital penalties unrelated to their relative exposure because investors do not have the information required to assess relative exposure levels and so impose cost-of-capital penalties that are roughly constant across smaller firms. Such penalties would not be detectable with our methods which rely on interfirm variation in exposure.[49]

Our results also point to an economic aspect of Superfund that has received little attention: the social cost of bearing the associated financial risk. We estimate that these costs are on the order of $200 to $800 million per year for the chemical industry (Table VIII). Because cleanup costs for chemical-manufacturing NPL sites are estimated to be roughly $40 million per site [37], the annual social cost of bearing financial risk may be comparable to the cost of cleaning up 5 to 20 sites. We emphasize, however, that the underlying sources of these risks remain uncertain, and that we are unable to compare the social risk costs associated with the current Superfund program with those that would be incurred using other approaches to cleaning up inactive waste sites. In particular, we cannot decompose the estimated social risk costs into those associated with site cleanup per se and those that depend on how cleanups are financed. Nonetheless, our estimates suggest that the social costs of bearing financial risk associated with Superfund warrant consideration in an overall economic assessment of the program.

[48] Recall that our exposure measures are more highly correlated for the larger firms than the smaller ones (Table II).

[49] Addressing such a possibility empirically would seemingly require between-industry comparisons and separation of industry-wide effects of Superfund from other potential causes of interindustry differences in costs of capital.

290   GARBER AND HAMMITT

APPENDIX A

For data concerning the sample firms see Table A.I, and for descriptive statistics see Table A.II. A second Appendix follows and a third is available from the authors.

TABLE A.I

Sample Firms

Firm	#Sites	First obs.	Last obs.	Post-CERCLA Obs. High ME	Low ME	Real ME (1/87) ($ millions)
Air Products & Chemicals	21	Jan 76	Dec 92	109	0	1,417
Airgas	0	Dec 86	Dec 92	0	72	25
Allied Signal	10	Jan 76	Dec 92	123	0	4,929
American Cyanamid	31	Jan 76	Dec 92	134	0	2,523
Artra Group	2	Jan 76	Dec 92	0	134	50
Big Three Industries	2	Jan 76	Sep 86	0	0	* * *
Bio Rad Laboratories	0	Feb 80	Dec 92	0	134	68
Borg Warner	13	Jan 76	Jun 87	46	0	2,303
Buffton	1	Feb 88	Dec 92	0	58	* * *
C M X	0	Mar 80	Dec 88	0	86	4
Cabot	5	Jan 76	Dec 92	0	29	591
Cambrex	4	Nov 90	Dec 92	0	25	* * *
Canadian Occidental	0	Jan 76	Dec 92	0	49	402
Church & Dwight	0	Aug 90	Dec 92	0	28	* * *
Corcap	0	Jul 88	Jun 91	0	35	* * *
Crompton & Knowles	0	Jan 76	Dec 92	0	122	77
De Soto	6	Jan 76	Dec 92	0	134	129
Dexter	14	Jan 76	Dec 92	0	132	390
Diamond Shamrock	13	May 87	Dec 92	0	67	* * *
Dow Chemical	41	Jan 76	Dec 92	134	0	7,883
Du Pont	54	Jan 76	Dec 92	134	0	14,202
Epitope	0	Mar 90	Dec 92	0	33	* * *
Essex Chemical	0	Jan 76	Sep 88	0	83	92
Ethyl	11	Jan 76	Dec 92	81	0	1,667
Fairmount Chemical	0	Jan 76	Jul 86	0	60	* * *
Ferro	7	Jan 76	Dec 92	0	132	188
First Mississippi	5	Jan 76	Dec 92	0	133	88
G A F	28	Jan 76	Feb 89	0	58	919
Georgia Gulf	0	Nov 87	Dec 92	0	33	* * *
Grace W R	25	Jan 76	Dec 92	134	0	1,438
Great Lakes Chemicals	2	Jan 76	Dec 92	35	64	380
Grow Group	4	Jan 76	Dec 92	0	134	87
Guardsman Products	7	Jan 76	Dec 92	0	134	27
Hercules	20	Jan 76	Dec 92	101	0	1,953
Himont	0	Feb 87	Dec 89	34	0	* * *
International Flavors & Fragrances	4	Jan 76	Dec 92	73	0	986
Koppers	21	Jan 76	Oct 88	0	52	601
Lawter International	1	Jul 76	Dec 92	0	134	199
Loctite	2	Oct 76	Dec 92	0	95	304
Lubrizol	2	Jan 76	Dec 92	41	0	881
Maxus Energy	2	Jan 76	Dec 92	61	33	988
Medchem Products	0	May 88	Dec 92	0	55	* * *
Monsanto	49	Jan 76	Dec 92	134	0	4,186
Montedison S P A	0	Jul 87	Dec 92	63	0	* * *

SUPERFUND AND THE COST OF CAPITAL 291

TABLE A.I—*Continued*

Firm	#Sites	First obs.	Last obs.	Post-CERCLA Obs. High ME	Low ME	Real ME (1/87) ($ millions)
N L Industries	24	Jan 76	Dec 92	25	52	213
Nabors Industries	0	Jan 76	Dec 92	0	131	7
Nalco Chemical	4	Jan 76	Dec 92	47	0	757
Olin	27	Jan 76	Dec 92	0	38	618
Pantasote	0	Jan 76	Aug 89	0	94	25
Pennwalt	11	Jan 76	Jul 89	0	81	358
Pratt & Lambert	8	Jan 76	Dec 92	0	134	57
Premier Industrial	1	Jan 76	Dec 92	0	42	605
Products Research & Chemicals	0	Jan 76	Jul 89	0	93	108
Publicker Industries	1	Jan 76	Dec 92	0	134	29
Rexene	1	Jul 88	Aug 92	0	49	* * *
Rohm & Haas	23	Jan 76	Dec 92	106	0	1,695
Sequa	5	Jan 87	Dec 92	0	66	* * *
Sherwin Williams	19	Jan 76	Dec 92	35	43	858
Sierra Spring Water	0	Apr 85	Apr 88	0	26	29
Thiokol	12	Jan 76	Dec 92	50	63	1,234
Tredegar Industries	1	Jul 89	Dec 92	0	41	* * *
Tyler	1	Jan 76	Dec 92	0	131	152
U S R Industries	2	Jan 76	Dec 87	0	74	1
Union Carbide	38	Jan 76	Dec 92	132	0	2,024
United Capital	0	Jan 76	Dec 92	0	50	* * *
United Guardian	0	Apr 90	Dec 92	0	32	* * *
Valspar	10	Jan 76	Dec 92	0	134	166
Vulcan Materials	5	Jan 76	Dec 92	39	0	963
Wellman	0	Sep 88	Dec 92	0	34	* * *
Whittaker	8	Jan 76	Dec 92	0	127	172
Witco	20	Jan 76	Dec 92	0	81	606
Wynns International	10	Jan 76	Dec 92	0	134	53
Zemex	0	Jan 76	Dec 92	0	134	15

Note. * * * no market equity data in 1/87.

TABLE A.II

Descriptive Statistics

Variable	Post-CERCLA (1981–1992) Mean	Std. dev.	Full sample (1976–1992) Mean	Std. dev.	Min	Max
		Full sample (73 firms, 7,624 observations)				
F#SITES	9.670	12.775	6.883	11.634	0	54.000
F#/OWNEQ	3.896	11.452	2.773	9.822	0	291.995
FEQSHR	98.613	616.624	70.198	522.160	0	14,599.800
M#SITES	7.923	10.955	5.640	9.915	0	54.000
M#/OWNEQ	3.215	10.452	2.289	8.938	0	291.995
MEQSHR	71.320	548.551	50.770	463.939	0	14,599.800
r	6.450	109.003	8.631	107.367	−670.867	1,196.200
RM	5.131	44.746	5.624	44.233	−224.306	125.031
CHMSHK	−1.167	25.856	−2.346	25.292	−71.891	80.250
ME	1,102	2,566	994	2,308	0.333	24,990

292　　　　　　　　　　　　GARBER AND HAMMITT

TABLE A.II—*Continued*

	Post-CERCLA (1981–1992)		Full sample (1976–1992)			
Variable	Mean	Std. dev.	Mean	Std. dev.	Min	Max
		High ME (23 firms, 1,871 observations)				
F#SITES	22.156	16.921	13.420	17.049	0	54.000
F#/OWNEQ	0.907	0.684	0.549	0.693	0	3.524
FEQSHR	12.803	9.545	7.755	9.712	0	44.568
M#SITES	18.374	14.822	11.129	14.618	0	54.000
M#/OWNEQ	0.755	0.603	0.457	0.597	0	3.524
MEQSHR	7.981	6.830	4.834	6.593	0	34.020
r	3.764	80.101	4.837	79.247	−372.667	473.966
RM	4.504	45.002	5.459	44.221	−224.306	125.031
CHMSHK	−1.104	26.061	−2.699	25.262	−71.891	80.250
ME	3,618	4,265	2,822	3,685	116	24,990
		Low ME (54 firms, 4,356 observations)				
F#SITES	4.656	6.422	3.142	5.708	0	28.000
F#/OWNEQ	6.026	14.768	4.066	12.454	0	291.995
FEQSHR	162.319	809.863	109.520	669.541	0	14,599.800
M#SITES	3.774	5.272	2.547	4.677	0	27.000
M#/OWNEQ	4.983	13.536	3.362	11.361	0	291.995
MEQSHR	118.464	722.084	79.930	595.699	0	14,599.800
r	7.750	125.453	11.195	121.886	−670.867	1,196.200
RM	5.473	44.590	5.906	44.051	−224.306	125.031
CHMSHK	−1.247	25.792	−2.577	25.145	−63.353	74.846
ME	143	139	160	197	0.333	1,796

Notes. Statistics reflect scaling of variables detailed in Table I.

APPENDIX B

Sensitivity of CAPM Results to Model Specification

The CAPM model was estimated for each of the six exposure measures, including and excluding CHMSHK, by OLS and by GLS. As shown in Table VII of the text, the implied changes in cost of equity capital for the high-market equity subsample are reasonably consistent across these specifications, while the results for the low-market equity subsample are sensitive to the exposure measure used and to whether random monthly effects are included (using a GLS estimator) or excluded (using the OLS estimator). In the following table, we report the estimated value of γ--the regression coefficient relating equity beta to Superfund exposure for each of the alternative specifications--and its dependence on the inclusion of CHMSHK and the choice between OLS and GLS estimates for the two subsamples and for the full sample of 73 firms. For the high-market equity subsample, the coefficient is insensitive to these variations, but for the full sample and for the low-market equity subsamples, the estimate is sensitive to the inclusion of monthly random effects, but not to the inclusion of CHMSHK.

SUPERFUND AND THE COST OF CAPITAL 293

TABLE B.I

Sensitivity of Estimated γ to Inclusion of CHMSHK and Estimation Technique
(t-statistic)

	F#SITES	F#/OWNEQ	FEQSHR	M#SITES	M#/OWNEQ	MEQSHR
	\multicolumn{6}{c}{Exposure Measure}					
	\multicolumn{6}{c}{All Firms}					
GLS including CHMSHK						
X-RM (γ)	8.30E-03	-2.42E-03	-5.87E-05	8.27E-03	-1.72E-03	-5.37E-05
	(2.71)	(-1.31)	(-1.42)	(2.40)	(-0.90)	(-1.38)
GLS excluding CHMSHK						
X-RM (γ)	8.76E-03	-2.39E-03	-5.83E-05	8.76E-03	-1.69E-03	-5.37E-05
	(2.84)	(-1.30)	(-1.42)	(2.52)	(-0.89)	(-1.39)
OLS including CHMSHK						
X-RM (γ)	2.04E-03	-3.15E-03	-6.82E-05	2.44E-03	-2.21E-03	-5.39E-05
	(0.79)	(-1.69)	(-1.61)	(0.84)	(-1.14)	(-1.35)
OLS excluding CHMSHK						
X-RM (γ)	2.62E-03	-3.00E-03	-6.74E-05	2.76E-03	-2.15E-03	-5.32E-05
	(1.01)	(-1.60)	(-1.59)	(0.95)	(-1.10)	(-1.33)
	\multicolumn{6}{c}{High Market Equity Sample}					
OLS including CHMSHK						
X-RM (γ)	5.06E-03	1.25E-01	5.52E-03	5.65E-03	1.56E-01	1.20E-02
	(2.75)	(3.02)	(1.80)	(2.72)	(3.17)	(2.62)
OLS excluding CHMSHK						
X-RM (γ)	5.44E-03	1.33E-01	5.15E-03	5.78E-03	1.58E-01	1.16E-02
	(2.89)	(3.13)	(1.64)	(2.72)	(3.15)	(2.49)
GLS excluding CHMSHK						
X-RM (γ)	5.03E-03	1.31E-01	3.84E-03	5.61E-03	1.64E-01	1.07E-02
	(2.16)	(2.52)	(1.00)	(2.13)	(2.68)	(1.92)
	\multicolumn{6}{c}{Low Market Equity Sample}					
GLS including CHMSHK						
X-RM (γ)	6.74E-03	-1.94E-03	-5.04E-05	7.17E-03	-1.24E-03	-4.92E-05
	(0.83)	(-0.90)	(-1.06)	(0.71)	(-0.56)	(-1.09)
GLS excluding CHMSHK						
X-RM (γ)	7.04E-03	-1.91E-03	-5.02E-05	7.47E-03	-1.23E-03	-4.91E-05
	(0.87)	(-0.89)	(-1.05)	(0.74)	(-0.55)	(-1.09)
OLS including CHMSHK						
X-RM (γ)	-8.45E-03	-3.25E-03	-6.80E-05	-1.00E-02	-2.31E-03	-5.38E-05
	(-1.20)	(-1.48)	(-1.37)	(-1.14)	(-1.01)	(-1.15)
OLS excluding CHMSHK						
X-RM (γ)	-7.74E-03	-3.15E-03	-6.74E-05	-9.67E-03	-2.27E-03	-5.34E-05
	(-1.10)	(-1.43)	(-1.36)	(-1.10)	(-0.99)	(-1.14)

Notes: Estimates reflect scaling of variables detailed in Table 1.

294   GARBER AND HAMMITT

REFERENCES

1. J. Acton, "Understanding Superfund: A Progress Report," RAND R-3838-ICJ, Santa Monica (1989).
2. J. Acton and L. S. Dixon, "Superfund and Transaction Costs," RAND R-4132-ICJ, Santa Monica (1992).
3. T. B. Atkeson, S. Goldberg, F. E. Ellrod III, and S. L. Conners, An annotated legislative history of the superfund amendments and reauthorization act of 1986 (SARA), *Environmental Law Reporter* 10,360–10,419 (Dec. 1986).
4. L. M. Barr, CERCLA made simple: An analysis of the cases under the comprehensive environmental response, compensation and liability act of 1980, *The Business Lawyer* 923–1001 (May 1990).
5. M. E. Barth and M. F. McNichols, Estimation and market valuation of environmental liabilities relating to superfund sites, *J. Accounting Res.* **32**, 177–209 (1994).
6. M. E. Barth, M. F. McNichols, and G. P. Wilson, "Factors Influencing Firms' Disclosures about Environmental Liabilities," research paper No. 1358, Graduate School of Business, Stanford University (Oct. 1995).
7. J. J. Binder, Measuring the effects of regulation with stock price data, *Rand J. Econom.* **16**, 167–183 (1985).
8. T. Breusch and A. Pagan, The Lagrange multiplier test and its applications to model specification in econometrics, *Rev. Econom. Stud.* **47**, 239–253 (1980).
9. K. C. Chan and N.-F. Chen, Structural and return characteristics of small and large firms, *J. Finance* **46**, 1467–1484 (1991).
10. K. C. Chan, N.-F. Chen, and D. A. Hsieh, An exploratory investigation of the firm size effect, *J. Financial Econom.* **14**, 451–471 (1985).
11. B. Dalton, D. Riggs, and B. Yandle, The political production of superfund: Some financial market results, *Eastern Econom. J.* **22**, 75–87 (1996).
12. Dialog Information Services Inc., *Database Catalogue* (1994).
13. Disclosure Information Service, Corporate information on public companies filing with the SEC, CD-ROM, Bethesda, MD (1993).
14. L. S. Dixon, D. S. Drezner, and J. K. Hammitt, "Private-Sector Cleanup Expenditures and Transaction Costs at 18 Superfund Sites," RAND MR-204-EPA/RC, Santa Monica (1993).
15. E. F. Fama and K. R. French, The cross-section of expected stock returns, *J. Finance* **47**, 427–465 (1992).
16. S. Farber, Nuclear power, systematic risk, and the cost of capital, *Contemporary Policy Issues* **9**, 73–82 (1991).
17. *Fortune*, "The Fortune 500 Ranked by Industry," p. 264 (Apr. 20, 1992).
18. *Fortune*, "The Fortune 500 Ranked by Industry," p. 228 (Apr. 19, 1993).
19. G. C. Freeman, Jr., Inappropriate and unconstitutional retroactive application of superfund liability, *The Business Lawyer* **42**, 215–248 (Nov. 1986).
20. E. A. G. Geltman, Disclosure of contingent environmental liabilities by public companies under the federal securities laws, *Harvard Environ. Law Rev.* **16**, 129–173 (1992).
21. E. L. Goldman, Buried toxins are ripe for SEC discovery, *The Recorder* 8–9 (June 15, 1993).
22. W. H. Greene, "Econometric Analysis," MacMillan, New York (1990).
23. S. Gupta, G. Van Houtven, and M. Cropper, Paying for permanence: An economic analysis of EPA's cleanup decisions at superfund sites, *RAND J. Econom.* **27**, 563–582 (1996).
24. J. T. Hamilton and W. K. Viscusi, The benefits and costs of regulatory reforms for superfund, *Stanford Environ. Law J.* **16**, 159–198 (1997).
25. J. A. Hausman, Specification tests in econometrics, *Econometrica* **46**, 69–85 (1978).
26. R. K. Harper and S. C. Adams, CERCLA and deep pockets: Market response to the superfund program, *Contemporary Econom. Policy* **14**, 107–115 (1996).
27. T. L. Hazen, "Federal Securities Law," Federal Judicial Center, Washington, DC (1993).
28. Ibbotson Associates, "Stocks, Bonds, Bills, and Inflation 1993 Yearbook," Chicago (1993).
29. Investor Responsibility Research Center, "Corporate Environmental Profiles Directory 1992," Washington, DC (1992).
30. D. E. Jones and K. E. McSlarrow, ...But were afraid to ask, *Environ. Law Reporter* 10,430–10,457 (Oct. 1989).

SUPERFUND AND THE COST OF CAPITAL 295

31. G. G. Judge, W. E. Griffiths, R. C. Hill, H. Lutkepohl, and T.-C. Lee, "The Theory and Practice of Econometrics," Wiley, New York (1985).
32. J. A. Klein, "Superfund Project—Industry Report," Kidder, Peabody & Company, Inc., New York (Jan. 9, 1985).
33. A. D. Marcus, "Firms Ordered to Come Clean About Pollution," *The Wall Street Journal* B1 (Nov. 16, 1989).
34. L. B. Mitchell, Comparability in accounting for contingencies: The case of superfund, manuscript, Claremont McKenna College (June 1995).
35. A. K. Naj, "See No Evil: Can $100 Billion Have 'No Material Effect' On Balance Sheets?" *The Wall Street Journal* 1 (May 11, 1988).
36. S. W. Norton, Regulation and systematic risk: The case of electric utilities, *J. Law Econom.* **28**, 671–686 (1985).
37. K. N. Probst, D. Fullerton, R. E. Litan, and P. R. Portney, "Footing the Bill for Superfund Cleanups," The Brookings Institution and Resources for the Future, Washington, DC (1995).
38. W. K. Reilly, "A Management Review of the Superfund Program," U.S. Environmental Protection Agency, Washington, DC (June 15, 1989).
39. S. A. Ross, R. W. Westerfield, and J. Jaffee, "Corporate Finance," 4th ed., Richard D. Irwin, Chicago, IL (1996).
40. M. E. Russell, W. Colglazier, and M. R. English, "Hazardous Waste Remediation: The Task Ahead," Waste Management Research and Education Institute, The University of Tennessee, Knoxville, TN (1991).
41. J. E. Sohl and W. E. Wetzel, Jr., Small firms and superfund: Assessing the impact, *J. Small Business Finance* **3**, 141–157 (1994).
42. W. K. Viscusi, Economic foundations of the current regulatory reform efforts, *J. Econom. Perspectives* **10**, 119–134 (1996).
43. U.S. Congressional Budget Office, "The Total Costs of Cleaning Up Nonfederal Superfund Sites," Washington, DC (1994).
44. U.S. Congressional Budget Office, "Analyzing the Duration of Cleanup at Sites on Superfund's National Priorities List," Washington, DC (1994).
45. U.S. Environmental Protection Agency, "Site Enforcement Tracking System (SETS)," NTIS Order Number PB92-592130, Washington, DC (Dec. 1992).
46. U.S. Environmental Protection Agency, "An Analysis of State Superfund Programs: 50-State Study, 1993 Update," Office of Solid Waste and Emergency Response, Publication 9375.6-08C, Washington, DC (Dec. 1993).
47. U.S. Environmental Protection Agency, "Background Information: National Priorities List, Final Rule," Office of Solid Waste and Emergency Response, Publication 9320.7-041, Washington, DC (May 1994).
48. U.S. Environmental Protection Agency, "Supplementary Materials: National Priorities List, Proposed Rule and Final Rule," Office of Solid Waste and Emergency Response, Publication 9320.7-051, Washington, DC (June 1996).

[21]

Strict Liability as a Deterrent in Toxic Waste Management: Empirical Evidence from Accident and Spill Data

Anna Alberini*

Economics Department, University of Colorado-Boulder, Boulder, Colorado 80309-0256

and

David H. Austin

Quality of the Environment Division, Resources for the Future, Washington, DC 20036

Received January 6, 1998; revised March 3, 1999

This paper examines whether strict liability imposed on polluters has reduced uncontrolled releases of toxics into the environment. We fit regressions relating spills of selected chemicals to the type of liability in force in a state and to state manufacturing activity. For some chemicals, spills are more numerous in states imposing strict liability. This could be due to unobserved state characteristics, with small firms being responsible for a disproportionate number of spills, regardless of the liability structure. Alternatively, separate regressions for the two liability regimes suggest that *only under strict liability* are small firms responsible for a disproportionate number of spills. © 1999 Academic Press

1. INTRODUCTION

The purpose of this paper is to explore the issue of whether strict liability imposed on polluters has served to reduce uncontrolled releases of toxics into the environment. Because it imposes pollution damages upon the polluter, strict liability should create additional incentives for firms to handle hazardous substances more carefully, thus reducing the future likelihood of such uncontrolled releases.

Provisions making polluters liable for the damages caused by their polluting activities have, in fact, been incorporated into a number of federal and state environmental laws passed over the last two decades, such as CERCLA (1980; reauthorized in 1986 and extended in 1991[1]), the hazardous waste cleanup laws of many states, and the Offshore Continental Shelf Act (1974), which deals with damages from off-shore spills occurring during drilling operations.

---

*To whom correspondence should be addressed. E-mail: alberini@colorado.edu.

[1]The Comprehensive Environmental Response, Compensation and Liability Act, commonly known as Superfund, instructs the U.S. Environmental Protection Agency to identify and list hazardous waste sites that pose a threat to human health and the environment, track down potentially responsible parties, and force them to clean up (or to reimburse the EPA for a cleanup already initiated by the agency). The EPA has generally interpreted the law to apply to closed and abandoned hazardous waste sites.

It has been argued that liability law is an important and promising policy tool for dealing with pollution problems (Tietenberg [20]). Economic theory, however, is ambivalent about its effects. Firms with relatively limited assets may be sheltered from the economic incentives created by strict liability (Shavell [18], Tietenberg [20]). Beard [4] and Larson [11] find that when firm assets are limited the effect of imposing strict liability remains, at best, uncertain. They dispel the notion that under strict liability the level of care taken by a firm to prevent accidental releases is always increasing in firm wealth and conclude that large, wealthy firms may or may not be safer than smaller ones.

Firms may even select their asset level or corporate financial structure to minimize payment of damages in the event of an accident (Pitchford [16]). Ringleb and Wiggins [17] provide evidence that imposition of strict liability may have in fact encouraged wealthier firms to spin off into, or subcontract risky operations to, smaller, judgment-proof companies in hopes of avoiding liability. Finally, the incentives created by liability can be altered by the availability and cost of pollution insurance.

In light of the many possible effects of imposing liability on polluters, it is rather surprising that so little empirical work has been done to date to examine firms' actual responses to environmental liability law. Opaluch and Grigalunas [15] present evidence that bids for tracts on the Outer Continental Shelf *do* reflect the environmental risks perceived by firms under the Offshore Continental Shelf Act, but we are not aware of any empirical studies examining the role of liability as a deterrent to uncontrolled releases of toxics into the environment.

In this paper, we set out to explore this issue, focusing specifically on firm liability for the cost of remediation at hazardous waste sites. Under the Federal Superfund law, certain parties—including waste generators and transporters and operators of waste sites—are held responsible for any cleanup costs at high-risk toxic waste sites, without requiring proof that they acted negligently or with intent (Fogleman [8]).[2] In addition, many states have established their own cleanup programs, with authorities and capabilities similar to those of the federal Superfund program. These state cleanup programs were authorized within a few years after the passage of the federal Superfund, in order to address the numerous sites which are not included on the National Priority List (NPL), and so do not qualify for federally financed remediation (Barnett [3]).[3] Their specific provisions, including the imposition of strict liability, vary across states, and many have evolved considerably since the program's inception. These differences, across states and over time, provide us with a natural experiment for assessing strict liability's effects on the handling of toxics.

We use data on accidents and spills involving hazardous substances to establish whether their frequency of occurrence has been systematically affected by the introduction of strict liability. The data come from a comprehensive database of events reported to the US EPA under their Emergency Response Notification

---

[2]The courts have interpreted Superfund as imposing joint and several liability, which holds all potentially responsible parties liable for the entire amount of the cleanup when it is not possible to determine their individual contributions.

[3]The state mini-Superfund programs also contain provisions for the funding of the state's share of the cost of cleanup at NPL sites. Such share is mandated by CERCLA.

System (ERNS). Because the ERNS begins in 1987, we are unable to establish whether the passage of the federal Superfund law has affected the occurrence of accidental releases. Instead, we examine whether the strict liability feature of state cleanup programs has had any *additional* influence on the number of accidental events, above and beyond that of the federal Superfund. In particular, we wish to see whether the effect of strict liability on firms' handling of toxic materials has been uniformly to reduce the incidence of toxic spills, or whether its effect is dependent on firm size and other factors.

To study this relationship, we estimate regressions relating the frequency of spills of selected chemicals used in manufacturing to the type of liability in force in a state. We control for the extent of manufacturing activity in the state and include in the regression other program features that might alter firms' expected outlays in the event of an accident, and thus affect firms' incentives to take care.

Results vary with the chemical being analyzed. For some chemicals, such as halogenated solvents, the presence of strict liability does not provide any additional explanatory power for the number of spills beyond what is achieved by the number of establishments and the sectoral composition of manufacturing. For other families of chemicals (acids, ammonia, and chlorine), spills appear to be more numerous where strict liability is imposed, even after we control for the extent and type of manufacturing. We present several alternative models and tests to shed light on this initial finding, looking for evidence about the effects of firm size.

The paper is organized as follows: Section 2 presents theoretical considerations. Section 3 describes our data on accidental releases of toxics. Section 4 discusses the state mini-Superfund programs and Section 5 discusses the role of pollution insurance. The econometric model, the variables, and the regression strategy are presented in Section 6. Section 7 presents the results and Section 8 concludes.

2. THEORETICAL CONSIDERATIONS

To provide a framework for our empirical work, in this section we examine models of firm care against uncontrolled releases of pollutants into the environment.

The simplest model (Shavell [18]) assumes that a firm faces a probability p of incurring an accident which results in damages for $\$D$. The firm can take precautions, at a cost x, to reduce such probability, $p = p(x)$, where $p'(x) < 0$ and $p''(x) > 0$. Under strict liability, the firm is responsible for payment of the damages in the event of an accident, and selects the level of care to minimize its expected expenditures; i.e., the sum of precaution costs and expected damages, $x + p(x) \cdot D$.

Assuming that the firm has assets sufficient to compensate the victims in the event of an accident and that it cannot escape suit, the firm's private objective function coincides with the social objective function. The social and the firm's private optimum is the level of care x^* such that its marginal cost (one dollar) is equal to the marginal benefit of care (the reduction in expected payments to victims).

Several factors may act to dilute the incentives posed to the firm by strict liability by reducing the expected disbursements in the event of an accident. Shavell [18] shows that—if the harm caused by some parties can exceed their assets, or if some parties can escape legal judgement—the level of care taken by a firm under strict liability is less than the socially optimal level. The privately optimal level of care, and hence the likelihood of an accident, should depend on the firm's total potential liability, D;[4] on its wealth, W; and on the probability of a suit, q. The firm's level of care increases with the size of the potential damages D it faces, but only so long as D is less than the wealth of the firm.

Variants of this model (Beard [4]; Larson [11]) do not necessarily support this hypothesis, dispelling the notion that, under strict liability, the level of care taken by a firm to prevent accidental releases is always increasing in firm wealth: Large, wealthy firms may or may not be safer than smaller ones.[5]

Under negligence-based liability, a firm is responsible for the payment of damages only if it can be shown to have taken a level of care less than the prescribed negligence standard, $\hat{x}$. Hence, as long as x exceeds or is equal to the standard $\hat{x}$, the only disbursements incurred by the firm are equal to x.

When D is less than the firm's assets and the probability of a suit is one, it can be shown (Tietenberg [20]) that under negligence the firm will always choose a level of care exactly equal to $\hat{x}$, as long as the standard $\hat{x}$ is less than x_0, where x_0 solves $x_0 = x^* + p(x^*) \cdot D$. In general, the resulting level of care and probability of accident will not be socially optimal, unless the negligence standard is set equal to the socially optimal level of care x^*. The probability of an accident is greater than the socially optimal probability of an accident if the court-established standards are lax relative to the socially optimal care and lower if they are more stringent. All else the same, different negligence standards should be expected to result in different accident rates.

Implicit in this reasoning is that the standard of negligence is directly observed by the firm. In practice, however, negligence standards are determined by the court on a case-by-case basis, suggesting that they might be surrounded by uncertainty and that firm behavior may be based on subjective expectations about such standards. Even if the negligence standard were perfectly known to the firm, limited assets or ability to escape prosecution may influence the level of care chosen by the firm.

To summarize, if firms are held fully accountable for damages, the difference in the level of care taken by a firm under the two alternative regimes should depend on how $\hat{x}$, the negligence standard established by the courts, compares with

---

[4]D includes, in the use of remediation at hazardous waste sites, cleanup costs, compensation to victims, and punitive damages (if prescribed by law).

[5]Beard allows the size of the damages from an accident to be random, so that there is a positive probability that the damages, in the event of an accident, exceed the firm's assets. While the probability of an accident is influenced by a firm's level of care, the distribution of the size of the damages is not. If the damages exceed the assets of the firms, disbursements are virtually "truncated" by bankruptcy. This makes the private benefits of care lower than the social benefits and the private costs of care lower than the social costs. In Beard's model, firms subject to strict liability may *either* over- or underinvest in care relative to the socially optimally level, depending on the distribution of accident size, and wealthy firms may *not* necessarily invest in more care than smaller firms. Larson [11] considers firms facing uncertainty about their profits in addition to uncertainty about accidental releases. Firms choose between allocating resources to production involving toxics and to riskless investments. A firm's level of care is shown to be increasing in wealth only for firms operating in "extremely hazardous" sectors (where an accident would always put the firm out of business).

24   ALBERINI AND AUSTIN

optimal care under strict liability (Tietenberg [20]). This difference may be altered by judgment-proofness,[6]

$$(P_N - P_S) = f(D, W, \hat{x}, q; I),\tag{1}$$

where P_I denotes the probability of an accidental release of toxics under regime I, $I \in \{N(\text{egligence}), S(\text{trict})\}$. Equation (1) informs our empirical analyses by suggesting that in addition to I, we control for potential liability, firm wealth, court-established standards of negligence, and the probability of environmental law suit. The effectiveness of investment in safety equipment (i.e., the slope of $p(x)$, here subsumed into $f(\bullet)$) may also be a determinant of such a difference.

In this paper, we explore the empirical issue of how strict liability has affected the level of care taken by firms to prevent unintended releases of pollutants into the environment. We examine the ultimate outcome of care, focusing on sudden and accidental releases that occurred over a relatively recent time period.[7] Datasets documenting individual spill events are publicly available, but in most cases do not contain information sufficient to identify the parties responsible for the spill. Hence, we aggregate the spill counts by state and year.

If economic theory does not offer unambiguous predictions of how *individual* firms adjust their level of care—and hence the likelihood of toxic spills—to the liability structure, matters become even more complicated when one examines total spills per state per year. Total spills may depend on individual firms' propensities to spill, the distribution of damages for firms of given size, the distribution of firm sizes, the effectiveness of safety equipment in reducing the risk of spills, the state's liability structure,[8] the negligence standards likely to be established by state courts, the availability and cost of pollution insurance, and the likelihood of detection and prosecution in the event of a chemical release. We use state-level variables proxying for all of these factors, and for the degree of heterogeneity among firms in the state, as predictors of the number of spills.

[7]We focus on spills and accidents involving chemicals for two reasons. First, chemical spills proxy for the level of care taken by firms to avoid liability, which is not observable. Second, many cases are documented where the accidental release of pollutants triggered a process that resulted in the placement of the site on the National Priorities List or on the list of sites eligible for the state cleanup program. This prospect should motivate firms to take precautions to avoid becoming liable for the cost of cleanup.

[8]Due to the simultaneous existence of the federal Superfund stature (imposing strict liability) and the state mini-Superfund programs (imposing negligence-based or strict liability, depending on the state), the state's liability structure should influence care, and hence the likelihood of an accident, especially for events resulting in moderate or low environmental and public health risk. For such events, placement on the NPL would not be granted, but remediation and/or placement of the state list may be required.

[6]To illustrate, suppose that for a small firm with assets, A, less than the damages, the privately optimal level of care minimizing $(p(x) \cdot A + x)$ is $x' < x^*$, and that the negligence standard is $\hat{x}$. Even if $\hat{x}$ is less than x^*, a firm choosing to comply with the negligence standard may experience a lower accident probability, as long as $\hat{x}$ is less than $p(x') \cdot A + x'$, the expected expenditures of the firm were it subject to strict liability.

3. THE SPILL AND ACCIDENT DATA

Our spill and accident figures come from the EPA's Emergency Response Notification System (ERNS) database.[9, 10] For each spill or release, the ERNS database reports the date and place where each discharge occurred; identifies the nature of the substance spilled, the statute under which the release was reported, and the medium into which the substance was released (air, etc.); and specifies whether the accident occurred during transportation or within a facility. It also attempts to identify the cause of the accident and provide a rough description of the circumstances surrounding the accident. Unfortunately, cause and description information are incomplete or missing for most spills.

Figures for the number of people injured, the number of fatalities, the number of people evacuated from a facility, and the estimated damage to property (in dollars) are also provided. Finally, the ERNS data indicate whether the party responsible is a private citizen, a firm, or a government agency. In most cases, however, firm names, addresses, and Dun & Bradstreet identification numbers are not available.

We were initially interested in estimating joint models of the *quantity* of chemicals released and the number of releases. We were concerned that strict liability would have affected the severity of spills, as well as their number. We found, however, that for many spills the quantity released data are missing or set to zero for lack of better information, making total quantities systematically underreported. Accordingly, in this paper we analyze the determinants of the *number* of spills per year in each state, from the beginning of 1987 to the end of 1995.

---

[9]Reporting requirements are spelled out in Superfund (CERCLA), the Emergency Planning and Community Right-to-Know Act (EPCRA) of 1986, the Hazardous Material Transportation Act (HMTA) of 1974, and the Clean Water Act. Reporting criteria vary, depending on the federal statute. CERCLA, Section 103, requires that any release of a CERCLA hazardous substance meeting or exceeding the reportable quantity prescribed in 40 CFR 302.4 be reported to the National Response Center. Several CERCLA toxic substances are also simultaneously defined as RCRA hazardous wastes, Clean Air Act hazardous air pollutants, and "imminently hazardous" substances addressed by the Toxic Substances Control Act. EPCRA requires that the release of a reportable quantity of an EPCRA extremely hazardous substance or a CERCLA hazardous substance (one pound or more, unless otherwise specified by regulation) resulting in exposure of people outside the boundary of the facility where the release occurs be reported to the State and local authorities. HMTA requires that the release of a DOT hazardous material during transportation be reported to the National Response Center under certain circumstances, such as death, injury, significant property damage, evacuation, or highway closure. Finally, the Clean Water Act requires that the release of oil be reported to the National Response Center if the release: (1) violates applicable quality standards; (2) causes a film, sheen, or discoloration of the water or adjoining shoreline; or (3) causes a sludge or an emulsion to be deposited beneath the surface of the water or upon the adjoining shoreline.

[10]Some of the spills reported to ERNS may also be covered by other environmental statutes. In practice, in litigation or action against the polluter, the agency will use the statute deemed relevant or the statute under which the agency can build the strongest case against the polluter. Since the level of care taken by firms should be motivated by *expected* liability, *ex post* events (whether the firm is eventually held liable, and under which statute) should not influence the level of care, and hence the likelihood that a firm experiences an accident. Moreover, some of the spills and accidents reported to ERNS may require immediate response, and hence fall under the auspices of the federal Superfund Removal program, triggering strict liability for the response costs. However, spills requiring immediate cleanup are only a very small fraction of all spills in our sample, suggesting that our analysis, which focuses on the additional effect of state-level liability, is appropriate.

26   ALBERINI AND AUSTIN

Since our data are aggregated to the number of spills and accidents per state per year, we need a way of controlling for differing patterns in the way various chemicals are used in manufacturing, which may influence the seriousness of the damages from the spills. We control for differences in how each chemical is used by organizing our analyses along more or less narrow chemical divisions. This approach also has the advantage of controlling for differences in the ways such substances may be regulated and in ERNS reporting requirements.

Specifically, we focus on spills involving selected substances or groups of relatively similar, highly toxic, CERCLA-regulated substances used in manufacturing: (1) acids; (2) chlorine and chlorine dioxide; (3) anhydrous ammonia; (4) four halogenated solvents, methylene chloride (METH), perchloroethylene (PERC), trichloroethylene (TCE), and 1,1,1- or 1,1,2-trichloroethane (TCA); and (5) a broader group of halogenated solvents that adds methyl ethyl ketone, chloroform, and carbon tetrachloride to the four solvents already mentioned. (See Appendix A for information about these chemicals.)

Most of the spill events here analyzed involved relatively low-level releases, rarely resulted in deaths and infrequently required remediation. Of the 12,662 ERNS-reported accidents involving releases of acids between 1987 and 1995, more than 22% involved sulfuric acid, and over 14% involved hydrochloric acid. A significant fraction of these spills occurred in California, which between 1987 and 1995 had 2354 spills reported to the ERNS, followed by Texas (2027), Louisiana (720), and Pennsylvania and Illinois (453 each), as shown in Fig. 1. About 51.4% of these spills are classified as primarily affecting land, another 25.5% affected air, 15.4% water; 3.4% of the spills were contained within a firm's facility, and 1.3%

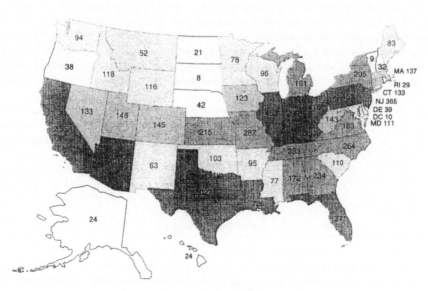

FIG. 1. Total number of acid spills, 1987–1995.

affected groundwater. Most of the spills occurred at a firm's facility (70%),[11] with highway and railroad spills accounting for another approximately 11.6 and 10.7% of the spills, respectively.

Among the chemical families we examined, acid spills were by far the most common type of accident in the ERNS data. By contrast, over the nine years between 1987 and 1995 there were 3412 releases of chlorine or chlorine dioxide and 5995 accidental releases of anhydrous ammonia. Over three-quarters of these releases occurred into air. We counted more than 2000 accidents involving METH, PERC, TCE, and TCA (air releases slightly outnumbering spills on land, 43 to 38%, with the remainder distributed 12% in water, 2.8% in groundwater, and 1.6% contained within the facility). Even more so than with acid spills, most of these releases (over 85%) occurred at a fixed facility, as opposed to during transport. The remainder of the releases were about equally distributed among highway and railroad spills.

For all of the families of chemicals considered here, the geographic distribution of the spills is qualitatively very similar to that displayed in Fig. 1 for acids, suggesting that accidental releases tend to be most common in large states with strong manufacturing economies, and especially in states with a significant amount of activity in the chemical sectors. The number of spills should, therefore, be related to the number of firms and to production levels in the manufacturing and chemical-intensive sectors of each state. Because chemical transport is regulated by a complex web of federal, state, and local regulations (Wentz [25]), our analyses are limited to the spills and accidents that occur at fixed facilities, such as manufacturing plants or storage facilities.

4. STATE MINI-SUPERFUND PROGRAMS

Since the early 1980s, many states have enacted laws and developed programs similar to the federal Superfund program, providing for emergency response actions and long-term remediation at hazardous waste sites. These statutes often establish a financing mechanism to pay for initial feasibility studies and remediation activities, spell out the conditions under which monies from such funds are to be used, and contain provisions conferring authority to force responsible parties to conduct feasibility studies and cleanups and/or pay for them (EPA, 1989, 1990, 1991; ELI, 1993, 1995).

By 1989, 39 states had created such funding and enforcement authorities. This number had climbed to 45 by 1995, as shown in Fig. 2. The 5 states without separate mini-Superfund programs addressed hazardous waste issues using other regulations.

One important difference between the Federal Superfund program and many state mini-Superfund programs lies in the liability standards imposed on the responsible parties: Liability under the federal Superfund is strict and joint-and-several, but this is not necessarily the case for many of the state programs. As of 1987, only 27 states had instituted strict liability; by 1995 this number had climbed to 40.

---

[11] Note the difference between a spill at a firm's facility (70 percent of all spills), and one that was successfully contained within the facility (without spilling on the ground or into air or water; only 3.4% of all spills).

28   ALBERINI AND AUSTIN

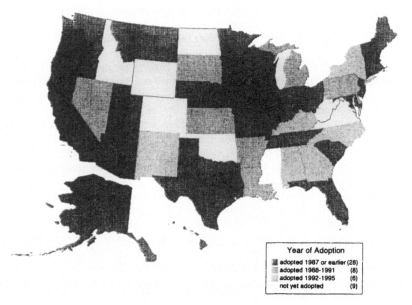

FIG. 2. States' adoption of strict liability.

The state mini-Superfund programs may enable states to initiate cleanup when the responsible parties are uncooperative and to seek to recover cleanup costs from them. State mini-Superfund laws may also include provisions allowing private citizens, as opposed to government agencies, to file civil actions requiring that the responsible party prevent further damage or take corrective action if citizens have been adversely affected. In some states (15 in 1995) responsible parties must compensate those who are affected by the release of the toxic substances. Compensation is usually limited to paying for alternative drinking water supplies or for temporary relocation.

5. THE ROLE OF POLLUTION INSURANCE

The ability of private firms to insure themselves against their potential environmental liabilities would, under the right conditions, mute the incentives of liability we wish to observe. In particular, were insurers required to sell environmental insurance to all who demanded it, and were they unable to monitor firms' level of care, the only incentives firms would have to take efficient levels of care would be reputational and moral.

The actual situation with environmental insurance differs sufficiently from this extreme scenario so that firms' incentives to avoid environmental liabilities remain robust. Perhaps the central issue governing firms' incentives is the ability of insurers to exclude pollution liability claims from their commercial general liability (CGL) policies. Pre-1986 CGL policies did exclude pollution coverage except for "sudden and accidental" spills. After 1986, however, firms had to purchase all of their pollution coverage separately (the so-called "absolute pollution exclusion"). The insurance industry, concerned about the potentially huge environmental liabilities, imposes rigorous documentary requirements on their policyholders (Gastel [9]).

Still, pollution insurance can be financially beyond reach for some firms and some types of activities. Unavailability of insurance for hazardous waste treatment, storage, and disposal facilities (TSDFs) has been particularly hard on landfills and surface impoundments, which are required by the Resource Conservation and Recovery Act to carry insurance for nonsudden accidental releases (GAO [24]). Insurance for generators of hazardous wastes and toxics also has been hard to find, and insurance policies and pollution exclusions have been an important source of contention (and transaction costs) between the insured, the insurance companies, and their reinsurers (Acton and Dixon [1]).

On the other hand, the 1986 absolute pollution exclusion has not gone unchallenged. Numerous states have failed to enforce the pollution exclusion. The temporal language of "sudden and accidental" has been interpreted broadly in such states, as with New Jersey's ruling that "insurers are liable for cleanup if the pollution discharge was accidental and unintended" (Gastel [9]).

Ideally, then, our analysis would control for states' differing interpretations of the pollution exclusion, total environmental insurance coverage by state and year, and insurers' safety requirements imposed upon the prospective insured. However, we were unable to find this information.

A lack of data about the availability and extent of pollution insurance forced the Government Accounting Office (GAO) to survey insurance providers in an effort to ascertain how hazardous waste legislation had affected the availability of insurance and claims paid out to the insured [24]. The survey revealed that in 1985 specialized pollution insurance made up only 0.5% of total premia paid for property/casualty insurance and that the median claim paid out to the insured was approximately $5000.

Insurers interviewed as part of the GAO study did assert that "CERCLA's standards of liability not only have reduced the availability of pollution insurance, but also have affected the standard of care owed by generators, transporters, and owners/operators of TSDFs." They further maintained that "liability standards undermine these parties' incentives to exercise due care to prevent pollution because the standard of care is not related to the potential for liability." According to the GAO report, however, this view contrasts sharply with the opinion expressed by other parties, such as an official of the largest commercial waste disposal company who thought that "the standards of liability have in fact increased the standard of care taken by the industry."

6. REGRESSION MODELS

To check whether a state's liability structure influences the frequency of accidents, we exploit differences in the provisions of the various state mini-Superfund programs. In this paper, we focus on spills occurring at fixed facilities and separately analyze each chemical family, explaining *numbers* of spills. For the two chemical families with an abundance of spills per year—acids and ammonia—we use linear regression models. For the other families with fewer spills, we use Poisson models.

30   ALBERINI AND AUSTIN

TABLE I

Descriptive Statistics

Label	Description	Mean	SD
AREA	Total area of the state (square miles)	72,824	90,072
POPUL	State population (thousands)	4945.76	5460.24
ALL_MIN	Number of mining establishments in the state	583.55	1091.20
MFGESTAB	Number of manufacturing establishments in the state	7211.52	8472.52
SMLMFG	Number of manufacturing establishments with fewer than 20 employees in the state	4763.28	5747.49
LGMFG	Number of manufacturing establishments with 20 or more employees in the state	2366.13	2731.75
SMLMINE	Number of mining establishments with fewer than 20 employees in the state	466.80	912.28
LGMINE	Number of mining establishments with 20 or more employees in the state	116.77	187.98
ENVORG	Number of in-state members of three major environmental organizations, per 1000 residents	8.49	3.54
HAZWASTE	Quantity of hazardous waste per capita generated in the state (thousands of lbs)	1.58	2.91
ACID spills	Number of reported acids spills per state per year	18.54	34.67
AMMONIA spills	Number of reported ammonia spills	10.98	16.55
HALOGENATED SOLVENTS spills I	Number of spills of TCA, TCE, METH and PERC	2.44	3.47
HALOGENATED SOLVENTS spills II	Number of spills of broader group of halogenated solvents	4.70	12.54
CHLORINE spills	Number of spills of chlorine/chlorine dioxide	6.27	9.33
STRICT	State program imposes strict liability	.68	.47
CITSUIT	State program allows citizen suit	.31	.46
PUNDAMAG	Punitive damages charged to uncooperative firms	.56	.50
VICTCOMP	Firms required to compensate victims of release	.24	.43
LAWYER	Number of lawyers working on state mini-superfund cases per million state residents	1.38	1.73
CORTEFF	% civil cases disposed of out of total civil cases filed	95.25	9.73
PCTDEMPR	% votes for democratic candidate in most recent presidential elections	48.04	9.14

For spills of acids and ammonia, we estimate the regression equations

$$\log(y_{it} + 1) = x_{it}\beta + \varepsilon_{it}, \qquad (2)$$

where y is the number of accidental releases of these chemicals in state i in year t. The vector x contains factors that are thought to be predictors of the number of spills and that proxy for the elements in Eq. (1). β is a vector of parameters and ε is an i.i.d. error term. There are 51 "states" in the analysis, including the District of Columbia; the year ranges between 1987 and 1995.

For the chlorine/chlorine dioxide and halogenated solvents families, there are far fewer spills (see Table I), and many states have no spills in a given year. To handle this, we fit Poisson regression models, estimated by maximum likelihood.

These regressions assume that the probability of experiencing y spills in year t is

$$\Pr(Y_{it} = y_{it}) = \frac{e^{-\lambda_{it}}\lambda_{it}^{y_{it}}}{y_{it}!}, \tag{3}$$

where $\lambda_{it} = \exp(x_{it}\,\beta)$, and that both the expected number of spills and their variance are equal to λ_{it}.

The Choice of Independent Variables

How a firm responds to the imposition of liability should depend, among other things, on its ability to deflect payment of some or all of the damages to its insurance companies. Aggregate spills rates should, therefore, depend on how insurers react to firms' demand for pollution insurance.

Ideally, we would like to account for these effects by specifying a system of two simultaneous equations, in which the dependent variables are (i) the number of spills, and (ii) the extent of pollution insurance coverage purchased by firms. Unfortunately, data on pollution insurance purchased by firms, and claims paid to firms in relation to spills and contaminated sites, are not available. This forces us to focus on single, reduced-form equations for spill counts (Eqs. (2) and (3)), in which the right-hand side variables are exogenous factors influencing care, and hence spills, either directly or through the demand and supply for pollution insurance.

The variables x, therefore, include measures of the state's economic and manufacturing activities; hazardous waste generation per capita; population characteristics (density, membership in environmental organizations); and program characteristics (indicators of presence of provisions for victim compensation, citizen suit, punitive damages, and strict liability).

The number of toxic spills should depend on the extent of economic activity involving chemicals. We capture this and the breakdown of industrial activity by firm size with the numbers of production units in the industrial and extractive sectors in the state, both at the aggregate level and broken down into "large" and "small" plants. We are forced to use the number of employees to define small and large establishments, since data on the number of firms by *asset* size are not available at the state level. In this paper, we report results obtained by defining small establishments as those with fewer than 20 employees.[12] We take log transformations of these variables to allow the number of spills to grow at either a decreasing or an increasing rate with the number of firms.

To further capture damages D, we create a pair of indicator variables, VICTCOMP and PUNDAMAGE, for, respectively, the presence of provisions for victim compensation in the state mini-Superfund program, and whether a state initiating cleanup in the presence of recalcitrant responsible parties may impose punitive damages.

To account for the probability q of being targeted by the agency, we construct a dummy (CITSUIT) for whether private citizens can initiate actions against parties

---

[12]Although establishments with fewer than 20 employees account for only about 2% of the total value of shipments from manufacturing firms, they are very numerous, making up about two-thirds of the total number of establishments. We repeated our analyses for other breakdowns into smaller and larger establishments (e.g., establishments with fewer and more than 50 or 100 employees) and obtained qualitatively similar results.

responsible for toxic releases. We treat this provision as an effective broadening of the reach of the state environmental agency because it increases the ability of private citizens to serve as "deputies" for the agency, possibly permitting closer oversight over firm behavior than the agency could achieve by itself.

The regressor at the heart of this paper is, of course, STRICT, our indicator for whether the mini-Superfund program prescribes strict liability. We note that STRICT could also influence firms' perceived probabilities of being targeted by the agency. In the absence of strict liability, the agency may have only limited control over potentially responsible parties (EPA [21]).

In most cases, liability standards are subject to interpretation by the state courts, based on the statutory language, the statutory structure, and the common law arguments advanced by the state (ELI [6]). State laws interpreted to impose strict liability on responsible parties typically give enforcement authority to the state agency, making it possible for the agency to issue unilateral orders to responsible parties, and to refer cases with recalcitrant responsible parties to the state general attorney. The burden of proof is placed on the defendant (the firm alleged to be responsible for the release).

By contrast, under negligence-based liability the burden of proof is on the plaintiff (the state agency), which must show that the responsible party committed a negligent, reckless, or intentionally wrongful act. It is up to the courts to establish the standards of negligence case by case. It is generally argued that, under negligence-based liability, the state agency will have to spend more resources investigating the intent of parties involved at a contaminated site and will face a smaller universe of parties on which liability may attach. This may lessen the incentive of firms to take care (ELI [6]).

While many responsible parties reach consent agreements with the state agency, making litigation necessary over only a fraction of all hazardous waste sites on the agency's priority list, the incentives faced by firms should be influenced by the expected outcome of litigation. This may depend on the aggressiveness of the state agency, which we measure as the number of lawyers working on state superfund cases per million residents (LAWYER); on the perceived efficiency of the state court system, and on the perception of the courts' general tendency to rule in favor of the defendant or the plaintiff in toxic tort lawsuits. We measure state court efficiency by the ratio of all civil cases disposed of to all civil cases filed (CORTEFF).[13] Lacking better statistics on state court rulings, we assume that state

---

[13] Data from *Court Statistics Project*, National Center for Court Statistics, Williamsburg, VA. By this measure, state court efficiency is lowest in Florida and Connecticut and is highest in Iowa. Interestingly, there appears to be a small, but negative and significant, correlation between state court efficiency and strict liability: States imposing strict liability appear to have less efficient court systems. Since the litigation generated under the state mini-Superfund program is likely to be only a small portion of total civil litigation, we do not believe that a lower degree of court system efficiency is necessarily caused by the additional litigation promoted by the liability structure. It is possible that some states plagued by an inefficient court system may have envisioned strict liability as a way of avoiding lengthy and costly litigation at state Superfund sites (strict liability does not place the burden of proof on the plantiff, reducing the states' costs in preparation for litigation; potentially responsible parties may be lured into out-of-court settlements, effectively bypassing a slow and inefficient court system). As one reviewer suggests, this negative correlation may reflect pressure by interest groups on state legislators: state legislation may pass a more stringent liability standard to please residents and environmental groups, while in reality the inefficient state court system helps potentially responsible parties delay payment of cleanup costs. On balance, these two arguments leave the sign of the coefficient of the state court system efficiency variable unknown *a priori*.

court preferences for business activity and environmental quality are similar to preferences of the state, and proxy them with the percentage of votes for the Democratic candidate in the most recent presidential elections (PCTDEMPR), a widely used political variable.[14]

To control for possible differences in state propensities to report spills to the ERNS, we include in the regression model two variables that we believe influence the *reporting* of spills: population density (accidents may be more difficult to conceal in highly populated places) and membership, per 1000 residents, in any of three major environmental organizations (environmental awareness of the population may affect the level of scrutiny and reporting). However, population density may also influence the extent and cost of cleanup and may encourage firms to avoid releases for fear that they will be reported to authorities by community residents, making the sign of the coefficient of population density unknown *a priori*. Similar considerations apply to the sign of the coefficient of ENVORG (membership in environmental organizations). Finally, we include among the regressors the amount of hazardous waste per capita generated in the state.

For both the linear and the Poisson regressions, our first order of business is to determine whether strict liability and the other attributes of a state's mini-Superfund program explain the number of spills beyond what is predicted by the extent and type of manufacturing and the reporting variables. To do so, we regress the number of accidental releases in a state on manufacturing and reporting variables and state program dummies, simply entered additively in the right-hand side of the model. We lag the dummy variables for strict liability, citizen suit, victim compensation, and punitive damages one year to try to avoid possible endogeneity with the dependent variable (number of spills), and to account for the lag, if any, in firms' behavioral responses to new laws.[15]

After establishing these relationships, we attempt to control for unobserved heterogeneity, and then, to see if behavioral responses of firms are structurally different under the two alternative liability regimes, we run separate regressions for states and years with and without strict liability.

7. RESULTS

We first report our initial OLS and Poisson regressions, testing the strict liability effect while controlling for state industrial activity (by firm size or sector), population, other program features, and proxies for environmental protection. The results are suggestive, but have several possible explanations. To eliminate possibilities, we estimate fixed effects models (to see if the effects are due to unobserved heterogeneity) and random effects (where the fixed effects models prove unsatisfactory). Finally, we split the sample according to liability regime and test for reporting effects and for the appropriateness of our basic econometric specification.

---

[14] To capture some of the possible effects of pollution insurance coverage, we also ran some initial regressions that included a dummy for whether the CGL pollution exclusion in that state has been successfully challenged. The coefficient of the dummy variable was close to zero and insignificant. We therefore omit this variable from the specifications we report in the paper.

[15] We present a simple test of endogeneity of strict liability in Appendix B.

34   ALBERINI AND AUSTIN

A. Initial Regressions

As shown in Table II, the number of spills a state experiences in a year is
generally well predicted by the numbers of manufacturing and mining establishments located there, the amount of hazardous waste generated in the state, the
degree of environmental awareness of the public, population density, and the
policy dummies. Jointly considered, these regressors are significant predictors of
the numbers of spills at the conventional significance levels and explain a reason-

TABLE II

Spills in Fixed Facilities: Basic Specifications[a]

Variable	OLS Acids Dep. Var.: log(count + 1)		OLS Ammonia Dep. Var.: log(count + 1)		Poisson Chlorine Dep. Var.: count	
	A	B	A	B	A	B
Intercept	−1.7198	−0.1647	−3.6768	−4.2993	−5.1263	−5.5867
	(−3.805)	(−0.269)	(−7.048)	(−5.777)	(−19.668)	(−6.686)
Log manufact. firms	−0.2766	−0.3643	0.2106	0.4209	−0.8101	−0.2815
20+	(−1.841)	(−2.214)	(1.125)	(1.999)	(−8.628)	(−1.537)
Log manufact. firms	0.5975	0.7377	0.4792	0.2468	1.5596	1.1258
< 20	(3.585)	(4.150)	(2.398)	(1.138)	(15.854)	(6.060)
Log mining firms	0.3214	0.1357				
20+	(4.515)	(1.736)				
Log mining firms	0.1082	0.2532				
< 20	(1.491)	(3.183)				
HAZWASTE	0.0100	0.0267	0.0440	0.0286	0.1219	0.1125
	(0.687)	(1.615)	(2.632)	(1.507)	(8.524)	(7.758)
Log pop. Density	−0.0269	0.2581	−0.2111	−0.2511	−0.0013	−0.1582
	(−2.004)	(5.094)	(−4.168)	(−4.149)	(−0.046)	(−2.228)
ENVORG	0.2446	−0.0063	−0.0864	−0.0816	−0.0970	0.0087
	(5.474)	(−0.400)	(−5.579)	(−4.274)	(−11.011)	(0.481)
Strict (lagged)	0.4408	0.3510	0.3138	0.2797	0.7392	0.5051
	(5.214)	(3.708)	(3.008)	(2.443)	(12.706)	(4.792)
Citizen suit (lagged)	−0.2475	0.2567	0.2568	0.1407	0.4066	−0.1029
	(−2.503)	(3.411)	(2.246)	(1.457)	(9.208)	(−1.030)
Punitive damages	−0.0744	0.1767	0.1986	0.0488	−0.1982	−0.0967
(lagged)	(−0.866)	(1.792)	(1.830)	(0.388)	(−4.186)	(−0.858)
Victim compens.	0.2692	−0.1235	0.2568	0.2426	−0.0998	0.1591
(lagged)	(3.711)	(−1.184)	(2.099)	(1.898)	(−0.557)	(1.367)
LAWYER		−0.0303		−0.0385		−0.1082
		(−1.349)		(−1.346)		(−2.698)
CORTEFF		−0.2320		−0.1407		0.5336
		(−0.597)		(−0.288)		(1.2753)
PCTDEMPR		−4.2266		2.2904		−2.8074
		(−5.752)		(2.467)		(−3.338)
Adj. R^2	0.6649	0.6762	0.4684	0.4912		
F statistic	70.252	49.321	39.281	27.311		
Log likelihood					−3366.59	−2635.70
N	384	325	392	328	391	328

TABLE II—*Continued*

Variable	Poisson Halogenated Solvents Dep. Var.: count		Poisson TCA, TCE, METH, PERC Dep. Var.: count	
	A	B	A	B
Intercept	−4.5603	−8.3095	−6.1816	−5.2316
	(−2.669)	(−8.271)	(−8.801)	(−5.464)
Log manufact. firms 20 +	0.1575	0.5193	0.4691	1.0483
	(0.395)	(2.027)	(1.666)	(4.055)
Log manufact. firms < 20	0.7071	0.7040	0.3823	−0.0829
	(1.557)	(2.623)	(1.411)	(−0.334)
HAZWASTE	0.0731	0.0838	0.0495	0.0137
	(3.008)	(3.138)	(2.492)	(0.723)
Log pop. density	0.1073	−0.1970	0.0960	0.0516
	(0.822)	(−1.927)	(1.209)	(0.560)
ENVORG	−0.1548	0.0087	0.0078	0.0910
	(−2.871)	(0.287)	(0.325)	(3.473)
Strict (lagged)	0.2631	0.5457	0.5392	0.2082
	(0.547)	(3.599)	(3.529)	(1.586)
Citizen suit (lagged)	0.7798	−0.1467	0.2625	0.0053
	(1.914)	(−1.189)	(1.941)	(0.035)
Punitive damages (lagged)	−0.2843	−0.0776	−0.4124	−0.0065
	(−1.690)	(−0.433)	(−2.912)	(−0.042)
Victim compens. (lagged)	−0.3088	−0.3890	−0.5205	−0.4198
	(−1.518)	(−2.532)	(−4.089)	(−2.881)
LAWYER		0.0048		−0.0074
		(0.094)		(−0.174)
CORTEFF		0.6026		0.2779
		(0.706)		(0.366)
PCTDEMPR		−3.8122		−4.9037
		(−2.934)		(−3.875)
Log likelihood	−2216.34	−1452.65	−251.23	−281.84
n	392	328	392	328

[a] *T* statistics in parentheses. Poisson regression: misspecification-consistent *t* statistics.

able portion of the variability in the dependent variable. The adjusted R^2 values in the models for acid and ammonia spills are 67 and 49%, respectively.[16]

Looking at the results for the attributes of the state mini-Superfund programs (Table II, regressions A), we find that the coefficient of strict liability is positive and significant: states that adopt strict liability continue to have higher rates of toxic spills. Further controlling for prosecutorial discretion of the state agency and likely outcome of litigation through the state court system (regressions B) does not

---

[16] For the Poisson regressions, we compute the *t* statistics based on misspecification-robust standard errors. The misspecification robust covariance matrix is $(F^{-1}VF^{-1})$, where V is the Fisher information matrix for the Poisson model and F is the expected value of the outer product of the score, the score being the vector of first derivatives of the model (see Fahrmeir and Tutz [7]).

change this result. The effect is robust across different chemical families and specifications and can be quite large.[17]

The effects of other attributes of the state programs appear to vary with the specification and with the chemical being analyzed. Excluding the dummy variables that capture the other aspects of the state programs generally does not change the coefficients of strict liability very much, nor their statistical significance.

The coefficients of population density and membership in leading environmental organizations frequently switch sign from one regression to the next, probably as a result of the moderate, but significant, correlation between these variables. By contrast, the quantity of hazardous waste generated per resident is almost always significantly and positively related to the frequency of spills. With values ranging from 0.04 to 0.12, however, the effect of HAZWASTE, which serves as a control for the amount of activity involving substances actually classified as toxic waste, is not very large.

Of particular interest is the possible firm-size effect. To find whether the number of small and large establishments have different effects on spills, we performed F tests (for ammonia and acid spills) and likelihood ratio tests (for the Poisson models) of the null hypothesis that, in each equation A of Table II, the coefficients of large firms are equal to their small-firm counterparts. We reject the null for spills of acids, chlorine, and the broader halogenated solvent family. For these families, the number of small firms is positively and significantly associated with the number of accidents, but the number of large firms is not. But the contributions of small and large firms to the frequency of ammonia spills and the four halogenated solvents are not statistically different.

Adding variables that account for the aggressiveness of the state in forcing responsible parties to pay for cleanup and that account for the expected outcome of litigation over responsibility at contaminated sites (regressions B) does not alter the basic results about the sign and magnitude of the coefficient of strict liability. F tests (for the linear regressions) and Wald tests (for the Poisson regressions) indicate that these additional variables as a whole significantly improve the fit of the model. In most regressions, the number of mini-Superfund case lawyers has the expected negative effect on spills, whereas the coefficient of the court efficiency variable tends to switch sign, depending on the chemical family. However, t statistics indicate that the coefficients of the latter variable are, for the most part, insignificant at the conventional levels. Popular support for Democratic presidential candidates generally has a strong and negative effect on the number of spills.

Regression results from controlling for the composition of production activities are reported in Table III. We control for the composition of manufacturing in the state by including as explanatory variables the number of plants, in logs, for industries that are major users of the chemicals. For instance, we predict annual chlorine gas and chlorine dioxide spills using the numbers of chemical plants (chlorine being a feedstock for other intermediate and finished chemical products), paper and allied products plants, food processing establishments, and textiles plants, all of which use these substances for bleaching purposes. Similarly, chlorinated solvents are used as a chemical feedstock, for metal cleaning purposes in

---

[17]The regressions using the broad halogenated solvents data suggest that the number of spills of these chemicals are up to 200 percent greater in strict liability states than what would be predicted by the other independent variables alone.

TABLE III

Spills in Fixed Facilities: Composition of Manufacturing[a]

Variable	OLS Anhydrous ammonia	Poisson Chlorine	Poisson Halogenated solvents	Poisson TCA, TCE, METH, PERC
Intercept	−2.6282	−3.3646	−2.9812	−4.1433
	(−5.892)	(−7.186)	(3.349)	(−1.050)
HAZWASTE	0.0600	0.0143	0.0494	0.0293
	(3.469)	(7.783)	(2.093)	(1.279)
Log chemical plants	−0.0518	0.6728	0.8086	0.3805
	(−0.370)	(5.272)	(2.226)	(1.957)
Log food processing plants	0.7239	0.5970		
	(6.730)	(4.083)		
Log textiles plants		−0.0599		
		(−0.972)		
Log furniture plants			−1.5308	−0.8461
			(−6.543)	(−5.441)
Log paper & allied products plants		−0.4003		
		(−2.484)		
Log rubber & plastics plants			−0.6171	−0.6522
			(−1.419)	(−2.365)
Log primary metals plants	−0.2386			
	(−1.815)			
Log fabricated metals plants	0.3267		0.3296	−0.5482
	(1.756)		(0.499)	(−1.234)
Log industrial machinery plants			−0.4671	0.7218
			(−1.088)	(1.505)
Log electronic & electric plants			3.3622	1.2874
			(3.885)	(4.679)
Log transportation equipment plants			0.7852	1.0217
			(3.623)	(6.735)
Log instruments plants			−1.7109	−0.4646
			(−3.543)	(−2.214)
Log pop. Density	−0.0322	0.0029	0.1451	0.2809
	(−0.661)	(0.037)	(1.401)	(2.857)
Env. Organization membership	−0.0768	−0.0584	−0.1576	0.0046
	(−5.244)	(−2.920)	(−2.039)	(0.170)
Strict (lagged)	0.2582	0.4847	−0.2970	0.1925
	(2.666)	(4.032)	(−0.883)	(1.373)
Citizen suit (lagged)	0.1429	0.1842	0.4738	−0.0708
	(1.633)	(1.800)	(1.499)	(−0.670)
Punitive damages (lagged)	0.2862	−0.0663	−0.1766	−0.5078
	(2.955)	(−0.596)	(−1.227)	(−4.514)
Victim compens. (lagged)	0.0849	0.0626	−0.1994	−0.6702
	(0.759)	(0.380)	(−0.861)	(−4.587)
adj. R^2	0.5585			
s^2	0.5327			
F-statistic	43.777			
Log likelihood		−3405.85	−2676.01	−344.98
n	373	391	390	390

[a] T statistics in parentheses. Poisson regressions: misspecification-consistent *t* statistics.

manufacturing, and in the furniture and plastics industries. Although they are also widely used for dry cleaning and in the service/repair industry, we do not try to control explicitly for the businesses in the latter sectors: population density should capture their numbers.[18]

In general, this improves the predictive power of the models, but has a mixed effect on the strict liability dummy. For spills involving halogenated solvents, the coefficient of the strict liability dummy becomes insignificant. One possible explanation for this finding is that the presence of other environmental regulations for these substances overwhelms the incentives posed by liability. When we included state regulations and standards for emissions of halogenated solvents (reported in Sigman [19]), though, we found no evidence of a significant correlation with the number of spills involving these substances. Other provisions of the state program (victim compensation and punitive damages) appear still to be associated with a lower number of spills.[19, 20]

For ammonia and chlorine spills, strict liability continues to be positively and significantly associated with the number of spills, over and above what is predicted by the amount of manufacturing in the various industries. Hence, we focus on these chemicals, as well as on acid spills, in our next analyses.

B. Interpreting Initial Results

That the presence of strict liability is a positive and significant predictor of spills is consistent with several possible explanations.

First, the effect could be real: strict liability could give firms fewer incentives to take care than a negligence standard, depending on how the negligence standard compares with the level of care chosen by firms under strict liability, how effective safety investment is in reducing the likelihood of spills, and the wealth of firms.

Second, the estimated coefficient of strict liability may capture the effects of other omitted factors influencing the number of spills. To account for unobserved heterogeneity, we respecify our models to include fixed and random effects.

Third, it is possible that the strict liability dummy captures a heightened reporting effect on the part of both firms and authorities—that states which have adopted strict liability are populated by individuals, firms, and government officials with a higher propensity to report spills. Fourth, the positive and statistically significant coefficient of the strict liability dummy may be an artifact of the econometric specification. For instance, if the true coefficients of the major variables in the model differ across states that do and do not have strict liability provisions, imposing that they be equal may result in biased estimates.

---

[18] Table III excludes acids. Because of their widespread use in manufacturing and mining, we do not try to control for the composition of the industrial sector.

[19] Excluding these other attributes makes the strict liability dummy negative but insignificant.

[20] The coefficients of the variables measuring the number of firms in the various manufacturing sectors often have counterintuitive signs in the halogenated solvents equations of Table III. We blame this result on the high degree of collinearity between these regressors: the coefficient of correlation between counts of plants varies between 0.83 and 0.94. When we go beyond controlling for manufacturing composition to also include firm size, there is little effect on the predictive power of our regression models, and the sign, magnitude, and significance of the coefficient of the strict liability dummy does not change much.

Formal testing of the third and fourth explanations requires that we split the data into two separate sets and fit separate regressions for observations from states and years with and without strict liability hazardous waste laws. Based on these separate regressions, we perform two Wald tests. The first is a test of the "reporting effect," the null hypothesis of which is that the coefficients of EN-VORG and population density are equal across the two regimes.

The second Wald test seeks evidence that, under strict liability, small plants contribute disproportionately to the number of spills—as would be the case if, for example, strict liability resulted in risky operations being shifted to smaller firms. The null hypothesis of the second Wald test is, therefore, that the variables measuring small-plant effects and those measuring large-plant effects have equal coefficients under the two regimes.

In the next section we report on the regressions accounting for unobserved heterogeneity. Following that, we present the tests of the reporting effect and of the firm-size effect.

C. Unobserved Heterogeneity

It is possible that spill counts are influenced by unobserved state characteristics that persist over time, such as the state regulatory stringency, the state's experience in dealing with toxic pollution problems, and insurers' reactions to liability. To account for unobserved heterogeneity in our data, we respecify our regression equations to include fixed effects and random effects.

In the case of acids and ammonia, the fixed effects model is

$$\log(y_{it} + 1) = \alpha_i + \tilde{x}_{it}\beta + \varepsilon_{it}, \tag{4}$$

where the αs are state-specific intercepts and $\tilde{x}$ includes only time-varying regressors (see Greene [10]).

Results from the fixed effects models for acid and ammonia spills are reported in Table IV. Although an F test supports the fixed effects model as opposed to a model with a common intercept, and a Hausman test supports the fixed effects model over the relevant random effects model,[21] it is hard to make out much from the fixed effects model for acid spills. All coefficients are insignificant, including that of strict liability, which is negative.

The fixed effects model is better behaved for ammonia spills. In this model, four coefficients are individually significant at the 10% level or better: the coefficients of small manufacturing plants, the citizen suit dummy, state superfund lawyers per million residents, and the percentage of popular votes cast for the Democratic presidential candidate. The coefficient of strict liability is now negative and insignificant.

To gain further insight into unobserved heterogeneity, we also fit random effects models.[22] For the acid and ammonia spills, the random effects follow the usual assumption of normality (see Greene [10]).

---

[21] Here, the relevant random effects model is a model that, like the fixed effects model, only includes time-varying regressors.

[22] One important difference between random effects and fixed effects models is that, in contrast to fixed effects models, random effects models rely on the assumption that the causes of unobserved heterogeneity are uncorrelated with the independent variables included in the model.

40   ALBERINI AND AUSTIN

TABLE IV

Spills in Fixed Facilities: Panel Data Models (T statistics in parentheses)

Variable	Acids		Ammonia	
	State random effects	State fixed effects	State random effects	State fixed effects
Intercept	−1.3082	–	−6.7930	–
	(−1.310)		(−5.321)	
Log manufact. firms 20 +	−0.2657	0.3210	−0.2293	−0.2440
	(−0.955)	(0.479)	(−0.652)	(−0.325)
Log manufact. firms <20	0.7406	0.7022	1.0638	3.2112
	(2.428)	(0.834)	(2.913)	(3.247)
Log mining firms 20 +	0.0669	0.0261		
	(0.673)	(0.161)		
Log mining firms <20	0.2434	0.4403		
	(2.098)	(1.209)		
HAZWASTE	0.0122	–	0.0218	–
	(0.394)		(0.553)	
Log pop. Density	0.2311	0.5845	−0.2067	−2.0714
	(2.412)	(0.356)	(−1.807)	(−1.062)
ENVORG	−0.0223	–	−0.8138	–
	(−0.805)		(−2.258)	
Strict (lagged)	0.0281	−0.0927	0.1483	−0.0402
	(0.278)	(−0.702)	(1.357)	(−0.264)
Citizen suit (lagged)	0.2284	0.2823	0.3795	0.6030
	(1.865)	(1.355)	(2.577)	(2.412)
Punitive damages (lagged)	−0.1577	−0.1657	−0.1164	−0.1389
	(−1.122)	(−1.568)	(−1.251)	(−1.085)
Victim compens. (lagged)	−0.8147	−0.1980	−0.3070	−0.3459
	(−0.969)	(−0.948)	(−1.889)	(−1.383)
LAWYER	−0.0273	−0.0063	−0.0434	−0.0471
	(−0.153)	(−0.285)	(−2.234)	(−1.834)
CORTEFF	0.0902	0.1344	−0.3981	−0.2707
	(0.331)	(0.417)	(−1.349)	(−0.699)
PCTDEMPR	−2.6344	−1.8028	4.6656	3.0902
	(−2.914)	(−1.299)	(4.537)	(1.912)
adj. R^2	0.6555	0.8334	0.4293	0.7744
F statistic		29.46		21.29
Log likelihood				
N	325	331	325	338

The results of the random effects models are also reported in Table IV and are quite instructive. In the acid and ammonia equations, strict liability is still positively associated with the number of spills, but its coefficient is no longer significant. Small firms are always positively and significantly associated with spills, but the coefficient of large firms is negative and insignificant.[23]

[23] Count data models, like the Poisson and the negative binomial, lend themselves to state-specific fixed and random effects. Unfortunately, the estimation routine did not converge for either variant for the chlorine spills. When we fit a regular negative binomial model, which allows for extra-Poisson variation (i.e., Var(y_{it}) can be greater than λ_{it}, where $\lambda_{it} = \exp(x_{it}\,\beta)$; Fahrmeir and Tutz [7]), but does not incorporate state-specific random effects, the coefficient of strict liability remains positive and significant. In addition, much as in the fixed effects models for acids and ammonia spills, the coefficient of small manufacturing firms is positive and strongly significant, and the coefficient of large manufacturing firms is negative and insignificant.

To summarize, three important results emerge from the models allowing for unobserved heterogeneity. First, unobserved heterogeneity *may* be a possible explanation for our earlier results about the effects of strict liability. Second, the coefficients of two program attributes interpreted as increasing firms' liability—provisions for punitive damages and for victim compensation—are now almost always *negatively* associated with spills, although the significance of their respective coefficients vary with the chemical family and model. The coefficient of provisions allowing for citizen suits is positive, suggesting that such provisions have made citizens more aware of spills. Third, regardless of the sign of the lagged strict liability dummy, small manufacturing firms appear to be consistently associated with more numerous spills.

D. Reporting Effect and Structural Change

In Table V we report the results of regressions for acids, ammonia, and chlorine spills that isolate the observations from states and years with strict liability from those with negligence-based liability.[24, 25]

The null hypothesis of equal propensities to report spills in states and years with versus without strict liability implies the equality of the coefficients on population density and environmental awareness. The Wald test clearly rejects this null hypothesis in the acids and chlorine regressions, but the sign of the coefficient of membership in environmental organization is negative—the opposite of what we had expected, were our proposed explanation ((iii) in Section 5 B) correct. If an environmentally sensitive populace truly increases reporting, then this tendency must have been more than compensated for by firms' tendency to increase safety precautions for fear of being reported.

This evidence and the fact that patterns are difficult to recognize for population density and for both variables in states with negligence-based liability suggest that enhanced reporting is probably not the reason that all else the same, states with strict liability appear to have more numerous spills.

Table V also displays the results of the Wald test of the hypothesis about firm size. With the exception only of ammonia spills, the Wald test rejects the null hypothesis that the coefficients of small and large plants are the same across the two liability regimes. The estimation results show clearly that, in strict liability regimes, the number of spills increases with the number of *smaller* plants. By contrast, the number of larger plants is typically not significantly associated with the number of spills. In negligence-based regimes, this result is reversed in the acids regressions, while neither firm-size variable is a significant predictor of the number of ammonia and chlorine spills.

The estimated equations of Table V predict that the "average" state (i.e., a state with average numbers of small and large manufacturing establishments) should have approximately the same number of spills under either liability regime. For instance, in the case of acids the predicted median number of spills is 9.5 under

---

[24] States which adopted strict liability after 1987 have observations in both sets of regressions. The liability rules in force at the beginning of each year determine to which regression an observation is assigned.

[25] To save space, we only report results from specifications that omit variables capturing prosecutorial discretion of the state agency and likely outcome of litigation. Results are qualitatively very similar when these variables are added in the model.

42   ALBERINI AND AUSTIN

TABLE V

Spills in Fixed Facilities: Separate Regressions[a]

	Acids (OLS)	Ammonia (OLS)	Chlorine (Poisson[b])
Strict liability (n = 277)			
Constant	− 3.4209	− 3.9280	− 4.4401
	(− 6.361)	(− 6.415)	(− 3.677)
Log population density	0.0579	− 0.1615	− 0.0082
	(1.289)	(− 3.206)	(− 0.076)
ENVORG	− 0.0858	− 0.0677	− 0.0821
	(− 5.443)	(− 3.829)	(− 2.615)
HAZWASTE	0.0110	0.0750	0.1234
	(4.408)	(2.555)	(4.009)
Log manufac. 20 +	− 0.2947	0.0455	− 0.8090
	(− 1.632)	(0.225)	(− 3.578)
Log manufac. < 20	1.0810	0.7141	1.5528
	(5.581)	(3.288)	(8.384)
Negligence-based liability (n = 115)			
Constant	0.0523	− 1.5881	0.5775
	(0.055)	(− 1.156)	(0.741)
Log population density	− 0.1379	0.0069	0.2511
	(− 1.1934)	(0.041)	(1.967)
ENVORG	0.0621	− 0.1275	− 4.41e-5
	(2.487)	(− 3.507)	(− 0.001)
HAZWASTE	0.0380	0.0110	0.0516
	(2.454)	(0.471)	(3.850)
Log manufac. 20 +	1.0855	− 0.3400	0.3337
	(3.329)	(− 0.717)	(0.854)
Log manufac. < 20	− 0.7985	0.8438	− 0.1300
	(− 2.471)	(1.795)	(− 0.340)
Wald test on reporting variables	25.50	2.32	21.00
Wald test on small and large plants	40.53	3.43	36.97

[a] *Wald test on reporting variables* test the null hypothesis that the coefficients of LPOPDENS and ENVORG are equal across the two liability regimes. The *Wald test on small and large plants* tests the null hypothesis that the coefficients of log small and log large plants are equal across the two liability regimes. For large samples, both tests are distributed as chi squares with 2 degrees of freedom under the null hypothesis. At the 5% significance level, the critical value is 5.99.

[b] T stats in parentheses. Poisson regression: misspecification-consistent t statistics.

strict liability and 10.9 with negligence-based liability; the two figures are not statistically distinguishable.

However, states that have adopted strict liability provisions differ from other states in one important respect: they typically have more manufacturing establishments. States with strict liability boast an average of 5402 small establishments (against 3792 for negligence states), and 2618 larger plants (against 1895). (In both types of states, the proportion of small to large plants is roughly 2 to 1.)

Taking these differences into account, the two separate regression equations in Table V imply that the predicted number of spills in a year *is* significantly greater in states with strict liability. When differences in the actual numbers of plants are allowed for, the predicted median number of acid spills in strict liability states becomes 15.6, versus 11.9 in negligence states. This is consistent with the results of Table II, where states with strict liability were seen to experience more spills. The other chemical families produce similar results. We conclude that *differences in the number of plants* and *in the higher propensity of small firms to experience spills* may be one reason accidents appear to be more frequent in states with strict liability.

8. DISCUSSION AND CONCLUSIONS

We have analyzed the patterns of spills and accidents involving chemicals in an effort to answer the question: Has strict liability encouraged firms to take care and thus reduced the number of accidents and spills? Because the predictions from the theoretical literature are ambiguous, we have turned to an empirical analysis of this issue. We have exploited the variation in the liability provisions of state Superfund programs, looking for additional effects over and above those created by the federal Superfund program.

Our results vary with the chemicals analyzed. This is reasonable given the various regulations and uses of the chemicals and the diverse industries in which they are used. For some of these chemicals (halogenated solvents), there does not seem to be much difference in spill rates between states with and without strict liability provisions in their cleanup programs, after we account for the number of plants and for the composition of manufacturing.

For other chemicals (acids, chlorine, and ammonia) our initial empirical evidence suggests that, even after accounting for manufacturing and population variables, spills may be more numerous in states that have adopted strict liability. Further investigation suggests that for some chemical families, this difference may be the result of unobserved state-level heterogeneity, the liability structure *per se* being insignificant. This could be due to the different industrial activities that use the specified chemicals, to their different market structures, locations, and interaction with state regulatory agencies, and possibly to different environmental standards. These same panel-data regressions also suggest that small firms might be positively associated with spills, regardless of the liability structure, a result that is consistent with the existence of economies of scale in safety or with the possibility that the liability regime cannot alter small firms' expected disbursements for pollution releases.

By contrast, an alternative explanation, supported by the results of separate regressions for states with and without strict liability, is that small and large plants (our proxy for small and large firms) may contribute differently to spill rates, depending on whether the state's hazardous wastes policy is based on strict liability or negligence. Specifically, in states that have adopted strict liability, small firms appear responsible for a larger share of spills involving these chemicals. Since states that have adopted strict liability have, on average, more manufacturing firms and more small firms (in absolute terms), this effect is magnified, leading to greater numbers of spills in states with strict liability laws in place.

The small-firm finding could be the result of deliberate firm decisions about privately optimal levels of care under different liability regimes. As earlier argued, depending on the particular mix of possible damage sizes and asset levels of small firms, firms with limited assets operating in states with negligence-based liability may choose a higher level of care than a similar firm operating in a strict-liability state. That might be the case, for instance, if the negligence standard established by the courts were somewhat more stringent than the level of care that the firm would spontaneously choose to minimize its expected disbursements.

The result may also be explained by larger firms in strict liability states subcontracting riskier operations to smaller, more judgment-proof firms—or setting up formally separate, limited-asset corporations to handle such operations—in hopes of avoiding exposure to liability. Ringleb and Wiggins [17] find empirical evidence consistent with this phenomenon after firms began to be held strictly liable for long-term health damages to workers exposed to dangerous chemicals. It is possible that a similar phenomenon is at work here. In a negligence system, firms would have less incentive to spin off risky operations because their expected disbursement, beyond the least level of care that is deemed nonnegligent, would be zero. Riskier operations and limited investment in safety would increase the probability of accidents for smaller firms under strict liability.

It is also possible that small firms in states with strict liability have tended to specialize in operations for which $p(x)$, the function linking investment in safety and probability of an accident, is very flat. These are operations for which incremental expenditures would only modestly lower the firm's *ex ante* costs: perhaps large investments in capital equipment or in more highly skilled labor would be required to appreciably lower the probability of an accident. Such specialization in strict-liability states might occur precisely because of the Shavell result: shielded from full liability by their limited assets, small firms would find it more attractive to locate such operations in a strict-liability state, where their expected disbursements may be less than those incurred when complying with the negligence standards imposed by states upholding negligence-based liability. A firm facing a flat $p(x)$ would, therefore, be very reluctant to invest in safety.

A similar conclusion could be drawn if the damages, D, for typical *small*-firm operations were very low relative to the investment required to reduce spills. This would be the case if the spills are likely to be of little consequence to public health or to the firm responsible for them. In this case it would be privately optimal for small firms to invest little in safety; the outcome, in a strict liability state, would be more (but nondamaging) spills than in a negligence state that fails to recognize the nonharmful nature of those spills in setting its negligence standard. Unfortunately, the information we have in the ERNS database, concerning the quantity of chemicals released into the environment and the seriousness of the spill, is incomplete and does not allow us to explore this possibility.

To summarize, we have found evidence that strict liability *may* increase the frequency of accidental releases of toxic into the environment. Further research, preferably based on firm-level data, is needed to ascertain why such effects are seen for some chemicals but not others, whether risky production processes are indeed shifted to smaller firms, and whether a state's adoption of strict liability is potentially endogenous with the incidence of toxic spills in that state.

APPENDIX A: PROPERTIES OF CHEMICALS

Chlorine is a naturally occurring, greenish yellow gas with an irritating odor or is present in liquid solutions. It is used in making solvents, many chemicals, synthetic rubber, plastics, disinfectants, and chlorine bleach cleaners. Chlorine is acutely toxic to aquatic life. Chlorine dioxide is a gas with a pungent odor, and is normally diluted to less than 10% in cold solution to reduce its explosive properties. It is sold as a hydrate in frozen form and is used for bleaching wood pulp, oils, textiles, and flour and in water treatment. Both of these gases can cause irritation and severe burning of the eyes, nose, and throat, tearing, coughing, and chest pain. Higher levels burn the lungs and can cause a buildup of fluid in the lungs (pulmonary edema) and death. Both gases are highly reactive and explosive in fire.

Ammonia is a highly corrosive and reactive gas that can severely irritate the lungs and burn the skin and the eyes, leading to permanent damage. It is found as a colorless gas and in water solution and is used in making fertilizers, plastics, dyes, synthetic fibers, glues, animal foods and explosives. It is also used in the treatment and refining of metals.

METH is a colorless volatile liquid used in food, furniture and plastics processing, in paint removers, and in degreasing and cleaning fluids. TCE is used as a solvent for degreasing and dry cleaning and in printing inks, paints, lacquers, varnishes, and adhesives. TCA is used in making other chemicals and adhesives and as a solvent in cleaning metal and in cleaning plastic molds. It is also used to make other organic chemicals. These halogenated solvents tend to cause unconsciousness, and irregular heartbeat and may result in death at high exposures. Long term or extremely high exposures may damage the liver and brain and cause skin damage or burns. They are suspected carcinogens in humans, and trichloroethylene has been associated with reproductive problems. These chemicals are subject to a variety of federal statutes (see Macauley *et al.* [12]), including the Clean Air Act, which lists them as hazardous air pollutants. The National Research Council [14] lists TCE, PERC, METH, and TCA among the 25 most frequently detected substances at sites with contaminated ground water. TCE and PERC are ranked first and third, respectively.

Cleanup of groundwater contaminated by halogenated solvents is particularly difficult. Traditional pump-and-treat techniques tend to "miss" them due to their high density and tendency to form "columns" or "fingers" that do not easily mix with the surrounding groundwater and can recontaminate the groundwater as pumping and treatment take place (National Research Council [14]). Bioremediation options for this kind of solvents are also limited (National Research Council [13]).

The additional chlorinated solvents in the more comprehensive group of halogenated solvents have uses similar to those of METH, PERC, TCA, and TCE.

APPENDIX B: TESTING ENDOGENEITY OF STRICT LIABILITY

To test whether strict liability is endogenous to the number of spill events (the dependent variable in the models we estimate in this paper) we propose the following test procedure. We assume that log spills, y_{it}, depend on a set of variables measuring economic activity and generation of toxics in the state and on a variable, z_{it}^*, measuring state propensity to adopt strict liability,

$$y_{it} = x_{it}\beta + z_{it}^*\gamma + \varepsilon_{it}, \tag{B1}$$

where ε is a normally distributed i.i.d. error term. Following Alberini and Austin [2], we assume that z_{it}^*, state propensity to maintain strict liability, depends on a set

46 ALBERINI AND AUSTIN

of variables proxying the net benefits of strict liability over the alternative regime. Specifically, we assume that

$$z_{it}^* = w_{it}\delta + \eta_{it}, \tag{B2}$$

where w_{it} is a vector of state characteristics influencing the net benefits of strict liability and η is a standard normal error term. Strict liability is present in state i at time t ($z_{it} = 1$) if $z_{it}^* > 0$, and is absent ($z_{it} = 0$) otherwise. The error terms of the two equations are allowed to be correlated with one another for equal i and t, resulting in endogeneity of z_{it}^* (and hence z_{it}) and y_{it}.

To develop our endogeneity test, we factor the joint distribution of z_{it}^* and y_{it} into the marginal distribution of z_{it}^* (which is a standard normal) and the distribution of y_{it}, conditional on z_{it}^* (which is a normal). We use such factorization to compute the joint likelihood of liability configuration and number of spills. The joint likelihood is the probability that $z_{it}^* > 0$ (and hence strict liability is observed) or that $z_{it}^* \le 0$ (negligence-based liability is observed), times the density of y_{it}, conditional on strict liability or negligence-based liability. The probability that strict liability is observed is then $\Phi(w_{it}\delta)$, whereas the expected value of log spills, conditional on strict liability being in place is $x_{it}\beta + z_{it}\gamma + \sigma_{12}\phi(w_{it}\delta)/\Phi(w_{it}\delta)$. The expected value of log spills, conditional on liability not being in place, is $x_{it}\beta + z_{it}\gamma - \sigma_{12}\phi(w_{it}\delta)/(1 - \Phi(w_{it}\delta))$. This leads to an "augmented" regression for chemical spills.

The test procedure is as follows:

A. Fit a probit model in which the dependent variable is z_{it} and the set of right-hand variables is w_{it} to get $\hat{\delta}$.

B. Run OLS on the "augmented" regression in which the dependent variable is log spills, y_{it}, and the independent variables are x_{it}, z_{it}, and λ_{it}, where $\lambda_{it} = \phi(w_{it}\hat{\delta})/\Phi(w_{it}\hat{\delta})$ if $z_{it} = 1$ and $\lambda_{it} = -\phi(w_{it}\hat{\delta})/(1 - \Phi(w_{it}\delta))$ if $z_{it} = 0$. It can be shown that the coefficient of λ_{it} in the augmented regression is an estimate of σ_{12}, the covariance between ε and η.

C. Let ξ denote the square of the asymptotic t statistic for $\hat{\lambda}_{it}$ from step B. ξ serves as our test of endogeneity. Under the null hypothesis that $\delta_{12} = 0$ (z_{it} is not endogenous with log spills), ξ is distributed as a chi-squared with one degree of freedom.

We applied this procedure to the acids and ammonia spills. We select z_{it} to be the indicator for strict liability in the previous year, and following Alberini and Austin [2], we specify w_{it} to include (a) the lagged values of manufacturing and mining establishments with more and less than 20 employees; (b) measures of effectiveness of the state water and air quality programs; (c) measures of educational attainment of state residents; (d) estimates of the number of hazardous waste sites in the state; (e) state expenditure per capita, and percent of state budget dedicated to environmental programs; and (f) percent of votes for the Democratic candidate in the most recent presidential elections. Alberini and Austin argue that these variables capture the net benefits of the program, defined as the reduction in the expected health damages incurred by the population exposed to accidental releases of toxics at contaminated sites where mitigation is subsequently undertaken, minus the costs of the program. The cost of the program should be affected by the liability regime and program attributes, and by the type (size) of firms in the state.

The vector x_{it} includes log manufacturing and mining establishments with more and less than 20 employees, log population density, HAZWASTE, ENVORG, the number of lawyers working on state superfund cases per million state residents, our measure of efficiency of the state court system, and PCTDEMPR.

For the acids regression, ξ is equal to 4.71, which falls in the rejection region of the chi square with one degree of freedom, whereas for the ammonia regression ξ is equal to 1.488, leading us to conclude that liability is not endogenous with ammonia spill events. Based on these mixed results, for the purposes of this paper we keep the lagged strict liability indicator among the independent variables of the spill equations and leave further investigation of the endogeneity problem for future research.

REFERENCES

1. J. P. Action and L. Dixon, "Superfund and Transaction Costs. The Experiences of Insurers and Very Large Industrial Firms," RAND, Santa Monica, CA (1992).
2. A. Alberini and D. Austin, Off and on the liability bandwagon: Explaining state adoptions of strict liability in hazardous waste programs, *J. Regulatory Econom.* 15, 41–63 (1999).
3. H. Barnett, "Toxic Debts and the Superfund Dilemma," Univ. of North Carolina Press, Chapel Hill, NC (1994).
4. R. T. Beard, Bankruptcy and care choice, *RAND J. Econom.* 21, No. 4, 626–634 (1990).
5. Environmental Law Institute, "An Analysis of State Superfund Programs: 50-State Study. 1993 Update," prepared for the US Environmental Protection Agency, Washington, DC (1993).
6. Environmental Law Institute, "An Analysis of State Superfund Programs: 50-State Study. 1995 Update," prepared for the US Environmental Protection Agency, Washington, DC (1995).
7. L. Fahrmeir and G. Tutz, "Multivariate Statistical Modelling Based on Generalized Linear Models," Springer-Verlag, New York (1994).
8. V. M. Fogleman, "Hazardous Waste Cleanup, Liability, and Litigation," Quorum, Westport, CT (1992).
9. R. Gastel, "Environmental Pollution: Insurance Issues," Insurance Information Association, Washington, DC (1998).
10. W. H. Greene, "Econometric Analysis," 3rd ed., Prentice-Hall, Englewood Cliffs, NJ (1997).
11. B. A. Larson, Environmental policy based on strict liability: Implications of uncertainty and bankruptcy, *Land Econom.* 72 No. 1, 33–42 (1996).
12. M. K. Macauley, M. D. Bowes, and K. L. Palmer, "Using Economic Incentives to Regulate Toxic Substances," Resources for the Future, Washington, DC (1992).
13. National Research Council, "*In Situ* Bioremediation: When Does It Work?" National Academy Press, Washington, DC (1993).
14. National Research Council, "Alternatives for Ground Water Cleanup," National Academy Press, Washington, DC (1994).
15. J. J. Opaluch and T. A. Grigalunas, Controlling stochastic pollution events through liability rules: Some evidence from OCS leasing, *RAND J. Econom.*, 1984, 15, No. 1, 142–151 (1984).
16. R. Pitchford, How liable should a lender be? The case of judgment-proof firms and environmental risk, *Amer. Econom. Rev.* 85, 1171–1186 (1995).
17. A. H. Ringleb and S. N. Wiggins, Liability and large-scale, long-term hazards, *J. Polit. Economy* 98, No. 31, 574–595 (1990).
18. S. Shavell, A model of the optimal use of liability and safety regulation, *RAND J. Econom.* 15, 271–280 (1984).
19. H. Sigman, Cross-media pollution: Responses to restrictions on chlorinated solvent releases, *Land Econom.* 72, No. 3, 298–312 (1996).

20. T. H. Tietenberg, Indivisible toxic torts: The economics of joint and several liability, *Land Econom.* **65**, No. 4, 305–319 (1989).

21. U.S. Environmental Protection Agency, Office of Emergency and Remedial Response, "An Analysis of State Superfund Programs: 50-State Study," Washington, D.C. (1989).

22. U.S. Environmental Protection Agency, Office of Emergency and Remedial Response, "An Analysis of State Superfund Programs: 50-State Study. 1990 Update," Washington, D.C. (1990).

23. U.S. Environmental Protection Agency, Office of Emergency and Remedial Response, "An Analysis of State Superfund Programs: 50-State Study. 1991 Update," Washington, DC (1991).

24. U.S. Government Accounting Office, "Hazardous Waste. Issues Surrounding Insurance Availability," Report to the Congress, PB88-123138, Washington, DC (1987).

25. C. A. Wentz, "Waste Management," McGraw–Hill, New York (1989).

[22]

Liability and Large-Scale, Long-Term Hazards

Al H. Ringleb

Clemson University

Steven N. Wiggins

Texas A&M University

This paper analyzes the application of liability to large-scale, long-term hazards. The key features distinguishing such hazards are the long temporal separation between exposure to a hazard and disease and the large damages when injuries finally emerge. The large scale of damages creates a strong incentive to avoid liability payments, and the long temporal separation creates numerous avenues through which parties can avoid paying possible damage awards. The analysis focuses on the incentive to avoid paying damages by vertically divesting production tasks associated with serious occupational risks. Such divestiture can lower liability costs if the small firm operating the risky stage goes out of business before latent injuries emerge or has insufficient assets to pay damages and declares bankruptcy when suits are filed. The paper then presents an empirical regression analysis of small-firm entry into the U.S. economy between 1967 and 1980, the period in which liability laws were changing. The point estimate is that, ceteris paribus, liability changes appear to have led to a large increase in small corporations in hazardous sectors. Hence the empirical analysis shows widespread attempts to avoid liability by shielding assets through divestiture.

Helpful comments were provided by two anonymous referees, numerous colleagues at Texas A&M, Armen Alchian, Michael Baye, Steven Fazzari, James Griffin, Dan Levin, Allan Meltzer, Steve Pejovich, Sam Peltzman, W. Robert Reed, participants in the first annual Hayek seminar in Freiburg, Germany, and participants in seminars at Chicago, UCLA, Houston, Texas, Virginia Commonwealth, and George Mason. Special thanks go to Thomas R. Saving. Support for Wiggins's research through the Rex B. Grey Professorship and the Institute for Innovation and Design in Engineering at Texas A&M University is gratefully acknowledged.

I. Introduction

Exposure to large-scale, long-term hazards has recently emerged as a pressing policy concern. Consumers and workers have been exposed to health risks associated with radiation, DES, cigarette smoking, saccharin, occupational carcinogens, asbestos, dioxin, vinyl chloride, PCB, beta-napthylamine, benzidine, coke-oven emissions, and numerous other latent hazards. Recent studies have also linked occupational cancer to such basic materials as petroleum, coal, paraffin, wood, leather, iron ore, nickel, and chromium, all of which are fundamental inputs to production (Cole and Merletti 1980). These linkages suggest the likely exposure of hundreds of thousands of workers to possible and known carcinogens. Given the pervasive nature of the problem, an important economic question is how to institutionally govern compensation for workers injured by exposure to such hazards.

Tort liability, for good or ill, is quickly emerging as a primary institutional form.[1] A key advantage of a liability system is that such a system is injury-based.[2] Such a system permits compensation for injuries to be made after parties determine the extent of damages associated with hazardous products, and other activities. Accordingly, liability can produce both appropriate incentives for firms to provide safety and implicit insurance to injured workers or consumers (Spence 1977).

With latent hazards, liability appears particularly attractive because it permits injury-based compensation in an area in which dangers are (arguably) difficult to foresee. Despite its increasingly widespread adoption, however, there has been little evaluation of liability in a latent hazard setting. As a result, our understanding of how liability will perform rests largely on a simple extrapolation of analyses in acute injury settings (see, e.g., Oi 1973; Spence 1977).

This paper analyzes the use of a liability system in the latent hazard setting. The paper argues that the attractiveness of liability is somewhat superficial because the injury-based nature of the system leads to unique enforcement problems. In particular, the paper argues that a major option to minimize liability exposure is for firms to segregate risky activities in small corporations. Such segregation becomes valuable when latent injuries later manifest themselves and the claimants

---

[1] A number of other arrangements could also be used, including simple wage premiums, insurance, federal compensational programs, and direct regulation. See Wiggins and Ringleb (1989) for a more comprehensive discussion of the alternative institutional forms.

[2] According to Wright (1944, p. 238), "the purpose of the law of torts is to adjust losses, and to afford compensation for injuries sustained by one person as the result of the conduct of another."

are restricted to the assets of the small corporation to pay the associated liability damages.

The primary focus of the paper is to present empirical evidence that suggests that such firm efforts to avoid liability are widespread. This empirical evidence is generated by econometrically analyzing the pattern of entry by small corporations into the U.S. economy over the period 1967–80. The analysis shows that changes in potential liability appear to be closely linked to substantial increases in the number of small firms operating in hazardous sectors. The entry of these small firms, moreover, seems designed primarily to avoid liability. The implication is that liability, at least as currently imposed, may be difficult to enforce because these small firms have insufficient assets to pay substantial damage awards. Hence liability may not lead to large damage awards in long-run equilibrium, but instead may simply lead to a restructuring of enterprises to avoid damage payments. To the extent that this finding is verified, liability may perform significantly less well than existing analyses would suggest. The implication is that these enforcement problems need to be carefully addressed in continuing efforts to evaluate liability and to deal with the latent hazard problem.

The remainder of the paper is organized as follows. Section II discusses how latent hazards differ from other hazards and then shows how these differences create an incentive for firms to spin off hazardous activities to minimize the exposure of assets to liability claims. Section III then shows how the change in liability rules of the early 1970s created incentives for such divestiture during that period. The section then goes on to examine how changing liability rules are linked to substantial changes in the rate of entry of small corporations in risky sectors of the economy, suggesting that divestiture may be a significant problem. Section IV then summarizes the results and briefly examines several recent experiments designed to improve enforcement.

II. Latent Hazards, Small Firms, and the Enforcement of Liability

Latent hazards differ from other hazards both because of the severe nature of potential injuries and because of the long separation between exposure to substances and the manifestation of injury. Both of these distinguishing features contribute to enforcement problems for a liability system.

The hazards described in the introduction hold in common a significant potential to cause cancer, birth defects, and other major, life-threatening risks. The severity of these risks means that individual injuries are likely to be severe, and as a consequence each worker or consumer represents a potentially large damage award. Even a few suits can lead to formidable damage awards, and numerous suits can easily represent sums that are substantial relative to the assets of even large firms. The large size of these potential damage awards creates strong incentives to be concerned with liability and to make every effort to minimize potential damages.

Liability, moreover, is designed precisely to create such incentives; through efforts to reduce damage payments, firms provide increased safety. The problem with latent injuries, however, is that potential liabilities are sufficiently large that they can easily come to dwarf the assets of even large, profitable corporations (Epstein 1982, p. 8). When damages reach such a large scale, firms can easily become more concerned with structuring their affairs to minimize exposure rather than with improving safety.[3] These incentives to restructure can then undermine the otherwise attractive incentive properties of a liability system.

While large damage awards pose problems, what really sets latent hazards apart is the long temporal separation between exposure to a dangerous substance and the manifestation of injury. Latent injuries remain dormant for long periods, ranging anywhere from 4 to 40 years and averaging roughly 20 years (Armenien and Lilienfeld 1974). This latency period creates distinctive enforcement problems for traditional liability systems because such systems are injury-based. In other words, damages are generally assessed only for actual and not for speculative or hypothetical damages. Hence damages are assessed only after an injury manifests itself.[4]

The key advantage of such traditional tort systems is that they allow parties to observe actual injuries before damage payments are made. With ordinary injuries, moreover, such a system functions smoothly because damages are paid in the ordinary course of business as injuries occur during the production, sale, and use of products.[5]

With latent injuries, however, an injury-based system creates a long separation between the activities that lead to injury and damage

---

[3] More formally, when large damage awards lead to a large probability of bankruptcy, liability may lead to either increases or decreases in safety, but it creates an unambiguous incentive to avoid payments. See Wiggins and Ringleb (1989) for a formal model and an extensive theoretical analysis of the incentive properties of liability in a latent hazard setting.

[4] For case law supporting this position, see, e.g., Clutter v. Johns-Manville Corp., 646 F. 2d 1151 (6th Cir. 1981); Uvie v. Thompson, 337 U.S. 163 (1949); Barnes v. A. H. Robbins Co., 476 N.E. 2d 84 (Ind. 1984); Raymond v. Eli Lilly & Co., 117 N.N. 16Y, 371 A. 2d 170 (1977).

[5] With acute injuries it is also possible to use an occurrence form of liability insurance so that insurance premiums can be continuously updated as injuries occur. With latent hazards, injuries are typically delayed for 20 years, seriously undermining the ability to use an occurrence form of liability insurance.

awards. This separation creates severe enforcement problems because it means that damage obligations accrue for many years. As time passes, the accumulated damages can become formidable. This accumulation is then exacerbated by the severe nature of the associated injuries. The net result is a large incentive to escape payment.

Besides just producing an incentive to avoid payments, however, this long separation also provides the potential opportunity. The long delay between exposure and injury means that agents can engage in risky activities and reap the associated returns, while remaining confident that potential damage awards lie many years in the future. Hence firms can often produce for substantial periods with relative impunity. Then before liability obligations appear, such agents can simply go out of business and enter entirely separate lines of work. Successful pursuit of such a strategy will leave few assets exposed to damage awards when injuries appear.

A primary way firms implement such a strategy is by shutting down or divesting their interest in hazardous portions of their production processes and then purchasing the required input from a specialized producer (see, e.g., Stone 1980, p. 71; "Why Small Companies Will Survive" [1982, p. 63]; Kraakman 1984, p. 872). Under such an arrangement, the purchasing firm is not liable for injuries associated with the manufacture and use of the product made by the specialized producer.[6]

Hence in normal circumstances the responsibility for the safety of workers directly associated with the hazardous process is generally assumed to be a natural part of a firm's legal responsibility to direct and monitor the production process. The simple rationale behind such a rule is that a firm purchasing inputs cannot generally dictate or monitor the working conditions and safety precautions of the firm from which it purchases inputs; such a requirement would effectively

---

[6] There are several exceptions to this general rule. For example, liability may not be avoided if the specialized producer is an employee of the purchasing firm (Keeton 1984, pp. 501–8), if the specialized producer is an independent contractor for whom the purchasing firm has failed to provide sufficient information regarding the hazard process to take the necessary precautions (pp. 509–16), or finally if the product produced by the specialized producer is itself hazardous and the purchasing firm incorporates the product into its own product and then fails to warn its consumers of the risks involved in the use of the product. See, e.g., Michalko v. Cooke Color and Chemical Corp., 91 N.J. 386, A. 2d 179, 181–83 (1982) (the defendant independent contractor did not design or sell the product, but only manufactured it; the defendant manufacturer was held strictly liable for failing to warn buyers of defects). Several other arrangements are yet to be tested in the courts. For example, firms have established special subsidiaries, spin-offs, product manufacturing by contract, purchase of products from specialized producers, and other similar arrangements in an apparent effort to avoid potential liability (see, e.g., Scredon and Glaberson 1985, pp. 58–59; Roe 1986).

break down arm's-length market exchange. The legal responsibility for safety then generally falls on the firm whose workers are exposed to the hazardous process. In addition, if the product produced is itself hazardous, then the specialized producer will be liable for injuries to workers in those firms using the product as an input, if it has failed to warn of the risks associated with the product's use (see, e.g., *Borel v. Fiberboard Products Corp.*, 493 F. 2d 1076 [5th Cir. 1973], *cert. denied*, 419 U.S. 869 [1974]).

The primary disadvantage of using divestiture to avoid liability is that under such a strategy firms sacrifice potential economies of internal organization. When these economies are small relative to the potential liability damage awards, however, the small independent corporation becomes the cost-minimizing way to operate in a latent liability environment. Hence large firms can often minimize the cost of obtaining inputs whose manufacture is risky by purchasing such inputs from small corporations with few assets.

When such implicit divestiture is the cost-minimizing response to liability, such a system simply leads to an equilibrium in which small corporations handle hazards. These firms then turn over at a high rate to avoid damage payments. Under such an equilibrium, liability leads neither to substantial incentives for safety nor to appropriate compensation for injury. In fact one can show that individual worker compensation can easily fall, safety can rise or fall, and more workers may well be exposed to hazards as small, labor-intensive firms take over production.[7]

Such implicit divestiture is a potentially significant problem because in many sectors the most serious latent risks are concentrated in a relatively small set of specific tasks. In chemical manufacture, for example, the most serious risks are often associated with specialty chemicals and processes (see, e.g., "Why Small Companies" [1982, p. 63]) or occur when potent raw chemicals are combined to create a finished or secondary product (*Moore v. Allied Chemical Corp.* 480 F. Supp. 364 [1979]; *Wall Street Journal*, October 6, 1976; Goldfarb 1977). Handling of the chemicals and other products produced by these hazardous tasks, both before and after the hazardous activity, is then relatively safe. Similarly, the general operation of a nuclear reactor is quite safe and involves minimal health hazards to the relevant set of workers. In contrast, the *cleaning* of the reactor vessel involves intense exposure to workers over short periods of time; hazards in this task are severe (*Wall Street Journal*, October 12, 1983). As another

---

[7] See Wiggins and Ringleb (1989) for formal proofs of these claims and a more complete discussion of these theoretical issues. The labor intensity of small firms emerges because capital is less valuable to such firms because of the likelihood that capital will lose its value to shareholders if it is claimed as part of a damage settlement.

example, instrument manufacture involves intensive exposure to heavy metals and other carcinogens, but once the instruments are completed, ordinary handling is quite safe (Hickey and Kearney 1977). The implication is that hazardous tasks are often distinct from other, safer activities.

Even when the tasks are difficult to separate, moreover, the large scale of potential liability creates significant incentives for firms to take extraordinary measures in an attempt to segregate risky activities from the assets associated with the safer activities of a large firm.

The implication of these arguments is that large, integrated firms have an incentive to divest risky activities and minimize the exposure of assets to potential liability claims. The disadvantage of this arrangement is that firms must forgo economies of internal organization, and hazardous tasks must be segregated in small corporations.

The key issue then becomes the empirical question of how steep the trade-off is regarding the cost of vertical divestiture compared with the benefit of avoiding liability payments. When there are large cost savings from avoiding liability, then divestiture will be common. When it is technologically difficult to separate risky tasks, divestiture will be rare. When divestiture is common, the implication is that firms must believe that there are significant cost savings from reduced expected liability payments. Hence if divestiture is common, the implication is that the liability will not generate appropriate incentives for safety or compensation to the injured. Instead liability merely leads to corporate restructuring, small-firm operation of hazardous tasks, and high firm turnover rates. The result is a system with questionable incentive properties. The key to the evaluation of the liability system, then, is to examine the extent of divestiture. Attention is now turned to this empirical trade-off.

III. Empirical Tests

A. An Econometric Model

The key empirical issue is to determine how firms are responding to recent changes in the liability system. The issue is to determine whether hazards are sufficiently concentrated in particular tasks to enable firms to segregate hazards in small corporations on a substantial scale. The natural way to examine divestiture is to examine how recent changes in the liability system have affected the structure of organizations in risky sectors of the economy. The obvious period to examine for these effects is 1967–80, the period surrounding rapid changes in liability law.

Prior to the mid-1960s, the law offered substantial obstacles to workers seeking damages for latent injuries. State workers' compensation programs routinely rejected claims for latent injuries, particularly when the latency period was long and the injury seemed similar to "the ordinary diseases of life." Further, the workers' compensation statutes in nearly all states precluded workers from seeking redress through the court system under tort law, affording employers strong protection from liability suits in the large majority of cases.[8] In those circumstances in which employees were able to sue, the evidentiary requirements under then existing tort law posed formidable additional barriers to recovery.

Beginning in the late 1960s, numerous changes in the legal environment caused these obstacles to worker recovery to begin to unravel. The most fundamental changes involved inroads made in third-party liability and against the workers' compensation exclusivity rule; these changes allowed workers to more easily seek compensation for injuries under tort law.[9] The advent of strict liability in tort in latent injury cases also allowed workers suffering from latent injuries

[8] All workers' compensation statutes provide that "the Compensation remedy is exclusive of all other remedies by the employee or his dependents against the employer and insurance carrier for the same injury, if the injury falls within the coverage formula of the Act" (Larson 1976, sec. 65.00).

[9] Recent cases have recognized several exceptions to the exclusivity rule. The most obvious exception is that the worker must be in that class of worker subject to workers' compensation; employees outside this class may pursue common law remedies (see Prosser 1971, p. 526). In almost all jurisdictions, an exception to the exclusivity rule is recognized for intentional torts (see Larson [1976, sec. 68.13, p. 13-5] and cases cited in his n. 11). A growing number of jurisdictions are beginning to define intentional torts more broadly to include those situations in which the employer was knowledgeable about the hazardous nature of the employment (see, e.g., Boudeloche v. Grow Chemical Coating Corp., 728 F. 2d 759 [5th Cir. 1984]). A number of courts have held the firm liable for workers' injuries resulting from the employer's "willful, wanton, and reckless misconduct": Mandolidas v. Elkins Industries, Inc., 246 S.E. 2d 907 (1978); Blankenship v. Cincinnati Milacron Chem. Inc., 433 N.E. 2d 572 (1982); Wade v. Johnson Controls, Inc., 693 F. 2d 19 (2d Cir. 1982) (Vermont law applied). Workers have been allowed to recover in those situations in which the firm fraudulently conceals from workers the fact that they are suffering from an occupational disease (see Johns-Manville Products Corp. v. Superior Court, 612 F. 2d 948 [1980] [lung cancer]; Del Monte v. Unitcast Division of Midland Ross Corp., 411 N.E. 2d 814 [1978] [silicosis]). In a minority of jurisdictions, workers may sue the employer if the employer has breached a duty independent of those imposed on it by virtue of being an employer, so-called dual-capacity situations. Dual-capacity liability generally arises in torts involving product liability or medical malpractice. In the product liability cases, an injured worker maintains an action against the firm based on injuries or illnesses caused by the product the firm manufactures if the product is manufactured for sale to the public. See, generally, "Dual Capacity Doctrine" (1979). Plaintiffs are allowed to bring suit in several jurisdictions if it can be demonstrated that corporate strategy existed for concealing workplace-related diseases discovered in company examinations (see, e.g., Johns-Manville Products Corp. v. Contra Costa Superior Court, 27 Cal. 3d 465, 612 P. 2d 948, 165 Cal. Rptr. 858 [1980]; Millison v. E. I. duPont de Nemours & Co., 501 A. 2d 505, 101 N.J. 161 [1987]). Medical malpractice may apply depending on whether or not the physician is an employee of the firm (see Proctor v. Ford Motor Co., 302 N.W. 2d 580 [1973]) and to whom the benefit of those medical services accrues (physician-patient relationship required; see Rogers v. Horvath, 237 N.W. 2d 595 [1975]). See, generally, Blum (1978, p. 433).

to press tort actions under substantially lower evidentiary require-ments, which led to increased success (see, e.g., *Borel v. Fiberboard Products Corp.*, cited in Sec. II). Damage awards in successful tort cases also came to dwarf those found under workers' compensation, sub-stantially raising firm costs. At the same time, judicial experiments emerged regarding statutes of limitations, causation, the application of joint and several liability, and others, all of which further reduced barriers to worker recovery.[10]

Concurrently, substantial medical and scientific evidence linking occupational exposures to latent disease began to emerge. These scientific findings reinforced the impact of judicial changes. Medical results ever more closely linked hazardous substances to latent occu-pational injuries. When combined with changes in firms' legal respon-sibilities at tort, these medical changes substantially increased firms' potential liability exposure for latent injuries. Prior to these develop-ments, firms had little reason to be concerned with possible damage awards for latent occupational injuries; afterward expected liabilities became a major concern. Hence these changes in legal structure and in medical opinion led to large increases in potential liability costs for firms operating in hazardous sectors of the economy.

If divestiture is an important response to liability, then these changes in liability should lead to substantial increases in the number of small corporations operating in hazardous sectors of the econ-omy.[11] This entry will occur as large firms cease production associated with hazards and then seek outside suppliers that have lower ex-pected liability costs, an implicit form of divestiture.[12] Since hazard-

[10] See, e.g., Sindell v. Abbott Labs., 26 Cal. 3d 588, 607 P. 2d 924, 163 Cal. Rpt. 132, *cert. denied*, 101 S. Ct. 268 (1980) (liability was assessed on the basis of each firm's market share within the industry in a case in which the plaintiff could not identify the responsi-ble firm).

[11] Divestiture is likely to be in the form of a corporation. According to the general rule of corporate limited liability, shareholders are not liable for the torts of the corpo-ration (see, e.g., Zubik v. Zubik, 384 F. 2d 267 [3d Cir. 1967], *cert. denied*, 390 U.S. 988 [1968]). Limited liability will be sustained by the courts as long as the corporate entity is not used by its owners to perpetuate a fraud, evade an existing obligation, or circum-vent the law (Henn 1970, p. 146). If the corporate form of organization is used for such purposes, the court will ignore the corporate structure by "piercing the corporate veil" and holding the shareholders liable personally. In context, this means that the corpo-rate form of organization cannot provide an ex post shield from tort liabilities arising from worker injuries. Rather, the corporation will need to have been selected and put into place by the owners well in advance of any tort claims arising from the use or production of their products to avoid personal liability.

[12] This implicit form of divestiture will often be chosen so that the firm can avoid any possible legal entanglements with continuing hazardous production. At present a firm is not generally responsible for hazardous exposures that occur after a subsidiary is sold, but as the courts continue to modify rules, prudent firms may choose to shut down rather than spin off hazardous units. The reader should note that in either event, spinning off or shutting down a unit does not generally shield the firm from liability for past activities.

ous activities are often a specialized portion of production, moreover, the best way to measure these effects is to examine changes in the *number* of small firms. Pure numbers of firms are likely to be more sensitive than value-added measures because of the specialized nature of the tasks in which exposure to hazards is severe.

On the other hand, if divestiture does not provide an effective shield from liability, increases in liability costs should not affect the number of small corporations. Finally, regardless of the effect on small firms, changes in liability should not generally affect the number of medium and large firms because such firms will divest only small, hazardous portions of production.

Accordingly, data were gathered for the number of small corporations operating in various sectors of the economy for the years 1967 and 1980. The year 1967 was chosen to precede the rapid changes in the liability system, which occurred primarily in the first half of the 1970s, while 1980 was chosen to enable firms sufficient time to respond to the changes. Small corporations were defined as ones with assets of less than $250,000 in 1980 dollars (= $100,000 in 1967 dollars). Since such small corporations are relatively homogeneous, moreover, increased numbers ought also to be closely linked to increased value-added but the number of firms is likely to be more sensitive. The data are derived for manufacturing industries using Internal Revenue Service (IRS) data.[13]

The primary empirical task is to determine the effect of changing liability costs on the rate of entry of these small corporations. Changing liability costs are created by worker exposures to carcinogens, which translated into increased expected liability costs when workers were given more ready access to tort actions. Accordingly, one way to measure expected liability costs is to measure the exposure of workers to carcinogens in the workplace.

By measuring worker exposure to carcinogens, the analysis measures the incentive of firms to avoid prospective future liabilities that firms would expect if they continued to be associated with hazards. Hence worker exposure in, say, the early 1970s measures prospective

---

[13] The sources of the data are *Statistics of Income* (1967), *Corporate Income Tax Returns* (1968), and *Corporation Source Book of Statistics of Income* (1980). The 1980 end point for the period was chosen because it provided ample time for firms to respond to liability changes and because of the way the IRS data are reported. The IRS reports brackets of $100,000 and $250,000 ($250,000 in 1980 dollars is equal to $100,000 in 1967 dollars). Hence by using 1980 as the end point, we had available a constant-dollars measure of the number of firms at the end of the period. The beginning date was chosen to predate changes in liability and to correspond with the publication of a *Census of Manufactures* so that other variables would be available. The data sources did not provide data for tobacco manufacturers because of confidentiality constraints, and so this industry had to be excluded from the data set.

future liabilities that would become apparent in the late 1980s or early 1990s. In contrast, reorganization is unlikely to avoid past liabilities. The reason is that reorganization would not generally relieve firms of their legal responsibility for injuries to their workers that were already incurred before the changes in liability rules.[14] Hence the primary motive for divestiture would be for firms to avoid liability associated with future activities.

There are numerous ways worker exposure to carcinogens can be measured, but perhaps the best data were developed in a study by Hickey and Kearney (1977). In determining the number of workers exposed to a given substance, they relied on the 1972–74 National Occupational Hazard Survey (National Institute for Occupational Safety and Health 1974). These data, collected within the manufacturing sector for 86 carcinogenic and suspected carcinogenic chemicals, are presented in table 1.

These data differ from those in other studies because Hickey and Kearney measure the frequency of exposures of *individual* workers to a large number of carcinogenic and suspected carcinogenic agents. In contrast, alternative data sources often simply use the volume of hazardous substances an industry produces, under the unrealistic assumption that human exposures are directly proportional to production. Still other sources use census data that classify all workers in a plant as having been exposed, regardless of whether they are directly involved with the process in which the carcinogen is used. Both alternatives are qualitatively inferior to the Hickey-Kearney methodology, which attempts to measure exposures at the worker level. Unfortunately the Hickey and Kearney data are available only at the two-digit Standard Industrial Classification level. Accordingly, the econometric analysis must be carried out using two-digit data.

To estimate the relationship between entry of small corporations and worker exposure to latent hazards, it is important to develop a fully specified model of entry. Let entry by small firms be

$$E_i = g(H_i, X_i, \epsilon_i), \tag{1}$$

where E_i is the rate of entry of small corporations in industry i between 1967 and 1980, H_i is worker exposure to carcinogens in the

---

[14] While the rule cited in the text is typical, it is important to note that legal precedents in this area remain unsettled. Accordingly, some firms also seem to be attempting to restructure to avoid past liabilities on the off chance that such a strategy will be successful. For example, Roe (1986) argues that if the base firm has already marketed the product, a subsequent transfer or spin-off should not relieve the base firm of liability for injury. The liability issue is clouded, however, if, at the time of transfer or spin-off, the dangerous product had not yet produced substantial injury or if the product development was at that time incomplete. The analysis here will reflect restructuring that is motivated by either of these efforts to avoid liability.

TABLE 1

FREQUENCY OF WORKER EXPOSURES TO CARCINOGENS AND SUSPECTED CARCINOGENS
FOR TWO-DIGIT INDUSTRIES IN THE MANUFACTURING SECTOR

Standard Industrial Classification	Industry	Worker Exposures to Carcinogens
20	Food and kindred products	2,874
21	Tobacco manufacturers	13,885
22	Textile mills	2,607
23	Apparel	7,591
24	Lumber and wood products	5,588
25	Furniture and fixtures	4,309
26	Paper and allied products	14,205
27	Printing and publishing	19,625
28	Chemical and allied products	25,984
29	Petroleum and coal products	38,398
30	Rubber and plastics	16,987
31	Leather and leather products	40,599
32	Stone, clay, and glass	11,985
33	Primary metals	24,367
34	Fabricated metals	90,428
35	Machinery (except electrical)	51,927
36	Electrical machinery	81,533
37	Transportation equipment	53,574
38	Instruments	107,023

SOURCE.—Hickey and Kearney (1977, p. 29, table 7).

workplace in industry i, X_i is a set of other factors affecting entry rates of small firms, and ϵ_i is a random error term that is assumed to have zero mean and finite variance and to be independent of the right-hand-side variables.

If the number of small firms was in long-run equilibrium in 1967 and if $g(\cdot)$ and X are properly specified, then the coefficient of H_i will measure the effect of changing liability costs on the rate of entry by small corporations. To see why, note that if one begins in a long-run equilibrium, systematic changes in the number of small corporations can be traced either to changes in ordinary market conditions or to firm efforts to evade liability. If proper account is then taken of these changing market conditions, the coefficient of H_i will measure the partial effect of changes in liability costs on the number of small firms.

More generally, even if the number of small firms was not in long-run equilibrium in 1967, the interpretation of the coefficient of H_i will still be correct, as long as the source of the disequilibrium was not statistically correlated with the independent variables. The goal, then, is to account for other market factors that might influence entry to ensure an unbiased estimate of the effects of exposure to hazards and liability.

Industry growth is the first important structural factor to account for percentage changes in the number of small corporations. If the industry began in equilibrium, then an increase in an industry's value-added will generally increase the number of firms of all sizes, including small firms. Put differently, with constant market shares for large and small firms, growth will increase the number of small firms. To account for this influence on the number of small firms, industry growth rates in value-added were calculated from *Census of Manufactures* data for the period 1967–77.

In addition, however, there may be systematic increases or decreases in the market share of small firms over the sample period. Such changes could be traced to changes in government policy or other economywide factors. Such considerations would generate a systematic change in the number of small firms across all markets, which can be accounted for by using a constant term in the regressions.[15] Such a term will measure the average percentage change in small firms in the economy as a whole. Hence, the growth variable will account for changes in a particular industry's size, which might lead to a change in the number of small firms, while the constant term will account for systematic economywide influences on the number of small firms.

Other factors might also change the rate of entry of small firms in an industry, and previous studies of entry were used to assist in determining the set of factors to be examined. These studies identify several determinants of changes in the number of small firms over time.[16] One such factor is energy costs. Energy costs rose sharply during the 1967–80 period, and large and small firms differ systematically in their energy intensities. Hence, energy cost increases during the period should bring about increased small-firm entry. Pashigian (1984) developed a measure of the relative energy costs of large and small firms from unpublished Bureau of Census tables. That measure is used here.

In addition, more traditional structural conditions may lead to changes in the number of small firms in the period in question. These

---

[15] In addition, major policy changes were investigated within individual sectors. During the period there were important policy changes in petroleum and coal products that lowered the costs of small firms relative to large firms. Most important of these policies was the small refiner bias in the fuel entitlement program: refiners using less than 175,000 barrels of oil per day were heavily subsidized. In addition, there were major policy changes in the tobacco industry that favored small firms. Given the purely cross-sectional nature of the estimating equation, there was no statistical mechanism to account for these policies other than a dummy variable, which would have eliminated any influence of this observation on the remaining coefficients. Hence, these observations were omitted.

[16] Some of the more prominent previous studies of entry include Mansfield (1962), Peltzman (1965), and Orr (1974).

TABLE 2

DESCRIPTIONS AND MEANS OF DEPENDENT AND INDEPENDENT VARIABLES

Variable	Mean
Dependent variable:	
Entry rates of small corporations (%) (entry)	39.2
Independent variables:	
Hickey and Kearney index (expected disease liability)	33,010
Industry growth rate (%) (growth)	33.09
Reciprocal of distances goods are shipped (regional market)	384.4
Relative energy costs of large and small firms (%) (energy)	88.02
Weighted-average four-digit concentration ratios (%) (CR_4)	34.06
Advertising to sales ratio (%) (AD/sale)	1.0

NOTE.—The names of variables used in the regression tables are in parentheses.

factors include the level of concentration and the advertising to sales ratios. Concentration is measured at the two-digit level by using a weighted average of the four-digit concentration levels (see Collins and Preston 1968).[17] The advertising to sales ratio is used to measure product differentiation as a barrier to small-firm entry (see Comanor and Wilson 1967). The latter measure is introduced both directly and with a slope dummy that allows for a different relationship between advertising and entry in producer and consumer goods industries.[18]

Finally, a regional market variable was also included in the model. Since changes in market shares of small firms may differ systematically in geographically segmented markets, a measure was included to control for such factors. The variable, developed by Weiss (1972), is the reciprocal of the distance goods are shipped, as reported in the Commodity Transport Surveys of the 1977 *Census of Transportation.* Simple statistics for the variables are reported in table 2.

B. Estimation and Results

Table 3 reports six different specifications of the basic estimating equation so that the reader can examine the impact of alternative specifications.[19] The null hypothesis is that worker exposure to occu-

[17] Averages of the four-firm concentration ratios in 1967, weighted by the value of shipments of each industry, were used to estimate concentration level. Data were derived from the 1967 *Census of Manufactures.* This ratio is similar to that employed by Collins and Preston (1968).

[18] In constructing the advertising to sales ratio, we used the average of advertising to sales ratios from 1972 to 1975. A differential slope for consumer goods was introduced by multiplying the original variable times a zero-one dummy, which assumed a value of one in consumer goods industries. This is to allow for the possibility that the role advertising plays in entry differs between producer and consumer goods industries.

[19] The regressions reported in table 3 are simple additive specifications. In addition, a number of double log specifications were run. We report the additive specifications

TABLE 3
DETERMINANTS OF SMALL-FIRM ENTRY, 1967–80

$$E_i = \left(\frac{SC_{i,1980}}{SC_{i,1967}} - 1\right) \cdot 100$$

RIGHT-HAND-SIDE VARIABLE	EQUATION					
	(1)	(2)	(3)	(4)	(5)	(6)
Intercept	3,993.0	−4,488.0	−3,009.0	−3,733.0	−3,212.0	−3,439.0
	(3,127.0)	(2,895.0)	(2,489.0)	(2,711.0)	(2,875.0)	(1,957.0)
Expected disease liability	.060	.053	.061	.062	.060	.057
	(.028)*	(.024)*	(.025)*	(.025)*	(.027)*	(.020)
Growth	78.0	80.0	79.0	77.0	80.0	80.0
	(23.0)*	(27.0)**	(26.0)**	(27.0)**	(28.0)**	(25.0)*
Energy	41.5	38.6	35.3	41.5	35.2	34.7
	(23.4)	(22.1)	(20.4)	(22.4)*	(21.3)	(19.6)
Regional market	−3.2	...	−1.5	−3.1	−1.6	...
	(5.8)		(5.0)	(5.0)	(5.3)	
CR_4	10.3	7.3	...	...	8.4	...
	(52.1)	(50.1)			(50.9)	
AD/sale	7.3	5.3	...	7.2	...	...
	(10.0)	(9.0)		(9.6)		
R^2	.71	.70	.69	.71	.69	.69
F	4.05	5.13	6.75	5.32	4.96	9.64

NOTE.—Standard errors are in parentheses. The mean of the dependent variable is 39.2 percent. $SC_{i,j}$ = corporations with less than $250,000 in assets, in 1980 dollars, in industry i, year j.
* Significant at the 5 percent level.
** Significant at the 1 percent level.

588

pational hazards will be unrelated to the entry of small firms. This hypothesis corresponds to the theoretical proposition that changing liability rules did not affect the number of small corporations, which means that divestiture provides little protection from latent hazard liabilities. The alternative hypothesis is that worker exposure has a significant effect on entry by small corporations, implying that corporate limited liability offers substantial protection from liability costs.

The statistical results strongly reject the hypothesis that expected disease liability, as measured by the exposure of workers to carcinogens, has no effect on entry by small corporations. The coefficient of the expected liability variable is large and statistically significant in all the specifications in table 3. The coefficient estimate is also virtually independent of the specification of the estimating equation across the six specifications reported in table 3. In these estimations, the median coefficient of the hazard variable is .060, its standard error is roughly .028, and it is uniformly significant at the 5 percent level. The estimated hazard variable coefficients all lie roughly within one-half of one standard error of the median coefficient; the estimated relationship between worker exposure to hazards and entry is remarkably insensitive to the specification of the basic estimating equation. Hence, the data show a robust, statistically significant relationship between entry rates and potential liability costs.

In addition to being highly statistically significant, the results show that hazard exposure is a major determinant of small-firm entry. To assess its importance, consider equation 1, the most fully specified equation in table 3. The portion of entry that can be attributed to the avoidance of liability can be found by multiplying the estimated coefficient 0.060 percent (.00060) times the sample mean of the hazard variable (33,010), which yields 19.8 percent. In other words, the incentive to evade liability has led to roughly a 20 percent increase in the number of small corporations in the U.S. economy. Since there was an average 39.2 percent increase in the number of small corporations over the period, the data show that roughly one-half of the entry of small corporations over the period is linked statistically to the exposure of workers to occupational carcinogens.

In pure numbers, the incentive effects of liability on small-firm entry appear to be substantial. The percentage increase corresponds to an increase of more than 25,000 small corporations whose entry is

---

because there are negative values for some observations, requiring some kind of ad hoc adjustment in the log specifications. Some of the log specifications were run omitting observations in which one or more values were negative, and others were run adding 100 units to all the values of a variable before taking logs so that there would be no negative values. In all cases the log specifications yielded results qualitatively similar to those reported in table 3.

tied statistically to changing liability rules. The magnitude of these effects suggests substantial efforts by firms to avoid possible liability costs associated with latent hazards.

The findings then suggest that liability has led to a significant transformation in the organization of hazardous production processes. Large numbers of small firms are entering hazardous sectors. The large magnitude of these effects, moreover, suggests that at least in significant sectors the sacrifice of economies of internal organization appears to be small relative to liability costs. Hence restructuring appears to be a path that firms are pursuing in significant numbers in efforts to avoid liability.

These findings raise substantial questions about likely future problems in enforcement for tort liability in the case of latent hazards. Before we examine the policy implications and alternatives, however, it is also important to evaluate the basic regression model more fully to assess the reliability of the results.

One way to carry out such an evaluation is to note that in other ways the regressions seem to provide plausible results. As theory would predict, for example, the variables measuring small-firm energy cost advantages and industry growth seem to be closely related to the rate of entry of small firms in an industry. The variable measuring small-firm energy cost advantages shows significant increases in small firms in industries in which small firms are comparatively less energy intensive than larger ones. Industry growth should also lead to a significant percentage increase in the number of small firms, and this hypothesis is generally confirmed in the various specifications presented in table 3. In contrast, the entry barrier variables are not generally significant, though the two-digit level of aggregation does not provide a powerful test of the entry barrier hypothesis.

An alternative check on the reliability of the basic equations is to replicate the statistical analysis for an earlier period. The empirical analysis implicitly presumes that the number of small corporations was in long-run equilibrium in 1967. An alternative possibility is that instead there has been a long, systematic increase in the number of small firms in hazardous sectors; despite large *t*-values, the data may merely reflect a spurious historical relationship.

To investigate this possibility, data were gathered so that the model could be estimated over the period 1957–67. Data could be collected for all variables except the hazard variable. Concern with hazards and the investigation of exposures in the workplace are relatively recent phenomena, and we are unaware of reliable hazard data for this earlier period. On the other hand, it is unlikely that there would be much change in hazardous exposures between the Hickey and Kearney study using data from the early 1970s and exposures during the

1960s. Concern with hazards emerged only in the early 1970s, and levels of hazards were likely determined by standard manufacturing practices across industries. Given an absence of concern over hazards during the 1960s, it is unlikely that hazard levels changed substantially across industries during this period. Accordingly, the hazard variable used was the same as that for the original set of regressions.

The model was then reestimated to see if there had existed previously a relationship between small-firm entry and exposure to hazards. These regressions were run for corporations with $100,000 in assets, and the results are reported in table 4.[20] Inspection of the table shows that there is no evidence of a historical relationship. The signs of the coefficients are negative and statistically insignificant.

The evidence then shows that the strong, positive relationship between small corporate entry and hazardous exposures emerged only after liability laws were changed during the sample period. The strong suggestion is that the relationship between entry and hazards is directly linked to changes in liability laws.

Finally, to explain our results, it might be argued that small firms are simply lower-cost producers of hazardous products. Such an explanation, however, does not explain why such a cost advantage would have emerged in the late 1960s or early 1970s, which is necessary to explain the change in the number of small corporations that occurred during that particular period. Hence, there do not appear to be simple, competing explanations of the econometric findings. The implication is that the empirical evidence suggests a large-scale effort by firms to structure hazardous production processes to avoid liability.

IV. Interpretations, Policy Options, and Conclusions

The empirical results indicate that liability has led to a substantial restructuring of production in hazardous sectors of the economy. The implication of these findings is that expected liability costs seem to outweigh the returns to internal organization for hazardous activities, and as a result small firms are playing an increasingly important role in hazardous sectors. This finding suggests that there may be

---

[20] Recall that in the primary estimations we used $100,000 in 1967 dollars and $250,000 in 1980 dollars as our size boundaries. The low inflation rates of the late 1950s and early to mid 1960s precluded use of a similar procedure in these regressions. The constant term in the regressions, however, will capture any systematic samplewide changes in the number of small firms. Hence, changes in the classification of firms due to price inflation, which should be (roughly) uniformly distributed throughout the sample, will be captured by the constant term in the regression.

TABLE 4

DETERMINANTS OF SMALL-FIRM ENTRY, 1957–67

Dependent Variable = Entry	(1)	(2)	(3)	(4)	(5)	(6)
Intercept	-626.15	-277.57	-588.14	-530.02	-600.27	-475.73
	(346.48)	(362.41)	(312.57)	(302.16)	(306.38)	(340.94)
Expected disease liability	-.0014	-.0046	-.0040	-.0035	-.0042	-.0014
	(.0028)	(.00335)	(.0027)	(.0026)	(.0026)	(.0020)
Growth	10.2	12.5	10.4	9.0	10.9	...
	(7.6)	(8.9)	(7.3)	(7.2)	(6.5)	
Energy	1.4	1.6	1.2	...	1.6	.07
	(2.2)	(2.6)	(2.0)		(2.0)	(2.3)
Regional market	11.4	-18.4	12.7	25.1	...	44.1
	(56.4)	(64.3)	(53.7)	(50.5)		(52.9)
CR_4	8.1	...	8.2	8.2	7.9	8.8
	(3.7)		(3.5)	(3.6)	(3.4)	(3.8)
AD/sale	26.1	33.6	...	10.4	27.1	32.4
	(77.8)	(91.4)		(71.5)	(73.8)	(80.7)
R^2	.48	.36	.37	.48	.46	.47
F	1.38	1.11	1.19	1.82	1.67	1.79

substantial enforcement problems associated with the use of tort liability as a solution to problems of latent hazards.

Accordingly, when one is evaluating the desirability of liability as a policy option, it becomes important to consider both the problems posed by enforcement and the net incentive effects of corporate restructuring. With latent hazards, liability can be difficult to enforce because the injury-based nature of claims provides agents with substantial opportunities to avoid payment during the latency period. When firms successfully avoid payment, liability provides neither the incentives for care nor the insurance function normally attributed to it. Moreover, when liability leads to a preponderance of small firms and rapid turnover in hazardous sectors, it undermines the accumulation of experience in dealing with hazards, so that safety does not rise with the accumulated lessons of the past. The implication, then, is that liability for latent hazards differs substantially from its application in more traditional settings.

There are a number of ways in which the liability system can be modified in an effort to deal with these problems, but these too pose problems. One obvious solution is to assess damages earlier to prevent firms from avoiding damages. The difficulty with this solution is that it subverts the key distinguishing feature of liability. The key advantage of liability is to permit ex post compensation after injuries can be commonly observed. Imposing liability earlier would mean that injuries could not be observed, and so a liability system either degenerates into a simple lump-sum transfer to all workers or acts like a labor tax that is rebated to workers. Hence liability's essential feature of linking payments to ex post damages is lost, as is its implicit insurance function.

Another option is to attempt to apportion damages according to market share, which has been attempted in the DES cases (see also *Sindell v. Abbott Labs.*, cited in n. 10). The problem with this solution, however, is that payments are not conditioned on the individual firm's safety activities, and so it becomes essentially a form of social insurance. Finally, there have been numerous attempts in the asbestos cases to link insurance payments to the degree of worker exposure over time. This scheme, however, also implicitly permits liability obligations to accrue over many years, creating incentives to avoid liability similar to those found here.

The implication of these findings, then, is that liability for latent hazards differs substantially from other forms of liability because of the potentially significant problems posed by enforcement. Moreover, there does not appear to be a simple remedy to these enforcement problems that preserves liability's traditional incentive characteristics. The general implication, though, is that enforcement problems are a

594   JOURNAL OF POLITICAL ECONOMY

fundamental concern and need to be considered carefully in continuing efforts to deal with the latent hazard problem.

References

Armenien, Haroutune K., and Lilienfeld, Abraham M. "The Distribution of
  Incubation Periods of Neoplastic Diseases." *American J. Epidemiology* 99
  (February 1974): 92–100.
Blum, John D. "Corporate Liability for In-House Medical Malpractice." *St.
  Louis Univ. Law J.* 22 (1978): 433–51.
Cole, Philip, and Merletti, Franco. "Chemical Agents and Occupational Can-
  cer." *J. Environmental Pathology and Toxicity* 3 (March 1980): 399–417.
Collins, Norman R., and Preston, Lee E. *Concentration and Price-Cost Margins
  in Manufacturing Industries.* Berkeley: Univ. California Press, 1968.
Comanor, William S., and Wilson, Thomas A. "Advertising Market Structure
  and Performance." *Rev. Econ. and Statis.* 49 (November 1967): 423–40.
"Dual Capacity Doctrine: Third-Party Liability of Employer-Manufacturer in
  Products Liability Litigation." *Indiana Law Rev.* 12 (Fall 1979): 553–81.
Epstein, Richard A. "Manville: The Bankruptcy of Product Liability Law."
  Regulation 6 (September/October 1982).
Goldfarb, William. "Kepone: A Case Study." *Environmental Lawyer* 8 (Spring
  1977): 645–62.
Henn, H. *The Law of Corporations.* 2d ed. St. Paul, Minn.: West, 1970.
Hickey, J. L. S., and Kearney, J. J. *Engineering Control Research and Development
  Plan for Carcinogen Materials.* Cincinnati: Nat. Inst. Occupational Safety and
  Health, 1977.
Keeton, W. Page, ed. *Prosser and Keeton on the Law of Torts.* 5th ed. St. Paul,
  Minn.: West, 1984.
Kraakman, Reinier H. "Corporate Liability Strategies and the Costs of Legal
  Controls." *Yale Law J.* 93 (April 1984): 857–98.
Larson, Arthur. *Workmen's Compensation Law.* New York: Bender, 1976.
Mansfield, Edwin. "Entry, Gibrat's Law, Innovation, and the Growth of
  Firms." *A.E.R.* 52 (December 1962): 1023–51.
National Institute for Occupational Safety and Health. *National Occupational
  Hazard Survey.* Washington: Government Printing Office, 1974.
Oi, Walter Y. "The Economics of Product Safety." *Bell J. Econ. and Manage-
  ment Sci.* 4 (Spring 1973): 3–28.
Orr, Dale. "The Determinants of Entry: A Study of the Canadian Manufac-
  turing Industries." *Rev. Econ. and Statis.* 56 (February 1974): 58–66.
Pashigian, B. Peter. "The Effect of Environmental Regulation on Optimal
  Plant Size and Factor Shares." *J. Law and Econ.* 27 (April 1984): 1–28.
Peltzman, Sam. "Entry in Commercial Banking." *J. Law and Econ.* 8 (October
  1965): 11–60.
Prosser, William L. *Law of Torts.* 4th ed. St. Paul, Minn.: West, 1971.
Roe, Mark J. "Corporate Strategic Reaction to Mass Tort." *Virginia Law Rev.*
  72 (February 1986): 1–59.
Scredon, S., and Glaberson, W. "Tobacco Companies Are in the Fight for
  Their Lives." *Bus. Week* (November 11, 1985).
Spence, A. Michael. "Consumer Misperceptions, Product Failure and Pro-
  ducer Liability." *Rev. Econ. Studies* 44 (October 1977): 561–72.
Stone, Christopher D. "The Place of Enterprise Liability in the Control of
  Corporate Conduct." *Yale Law J.* 90 (November 1980): 1–77.

LIABILITY   595

Weiss, Leonard W. "The Geographic Size of Markets in Manufacturing." *Rev. Econ. and Statis.* 54 (August 1972): 245–57.

"Why Small Companies Will Survive." *Chemical Week* 131 (December 1, 1982): 60–67.

Wiggins, Steven N., and Ringleb, Al H. "Institutional Control for Large Scale, Latent Hazards." Manuscript. College Station: Texas A&M Univ., Depts. Management and Econ., 1989.

Wright, Cecil A. "Introduction to the Law of Torts." *Cambridge Law J.* 8, no. 3 (1944): 238–46.

Liability Reform

[23]

European Journal of Law and Economics, 3:39–60 (1996)
© 1996 Kluwer Academic Publishers

Environmental Liability Reform and Privatization in Central and Eastern Europe

JAMES BOYD
Resources for the Future, 1616 P Street NW, Washington, D.C. 20036

Abstract

The legacy of severe environmental degradation inherited by the new Central and Eastern European (CEE) economies requires liability reform to aid the cleanup of existing pollution sources and create incentives for future environmental risk reduction. The paper analyzes a host of liability approaches to meet these goals, given economic and institutional characteristics specific to the CEE nations, and explores the impact of environmental liability rules on privatization and foreign investment. A principal conclusion of the analysis is that, for a host of efficiency-based reasons, liability should not be retroactively applied to the new owners of privatized firms. Also, the paper advocates the use of national liability funds to finance the cost of existing liabilities, while highlighting dangers associated with their use. In addition to the desirability of alternative privatization mechanisms, the paper also analyzes alternative liability rules to govern prospective environmental hazards.

Keywords: liability, privatization

1. Introduction

Privatization and market reform in Central and Eastern Europe is occurring against a backdrop of severe environmental degradation left by decades of inadequate government attention to environmental conditions.[1] The new CEE governments must grapple with the health and ecological impacts of existing pollution and the effect of environmental problems on foreign investment and the domestic privatization process. Liability law reform is central to the pursuit of both environmental improvements and the efficient transfer of property from the state to the private sector.

The paper evaluates a variety of liability systems that can be used to govern legal responsibility for past and future environmental problems. These include state administered liability pools, retroactive liability, environmental escrow funds, and a variety of contractual mechanisms. In addition to the policies' effect on existing and future environmental conditions, the impact of these systems on the privatization process is emphasized. Also, while the experience of the United States and the European Economic Community (EEC) in dealing with environmental problems is instructive, the CEE economies are much weaker, environmental problems much greater, and legal and regulatory institutions much less developed than in the West. The analysis therefore stresses the importance of these unique factors in the evaluation of policy options.

One of the primary conclusions of the analysis is that liability should not be retroactively applied to new domestic or foreign property owners. Viewed from the standpoint of social equity, this conclusion is unsurprising. After all, responsibility for existing pollution lies with the government or former managers of industrial cooperatives, not with the properties' new owners. However, there are efficiency-based reasons for disfavoring retroactive liability as well. In particular, the analysis demonstrates that retroactive liability can reduce the efficiency of investments geared toward the reduction of future risks.

Privatization policies currently in use in the region attempt to separate legal responsibility for environmental risks present at the time of privatization and those created by new property owners. However, the analysis shows that these alternative mechanisms are not equivalent in their effects on either environmental conditions or the privatization process. In practice, there are both economic factors, such as information asymmetries, and institutional constraints that make state-funded liability pools a more desirable privatization policy than either purchase price reductions or environmental escrow funds. However, the analysis also highlights a set of dangers associated with pooled liability funds that should be addressed by governments that use such a mechanism.

The paper is organized as follows. Section 2 provides a brief overview that relates liability law to environmental cleanup incentives, the deterrence of future environmental risks, and the decisions of foreign and domestic investors. Section 3 develops a simple model to demonstrate the desirability of separating responsibility for retroactive and prospective environmental problems. Section 4 evaluates alternative privatization policies and motivates the desirability (and potential pitfalls) of state-sponsored liability funds. Finally, Section 5 considers policy options relating to prospective liability. This section considers regulatory complements to liability law and highlights a set of institutional requirements that are central to the implementation of effective legal deterrents to further environmental degradation in the region.

2. The importance of liability reform

This section motivates a set of broad justifications for environmental liability reform in the CEE economies. First, liability law acts as a deterrent to future environmental degradation. Second, liability law defines the allocation of responsibility for existing environmental problems and thereby influences the remediation of existing pollution sources. Third, liability rules affect privatization and investment decisions since they are a determinant of the environmental costs attached to property assets.

2.1. Liability deters future pollution

Liability rules help to define the system of property rights that underlie market transactions. In contrast to property rights, such as a land title, that are traded through voluntary *ex ante* negotiation, liability defines rules of compensation when a party has property rights seized involuntarily—that is, absent a market transaction. By requiring compensation to injured parties, liability rules force injurers to internalize the social costs of their behavior. In most cases when a polluting firm or hazardous product causes injury, the victim's right to health or safety is not voluntarily traded, and prices therefore do not fully reflect social costs. Many command and control regulations, such as effluent fees or gas taxes, are an *ex ante* mechanism to force the internalization of environmental costs. In contrast, liability rules lead to cost internalization by requiring *ex post* compensation for environmental degradation. In principle, the expectation that costs will be internalized motivates efficient risk reduction and leads to product prices that reflect expected social costs. For instance, strict liability (the prevailing rule in cases of environmental degradation in the United States) requires the full internalization of environmental costs caused by the producer. Under ideal circumstances, this leads to efficient risk reduction, prices that reflect social costs, and a distribution of risks that favors consumers and other potential victims.

2.2. Liability determines responsibility for the cleanup of existing pollution

While liability law affects future decision-making and environmental conditions, in the transitional economies it also defines responsibility for the costs of remediating existing pollution. Responsibility for these costs is particularly significant in the CEE economies due to the scale of existing environmental problems. While the costs of remediating existing pollution in the former Soviet Bloc cannot be precisely estimated, they are clearly huge.[2] Even in relatively healthier Western economies, past environmental costs have been borne only with great difficulty.

The assignment of liabilities is made more complicated in the CEE countries since many firms and property owners are in weak financial condition. Firms' financial strength is particularly important to the deterrent function of liability law. When firms lack the capital to compensate for risks *ex post*, liability law fails to provide adequate incentives for prospectively efficient behavior. Thus, the distribution of costs due to existing pollution can influence firms' incentives to take appropriate precaution against future environmental problems.

In addition, the scarcity of CEE resources means that environmental remediation expenditures should be prioritized so that the most serious problems are addressed first. As will be shown, liability rules affect not only who is responsible and for what amounts, but also the way in which funds are allocated to remediation.

2.3. Liability affects privatization and foreign investment

Liability rules have an immediate impact on privatization and investment decisions through their impact on the value of assets. The net value of privatized assets is clearly a function of liabilities attached to the property. Liabilities attached at the time of privatization are a function of environmental conditions and the contractual, regulatory, and legal rules governing responsibility for existing conditions. Moreover, there may be significant scientific and legal uncertainty regarding liabilities. To the extent that investors are risk averse, these types of uncertainty can depress the value of properties at the time of privatization. Are property owners to be liable for environmental costs associated with past use? What are the rules that define liabilities for future environmental problems? The answers to these questions directly affect the value and risk of property-right endowments for both domestic and foreign investors.

Potentially large-scale and hidden pollution costs are tied to almost any CEE property transaction due to decades of lax enforcement, a lack of lending and insurance institutions familiar with risk assessment, and virtually nonexistent accounting, zoning, or regulatory requirements for documentation of risk-generating processes or technologies.[3] As a result, concern over environmental responsibilities in the region ranks as high among potential Western investors as exchange rate or political risks (see Klavens and Zamparatti, 1992, described in Goldenman et al., 1994, pp. 24–25; see also Gruson and Thoma, 1991). While it is appealing to make new property owners (particularly foreign investors) liable for existing environmental problems, it is important that liability costs and risks do not inhibit investment.

3. The effect of retroactive liability on prospective deterrence

Liability reforms should address, but also be careful to distinguish between, the following two goals: (1) the definition and enforcement of policies to promote prospectively efficient environmental risk reduction and (2) the cleanup of existing sources of pollution. These are distinct social challenges. The first concerns creating incentives for efficient future behavior. The second is, on its face, a distributional question: namely, who should bear the costs of past, inefficient decisions? However, the assignment of responsibility for retroactive liabilities is not a purely distributional issue. In fact, as is now shown, the way in which *past* liabilities are treated can affect incentives for *future* risk reduction. To the extent that liability for past pollution weakens a firm's financial condition, it can reduce the incentive to make prospective risk-reduction investments.[4] Firms with assets eroded by retroactive liability may not expect to fully internalize future liability costs. In turn, liability for future pollution can fail as an effective deterrent against future risks.

Because existing environmental problems are a form of sunk cost, there is no intrinsic benefit to applying prospective liability rules to the cleanup of retrospective problems. Policy toward existing environmental problems should be geared toward the disposal of these sunk environmental costs in the least economically distorting manner.

A policy of retroactive liability for polluters and property owners has been adopted in several Western countries, including the United States, the Netherlands, Great Britain, and Germany. Independent of judgments on the performance of retroactive liability in these economies, such a system is less likely to be optimal in the CEE context.[5] Given the relatively weak condition of the CEE economies and, in particular, the scarcity of capital, retroactive liability can impose costs significant enough to force the bankruptcy and asset liquidation of many domestic producers. Bankruptcy and asset liquidation, during what is certain to be a lengthy transition to a market-based economy, is not desirable for either economic or political reasons. The magnitude of existing environmental hazards implies that the full internalization of costs based on a strict and retroactive application of liability might yield negative real asset values for a perhaps significant fraction of industrial properties.[6] These consequences are undesirable since bankruptcy and asset dissolution involve costs of their own in the form of abandoned capital, lost firm-specific human capital, and reduced competition. Moreover, as is now shown, forcing property owners to bear the costs of past pollution can weaken the law's deterrence of future pollution.

ENVIRONMENTAL LIABILITY REFORM IN CENTRAL AND EASTERN EUROPE 43

As discussed in the previous section, strict liability promotes efficiency to the extent that it leads potential polluters to internalize the environmental costs of their decisions. However, at the time of legal reform, should liability be strictly and *retroactively* applied? To address this issue, we employ a model that features both the prospective and retrospective imposition of liability on firms, some of whom may have existing liabilities. Particularly when these firms' financial condition is initially weak, this policy can be strictly less efficient than a policy that absolves firms of retroactive liability. For simplicity, the model initially ignores the privatization process and property transactions. As shown here, even when firms are already assumed to be privately owned, it is desirable to absolve them of retroactive liability. Section 4 considers the privatization process explicity and strengthen the argument against retroactive liability.

To analyze the problem, consider a model with a temporal structure featuring three periods, $t = -1, 0, 1$, corresponding to an historic, a current, and a future period, respectively. In the model, firms own property that may have existing pollution. Also assume that the likelihood of future environmental problems can be reduced by the firm via investments in environmental safety. Are the firm's incentives to invest in future environmental safety influenced by whether or not liability is retroactive? To answer this question, consider the following definitions:

D_{-1} = social costs of existing pollution, given remediation at $t = 0$,
$D_{-1,1}$ = social costs of existing pollution, given remediation delayed until $t = 1$,
D_1 = social cost of uncertain, future pollution, given no existing pollution at $t = 0$,
u = cost of reducing the likelihood of future pollution,
p_1^u = probability of future pollution given safety improvements,
p_1^n = probability of future pollution given no improvements in safety, and
A = firm value.

Assume that the costs of unremediated, existing pollution increase over time, so that $D_{-1,1} > D_{-1}$. For sites that have no contamination at $t = 0$, a future pollution cost D_1 occurs with probability p_1^n if the firm does not invest in environmental improvements and p_1^u if it does upgrade (where $p_1^n > p_1^u$). Also, assume that the total damage costs of not remediating existing pollution are greater than the costs of remediation plus the costs of future environmental damage, if it occurs ($D_{-1,1} > D_{-1} + D_1$). In other words, environmental damages will always be less if remediation at $t = 0$ occurs.

A denotes the gross value of the firm, including the value of capital investments, real estate, and expected future profits.[7] If the firm's liabilities exceed its value A, the firm is *insolvent* and will declare bankruptcy.[8]

Given existing pollution, immediate remediation and investment in risk reduction are effficient. Formally, this requires that

$$D_{-1,1} - [D_{-1} + p_1^u D_1] > u, \tag{1}$$

or the difference in expected environmental costs, given existing pollution, of not remediating and investing exceeds the costs of the investment u. Also, assume the investment u is efficient even when there is no existing pollution. This implies that

$$(p_1^n - p_1^u)D_1 > u. \tag{2}$$

Given retroactive liability, what are the firm's incentives to remediate and invest in future risk reduction? The firm's remediation and risk-reduction decision is a function of its value and whether or not it has historic liabilities. If the firm's value A is large (for example, so that $A \geq D_{-1} + D_1$), it has a dominant strategy to remediate existing liabilities and invest in risk reduction. This follows since valuable firms expect to fully internalize the benefits and costs of prospective investments in environmental safety. In contrast, firms with little value ($A \approx 0$) do not have an incentive to remediate or invest, since the costs of doing so exceed the firm's value. Given its existing and potential liabilities, the possibility of insolvency can induce inefficient risk reduction and remediation decisions.

Consider a firm that has existing liabilities (at $t = 0$). Clearly, if $A < D_{-1}$, then the firm knows that it will have no recoverable value remaining after settling claims due to its existing liability. There is therefore no private incentive to remediate. Even if $A > D_{-1}$, efficient remediation and investments in risk reduction may not occur. To explore the importance of historic liabilities to the firm's remediation and investment decision, we now derive the firm value A that leaves the firm indifferent between remediating and investing and not remediating and investing.

3.1. The decision to remediate and invest given historic liability

First, note that the firm's expected costs if it does not remediate and invest are equal to $\min\{D_{-1,1}, A\}$. However, if $D_{-1,1} < A$, the firm has assets sufficient to internalize even the largest possible social cost $D_{-1,1}$ and so will upgrade (since upgrade is efficient). Therefore, only the case where the firm's expected costs are bounded by A is of interest.

The firm faces the following choice when deciding whether or not to remediate and invest. If the firm remediates and invests, its expected costs are

$$EC^r = [D_{-1} + u] + [A - (D_{-1} + u)]p_1^u \tag{3}$$

The first term in brackets denotes the costs of retroactive liability and investment. The second term reflects the firm's expected future liability. With probability p_1^u the firm loses the value that remains after making its expenditures in period $t = 0$.[9]

In making its remediation decision the firm compares its costs if it does not remediate, A, to EC^r and chooses the cost-minimizing strategy. The condition $EC^r < A$ implies that the firm will remediate and invest and is equivalent to the condition that

$$A > D_{-1} + u. \tag{4}$$

This is intuitive. The firm bears a cost A if it does not remediate. Therefore, remediation and upgrade occur only if their combined costs are less than A. Put differently, the firm knows that it will only remediate if it has value remaining after incurring remediation costs. Note also that the condition expressed in equation (4) does not depend on the probability of future environmental liabilities, p_1^u. As long as condition (4) holds and there is some positive probability that there will be no future liability $(1 - p_1^u > 0)$, there is a positive probability that the firm will face costs less than A by remediating and investing at $t = 0$.

Denote as A^* the value that makes the firm indifferent between bearing these costs and not taking any action ($A^* = D_{-1} + u$).

ENVIRONMENTAL LIABILITY REFORM IN CENTRAL AND EASTERN EUROPE   45

3.2. The decision to remediate and invest given no historic liability

When there are no historic liabilities, the firm must still decide whether or not to upgrade. Let A^{**} denote the level of assets where a firm with no historic liability is indifferent between remediating and investing or not. The indifference level is determined by substituting A^{**} for D_1 in (2) yielding

$$(p_1^n - p_1^u)A^{**} = u. \tag{5}$$

In other words, if the firm's assets are sufficiently low, then it will prefer not to invest because the expected reduction in liability from this action is less than the investment.

In sum, the firm's decision to remediate and invest or not depends on both its value A and whether or not it is liable for existing pollution costs. Retroactive liability consumes firm resources, which reduces the amount of firm value that is exposed to future liability claims. In turn, this weakens prospective deterrence (that is, the incentive to make efficient investments u in risk reduction). Thus, retroactive liability can have a negative effect on investments geared toward future safety. Moreover, since A^* is normally greater than A^{**} more firms have an incentive *not* to remediate and invest when they have existing liabilities.[10] Of course, it is in just this situation that remediation and investment are most socially desirable.

Retroactive liability is also likely to have political consequences that reduce its desirability. The distributional impact of strict and retroactive liability poses a threat not only to the success and timeliness of cleanups of existing pollution but to the political viability of liability rules aimed at future pollution reduction. As in the West, environmental policies in Central and Eastern Europe will be derived and enforced in a political context, and their distributional impacts will largely determine their legislative and political success.[11] The fact that liability rules have large distributional and, hence political, consequences can influence the evolution and enforcement of environmental pollution law. Because the profitability (or existence) of new enterprises is potentially threatened by strict and retroactive liability, resources will be directed at the political system to redistribute costs. One natural way to do this is to seek changes in the liability rules themselves. Given the political context in which liability laws are formulated, it follows that rules dealing with future liabilities should be separated from rules dealing with retroactive liabilities in order to enhance political acceptance of a tough prospective liability system. A more equitable distribution of the costs arising from existing pollution makes laws aimed at future pollution reduction more politically and economically sustainable.

This section has provided an efficiency-based rationale for avoiding the retroactive application of liability to newly privatized enterprises. The next section elaborates on this point and demonstrates an additional set of reasons to create a legal separation between retroactive and prospective liabilities. As part of this analysis, the desirability of various privatization mechanisms is considered. A central question that must still be addressed is, if liability is not retroactive, how should historic liabilities best be financed?

4. Privatization and liability mechanisms

Ideally, during the CEE economies' period of economic and legal transition, existing environmental risks would be quickly identified and quantified. Quantification of existing pollution sources has several benefits. First, with existing risks quantified, the costs of remediation can be distributed in the least economically disruptive way. This point is underscored by the benefits of separating responsibility for retroactive and prospective liabilities described in the previous section. Second, privatization transactions can explicitly account for the costs implied by existing liability, thus reducing investor uncertainty—and enhancing privatization revenues and foreign investment.[12] Also, a precise delineation of past environmental problems ensures that legal responsibility for future environmental problems will unambiguously lie with the new property owners who create those risks.

While conceptually desirable, from a practical standpoint, the precise decoupling of existing and future risks is problematic and costly. Environmental auditing technologies are imperfect risk-assessment tools and can cost upwards of $100,000 for an industrial site. And note that these costs may have to be expended before a property transaction takes place and without the certainty that a transaction will take place. Moreover, risk assessment capabilities in the CEE economies lag those of their EEC and U.S. counterparts.[13] Experience in other countries has shown that a direct causal linkage of environmental damage to responsible parties is often problematic. "Joint and several" liability, which imposes full liability for damages that may have been created only in part by the producer, deemphasizes the importance of causality and fault in liability allocations. The rule's increased use in the United States is due in large part to the difficulty of establishing direct causal links between producers and environmental risks. When existing pollution is widespread but difficult to detect *ex ante* with conventional site-assessment methods, and advanced risk-assessment technologies and expertise are themselves in short supply, a bright line technical—let alone legal—separation of past from future risks is unrealistic. Even with exhaustive environmental auditing, foreign investors may shy away from deals because of the risk that undetected pollution sources (or sources migrating from neighboring properties) will be revealed at a later date.

If a clear separation of past and future risks is not practical, the question that remains is how to distribute the costs of past pollution while creating incentives for prospectively efficient behavior. The remainder of this section considers the way in which alternative privatization mechanisms address these goals.

We now turn to the description and analysis of three policy mechanisms for dealing with environmental liabilities at the time of privatization: purchase price reductions, environmental escrow accounts, and indemnity agreements with retroactive remediation costs borne by national liability funds. All three mechanisms attempt to address the investment and environmental issues created by pollution existing at the time of privatization. The mechanisms will be evaluated based on their ability to motivate (1) prioritized expenditure of limited remediation resources, (2) the deterrence of future pollution, and (3) efficient property transactions.

4.1. Purchase price reductions

Investors require purchase price reductions to reflect environmental liabilities when liability is transferred and retroactively applied to a privatized property.[14] This mechanism has several practical and theoretical drawbacks, however. First, purchase price reductions directly deprive the government of revenue, thus making this mechanism unpopular politically. Moreover, purchase price adjustments require an *ex ante* consensus between the government and purchaser regarding the magnitude of retroactive liabilities. Given imperfect information, agreement on these values may be impossible, and willingness to trade limited.

If liability is transferred with the property, buyers are in effect purchasing an asset of unknown quality—where quality in this sense refers to the liability inherited through purchase. Information asymmetries between the government and potential purchasers can generate an adverse selection problem that distorts investment decisions. As in a traditional "lemons" problem, investors will rationally discount their demand for properties based on an expectation of average environmental quality—and the implied liability cost of environmental conditions. This discount in demand—and willingness to pay—restricts the supply of high quality (relatively unpolluted) property. In turn, potential purchasers' discount is adjusted downward to reflect the rational expectation that clean properties will not be represented in the market. The result is an adverse selection problem—in which high-quality, but risky, properties are not brought to market.[15]

An additional, negative consequence of the adverse selection problem is that it can create a distortion toward the development of "greenfield" properties that are free from environmental risks because they have not been previously associated with industrial or commercial activity. To the extent that there is a failure in the market for environmentally risky properties, demand for these greenfield properties may be artificially high. The development of greenfield sites is not likely to be socially desirable since greenfield properties lack the infrastructure and proximity to labor of existing industrial sites and their development by definition results in increased environmental degradation.[16]

Reliance on purchase price reductions as a privatization mechanism is particularly undesirable due to the distorting effects of information asymmetries on property transactions and investment behavior. However, the adverse selection problem can be alleviated through the use of policy mechanisms that establish with the government a contractual responsibility for past environmental problems. Environmental escrow accounts and indemnity agreements are two policy mechanisms that do this.

Given the adverse selection problem that attends privatization, an optimal contract requires that the government provide insurance or a warranty against a level of product quality that is not observable to potential purchasers at the time of the transaction. This type of warranty can be implemented either through (1) an environmental escrow account that guarantees that the government will finance the cleanup of environmental problems that are revealed subsequent to the transaction or (2) an indemnity agreement that guarantees the government's liability for environmental conditions existing at the time of sale.[17]

Environmental escrow funds are time-limited accounts that can be drawn on to reimburse new owners for either previously agreed upon, or subsequently revealed, liabilities. The value of the account is variable but limited to no more than the asset's purchase price. While liabilities are transferred along with the property, the new owner is in effect insured against these costs by the independent administrator of the account. Escrow accounts are used particularly frequently in Poland and are the only statutorily approved mechanism in the Czech Republic.[18] Indemnity agreements are a form of contract that absolves the new owner of legal responsibility for existing environmental problems. This system is currently employed in the former Eastern Germany, where retroactive liability is retained by the government (see Kunth, 1992). A policy that features indemnity agreements requires a funding mechanism to bear the costs of remediating existing pollution. A possible funding mechanism is a cleanup fund supported through general government revenues or taxation of polluting products. Indeed, in the CEE economies several of these revenue sources already exist.[19]

Escrow funds and indemnity agreements can eliminate or mitigate adverse selection problems. However, these policy mechanisms can introduce a different set of inefficiencies due to moral hazard on the part of new owners. Understanding the incentives created by these mechanisms is central to the determination of an optimal privatization policy. As is argued below, on balance, indemnity agreements and national liability pools to finance existing liabilities are likely to result in more efficient expenditures on remediation than will an escrow fund policy. However, liability pools can, if not designed appropriately, fail to adequately deter future pollution.

4.2. Environmental escrow accounts

Moral hazard arises under the use of escrow accounts since new owners view the account as a costless source of funds for environmental restoration. The new owner's incentive, therefore, is to make the largest possible claims on escrow moneys. In effect, escrow accounts provide a costless subsidy to new owners' remediation activities. This tends to induce excessive remedial actions. Also, the new property owner is typically responsible for the risk assessment that forms the basis for escrow account claims. Given that claims are financed by the fund, new property owners have an incentive to overinvest in risk assessment.

One particularly negative consequence of this moral hazard problem for the CEE countries is that it leads to unprioritized expenditures on remediation of existing environmental problems. The funds placed in escrow are typically a function of the property's purchase price. This ensures that expenditures on remediation do not exceed the property's gross value. As a consequence, more money is available for remediation for more expensive or valuable property. However, there is no reason to expect that a property's gross value is related to the scale of existing environmental degradation.[20] Remediation expenditures will tend to be directed toward large, valuable enterprises and toward enterprises that are best able to scientifically and legally justify those expenditures. Expenditures will not be made on the basis of the social benefits and costs of remediation.

Given that environmental standards and a precise definition of liabilities are highly uncertain in the CEE economies, precise definitions of required levels of cleanup or reimbursable liabilities are impossible. As a result, the contracts that form the basis of escrow accounts must take account of new owners' incentive to make maximum use of the funds, while at the same time preserving the fund's function as a warranty against unforeseen environmental problems.[21] Also, new owners will not have an adequate incentive to ensure that remediation contractors minimize costs. This argues for government policing of bidding processes or the imposition of cost ceilings for specific cleanup procedures.

Because of their inability to lead to prioritized and benefit-justified expenditures on retrospective remediation, escrow funds are not the preferred system for dealing with liabilities at the time of privatization. A better system, but one with problems of its own, is the use of indemnity agreements and a national liability pool to finance retrospective remediation.

4.3. Indemnity agreements and national liability pools

An alternative policy mechanism is for the government to grant indemnity (a liability amnesty) to new property owners for environmental problems present at the time of privatization. In order to finance the remediation of existing pollution, the government would raise and disburse funds via a national liability pool. Liability funds, by widely distributing the costs of environmental cleanups, may represent the least economically disruptive mechanism for dealing with existing environmental problems. Because environmental cleanups are financed through general, public revenues, liability pools may be more politically attractive than liability assignments that focus the burden of cleanups on producers or landowners. The administration of such funds also allows for the coordination and rationalization of a nation's risk-reduction activities. With government control of expenditures on remediation, the remediation of problems presenting the greatest social costs could, in principle, receive priority.

The wide distribution of costs also reduces the likelihood of firms being made insolvent due to retroactive liability. As argued in Section 2, there are significant social costs associated with insolvency due to abandoned human or firm-specific capital, transaction costs, and reduced competition. Forcing enterprises going through the process of privatization to bear liabilities alone may lead to failed privatizations, abandonment, or insolvency. By improving the viability of newly privatized properties, the funds may also avert the possibility of pollution or inefficient investment created by firms that feel they have little to lose by polluting. Firms that expect large retroactive liabilities to ultimately force the closure of their enterprises pose a particularly serious pollution threat. If the enforcement of liability is delayed due to an overburdened legal system or lagging regulatory knowledge of pollution sources, such firms have no incentive to reduce pollution associated with their production in the period before enforcement occurs. Faced with the likely prospect of closure due to existing liabilities, it may be profit-maximizing for such firms to pollute until closure is forced by the imposition of liability. A benefit of liability amnesties, then, is that they increase the expected value of the firms, reduce the likelihood of closure due to retroactive liability claims, and thus lead firms to make safety investments based on the now realistic desire to continue operation. Since legal and regulatory enforcement of liability claims is likely to take some time in the former Soviet Bloc, this beneficial aspect of amnesties is particularly important.

There are potentially significant problems associated with the use of such funds, however. First, the hope that a government-controlled system of risk discovery, assessment, ranking, and cleanup would yield an efficient allocation of remediation expenditures may be overly optimistic. The informational and administrative costs of such a scheme will be large. Experience in countries such as the United States is instructive. The EPA's Superfund program, which is relatively well funded and technologically advanced, is criticized for failing to effectively set priorities for cleanups. Moreover, bureaucratic decision making is subject to political distortions in the expenditure of public funds.[22]

A more fundamental problem associated with liability pools is due to the difficulty in separating existing risks from those created during the lifetime of the fund. If indemnity for retroactive liability is granted, but the government is unable to distinguish between past and current risk generation, a new property owner might inflate the value of liabilities it claims to have inherited at the point of sale. In this way newly created hazards could be claimed as past hazards, and their costs be shifted to the government. Clearly, this provides the new owner with an inadequate incentive to avoid future environmental problems.

While liability pools may have desirable short-term benefits, it is undesirable for pools to become a permanent fixture in a government's environmental policy portfolio. The reason is that funds blunt the incentives for prospective risk reduction. If producers believe that all or even a fraction of their potential future liabilities will be borne by a subsidized government fund, then the private incentive to invest in costly risk reduction is reduced. Without the full, private internalization of social costs, inadequate preventive investments will be made and levels of pollution will be inefficiently high. With a pool to cover the costs of this pollution, excessive environmental costs are ultimately recovered through taxes. The implication is that risks are too large and product prices are inefficiently high.[23]

Liability pools provide one of the fundamental functions of a private insurance market, specifically *ex post* compensation for injured or insured parties. The crucial difference is that private insurance markets necessarily condition the costs of insurance on the actuarial profile of the insured, including the risk-reduction technologies in place. In private insurance markets, purchasers of insurance can reduce premiums by reducing risks through investments or changes in behavior. When liability insurance is required, insured firms internalize costs through insurance premiums and in this way can be led to make efficient investments in risk reduction.

While public liability pools can mimic this function of private insurance markets, in practice it is less common and in theory less likely. Private insurers provide a form of enforcement by (1) creating the premium-based incentives noted above, (2) denying coverage to uninsurable risks, and (3) withdrawing coverage from producers who fail to maintain adequate risk-reducing procedures or technologies. In a competitive market, private insurers must act as enforcers in this way in order to maximize profit and satisfy shareholders. The public administrators of liability pools do not face the same incentives.[24] Liability pools tend to be politically devised, often as a form of subsidy to the affected industries and thus are less likely to exclude participation or condition coverage on poor actuarial risks.

To explore the potentially undesirable characteristics of pooled funds more formally, consider the following models of the incentives created by funds. The models identify potential weaknesses in two distinct types of fund. The first example relates to a *short-horizon fund*— that is, a fund designed to finance only retroactive liabilities. The weakness that is explored in this type of fund is that the fund might subsidize future pollution created by new property owners if future pollution cannot be easily distinguished firom past pollution. The second example involves a *long-horizon fund* where both past and future environmental liabilities are financed by the fund, provided that the property owner makes efficient prospective investments in pollution abatement. The weakness of this type of policy is that the government may fail to make coverage conditional on compliance with efficient standards. If so, the fund subsidizes future pollution costs, leading to inadequate deterrence of future risks.

4.4. A short-horizon fund

We return to the notation and assumptions defined in Section 2. First, assume that while existing liabilities D_{-1} cannot be detected prior to sale, *ex post* they can be perfectly distinguished from risks created after the sale. Ideally, the government bears only the cost of existing liabilities D_{-1}. The new owner expects to bear the full cost of future liabilities D_1 and will therefore make efficient investments in pollution abatement.

Now consider the case where a new owner can falsely claim that pollution they caused was a preexisting condition of the property. This creates a form of moral hazard that can lead new property owners to not remediate existing pollution and fail to make efficient prospective abatement investments.

Denote as β the probability that such a false claim is successful. More specifically, there is a probability β that after period $t = 1$, the new owner successfully, but falsely, convinces the government to bear the costs of either (i) new damages D_1, if there was no preexisting liability or, if there were existing damages, (ii) both existing and incremental damages $D_{-1,1}$ due to the failure to remediate at $t = 0$.

If there was no preexisting liability, the new owner will invest in the efficient future abatement technology only if

$$(1 - \beta)D_1(p_1^n - p_1^u) > u, \tag{6}$$

or if the investment cost is less than its benefits due to a reduction in expected liability. Comparison with condition (2) indicates that the ability to shift future liability costs to the government means that efficient abatement investments will not necessarily be made.

Similarly, consider the case where the property was purchased with preexisting environmental contamination. If at $t = 0$, the new owner remediates, the government bears the expense D_{-1}. The new owner expects to bear future liability costs D_1 and therefore makes the efficient investment u. As a result, if the firm remediates at $t = 0$, its expected costs are $D_1 p_1^u + u$. What if the firm does not remediate at $t = 0$? In this case, the new owner expects that with probability β the government will bear the cost of both the preexisting condition and the incremental costs of failure to remediate at $t = 0$. In this case the firm will remediate at $t = 0$ only if

$$(1 - \beta)[D_{-1,1} - D_{-1}] > D_1 p_1^u + u. \tag{7}$$

The left-hand side denotes the expected costs to the new firm of not remediating at $t = 0$. Comparing (7) to condition (1) indicates that efficient remediation decisions will not necessarily occur when new owners can shift future liability costs to the government.[25]

Thus, a pooled fund's desirability is related to the magnitude of β, or the government's ability to differentiate between past and future sources of pollution. This underscores the desirability of government risk assessment efforts and capabilities. The ability to assess risks allows the government to limit the indemnities it offers to historic pollution sources.[26] This allows for the benefits of indemnity to be realized, without the long-term prospective moral hazard costs associated with a pool that subsidizes the costs of future environmental hazards.

4.5. A long-horizon fund

What incentives are created by a long-horizon fund? Like a short-horizon fund, a long-horizon fund absolves the firm of historic liability. However, because of the longer coverage horizon, a long-horizon fund also subsidizes the costs of cleanup for (1) leaks that occur during $t = 1$ and (2) unremediated historic pollution. This subsidy of future cleanup costs weakens the incentive to upgrade and remediate at $t = 0$. Since even firms with clean properties at $t = 0$ don't feel they will bear the full costs of future leaks, they may choose to not invest in the effficient risk reduction technology.

The incentive problem created by long-horizon coverage can be reduced or eliminated if coverage is made conditional on the firm making prospectively efficient abatement investments. For this to work, it is crucial that (1) compliance at $t = 0$ be verifiable *ex post* and (2) that exclusion of coverage given failure to comply with the investment criteria is a credible threat.

Consider the case where a firm with no historic contamination believes there is a probability γ that it will have coverage denied if it fails to upgrade. If the firm upgrades, its expected costs are

$$p_1^u D_1 + u, \tag{8}$$

or the probability of future pollution times its liability costs plus the cost of efficient abatement. If it does not effficiently abate, its expected costs are

$$\gamma p_1^n D_1. \tag{9}$$

These expected costs reflect the possibility that the firm will be provided with coverage even though it did not efficiently abate (which occurs with probability $(1 - \gamma)$).

Note that as γ tends to zero, the incentive to efficiently abate is removed, since (9) goes to zero. However, if $\gamma = 1$ (the regulator can perfectly exclude noncompliant firms from coverage), the firm expects efficient abatement to minimize its costs.[27] Thus, the disincentive to efficient prospective investment created by a long-horizon fund can be reduced if coverage is credibly conditioned on efficient investment decisions made at $t = 0$.

If funds are established and applied to future pollution sources, it is imperative that the coverage they provide to property owners be conditioned on compliance with environmental standards. Whether or not this is practical is an open question due to political pressures that will arise for the use of pool funds to finance future environmental problems. A more desirable policy is to establish short-horizon funds to address retroactive liabilities and enforce a system of prospective liability that makes property owners, rather than the government, bear the costs of future environmental degradation.

5. The choice of prospective liability rules

While the consequences of historic liabilities pose the most serious immediate threat to environmental safety in the CEE nations, it is also important that legal rules governing responsibility for future pollution be clearly defined at an early stage. A defined direction for the liability system will reduce uncertainty in investment and production decisions and foster the early growth of institutions and markets that will complement the system that is implemented. A basic question surrounding liability reform is whether strict liability or negligence is the more desirable to govern prospective environmental liabilities. This section addresses this question given the institutional, informational, and economic constraints that have been emphasized throughout the article. Also, analysis of the relative merits of strict liability and negligence highlights the importance of bureaucratic regulations to act as complements to environmental liability law.

Strict liability and negligence are common law legal concepts that are easily interpretable within the civil law traditions of the CEE. The essential difference between the two rules is that a negligence rule conditions the defendant's liability on fault, while strict liability does not. Despite this important difference, however, both rules tend to induce efficient risk-reduction behavior on the part of potential defendants. In the case of strict liability, this occurs since the defendant expects to fully internalize the costs of its actions. In the case of negligence, efficient behavior comes about because the defendant is induced by the threat of liability to comply with a presumably efficient standard of negligence. Environmental penalties that arise in civil law systems are akin to a negligence rule in that penalties are applied for violating statutorily defined standards or norms.[28]

There is a large literature that weighs the relative merits of strict liability and negligence rules.[29] The literature stresses differences based on the level of insurance provided by the rules, judicial transaction costs associated with them, and their effect on potentially insolvent defendants. On the basis of these considerations and others, the use of negligence rules appears on balance to be the preferred direction for environmental liability reform in the CEE nations. However, this holds only if negligence liability is based on clear, governmentally determined standards and is used in combination with environmental levies that provide victim insurance and correct for distortions in aggregate consumption.

Given an efficient negligence standard, both strict liability and negligence induce equivalent, efficient levels of care.[30] The primary difference between the two rules relates to insurance and aggregate consumption levels. Strict liability provides consumers or injured third parties with a form of insurance against risks, since losses are compensated *ex post* via the liability system, regardless of the defendant's care. In contrast, if a defendant is compliant with a negligence standard, rules can lead producers to make efficient care choices, but risks are not eliminated altogether. If due care is taken by producers then they are absolved of liability and the costs of injury are borne entirely by the injured party. In effect, victims under a negligence-based liability system are uninsured against product and environmental risks. If the consumers of products are also the victims of environmental risks, the need to self-insure may inhibit transactions due to risk aversion (as in Shavell, 1982).

Also, negligence-based rules imply product prices that do not reflect a good's residual social risks. If consumers bear the costs of injury and accurately gauge residual risks, they will "discount" that expected cost from their willingness to pay, and appropriate levels of consumption arise even though prices are not fully capturing expected hazard costs. However, in the case of most environmental hazards, consumers do not directly bear these costs, third-party victims do. As a result, negligence rules can lead to over-consumption of environmentally risky goods.

These drawbacks to the use of negligence rules—uninsured victims and excessive consumption—constitute the greatest potential drawback to the use of the rule. It should therefore be emphasized that the use of negligence rules should be accompanied by complementary (1) tax-based or (2) mandated insurance regulations. First-best aggregate consumption and victim insurance can be provided through the use of environmental levies that increase product prices to reflect expected hazard costs and provide a source of funds for victim compensation. In this type of system, all producers are levied this baseline tax, while noncompliant firms are fully liable for all environmental damages they cause.[31] Mandatory environmental insurance provides victim compensation and, by forcing the internalization of such insurance costs, leads to prices that reflect full expected social costs. This type of regulatory intervention is akin to financial responsibility requirements that have been included in U. S. and draft European statutes governing environmental liability.[32] Through the use of this type of complementary regulatory intervention, the insurance- and consumption-based drawbacks to a negligence-based system can be addressed.

The rationale for favoring a negligence-based system in the first place is that negligence is preferred to strict liability when potential defendants are shallow pocketed. As discussed earlier, the possibility of defendant bankruptcy reduces the law's deterrent effect (see note 5). When firms are potentially insolvent, negligence outperforms strict liability in its ability to motivate efficient risk reduction (see Shavell, 1986; Landes and Posner, 1987; Landes, 1990). Strict liability fails to induce efficient abatement whenever the firm's recoverable capital value—the amount that can be seized in liability actions—falls short of the scale of liabilities it can create. Negligence rules, by absolving defendants of liability if they comply, can motivate efficient care even from undercapitalized firms. In the CEE context, this advantage of negligence rules is particularly important. The weak financial condition of newly privatized CEE enterprises makes liability-induced insolvency a real possibility and argues for the use of negligence rules.[33]

Strict liability and negligence also differ in the transaction and information costs associated with them. By deemphasizing the role of fault, strict liability is typically thought to economize on the costs of jurisprudence, since arguments over what level of precaution was taken by the producer, or whether the producer's action comply with standards of nonnegligence, are irrelevant. Under a negligence rule, the court must first determine what the standard of negligence is and then ascertain whether or not the defendant's conduct conformed to that standard.[34] However, strict liability leads to more claims, since all tort victims have an incentive to petition the legal system for compensation. Under a negligence rule, only those injured by an arguably negligent producer see it in their interest to bring suit. Moreover, this does not represent a complete accounting of transaction costs associated with the rules. In particular, given strict liability, what are the costs to firms of determining privately optimal investments, given that they will be fully and strictly liable? Second, can regulatory standards be used in conjunction with a negligence rule to set and communicate appropriate standards of conduct?

Strict liability and negligence place different informational requirements on producers. Under a strict liability rule, a producer must balance the costs of current risk reduction efforts against the expected benefits of reduced liability in the future. This process requires (1) an unbiased view of hazard probabilities, (2) an unbiased view of losses associated with an accident, release, or product failure, and (3) the ability to estimate the marginal impact of safety investments on loss probabilities and scale. In other words, the informational requirements that justify the assumption that strict liability will induce efficient pollution prevention are significant. This is particularly true in the CEE economies since private sector experience with risk assessment is limited.

Under a negligence-based rule, the managers' task may be simpler: namely, to comply with standards of conduct that are commonly known or governmentally determined. Reliance on negligence-based standards can shift the locus of risk assessment away from private managers and toward the government. A centralized, bureaucratic approach to standards definition can in principle economize on the costs of risk assessment and reduce uncertainty since risk assessment is in some cases a public good. Also, a standards-based negligence system is reminiscent of civil law approaches already used in the CEE that impose damages almost exclusively in cases where there has been a violation of a government standard or regulation.

Of course, the tradeoff is that governmental, centralized standards creation is inflexible and ignores site-or firm-specific considerations. Also, the desirability of standard-based systems hinges on whether the standards used are in fact efficient and appropriately enforced. Given this, and given the fledgling nature of CEE legal systems, it is important to note that legal rules that require relatively more discretion or interpretation to enforce expand the scope of possible corruption. While strict liability maximizes the number of cases brought to the legal system for adjudication, the rule also minimizes the need for judicial discretion by limiting the importance of fault. A negligence rule, requiring as it does greater judgment regarding actions taken and applicable standards, may be less desirable in situations where greater discretion is called for and possible corruption is a realistic threat. The potential desirability of limiting judicial discretion also underscores the potential desirability of tying the use of negligence standards to governmentally derived standards of conduct. While there is nothing to guarantee that standards will be optimally defined if derived by the government, they are more available to public scrutiny and therefore less subject to abuse.[35]

Whatever the specific rule, negligence or strict liability, liability law can help deter future environmental hazards. Because a negligence rule deters undercapitalized firms more effectively and results in fewer claims than strict liability it is the preferable rule in the CEE context. However, this is subject to important caveats: that a negligence rule be combined with (1) taxation or mandatory insurance to overcome a negligence rule's inability to compensate victims and induce efficient consumption and (2) standards that are defined and communicated by the government in order to economize on information costs and limit judicial corruption.

Several of the issues discussed above also bear on the question of whether liability law or command and control regulation is the most desirable form of government intervention to prevent future environmental hazards. For instance, to the extent that liability fails to induce efficient abatement due to potential defendant insolvency, the case for *ex ante* performance or technology standards, rather than liability, is strengthened. In addition, the relative familiarity of CEE governments and managers with command and control regulations may argue for their use. An in-depth review of bureaucratic regulations is outside the scope of this analysis. However, the interaction between liability law and these other forms of regulation is an important and relatively unexplored area in environmental policy scholarship.[36]

6. Conclusions

This analysis has explored a set of issues that are of potential importance to policy makers interested in the design of liability rules and legal institutions to address both existing and future environmental pollution in Central and Eastern Europe. With emphasis placed on the constraints faced by emerging CEE legal institutions, a set of prescriptions is offered. Chief among them is the importance of not applying liability retroactively to new property owners. The analysis demonstrates that retroactive liability can have an undesirable impact, not only on the efficiency of property privatizations but on the deterrence of future environmental risks as well. The analysis also emphasizes the need for a prompt assessment and priority-based approach to existing pollution sources. Given the limited resources that can be devoted to pollution mitigation, it is imperative for CEE regulators to focus expenditures on those risks that pose the greatest immediate threat to health and the environment. This is by no means a small task, as is evidenced by failures to effectively prioritize risk abatement activities in more developed nations.

While a retroactive application of liability is undesirable, the costs of remediating existing pollution must be distributed somehow. The paper has argued that the use of liability pools is likely to be the most economically and politically effective mechanism for addressing these goals. Subject to important safeguards—specifically, a limited duration of coverage and technical compliance conditions placed on participation (such as required installation of pollution reduction technologies)—the funds are a necessary compromise between strict retroactive liability and unrealistic attempts to perfectly and quickly separate past from future pollution sources.

By reducing the distributional impact of large-scale liabilities in the short term, liability pools have the virtue of making tough future liability rules more palatable to those affected. With time given to adjust to new legal standards, and without those standards being applied retroactively, effective liability rules and institutions designed to induce efficient pollution reduction are a more realistic possibility. With regard to these future liability rules, a number of factors—such as the large fraction of undercapitalized enterprises and an overburdened judicial system—argue for the use of negligence-based rather than strict liability. An efficient future liability system will also rely to a large degree on the formation of competitive and modern insurance markets and a regulatory system that can communicate and evaluate standards of appropriate environmental conduct. Finally, it must be acknowledged that the above prescriptions define a very ambitious agenda. Realistic expectations for the formation of new legal and regulatory institutions are required, and, if anything, confidence in the law as a motivator of appropriate environmental behavior should be given the greatest emphasis of all.

Notes

1. While the analysis focuses on legal reform in Central and Eastern Europe, the environmental and economic issues discussed are of relevance to all of the former Soviet-bloc economies.

2. In Hungary, one estimate places the cost of environmental cleanups for privatized enterprises at around 5 percent of their total value (Urban, 1992), and it is estimated that $100 billion would be required to bring East German environmental conditions in line with current West German standards (Gelb and Gray, 1991). Studies of the Polish economy have suggested a 3 to 4 percent loss of GDP due to environmental degradation, and estimates of Poland's cleanup costs alone are put at between $100 and $300 billion (Marshall, 1991). For estimates of cleanup costs that range into the hundreds of billions of dollars see Berz and Connolly (1992) and Cole (1991).

3. To illustrate the pervasiveness of the problems, Eastern Germany has 60,000 suspected contaminated sites, according to the German Environment Ministry (*International Environment Reporter*, p. 706, 11/4/92). Also a study found that 80 percent of 400,000 tons of hazardous waste generated in Prague could not subsequently be traced (French, 1990).

4. Liability law fails as a deterrent when potential liabilities exceed a potential defendant's ability to satisfy them. Insolvency truncates the penalties borne by tort defendants, since liabilities are dischargeable debts in bankruptcy. For analyses that explore or employ this idea more fully see Schwartz (1985), Shavell (1986), and Boyd and Ingberman (1994).

5. For a country-by-country description of approaches to retroactive liability see Goldenman et al. (1994). Liability reform in the United States and its keystone statute CERCLA (the Comprehensive Environmental Response, Compensation, and Liability Act) imposed liability retroactively on enterprises and property owners. For more detailed analysis and criticism of this type of liability reform see Church and Nakamura (1993), Probst and Portney (1992), and Revesz and Stewart (1995).

6. An estimate suggests that in 1990 Hungary, with roughly 2,000 state enterprises, had 400 significant "loss-makers," half of which faced liquidation (a 10 percent liquidation rate for state enterprises). And note that this is absent strict liability enforcement.

7. The value A should be though of as recoverable value only—that is, value that can be converted into payments used to satisfy liability obligations or used as collateral. A does not represent value that is lost in the event of bankruptcy, such as human capital or firm-specific reputational capital.

8. In most Western countries, tort claims are considered debts that can be discharged in bankruptcy. New CEE bankruptcy laws, while currently untested on this issue, will likely have the same feature.

9. The key point is that the firm's need to finance the expenditures D_{-1} and u reduces its value, either by requiring cash outlays or a stream of debt payments to creditors.

10. Comparison of equations (3) and (4) confirms that $A^{**} < A^*$ whenever $D_{-1} > D_1$. The condition that $D_{-1} > D_1$ is likely to hold in most cases, since the social costs of pollution from technologies that feature efficient prospective safety, D_1, will tend to be smaller than the social costs of existing environmental problems D_{-1}.

11. See Becker (1985) for the argument that policies' distributional impacts largely determine their legislative and political success.

12. See Thomas (1994) who uses auction theory to emphasize the importance of environmental auditing to property transfers and the maximization of privatization revenues.

13. Site assessments in the United States typically employ title searches, building permit audits, and regulatory compliance documentation to determine past property use and potential sources of contamination or waste. This type of auditing input is in most cases not available in the CEE nations.

14. Hungary currently allows for purchase price reductions in deals that involve foreign investors. In contrast, the Czech Republic explicitly outlaws this method of adjusting for the transfer of liability.

15. Akerlof (1970) is the seminal description of this problem.

16. For a discussion of the "greenfield" problem—distortions in land use by environmental liabilities— see Boyd, Harrington, and Macauley (1996).

17. A third alternative is enforcement of "duty to warn" laws that impose liability on the government for misrepresentation of the environmental condition of the property. This option is of less direct relevance, however, since the government itself suffers from imperfect information regarding environmental conditions.

18. Czech Republic, Resolution Concerning Environmental Liabilities During the Privatization Process (123/1993). The legislation instructs the Czech National Property Fund "to compensate the [property purchaser] for the costs reasonably incurred by the [purchaser] as a result of discharging environmental liabilities" up to 100 percent of the purchase price. Coverage typically applies to both undiscovered environmental problems and problems identified in the transaction contract. For a detailed account and analysis of the Polish system see Bell and Kolaja (1993).

19. Poland and the Czech and Slovak Republics have established environmental funds, with revenues supplied through taxes, fees, and fines. Germany has proposed a fund to be dedicated explicitly to the financing of government liabilities arising from indemnity agreements, though it has not yet been established (Kunth, 1992). Draft Hungarian and Romanian laws provide for similiar instruments (see Bowman and Hunter, 1992). In the United States, liability for the cleanup of leaking underground fuel tanks is financed through the taxation of fuel sales and deliveries. Private tank owners do not directly bear liability for these risks.

20. The gross value is the firm's value absent environmental liabilities.
21. Czech policy attempts to address these issues. Resolution 123/1993, for instance, requires that the new owner "in selecting the subcontractor who will implement the cleanup measures, shall request the opinion of the ministry of Environment regarding the cleanup project." In Poland, the government generally is willing to allow use of escrow funds only for problems identified and agreed upon prior to sale. While this guards against buyer moral hazard, it fails to provide the buyer with a warranty against unobservable liabilities.
22. To illustrate, there have been reports that Polish environmental funds have been abused by local officials responsible for their disbursement. A fund director explained the use of environmental moneys to open a local library by saying, "there are many ecological books in the library now" (*International Environment Reporter*, p. 221, March 24, 1993).
23. If liability pool taxes cover the full costs of environmental damage, the product price (including the tax) will reflect the inefficient, nonsocial cost-minimizing choices of firms. And of course, with prices set inefficiently high, aggregate market consumption of these goods will be inefficiently low.
24. The costs of environmental liability are passed on to the (presumably less vigilant) consumer, rather than shareholders.
25. An additional source of moral hazard can arise when future damages are affected by the type or extent of development. This can happen, for example, if new structures built at the site make cleanup more difficult, or if more intensive use of the site increases the number of persons exposed to contaminants. Perhaps the most problematic case occurs if contamination, severe enough to enjoin further use of the site, is discovered after nonmoveable investments at the site are made. In that case the government may be liable for original (predevelopment) losses plus the new owner's lost, sunk investment.
26. Privatization laws in Hungary, the Czech Republic, and Poland, among others, require at least a baseline environmental assessment at the time of privatization. For instance, language in the Polish privatization act has been interpreted to require an environmental audit: an "economic and financial study shall be prepared for the purpose of asset valuation as well as establishing whether the implementation of organizational, economic, or technical changes is required." 13 July 1990 Act on the Privatization of State Owned Enterprsies (Dz.U Nr 51, poz. 298), art. 20, para. 1.
27. This follows since $(p_1^n - p_1^u)D_1 > u$, by construction.
28. For instance, in Russia producers are held liable when found to have "violated legislation" (see Article 84 of the 1991 Law on Environmental Protection).
29. For good examples, see Shavell (1980) and Landes and Posner (1987).
30. It should be noted that negligence standards need not be efficient. When they are not—they may be over- or under restrictive—the assumption that efficient levels of care will be induced by compliant firms is clearly invalidated. Courts with objectives that include distributional preferences (such as a desire for victim compensation) or that are subject to political influence or corruption should not be expected to employ standards corresponding to efficient firm behavior. The likelihood that negligence-based rules will be used by courts in this way is elaborated in the legal institutions section below.
31. In practice, this resembles the fee/fine environmental penalty system historically used by regulators in the CEE countries. In this case, the *fee* corresponds to the Pigouvian tax given efficient investment in safety, while the *fine* corresponds to the liability of a negligent producer.
32. Financial responsibility rules guarantee capital availability when tort claims arise. The Resource Conservation and Recovery Act (42 U.S.C. §§ 6901–6992) requires financial responsibility for the owners of underground petroleum tanks, and the Oil Pollution Act (33 U.S.C. §§ 2701–2761) requires it for oil tankers and offshore facilities. Germany's 1990 Act on Liability and Environmental Damage (art. 19) includes pollution insurance or other financial guarantee requirements for firms subject to strict environmental liability. The Danish Justice Ministry in 1992 recommended mandatory financial responsibility for high-risk industries.
33. Irrespective of whether negligence or strict liability is the prevailing rule, the use of liability law to motivate environmental safety creates an incentive for firms to divest themselves of capital. A study by Ringleb and Wiggins (1990) supports the hypothesis that U.S. firms have attempted to escape liability through divestiture or undercapitalization. This type of result emphasizes the desirability of financial responsibility regulations when liability is used to motivate environmental safety.

    It also underscores the desirability of removing a set of current CEE commercial and civil law provisions that create an incentive to undercapitalize, apart from the incentive to divest liablities. For instance, in Poland equity capital is taxed during a notary approval process and in the form of "stamp duties" at the time of incorporation. The fees are significant. Notary fees are assessed at 3 percent of equity capital up to 250M zlotys and .01 percent for value above that. The stamp duties are 2 percent up to 50M, 1 percent for 50–100M, .5 percent for 100–200M, and .1 percent for value greater than 200M. These forms of taxation tend to encourage thinly capitalized firms.

34. Ideally, the negligence standard is defined by the level of care that equates the marginal social benefits and costs of care. In practice, of course, this may be difficult to determine precisely.

35. New environmental legislation in the CEE makes explicit provision for the public's right to environmental risk information and participation in environmental policy formation (see Czech and Slovak Republic Act 17/1992, Environmental Protection Code of Hungary, draft, Jan. 1992; Bulgarian Environmental Protection Act, Oct. 1991). Bowman and Hunter (1992) provide a more complete description of these provisions.

36. For an analysis that features a choice between liability and *ex ante* command and control regulation, see Shavell (1984). In it, he contrasts liability, which may fail due to the incomplete internalization of costs by insolvent defendants, with direct, *ex ante* regulation that can be inefficient due to incomplete regulator information. He concludes that a system featuring both regulatory mechanisms will in general be optimal.

References

Akerlof, G. (1970). "The Market for 'Lemons': Qualitative Uncertainty and the Market Mechanism." *Quarterly Journal of Economics* 84, 488–500.

Becker, G. (1985). "Pressure Groups and Political Behavior." In R. Coe and C. Wilber (eds.), *Capitalism and Democracy: Schumpeter Revisited*. Notre Dame, Ind.: Univ. of Notre Dame Press.

Bell, R., and T. Kolaja. (1993). "Capital Privatization and Environmental Liability in Poland." *Business Lawyer* 48, 943, 961.

Berz, D., and A. Connolly. (1992). "The Economics of Cleaning Up the Countries of the Eastern Bloc." *Recorder*, Dec. 30, p. 6.

Bowman, M., and D. Hunter. (1992). "Environmental Reforms in Post-Communist Central Europe: From High Hopes to Hard Reality." *Michigan Journal of International Law* (Summer), 921–980.

Boyd, J., W. Harrington, and M. Macauley. (1996). "The Effects of Environmental Liability on Industrial Real Estate Development." Vol. 12 *Journal of Real Estate Finance and Economics*, pp. 37–58.

Boyd, J., and D. Ingberman. (1994). "Non-Compensatory Damages and Potential Insolvency." *Journal of Legal Studies* 23, 895–910.

Church, T., and R. Nakamura. (1993). *Cleaning Up the Mess: Implementation Strategies in Superfund*. Washington, DC: Brookings Institution.

Cole, D. (1991). "Cleaning Up Krakow: Poland's Ecological Crisis and the Political Economy of International Environmental Assistance." *Colorado Journal of International Environmental Law and Policy* 2, 205, 234.

French, H. (1990). "Green Revolutions: Environmental Reconstruction in Eastern Europe and the Soviet Union." *Worldwatch Paper* No. 99.

Gelb, A., and C. Gray. (1991). "The Transformation of Economies in Central and Eastern Europe: Issues, Progress, and Prospects." World Bank Policy and Research Series, Washington, DC.

Goldenman, G., et al. (1994). *Environmental Liability and Privatization in Central and Eastern Europe*. Norwell, MA: Kluwer.

Gruson, M., and G. Thoma. (1991). "Investments in the Territory of the Former German Democratic Republic: A Change of Direction." *Fordham International Law Journal* 14, 1139, 1154.

Klarens, J., and A. Zamparutti. (1992). *OECD/World Bank Survey on Western Direct Investment and Environment Issues in Central and Eastern Europe*. Washington, D.C.: The World Bank.

Kunth, B. (1992). "Environmental Law of Germany." In J. Schlickman et al. (eds.), *International Environmental Law and Regulation* (pp. 26–27). Washington, D.C.: The World Bank.

Landes, W. (1990). "Insolvency and Joint Torts: A Comment." *Journal of Legal Studies* 19, 679.

Landes, W., and R. Posner. (1987). *The Economic Structure of Tort Law*. Cambridge, MA: Harvard University Press.

Marshall, P. (1991). "The Greening of Eastern Europe." *CQ Researcher*, Nov. 15, p. 851.

Probst, K., and P. Portney. (1992). *Assigning Liability for Superfund Cleanups: An Analysis of Policy Options*. Washington, DC: Resources for the Future.

Revesz, R., and R. Stewart (eds.). (1995). *Analyzing Superfund: Economics, Science, and Law.* Washington, DC: Resources for the Future.

Ringleb, A., and S. Wiggins. (1992). "Liability and Large-Scale, Long-Term Hazards." *Journal of Political Economy* 98, 574–595.

Schwartz, A. (1985). "Products Liability, Corporate Structure, and Bankruptcy: Toxic Substances and the Remote Risk Relationship." *Journal of Legal Studies* 4, 689–736.

Shavell, S. (1980). "Strict Liability versus Negligence." *Journal of Legal Studies* 9, 1–25.

Shavell, S. (1982). "On Liability and Insurance." *Bell Journal of Economics* 13, 120.

Shavell, S. (1984). "A Model of the Optimal Use of Liability and Safety Regulation." *Rand Journal of Economics* 15(2), 271–280.

Shavell, S. (1986). "The Judgment-Proof Problem." *International Review of Law and Economics* 6, 45–58.

Thomas, R. (1994). "The Impact of Environmental Liabilities on Privatization in Central and Eastern Europe: A Case Study of Poland." *University of California Davis Law Review* 28, 165, 217.

Urban, L. (1992). "Public Institutions and the Preparation and Implementation of Privatization in Hungary." Discussion paper, Eotvos University of Budapest.

[24]

European Journal of Law and Economics, 2:21–43 (1995)
© 1995 Kluwer Academic Publishers

Economic Models of Compensation for Damage Caused by Nuclear Accidents: Some Lessons for the Revision of the Paris and Vienna Conventions

MICHAEL FAURE
Institute for Transnational Legal Research, University of Limburg, P.O. Box 616, 6200 MD Maastricht, The Netherlands

Abstract

In this paper the economic analysis of accident law is used to examine the liability for nuclear accidents. It is argued that the classic system of individual liability of a nuclear power plant operator with a financial cap on compensation and individual insurance by national pools is not effective. The current system leads to a too low compensation for victims and lacks an adequate internalization of the nuclear risk. Hence, it is argued that the economic analysis of law can provide useful insights for the revision of the Paris and Vienna Conventions on the liability for nuclear accidents. It is also argued that higher amounts of compensation can be generated only if the idea is accepted that all plants share the costs of an accident wherever it occurs. This could be realized through a mutual pooling system. Such a system could also be fitted into the revision of the Paris and Vienna Conventions.

1. Introduction

The rights of victims of a nuclear accident to be compensated for losses are governed by international conventions. The conventions make the licensee of a nuclear plant strictly liable and introduce compulsory insurance. However, the maximum amount of compensation is limited, and short statutes of limitations apply. The conventions provide that the signatory states should implement a minimum compensation to victims, but, within the limits set by the convention, the states are free to set the maximum amount of compensation.

After the accidents of Harrisburg and Chernobyl it has become clear that the amounts provided for in the various national statutes implementing the conventions are not sufficient to cover the damage caused by such an accident. Hence, among lawyers, and also within the Organization for Economic Corporation and Development (OECD), the Nuclear Energy Agency (NEA), and the International Atomic Energy Association (IAEA), plans are being discussed to find new systems that could provide higher amounts of compensation than is presently the case.

In this respect it is interesting to look at the economic literature on accidents and on compensation for nuclear accidents in particular. The area of nuclear accidents has recently attracted interest from economists and in particular those interested in the economic analysis of law. They have argued that liability should be strict and in principle unlimited, but combined with safety regulation. Attention has also been paid by economists to the negative effects of the actual limits in the existing conventions. It has been argued that setting the financial cap on compensation at levels lower than the actual costs of an average nuclear accident leads to problems of underdeterrence and may cause disruption of the financial system. Hence, authors have proposed alternative systems of compensation for damages caused by nuclear accidents. In this respect the question merits attention whether these alternative models of compensation discussed in the economic literature could be implemented when discussing the revision of the Paris and Vienna Conventions. Indeed, the revision of the conventions will probably lead to an increase in the liability of the licensee of a nuclear plant. However, in addition, systems to cover the risks exceeding the financial possibilities of the licensee and his insurer should be considered. In that respect risk-sharing agreements between nuclear power plant operators should be examined as a serious alternative.

The paper is structured as follows: after an introduction (1) the economic principles of accident law are outlined (2); then the findings of this economic literature are contrasted with the existing liability schemes in the conventions and the structure of the insurance market (3). This is followed by a critical appraisal of the conventions and the functioning of the insurance through the pooling system (4). Then an alternative model of compensation is outlined (5), and the question is asked whether such an alternative model can be implemented in the revised Paris and Vienna Conventions (6). The paper is concluded by a few final remarks (7).

2. Economic principles of accident law

The regulation of nuclear accidents may aim at two goals: an optimal prevention of nuclear accidents and an optimal compensation of losses. These two goals cannot be seen separately from each other. The first goal is to minimize the social costs of nuclear accidents by taking preventive measures. The second is often referred to as the victim-protection goal, but the first goal also serves the victim, since it is in his interest that the occurrence of an accident will be avoided.

In the law and economics literature much attention has been paid to the optimal legal mechanisms to prevent accidents.[1] A legal mechanism that aims at preventing nuclear accidents should give incentives to the plant owner to take efficient preventive measures. It is well known in the economic analysis of tort law that liability rules can induce a potential injurer to take optimal care (see Brown, 1973). Efficient care can be found where marginal costs of care equal marginal benefits in accident reduction, assuming risk neutrality. This point is referred to in the basic economic model of tort law as y^*, the optimal care to be taken by the potential injurer (see Shavell, 1980). One possible liability rule that will give the injurer an incentive to spend on care to reach the efficient level y^* is to use a negligence rule. Assuming that under a negligence rule the injurer will have to pay compensation only if he spends less on care than the legal system wants him to (due care), the injurer will have an incentive to spend on care, since it is a way to avoid liability, which will maximize his utility. Provided that the legal system defines the due-care level as the efficient care y^*, a negligence rule will therefore give the injurer incentives to follow the efficient-care level. Also a strict liability rule will lead to optimal incentives for care taking for the injurer, since taking efficient care will minimize the expected accident costs that the injurer has to bear under a strict liability system. Therefore, the literature generally accepts that both a negligence rule and a strict liability rule will provide a potential injurer with incentives to take the efficient care level (see Faure and Van den Bergh, 1987). However, this is valid only in a unilateral accident setting—that is, an accident whereby only the injurer can influence the accident risk. If victims were also given incentives for accident reduction, a contributory negligence defense should be added to the strict liability rule. Under negligence victims will always have an incentive to take efficient care as well since they will in principle not be compensated by the injurer, who, under a negligence rule, will take efficient care to avoid liability.

However, the accident risk is influenced not only by the level of care but also by the number of times that the parties are involved in the risky activity—that is, the activity level. Hence, an optimal liability rule should also give the parties in a potential accident setting incentives to adopt an optimal activity level (see Diamond, 1974; Adams, 1989). A negligence rule will not give optimal incentives to the injurer to adopt an optimal activity level since the activity level is not incorporated in the due-care standard that the court applies. Hence, under a negligence rule the injurer has an incentive to take efficient care (to escape liability) but not to adopt an efficient activity level. Under a strict liability rule, on the contrary, an injurer has an incentive to adopt an efficient activity level since this is also a way to minimize the total expected accident costs that he has to bear. In a unilateral accident model (whereby only the behavior of the injurer influences the accident risk) strict liability is the efficient liability rule since it leads both to efficient care and to an optimal activity level.

It has, however, been pointed out that liability rules can sometimes fail to have a deterrent effect since there can be a time lapse between the tort and the occurrence of the harm or causation problems can occur. In those cases, safety regulation is advanced as an alternative to the tort system (Shavell, 1984), and the standard of efficient care is fixed ex ante by government regulation. The violation of this regulatory standard is penalized with administrative or criminal sanctions, irrespective of the occurrence of the harm. Of course, tort rules are also combined with safety regulation.

It also should be noted that in the economic literature on accident law deterrence efficiency is advanced as the goal of liability rules. Liability rules should in the first place aim at a reduction of the total costs of accidents and not necessarily at victim compensation. In a way, victim compensation is only considered to be a means to give the potential injurer incentives to take efficient care. Therefore, strict liability is often advanced in the economic literature as a means to provide optimal accident prevention since it will also give incentives for an optimal activity level. In most legal literature, on the contrary, the strict liability rule is often advanced for its distributional advantage of always providing compensation to the victim.

In the economic literature the optimal distribution of losses is also examined. In that respect the comparative benefits of liability rules with private insurance on the one hand, and safety regulation with social insurance (or compensation funds) on the other, are often discussed (see Skogh, 1982; Hanson and Skogh, 1987).

We will now turn from a discussion of the principles of the economic analysis of accident law to the existing conventions on liability and insurance for nuclear accidents (3) and the efficiency of the existing liability and insurance schemes (4).

3. The liability and insurance for nuclear accidents

3.1. The legal situation

Most of the conventions regulating liability and insurance for damage caused by nuclear accidents originated through the ENEA of the OECD and the IAEA in Vienna. The contents of these conventions are well known. In this paper we can therefore limit ourselves to a brief summary of these principles. We especially note the features of the liability under the conventions that deviate from the general rules of tort law and that are of relevance for the economic principles of accident law.

Article 3 of the convention of Paris of July 29, 1960 provides that the licensee of a nuclear power plant is liable for all damage caused to persons and for all property damage (with a few exceptions) where it can be proved that the losses are caused by a nuclear accident.[2] Article 6 of the convention of Paris expressly states that a lawsuit can be brought only against the licensee who is liable according to the provisions of the conventions or, if possible, under national law against the insurer of the licensee. The same article provides that no one other than the licensee of the nuclear plant will be held liable. This is the so-called channeling of liability. The right of redress of the licensee against third parties who may be liable for causing the accident is also seriously limited: Article 6(f) provides that recourse is only possible if the third party intentionally caused the harm or if a right of redress was made possible through a contractual arrangement.

Article 7 of the convention of Paris provides that the liability of the licensee shall be limited to 15 million currency units, but it is left to the law of the signatory states to increase or decrease this amount. Article 7(b) expressly mentions that the possibility of obtaining insurance coverage should be taken into account in fixing the amount of liability of the licensee. However, the exposure to liability of the licensee may never be lower than 5 million currency units.

Article 8 stipulates that the entitlement on compensation lapses if a lawsuit has not been filed within ten years of the nuclear accident. In addition, Article 8 allows the national legislation to introduce an additional time bar of two years from the moment that the victim knew the damage and the identity of the licensee who is liable for the accident. However, even with the introduction of this time bar of two years, the aforementioned statute of limitations of ten years may not be passed. Article 8(c) provides that national legislation can fix a term longer than ten years if the liability of the licensee is also covered after the ten-year period.

Particularly important is Article 10, which provides that the liability according to the convention should be covered by insurance or another kind of guarantee for the amount fixed according to Article 7.

The convention of Paris has been complemented by a supplementary convention of Brussels of January 31, 1963. In Article 3 of this convention of Brussels, the signatory states agree to cover losses caused by nuclear accidents to an amount of 120 million currency units per accident. The compensation should take place as follows:

- Up to 5 million currency units (the exact amount must be fixed by the legislation of the signatory states), the damages must be covered by the licensee who is liable for the accident and who should have insurance to cover this amount;

- Between the amount to be paid by (the insurance of) the licensee and 70 million currency units, the state in which the nuclear power plant that caused the accident is located must pay the damages;
- Between 70 million and 120 million currency units, all the signatory states will contribute to the compensation of the damages, according to a division that is provided in Article 12 of the convention of Paris.

The convention of Brussels was amended by two protocols of Paris of November 16, 1982. One of the consequences of these protocols was that the maximum amounts of compensation for nuclear damages were changed from currency units to IMF Special Drawing Rights. The maximum amount of the liability of the licensee was fixed at 15 million Special Drawing Rights. The states can change this amount, but it can never be lower than 5 million Special Drawing Rights. The additional protocol also changed the amount, referred to in the convention of Brussels, into Special Drawing Rights. The maximum amount available for compensation of losses caused by a nuclear accident is now 300 million Special Drawing Rights. This is the amount up to which all signatory states will intervene according to a division provided for in the convention.

The International Atomic Energy Agency in Vienna also drafted a convention on civil liability for nuclear damages on May 21, 1963. However, far fewer countries joined this Vienna convention than adhered to the Paris convention. Von Busekist noted in 1989 that of a total number of power plants worldwide of 414 only three were covered by the Vienna convention, 139 by the Paris and Brussels conventions, while for 272 power plants neither of these conventions was applicable (Von Busekist, 1989). As a consequence of the Chernobyl accident on September 21, 1988, a joint protocol was adopted relating to the application of the Vienna convention and the Paris convention.[3] This joint protocol has built a bridge between the two conventions on liability for nuclear damage in that the operator of a nuclear installation situated in the territory of a party to either the Vienna or the Paris conventions shall be liable in accordance with those conventions for nuclear damage suffered in the territory of a party to the other convention. This reciprocity principle means that the application of both conventions has been enlarged by the territory of the parties to the other convention.

The conventions have been implemented by the various contracting states. All the conventions had to introduce strict liability for the licensee of a nuclear power plant and some type of compulsory insurance or guarantee for the liability exposure of the licensee. In practice there is a lot of difference between the states, especially as far as the amount of damages to be compensated by the licensee is concerned. Some states have even introduced unlimited liability of the licensee but have limited the duty to insure to a certain amount.[4]

3.2. The insurance of the nuclear risk

The insurance of the nuclear risk is provided by the nuclear pools. Since the risks faced are considered to be very serious, the major national insurance companies in every nuclear country decided to pool their resources in the 1950s on a noncompetitive basis in order to be able to provide coverage for the nuclear risk (see Faure and Van den Bergh, 1990). The result of this pooling arrangement is that at the beginning of each year the insurers determine the amount that they are prepared to commit for every nuclear installation. The total of contributions made by the participating insurers at the beginning of the year constitutes the capacity of the national pools involved. Pools are organized on a national basis. Reinsurance is obtained from similar pools or syndicates in other countries. Nowadays twenty-eight pools exist worldwide (Reitsma, 1992). Through this organization of the reinsurance with other pools, the whole nuclear insurance is connected worldwide (see Dow, 1985). Therefore, for example, Belgian insurance companies that joined the Belgian nuclear pool SYBAN intervened in paying the damage caused by the nuclear accident at Three Mile Island in the United States.

These pools do not only provide for coverage for third-party liability but also first-party insurance for the damage caused to the nuclear power plant itself. This is an aspect of considerable importance since the amount available for third-party liability insurance is limited by the amounts made available for the first party insurance for the nuclear power plant. In some literature it is even argued that the amounts that should be available for coverage of the nuclear power plant should be much higher than the amounts to be made available for the liability of the licensee of the power plant toward third parties (see Dow, 1985, p. 180). According to some authors, first-party insurance even has priority over third-party liability insurance since a nuclear accident will probably first affect the installation itself and only then the surrounding area.[5] This combination of first-party and third-party liability insurance through the nuclear pools therefore leads to a limitation of the amount available for third-party liability insurance. It is also remarkable that brokers argued during an OECD conference in München in 1984 that the first-party insurance should be removed from the pools; the premiums would be relatively high due to the monopoly. They also argued that an exclusion of competition was possibly justified thirty years ago at the beginning of the nuclear age but could not be defended nowadays.[6] Given this high concentration on the nuclear insurance market in some countries initiatives have been taken by the nuclear industry, in cooperation with some brokers, to withdraw the first-party insurance from the nuclear pools and to cover this through a new mutual insurance fund of nuclear power plant operators.[7]

4. A (critical) economic analysis of the current liability for and insurance of nuclear damage

We now compare the existing liability and insurance schemes for nuclear accidents with the economic principles of accident law described under Section 2.

First, some of the economic principles of accident law are compared with the liability of the licensee as set out in the convention (4.1), then the costs of a nuclear accident is discussed (4.2). The structure of the existing insurance model is analyzed (4.3), and the question as to whether some of the inefficiencies of the existing model might be explained through the economics of interest groups is addressed (4.4).

4.1. An economic analysis of the liability of the licensee of a nuclear power plant

A first aspect to look at in nuclear liability law is whether the licensee of a nuclear power plant should be held strictly liable. In many statutes implementing the international conventions it is stated that *strict liability* will help the victim in obtaining compensation since he is released from the heavy burden of proving fault under the negligence rule. As was mentioned earlier, from an economic point of view victim compensation is not as such a goal of accident law. The duty of the injurer to compensate his victim is only an instrument to reach deterrence efficiency. Moreover, the victim-compensation argument to introduce strict liability for nuclear accidents is not that convincing. Indeed, many legal systems qualify every violation of a statutory or regulatory norm as a civil fault. The nuclear industry is subjected to extensive safety regulation. Hence, the victim only has to prove the violation of one of these regulations to establish a fault. If, in addition, the victim can prove a causal relationship with the loss suffered, he will be able to claim compensation. In many accident cases this burden of proof will therefore not be as heavy as has been argued. It is, therefore, at least questionable whether a strict liability rule substantially improves the situation of the victim in comparison with an already existing broadly interpreted civil fault regime. It should also not be overlooked that under the general-fault regime of tort law no limitations apply and the victim is entitled to full compensation.

Although we argue that the victim-compensation argument as such cannot justify the introduction of strict liability for nuclear accidents, there are economic reasons based on deterrence efficiency for introducing a strict liability rule. A nuclear accident can certainly be considered a unilateral accident—that is, an accident whereby only the injurer can influence the accident risk. In this case we noted that the advantage of the strict liability rule is that it will give the injurer an incentive both to adopt an optimal activity level and to take efficient care. Since the victim cannot influence the accident risk, strict liability seems to be the first best solution to give the injurer optimal incentives for accident reduction.

An important condition, however, for a strict liability rule to be efficient is that the amount of compensation to be paid to the victim should be equal to the actual costs incurred by the victim. This brings us to a second feature of the nuclear liability regime under the conventions: the *limitation of compensation*. An obvious disadvantage is that this seriously impairs the rights of the victim to full compensation. In the next section we will discuss whether the current limitations in the national legislations are set at a lower amount than the expected losses of an average nuclear accident. If this were the case, not only would the right of victims to compensation be seriously limited, but there would also not be a full internalization of the externality caused by the nuclear risk. Indeed, if the legislator limits the compensation due to victims the energy prices for nuclear power will not reflect the true social costs of nuclear power. This will lead to an overconsumption of nuclear power—a consumption that is higher than the socially optimal amount. From an economic point of view a limitation of the compensation is therefore a serious problem, since it will not lead to an internalization of this risky activity. In fact, if the nuclear power industry is protected by a statutory limitation of compensation, this also constitutes an indirect subsidization of the nuclear power industry. This point was also raised in the Netherlands during the parliamentary debate preceding a recent statutory change of the nuclear liability statute. The amount of guarantee provided by the Dutch state was increased to the exceptional amount of 5 billion Dutch guilders. It was mentioned in the legislation that the ministry of finance will have to charge the licensee of a nuclear power plant for this guarantee provided by the state. If this would not be the case the nuclear energy would remain too cheap, since the energy price would not reflect the true costs of the nuclear risk.[8] Of course this problem of "overconsumption of nuclear power" would be reduced if other energy producers would enjoy a limitation of liability as well. In that case a second-best solution could be achieved. However, it seems nuclear energy producers are the only ones enjoying this benefit of the limitation of liability.

If one believes that the exposure to liability has a deterrent effect, a limitation of the amount of compensation due to victims poses another problem. There is direct linear relationship between the magnitude of the accident risk and the amount spent on care by the potential injurer (Landes and Posner, 1984, p. 417). If the liability therefore is limited to a certain amount, the potential injurer will consider the accident as one with a magnitude of the limited amount. Hence, he will spend on care to avoid that an accident will be caused with a magnitude equal to the limited amount, and he will not spend the care necessary to reduce the total accident costs. Obviously, the amount of care spent by the potential injurer will be lower and a problem of underdeterrence arises. The amount of optimal care, y^*, being the care necessary to reduce the total accident costs efficiently, will be higher than the amount the potential injurer will spend to avoid an accident equal to the statutory limited amount.

Another deviation from the general tort rules is the *channeling of liability*. This means that the victim of a nuclear accident can sue only the licensee of the nuclear plant and cannot sue a third party, even if the loss was actually caused by him. Some statutes implementing the convention even exclude the possibility for the victim to sue either the licensee or a third party under the common-fault regime to claim full compensation. This channeling of liability clearly limits the rights of the victim to full compensation, but it can also have negative effects for the incentives to take efficient care. Since channeling leads to the liability of only one injurer who can be sued by the victim, other parties that could also influence the accident risk might have insufficient incentives to take efficient care.

Also the short *periods of limitation* and the special terms in which the suit has to be brought impair the situation of the victim.[9] If the risk that an injurer will be held liable decreases as a consequence of time bars, this can have a negative effect on his incentives to take care. If the consequences of damage manifest themselves only after the statute of limitations has expired, the licensee will not be held liable and will therefore have reduced incentives for accident reduction.

In sum, through these deviations from the general rules of tort law liability rules will not optimally deter nuclear accidents. As we have mentioned above, *safety regulation* could compensate for this problem of underdeterrence. Indeed, especially in the field of nuclear energy, one notices an extensive field of safety regulation aiming at a reduction of the accident risk. In this respect it should also be mentioned that the classic assumption of risk neutrality does, of course, not hold in case of nuclear accidents. In fact, most persons are extremely averse toward the risk of a major nuclear accident.[10] Risk can be removed from persons who are risk averse through insurance. Another point is that under risk aversion the socially optimal amount of care, y^*, increases. One can therefore note that in nuclear safety devices are often required from the licensee of a nuclear power plant for which the marginal costs are certainly higher than the marginal benefits in additional accident reduction. However, such an additional investment in safety might be efficient given the high degree of risk aversion of the general public toward nuclear accidents.

One should, however, not think that the mentioned inefficiencies of the liability rules with respect to nuclear accidents can be completely outweighed by extensive safety regulation. The effectiveness of safety regulation is dependent, among other, on the capacity of the regulator or administrative authority to set the optimal safety standards ex ante and on an effective control with respect to compliance. Administrative control of the compliance with safety regulations is still a weak point in many countries. Therefore the safety of nuclear power plants should be dependent not only on government safety regulation but also on the incentives given by liability rules for an optimal reduction of the accident risk by the licensee of a nuclear power plant. This has, moreover, the advantage that the licensee of a nuclear power plant possesses better information on the optimal techniques of accident reduction and increased safety than the government or a regulatory authority. Strict liability can give optimal incentives for the operator of a nuclear power plant to invest in research to discover the optimal safety measures to reduce the accident risk. This, however, assumes a strict liability of the operator of a nuclear power plant for the total accident costs and not just a limited amount.

4.2. The costs of a nuclear accident

The estimates of the risk of core meltdown have varied enormously between studies and have changed substantially over time (Evans and Hope, 1984). However, in a 1986 article, Islam and Lindgren estimated that with the then existing nuclear power plants (374 in the whole world) there was an 86 percent probability that a new nuclear accident would occur within the next ten years (or 70 percent that it would occur within the following 5.4 years) assuming that from 1986 onward no new power plant would be built (Islam and Lindgren, 1986). It is therefore most important to examine whether losses caused by a major nuclear accident could be covered within the existing statutory limitations.

An indication of the potential costs of a nuclear accident is given in the Sandia Siting study of 1982 (also called the Sandia Report).[11] The study examined the consequences of an accident that could have happened in any of the American nuclear power plants. It made a distinction between an accident with "average" consequences and a large accident. The only costs measured are the costs of deaths, injuries, and potential cancer cases and property damage. They produce the results shown in Table 1.[12]

Of course, one could discuss why the drafters of the Sandia report have chosen certain weights to compare deaths, injured, and cancer affected. More important than criticizing the details of this estimation seems to be the fact that these estimations indicate that even the costs of an average nuclear accident could largely outweigh the amount available for compensation of victims. It is only to show this point that the Sandia report is used in this paper.

There are also estimations of the costs of the nuclear accidents that have already occurred. For the Three Mile Island accident of March 28, 1979, insurers reported that they had paid $29 million (U.S.) up to June 1983. The amount the insurers paid covers only a part of the losses and gives no indication of the total social costs of the accident. Evans and Hope show that there are many hidden costs of the accident at Three Mile Island. The direct costs of the clean-up operation were estimated at $975 million to $1.034 billion (U.S.).

Table 1. Costs of a nuclear accident according to the Sandia Report (millions of dollars).

1. Average accident			
• 700 to 1,300 deaths on the spot			
• 2,400 to 5,000 injured			
• 7,600 to 9,600 potential cancer cases			
Deaths	5 × 700 to 1,300 =	3,500	6,500
Injured	0.1 × 2,400 to 5,000 =	240	500
Cancer cases	1 × 7,600 to 9,300 =	7,600	9,300
Subtotal		11,340	16,300
Property damage		10,000	10,000
Total		21,340	26,300
2. Large accident			
• 56,600 deaths			
• 227,000 injured			
• 15,600 potential cancer cases			
Deaths	5 × 56,600 =	283,000	
Injured	0.1 × 227,000 =	22,700	
Cancer	1 × 15,600 =	15,600	
Subtotal		321,300	
Property damage		374,000	
Total		695,000	

In addition to these costs, the costs of writing off what was essentially a new reactor should also be taken into account. The figure involved is somewhere in the range of $1 to 3 billion (U.S.) (Evans and Hope, 1984). The press reports on the Chernobyl accident of April 26, 1986 give some indiction of the costs of that accident: 250 persons died as a direct result of the accident; in an area of 30 km around the plant 135,000 persons had to be evacuated, and after three years 600,000 persons had complained of health problems due to exposure to radiation. The direct loss caused by the accident is estimated at $15 billion (U.S.) in the Soviet Union alone. The effects were, of course, not limited to Russia. For instance, in Norway, between 1987 and 1989, 30 percent of all cattle were contaminated through radioactive exposure (Morrens, 1990, pp. 14–15). In other studies attention is also paid to the impact of the accident on the environment, on agriculture, and on health in the Soviet Union (see Hayes and Bojcun, 1988; Marples, 1988; Medvedev, 1990).

For Canada an estimation of the financial consequences of a severe nuclear accident has been carried out by Lonergan, Goble, and Cororaton (1990). The objective of their study was to estimate the off-site financial consequences of a severe accident. As far as health effects are concerned, they estimate the costs of immediate fatalities at $22.66 million (Canadian), the total costs of cancer deaths at $200.77 million (Canadian). The costs of emergency actions, milk loss, crop loss, and so on were estimated at $2.03 billion (Canadian), not taking into account the evacuation costs and the property damage.

   This Canadian study, the results of the Sandia report and the costs estimations with respect to the accidents at Three Mile Island and Chernobyl justify the conclusion that the costs of an average nuclear accident will be much higher than the limited amount of liability of the operator of a nuclear power plant. Of course, there are serious differences between the national legislations implementing the conventions. But in most countries the legal scholars and some members of parliament are aware that even when the limitations are set at a relatively high amount it will never be sufficient to cover the average costs of a nuclear accident. For instance, in Belgium it was clearly stated by some members of parliament during the Parliamentary Proceedings that the limitation of liability was set at a much lower amount than the expected losses of an average nuclear accident. Indeed, according to the Sandia study, quoted in the Parliamentary Proceedings in Belgium, the costs of an average nuclear accident could amount to 600 to 900 billion Belgian francs. The amount of 4 billion Belgian francs to which the liability of the licensee is limited therefore reduces the victims right to compensation to less than 1 percent of the average costs of an accident.[13] Also in the Netherlands, where a state guarantee of 5 billion Dutch guilders was introduced with the statute of June 26, 1991, both the minister and members of parliament agree that even this—relatively high—amount cannot provide real compensation for the costs of a serious nuclear accident. In this respect minister Kok noted that although the Dutch amount is also high in an international comparison, no amount might be enough to cover the nuclear risk.[14] A member of parliament estimated the average costs of a nuclear accident between 14 and 30 billion Dutch guilders.[15] This means that the state guarantee of 5 billion Dutch guilders will not be sufficient but that the limited liability of the operator of the power plant (500 million Dutch guilders) will in any case be too low.

   Hence, the conclusion seems justified that the above-mentioned disadvantages of a limitation of liability do constitute a serious problem in most legislations implementing the international nuclear liability conventions. Since most of these limitations were introduced given the limited availability of insurance coverage, the structure of the insurance market for the nuclear risk merits a critical analysis.

4.3. The structure of the insurance market for the nuclear risk: A critical analysis

A first problem with the insurance of the nuclear power plants through the pooling system is that these pooling arrangements exclude the normal competition on the insurance market.[16] Such a pooling of risks could be justified in high-risk lines—for example, for catastrophical risks—since pooling permits small insurance companies to participate in a particular market. Therefore, pooling arrangements make insurance on a larger scale possible and might even contribute to an increased level of competition. If pooling arrangements were absent, only a few large insurance companies would be able to provide insurance coverage for specialized and risky activities. Allowing smaller firms to pool will therefore increase the number of competitors (Havens and Theisen, 1986; Finsinger, 1988). However, if pooling is combined with further restrictions that are not necessitated by insurance techniques, the final users will not receive a fair share of the resulting benefits and inefficiencies may appear. In the case of nuclear insurance the national pools are clearly a monopoly that excludes all competition. The national pools do indeed (except for reinsurance) in principle only insure the nuclear installations on their own territory; there is therefore no competition between the various national pools. Also, the European Commission has recognized the danger of pooling arrangements, which might lead to restrictions on price competition (premiums). A recent EC regulation 3932/92[17] provides for an exemption from the cartel prohibition for the insurance industry. But Article 11 of this regulation provides that the exemption only applies if the insurance products underwritten by the participating undertakings do not represent more than 10 percent of the market in case of coinsurance or 15 percent of the market in case of coreinsurance (see Faure and Van den Bergh, 1993).

As this regulation does not provide for an exception for the nuclear insurance, the question arises how the European Nuclear Insurance Pools will deal with this regulation now that they clearly fall under the cartel prohibition of Article 85 of the EEC Treaty.

The fact that the nuclear insurance market is noncompetitive will, of course, have the expected effect on the amount of the premiums. It depends on the structure of the demand side of the insurance market whether the monopolistic insurer will be able to force his conditions on the insured. If the nuclear industry also shows a high amount of concentration—which is, due to regulation, the case in many countries—there will often be a bilateral monopoly that will preclude the nuclear insurer from realizing his full monopoly profits.[18] In this respect we should remember the remark of some brokers who attempt to remove the first-party property insurance from the nuclear insurance pools because the premiums charged by the pools would be too high. This seems to confirm the expectation of monopolistic premium setting by the insurance pools.

From a legislative and regulatory point of view a major objective against the high amount of concentration on the nuclear insurance market is that the legislator becomes totally dependent on the information given by a monopolistic insurer to judge the insurability of a certain risk. Especially in the case of the nuclear risk the exposure to liability is very much dependent on the insurability of the liability of the nuclear power plant operator. It has often been argued in the many national parliaments that had to decide on the amount of liability of the nuclear power plant operator that the liability should be limited, taking into account the limited availability of insurance. The problem is that the insurability of the nuclear risk is usually not based on an objective actuarial study but on the willingness of the monopolistic insurer to cover a certain risk. The information that is provided by the national insurance pools is not always highly reliable. An example can be found in the Belgian Act of July 22, 1985, which limits the liability of the licensee to 4 billion Belgian francs. This was based on the unwillingness of the Belgian monopolist insurer, SYBAN, to provide coverage for an amount above 4 billion Belgian francs. This information given by SYBAN is unreliable because of the lack of competition on the relevant insurance market. In foreign insurance markets third-party nuclear risks are insured for much higher amounts, and moreover the value of the nuclear power plant itself in Belgium is insured by the same pool (SYBAN) for more than 40 billion Belgian francs (Faure and Van den Bergh, 1990). It is unclear why for third-party liability insurance only an amount of 4 billion Belgian francs can be made available, whereas the installation itself can be insured to 40 billion Belgian francs.

This leads to several conclusions:

• The exposure to liability of the operator of a nuclear power plant should not depend on the willingness of a monopolistic insurer to provide coverage; eventually one could consider making the liability of the operator unlimited, which is more consistent with the economic model and which has been approved in several countries, and to limit the duty to insure to a certain amount.

- There seems to be no justification for the practice of many nuclear insurance pools of providing much higher amounts for the first-party insurance of the power plant than for third-party liability insurance.
- The availability of coverage should not be judged merely by looking at national nuclear insurance pools. Since the pools are connected through international reinsurance, it cannot be understood why in one country much higher amounts can be made available by the national pools than in other countries.
- In general, legislators should not base their decision with respect to the exposure to liability of the nuclear power plant operator on the willingness to insure of a monopolistic insurer.

4.4. An interest-group perspective

Until now we adopted the relatively unrealistic assumption that politicians act in the public interest and will therefore promulgate legislation only with respect to liability rules and safety regulation if this is welfare maximizing. We, however, noted that some of the features of the nuclear liability legislation are inefficient and therefore not in the public interest. This argument could even be strengthened by looking at several of the national implementation legislations, which make clear that the victim-protection argument is a very weak defense for the existing liability schemes.[19] Given the low limitations in some countries the conclusion seems justified that in some cases the victims were better "protected" before the implementation of the nuclear liability legislation than after.

Many economists and political scientists have developed theories to explain those inefficiencies. In these theories the behavior of politicians as individual wealth maximizers is analyzed. Regulation is seen as the product of a demand for regulation by interest groups and a supply by wealth-maximizing politicians. In that respect the work of Nobel Prize winner Buchanan and other scholars of the public-choice school (Buchanan and Tullock, 1962; McCormick and Tollison, 1982; Olson, 1971) and the work of Nobel Prize winner George Stigler and other scholars interested in the economic theory of regulation (see Stigler, 1971; Peltzman, 1976; Posner, 1974) is well-known. Regulation is generally seen as the result of rent seeking by interest groups, which imposes a welfare loss on the general public.

The regulation introducing liability rules and financial caps on liability might also be explained to a large extent by the influence of pressure groups. This is probably true both for the contents of the nuclear liability conventions and for the implementing legislation in some states.

The regulation of nuclear accidents originated in the 1950s from a demand for regulation from the nuclear industry and possibly also from "the public." The nuclear risk was, and still is, a very sensitive issue for public opinion. In the field of nuclear risks there was probably a rather vague demand from the public "to do something about it." This demand for regulation was not represented by well-defined and active particular interest groups. Potential victims of a nuclear accident could be seen as members of a "shadow interest group" (Keenan and Rubin, 1988). A *shadow interest group* can be defined as a group that would have members and come into being if an accident occurred; potential victims of a nuclear accident can thus be seen as members of this latent interest group. Knowing that shadow interest groups have the potential to become an effective lobby if an accident occurs, rational politicians will respond to this group in the same way that they will respond to normal interest groups, even though the shadow interest group has not yet been organized (Keenan and Rubin, 1988, p. 22). On the other hand, the interests of the nuclear industry in having protective regulation are clear. In the 1950s the nuclear industry feared that the future of nuclear power could be endangered by unlimited liability. In the preparatory documents preceding the Paris Convention it can be clearly seen that the goal of the regulation of nuclear liability was not so much the protection of victims but the protection of the nuclear industry itself. There is qualitative evidence of the influence of the nuclear industry both in the drafting of the international conventions and especially in the national implementing legislation. At first glance the introduction of strict liability and compulsory insurance does not seem to benefit the nuclear industry. However, due to the sensitivity of the issue in the public opinion some legislative intervention seemed unavoidable. The economic theory of regulation suggests that in those circumstances the interest group involved will accept the general principle of regulation but will strive to change its scope to its advantage (Pelzman, 1976). The interest groups will realize that regulation may enhance producer wealth, while it simultaneously corrects an externality problem. This outcome has been stressed by Maloney and McCormick (1982) with respect to environmental quality regulation.

As far as the qualitative evidence for the success of the interest groups is concerned, one can point to the fact that strict liability is introduced, although this does not really increase the exposure to liability in a serious way given the already broadly interpreted negligence standard. A duty to insure is introduced, but in most legislations the amount of liability is limited. Short periods of limitation are laid down. Through this regulation the public is "reassured" that compensation will always be paid when a nuclear accident occurs. On the other hand, the interests of the nuclear industry are better protected than before the regulation.

The interests of the politicians, acting as utility maximizers, are the following: they face incentives to produce "public-interest" legislation together with incentives to broker wealth transfers favoring small interest groups. The politicians will strive for public-interest regulation because such regulation increases political support (votes) in the long run. Simultaneously they may wish to serve established interest groups. The most effective lobbyists are small groups that are well-organized and can therefore realize wealth transfers to the members because of low transaction costs. The success of interest groups is also to a large extent due to the high information costs on the side of both the public (the potential victims) and the legislator. The regulation of liability for nuclear accidents is very complicated: strict liability, compulsory insurance, limits to compensation, and short periods of limitation. These complexities lead to the fact that prima facie it would seem that the regulation does not transfer wealth to the interest groups and serves the interests of the victim. Only after a critical analysis does one understand that the victim is in fact worse off with than without the regulation.

Finally, one can also point to the influence of the monopolistic insurers on the national legislatures. The insurance industry, as well as the nuclear industry, enjoys important political power and has strong connections with the politicians of the governing parties in most countries. As we mentioned above, the market structure is a bilateral monopoly since both the insurance and the nuclear industry are monopolized. Characteristic of a bilateral monopoly is that a joint profit-maximizing strategy will be followed (see Scherer, 1970). One can see that at the national level the interests of the insurer and the nuclear industry are mixed. Both have an interest in a limitation of the compensation. For the nuclear industry this would lower the premiums. The latter will also have an interest in limiting its liability to the insured amount available; this means that the licensee of a nuclear plant would bear no liability apart from the insured amounts. It seems also in the interests of both to have short periods of limitation in order to limit the risk-exposure for the insurer and the exposure to liability for the nuclear industry. At first glance it might seem strange that the insurance industry also favored a reduction of the liability of the operator of a power plant, since this also reduces the demand for insurance. However, one can clearly note in many national parliaments that the insurance industry lobbied for a limitation of the third-party liability of the operator to the "insurable" amount. One possible explanation is that, because of the unpredictability of the loss, premium calculation in a profit-maximizing manner is impossible, whereas premiums in other classes of insurance are profitable. Indeed, we have mentioned that the insurer of the nuclear risk prefers to cover property damage instead of third-party liability. One possible reason for this preference might be the fact that administrative costs can be much higher in a third-party nuclear insurance. This seems to be a plausible additional explanation for the lobbying in favor of a reduced third-party liability by the insurance industry.

Evidence of the influence of the insurance industry in the regulatory process can be observed in the parliamentary proceedings in many countries. For instance, in Belgium, when an amendment was introduced to increase the amount of the limited liability, the minister expressly stated that it was first necessary to ascertain whether this amount could be insured by SYBAN. After a negative response from SYBAN, the majority parties voted against the proposal.[20] Also in the Netherlands the Dutch legislature blindly trusted the information of the Dutch nuclear pool with respect to the availability of coverage for third-party insurance. During the parliamentary debate Minister Kok declared that throughout the whole period of preparation for the bill negotiations took place with the nuclear insurance pool. He confirmed that in all cases the nuclear pool agreed with the proposals.[21] Some critics asked whether the financial limitation on liability for the operator of 500 million Dutch guilders should not be compared with the increasing possibilities of coverage on the international market, but in the end the information given by the nuclear insurance pool was decisive for the exposure to liability of the operator of the power plant.[22]

In sum, some of the inefficiencies or deviations from the economic model of accident law, both in the conventions and especially in national implementation legislation might be explained through the influence of pressure groups. We will, however, argue that where these low limitations might have been in the interest of the nuclear industry in the 1960s and acceptable for politicians, this might not be the case nowadays, especially after the experiences with the Three Mile Island and Chernobyl accidents. We believe that the nuclear industry itself now has an interest in working out a compensation scheme for the costs of nuclear accidents that provides for substantially higher amounts than is the case nowadays. These new compensation schemes might be worked out with or without the classic nuclear insurance pools. It might therefore not be in their direct interest to change the existing system. How such an alternative compensation scheme could look will be explained in the following paragraph.

5. A risk-sharing agreement

As has been mentioned above, substantial disadvantages of the actual system of liability and insurance are that the insurance pools still operate on a national level, differences exist between the amounts available in third-party liability insurance, and the pools have a large influence on the national legislators in fixing the exposure to liability of the operator of a nuclear power plant. This has been partially caused by the fact that the Paris Convention was drafted in a period when the concern was not so much with victim compensation but with keeping the risks for the operator within acceptable limits. Given the relatively large extent of the costs of a potential nuclear accident, economists have considered the question of whether it would be possible to introduce more efficient systems of compensation that would allow the generation of higher amounts to cover the costs of a potential nuclear accident. One proposal has been produced by two Swiss scholars, Jean-Robert Tyran and Peter Zweifel (1993). They begin with the statement that the third-party liability as it exists fails to internalize the externality caused by the nuclear risk. They also criticize the argument of the uninsurability of the nuclear risk, noting that earthquakes are also not predictable and have devastating consequences but that insurance coverage for earthquake is common, even for large amounts.[23] They also point to the disadvantages of the pooling system: the cartels charge excessive premiums. In addition they criticize the limitation of liability to a value that falls far short of a possible loss, since this constitutes a subsidization of nuclear power. They then produce an alternative that is the use of capital markets to provide additional coverage for liability. Rather than turning to nuclear insurance pools, Tyran and Zweifel suggest that plant operators should be permitted to take risk-participation shares on capital markets. Investors would have the opportunity of buying such a share against deposit of financial assets, creating a warrant in favor of the plant of their choice. This warrant can be exercised by the agency when liability claims are presented. Since operators must have sufficient coverage, they will compete for coverage capital and bad risks will not be able to get coverage. Hence Tyran and Zweifel argue that their ERICAM system can correct the market failure and provide for higher coverage of the nuclear risk and improved safety.

The idea of ERICAM is that the interest rate on the bonds issued reflects the accident rate. In so far as the care of operators is observable, it will be reflected in interest rates. But when the accidents are a rare experience, rating will be impossible and government regulation will still be necessary. The ERICAM system has advantages compared to the current system of limited liability and noncompeting insurance pools.

Together with Göran Skogh, I have proposed still another alternative compensation scheme based on risk pooling by plant operators. It can be summarized as follows (see Faure and Skogh, 1992).

Although large risks may be uninsurable on the traditional insurance market, these large risks might be shared by ex ante agreements. Those ex ante agreements are often used in cases where the risk is uncertain and possibly difficult to estimate, at least initially before information on probability and possible magnitude of the accident is available. The risk sharing could be realized through an international convention in order to get as many plant owners involved as possible. It could, however, also function within the existing conventions on a voluntary basis. The risk-sharing agreement would function according to the following points:

- The owner of a nuclear power plant is strictly liable for losses caused by an accident, including third-party liability.
- In principle, as was mentioned above, strict liability should be unlimited. It may, however, be necessary to limit initially the liability to $100 billion (U.S.), which would already be substantially larger than the size of the liability today. This would also allow for compensation for medium-size accidents.
- Every plant owner should contribute to a mutual guarantee fund. This mutual pool covers the liability in case of an accident. If there are 100 nuclear power plants involved in the pool and thus 100 members, each plant onwer has to contribute $1 billion (U.S.) in case of an accident with costs rising to $100 billion (U.S.).
- The maximum potential claim on each plant is therefore $1 billion (U.S.). This makes reinsurance necessary. A fraction of the desired coverage can be provided by the international insurance market; another part can be obtained through reinsurance from the states.

A major difference in the existing system is that, in the proposed risk-sharing agreement, all plants share the costs of accidents wherever they occur in signatory states. This makes nuclear safety a collective economic responsibility for the industry. The liability is to a large part transferred from the single plant owner to the collective guarantee fund mutually owned by the nuclear industry in the contracting states. The mutual fund will face moral-hazard problems caused by the individual members. It will therefore be in the interest of the fund to control its members and to reduce risks, for instance, by imposing requirements before being accepted as a member. Hence, the industry will be forced to take preventive measures by the mutual fund as a condition of being accepted as a member.

Thus an important effect of this risk-sharing agreement would be that accident prevention would gain a new economic dimension. Unlimited liability of plant owners in combination with a mutual guarantee fund will create a collective interest of the industry in reducing risks and controlling pool members.

The working of this ex ante agreement can be illustrated by one example. Assume, for instance, that there is an accident in France that causes $60 billion (U.S.) damages in France, Belgium, and Germany. Each of the 100 plant owners will then contribute $600 million (U.S.). The twelve plants in Sweden would have to cover $7.2 billion (U.S.) of losses. A large part of these costs would be insured by the insurance market (and maybe by the existing nuclear insurance pools), and there would be reinsurance by the states and to some extent by the international insurance market. The possibility of reinsurance by the state is already covered under the Paris Convention. For instance, in the Netherlands the Dutch state provides for a guarantee of 5 billion Dutch guilders (almost $3 billion (U.S.)). This illustrates that although it might be impossible to receive insurance coverage up to $1 billion (U.S.) for each plant, an ex ante commitment by each power plant to intervene in the costs of a nuclear accident up to a maximum amount of $1 billion (U.S.) might well be given if it is supported by insurance, reinsurance, and a state guarantee.

6. Chances of an implementation of economic models in the Paris and Vienna Conventions

The statements made above that the existing limitations on liability neither provide for adequate compensation of losses nor for full internalization of the nuclear risk are not new.

Also within the IAEA and the Nuclear Energy Agency of the OECD an increase of the amounts available is seen as a necessary change to the conventions, especially in the light of the Chernobyl accident. We also have reason to believe that it is in the interest of the nuclear industry today not to oppose these increases. With the current limitations, property damage will to a large extent be uncovered by insurance and the international conventions. A nuclear accident in Central Europe may destroy land or property in surrounding nations with serious diplomatic controversies as a consequence. An accident that makes an abandonment of the area around a plant necessary may also cause immense losses of land and property. The effects of these losses on the financial system are often overlooked. Since most credits are guaranteed by real estate, a lot of creditors will not recover their loans. The consequence can be the bankruptcy of many financial institutions, which may disturb the international financial system. The impact on public budgets may therefore be large. Since not all the losses will be compensated, the distribution of the available compensation will be a political matter. In general, the undercompensation will lead to a general distrust in nuclear power, which will cause a considerable pressure on politicians to reduce the use of nuclear power to an even greater extent. This can be avoided only if the nuclear industry can come up with an arrangement that provides at least for adequate compensation if an accident happens. The classic system of individual liability of a nuclear power plant operator with individual insurance by the national pools has not proven able to generate sufficient amounts. As we have demonstrated, an ex ante risk-sharing agreement on an international level might provide more adequate victim compensation. In a way the ex ante agreement is simply a decision on how to distribute the costs of a potential accident ex ante. An accident today could lead to random victimization, political conflicts, and large economic disturbances. An ex ante regulation is therefore in the public interest but also in the interest of the industry. Such a risk-sharing agreement will reduce the public's disutility of risk aversion and thus the fear of nuclear power in general. The ex ante agreement will also reduce the risk for the nuclear industry of political failures due to sudden opinions, poorly informed politicians, and so forth.

An opinion in favor of an ex ante risk-sharing agreement may be established. First, countries without nuclear power will only benefit from the system. Second, countries with nuclear power may have very large losses. It is therefore in the interest of these countries to clarify the liability and the sharing of the potential costs ex ante. Third, pressure groups that are very strong economically have much to gain from this ex ante risk-sharing agreement, especially creditors and insurance with a lot of real estate in their portfolio or as surety.

The implementation of such a risk-sharing agreement should not be considered as impossible at all for several reasons. In this respect we can point to the fact that a comparable, although not identical, system has been introduced by the most recent amendment to the American Price-Anderson Act. The principle in U.S. law is still individual liability of the operator of the power plant up to an amount of $200 million (U.S.), for which the operator will seek insurance coverage with the classic nuclear insurance pools. If the damage is higher than $200 million all nuclear power plants in the United States will share on a pro rata basis up to a total amount for the 114 American power plants of $8.96 billion.[24] This American example shows that through a risk spreading between all nuclear power plants, considerably higher amounts can be made available than with a liability limit that is set on the basis of the insurability of the risk by a national insurance pool. Also in other fields of liability risk-sharing agreements are well known. For instance, marine oil pollution is insured by the so-called Protection and Indemnity Clubs (P&I Clubs). The members of these clubs are the tanker owners. They provide insurance on a nonprofit basis for the members. At the beginning of each year a "call" is made that should cover the claims and administrative costs (see Bongaerts and Debièvre, 1987; Coghlin, 1984). These P&I Clubs function as a mutual insurance company. Profits and losses are shared among the members. If the receipts of a year were insufficient to cover the losses, an additional call can be asked for from the members.

Also within the revision of the Paris and Vienna Conventions, the drafting committees have discussed several alternatives to produce higher amounts of coverage. In this respect a proposal by the delegations of the United Kingdom and France is worth mentioning. They proposed a four-tier system whereby the compensation would be provided as follows:

a. up to the amount provided under the legislation of a contracting party, by insurance or other financial security of the operator liable in accordance with the Vienna or the Paris conventions;
b. between that amount and (A) million Special Drawing Rights, out of funds provided by the operator liable which, subject to §4 of this article, the operator shall have secured through his membership of a risk pool established by free association of operators;
c. between (A) and (B) million Special Drawing Rights, out of public funds to be made available by the contracting party in whose territory the nuclear installation of the operator liable is situated;
d. between (B) and (C) million Special Drawing Rights, out of public funds to be made available by the contracting parties according to the formula for contributions specified in article 5.

The proposal moreover stipulates that the risk pool shall secure the availability of the funds through contracts binding on all participants and shall allow for the accession of new participants on agreed terms that may take account, inter alia, of risk.

It seems clear that this French and English proposal goes very much in the direction of the risk-sharing agreement we have proposed under Section 5.

7. Concluding remarks

In this paper we have made a modest attempt to contribute to the discussion on the revision of the Paris and Vienna Conventions on the liability for nuclear accidents by illustrating the usefulness of the economic analysis of law. Especially in the field of nuclear accidents it might be clear that an interdisciplinary approach using both legal and economic tools might be fruitful to understand the functioning of liability rules. After a description of the basic concepts of the economic analysis of accident law and the structure of the liability for nuclear accidents today, we have shown that both the liability based on the conventions and the insurance through the national nuclear insurance pools cause various inefficiencies. The classic system of individual liability of a nuclear power plant operator with a financial cap on compensation and individual insurance by national pools has not proven to be very effective. Hence, the economic analysis of law can provide additional arguments in favor of a revision of the Paris and Vienna Conventions, which would lead to higher amounts of liability of the nuclear power plant operator. Indeed, the current system not only leads to too little victim compensation but also lacks adequate internalization of the nuclear risk and might eventually even lead to a too low level of care by the nuclear power plant operator.

We have also shown that a revision of the conventions, which would consist mainly in an increase of the amounts of liability, would amount to "more of the same" but would not take away the principal objections to the current system. Indeed, we believe that it is possible to generate a sufficient amount of coverage for the costs of a nuclear accident only if the idea is accepted that all plants share the costs of an accident wherever it occurred through a mutual pooling system. Such a system might lead not only to higher amounts of victim compensation but also to a more adequate system of control and therefore to accident prevention.

We believe that apart from the economic arguments there should in any case be a substantial increase in the amount of liability of the nuclear power plant owner. We have shown that this might be reached through an ex ante risk-sharing agreement, but possibly other economic tools, such as capital markets, can also lead to an increase in the amounts available for victim compensation. It is, in any case, necessary that the amounts available will be considerably increased to reassure the credibility of the nuclear industry. We believe that there is a certain future for nuclear power only if the industry shows itself to be able to cover at least a substantial part of the costs of an accident when it happens. An ex ante pooling system might help to achieve that end.

Acknowledgments

I would like to thank Jürgen Backhaus and two anonymous referees for useful comments.

Notes

1. For an overview of this literature, see Shavell (1987).
2. For an overview of the contents of these conventions, see, inter alia, the excellent recent dissertation by Domsdorf and Faure and Van den Bergh (1989, p. 284 onward).
3. See *Nuclear Law Bulletin* 42 (December 1988), 56–72.
4. For an overview of these various amounts provided for in the national legislations implementing the conventions, see Domsdorf, (1993, p. 682). In addition to the civil liability of the licensee of a nuclear power plant, one could also examine the possibility of a state liability for a nuclear accident that occurred on the state's territory. See, for these aspects that go beyond the scope of this paper, Rest (1989, p. 609).
5. Muller (1985, p. 171) notes in this respect: "In view of the rising cost of erecting nuclear energy plants, nuclear property insurance, which is likewise borne by the nuclear pools, is under considerable pressure and, in turn, represents an involvement by the insurance industry to the machinery insurance which, in the case of a nuclear power plant, also goes into the billions. Both forms of cover have priority over liability insurance, since a theoretical large scale nuclear occurrence would probably first affect the material assets within the plant, then the surrounding area.

   "It is naive to consider only the third party suffering loss or damage—as occasionally happens—and to regard property insurance as an unnecessary appendage which only absorbs capacity. Every reasonable person knows that a nuclear power plant requires a heavy investment and that not only the operators, but also their creditors, should be protected. It is quite simply foolish to regard the loss of this investment as a sort of

ECONOMIC MODELS OF COMPENSATION FOR DAMAGE 41

'punishment' for having brought about a nuclear occurrence and to ignore the interests of the power supply company and the investors in safeguarding their material assets."

6. See the discussion in *Nuclear Third Party Liability and Insurance, Munich Symposium, Status and Prospects,* 192-196.

7. In Belgium a European Mutual Association for Nuclear Insurance (EMANI) was funded in 1978, which by 1984 covered 1.4 billion Belgian francs of the property damage to nuclear power plants per installation in Belgium.

8. A member of parliament (Rosenmüller) therefore noted that an inadequate pricing of this state guarantee could lead to a subsidization of nuclear energy, *Parliamentary Documents of the Second Chamber of Representatives,* 23 April 1991, 72-4054.

9. Due to latency problems, diseases might appear several years after the nuclear accident. Therefore, the short periods of limitation and special time bars might seriously limit the victims' right to compensation.

10. Experimental psychologists have argued that persons generally have a high degree of risk aversion against risks with a low probability but a large potential magnitude (see Kahneman and Tversky, 1979; Kahneman, Slovic and Tversky 1982).

11. The results of this study are also summarized in the Appendix of a Belgian proposal to increase the insured amount substantially (*Parliamentary Proceedings of the Belgian Senate,* 1986-87, 402/1, pp. 6-7) and in a proposed amendment to the Belgian Act of July 22, 1985 (*Parliamentary Proceedings of the Belgian Senate,* 1983-84, 593/4, p. 2).

12. This study was ordered by the Nuclear Regulatory Commission, an American federal agency for nuclear energy. As a result of this study the NRC proposed an amendment of the Price-Anderson Act regulating liability for nuclear accidents in the United States in order to increase the amount of liability.

13. See the amendment by Trussart, *Parliamentary Documents of the Belgian Senate,* 1983-84, 593/4, pp. 1-2, amendment of Mr. De Wasseige, *Parliamentary Documents of the Belgian Senate,* 1983-84, 593/5, p. 1, and the amendment by Mr. De Batselier, *Partliamentary Documents of the Belgian Chamber of Representatives,* 1984-85, 1207/7, p. 1.

14. See *Parliamentary Documents of the Dutch Chamber of Representatives,* 23 April 1991, 72-4062.

15. See the remarks of Mr. Tommel in *Parliamentary Documents of the Dutch Chamber of Representatives,* 23 April 1991, 72-4050.

16. This monopoly position of the nuclear insurance pool was recognized by the Dutch legislator and advanced as an argument for the state to act as insurer as well (see Hamburger 1986, p. 1340).

17. Official Journal of the EC of 31.12.1992.

18. With respect to the bilateral monopoly, see Scherer (1970, pp. 242-245).

19. For such an interest-group analysis, see Faure and Van den Bergh (1990).

20. *Parliamentary Documents of the Belgian Senate,* 1983-84, 593/3, p. 11.

21. *Parliamentary Documents of the Dutch Chamber of Representatives,* 23 April 1991, 72-4064.

22. See the questions by Ms. Van Rijn-Vellekoop, *Parliamentary Documents of the Dutch Chamber of Representatives,* 23 April 1991, 72-4046 and of Mr. De Korte, *Parliamentary Documents of the Dutch Chamber of Representatives,* 23 April 1991, 72-4052.

23. Tyran and Zweifel (1993, p. 433) report that the 1906 San Francisco earthquake caused insured damages to $39.5 billion (U.S.). This sum is 100 times greater than the maximum nuclear coverage granted by private insurers. Other examples can be given where the probabilities of an accident are unknown, the expected accident costs are large, but nevertheless large amounts of insurance coverage are provided.

24. For a description of the American system, see Marrone (1993, pp. 361-381), Heimann (1993, pp. 417-425), Robesin (1987, pp. 228-229), and Rowden, Kraemer, and Cuoco (1988, pp. 79-101). The amount in the Price-Anderson Act of 1988 of $7.2 billion (U.S.) was increased to $8.96 billion (U.S.) to adopt to inflation in August 1993.

References

Adams, M. (1989). "New Activities and the Efficient Liability Rules." In M. Faure and R. Van den Bergh (eds.), *Essays in Law and Economics* (pp. 103-107). Antwerp: Maklu.

Bongaerts, J., and A. Debievre. (1987). "Insurance for Civil Liability for Marine Oil Pollution Damages." *Geneva Papers on Risk and Insurance*, 145–187.

Brown, J.P. (1973). "Towards an Economic Theory of Liability." *Journal of Legal Studies*, 323–349.

Buchanan, J.M., and G. Tullock. (1962). *The Calculus of Consent.* Ann Arbor: University of Michigan Press.

Coghlin, T.G. (1984). "Protection and Indemnity Clubs." *Lloyd's Maritime and Commercial Law Quarterly*, 403–416.

Diamond, P. (1974). "Single Activity Accidents." *Journal of Legal Studies*, 107–164.

Domsdorft, E.P.M.W. (1993). *Internationaal Atoomenergierecht, De betrokkenheid van Nederland bij meer dan 100 verdragen.* Zwolle: Tjeenk Willink.

Dow, J. (1985). "The Organisation and Development of International Liability Capacity and National Market Pools, with Special Reference to New 'Nuclear Countries.'" In *Nuclear Third Party Liability and Insurance, Munich Symposium, Status and Prospects* (pp. 172–182). Paris: OECD.

Evans, N., and C. Hope (1984). *Nuclear Power: Future, Costs and Benefits.* Cambridge: Cambridge University Press.

Faure, M., and G. Skogh. (1992). "Compensation for Damages Caused by Nuclear Accidents: A Convention as Insurance." *Geneva Papers on Risk and Insurance*, 499–513.

Faure, M., and R. Van den Bergh. (1987). "Negligence, Strict Liability and Regulation of Safety Under Belgian Law: An Introductory Economic Analysis." *Geneva Papers on Risk and Insurance*, 95–114.

Faure, M., and R. Van den Bergh. (1989). *Objectieve aansprakelijkheid, Verplichte verzekering en Veiligheidsregulering.* Antwerp: Maklu.

Faure, M., and R. Van den Bergh. (1990). "Liability for Nuclear Accidents in Belgium from an Interest Group Perspective." *International Review of Law and Economics* 241, 254.

Faure, M., and R. Van den Bergh. (1993). "Het toelaten van kartels op de Europese verzekeringsmarkt: hogere premies, lagere kwaliteit en meer ongevallen." *Nederlands Juristenblad* (February 25), 262–267.

Finsinger, J. (1988). *Verbraucherschutz auf Versicherungsmarkten.* Munich: Florentz.

Hamburger, M. (1986). "De aansprakelijkheidsverzekering in Nederland voor schade door kernongevallen in West-Europa." *NJB*, 1335–1341.

Hansson, I., and G. Skogh. (1987). "Moral Hazard and Safety Regulation." *Geneva Papers on Risk and Insurance*, 132–144.

Havens III, J.C.W., and R.M. Theisen. (1986). "The Application of United States and EEC Antitrust Laws to Reinsurance and Insurance Pooling Arrangements." *Antitrust Bulletin*, 1301.

Haynes, V., and B. Bojcun. (1988). *The Tsjernobyl Disaster.* London: Hogarth Press.

Heimann, F. (1993). "The U.S. Liability Protection System for Nuclear Power Plants." *Nuclear Accidents, Liability and Guarantees* (pp. 417–425). Paris: OECD.

Islam, S., and K. Lindgren. (1986). "How Many Reactor Accidents Will There Be?" *Nature* 21 (August).

Kahneman, D., P. Slovic, and A. Tversky. (1982). *Judgement Under Uncertainty: Heuristics and Biases.* Cambridge: Cambridge University Press.

Kahneman, D., and A. Tversky. (1979). "Prospect Theory: An Analysis of Decision Under Risk." *Econometrica*, 263–291.

Keenan, D., and P. Rubin. (1988). "Shadow Interest Groups and Safety Regulation." *International Review of Law and Economics*, 21–36.

Landes, W., and R. Posner. (1984). "Tort Law as a Regulatory Regime for Catastrophic Personal Injuries." *Journal of Legal Studies*, 417–434.

Lonergan, S., R. Gobel, and C. Cororaton. (1990). "Estimating the Financial Consequences of a Severe Nuclear Accident in Canada." *Energy* 15(6), 507–522.

Maloney, M., and R. McCormick. (1982). "A Positive Theory of Environmental Quality Regulation." *Journal of Law and Economics* 99–123.

Marples, D. (1988). *The Social Impact of the Tsjernobyl Disaster.* London: MacMillan.

Marrone, J. (1993). "Closing the Circle of Protection for the Public: The Evolution of the System in the United States." In *Nuclear Accidents, Liability and Guarantees* (pp. 361–381). Paris: OECD

McCormick, R., and R. Tollison. (1982). *Politicians, Legislation and the Economy: An Inquiry into the Interest Group Theory of Government.*

Medvedev, Z. (1990). *The Legacy of Tsjernobyl.* New York: Norton.

Morrens, P. (1990). *De Golf en de Zwemmer. Bedenkingen bij de leefimilieuproblematiek.* Antwerp: Standard.

Muller, W. (1985). "The Role of Insurance Industry in Covering Nuclear Third Party Liability Risks." In *Nuclear Third Party Liability and Insurance, Munich Symposium, Status and Prospects.* Paris: OECD.

Olson, M. (1971). *The Logic of Collective Action*. Cambridge, MA: Harvard University Press.

Peltzman, S. (1976). "Toward a More General Theory of Regulation." *Journal of Law and Economics*, 211–240.

Posner, R. (1974). "Theories of Economic Regulation." *Bell Journal of Economics*, 335–358.

Reitsma, S.M.S. (1992). "Nuclear Insurance Pools: History and Development." Paper presented at the OECD Symposium on Nuclear Accidents, Liabilities and Guarantees, Helsinki, Finland, September.

Rest, A. (1989). "Tschjernobyl und die Internationale Haftung: volkerrechtliche Aspekte." *Verischerungsrecht*, 609.

Robesin, M. (1987). "Aansprakelijkheid voor kernongevallen, ruim een jaar na Tsjernobyl." *Milieu en Recht* 228–229.

Rowden, M., J. Kraemer, and L. Cuoco. (1988). "La revision de 1988 de la loi Price-Anderson ou mieux vaut tard que jamais." *Bulletin de droit nucleaire* 42, 79–101.

Scherer, F.M. (1970). *Industrial Market Structure and Economic Performance*. Chicago: McNally.

Shavell, S. (1980). "Strict Liability Versus Negligence." *Journal of Legal Studies* 1–25.

Shavell, S. (1984). "Liability for Harm Versus Regulation of Safety." *Journal of Legal Studies*, 357–374.

Shavell, S. (1987). *Economic Analysis of Accident Law*. Cambridge, MA: Harvard University Press.

Skogh, G. (1982). "Public Insurance and Accident Prevention." *International Review of Law and Economics* 67–80.

Stigler, G. (1971). "The Theory of Economic Regulation." *Bell Journal of Economics* 3–21.

Tyran, J.-R., and and P. Zweifel. (1993). "Environmental Risk Internationalization Through Capital Markets (ERICAM): The Case of Nuclear Power." *International Review of Law and Economics*, 431–444.

Von Busekist, O. (1989). "A Bridge Between Two Conventions on Civil Liability for Nuclear Damages: The Joint Protocol Relating to the Application of the Vienna Convention and the Paris Convention." *Nuclear Law Bulletin* 43 (June), 10–39.

Name Index

For Product Safety Concerns and Information please contact our EU representative GPSR@taylorandfrancis.com Taylor & Francis Verlag GmbH, Kaufingerstraße 24, 80331 München, Germany

T - #0101 - 230425 - C0 - 244/170/28 - PB - 9781138730601 - Gloss Lamination